The Cycles of
American History

BOOKS BY ARTHUR M. SCHLESINGER, JR.

Orestes A. Brownson
A Pilgrim's Progress

The Age of Jackson

The Vital Center

The General and the President
(with Richard H. Rovere)

The Age of Roosevelt
I. The Crisis of the Old Order, 1919–1933
II. The Coming of the New Deal
III. The Politics of Upheaval

The Politics of Hope

A Thousand Days
John F. Kennedy in the White House

The Bitter Heritage
Vietnam and American Democracy, 1941–1966

The Crisis of Confidence
Ideas, Power and Violence in America

The Imperial Presidency

Robert Kennedy and His Times

The Cycles of American History

ARTHUR M. SCHLESINGER, JR.

The Cycles of
American History

HOUGHTON MIFFLIN COMPANY
Boston/1986

Library of Congress Cataloging-in-Publication Data

Schlesinger, Arthur Meier, 1917–
The cycles of American history.

Bibliography: p.
Includes index.
1. United States—Foreign relations—Philosophy.
2. United States—Politics and government—Philosophy.
3. Cycles.   I. Title.
E183.7.S373   1986   973   86-7706
ISBN 0-395-37887-7

Printed in the United States of America

Q 10 9 8 7 6 5 4 3 2 1

For

AVERELL HARRIMAN

who has seen the cycles pass, and turn again

Contents

Foreword

———————— ✦ ————————

THIS BOOK offers a historian's reflection on the past and the future of the American experiment. The word 'experiment' is used advisedly. The men who established the United States of America believed that they were trying something new under the sun. The idea that a democratic republic might endure ran against all the teachings of history. The vindication of this idea, said Washington in his first inaugural, was "an experiment intrusted to the hands of the American people." The Founders were far from sure of success. Can we be certain even today that the experiment has succeeded? At least it has lasted for two centuries, and that is something.

Section I of this book raises general questions about the ebb and flow of American history. One essay describes the continuing tension between two divergent conceptions of the nation: does America mean commitment to a national experiment? or consecration of a national destiny? A second essay outlines a theory of the cyclical rhythms that characterize American politics. Section II deals with the United States and the great world beyond — foreign policy and the American character; national interests, moral absolutes and human rights; the rise of the American empire and the causes of the Cold War. Section III deals with the United States as a domestic polity — the role and the prospects of government, of political parties and of the Presidency.

Underlying these reflections is the conviction that the cumulative increase in the rate of change has been decisive in the making of the modern world. The last three centuries have seen dazzling revolutions in scientific theory and dazzling advances in the translation of theory into technology. The world has moved faster than ever before, and until recently it has moved fastest of all in the United States.

The American Revolution and the Industrial Revolution began at about the same time. From the start Americans have rejoiced in unremitting technological change. Innovation was unrestrained by custom or tradition or timidity. "I simply experiment," said Emerson, the quintessential American, "an endless seeker, with no Past at my back."[1] It is hardly surprising that the first historian to emphasize the accelerating velocity of history should have been an American. "The world did not double or treble its movement between 1800 and 1900," Henry Adams wrote in 1909, "but, measured by any standard known to science — by horsepower, calories, volts, mass in any shape, — the tension and vibration and volume and so-called progression of society were fully a thousand times greater in 1900 than in 1800."[2] Acceleration left man and mind far behind. Adams's own education, the best an American could get in the nineteenth century, was, he concluded in the early twentieth century, a total waste; the Harvard freshman he was in 1854 probably stood nearer to the thought of the year 1 than to that of the year 1904. "The law of acceleration," Adams said, "definite and constant as any law of mechanics, cannot be supposed to relax its energy to suit the convenience of man."[3]

Adams's appeal to scientific law was both romantic and ironic. His notion that history could be reduced to mathematical physics was a delusion, or perhaps an elaborate joke. Still, as metaphor, his point is powerful. William James, who patiently explained to Adams why the second law of thermodynamics did not apply to history, agreed that humanity had experienced only the most preliminary impact of science and technology. "Think how many absolutely new scientific conceptions have arisen in our own generation," he wrote, "how many new problems have been formulated that were never thought of before, and then cast an eye upon the brevity of science's career. . . . Is it credible that such a mushroom growth overnight as this *can* represent more than the minutest glimpse of what the universe will really prove to be when adequately understood? No! our science is a drop, our ignorance a sea."[4]

Humans have lived on earth for possibly eight hundred lifetimes, most of which they spent in caves. "Some five or six score people," James said, "if each . . . could speak for his own generation, would carry us back to the black unknown of the human species, to days without a document or monument to tell their tale."[5] Movable type appeared only eight lifetimes ago, industrialization in the last three lifetimes. The static societies that consumed most of human history perceived no great difference between present and past. Society subsisted on the existing stock of wisdom for a long time. The functional need for new ideas was limited. Tradition was sacred and controlling.

The last two lifetimes have seen more scientific and technological achievement than the first 798 put together. The shift to a swiftly changing society has not greatly affected the surfaces of daily living. The New York of the 1980s resembles the New York of the 1930s more than the New York of the 1930s resembled the New York of the 1880s. But the shift has profoundly altered inner perceptions and expectations. It has placed traditional roles and institutions under severe and incomprehensible strain. It has cast off reference points and rituals that had stabilized and sanctified life for generations. It has left the experience of elders useless to the tribulations of the young. Children, knowing how different their own lives will be, no longer look to parents as models and authorities; rather, parents now learn from their children.

The pace of change grows ever faster. A boy who saw the Wright brothers fly for a few seconds at Kitty Hawk in 1903 could have watched *Apollo II* land on the moon in 1969. The first rockets were launched during the Second World War; today astronauts roam outer space. The first electronic computer was built in 1946; today the world rushes from the mechanical into the electronic age. The double helix was first unveiled in 1953; today biotechnology threatens to remake mankind. The first atomic bomb fell in 1945; today the world shudders under the threat of nuclear obliteration.

The acceleration of change compels us to perceive life as motion, not as order; the universe not as complete but as unfinished. For people of buoyant courage like William James the prospect was exhilarating. Henry Adams saw change as irreversible, but contemplated the future with foreboding. Others, in the midst of flounder and flux, strive to resurrect the old ways.

The hunger for stability is entirely natural. Change is scary; uncharted change, demoralizing. If the law of acceleration is not to spin the world out of control, society must cherish its lifelines into the past. That is why, even in this age of whirl, so much of the old abides. People instinctively defend the self against disruption. "In this matter of belief," said James, "we are all extreme conservatives." When new facts finally drive out old opinions, we take care to graft the new perception on the ancient stock with "a minimum of jolt, a maximum of continuity."[6] Everyone becomes his own Landmarks Preservation Commission. We seek with Eliot the still point in the turning world.

Traditions endure, from which, consciously or not, we draw sustenance. It is not fashionable these days for historians to talk about
'national character.' But of course persisting traits, values, folkways,
create a palpable national identity. The reader of Tocqueville is constantly astonished to recognize the lineaments of modern America in
his great work, though Tocqueville visited a predominantly agricultural nation of thirteen million people a century and a half ago. Even
Crèvecoeur still astonishes by the contemporaneity of his eighteenth-
century answer to his own famous question: "What then is the American, this new man?"*

The law of acceleration hurtles us into the inscrutable future. But
it cannot wipe the slate of the past. History haunts even generations
who refuse to learn history. Rhythms, patterns, continuities, drift out
of time long forgotten to mold the present and to color the shape of
things to come. Science and technology revolutionize our lives, but
memory, tradition and myth frame our response. Expelled from individual consciousness by the rush of change, history finds its revenge
by stamping the collective unconscious with habits, values, expectations, dreams. The dialectic between past and future will continue to
form our lives.

These reflections are not presented in any confidence that history is
the cure for all that ails us. Still the past helps explain where we are
today and how we got there. Knowledge of what Americans have
been through in earlier times will do us no harm as we grope through
the darkness of our own days. During the Soviet blockade of Berlin
in 1948, when forebodings of a Third World War swept Washington,
a young assistant secretary exclaimed to Secretary of State George C.
Marshall at a panicky staff meeting, "How in the world can you remain so calm during this appalling crisis?" Marshall replied, calmly,
"I've seen worse."

Americans have indeed seen worse. History, by putting crisis in perspective, supplies the antidote to every generation's illusion that its

---

*"*He* is an American, who, leaving behind him all his ancient prejudices and manners,
receives new ones from the new mode of life he has embraced, the new government he
obeys, and the new rank he holds. . . . Here individuals of all nations are melted into a
new race of men, whose labours and posterities will one day cause great changes in the
world. Americans are the western pilgrims, who are carrying with them that great mass
of arts, sciences, vigour, and industry which began long since in the east; they will finish
the great circle. . . . The American is a new man, who acts upon new principles; he
must therefore entertain new ideas, and form new opinions." J. Hector St. John de
Crèvecoeur, *Letters from an American Farmer* (1782), Letter III.

own problems are uniquely oppressive. Troubles impending always seem worse than troubles surmounted, but this does not prove that they really are. Nuclear weapons excepted, the problems of the 1980s are modest compared to the problems that confronted Washington's generation in achieving independence and fashioning a free state, or to the problems that confronted Lincoln's generation in bringing the republic through the glare of civil war, or to the problems that confronted Franklin Roosevelt's generation in surviving the worst depression and winning the greatest war in American history. "So hot? my little Sir," said Emerson, warning us not to mistake the sound of a popgun for the crack of doom.

Nuclear weapons, however, are the fatal exception. They introduce a qualitatively new factor into the historical process. For the first time in the life of humanity the crack of doom becomes a realistic possibility. So history embraces discontinuity as well as continuity. Knowledge of the past should inoculate against hysteria but should not instill complacency. History walks on a knife edge.

No one knew the risks of history better than Henry Adams, whose name is invoked more than once in the pages that follow. Humanity, Adams well understood, had been subjected to a succession of technological shocks, each of which by itself would have taken decades to digest and control. Every shock increased the velocity of history. The nuclear shock threatens the end of history. "Man has mounted science and is now run away with," Adams wrote to his brother on 11 April 1862, a few days after the Battle of Shiloh, while the *Monitor* and the *Merrimac* were maneuvering around Newport News. "I firmly believe that before many centuries more, science will be the master of man. The engines he will have invented will be beyond his strength to control. Some day science shall have the existence of mankind in its power, and the human race commit suicide by blowing up the world."[7]

Arthur M. Schlesinger, Jr.

Acknowledgments

———◆·◆———

S OME OF THESE ESSAYS have appeared in different forms; for their provenance, see the endnotes. All essays heretofore published, except for the first part of chapter 8, have been extensively revised. The other essays were written expressly for this book. I thank Albert O. Hirschman, Frank L. Klingberg and Barbara Wendell Kerr for comments on the essay on cycles, McGeorge Bundy for comments on that essay and on the revaluation of Eisenhower and Joseph L. Rauh, Jr., for comments on the essays on affirmative government and on the Presidency. I am indebted to Robert Johnson for suggesting the book, to Nan Talese and Austin Olney for intelligent and helpful comment on the manuscript, to Luise Erdmann for meticulous copy editing and to Irving Tullar for the excellent index. I must express everlasting gratitude to the expert secretaries who typed this material in a series of versions — Dianne L. Sikorski, Elizabeth Hogan, Mary Chiffriller and especially the late Gretchen Stewart. My appreciation for the forbearance of Alexandra Emmet Schlesinger and of our children during the ordeal of composition is beyond expression.

PART I

ONE

The Theory of America:
Experiment or Destiny?

———◆———

IN THE BICENTENNIAL YEAR of American independence, almost two centuries after Crèvecoeur propounded his notorious question, an American Indian writing on the subject "The North American" in a magazine addressed to American blacks concluded: "No one really knows at the present time what America really is."[1] Surely no observer had more right to wonder at this continuing mystery than a descendant of the original Americans. Surely no readers had more right to share the bafflement than the descendants of slaves. Nor indeed does the mystery have a final answer. There is no solution in the last chapter; there is no last chapter. The best the interpreter can do is to trace figures in the carpet, recognizing as he must that other interpreters will trace other figures.

I

The American carpet has many figures. Two strands, intertwined since the time when English-speaking white men first invaded the western continent, represent themes in recurrent contention over the meaning of America. Both themes had their origins in the Calvinist ethos. Both were subsequently renewed by secular infusions. Both have dwelt within the American mind and struggled for its possession through the course of American history. Their competition will doubtless continue for the rest of the life of the nation.

I will call one theme the tradition and the other the counter-tradition, thereby betraying at once my own bias. Other historians might reverse the terms. I would not quarrel too much about that. Let them betray their own biases. In any event, the tradition, as I prefer to style it, sprang initially from historic Christianity as mediated by Augustine and Calvin. The Calvinist ethos was suffused with convictions of the depravity of man, of the awful precariousness of human existence, of the vanity of mortals under the judgment of a pitiless and wrathful deity. Harriet Beecher Stowe recalled the atmosphere in *Oldtown Folks:* "The underlying foundation of life . . . in New England, was one of profound, unutterable, and therefore unuttered melancholy, which regarded human existence itself as a ghastly risk, and, in the case of the vast majority of human beings, an inconceivable misfortune."[2] "Natural men," cried Jonathan Edwards, "are held in the hand of God, over the pit of hell. . . . The devil is waiting for them, hell is gaping for them, the flames gather and flash about them, and would fain lay hold on them, and swallow them up; the fire pent up in their own hearts is struggling to break out. . . . You have nothing to stand upon, nor any thing to take hold of; there is nothing between you and hell but the air."[3] The language rings melodramatically in twentieth-century ears. Perhaps we moderns can more easily accept it as a metaphorical rendering of what those for whom God is dead call the existential crisis.

So terrible a sense of the nakedness of the human condition turned all life into an endless and implacable process of testing. "We must look upon our selves," said William Stoughton, the chief justice of the court that condemned the Salem witches, "as under a *solemn divine Probation;* it hath been and it is a Probation-time, even to this whole people. . . . This hath been and is a time and season of eminent trial to us."[4] So had it been at all times for all people. Most had failed the test. Were the American colonists immune to the universal law? In this aspect, the Calvinist notion of "providential history" argued against American exceptionalism. In the Puritan cosmos, Perry Miller has written, "God is not a being of whims and caprices, He is not less powerful at one moment than another; therefore in a certain sense any event is just as significant as any other."[5] This facet of the Calvinist outlook came close to the view of the Lutheran Ranke in the nineteenth century that "every epoch is immediate to God."[6]

The idea of "providential history" supposed that all secular communities were finite and problematic; all flourished and all decayed; all had a beginning and an end. For Christians this idea had its locus classicus in Augustine's great attempt to solve the problem of the decline and fall of Rome—the problem that more than any other transfixed the serious historical minds of the west for thirteen centuries after the appearance of *The City of God.* This obsession with the classical catastrophe provided a link between the sacred and the profane in the American colonies—between seventeenth-century Americans who read the Christian fathers and eighteenth-century Americans who read Polybius, Plutarch, Cicero, Sallust, Tacitus.

By the time the revolutionaries came to Philadelphia in 1776, the flames of Calvinism were burning low. Hell was dwindling into an epithet. Original sin, not yet abandoned, was, like everything else, secularized. Still, for the fathers of the republic as for the fathers of the Church, the history of Rome, in the words of Jaroslav Pelikan, remained the "textbook to which to turn for instruction about the course of human affairs, the development of freedom and the fate of despotism."[7] And, from different premises, Calvinists and classicists reached similar conclusions about the fragility of human striving.

Antiquity haunted the federal imagination. Robert Frost's poem about "the glory of a next Augustan age. . . . A golden age of poetry and power" would have been more widely understood at George Washington's inauguration than at John Kennedy's. The Founding Fathers had embarked on a singular adventure—the adventure of a *republic*. For landmarks on a perilous voyage they peered across the gulf of centuries to Greece and especially to Rome, which they saw as the noblest achievement of free men aspiring to govern themselves. "The Roman republic," Alexander Hamilton wrote in *The Federalist*, "attained to the utmost height of human greatness."[8] In this conviction the first generation of the American republic called the upper chamber of its legislature the Senate, signed its greatest political treatise "Publius," sculpted its heroes in togas, named new communities Rome and Athens, Utica and Ithaca and Syracuse, organized the Society of the Cincinnati, and assigned Latin texts to the young. "One is hagridden," complained Edmund Trowbridge Dana in 1805, ". . . with nothing but the classicks, the classicks, the classicks!" (In consequence of this heretical attitude, Dana was denied his A.B. degree, receiving it posthumously in 1879 as of the class of 1799.)[9]

There was plausibility in the parallel. Alfred North Whitehead later said that the two occasions in history "when the people in power did what needed to be done about as well as you can imagine its being possible" were the age of Augustus and the framing of the American Constitution.[10] There was also warning. For the grandeur that was Rome had come to an inglorious end. Could the United States of America hope to do better?*

*The careful reader will note that some of the Founders' allusions are to Rome as a republic, some to Rome as an empire. They drew no sharp distinction between these phases in Roman history. See, for example, Fisher Ames: "Rome was a republic from its very birth. It is true, for two hundred and forty-four years it was subject to its kings;

II

The Founding Fathers passionately ransacked the classical historians for ways to escape the classical fate. One cannot easily overstate the anxiety that attended this search or the relevance they found in the ancient texts. Thomas Jefferson thought Tacitus "the first writer of the world without a single exception. His book is a compound of history and morality of which we have no other example." "To live without having a Cicero and a Tacitus at hand," said John Quincy Adams, a founding son, "seems to me as if it was a privation of one of my limbs." [11] As Adams's cousin William Smith Shaw put it, "The writings of Tacitus display the weakness of a falling empire and the morals of a degenerate age. . . . They form the subject of deep meditation for all statesmen who wish to raise their country to glory; to continue it in power, or preserve it from ruin." [12] Polybius was almost as crucial — for delineating the cycle of birth, growth, and decay that constituted the destiny of states; and for shadowing forth the mixed constitution with balanced powers that the Founding Fathers seized as remedy. [13]

The classical indoctrination reinforced the Calvinist judgment that life was a ghastly risk and that this was a time of probation for America. For the history of antiquity did not teach the inevitability of progress. It taught the perishability of republics, the transience of glory, the mutability of human affairs. The traditional emphasis on John Locke as the father of us all obscures the darker strain in the thought of the Founders recently recalled by J. G. A. Pocock—the strain of classical republicanism and civic humanism that led from Machiavelli's *Discourses on Livy* through Harrington, the English country party and Montesquieu to the Constitutional Convention. [14] This tradition argued that republics lived and died by virtue—and that in the fullness of time power and luxury inexorably brought corruption and decay. "The Machiavellian moment," according to Pocock, was the moment in which a republic confronted its own mortality.

This apprehension of the mortality of republics pervaded Philadelphia in 1787. Not only was man vulnerable through his propensity to sin, but republics were vulnerable through their propensity to corruption. History showed that, in the unceasing contest between corruption and virtue, corruption had always—up at least to 1776— triumphed. "It is not at all easy to bring home to the men of the

---

but the spirit of liberty was never more lofty at any period of its long troubled life than when Rome was governed by kings. They were, in war, generals; in peace, only magistrates. For seven hundred years Rome remained a republic." Seth Ames, ed., *The Works of Fisher Ames* (Boston, 1854), II, 332–333.

present day," wrote Sir Henry Maine in 1885, "how low the credit of republics had sunk before the establishment of the United States." The authors of *The Federalist* were "deeply troubled by the ill success and ill repute of the only form of government which was possible for them."[15]

The Founding Fathers had an intense conviction of the improbability of their undertaking. Such assets as they possessed came in their view from geographic and demographic advantage, not from divine intercession. Benjamin Franklin ascribed the inevitability of American independence to such mundane factors as population increase and vacant lands, not to providential design.[16] But even these assets could not be counted on to prevail against human nature. "The tendency of things will be to depart from the republican standard," Hamilton told the New York ratifying convention. "This is the real disposition of human nature." Nor did history hold out greater hope. "Every republic at all times," Hamilton said (always the classical analogy), "has its Catilines and its Caesars. . . . If we have an embryo-Caesar in the United States, 'tis Burr."[17] Jefferson and John Adams no doubt thought it was Hamilton.

If Hamilton be discounted as a temperamental pessimist or a disaffected adventurer, his great adversaries were not always more sanguine about the republic's future. "Commerce, luxury, and avarice have destroyed every republican government," Adams wrote Benjamin Rush in 1808. "We mortals cannot work miracles; we struggle in vain against the constitution and course of nature."[18] "I tremble for my country," Jefferson had said in the 1780s, "when I reflect that God is just."[19] Though he was trembling at this point—rightly and presciently—over the problem of slavery, he also trembled chronically in the nineties over the unlikely prospect of "monarchy." In 1798 he saw the Alien and Sedition Acts as tending to drive the states "into revolution and blood, and [to] furnish new calumnies against Republican government, and new pretexts for those who wish it to be believed, that man cannot be governed but by a rod of iron."[20] As President, Jefferson trembled himself into panic over the murky dreams of Aaron Burr, that embryo forever struggling to become Caesar. From the next generation William Wirt asked in 1809, "Can any man who looks upon the state of public virtue in this country . . . believe that this confederated republic is to last forever?"[21]

III

This pervasive self-doubt, this urgent sense of the precariousness of the national existence, was nourished by European assessments of the American prospect. For influential Europeans regarded the new world, not as an idyll of Lockean felicity—"in the beginning, all the world was America"[22]—but as a scene of disgusting degeneracy.

In the middle of the eighteenth century the famous Georges Buffon lent scientific weight to the proposition that life in the western hemisphere was consigned to biological inferiority. American animals, he wrote, were smaller and weaker; European animals shrank when transported across the Atlantic except, Buffon specified, for the fortunate pig. As for the natives of the fallen continent, they too were small and weak, passive and backward. Soon Abbé de Pauw converted Buffon's pseudoscience into derisive polemic. Horace Walpole drew the inevitable conclusion: "Buffon says, that European animals degenerate across the Atlantic; perhaps its migrating inhabitants may be in the same predicament."[23] As William Robertson, the Historiographer Royal for Scotland, rendered it in his widely read *History of America,* published the year after the Declaration of Independence, "The same qualities in the climate of America which stunted the growth . . . of its native animals proved pernicious to such as have migrated into it voluntarily."[24] In Britain Oliver Goldsmith portrayed America as a gray and gloomy land where no dogs barked and no birds sang.

No one made this case more irritatingly than Abbé Raynal in France. Buffon, Jefferson observed, had never quite said that Europeans degenerated in America: "He goes indeed within one step of it, but he stops there. The Abbé Raynal alone has taken that step."[25] Raynal's popular *Philosophical and Political History of the Settlements and of the Commerce of Europeans in the Two Indies,* first published in 1770 and much reprinted thereafter, explained how European innocence was threatened by American depravity. America, Raynal wrote, "poured all the sources of corruption on Europe." The search for American riches brutalized the European intruder. The climate and soil of America caused the European species, human as well as animal, to deteriorate. "The men have less strength and less courage . . . and are but little susceptible of the lively and powerful sentiment of love"—a comment that perhaps revealed Raynal as in the end more a Frenchman than an abbé. "Let me stop here," Raynal said in summation,

and consider ourselves as existing at the time when America and India were unknown. Let me suppose that I address myself to the most cruel of Europeans in the following terms. There exist regions which will furnish thee with rich metals, agreeable clothing, and delicious food. But read this history, and behold at what price the discovery is promised to thee. Does thou wish or not that it should be made? Is it to be imagined that there exists a being infernal enough to answer this question in the affirmative! *Let it be remembered, that there will not be a single instant in futurity, when my question will not have the same force.* [Emphasis added.]

After the Declaration of Independence, Raynal added insult to injury. He was passing through Lyons on a journey from Paris to Geneva. The local academy, apprised of his presence, made him a member. In return, Raynal established a prize of 1200 francs to be awarded by the Academy of Lyons for the best essay on the arresting topic: "Was the discovery of America a blessing or a curse to mankind? If it was a blessing, by what means are we to conserve and enhance its benefits? If it was a curse, by what means are we to repair the damage?"[26]

The Founding Fathers were predictably sensitive to the proposition that America was a mistake. Franklin, who thought Raynal an "ill-informed and evil-minded Writer," once had to endure at his own dinner table in Paris a monologue by the diminutive abbé on the inferiority of the Americans. "Let us try this question by the fact before us," said Franklin, calling on his guests to stand up and measure themselves back to back. "There was not one American present," wrote Jefferson, who was also there, "who could not have tost out of the Windows any one or two of the rest of the Company."[27] Jefferson himself devoted long passages in his *Notes on Virginia* to the refutation of Buffon on animals and of Raynal on human beings. Europeans "admired as profound philosophers," Hamilton wrote scornfully in *The Federalist,* "have gravely asserted that all animals, and with them the human species, degenerate in America—that even dogs cease to bark after having breathed a while in our atmosphere."[28] Tom Paine joined the fight; and John Adams noted in his *Defence of the Constitutions of the United States* his delight in the way Paine had "exposed the mistakes of Raynal, and Jefferson those of Buffon, so unphilosophically borrowed from the despicable dreams of De Pau [*sic*]."[29]

Though the Founders were vigorous in rebuttal, the nature of the attack could hardly have increased their confidence in the prospects of their adventure. The European doubt, along with the Calvinist judgment and the Machiavellian moment, made them acutely aware of the chanciness of an extraordinary enterprise. The fate of the Greek city-states and the fall of the Roman Empire cast somber light on the future of the American republic. The Founders had no illusions about the inviolability of America to history, supposing all states, including the American, immediate to history, as a consistent Calvinist should have supposed all states immediate to God. "Have we not already seen enough," wrote Hamilton, "of the fallacy and extrava-

gance of those idle theories which have amused us with promises of
an exemption from the imperfections, weaknesses, and evils incident
to society in every shape? Is it not time to awake from the deceitful
dream of a golden age, and to adopt as a practical maxim for the
direction of our political conduct that we, as well as the other inhabitants of the globe, are yet remote from the happy empire of perfect
wisdom and perfect virtue?"[30]

IV

We carelessly apply the phrase "end of innocence" to one or another
stage of American history. This is an amiable flourish when not a
pernicious delusion. How many times can a nation lose its innocence?
No people reared on Calvin and Tacitus could ever have been very
innocent. No nation founded on invasion, conquest and slaughter
was innocent. No people who systematically enslaved black men and
killed red men were innocent. No state established by revolution and
thereafter rent by civil war was innocent. The Constitution did not
assume the innocence of man, not even of those men blessed enough
to be Americans. It was, James Bryce well said, "the work of men who
believed in original sin and were resolved to leave open for trans-
gressors no door which they could possibly shut."[31] Nor did the
Founding Fathers see themselves as a band of saints anointed by
Providence. They were brave and imperturbable realists committed,
in defiance of history and theology, to a monumental gamble.

This is why Hamilton, in the third sentence of the 1st *Federalist*,
formulated the issue as he did. The American people, he wrote, had
the opportunity "by their conduct and example, to decide the important question, whether societies of men are really capable or not of
establishing good government from reflection and choice, or whether
they are forever destined to depend for their political constitutions
on accident and force." So Washington defined the American opportunity in his first inaugural address: "The preservation of the sacred
fire of liberty and the destiny of the republican model of government
are justly considered, perhaps, as *deeply*, as *finally*, staked on the experiment intrusted to the hands of the American people." The first
generation of independence, said Woodrow Wilson, "looked upon
the new federal organization as an experiment, and thought it likely
it might not last."[32]

The Founding Fathers saw the American republic not as a divine
consecration but as the test against history of a hypothesis. Yet the
very faith in experiment implied the rejection of the classical republican dogma that time guaranteed decay. "The men who made the

Constitution," wrote Henry Adams, "intended to make by its means an issue with antiquity."[33] They dismissed republican forebodings as mere speculation. In his Farewell Address, Washington countered the Machiavellian moment by arguing that, when there was a doubt, "Let experience solve it. To listen to speculation in such a case is criminal. . . . It is well worth a full and fair experiment." In the last *Federalist* paper, Hamilton quoted Hume about the difficulty of erecting a large state on general laws: "The judgments of many must unite in the work; experience must guide their labor; time must . . . correct the mistakes which they *inevitably* fall into in their first trials and experiments." In the words of John P. Diggins, "Whereas the Machiavellian thesis assumes that virtue can only reign over time and that time also threatens virtue, the Federalist thesis assumes that time was basically redemptive rather than destructive. . . . The Machiavellian framework presupposes the futility of time, the Madisonian its fertility."[34]

So experiment was the way of escape from classical republican doom. Washington's successors, with mingled anxiety and hope, issued periodic reports on the experiment's fortunes. In his last message to Congress, James Madison permitted himself "the proud reflection that the American people have reached in safety and success their fortieth year as an independent nation." This, the Presidents believed, had more than local significance. "Our institutions," said James Monroe in his last message, "form an important epoch in the history of the civilized world. On their preservation and in their utmost purity everything will depend." Washington, said Andrew Jackson in his own Farewell Address, regarded the Constitution "as an experiment" and "was prepared to lay down his life, if necessary, to secure it a full and a fair trial. The trial has been made. It has succeeded beyond the proudest hopes of those who framed it." Still Jackson discerned threats to the experiment—in the "moneyed power" and even more in the dissolution of the union itself, where chaos, he supposed, might lead the people "to submit to the absolute dominion of any military adventurer and to surrender their liberty for the sake of repose."[35]

Nevertheless, confidence—or at least the simulation of confidence — grew. "The present year," Martin Van Buren said in 1838, "closes the first half century of our Federal institutions. . . . It was reserved for the American Union to test the advantages of a government entirely dependent on the continual exercise of the popular will." "After an existence of near three-fourths of a century as a free and independent Republic," said James Polk in the next decade, "the problem no longer remains to be solved whether man is capable of self-government. The success of our admirable system is a conclusive refutation of the theories of those in other countries who maintain that a 'favored few' are born to rule and that the mass of mankind must be governed by force." The Mexican War, Polk soon added, "evinces beyond any doubt that a popular representative government is equal to any emergency." Sixty years after the Constitution, Zachary Taylor pronounced the United States of America "the most stable and permanent Government on earth."[36]

How is one to account for this rising optimism? It was partly a tribute, reasonable enough, to survival. It was partly the spread-eagleism and vainglory congenial to a youthful nationalism. It was no doubt also in part admonitory exhortation—let us not throw away what we have so precariously achieved. For the Presidents of the middle period must have known in their bones that the American experiment was confronting its fiercest internal trial. No one understood the risks more profoundly than the young man who spoke in 1838 on "The Perpetuation of our Political Institutions" before the Young Men's Lyceum of Springfield, Illinois. Over most of the first half century, Abraham Lincoln said, America had been felt "to be an undecided experiment; now, it is understood to be a successful one." But success contained its own perils; "with the catching, end the pleasures of the chase." As the memory of the Revolution receded, the pillars of the temple of liberty were crumbling away. "That temple must fall, unless we . . . supply their places with other pillars, hewn from the solid quarry of sober reason."

The conviction of the incertitude of life informed Lincoln's Presidency—and explained its greatness. His first message to Congress asked whether all republics had an "inherent and fatal weakness." At the Gettysburg cemetery he described the great civil war as "testing" whether any nation conceived in liberty and dedicated to the proposition that men are created equal "can long endure."[37]

V

This was a dominant theme of the early republic—the idea of America as an experiment, undertaken in defiance of history, fraught with risk, problematic in outcome. But a counter-tradition was also emerging—and, as the mounting presidential optimism suggests, with accumulating momentum. The counter-tradition too had roots in the Calvinist ethos.

Historic Christianity embraced two divergent thoughts: that all people were immediate to God; and that some were more immediate than others. At first, Calvin had written in the *Institutes*, God "chose the Jews as his very own flock"; the "covenant of salvation . . . belonged only to the Jews until the wall was torn down."[38] Then, with what Jonathan Edwards called "the abolishing of the *Jewish dispensation*," the wall was "broken down to make way for the more extensive success of the gospel."[39] The chosen people thereafter were the elect as against the reprobate. In time the idea of saints identifiable within history disappeared into the transcendency of the posthistorical City of God.

So Augustine set alongside "providential history"—the rise and decline of secular communities within history—the idea of "redemptive history"—the journey of the elect to salvation beyond history. The age that sent the Calvinists to New England also saw a revival of the primitive millennialism of the first century. The New Englanders felt they had been called from hearth and home to endure unimaginable rigor and ordeal in a dangerous land; so they supposed someone of importance had called them, and for important reasons. Their very tribulations seemed proof of a role in redemptive history. "God hath covenanted with his people," said Increase Mather, "that sanctified afflictions shall be their portion. . . . The usual method of divine Providence [is] by the greatest Miseries to prepare for the greatest Mercies. . . . *Without doubt, the Lord Jesus hath a peculiar respect unto this place, and for this people.*"[40]

It was not only that they were, in John Winthrop's words, as a City upon a Hill, with the eyes of all people upon them. It was that they had been despatched to New England, as Edward Johnson said, by a wonder-working Providence because "this is the place where the Lord will create a new Heaven, and a new Earth." The "Lord Christ" intended "to make his New England Souldiers the very wonder of this Age."[41] The Reverend Arthur Dimmesdale's last sermon, Nathaniel Hawthorne told us, dealt with "the relation between the Deity and the communities of mankind, with a special reference to the New England which they were here planting in the wilderness." But, where the Jewish prophets had foreseen ruin for their country, Dimmesdale's mission was "to foretell a high and glorious destiny for the newly gathered people of the Lord."[42] The great Edwards concluded that "the Latter-Day Glory is probably to begin in America."[43]

This geopolitical specification of the millennium—this identification of the New Jerusalem with a particular place and people—was rare, even in a time of millennial fervor. "What in England, Holland, Germany and Geneva," Sacvan Bercovitch writes, "was an *a priori* antithesis [between the saints and the state] became in America the twin pillars of a unique federal eschatology." For the old world was steeped in iniquity, one more shameful episode in the long shame of providential history. The fact that God had withheld America so long—until the Reformation purified the church, until the invention of printing spread Scripture among the people—argued that He had been saving the new land for some ultimate manifestation of His grace. God, said Winthrop, having "smitten all the other Churches before our eyes," had reserved America for those whom He meant *"to save out of his generall callamitie,"* as he had once sent the ark to save Noah. The new land was certainly a part, perhaps the climax, of redemptive history; America was divine prophecy fulfilled.[44]

The covenant of salvation, it seemed, had passed from the Jews to the American colonists. Like original sin, this proposition underwent secularization in the eighteenth century. Before the Revolution, John Adams, reading his "Dissertation on the Canon and Feudal Law" to a club of Boston lawyers, indulged in a well-known rhetorical flight: "I always consider the settlement of America with reverence, as the opening of a grand scene and design in Providence for the illumination of the ignorant and the emancipation of the slavish part of mankind all over the earth." On reflection Adams repented this sentiment and deleted it before he published the paper. By the 1780s he concluded that there was "no special providence for Americans, and their nature is the same with that of others." But John Quincy Adams seized on the thought his father had abandoned: "Who does not now see that the accomplishment of this great object is already placed beyond all possibility of doubt?" And J. Q. Adams's son Charles Francis Adams called the passage his grandfather cut "the most deserving of any to be remembered."[45] So within a single family the secular idea of experiment began to yield to the mystical idea of an American national destiny.

VI

Independence gave new status to the theory of America as an "elect nation" (Bercovitch) or a "redeemer nation" (E. L. Tuveson),[46] entrusted by the Almighty with the charge of carrying its light to the unregenerate world. The Reverend Timothy Dwight, Jonathan Edwards's grandson, called Americans "this chosen race."[47] "God's mercies to New England," wrote Harriet Beecher Stowe, daughter of one minister and wife of another, foreshadowed "the glorious future of the United States . . . commissioned to bear the light of liberty and religion through all the earth and to bring in the great millennial day, when wars should cease and the whole world, released from the thralldom of evil, should rejoice in the light of the Lord."[48]

Patriotic fervor bore far beyond the evangelical community the idea of Americans as chosen people charged with a divine mission. Jefferson thought the Great Seal of the United States should portray the children of Israel led by a pillar of light.[49] "Here Paradise anew shall flourish," wrote Philip Freneau in an early statement of the myth of American innocence,

> *by no second Adam lost*
> *No dangerous tree or deathful fruit shall grow,*
> *No tempting servant to allure the soul*
> *From native innocence. . . .*[50]

"We Americans," wrote the youthful Herman Melville, "are the peculiar, chosen people — the Israel of our time; we bear the ark of the liberties of the world. . . . God has predestinated, mankind expects, great things from our race; and great things we feel in our souls. The rest of the nations must soon be in our rear. . . . Long enough have we been sceptics with regard to ourselves, and doubted whether, indeed, the political Messiah had come. But he has come in *us*."[51]

The belief that Americans were a chosen people did not imply a sure and tranquil journey to salvation. As the Bible made amply clear, chosen people underwent the harshest trials and assumed the most grievous burdens. The rival propositions — America as experiment, America as destiny — thus shared a belief in the process of testing. But one tested works, the other faith. So Lincoln and Mrs. Stowe agreed from different standpoints in seeing the Civil War as the climactic trial. The northern victory, however, strengthened the conviction of providential appointment. "Now that God has smitten slavery unto death," Mrs. Stowe's brother Edward wrote in 1865, "he has opened the way for the redemption and sanctification of our whole social system."[52]

The Kingdom of God was deemed both imminent in time and immanent in America. It was a short step from salvation at home to the salvation of the world. The Hebrews, the Greeks, and the Romans, wrote the Reverend Josiah Strong, had separately developed the spiritual, intellectual, and physical qualities of man. "Now for the first time in the history of mankind the three great strands pass through the fingers of one predominant race to be braided into a single supreme civilization in the new era, the perfection of which will be the Kingdom fully come. . . . All unite in the one Anglo-Saxon race, indicating that this race is pre-eminently fitted, and therefore chosen of God, to prepare the way for the full coming of His kingdom in the earth."[53] It was another short step from this to what the Reverend Alexander Blackburn, who had been wounded at Chickamauga, called in 1898 "the imperialism of righteousness";[54] and from Blackburn to the messianic demagoguery of Albert J. Beveridge, "God has not been preparing the English-speaking and Teutonic peoples for a thousand years for nothing but vain and idle self-contemplation. . . . And of all our race He has marked the American people as His chosen nation to finally lead in the regeneration of the world."[55]

So the impression developed that in the United States of America the Almighty had contrived a nation unique in its virtue and magnanimity, exempt from the motives that governed all other states. "America is the only idealistic nation in the world," Woodrow Wilson said on his pilgrimage to the West in 1919. "The heart of this people is pure. The heart of this people is true. . . . It is the great idealistic force of history. . . . I, for one, believe more profoundly than in anything else human in the destiny of the United States. I believe that she has a spiritual energy in her which no other nation can contribute to the liberation of mankind. . . . [In the great war] America had the infinite privilege of fulfilling her destiny and saving the world."[56]

In another forty years the theory of America as the savior of the world received the lordly imprimatur of John Foster Dulles, another Presbyterian elder, and from there the country roared on to the horrors of Vietnam. "History and our own achievements," President Johnson proclaimed in 1965, "have thrust upon us the principal responsibility for protection of freedom on earth."[57] So the hallucination brought the republic from the original idea of America as exemplary experiment to the recent idea of America as mankind's designated judge, jury and executioner. Nor did Vietnam cure the infatuation. "I have always believed," President Reagan said in 1982, "that this anointed land was set apart in an uncommon way, that a divine plan placed this great continent here between the oceans to be found by people from every corner of the earth who had a special love of faith and freedom."[58]

VII

Why did the conviction of the corruptibility of men and the vulnerability of states—and the consequent idea of America as experiment — give way to the delusion of a sacred mission and a sanctified destiny? The original conviction was rooted in realistic conceptions of history and of human nature—conceptions that waned as the republic prospered. The intense historical-mindedness of the Founding Fathers did not endure. Though the first generation came to Philadelphia loaded down with historical examples and memories, its function was precisely to liberate its progeny from history. Once the

Founders had done their work, history commenced on a new foundation and in American terms. "We have it in our power," Tom Paine said in *Common Sense*, "to begin the world all over again." Emerson defined himself as the endless seeker, with no Past at his back. "The Past," Melville said in *White-Jacket*, "is dead, and has no resurrection; but the Future is endowed with such a life, that it lives to us even in anticipation."[59]

The process of narcissistic withdrawal from history, much commented on by foreign travelers, was sustained by the simultaneous withdrawal, after 1815, from the power embroilments of the old world. The new nation was largely populated by people torn from, fleeing from, or in revolt against their own histories. This also helped take the republic out of the movement and motive of secular history. "Probably no other civilised nation," said the *Democratic Review* in 1842, "has . . . so completely thrown off its allegiance to the past as the American."[60]

But the nineteenth century was steeped in history compared to the twentieth. Today, for all the preservation of landmarks and the show biz of bicentennials, we have become, so far as interest and knowledge are concerned, an essentially historyless people. Businessmen agree with the elder Henry Ford that history is bunk. The young no longer study history. Academics turn their backs on history in the enthusiasm for the ahistorical behavioral "sciences." As the American historical consciousness has thinned out, the messianic hope has flowed into the vacuum. And, as Christianity turned liberal, shucking off such cardinal doctrines as original sin, one more impediment was removed to belief in national virtue and perfectibility. Experiment gave ground to destiny as the premise of national life.

All this, of course, was both provoked and fortified by latter-day exertions of national power. All nations succumb to fantasies of innate superiority. When they act on these fantasies, as the Spanish did in the sixteenth century, the French in the seventeenth, the English in the eighteenth, the Germans and Japanese and Russians and Americans in the twentieth, they tend to become international menaces. The American hallucination took root during the long holiday from the world of reality. When America reentered that world, overwhelming power confirmed the hallucination.

So the theory of the elect nation, the redeemer nation, almost became the official creed. Yet, while the counter-tradition prospered, the tradition did not quite expire. Some continued to regard the idea of the happy empire of perfect wisdom and perfect virtue as the deceitful dream of a golden age, wondering perhaps why the Almighty should have singled out the Americans. "The Almighty," Lincoln insisted at his second inaugural, "has His own purposes." He clearly knew what he was saying, because he wrote soon thereafter to a fellow ironist, Thurlow Weed: "Men are not flattered by being shown that there has been a difference of purpose between the Almighty and them. To deny it, however, . . . is to deny that there is a God governing the world."[61]

After the war, Walt Whitman, once the joyous poet of democratic faith, perceived a dark and threatening future. The experiment was in jeopardy. These States had become a "battle, advancing, retreating, between democracy's convictions, aspirations, and the people's crudeness, vice, caprices." America, Whitman apprehended, might well "prove the most tremendous failure of time."[62] Emerson too lost his early confidence in the experiment. "'Tis a wild democracy," he said in his last public address; "the riot of mediocrities and dishonesties and fudges."[63]

There is prosopographical felicity in the fact that a fourth generation of Adamses raised the keenest doubts whether Providence in settling America had after all opened a grand design to emancipate mankind. For Henry Adams, the failure of Jefferson's embargo marked the end of innocence. "America began slowly to struggle, under the consciousness of pain," he wrote, "toward a conviction that she must bear the common burdens of humanity, and fight with the weapons of other races in the same bloody arena; that she could not much longer delude herself with hopes of evading laws of Nature and instincts of life."[64] He thus reaffirmed a century later his great-grandfather's conclusion that there was no special providence for Americans.

His fellow countrymen resisted the conclusion. "You Americans believe yourselves to be exempted from the operation of general laws," the cynical Baron Jacobi growled in Adams's *Democracy*.[65] But Henry's brother Brooks, juggling equations of energy, centralization and social velocity, doubted that any nation was exempt from the law of civilization and decay. Henry, seizing his brother's clue, tried to pursue thought "to the limit of its possibilities," a point he predicted would arrive in the year 1921[66]—the year, Professor James A. Field, Jr., reminds me, that gave the republic Warren G. Harding. Henry Adams ended a reverse millennialist, convinced that science and technology were rushing the planet toward an apocalypse unredeemed by a Day of Judgment.

"At the rate of increase of speed and momentum, as calculated on the last fifty years," he wrote Brooks in 1901, "the present society

must break its damn neck in a definite, but remote, time, not exceed-
ing fifty years more." It was a queer sensation, he felt—"this secret
belief that one stands on the brink of the world's greatest catastrophe.
For it means the fall of Western Europe, as it fell in the fourth century."[67] He began to see himself as Augustine—a failed Augustine,
of course ("I aspire to be bound up with St. Augustine. . . . My idea
of what it should be proved beyond my powers. Only St. Augustine
ever realised it"). Augustine had the consolation of the City of God.
The second law of thermodynamics left room only for the City of
Chaos. The United States, like everything else, was finished. In the
end Adams too abandoned experiment for destiny; but destiny for
him was not only manifest but malign. "No one anywhere," he wrote
a few weeks before the outbreak of the First World War, ". . . expects
a future. The life is that of the fourth century, without St. Augustine."[68]

The forever sane William James retained the experimental faith.
He abhorred the fatalisms and absolutes implied by "the idol of a
national destiny . . . which for some inscrutable reason it has become
infamous to disbelieve in or refuse." We are instructed, James said,
"to be missionaries of civilization. . . . We must sow our ideals, plant
our order, impose our God. The individual lives are nothing. Our
duty and our destiny call, and civilization must go on. Could there be
a more damning indictment of that whole bloated idol termed 'modern civilization'?" The apotheosis of America had come about too fast
"for the older American nature not to feel the shock." One cannot
know for sure what James meant by "the older American nature";
but he plainly rejected the supposition that American motives were,
by definition, pure, and that the United States enjoyed a divine immunity to temptation and corruption. "Angelic impulses and predatory lusts," he precisely wrote, "divide our heart exactly as they divide
the heart of other countries."[69]

VIII

So the warfare between realism and messianism, between experiment
and destiny, continued to our own day. No recent critic of the
counter-tradition was more effective than Reinhold Niebuhr with his
devastating Christian polemic against the whole idea of "salvation
through history."[70] The United States embodied the illusions of liberal culture, Niebuhr supposed, because "we had a religious version
of our national destiny which interpreted the meaning of our nation-
hood as God's effort to make a new beginning in the history of mankind." The Puritans had gradually shifted from emphasis on the di-

vine favor shown to the nation to emphasis on the virtue the nation allegedly acquired through divine favor. Niebuhr defined messianism as "a corrupt expression of man's search for the ultimate within the vicissitudes and hazards of time" and warned against the "deep layer of Messianic consciousness in the mind of America." The myth of innocence was fatal to wisdom and prudence. "Nations, as individuals, who are completely innocent in their own esteem, are insufferable in their human contacts." Let the righteous nation understand the divine judgment that waits on human pretension—and never forget "the depth of evil to which individuals and communities may sink, particularly when they try to play the role of God in history."[71] So, in an ultimate irony of American history, Niebuhr used religion to refute the religious version of the national destiny.

Men were corruptible, states perishable: like all other nations, America was forever on probation-time. If some political leaders were messianists, others saw an experiment conducted without divine guarantee by mortals of limited wisdom and power. The second Roosevelt regarded life as uncertain and the national destiny at risk. The republic still demanded "bold, persistent experimentation. It is common sense to take a method and try it: If it fails, admit it frankly and try another. But above all, try something."[72] John F. Kennedy combined a premonition of the Machiavellian moment with an ancestral religion that understood the limits of human striving. "Before my term has ended," he said in his first annual message, "we shall have to test anew whether a nation organized and governed such as ours can endure. The outcome is by no means certain."[73]

This evoked the mood of the Founding Fathers. But the belief in national righteousness and providential destiny remains strong.* One cannot but feel that this belief has encouraged American excesses in the world and that the republic has lost much by forgetting what James called "the older American nature." For messianism is an illusion. No nation is sacred and unique, the United States or any other. All nations are immediate to God. America, like every country, has interests real and fictitious, concerns generous and selfish, mo-

---

*Not perhaps so strong, though, as people sometimes think—at least to judge by a recent survey of eighty members of the Ninety-sixth Congress (1979–81). Presented with the statement "God has blessed America more than other nations," 38 percent of the respondents pronounced the statement false and only 32 percent thought it true. Asked whether God had chosen America to be "a light to the world," 49 percent said "not true" and only 7 percent, "true." Asked how close America was to meeting God's standards, 7 percent said very close and 57 percent said "very far from fulfilling God's expectations." P. L. Benson and D. L. Williams, *Religion on Capitol Hill: Myths and Realities* (San Francisco, 1982), 95–97.

tives honorable and squalid. Providence has not set Americans apart from lesser breeds. We too are part of history's seamless web.

Yet we retain one signal advantage over most nations—an entirely secular advantage, conferred upon us by those quite astonishing Founding Fathers. For they bequeathed us standards by which to set our course and judge our performance—and, since they were exceptional men, the standards have not been rendered obsolescent even by the second law of thermodynamics. The Declaration of Independence and the Constitution establish goals, imply commitments, and measure failures. The men who signed the Declaration, said Lincoln, "meant to set up a standard maxim for a free society which should be familiar to all, and revered by all; constantly looked to, constantly labored for, and even though not perfectly attained, constantly approximated, and thereby constantly spreading and deepening its influence and augmenting the happiness and value of life to all people of all colors everywhere."[74] Where the Declaration set forth ends, the Constitution prescribed means. The values embodied in these remarkable documents constitute what Gunnar Myrdal has called the "American Creed": "The schools teach them, the churches preach them. The courts pronounce their judicial decisions in their terms." The conflict between creed and reality has been a powerful motive in the quest for justice. "America," said Myrdal, "is continuously struggling for its soul."[75]

Charles Dickens was no admirer of the United States, but even this skeptic was impressed by the power America might draw from the exercise of living up to its own best standards. Mark Tapley, Martin Chuzzlewit's servant, wondered on the voyage back to Britain how, if he were an artist, he would paint the American eagle. His master replied:

"Paint it as like an Eagle as you could, I suppose."
"No," said Mark. "That wouldn't do for me, sir. I should want to draw it like a Bat, for its short-sightedness; like a Bantam, for its bragging; like a Magpie, for its honesty; like a Peacock, for its vanity; like an Ostrich, for its putting its head in the mud, and thinking nobody sees it —"
"And like a Phoenix, for its power of springing from the ashes of its faults and vices, and soaring up anew into the sky!" said Martin. "Well, Mark. Let us hope so."[76]

Let us all hope so. For Americans can take pride in their nation, not as they claim a commission from God and a sacred destiny, but as they fulfill their deepest values in an enigmatic world. America remains an experiment. Only hard work at the experiment will achieve the destiny. The outcome is by no means certain. The possibility lingers that the republic will end like Gatsby in F. Scott Fitzgerald's emblematic fable—Gatsby, who had come so long a way and whose "dream must have seemed so close that he could hardly fail to grasp it. He did not know that it was already behind him, somewhere back in that vast obscurity beyond the city, where the dark fields of the republic rolled on under the night.

"Gatsby believed in the green light, the orgastic future that year by year recedes before us. It eluded us then, but that's no matter—tomorrow we will run faster, stretch out our arms farther. . . . And one fine morning —

"So we beat on, boats against the current, borne back ceaselessly into the past."[77]

TWO

The Cycles of American Politics

———————◆•◆———————

WISE MEN have remarked on patterns of alternation, of ebb and of flow, in human history. "The two parties which divide the state, the party of Conservatism and that of Innovation," wrote Emerson in 1841, "are very old, and have disputed the possession of the world ever since it was made. . . . Now one, now the other gets the day, and still the fight renews itself as if for the first time, under new names and hot personalities." Innovation presses ever forward; Conservatism holds ever back. We are reformers spring and summer, in autumn and winter we stand by the old; reformers in the morning, conservers at night. "Innovation is the salient energy; Conservatism the pause on the last movement."[1]

I

Half a century later, Henry Adams applied a more precise version of the cyclical thesis to the first years of the American republic. "A period of about twelve years," he wrote, "measured the beat of the pendulum. After the Declaration of Independence, twelve years had been needed to create an efficient Constitution; another twelve years of energy brought a reaction against the government then created; a third period of twelve years was ending in a sweep toward still greater energy; and already a child could calculate the result of a few more such returns."[2]

Adams's cycle described alternating currents in the domestic affairs of the new nation, and his pendulum swung back and forth between the centralization and diffusion of national energy. The broad rhythms he discerned in the first thirty-six years of American independence continue to be discernible in the long years since. I inherit an alternative interpretation of this cyclical phenomenon from my father, who defined the swing as between conservatism and liberalism, between periods of concern for the rights of the few and periods of concern for the wrongs of the many.[3]

In a 1949 essay, my father identified eleven such alternations. His first three periods correspond more or less to the three beats of Henry Adams's pendulum. There follow the period of Jeffersonian retreat after the War of 1812; the democratizing age of Jackson, 1829–1841; increasing domination of the national government by slaveholders, 1841–1861; abolition of slavery, 1861–1869; conservative rule, 1869–1901; the Progressive era, 1901–1919; the Republican restoration, 1919–1931; the New Deal era, 1931–1947.

In six of the periods the object was to increase democracy; in five, to contain it. The average length of the eleven periods was sixteen and a half years. The major deviation came in the years 1861–1901, when an eight-year burst of convulsive change was followed by thirty-two years of regression and reaction. This deviation took place, my father thought, because the Civil War and Reconstruction speeded the tempo and widened the sweep of reform, achieving in a short time deep and exhausting changes that would otherwise have taken far longer; "the prolongation of the countermovement in the next period was a form of compensation to restore the rhythm."[4]

My father, like Adams, conceived the political cycle in domestic terms. He diverged from Adams in the characterization of the phases and (slightly) in periodicity. He also rejected the image of the pendulum because it implied oscillation between two fixed points. The cycle, he pointed out, did not return the nation to the status quo ante. Liberal reforms usually survived after conservatives regained power. The appropriate image, my father said, was the spiral, in which the alternation proceeded at successively higher levels and allowed for the cumulation of change.[5]

The Schlesinger formulation, when first set forth in a 1924 lecture, included the prediction that Coolidge-style conservatism would last till about 1932 — a thought that elicited an anguished cry of "My God!" from a member of the audience. (The crier, David K. Niles, served in the next liberal period as a special assistant to Roosevelt and Truman.) The first published version — "Tides of American Politics," in the *Yale Review* of December 1939 — predicted that the then prevailing liberal mood would run its course in about 1947. When my father brought the argument up to date in *Paths to the Present* in 1949, he wrote, "The recession from liberalism which began in 1947 [with the arrival of what Truman called the "do-nothing, good-for-nothing" Eightieth Congress] was due to end in 1962, with a possible margin of a year or two in either direction. On this basis the next conservative epoch will commence around 1978."[6]

II

Predictive success creates a presumption in favor of a hypothesis. But, as the legatee, I found myself troubled by the question of characterizing the cyclical alternations.

Emerson's formulation—conservatism versus innovation—presents problems. "The castle which conservatism is set to defend," Emerson wrote, "is the actual state of things, good and bad. . . . Conservatism never puts the foot forward; in the hour when it does that, it is not establishment, but reform."[7] Identifying conservatism with the status quo fits Buchanan and Hayes, Coolidge and Eisenhower. But where does it leave Alexander Hamilton, no friend of democracy but the great innovator of his time, or, for that matter, Ronald Reagan, avowedly a conservative but one who disliked the "actual state of things," condemned the establishment and was in his own way a reformer?

As for the Adams formulation—diffusion versus centralization of national energy—this works for the three periods to which he applied it and works for the twentieth century; but it is not quite right for most of the nineteenth century. My father's formulation—conservatism versus liberalism—works all the time in a general way; but the operative terms are subject to too many varying definitions.

The economist Albert O. Hirschman in his book of 1982, *Shifting Involvements,* proposes another cyclical pattern. In an extension of consumption theory to politics, Hirschman argues that western society since the Industrial Revolution has regularly shifted its involvements between the divergent goals of private and public happiness. In the Hirschman cycle, society passes back and forth between times of absorption in private affairs and times of preoccupation with public issues; a periodic alternation, in his words, between "private interest" and "public action."[8]

The 1984 book by the political scientists Herbert McClosky and John Zaller, *The American Ethos,* offers further specification. While McClosky and Zaller do not cast their analysis in cyclical terms, their account of the tension in American society between capitalism and democracy illuminates the cycle. Drawing on public opinion polls as well as on history, they find a continuing struggle between capitalist values—the sanctity of private property, the maximization of profit, the cult of the free market, the survival of the fittest—and democratic values—equality, freedom, social responsibility and the general welfare, ends to be promoted when necessary by public action regulating property and restricting profit. This remains a tension rather than a mortal antagonism. Capitalism and democracy began as allies in the revolution against absolute monarchy and feudal aristocracy, and they continue to share a faith in individual freedom, popular sovereignty, limited government and equality before the law. In America capitalism includes democracy, and democracy includes capitalism. Yet the two creeds point in different directions. Survey research is "unequivocal," McClosky and Zaller write, in showing that, while neither side wants to abolish the other, those most firmly attached to democratic values exhibit least support for capitalism and those most firmly attached to capitalist values exhibit least support for democracy.[9]

The polarity between public action and private interest, democracy and capitalism, still does not solve the problems of the early republic. Where to place Hamilton, who believed that private accumulation must be guided by public purpose? Jefferson, who mistrusted government (except when he headed it) and placed his faith in private interest? But the early republic was a time of transition when public action in the mercantilist mode was the ally of capitalism and private interest in the agrarian mode, the ally of democracy. And the polarity, even if it does not tidily locate Hamilton and Jefferson, does correspond to the conflict that has recently preoccupied American historians between 'republican' and 'liberal' (i.e., free enterprise) traditions in the formation of the nation.

Classical republicans regarded virtue as the lifeblood of free republics and feared the degeneration perennially brought about, as they read history, by self-interest and private gain. No doubt scholars, in the enthusiasm of discovery, have overdone the republican component in American thought.[10] Still republicanism was a strain in the inheritance; and the eighteenth-century dialectic between virtue and commerce, between commonwealth and property, was born again in the later dialectic between democracy and capitalism, between public purpose and private interest.

Does this dialectic correspond in addition to the historic argument over the theory of America—the divergence between the pragmatic conception of America as a nation of history, one among many, engaged in a risky experiment, and the mystical vision of America as a nation of destiny appointed by the Almighty to save unregenerate humanity? The public-private equation and the experiment-destiny equation overlap rather than coincide. Experimentalists like the two Roosevelts and predestinarians like Wilson were alike devotees of public purpose. Practical men like Eisenhower and ideologues like Reagan were alike devotees of private interest. The two equations interweave in forming the complex fabric of American history.

III

Let us define the cycle then as a continuing shift in national involvement, between public purpose and private interest. But definition is not explanation. Why does the cycle move as it does? What causes these periodic alternations, this ebb and this flow, in national priorities?

If it is a genuine cycle, the explanation must be primarily internal. Each new phase must flow out of the conditions—and contradictions — of the phase before and then itself prepare the way for the next recurrence. A true cycle, in other words, is self-generating. It cannot be determined, short of catastrophe, by external events. War, depressions, inflations, may heighten or complicate moods, but the cycle itself rolls on, self-contained, self-sufficient and autonomous. The independence of the political cycle is confirmed by the absence of correlation with even something so potent in impact as the business cycle. The depression ushered in the New Deal, but the Progressive era began in a time of general prosperity, and two grinding depressions took place in the 1869–1901 period without reversing the ground swell of conservatism.

The roots of this cyclical self-sufficiency doubtless lie deep in the natural life of humanity. There is a cyclical pattern in organic nature — in the tides, in the seasons, in night and day, in the systole and diastole of the human heart. The physiologist Walter B. Cannon half a century ago demonstrated that automatic corrective reactions take place in the human body when a shift from the stable state is threatened and thereafter speculated that a similar "homeostasis" may be at work in the social organism.[11]

There is also a cyclical basis in the very psychology of modernity. With the acceleration in the rate of social change, humans become creatures characterized by inextinguishable discontent. Wishes are boundless and therefore can never be fully satisfied. Adam Smith celebrated "the desire of bettering our condition, a desire which . . . comes with us from the womb, and never leaves us till we go into the grave. In the whole interval which separates those two moments, there is scarce perhaps a single instant in which any man is so perfectly and completely satisfied with his situation, as to be without any wish of alteration or improvement."[12] Hirschman recalls Kant's remark to Karamzin, the Russian historian: "Give a man everything he desires and yet at this very moment he will feel that this *everything* is not *everything*."[13] Disappointment is the universal modern malady.

It is also a basic spring of political change. People can never be fulfilled for long either in the public or in the private sphere. We try one, then the other, and frustration compels a change in course. Moreover, however effective a particular course may be in meeting one set of troubles, it generally falters and fails when new troubles arise. And many troubles are inherently insoluble. As political eras, whether dominated by public purpose or by private interest, run their course, they infallibly generate the desire for something different. It always becomes after a while 'time for a change.'

Each phase breeds its distinctive contradictions. Public action, in its effort to better our condition, piles up a lot of change in rather short order. Reform in the United States tends to come in bursts. The model is the Hundred Days of Franklin Roosevelt. Finally the rush of innovation begins to choke the body politic, which demands time for digestion. As Emerson said, "A good deal of our politics is physiological."[14] Sustained public action, moreover, is emotionally exhausting. A nation's capacity for high-tension political commitment is limited. Nature insists on a respite. People can no longer gird themselves for heroic effort. They yearn to immerse themselves in the privacies of life. Worn out by the constant summons to battle, weary of ceaseless national activity, disillusioned by the results, they seek a new dispensation, an interlude of rest and recuperation.

So public action, passion, idealism and reform recede. Public problems are turned over to the invisible hand of the market. "Everything was slack-water," Henry Adams said of the 1890s.[15] The pursuit of private interest is seen as the means of social salvation. These are times of 'privatization' (barbarous but useful word), of materialism, hedonism, and the overriding quest for personal gratification. Class and interest politics subside; cultural politics—ethnicity, religion, social status, morality—come to the fore. These are also often times of consolidation, in which innovations of the previous period are absorbed and legitimized.

And they are times of preparation. Epochs of private interest breed contradictions too. Such periods are characterized by undercurrents of dissatisfaction, criticism, ferment, protest. Segments of the population fall behind in the acquisitive race. Intellectuals are estranged. Problems neglected become acute, threaten to become unmanageable and demand remedy. People grow bored with selfish motives and vistas, weary of materialism as the ultimate goal. The vacation from public responsibility replenishes the national energies and recharges the national batteries. People begin to seek meaning in life beyond themselves. They ask not what their country can do for them but what they can do for their country. They are ready for a trumpet to sound. A detonating issue—some problem growing in magnitude and menace and beyond the capacity of the market's invisible hand to solve—at last leads to a breakthrough into a new political epoch. As they used to say during the Chou dynasty in China a thousand years before Christ, "The Mandate of Heaven is not forever."

IV

One as yet unremarked dimension of the cyclical process deserves particular attention. For in basic respects it is the generational experience that serves as the mainspring of the political cycle.

The concept of generation has only recently emerged as a unit of historical analysis. In traditional societies, where change was imperceptible and each generation lived as its parents and grandparents had lived before it, the passage of generations made little difference. But, with the acceleration in the velocity of history, new generations began to undergo novel experiences and thereby to achieve distinctive outlooks. At the same time, the rise of democracy enfeebled the social identifications left over from feudalism and made generation a convenient way to place people in the indiscriminate flux. Age replaced status as a social indicator. This effect was particularly marked in the United States, which had never known feudalism. "Among democratic nations," wrote Tocqueville, "each generation is a new people." [16]

Auguste Comte was the first to recognize the historical significance of the generational procession. The observations in the fourth volume of his *Cours de Philosophie Positive* (1839) led John Stuart Mill to decree four years later that historical change is to be measured in "intervals of one generation, during which a new set of human beings have been educated, have grown up from childhood, and taken possession of society." [17]

The concept of generation provokes obvious objections. Since babies are born continuously, the division of people into generations seems arbitrary. But then so, it must be said, is most categorization, including the division of people into economic classes. Like economic classes, generations overlap and intertwine. Yet epochal historical events establish boundaries between generations. Common experience precipitates common perceptions and outlooks. The leading twentieth-century theorist of generations, Ortega y Gasset, viewed each generation as "a new integration of the social body" and "the pivot responsible for the movements of historical evolution."[18]

Still, even conceding that generations are broadly distinguishable (the Lost Generation, the silent generation of the 1950s, the noisy generation of the 1960s, and so on), surely members of the same generation often hold antipathetic views. Ortega denied that this objection invalidates the concept. "Under the most violent opposition of 'pros' and 'antis,'" he argued, "it is easy to perceive a real union of interests. Both parties consist of men of their own time; and great as their differences may be their mutual resemblances are still greater. The reactionary and the revolutionary of the nineteenth century are much nearer to one another than either is to any man of our own age." Different individuals respond differently to the same stimuli. But shared stimuli give each generation, if not a uniform ideology, at least a collective identity. Members of the same generation, in Karl Mannheim's words, occupy "a common location in the historical dimension of the social process."[19]

How long is a generation? For Ortega and Mannheim, a generation's political life lasts about thirty years. Each generation spends its first fifteen years after coming of political age in challenging the generation already entrenched in power. Then the new generation comes to power itself for another fifteen years, after which its policies pall and the generation coming up behind claims the succession.[20] The Ortega-Mannheim fifteen-year oscillations roughly match Henry Adams's twelve years in the early republic (when life expectancy was shorter) and my father's sixteen and a half years.

Ortega and Mannheim could have strengthened the analysis by noting the element of recurrence in the generational succession. For people tend to be shaped throughout their lives by the events and ideals dominating the time when they arrived at political consciousness. There is a feedback from the generation in power to the generation coming of political age, while in between an antagonistic generation clamors for change. Each new generation, when it attains power, tends to repudiate the work of the generation it has displaced and to reenact the ideals of its own formative days thirty years before.

There is no arithmetical inevitability in the generational sequence. A generation is a rough, not an exact, unit; almost a metaphor. Nor are the cycles involved the grandiose and immutable cycles beloved by Toynbee or Spengler. They are only fluctuations, rhythms, in the short-run politics of a single country. They may foreshadow but do not control the shape of things to come. Because the cycle is not a pendulum swinging between fixed points but a spiral, it admits novelties and therefore escapes determinism (and confounds prophecy). And the historical cycle is always relative to the historian.

"The historical cycle," wrote R. G. Collingwood, the philosopher of history, "is a permanent feature of all historical thought; but wherever it occurs, it is incidental to a point of view. The cycle is the historian's field of vision at a given moment. . . . Some system of cycles there must always be for every historical student, as every man's shadow must fall somewhere on his own landscape; but as his shadow moves with every movement he makes, so his cyclical view of history will shift and dissolve, decompose and recompose itself anew, with every advance in the historical knowledge of the individual and the race."[21]

V

How does the model of a thirty-year alternation between public purpose and private interest fit the political history of the United States in the twentieth century?

The opening decades of the century were the years of the Progressive movement and the First World War. Two demanding Presidents, Theodore Roosevelt and Woodrow Wilson, exhorted the American people to democratize their political and economic institutions at home and then to make the great world outside safe for democracy. After two decades of unrelenting public action, the American people were worn out. Their capacity for further response to crisis was spent. They were disenchanted with discipline, sacrifice and intangible goals. They had had their fill of crusades. "It is only once in a generation that a people can be lifted above material things," Wilson remarked to his Assistant Secretary of the Navy. "That is why conservative government is in the saddle two-thirds of the time." The Assistant Secretary of the Navy became the Democratic vice presidential candidate in 1920. After the Democratic defeat, Franklin D. Roosevelt mused, "People tire quickly of ideals and we are now repeating history."[22]

"Americans tire, after twenty years," wrote H. L. Mencken from another viewpoint, "of a steady diet of . . . highfalutin and meaningless words; they sicken of an idealism that is oblique, confusing, dishonest and ferocious. . . . Tired to death of intellectual charlatanry, [the citizen] turns to honest imbecility."[23] The new President summed up the new mood. The nation, said Warren G. Harding, wants "not heroics but healing, not nostrums but normalcy, not revolution but restoration, not agitation but adjustment, not surgery but serenity. . . ."[24] He should have added: not action but alliteration. The politics of public purpose gave way to the politics of private interest; virtue surrendered to commerce. The New Era was the decade of the free market run riot, with the business of America presidentially defined as business—the decade that culminated in the Great Depression.

Then came two more decades of action and passion, of idealism and reform: Franklin Roosevelt and the New Deal; the Second World War; Harry Truman and the Fair Deal. During the 1930s and 1940s Americans experienced the worst depression of their history, their worst hot war, their worst cold war, their most frustrating limited war (to that point). Years of crisis once again left the people drained, all passion spent. Dwight Eisenhower became President, as Walter Lippmann wrote at the time, when "this country and the Western World had had all the dynamism, all the innovation, all the crusading that human nature can take."[25] In the 1950s, as in the 1920s, public purpose receded, private motives predominated. The Eisenhower years provided a needed respite amidst the storms of the twentieth century.

As the decade passed, Americans felt once more the need to get the country moving again. As the private interest of the 1920s had led to the public action of the 1930s, the 1950s now led into the 1960s and a new rush of commitment: Kennedy and the New Frontier; Johnson and the Great Society; the racial revolution, the war on poverty. This time desperate events gave the cyclical swing an ominous turn, an edge of hysteria—first the assassination at Dallas, then the war in Vietnam. Objectives embraced with fervent hope—racial integration, community action, urban renewal, environmental protection—caused unanticipated disruptions. Energies released turned destructive—riots in the cities, turmoil on the campuses, two more terrible assassinations, drugs and violence, Watergate and the fall of a President—until the social fabric itself seemed to be unraveling. So much trauma compressed in so short a time produced national disillusion and exhaustion in less than the customary two decades. By the later 1970s Americans were once more, as they had been in the 1950s and 1920s, fed up with public action and disenchanted by its consequences. The compass needle now swung toward private interest and the fulfillment of self. The time received its appropriate names—the 'me' decade; the 'culture of narcissism.' The reaction reached its culmination in the age of Reagan in the 1980s.

Each swing of the cycle produced Presidents responsive to the national mood, sometimes against their own inclination. The conservative William Howard Taft in 1908 provided an interlude between two belligerently progressive Presidents; but he was carried forward by the flow of the times and actually launched more antitrust prosecutions than Theodore Roosevelt, his flamboyant predecessor. Richard Nixon in 1968 may seem another anomaly. But Nixon received only 43 percent of the popular vote, and the liberal tide of the sixties, still running strong, shaped his early domestic legislation. The Environmental Protection Act, the Occupational Safety and Health Act, the Comprehensive Employment and Training Act and its federal employment program were all enacted during the Nixon administration. Nixon even proposed a guaranteed minimum income in his Family Assistance Program, indexed social security benefits, imposed price and wage controls and presided over the fastest increase in social payments since the New Deal.

The election of a Democrat in 1976 may also seem anomalous. But Jimmy Carter rejected the commitment of the modern Democratic party to affirmative government and became the most conservative Democratic President since Grover Cleveland a century earlier. He derided the federal service, advocated deregulation, promised to balance the budget, combatted inflation by high interest rates and recession and encouraged the injection of religion into public affairs. From a longer perspective, the differences between Carter and Reagan will seem less consequential than the continuities. Both Presidents responded with ardor to a perceived conservative surge in the nation.

Each period of public purpose had its detonating issue. In the early decades of the century, the concentration of economic power in the trusts sparked the cycle. In the 1930s the detonating issue was depression. In the 1960s it was racial justice. As the republic gathered its forces to meet each detonating issue, it discharged energies of reform across the board.

One notes too the generational self-consciousness of the twentieth century. Theodore Roosevelt, it was widely remarked, was the youngest President in American history. Franklin Roosevelt, accepting renomination in 1936, proclaimed, "This generation of Americans has a rendezvous with destiny." John Kennedy, the youngest elected President, said in his inaugural address, "The torch has passed to a new generation of Americans."

Each of these leaders, moreover, molded a new political generation in his own image. Young men and women whose ideals were formed by TR and Wilson—Franklin and Eleanor Roosevelt, Harry Truman — produced the New and Fair Deals in their own maturity. The generation whose ideals were formed by FDR—John Kennedy and Lyndon Johnson—produced in their maturity the New Frontier and the Great Society. In the same way the age of Kennedy touched and inspired a new generation. That generation's time is yet to come.

One notes finally that the thirty-year cycle accounts both for the eras of public purpose—TR in 1901, FDR in 1933, JFK in 1961— and for the high tides of conservative restoration—the 1920s, the 1950s, the 1980s.

VI

The conservative tide ran high indeed in the 1984 election—so high that many conservatives and some liberals thought it might establish a new electoral majority and an enduring period of conservative ascendancy. This expectation was based on an alternative cyclical interpretation of American political history—the theory of periodic party realignment.

According to the realignment model, the American party system consists characteristically of a majority party and a minority party, both oriented around a particular set of problems. In time, exigent new problems emerge. Issues that once galvanized the electorate fade into irrelevance. The new issues cut across party lines, split each party internally and confront the established system with questions it struggles to dodge or ignore. Frustration produces voter restiveness, awakens new constituencies, leads to ideological division, third parties and high-intensity politics. The process culminates when a crucial event produces a fundamental shift in the pattern of voting and in the direction of national policy. The result is a new party system founded on a new line-up of political forces and a new rationale of party division.

The realignment model was first launched by Samuel Lubell in 1952 with a famous astronomical metaphor. The American political solar system, Lubell suggested, has been marked "not by two equally competing suns, but by a sun and a moon. It is within the majority party that the issues of any particular period are fought out; while the minority party shines in reflected radiance of the heat thus generated. . . . Each time one majority sun sets and a new sun arises, the drama of American politics is transformed. Figuratively and literally a new political era begins. For each new majority party brings its own orbit of conflict, its own peculiar rhythm of ethnic antagonisms, its own economic equilibrium, its own sectional balance."[26]

As elaborated by political scientists, notably V. O. Key, James L. Sundquist and Walter Dean Burnham, the realignment model identifies five party systems or electoral eras in American political history.

The election of 1800 created the first rudimentary system. The failure of this original system to contain the new politics of mass democracy led after the election of 1828 to the second party system. The Jacksonian coalition then dominated national politics until the pressure of the slavery issue in the 1850s upset the second system. The Whig party disappeared, and the rise of the Republicans ushered in a new political era.

The third party system, running from the 1850s to the 1890s, deviated from the model, because it was a time of close party competition rather than of one-party domination. Then the election of 1896 established the fourth system, in which the Democratic party retreated to the Solid South and the Republicans gained the national majority. Battered by the Great Depression, the fourth system collapsed in the 1930s, giving way to the Roosevelt coalition and the fifth system.

Over the last century and a quarter, each realignment cycle has run about forty years—the 1850s, the 1890s, the 1930s. The sixth party system is thus presumably overdue in the 1980s. Indeed, some analysts—Kevin Phillips, for example—think that the realigning election in fact took place in 1968, when Richard Nixon and George Wallace together won 57 percent of the popular vote, but that Watergate prevented the subsequent consolidation of a new conservative majority. Nevertheless, Phillips points out, the party ascending to power in 1968 controlled the White House, as in previous realignments, for sixteen of the twenty years after the critical election. According to this reading, the conservative period is by the mid-1980s in late middle age.[27]

An alternative reading dates the start of realignment in 1981, with Ronald Reagan as the founder of the sixth party system and the Reagan coalition replacing the Roosevelt coalition as the new sun shining over American politics. In explaining the stretch-out of the realignment cycle, the theorists might (though they don't) call on the American school of neo-Marxist economists who find a crisis every thirty-five to fifty years in the "social structure of accumulation."[28] These crises, it is argued, demand drastic revisions of institutional and legislative incentives in order to bring about the resumption of capital accumulation. Each accumulation crisis since the 1850s corresponds to a time of party realignment. The Reagan economic policies of the 1980s were designed precisely to stimulate capital accumulation; and it is a happy irony that Republican realignment expectations rest analytically on a Marxist theory of capitalist development.

There remains, however, a devastating doubt about the whole realignment hypothesis. For the realignment cycle assumes party to be the constitutive unit of American politics. But parties aren't what they used to be.* They no longer command the voters as they did in the nineteenth century. Party affiliation has never been more casual, party loyalty more fleeting. The stigmata of decay are everywhere. The operational premise of the realignment model is very likely defunct. One doubts that either party can organize an enduring majority in the electronic age. The prospect for the future is surely not realignment but dealignment.

VII

Nevertheless, even if parties have become imperfect vehicles, do not portents remain foretelling a sea change in the national mood? By 1984 Republicans had won four of the last five presidential elections, and the fifth was won by the most conservative Democratic President of the century. Even if Reagan did not in reelection sweep both houses of Congress as Roosevelt had done in 1936, he had succeeded brilliantly in capturing the policy agenda and redefining the terms of political debate. After the 1984 election almost as many voters called themselves Republicans as Democrats, including many who had called themselves Democrats only a short time before.

Reagan's ingratiating vision of the Republican party as the party of optimism, patriotism, national confidence and individual opportunity reached across traditional political lines. Reaganism, its adherents said, was a 'populist' movement, appealing to intellectuals, to a fervent evangelical constituency, to blue-collar workers, to Catholics, to voters of East European descent, to the suburbs, to the sunbelt, the fastest growing part of the country, and to the young. The appropriation by Republicans of the word 'populist,' a term originally applied in the 1890s to farmers seeking a redistribution of wealth and power against the business community, struck historians as bizarre. Representative Newt Gingrich of Georgia, a self-styled populist of the right, achieved a high point of historiographical perversity when he proclaimed himself the inheritor of "the six successful American revolutions" and listed the McKinley victory of 1896 as one of them.[29] If McKinley was a populist, what in the world was his impassioned opponent William Jennings Bryan? what were the Populists? Still one understands the groping after new terminology. For Reagan's appeal carried the conservative movement impressively beyond its historic base in the business community.

*For an extended discussion, see "The Short Happy Life of American Political Parties" later in this volume.

And his policies aimed to redraw the political map of the republic. Unprecedented budget deficits, deliberately contrived for the purpose, denied the national government and the liberal opposition the prospect of new social initiatives requiring large appropriations. The Reaganization of the regulatory agencies and of the federal judiciary strengthened the power of business at the expense of consumers, organized labor and racial minorities. Republican devotion to tax reduction and venture capital attracted the Yuppies of the high-technology age a good deal more than Democratic emphasis on protecting the steel and automotive industries. The proposed elimination of federal income tax deductions for state and local taxes would help the conservative low-tax sunbelt and hurt the more liberal high-tax frostbelt. The proposed elimination of public financing of presidential campaigns would help the party of the rich and hurt the party of the poor. The Reagan program was shrewdly designed to cripple permanently the organizational foundations of the New Deal coalition.

Some of the Republican gains were doubtless transient. In the United States as in most democracies, the economic situation is a prime determinant of electoral outcomes. Working-class people applauded Reagan's unabashed flag-waving and moralism; but, had he run for reelection in 1982 with 11 percent unemployment, he would hardly have commanded the working-class vote. Nineteen eighty-four, however, was a time of economic recovery, with unemployment declining, gross national product rising and inflation remaining low. Sailing seas of economic well-being, voters saw no reason to rock the boat. The onset of new economic turbulence would quickly detach blue-collar voters from conservative policies. After all, John L. Lewis was an ardent Republican in the 1920s and pronounced Herbert Hoover in 1928 "the foremost industrial statesman of modern times."[30] A decade later he was the business community's public enemy number one. The recurrence of economic trouble will even reduce the laissez-faire unction of the sunbelt.

The conservative claim to the future rested more convincingly on the theory of the Republicans as the party of new ideas, of the old morality and of the young. But all these items turn out on closer examination to be predictable features of the political cycle in its private-interest phase.

VIII

Consider, for example, the theory of conservatism as the party of new ideas. I came the other day on the following observation:

No intellectual phenomenon has been more surprising in recent years than the revival in the United States of conservatism as a respectable social philosophy. For decades liberalism seemed to have everything its way. The bright young men were always liberals; the thoughtful professors were generally liberals. . . . But in the last year or two, it has all seemed to change. Fashionable intellectual circles now dismiss liberalism as naive, ritualistic, sentimental, shallow. With a whoop and a roar, a number of conservative prophets have materialized out of the wilderness, exhuming conservatism, revisiting it, revitalizing it, preaching it. . . . Today, we are told, the bright young men are conservatives; the thoughtful professors are conservatives; even a few liberals, in their own cycle of despair, are beginning to avow themselves conservatives.

This quotation is true enough for 1986. It was just as true when I first wrote it more than thirty years ago (in the *Reporter*, 16 June 1955).[31] Every conservative period throws up its philosophy of self-approbation. The neo-conservatism of the 1980s is a replay of the New Conservatism of the 1950s, which was itself a replay of the New Era philosophy of the 1920s.

As practical criticism, contemporary neo-conservatism often offers (in magazines like Irving Kristol's excellent if misnamed *Public Interest*) penetrating assessments of liberal institutions and illusions. As program, however, neo-conservatism is very much *recherche du temps perdu*. It repeats conservative themes not just of the 1950s and 1920s but of the 1890s and before: the exaltation of laissez-faire and the unfettered market (Herbert Spencer's *Social Statics*, 1850); the crusade against government regulation (which began after the passage of the Interstate Commerce Act in 1887); the faith in trickle-down, now rebaptized supply-side, economics (Calvin Coolidge and Andrew Mellon); the call for the devolution of authority from Washington to the states (Eisenhower). Far from being bold new ideas, these constitute the boilerplate of every epoch of private interest. Neo-conservative zealots even want to return to the gold standard—and succeeded in inserting that thought into the 1984 Republican platform.

The social philosophy of private-interest periods characteristically exists on two discordant levels: not only the intellectual pretensions of neo-conservatism but the evangelical passions of those who in the 1980s call themselves the Moral Majority. Here too one notes the cyclical recurrence. The Moral Majority, in its efforts to dictate private behavior, is a reenactment of the fundamentalist movement that sixty years ago imposed prohibition on a hapless country and tried to expel Darwin from Tennessee classrooms. The twenties were the heyday of Billy Sunday, Aimee Semple McPherson and the types that Sinclair Lewis celebrated in *Elmer Gantry*. The next great outburst of evangelical moralism came thirty years later, when Norman Vincent Peale and Billy Graham in the 1950s appointed themselves the nation's moral arbiters.

Economic conservatism and evangelical moralism have always been uneasy partners. They have different fish to fry. The economic conservatives of the 1980s want primarily to reduce government regulation and taxes. The evangelical moralists want to ban liberated women, abortion, secular humanism, pot and sexual candor; to restore authority to the male and prayer to the public school. One group enjoys the permissive society. The other demands its abolition. Economic conservatives want to get government off our backs. Evangelical moralists want to put government into our beds. Just as business leaders and their intellectual apologists in the 1920s defied prohibition and accepted evolution, so sophisticated conservatives today regard the indignations of the Moral Majority with acute discomfort. The more militant the Moral Majority becomes, the more it will split the conservative coalition. In any event, the Moral Majority, far from signaling a permanent change in the national mood, is an entirely predictable by-product of the cyclical swing.

Of all the portents claimed to herald a new conservative era, none appeared more convincing than the wide and eager support the oldest President in American history received from the youngest voters of 1984. Realignment forecasts rest heavily on the anticipated politics of the 'baby boom' generation—the nearly 80 million Americans, more than a third of the population, born in the years from 1946 to 1966.

It is misleading, though, to define this group as constituting a single generation. For those born between 1946 and, say, 1957 (the year the birth rate turned down again) are children of the generation that came of political age under Franklin Roosevelt and Truman; they are grandchildren of the generation that came of political age under Theodore Roosevelt and Wilson. They themselves arrived at political consciousness in the Kennedy-Johnson years.

Young people born after 1957 had very different political conditioning. They are children of the Eisenhower generation and grandchildren of the generation that came of political age in the conservative twenties. The eighteen- to twenty-four-year-olds who flocked to Reagan in 1984 were born between 1960 and 1966. They have no memory of the Kennedy years and arrived at political consciousness in the conservative eighties. In political attitudes they predictably resemble their Eisenhower-generation parents and their Harding-Coolidge-Hoover grandparents. (Indeed, these grandparents—vot-

ers seventy-eight and over—are the group that, along with their eigh-
teen- to twenty-four-year-old grandchildren, voted most heavily for
Reagan in 1984.) The baby-boomers thus consist of two distinct generations, with 1957 as (roughly) the dividing line: the older generation attuned to democratic purpose, the younger to private interest.

In short, the conservatism found in the 1980s among intellectuals,
religious zealots and the young does not necessarily prove a fundamental transformation in the national mood. It is exactly what the
historian would expect during the private-interest swing of the political cycle.

IX

Private-interest eras display further recurrences. Such eras arise in
reaction against the demands of public purpose. For public-purpose
eras are importunate. They consume not only psychic energy but
time. There are not enough hours in the day both to save the nation
and to cherish one's family. Ultimately public action exhausts as well
as disappoints. People turn away from the public sphere in order to
concentrate on the privacies of existence.

This phenomenon was first identified in 1840 by Tocqueville, who
called it "individualism" and considered it a grave threat to democracy. By individualism Tocqueville meant something very different
from Emersonian self-reliance or Darwinian rugged individualism.
He meant something closer to the modern sociological concept of
'privatization.' For Tocqueville, individualism was not self-assertion
but self-withdrawal—the tendency of each member of the community "to draw apart with his family and friends, so that after he has
thus formed a little circle of his own, he willingly leaves society at
large to itself." Individualism fosters the isolation of men from one
another, "saps the virtues of public life" and makes it "difficult to
draw a man out of his own circle to interest him in the destiny of the
state."[32]

Privatization has its function in the systole and diastole of society.
It is a form of corrective action—homeostasis—within the body politic against excesses of public concern. It replenishes the self, the family and the private economy and renews defenses against mass society
and an aggressive state. But, as Tocqueville pointed out, privatization
also leads to excesses of its own, especially the exclusive pursuit of
present and material pleasures. The "love of wealth," he decided, is
"at the bottom of all that the Americans do."[33]

Private-interest eras rest on the principle that the individual in promoting his own interests promotes the general interest. Private vices, as Mandeville said, yield public benefits. The ethos of self-interest dominates all. In the 1980s, for example, the Reagan administration actually encouraged government scientists to sell their publicly financed defense research for private gain.[34] The ethos even affects espionage. Americans spying for the Soviet Union in this private-interest era do so not for ideology but for money.

This priority of wealth over commonwealth naturally nourishes a propensity to corruption in government. When public purpose dominates, government tends to be idealistic. Idealists have many faults, but they rarely steal. Under FDR's New Deal, the national government spent more money than ever before in peacetime and regulated the economy as never before; but there was a notable absence of corruption. Lyndon Johnson had been a notorious wheeler-dealer; but there was much less graft in his Great Society than in the conservative administrations of the 1920s, 1950s and 1980s. In liberal administrations corruption arises mostly at the tag end, after the idealists have moved on and the time-servers have taken over.

When private interest dominates, public morals are very different. Many businessmen who serve conservative governments are men of integrity. But some do not scruple to use public authority to feather their own nests. They do what comes naturally. Everyone remembers the Harding scandals of the 1920s. Eisenhower's administration was marked by scandals that forced the resignation of his Secretary of the Air Force, his chairman of the Interstate Commerce Commission, his General Services Administrator, his Public Buildings Administrator, the chairman of the Republican National Committee and even of the Assistant to the President himself. More than forty members of the Nixon administration underwent criminal prosecution. His Vice President, two cabinet members, a dozen members of the White House staff and fifteen others scattered through the executive branch pleaded guilty or were convicted after trial. The Reagan administration, as the list lengthened of its appointees under indictment or forced to resign under fire, added the word "sleaze" to the political vocabulary. ("Sleaze" is not to be found in the 1978 edition of *Safire's Political Dictionary.*)

"There is absolutely nothing to be said," Theodore Roosevelt observed, "for government by a plutocracy, for government by men very powerful in certain lines and gifted with 'the money touch,' but with ideals which in their essence are merely those of so many glorified pawnbrokers."[35] Still, voters exhibited no more distress over corruption in government in the 1980s than they had exhibited in the 1920s and 1950s. The much-remarked Teflon effect—the shedding by Presidents of responsibility for the misdeeds of their own administrations—is produced less by the genially imperturbable personalities of Presidents like Eisenhower and Reagan than by the withdrawal of popular attention from public affairs when the consuming absorption is in private interest.

X

Nor is privatization confined to politics. Literature turns inward, explores the psyche rather than society, employs experimental techniques to evoke the traumas of the isolated family and the even more isolated and fragmented self (the symbolism and stream of consciousness of the twenties, the fabulation of the eighties) and is committed to individual damnation and redemption. (No value judgment is here implied; literature thrives to a point on inwardness; what could have been more perishable than the proletarian fiction and poetry of the 1930s?)[36] Economics and political science too abandon a larger vision of history, retreat from public responsibility and become behavioral, quantitative, mathematical, antiseptic, 'value free.' History itself turns from delineations of conflict to myths of consensus.

What worried Tocqueville most were the long-run consequences when Americans construed "the principle of self-interest" too narrowly. Citizens who shut themselves off from "those great and powerful public emotions which perturb nations, but which develop them," Tocqueville said, may soon arrive at the state where they regard every new theory as a peril, every innovation as a steppingstone to revolution. "I dread, and I confess it," he wrote in a startlingly personal outburst, "lest they should at last so entirely give way to a cowardly love of present enjoyment as to lose sight of the interests of their future selves . . . rather than to make, when it is necessary, a strong and sudden effort to a higher purpose."[37]

If the intellectual consequence of individualism is stagnation, the political consequence could be despotism. People begin to see public obligations as a vexatious distraction from the scramble for money; and "the better to look after what they call their own business, they neglect their chief business, which is to remain their own masters." Privatization by promoting civic apathy invites tyranny. How to "ward off a disorder at once so natural to the frame of democratic society and so fatal"? Tocqueville saw "only one effectual remedy" for individualism—political freedom.[38]

Public action, he said, forces individuals to recognize that they live not just to themselves but in society. "Men attend to the interests of the public, first by necessity, afterwards by choice, what was intentional becomes an instinct, and by dint of working for the good of one's fellow citizens, the habit and the taste for serving them are at length acquired."[39] Politics, in short, is the great means of counteracting private interest, of reviving public virtue and of overcoming the apathy that prepares the way for despotism.

Tocqueville expounded his theory of individualism in the second volume of *Democracy in America* (1840), and commentators spot a contradiction between the portrait of democratic man in this volume as isolated, weak, docile, powerless, and the quite different portrait drawn in his first volume five years before. In 1835 Tocqueville had looked at democratic man and seen energy, participation, civic zeal, public commitment, even majority tyranny. "If an American were condemned to confine his activity to his own affairs," he wrote then, "he would be robbed of one half of his existence ... and his wretchedness would be unbearable."[40] Between Volumes I and II the democratic distemper changed from activism to anomie.

There is a solution to this apparent contradiction. With his marvelous antennae, Tocqueville perceived that American democracy comprehended both the aggressive individuals of his first volume and the withdrawn individualism of his second. And he came close to perceiving that public action and private interest exist in cyclical alternation. "An American attends to his private concerns as if he were alone in the world, and the next minute he gives himself to the common welfare as if he had forgotten them. At one time he seems animated by the most selfish cupidity; at another, by the most lively patriotism."[41] There was, in fact, no contradiction between the Tocqueville of 1835 and the Tocqueville of 1840; only cyclical change. As activism led on to anomie, so in due course the cowardly love of present enjoyment would give way to a strong and sudden effort to a higher purpose.

XI

A cyclical rhythm exists in foreign policy as well. Over thirty years ago Frank L. Klingberg analyzed what he called "the historical alternation of moods in American foreign policy." He uncovered a periodic swing between "extroversion"—a readiness to use direct diplomatic, military or economic pressure on other nations to gain American ends—and "introversion"—a concentration on concerns of the national community. Examining wars, annexations, armed expeditions, naval expenditures, presidential statements and party platforms, Klingberg in 1952 identified seven alternations since 1776:

Introvert	Extrovert
1776–1798	1798–1824
1824–1844	1844–1871
1871–1891	1891–1918
1918–1940	1940–

The Klingberg foreign policy cycle thus showed (as of 1952) four introvert phases averaging twenty-one years each and three extrovert phases averaging twenty-seven years each. The movement, he noted, is spiral in character, with involvement abroad increasing after each extrovert phase. He also noted the generational sequence: most of the Presidents lived the greater part of their formative years "under a phase similar to that of their Presidency, while in their early maturity they were able to see the opposite policy being followed and ultimately appearing to fail, at least in part." And he subjected his theory to the test of prediction. In 1952, at a high point of extroversion, he found it "logical to expect America to retreat, to some extent at least, from so much world involvement, and perhaps to do so sometime in the 1960's." So America did as it turned against the war in Vietnam. Klingberg further proposed that in this next introvert period the major problem "will carry heavy moral implications" — an interesting anticipation of the rise of human rights. Bringing his analysis up to date in 1978, Klingberg predicted that "the first signs of a shift toward extroversion" would be "apparent by, say, 1983."[42]

There is no evident correlation between the Klingberg and Schlesinger cycles*—which suggests that both cycles are to a considerable degree self-generating and thus true cycles. America has gone to war almost equally, for example, in private-interest and public-purpose eras. One would think that international crisis is peremptory and leaves national leaders little room for choice. This is not quite so. The nation will react one way to external challenge in a phase of introversion; very differently in a phase of extroversion. What an introvert age may observe with indifference, an extrovert age regards as a danger demanding a fierce response. In 1940, toward the end of an introvert phase, a powerful but declining minority of Americans regarded Hitler with complacency. A quarter century later, toward the end of an extrovert phase, another powerful and growing minority refused to see vital interests at risk in Vietnam.

*Private-interest eras show fifty-seven introvert years and fifty-five extrovert; public-purpose eras show forty-two introvert years and sixty-six extrovert. See Robert E. Elder, Jr., and Jack E. Holmes, "U.S. Foreign Policy Moods, Institutional Change, and Change in the International Economic Systems," paper prepared for the 1985 meeting of the American Political Science Association, 9.

Still, even if the foreign and domestic cycles do not coincide, there is a relation between the domestic cycle and foreign policy. For each phase of the domestic cycle defines the national interest in terms of its own values. Each uses foreign policy to project those values abroad. Public-purpose eras tend to incorporate into foreign policy ideas of democracy, reform, human rights, civil liberties, social change, affirmative government. Such eras display a preference abroad for democratic center-left regimes. Private-interest eras tend to conceive international affairs in terms of capitalism, private investment, the magic of the marketplace, the defense of American corporations doing business in foreign lands. Such eras display a preference abroad for right-wing and authoritarian regimes that promise protection for private capital.

So the conduct of foreign affairs breathes the spirit of the alternations in the domestic cycle, while the intensity in which this spirit is imposed on the world depends on phases in the foreign cycle.

XII

What is the view from 1985? How goes the cycle now? If the thirty-year rhythm holds, then the 1980s will witness the burnout of the most recent conservative ascendancy, and the age of Reagan, like its earlier versions in the 1950s, 1920s and 1890s, will fade into historical memory.

If the rhythm holds . . . but there is no mathematical determinism in history. The electronic age threatens to vaporize the parties;* will it vaporize the cycle as well? Probably not; propaganda, whether typographic or electronic, succeeds only as it harmonizes with the collective mood and is not likely by itself to reverse basic drifts of sentiment. But, within the cyclical pattern, it is conceivable that the brief, highly charged and highly traumatic phase of the 1960s may, like the brief, highly charged and highly traumatic phase of the 1860s, have sated the nation's appetite for public action for years to come, and that the countermovement will be prolonged as a form of compensation to restore the rhythm. The private-interest era after the intense days of Civil War, Reconstruction, presidential assassination and presidential impeachment lasted for more than thirty years.

As the cycle is not automatic, neither is it self-enforcing. It takes people to make the cycle work. Those who believe in public purpose must interpret events, press issues and devise remedies. They must rise above those worthy special interests—labor, women, blacks, old

*See "The Short Happy Life of American Political Parties."

folks and the rest—that have become their electoral refuge and re-
gain a commanding national vision of the problems and prospects of
the republic. The need for an authentically national policy is all the
more urgent in the 1980s. There are enormous potentialities for disintegration in contemporary America—the widening disparities in
income and opportunity; the multiplication of the poor and the underclass; the slowdown on racial justice; the structural propensity to
inflation; the decline of heavy industry before competition abroad
and the microchip at home; the deterioration of education; the pollution of the environment and the decay of infrastructure; the rotting
away of the great cities; the farm crisis; the mounting burden of public and private debt; the spread of crime and violence.

One can be certain that neither public purpose nor private interest,
neither affirmative government nor the free market, will do away with
these anguishing problems. This leads two of our most acute diag-
nosticians, Walter Dean Burnham on the left and Kevin Phillips on
the right, to pessimistic conclusions about the future of democracy
itself. In the popular perception, as they sense it, the liberal interventionist state had its chance, botched it and thereby provoked the Reagan counterrevolution. When the counterrevolution only deepens
national troubles, people will see a "double failure" of both welfare-
state and free-market alternatives. Feelings of frustration and impotence will intensify. The cyclical alternation will lose its legitimacy. Not
since the 1850s, Phillips remarks, has there been such a pattern of
double failure and double obsolescence, and we all know what happened then. The accumulation of discontent will subvert the traditional political order and rush American politics into new and dangerous times. Phillips expects not a revival of the liberal spirit of the
New Deal but rather a nationalist, right-wing–populist authoritarianism operating an activist and repressive state. Burnham darkly
foresees "an escalating crisis of rule—a crisis . . . in the foundations
of the constitutional regime."[43]

This may all be so. But one remains skeptical of apocalyptic forebodings. When a friend burst into Adam Smith's drawing room with
news of Burgoyne's surrender at Saratoga and cried that the nation
was ruined, Adam Smith replied (or so the story goes), "There is a
lot of ruin in a nation." Democratic values are deeply rooted in American life—more deeply, it would appear, than capitalist values. At
least when democracy and capitalism have diverged, democratic values have proved more potent. National swings back toward uncontrolled private interest are generally holding actions; swings in the
democratic direction tend to produce enduring change. The spiral

effect registers the continuing accretion of democratic reform. The Reagan counterrevolution left the New Deal, even the Great Society, substantially intact. The McClosky-Zaller analysis finds democratic values more solidly established than they were a century ago, capitalist values less so. Indeed, when capitalists defend themselves today, they no longer invoke traditional capitalist arguments—the sovereign virtue of self-interest and the sanctity of private property. Instead they invoke democratic arguments and present capitalism as the means of the greatest good for the greatest number. Conflicts between capitalism and democracy, McClosky and Zaller write, are "likely to be resolved in ways predominantly favorable to the democratic tradition."[44]

We may conclude that public purpose will have at least one more chance. At some point, shortly before or after the year 1990, there should come a sharp change in the national mood and direction—a change comparable to those bursts of innovation and reform that followed the accessions to office of Theodore Roosevelt in 1901, of Franklin Roosevelt in 1933 and of John Kennedy in 1961. The 1990s should be the turn in the generational succession for the young men and women who came of political age in the Kennedy years.

If public purpose holds enough problems at bay in the 1990s, this phase will continue until, perhaps toward the end of the first decade of the twenty-first century, the nation tires again of uplift and commitment and the young people who came of political age in the Reagan years have their turn in power. For, as Emerson pointed out, both conservatism and reform degenerate into excess. The conservative party, he wrote, "vindicates no right, it aspires to no real good, it brands no crime, it proposes no generous policy, it does not build, nor write, nor cherish the arts, nor foster religion, nor establish schools, nor encourage science, nor emancipate slaves, nor befriend the poor, or the Indian, or the imigrant." On the other hand, "Reform in its antagonism inclines to asinine resistance, to kick with hoofs; it runs to egotism and bloated self-conceit; it runs to a bodiless pretension, to unnatural refining and elevation which ends in hypocrisy."[45]

Yet in the American republic conservatism and reform, capitalism and democracy, private interest and public purpose, join to define the political tradition. The two jostling strains in American thought agree more than they 'disagree. Both are committed to individual liberty, the constitutional state and the rule of law. Both have their reciprocal functions in preserving the body politic. Both have their indispensable roles in the dialectic of public policy. They are indissoluble partners in the great adventure of democracy. Emerson, as usual, said it best: "It may be safely affirmed of these two metaphysical antagonists, that each is a good half, but an impossible whole. Each exposes the abuses of the other, but in a true society, in a true man, both must combine."[46]

Still, let us not be complacent. Should private interest fail today and public purpose fail thereafter, what rough beast, its hour come round at last, may be slouching toward Washington to be born?

PART II

THREE

Foreign Policy
and the American Character

————— ◆ —————

FOREIGN POLICY IS THE FACE a nation wears to the world. The aim is the same for all states—the protection of national integrity and interest. But the manner in which a state conceives and conducts its foreign policy is greatly affected by national peculiarities. Every unhappy nation is unhappy in its own way.

The United States contributes its share of peculiarities. As Henry James, an early American specialist in international relations, once put it, "It's a complex fate, being an American."[1] The American character is filled with contradiction and paradox. So in consequence is American foreign policy. The conduct of policy is subject to cyclical fluctuations of withdrawal and return. And American conceptions of foreign policy respond to the old argument between experiment and destiny—between the United States perceived as one nation among many, liable like all the others to angelic impulses and predatory lusts; and the United States perceived as a chosen nation anointed by Providence to redeem the fallen world. Each perception breeds its own cast of mind. The first derives from history and issues in an empirical approach to world affairs. The second derives from theology and issues in the secularization of theology, which is ideology. The conflict between the two approaches expresses the schism in the American soul between a commitment to experiment and a susceptibility to dogma.

I

On the one hand, Americans are famous for being a practical people, preferring fact to theory, finding the meaning of propositions in results, regarding trial and error, not deductive logic, as the path to truth. "In no country in the civilized world," wrote Tocqueville, "is less attention paid to philosophy than in the United States."[2] And, when Americans developed a distinctive philosophy, it was of course the pragmatism of William James. James described a pluralist universe where people can discover partial and limited truths, truths that work for them, but where no one can gain an absolute grip on ultimate truth. He rejected monism—the notion that the world can be understood from a single point of view. He stood against the assumption that all virtuous principles are in the end reconcilable; against capitulation to a single body of unified dogma; in short, against ideology.

Yet at the same time that Americans live by experiment, they also show a recurrent vulnerability to cosmic generalities. This is not altogether surprising. The American colonists, after all, were nurtured on one of the most profound and all-consuming intellectual systems ever devised—the theology of Calvin—and they passed on to their descendants an abiding relish in system and abstraction. The ideas of the Americans, as Tocqueville found in the 1830s, "are all either extremely minute and clear or extremely general and vague."[3] The Calvinist mind pronounced America the redeemer nation—in the eighteenth century in Jonathan Edwards's theology of Providence, in the nineteenth century in Josiah Strong's theology of expansion, in the twentieth century in Woodrow Wilson's gospel of world order and in John Foster Dulles's summons to a holy war against godless communism.

This tension between experiment and ideology offers one way of looking at the American experience in foreign policy. The Founding Fathers were hard-headed and clear-sighted men. They believed that states responded to specific national interests; indeed, were morally obliged to do so, if there was to be order in international affairs. "No nation," observed George Washington, "is to be trusted farther than it is bound by its interest."[4] They believed further that international order depended on preserving an equilibrium among competing national interests. "There is a Ballance of Power in Europe," wrote John Adams. "Nature has formed it. Practice and Habit have confirmed it, and it must exist forever. It may be disturbed for a time, by the accidental Removal of a Weight from one Scale to the other; but there will be a continual Effort to restore the Equilibrium. . . . Congress adopted these Principles and this System in its purity."[5] And Congress did so because it recognized that the maintenance of the European balance was the safeguard of American independence. "It never could be our interest," Adams wrote, "to unite with France in the destruction of England. . . . On the other hand, it could never be our duty to unite with Britain in too great a humiliation of France."[6]

The Jeffersonians, though sentimentally inclined to favor France against Britain, were equally hard-headed when national interest intervened. "We shall so take our distance between the two rival nations," wrote Thomas Jefferson in 1802, "as, remaining disengaged till necessity compels us, we may haul finally to the enemy of that which shall make it necessary." In 1814, with Britain waging war against America, seven months before the British captured Washington and burned the White House, Jefferson still could not bring himself to applaud Napoleon's success against Britain in Europe. "It cannot be to our interest that all Europe should be reduced to a single monarchy," he wrote. ". . . Were he again advanced to Moscow, I should again wish him such disaster as would prevent his reaching Petersburg. And were the consequences even to be the longer continuance of our war [with Britain], I would rather meet them than see the whole force of Europe wielded by a single hand."[7] In this last incisive phrase Jefferson defined the national interest that explains American intervention in the twentieth century's two world wars as well as in the subsequent Cold War.

I do not imply that the Founding Fathers were devoid of any belief in a special mission for the United States. It was precisely to protect that mission that they wished to preserve the balance of power in Europe. They hoped that the American experiment would in time regenerate the world. But they did not suppose that the republic was immune, in Alexander Hamilton's words, to the imperfections, weaknesses, and evils afflicting other nations. If America was to redeem the world, it would do so by perfecting its own institutions, not by moving into other countries and setting things straight; by example, not by intervention. "She goes not abroad in search of monsters to destroy," said John Quincy Adams.[8]

The realism of the revolutionary generation was founded in the harsh requirements of a struggle for precarious independence. It was founded too in rather pessimistic conceptions of human nature and of history. The Founding Fathers saw the new republic as a risky and doubtful experiment. And the idea of experiment, by directing attention to the relation between actions and consequences in specific context, strengthened the historical approach to public affairs. Yet — another paradox — the role of the Founding Fathers was to annul history for their descendants. Americans started to believe they really had it in their power to begin the world all over again (President Reagan quoted Tom Paine's famous proposition in his "evil empire" address to the evangelicals at Orlando). Experimenters themselves, the Founders helped prepare the way for ideology.

The realism of the revolutionary generation faded away in the century from Waterloo to Sarajevo when the European balance of power was maintained without American intervention. The exemption from the European cockpit nourished the myth of American innocence and the ideology of American righteousness. For many Americans, the very idea of power politics became repellent. Safe from responsibility, we became the world's moralists. Declarations replaced diplomacy as the means of American relationship to other states. "The American habit," Herbert Croly remarked in 1909, "is to proclaim doctrines and policies, without considering either the implications, the machinery necessary to carry them out, or the weight of the resulting responsibilities."[9]

When America rejoined the big game in the twentieth century, it did so with an exalted conviction of its destiny as the savior of the world, and no longer by example alone. The United States entered the First World War for balance of power reasons; but Woodrow Wilson could not bring himself to admit the national interest in preventing the whole force of Europe from being wielded by a single hand. Instead he made himself the prophet of a world beyond power politics where the bad old balance of power would give way to a radiant new community of power. The United States, Wilson said, had notified mankind at its birth: "We have come to redeem the world by giving it liberty and justice."[10]

So two strains have competed for the control of American foreign policy: one empirical, the other dogmatic; one viewing international relations in the perspective of history, the other in the perspective of ideology; one supposing that the United States shares the imperfections, weaknesses and evils incident to all societies, the other regarding the United States as the happy empire of perfect wisdom and perfect virtue, commissioned to save humanity.

The competition between realism and ideology was complicated in the twentieth century by two developments: by the fact that the United States became a world power; and by the fact that the balance of power faced the gravest possible threats. There was in 1940 a very real monster to destroy and after 1945 another very real monster to contain. But the growth of American power also confirmed the messianism of those who believed in America's divine anointment. That there were a couple of real monsters roaming the world encouraged a fearful tendency to look everywhere for new monsters to destroy.

II

This schematic account does not do justice to the obvious fact that any American President, in order to command assent for his policies, must appeal to both geopolitics and ideology—and that, to do this effectively, Presidents must combine the two strains not only in their speeches but in their souls. Franklin Roosevelt, the disciple at once of Admiral Mahan and of President Wilson, was supreme in marrying national interest to idealistic hope, though in the crunch interest always came first. Most postwar Presidents—Truman, Eisenhower, Kennedy, Nixon—shared a recognition, alert or grudging, of the priority of power politics over ideology.

But the Reagan administration represented a mighty comeback of messianism in foreign policy. Renouncing, in his language at least, the national-interest approach of the Founding Fathers, viewing international affairs through the prism not of history but of ideology, President Reagan revived the dream of the United States as the redeemer nation. An unabashed nationalist, Reagan repeatedly affirmed his faith that God had a divine purpose in placing America where people with a special love of freedom would find it. He had no doubt that the United States was the noblest country on earth. Nothing made him prouder than the "new patriotism" he believed he had kindled in the nation.

If the United States was infinitely virtuous, the Soviet Union was infinitely wicked. It was, Reagan said, "the focus of evil in the modern world." Everything followed by deductive logic from this premise. The world struggle was "between right and wrong and good and evil." When evil was loose in the world, "we are enjoined by scripture and the Lord Jesus to oppose it with all our might."[11] Soviet leaders "reserve unto themselves the right to commit any crime, to lie, to cheat."[12] They were personally responsible for the world's manifold ills. "Let us not delude ourselves. The Soviet Union underlies all the unrest that is going on. If they weren't engaged in this game of dominos, there wouldn't be any hot spots in the world."[13] Not content with the orchestration of crisis around the periphery, the Soviet Union, once it acquired the proper margin of numerical superiority in warheads, could be expected to launch a surprise nuclear attack on the United States itself. Safety lay only in the establishment of American military dominance. If this meant a nuclear arms race, that was Moscow's fault, not Washington's, because America's heart was pure.

The seizure of foreign policy by a boarding party of ideologues invites a host of dangers. Ideologues tend to get things wrong. The empirical approach sees the present as emerging from the past and moving toward the future. Its view of the world is concrete and historical. Ideology is counterhistorical. It lives by models and substitutes models for reality. No doubt as an intellectual exercise the construction of models may help in the delineation of problems—but not when ideal types are mistaken for descriptions of the real world. This is what Alfred North Whitehead called "the fallacy of misplaced concreteness." It explains why ideology infallibly gets statesmen into trouble, later if not sooner. The error of ideology is to prefer essence to existence. The result undermines the reality principle itself.

Ideology withdraws problems from the turbulent stream of change and treats them in abstraction from the whirl and contingency of life. So ideology portrays the Soviet Union as an unalterable monolith, immune to historical vicissitude and permutation, its behavior determined by immutable logic, the same yesterday, today and tomorrow; Sunday, Monday and always. We are forever in 1950, with a dictator in the Kremlin commanding an obedient network of communist parties and agents around the planet. In the light of ideology, the Soviet Union appears as a fanatic state carrying out with implacable zeal and cunning a master plan of world dominion.

Perhaps this is all so. But others see rather a weary, dreary country filled with cynicism and corruption, beset by insuperable problems at home and abroad, lurching uncertainly from crisis to crisis. The Soviet leadership, three quarters of a century after the glorious Bolshevik revolution, cannot provide the people with elementary items of consumer goods. It cannot count on the honesty of bureaucrats or the loyalty of scientists and writers. It confronts difficult ethnic challenges as the non-Russians in the Soviet Union, so miserably underrepresented in the organs of power, begin to outnumber the Russians. Every second child born in the Soviet Union is a Muslim. Abroad, the Soviet Union faces hostile Chinese to the east and unreliable satellites to the west, while to the south the great Red Army after seven years still cannot defeat ragged tribesmen fighting bravely in the hills of Afghanistan.

I don't want to overdo the picture of weakness. The Soviet Union remains a powerful state, with great and cruel capacity to repress consumption, to punish dissent and to build nuclear missiles. But there is enough to the reality of Soviet troubles to lead even the ideologues in Washington to conceive Soviet Russia as a nation at once so robust that it threatens the world and so frail that a couple of small pushes will shove its ramshackle economy into collapse.

The Soviet Union of course is far more under the domination of ideologues than the United States, even if Soviet ideology has got shopworn and ritualistic over the long years. It too sees the enemy as unchanging and unchangeable, a permanently evil empire vitiated through eternity by the original sin of private property. Each regime, reading its adversary ideologically rather than historically, deduces motive from imputed essence and attributes purpose, premeditation and plan where less besotted analysts would raise a hand for improvisation, accident, chance, ignorance, negligence and even sheer stupidity. We arrive at the predicament excellently described by Henry Kissinger: "The superpowers often behave like two heavily armed blind men feeling their way around a room, each believing himself in mortal peril from the other whom he assumes to have perfect vision. Each side should know that frequently uncertainty, compromise, and incoherence are the essence of policymaking. Yet each tends to ascribe to the other a consistency, foresight, and coherence that its own experience belies. Of course, over time, even two blind men can do enormous damage to each other, not to speak of the room."[14]

III

By construing every local imbroglio as a test of global will, ideology raises stakes in situations that cannot be easily controlled and threatens to transmute limited into unlimited conflicts. Moreover, ideology, if pursued to the end, excludes coexistence. President Reagan instructed us that we must oppose evil "with all our might." How can we compromise with evil without losing our immortal soul? Ideology summons the true believer to a *jihad*, a crusade of extermination against the infidel.

The Russians are in no position to complain about such language. It has been more or less their own line since 1917. Reagan was simply paraphrasing Khrushchev: "We will bury you." Still the holy war has always represented a rather drastic approach to human affairs. It seems singularly unpromising in the epoch of nuclear weapons. And the irony was that, while Soviet ideology had grown tired, cynical and venal, the new American crusade was fresh and militant; and the Washington ideologues thereby presented the Kremlin with an undeserved opportunity to appear reasonable and prudent. In particular, the American dash into ideology promoted a major Soviet objective, the turning away of Western Europe from the alliance with the United States. It fostered the picture, in the words of Jacques Delors, the head of the European Economic Community, of an "increasingly aggressive and ideological" American administration carrying "a bible in one hand and a revolver in the other."[15]

The American administration, paradoxically, has collaborated in the alienation of America's allies; for the Reaganite nationalist ideology is, among other things, a new form of historic American isolationism. Isolationism never meant American secession from the world. Its essence was the rejection of commitments to other states and insistence on unhampered national freedom of action; no "entangling alliances," as Jefferson said in his first inaugural. In the Jeffersonian sense, isolationism can characterize an extrovert as well as an introvert America. "Unilateralism, to coin one more gobbledygook term," Richard Rovere and I wrote in 1951, "has become the new isolationism. Go it alone; meet force with maximum counterforce; there is no substitute for victory; do not worry about consequences: these are the tenets of the new faith. It is a more vivid, more adventurous, more dangerous faith than the placid, small-town isolationism of Borah, Hiram Johnson and Herbert Hoover. It provides scope for men of global vision or of messianic bent." [16]

We were writing about Douglas MacArthur; but in Ronald Reagan isolationism, now reincarnated as global unilateralism, found its messiah. Reagan deemed America's writ to run around the planet. In executing that writ, America was on its own. No administration since the Second World War so systematically scorned the United Nations, defied the World Court, overrode the interests of allies, dismissed negotiation with adversaries. No administration prided itself more, as Reagan said when an American plane forced down Palestinian hijackers in Italy in 1985, on doing it "all by our little selves."

The rush of ideology and unilateralism to the American head was fortunately far from complete. The Reaganite world view was not necessarily shared in its purity even by all the members of the Reagan administration. It was definitely not shared by the Republican leadership in Congress or by broad public opinion. It might not have been altogether shared by Reagan himself. In general, it has been more vigorously translated into rhetoric than into action. The suspicion has even arisen that Reagan's more impassioned ideological flights were, in Wendell Willkie's old phrase, "campaign oratory," pap for right-wing zealots to conceal the administration's covert creep to the center. His quest for reelection in 1984 had a notably tempering effect. The overriding political need to heed public opinion slowed down the march toward intervention in Central America and stirred the President into unexpected enthusiasm for arms control.

The most dependable restraint on ideology comes from the nature of foreign policy itself. The realism of the Founding Fathers sprang from the ineluctable character of international relations. National interest in the end sets limits on messianic passions. This fact explained the Reagan administration's tendency to march up the ideological hill and then march down again, as in the case of the pipeline embargo of 1983. For the United States does not have the power, even if it had the wisdom, to achieve great objectives in the world by itself. The idea that the recovery of military superiority would enable us to work our will around the planet is a vast delusion. In the 1940s, America had a monopoly of nuclear weapons—a margin of superiority we will never attain again; but we could not stop the Soviet Union from taking over Eastern Europe or the Communists from taking over China. Because both American power and American wisdom are limited, an effective foreign policy requires the cooperation of allies—and gives allies a certain capacity, too sparingly exercised, to rein in American messianism.

The pipeline embargo was only one example of the modification of ideology by interest. Ideology opposed the idea of negotiation with Moscow; but interest enjoined an appearance at least of trying to check the nuclear arms race. Ideology favored a blank check for the right wing in Israel. Interest argued for the equitable approach to a Middle Eastern settlement that Reagan set forth in 1982. Ideology called for the support of Taiwan against mainland China. Interest argued for the Beijing connection. Ideology converted the civil war in Lebanon into a supreme test of American will. Interest required a hasty American retreat. Ideology called for the support of South Africa against black Africa. Interest argued against a course that left black Africa no friends save the Soviet Union. Ideology called for the excommunication of socialist regimes. Interest saw benefits in cheerful relations with France, Italy, Spain, Portugal, Sweden and Greece. Ideology called for the chastisement of debtor nations in the Third World. Interest led to new rollovers and new loans in an effort to subsidize Third World economic growth.

Ideology found expression in unrestrained rhetoric; interest in generally restrained action. The trumpet kept sounding, but troops marched only when the enemy, like Grenada, had no army, navy or air force. Reagan's foreign policy remained a long twilight struggle between bark and bite. The mix, it must be added, appeared to suit the American people. Militancy in rhetoric gratified their sense of Soviet iniquity and American power and virtue. Moderation in action reassured them that immoderate talk would not blow up the world.

IV

There remain sectors of policy where ideology still holds sway. One, for the season at least, is Central America. No one can be too sure over the longer run because the administration has marched up and down this particular hill more than once in the last five years. During the vicariate of General Haig, insurgency in Central America was deemed a major Soviet challenge demanding a mighty American response. Then, in the first tranquilizing days of Secretary Shultz, the impression was allowed to spread that perhaps the troubles had local origins and might be amenable to local remedies. Subsequently Secretary Shultz caught the ideological flu, and by 1986 we were back at the global test of will.

Unquestionably the United States faces tough problems in the region. For a century American business had dominated, developed and deformed Central America, leaving an explosive contrast between poverty and oligarchy. A generation ago the Alliance for Progress set out to deal with poverty and oligarchy. But the Alliance changed its character and abandoned concern with social reform after Kennedy's death. When revolution predictably burst out in Central America in the late 1970s, ideology rejected the notion of local origins and decreed that the Russians were back at their old game of dominos.

Ideology, it should be noted, offers a field day for self-fulfilling prophecies. If you shape policy to what you regard as a predestined result, chances are that you will get the result you predestine. Having decided a priori that the Nicaraguan revolution was a Soviet-Cuban conspiracy, Washington gave the Sandinistas no alternative but the Cubans and Russians. The French wanted to sell Nicaragua arms and send in a military mission. Washington, instead of welcoming a democratic presence that would have been reliably alert to Soviet deviltry, erupted in wrath. When the CIA set out to overthrow the government in Managua, Washington expressed indignation that this government dared seek arms to defend itself. Maybe it would have happened anyway, but the ideological policy made insurgent anti-Americanism inevitable.

Washington's present disposition in Central America is to globalize the stakes and to militarize the remedy. We are trying to provide the government of El Salvador with sufficient military aid to defeat the insurgency and to provide the insurgency in Nicaragua with sufficient military aid to defeat the government. If we don't act to stop Marxism in Central America, the argument runs, dominos will topple, and the Soviet Union will establish a bridgehead in the center of the western hemisphere. "Our credibility would collapse," Reagan said, "our alliances would crumble, and the safety of our homeland would be in jeopardy."[17]

Other views are possible. The historian is bound to note that unilateral military action by the United States in Latin America is nearly always a mistake. In the 1980s armed intervention will do more to spread Marxism than to retard it. But another by-product of ideology, along with the self-fulfilling prophecy, is the conviction that the anointed country, whether the United States these days or the Soviet Union in all days, knows the interests of other countries better than they know their own interests. In 1967 President Johnson sent Clark Clifford on an Asian tour, charging him to get the states of the South East Asia Treaty Organization to increase their contributions to the forces fighting communism in Vietnam. Clifford was astonished to discover that other Asian countries, though considerably more exposed to the danger, took it less tragically than the United States did and saw no need to send more troops. When he thereafter became Secretary of Defense, Clifford did his best to end American participation in the war.

If a Marxist Nicaragua (population 2.9 million) or El Salvador (population 4.5 million) is a threat to the hemisphere, they are more dire threats to Mexico, to Costa Rica, to Panama, to Venezuela, to Colombia than to the United States. These nations are a good deal more vulnerable politically, economically and militarily than the United States; they are closer to the scene and more knowledgeable about it; and their leaders are just as determined as the United States is on their behalf to resist their own overthrow. When the people on the spot don't see the threat as apocalyptically as Washington does, only ideologues can conclude with divine assurance that they are wrong and we are right.

In any event, ideology is a sure formula for hypocrisy, if not for disaster. Mr. Reagan righteously declared that we will not "protect the Nicaraguan government from the anger of its own people."[18] A fine sentiment—but why did it not apply equally to the government of El Salvador? Why did we condemn Nicaragua for postponing elections until 1984 while we condoned Chile, which postponed elections till 1989? Would the administration have displayed the same solicitude for free elections and human rights in Nicaragua if the Somozas were still running things?

Ideology insists on the escalation of local troubles into global crises. National interest would emphasize the indispensability of working with Latin Americans who know the territory far better than we do and without whose support we cannot gain our objectives. Let Mexico, Venezuela, Colombia and Panama—the so-called Contadora Group—take the lead, and back them to the hilt. Only if all agree on a military remedy will armed intervention do the United States more good than harm in the hemisphere. If it is too late for a negotiated settlement and our Latin friends reject collective intervention, then we may have to resign ourselves to turmoil in Central America for some time to come—turmoil beyond our power to correct and beyond our wisdom to cure.

V

Another sector where ideology still controls policy in Washington is, alas, the most menacing of all—the nuclear arms race. It is in this field that the substitution of models for reality has the most baneful effect. War games are played by general staffs with such intensity these days that they have come to be taken not as speculations but as predictions. The higher metaphysics of deterrence, by concentrating on the worst imaginable cases, such as a Soviet first strike against the United States or a surprise invasion of Western Europe, makes improbable events the governing force in budgetary, weapons and deployment decisions. History shows the Soviet Union to be cautious about risking direct military encounters with the United States; but ideology abolishes history. Reality evaporates in the hallucinatory world where strategic theologians calculate how many warheads can be balanced on the head of a pin. Little seems more dangerous than the current fantasy of controlled nuclear war, with generals calibrating nuclear escalation like grand masters at the chessboard. Let us not be bamboozled by models. Once the nuclear threshold is breached, the game is over.

One cannot dismiss the Soviet Union as a military threat. We have noted that one thing Russia apparently does well is to build nuclear missiles. But ideology, here as elsewhere, encourages exaggeration. The professional duty of generals is to guarantee the safety of their countries; and the professional instinct of generals is to ask for enough to meet the remotest contingency. As old Lord Salisbury once wrote, "No lesson seems to be so deeply inculcated by the experience of life as that you never should trust experts. If you believe the doctors, nothing is wholesome; if you believe the theologians, nothing is innocent; if you believe the soldiers, nothing is safe."[19] Like ideology, defense budgets demand ever more menacing enemies.

In Washington Pentagon officials take masochistic pleasure at regular intervals in crying that the Soviet Union is now stronger than the United States. These recurrent Pentagon panics range from the "missile gap," promulgated by the Gaither Report in 1958, to the "window of vulnerability," announced by Secretary of Defense Weinberger in 1981 and slammed shut by the Scowcroft Commission in 1983. One doubts that defense officials really believe their own lamentations; at least, I have never heard any of them offering to trade in the American for the Soviet defense establishment. When asked in Congress recently whether he would exchange places with his Soviet counterpart, the chairman of the American Joint Chiefs of Staff replied succinctly, "Not on your life." The ideologues achieve their dire effects by selective counting—by comparing theater nuclear weapons, for example, and omitting American superiority in the invulnerable sea-based deterrent. It is not required to take these lamentations too seriously, especially around budget time.

The irony is that the Pentagon and the Soviet Defense Ministry prosper symbiotically. There is no greater racket in the world today than generals claiming the other side is ahead in order to get bigger budgets for themselves. This tacit collusion, based on a common vested interest in crisis, remains a major obstacle in the search for peace. As President Kennedy remarked to Norman Cousins, the editor of the *Saturday Review*, in the spring of 1963, "Mr. Khrushchev and I occupy approximately the same political positions inside our governments. He would like to prevent a nuclear war but is under severe pressure from his hard-line crowd, which interprets every move in that direction as appeasement. I've got similar problems. . . . The hard-liners in the Soviet Union and the United States feed on one another."[20]

The existence of Soviet military might obviously requires effective counterbalance. It requires nuclear deterrence capable of retaliation against a first strike, and this the West has. It also requires conventional force capable of discouraging Soviet aspirations in Europe, and this the West may presently lack. The European democracies must understand that the delusion of rescue through limited nuclear war makes no sense in the age of nuclear stand-off. However destructive conventional war can be in modern times, it is infinitely less destructive than nuclear war would be. And the sure way to make the improbability of a Soviet attack across rebellious satellites on Western Europe even more improbable is to leave no doubt that the costs, even without nuclear response, would be intolerably high. This lies within the power of the European democracies to do.

VI

But what of the bomb itself? For we live today in a situation without precedent—a situation that transcends all history and threatens the end of history. I must confess that I have come late to this apocalyptic view. To set limits on the adventures of the human mind has always

seemed—still seems—the ultimate heresy, the denial of humanity itself. But freedom involves risk, and today the free mind has led us to
the edge of the ultimate abyss.

One had always supposed that, with the nuclear genie out of the
bottle, the prospect of blowing up the world would have a sobering
effect on those who possessed the tragic power to initiate nuclear war.
For most of the nuclear age this supposition has been roughly true.
Statesmen have generally understood, as President Kennedy said in
1961, "Mankind must put an end to war—or war will put an end to
mankind."[21] I saw how after the Cuban missile crisis a shaken Kennedy—and a shaken Khrushchev, too—moved purposefully toward
a partial ban on nuclear testing and a systematic reduction of international acrimony.

When policy falls under the sway of ideology, one has less confidence in the admonitory effect of the possession of nuclear weapons.
The bane of ideology is that it exalts abstractions over human beings.
It impoverishes our sense of reality, and it impoverishes our imagination too. It enfeebles our capacity to visualize the Doomsday horror. It conceals nightmare behind a screen of jargon. It inhibits us
from confronting the possibility that can no longer be denied: the
extermination of sentient life on this planet.

Under the hypnosis of dogma, ideologues in Washington today see
an unlimited nuclear arms race not as an appalling threat to all humanity but as a neat way to do the Russians in. Either the Russians
will try to keep up with us, which will wreck their economy, or they
will fail to keep up, which will leave us the decisive military advantage.
To have an arms control agreement, the ideologues believe, would be
to renounce our most potent weapon against the empire of evil.

Now they have developed the Star Wars fantasy as the great new
stimulus to the nuclear arms race. Research begun in the 1980s, the
Reagan administration contends, will produce in the early twenty-
first century a shield in space that would provide effective defense
against intercontinental ballistic missiles (though it would not defend
cities and people, and it would not stop low-altitude delivery systems).
Most scientists doubt that the goal is technically attainable even in the
long run. No one can doubt the consequences in the short run. For
there is by universal agreement no such thing as a totally impenetrable shield. The Soviet Union will do exactly what we would do if
the Soviet Union were flourishing Star Wars against us: build more
ICBMs in order to overwhelm the space shield; build more cruise
missiles, bombers and other low-flying weapons in order to go under
the shield; build more decoys and other penetration aids to confuse

and exhaust the shield. Since these countermeasures are technically simpler than building the shield and cost far less, they will be relatively easy to sustain. And the arms race will roar on.

Despite recent emphasis in defense doctrine on "prevailing" in a "controlled and protracted" nuclear war, I continue to find it hard to suppose that either superpower would deliberately embark on nuclear war *ab initio*. But it is not hard to foresee nuclear overreaction to the frustration or embarrassment of defeat in conventional warfare. It is still easier, with 50,000 warheads piling up in the hands of the superpowers and heaven knows how many more scattered or hidden or incipient in other hands, to foresee nuclear war precipitated by terrorists, or by madness, or by accident, or by misreading the flashes on a radar screen.

The stake is too great to permit this horror to grow. For the stake is supreme: it is life itself. Nor can the answer to the nightmare be unilateral nuclear disarmament by the West. The likely result would not be to prompt the Soviet leadership to do likewise but to place the democratic world at the mercy of Soviet communism. Mercy has not been a salient characteristic of any communist regime.

Neither the arms race nor unilateral disarmament provides refuge. The better 'ole is the revival of the vanishing art of diplomacy. American officials these days like to strike Churchillian poses. They remind one of Mark Twain's response when his wife tried to cure him of swearing by loosing a string of oaths herself: "You got the words right, Livy, but you don't know the tune." Our tank-town Churchills lack one of the things that made Churchill great: his power of historical discrimination.

"Those who are prone by temperament and character," Churchill wrote in *The Gathering Storm*, "to seek sharp and clear-cut solutions of difficult and obscure problems, who are ready to fight whenever some challenge comes from a foreign Power, have not always been right. On the other hand, those whose inclination is . . . to seek patiently and faithfully for peaceful compromise are not always wrong. On the contrary, in the majority of instances they may be right, not only morally but from a practical standpoint."[22]

Churchill himself in his last tour as Prime Minister argued in this spirit for negotiation and détente against the opposition both of the Eisenhower administration and of his own foreign office. Harold Macmillan as Prime Minister continued Churchill's fight and fortified John Kennedy in the determination to bring nuclear weapons testing to an end. Macmillan, Kennedy, probably Khrushchev too, all wanted a comprehensive test ban. The comprehensive ban foundered on the problem of on-site inspection. The Soviet Union was ready to permit three annual inspections of suspicious seismic disturbances. The British would have settled for that. The United States would not go below seven—not because the administration considered seven technically necessary to ensure verification but because it had been hard enough to argue the Joint Chiefs of Staff down from twenty and further reduction would have doomed the treaty in the Senate. The result was the limited test ban treaty of 1963. This is one of the great might-have-beens of modern history. If Kennedy, Macmillan and Khrushchev had succeeded in their desire to end nuclear tests underground as well as in the atmosphere and under water, the development of the new generations of multiwarhead nuclear weapons would have been halted. The world today would have been a safer place.

A comprehensive test ban remains a key to reining in the arms race. But in the mid-1980s the American military establishment was as determined as ever to carry forward its programs of weapons tests. As usual, it claimed it was behind the Soviet Union. If there was a testing gap, it could only have been because the military had squandered their opportunities. By 1985 the United States had conducted some two hundred more nuclear tests than the Soviet Union. Though the limited test ban treaty committed the signatories "to continue negotiations" in order "to achieve the discontinuance of all test explosions of nuclear weapons for all time," Reagan instead discontinued the negotiations in 1982 and unilaterally repudiated the treaty commitment.

Much else is possible. A ban on weapons in space is long overdue. President Eisenhower's Open Skies plan of 1955, proposing that the superpowers exchange blueprints of military establishments and permit reciprocal aerial photographic overflights, deserves revival, as France has tried to do with its recent suggestion of a United Nations international satellite agency. A joint U.S.-Soviet crisis center, where each side could monitor the other's radar screens and to which war rumors would go for swift resolution, would reduce the chances of accidental nuclear war. A reciprocal and verifiable freeze on the production, testing and deployment of nuclear weapons and delivery vehicles enjoys wide popular support. We should eschew launch-on-warning and announce a policy of no-early-first-use of nuclear weapons. Deep cuts in nuclear stockpiles should follow, designed to produce mutual security at the lowest possible force levels. Robert McNamara and Hans A. Bethe estimate that the present inventory of 50,000 warheads can be cut to perhaps 2000.[23] Humanity has no choice but to find ways to crawl back from the edge of the abyss. Better the extinction of the nuclear race than the extinction of the human race.

VII

What the world needs to bring this about is above all deliverance from ideology. This is not to suggest symmetry between the United States and the Soviet Union. In the United States, ideology is a lurking susceptibility, a periodic fling, fooling some of the people some of the time but profoundly alien to the Constitution and to the national spirit. Washington's current ideological frenzy is the result, not of popular demand or mandate, but of the superficial facts that in the 1980 election the voters, unable to abide the thought of four more years of what they had, had Reagan as the only practical alternative and that in 1984 a Keynesian economic recovery produced by a $200 billion budgetary deficit assured Reagan's reelection.

In the Soviet Union ideology remains the heart of the matter. It is not a susceptibility but a compulsion, inscribed in sacred texts and enforced by the brutal machinery of a still hard police state. Yet even in the Soviet Union one senses an erosion of the old ideological intensity until a good deal of what remains is simply the vocabulary in which Soviet leaders are accustomed to speak. Let not a spurt of American ideologizing breathe new life into the decadent Soviet ideology, especially by legitimizing the Russian fear of an American crusade aimed at the destruction of Russian society.

Ideology is the curse of public affairs because it converts politics into a branch of theology and sacrifices human beings on the altar of dogma. The simplifications of doctrine are forever at war with the complexity of reality. "Doctrines are the most frightful tyrants to which men are ever subject," said William Graham Sumner, the pungent late-nineteenth-century conservative, "because doctrines get inside of a man's own reason and betray him against himself. Civilized men have done their fiercest fighting for doctrines. . . . If you want war, nourish a doctrine."*

Ideology in the end is out of character for Americans. Dogma does the republic grievous damage, above all in foreign policy. In thinking about international relations, Americans would do well to sober up

---

*William Graham Sumner, "War," in *Selected Essays of William Graham Sumner*, ed. A. G. Keller and M. R. Davie (New Haven, 1924), 338. Cf. Harold Macmillan in his maiden speech as Earl of Stockton to the House of Lords: "Once you get a doctrine, that is the end of you. Pragmatic politics are the only good ones." *London Sunday Times*, 18 November 1984.

from the ideological binge and return to the cold, gray realism of the Founding Fathers, men who lucidly understood the role of interest and force in a dangerous world and thought that saving America was enough without trying to save all humanity as well.

The Founding Fathers recognized that nations, like people, are subject to delusions of grandeur. Seeking always for checks on power, they emphasized in the 63rd *Federalist* that "attention to the judgment of other nations" was indispensable to the American government for two reasons:

the one is, that, independently of the merits of any particular plan or measure, it is desirable, on various accounts, that it should appear to other nations as the offspring of a wise and honorable policy; the second is, that in doubtful cases, particularly where the national councils may be warped by some strong passion or momentary interest, the presumed or known opinion of the impartial world may be the best guide that can be followed.

What has not America lost by her want of character with foreign nations; and how many errors and follies would she not have avoided, if the justice and propriety of her measures had, in every instance, been previously tried by the light in which they would probably appear to the unbiased part of mankind?

Wise words then. Wise words now.

FOUR

National Interests and Moral Absolutes

———————◆•◆———————

FOR CENTURIES theologians have distinguished between just and unjust wars, jurists have propounded rules for international conduct, and moralists have pondered whether a state's course in foreign affairs was right or wrong. Yet the problem of the relationship between ethics and international politics remains perennially unsettled. It has been a particularly vexing problem in the United States, at least since the Mexican and Spanish-American wars and more than ever during the Vietnam War; for an Anglo-Saxon ancestry and a Calvinist heritage have endowed Americans with a mighty need for seeing their exercise of power as morally virtuous.

In recent years, Americans have debated with renewed urgency the ethics of power and the dilemmas that confront moral man in an immoral world. Above all, in this nuclear age, we are compelled to wonder, as Robert Kennedy did after the missile crisis of 1962, "What, if any, circumstances or justification gives . . . any government the moral right to bring its people and possibly all people under the shadow of nuclear destruction?"[1] Historians cannot hope to resolve questions that have stumped philosophers through the ages. Still, some historical notes on this hopelessly amorphous subject may have their uses.

I

William James said that temperaments determine philosophies. People who respond to international affairs divide temperamentally into two schools: those who first ask of a policy, "Is it morally right?" and those who first ask, "Will it work?"; those who see policies as good or evil, and those who see them as wise or foolish. One cannot presume an ultimate metaphysical antagonism between the moralist and the realist. No realist can wholly escape perceptions of good and evil, and no policy can wholly divorce ethical from geopolitical considerations. Nor in the impenetrability of human motives can we easily know when moral reasons are realistic concerns in disguise (very often the case) or when realistic reasons are moral concerns in disguise (more frequent than one might think; Israel is an obvious example). Still the very choice of disguise reveals something about temperaments—and about philosophies.

Let us begin with those who hold that moral values should control foreign policy. This was not the view of the Founding Fathers, who saw international affairs as a function of the balance of power. But in the century after 1815, as Americans turned their backs on the power struggles of Europe, they stopped thinking about power as the essence of international politics. The moralization of foreign policy became a national penchant, nor did the subsequent return of the republic to the world power game much enfeeble that cherished habit. Woodrow Wilson's mission was precisely to move the world beyond power politics. In our own day moralists on both right and left, while quarreling about everything else, concur in thinking that moral principles should dominate foreign policy. The key question, as Ronald Reagan said in his first 1984 debate and as many of his radical critics would agree, is: "Is it morally right? And on that basis, and that basis alone, we make a decision on every issue."[2]

Yet many foreign policy decisions remain questions of prudence and adjustment, not of good and evil. Even moralizers would probably go along with their searching critic George Kennan in doubting that "it matters greatly to God whether the free trade area or the Common Market prevails in Europe, whether the British fish or do not fish in Icelandic territorial waters, or even whether Indians or Pakistani run Kashmir. It might matter, but it is hard for us, with our limited vision, to know."[3] The raw material of foreign affairs is, a good deal of the time, morally neutral or ambiguous. In consequence, for the great majority of foreign policy transactions, moral principles cannot be decisive.

But these, it may be said, are technical transactions. On the great issues, surely moral principles should be controlling. Yet how are right and wrong to be defined in dealings among sovereign states? Here the moralist of foreign affairs has recourse to the moral code most familiar to him—the code that governs dealings among individuals. His contention is that states should be judged by principles of individual morality. As Wilson put it in his address to Congress on the declaration of war in 1917, "We are at the beginning of an age in which it will be insisted that the same standards of conduct and of responsibility for wrong done shall be observed among nations and their governments that are observed among the individual citizens of civilized states."[4] John Foster Dulles said it even more directly during the Second World War: "The broad principles that should govern our international conduct are not obscure. They grow out of the practice by the nations of the simple things Christ taught."[5]

The argument for the application of simple Christ-like principles to questions of foreign policy is thus that there is, or should be, an identity between the morality of individuals and the morality of states. The issues involved here are not easy. One cannot doubt, as I shall contend later, that there are cases in foreign affairs where moral judgment is not only possible but necessary. One may also suggest that these are extreme cases and do not warrant the routine use of personal moral criteria in making foreign policy judgments.

"The rule of morality," Alexander Hamilton pointed out in the early years of the American republic, ". . . is not precisely the same between nations as between individuals. The duty of making its own welfare the guide of its actions, is much stronger upon the former than upon the latter. Existing millions, and for the most part future generations, are concerned in the present measures of a government; while the consequences of the private action of an individual ordinarily terminate with himself, or are circumscribed with a narrow compass."[6]

Reinhold Niebuhr renewed the argument against the confusion of moral categories half a century ago in *Moral Man and Immoral Society.* The obligation of the individual, Niebuhr wrote, is to obey the law of love and sacrifice; "from the viewpoint of the author of an action, unselfishness must remain the criterion of the highest morality." But states cannot be sacrificial. Governments are not individuals. They are not principals but agents. They are trustees for the happiness and interest of others. Niebuhr quoted Hugh Cecil's argument that un-selfishness "is inappropriate to the action of a state. No one has a right to be unselfish with other people's interests."[7]

In short the individual's duty of self-sacrifice and the state's duty of self-preservation are in conflict. This makes it impossible to measure the action of states by a purely individualistic morality. "The Sermon on the Mount," said Winston Churchill, "is the last word in Christian ethics. . . . Still, it is not on those terms that Ministers assume their responsibilities of guiding states."[8]

This is not to say that might makes right. It is to say that the morality of states is inherently different from the morality of individuals. Max Weber noted the contrast between the "ethic of ultimate ends— that is, in religious terms, 'The Christian does rightly and leaves the results with the Lord'" and the "ethic of responsibility," which takes into account the foreseeable results of one's action.[9] Saints can be pure, but statesmen must be responsible. As trustees for others, they must defend interests and compromise principles. In consequence politics is a field where practical and prudential judgment must have priority over simple moral verdicts.

II

Now it may be urged against this view that the tension between individual morality and political necessity has been, to a considerable degree, bridged within national societies. This takes place when the moral sense of a community finds embodiment in positive law. But the shift of the argument from morality to law only strengthens the case against the facile intrusion of moral judgment into foreign affairs.

A nation's legal code can set down relatively clear standards of right and wrong in individual behavior because statutory law is the product of an imperfect but nonetheless authentic moral consensus. International life has no such broad or deep areas of moral consensus. It was once hoped that modern technology would create a common fund of moral imperatives transcending the concerns of particular nations — common concepts of interest, justice and comity—either because the revolution in communications would increase mutual understanding or because the revolution in weaponry would increase mutual fear. Such expectations have been disappointed. Until nations come to such a common morality, there can be no world law to regulate the behavior of states as there is law within nations to regulate the behavior of individuals. Nor can international institutions—the League of Nations or the United Nations—produce by sleight of hand a moral consensus where none exists. World law must express world community; it cannot create it.

This is not to ignore the growth of an international consensus. Humanity has begun to develop standards for conduct among nations — defined, for example, in customary international law, in the Hague Conventions of 1899 and 1907, in the Geneva Protocol of 1925 and the Geneva Conventions of 1949, in the Charter and Covenants of the United Nations, in the Charter, Judgment, and Principles of the Nuremberg Tribunal, and so on. Such standards outlaw actions that the civilized world has placed beyond the limits of permissible behavior. Within this restricted area a code emerges that makes moral judgment in international affairs possible up to a point. And within its scope this rudimentary code deserves, and must have, the most unflinching enforcement.

But these international rules deal with the limits rather than with the substance of policy. They seek to prevent abnormalities and excesses in the behavior of states, but they do not offer grounds for moral judgment on normal international transactions (including, it must be sorrowfully said, war itself, so long as war does not constitute aggression and so long as the rules of warfare are faithfully observed). These international accords may eventually lead to a planetary consensus. But, for the present, national, ideological, ethical and religious divisions remain as bitterly intractable as ever.

To summarize the argument to this point, I am constrained to doubt the easy relevance of personal moral criteria to most decisions in foreign policy, first, because few issues in foreign affairs lend themselves to categorical moral judgments; second, because governments in their nature must make decisions on different principles from those of personal morality; and third, because no international moral consensus exists in sufficient depth and strength to sustain a comprehensive and binding international morality.

III

The problem is not only that simplistic moral principles are of limited use in the making of foreign policy decisions. It is that a moralistic foreign policy may well add troubles of its own creation.

For many Americans, morality in foreign policy consists in the application to the world of a body of general precepts, a process accompanied by lectures to others and congratulations to ourselves. The assumption is that we are the anointed custodians of international behavior, and that the function of United States policy is to mark other states up and down according to their obedience to the rules as we see them. Laying down the moral law to sinning brethren from our seat of judgment no doubt pleases our own sense of rectitude. But it fosters dangerous misconceptions about the nature of foreign policy.

Moralizers prefer symbolic to serious politics. They tend to see foreign policy as a means of registering ideological attitudes, not of producing hard results in a hard world. Moralistic rhetoric, moreover, often masks the pursuit of national advantage—a situation we Americans recognize at once when foreign states pursue their selfish objectives under a cloak of moral universalism. Should we be surprised that foreigners are just as cynical about American claims to moral disinterestedness? In practice, moralistic declarations serve less as a restraint on self-serving action than as a pretext, generally transparent, for such action. The one law that rules all others, said Henry Adams, is that "masses of men invariably follow interests in deciding morals."[10]

The moralization of foreign policy creates still graver problems. Indeed, moral reasons cynically exploited may do the world less harm than moral reasons fervently believed. The compulsion to convert conflicts of interest into conflicts of good and evil undermines diplomacy. For diplomacy is above all the adjustment of conflicting interests. Moralization shifts international relations from the political mode, which is conditional, to the ideological mode, which is unconditional. And moralization often ends by combining the most lofty intentions with the most ghastly consequences. "I do not like to hit a village," an American pilot in Vietnam told a newspaperman. "You know you are hitting women and children. But you've got to decide that your cause is noble and that the work has to be done."[11] The more passionately people decide the cause is noble, the more likely they are to reject accommodation and seek the final victory of their principles. Little has been more pernicious in international politics than excessive righteousness.

The moralizing fever may, as noted, strike at any point along the political spectrum. From one standpoint, there is little difference between moralists on the right who see the Soviet Union as the focus of all evil and moralists on the left who ascribe all sin to the United States. They are equal victims of the same malady. Both regard foreign policy as a branch of theology. Both rush to judgment on erring humanity. They end as mirror images of each other. "Moral indignation," the Christian historian Sir Herbert Butterfield observed, "corrupts the agent who possesses it and is not calculated to reform the man who is the object of it."

Butterfield added: "The passing of what purports to be a moral judgment—particularly a judgment which amounts to the assertion that they are worse men than I am—is . . . really a demand for an illegitimate form of power. The attachment to it is based on its efficacy as a tactical weapon, its ability to rouse irrational fervour and extraordinary malevolence against some enemy."[12] "The English are indeed a great and noble people," said Gladstone, a Christian statesman if there ever was one; "but it adds nothing to their greatness or their nobleness that . . . we should trumpet forth our virtues in elaborate panegyrics and designate those who may not be wholly of our mind as a knot of foreign conspirators."[13]

In the conduct of foreign policy, moral absolutism leads on to crusades and the extermination of the infidel. Failure is blamed not on intractable obstacles or on mistaken judgment but on traitors (or war criminals) in high places. We hear much about the great need of the modern world for religious faith. But religion, far from serving as a check on international ferocity, is in the 1980s the prime cause of most of the killing taking place in the world: in the Middle East, in the Persian Gulf, in Ireland, in India, in Cyprus, in the Philippines, in Sri Lanka, throughout Africa—not to mention the havoc wrought by the totalitarian religions of the twentieth century. A fanatic, Mr. Dooley reminds us, "does what he thinks th' Lord wud do if He only knew th' facts in th' case."[14]

IV

If moral principles have only limited application in foreign affairs, and if moral absolutism breeds fanaticism, must we abandon the effort to bring about restraint in international relations? Is the world therefore condemned to jungle anarchy? Not necessarily; the argument moves rather to the conclusion that foreign policy decisions must generally be taken on other than moralistic grounds. It is necessary now to consider what these other grounds are.

Those "who act upon the Principles of disinterestedness," wrote George Washington during the American Revolution, "are, comparatively speaking, no more than a drop in the Ocean." Washington acknowledged the power of patriotism. "But I will venture to assert that a great and lasting War can never be supported on this principle alone. It must be aided by a prospect of Interest. . . . We must take the passions of Men as Nature has given them."[15] What was true for men, Washington believed, was even more true for nations: no nation was to be trusted farther than it is bound by its interest. In short, where the embryonic international community cannot regulate dealings among nations, the safer basis for decision in foreign policy lies not in attempts to determine right or wrong but in attempts to determine the national interest.

The idea of national interest faded from the national consciousness after the United States receded from the European power equation. When America made its return in 1917, Wilson, the international moralist par excellence, rejected national interest as an explanation for American entry into the First World War. Thirty years later, when the Cold War undermined the Wilsonian dream of a world beyond power politics, the revival of the national-interest perspective came almost as revelation. National interest seemed for a season the key to the foreign policy riddle. Its apostles styled themselves realists. They took the passions of nations as history had given them. They saw international politics as a struggle for power. They rejected cant and sentimentality. And George Washington had plainly been right in saying that every nation *must* respond to some conception of its interest. No nation that abandons self-preservation as the mainspring of its policy can survive; nor, indeed, can any nation be relied upon in international dealings that acts against its national interest. Without the magnetic compass of national interest there would be no order or predictability in international affairs.

Moreover, every nation has a set of fairly definite strategic interests. One has only to recall the continuities of Russian foreign policy, whether directed by czars or by commissars. When one moves on to politics, economics and culture, identification of national interest becomes more debatable. Still even here nations often retain, through changes of government and ideology, an impressive amount of continuity: consider France from de Gaulle to Mitterrand.

National interest is obviously not a figment of the imagination. But, as critics began in time to point out, neither is it a self-executing formula. In practice, we quarrel endlessly over what national interest prescribes in particular situations. Hans Morgenthau, the great theoretician of national interest, argued that German leaders had twice in one generation betrayed Germany's national interest; but that is hardly what the Kaiser and Hitler thought they were doing. In the United States in the 1960s, the prominent realists—Morgenthau, Kennan, Niebuhr, Walter Lippmann—condemned American participation in the Vietnam War as unwarranted by national interest. But Lyndon Johnson decided to Americanize the war because, he explained, "we felt our national interest required it."[16] History, it is true, has vindicated the realists; but who could *prove* at the time where the national interest truly lay? When indeed have statesmen ever believed that they were acting against the national interest of their countries? Not only government departments but corporations, trade unions, lobbies domestic and foreign, always present their parochial concerns as the national interest. The idea of national interest, critics concluded, is dangerously elastic. Far from providing clear answers to every international perplexity, national interest turns out to be subjective, ambiguous and susceptible to great abuse.

Moralizers have still deeper objections. They consider national interest a wicked idea on which to found national policy. It nourishes, they say, a nation's baser self. It becomes a license for international aggrandizement. The pursuit of exclusively national goals leads ineluctably to aggression, imperialism, war. As many follies have been committed in the name of national interest as in the name of national righteousness. National interest, in short, is a mandate for international amorality.

In practice, this is often so. In principle, however, national interest prescribes its own morality. After all, the order and predictability valued by George Washington in international affairs constitute the precondition for international moral standards. More important, national interest, consistently construed, is a self-limiting motive. Any rigorous defender of the idea must accept that other nations have their legitimate interests too. The recognition of equal claims sets bounds on aggression. Unless transformed by an injection of moral righteousness, the idea of national interest cannot produce ideological crusades for unlimited objectives.

This self-limiting factor does not rest only on recognition of other nations' interests. It is reinforced by self-correcting tendencies in the power equilibrium—tendencies that prevent national interest, at least when the disparity of power is not too great, from billowing up into unbridled national egoism. For national interest is linked with the idea of an international balance of power. History has shown how often the overweening behavior of an aggressive state leads to counteraction on the part of other states determined to restore a balance of power. National egomania turns out to be contrary to long-term national interest. States that throw their weight around are generally forced to revise their notions as to where their national interest truly lies. This has happened in this century to Germany and Japan. In time it may even happen to the Soviet Union and the United States.

For these reasons, it may be suggested that national interest, realistically construed, will promote enlightened rather than aggressive policy. So a realist like Hamilton said that his aim was not "to recommend a policy absolutely selfish or interested in nations; but to show, that a policy regulated by their own interest, *as far as justice and good faith permit,* is, and ought to be, their prevailing one" (emphasis added).[17]

V

The idea of national interest appears neither altogether subjective nor altogether amoral. But a further objection arises: may it not be obsolescent, an idea overtaken by the onward rush of history? Is not the realist view in fact an extrapolation from the pattern of interstate relations prevailing in Europe in the eighteenth and nineteenth centuries? Realism's operative ideas—national interest, the balance of power, *raisons d'état,* limited objectives, foreign policy conducted by professional elites and protected from the vagrant emotions of domestic politics—all may have been no more than the functions of a specific historical epoch, an era of absolute monarchies when states agreed on the rules of the game and citizens made no claim to democratic control of foreign policy. Realism may well be inadequate to a new age characterized by the democratization of foreign policy, by total war, by absolute weapons, by ideological crusades, by the crashing into the international equilibrium of new states that do not accept the rules of the game and by the rise of transnational forces, from international agencies to multinational corporations to terrorist gangs, all draining power from national states.

Of these changes, the democratization of foreign policy bears most fatefully on the idea of national interest. The classical balance of power was a mechanism operated by professional diplomats. In the nineteenth century, diplomacy was, in G. M. Young's phrase, "what one clerk said to another clerk."[18] "Governments were made to deal with Governments," observed young Henry Adams when he served as a secretary in the American legation in London during the Civil War, "not with private individuals or with the opinions of foreign society."[19] But when Adams returned to Washington a decade later, he found not one but three State Departments—the official one, nominally presided over by the Secretary of State (who in this case "seemed to have vanished"); a second on Capitol Hill in the Senate Foreign Relations Committee, which Charles Sumner ruled with a high hand; and a third in the War Department, with President Grant himself for chief.[20] Two decades later, Adams bemoaned the added influence of the foreign lobbies—the German and Russian legations and the Clan-na-Gael.[21]

By the twentieth century the professional monopoly was shattered beyond recall. The era of government as a unified entity in foreign affairs, rationally calculating costs and benefits, came to an end (to the extent that the 'rational-actor' model ever had much reality). Policy-makers in a democracy now had to take account of bureaucratic rivals within the executive branch; of skeptics in the legislative branch; of the press; of pressure groups, idealistic and crooked; of national and of foreign opinion. The increase in economic interdependence among nations and the spread of the idea that government was responsible for the economy multiplied the number of groups claiming the right to define the national interest in foreign affairs. A new scholarly literature examining 'bureaucratic politics' and 'domestic constraints' grew up to deal with the transformation of diplomacy.

The democratization of foreign policy no doubt complicates the management of foreign affairs. Professional diplomats echo more poignantly than ever Tocqueville's lament that foreign policy calls for exactly those qualities in which democracy is most deficient. "A democracy can only with great difficulty regulate the details of an important undertaking, persevere in a fixed design, and work out its execution in spite of serious obstacles. It cannot combine its measures with secrecy or await their consequences with patience."[22]

Yet democratization was, as Tocqueville well understood, inevitable. Is it really after all such a calamity? Is it a bad thing that those who will be ordered to kill and to die should have a voice in forming the policies that decide their fate? Nor for that matter does history demonstrate that the professionals are always right and the people always wrong. The requirement of consent may even make it easier for governments to sustain policies, to demand sacrifice, to persevere in a fixed design and to await consequences with patience.

Nor does the democratization of foreign policy necessarily mean the rejection of the realist emphasis on interest and power. Democratization no doubt exposes the conduct of foreign affairs to those gusts of moralizing demagoguery that turn expedients into crusades. Still the concept of national interest can provide the focus and framework within which the debate over the idea's application takes place. It is the debate itself that gives the idea its content and, in a democracy, its legitimacy. And the play of democratic pressures on foreign policy often strengthens the latent moral content in the idea of national interest. "Let the people get it into their heads that a policy is selfish and they will not follow it," A. J. P. Taylor has written. ". . . A democratic foreign policy has got to be idealistic; or at the very least it has to be justified in terms of great general principles."[23]

So a realist like Theodore Roosevelt could say, "It is neither wise nor right for a nation to disregard its own needs, and it is foolish — and may be wicked — to think that other nations will disregard theirs. But it is wicked for a nation only to regard its own interest, and foolish to believe that such is the sole motive that actuates any other nation. It should be our steady aim to raise the ethical standard of national action just as we strive to raise the ethical standard of individual action."[24]

All human actions are subject to moral judgment. And it may well be that the compulsion of nations to justify their actions by abstract moral principles is an involuntary tribute to the vision of a world pub-

lic opinion, a potential international consensus, that we must all hope
will one day be crystallized in law and institutions. This is what Jefferson had in mind when the Declaration of Independence enjoined
"a decent respect to the opinions of mankind."

VI

Despite the perils of absolutism, the moral critique of national policy
has its value. Wise statesmen understand the importance of preserving the distinction between what morality prescribes and what circumstances are held to compel—and thereby preserving the integrity
of ideals in a world of distasteful necessity. In 1962 a delegation from
the World Council of Churches presented President Kennedy with a
resolution calling for the cessation of nuclear tests. Kennedy responded by discussing the problem he faced now that the Soviet
Union had resumed testing. Impressed by his analysis, a member of
the delegation said, "Mr. President, if you do resume tests, how can
we help you?" Kennedy replied, "Perhaps you shouldn't." "This was
a very different reaction," the theologian John C. Bennett has commented, "from the common one of seeking more church support the
more one feels uneasy about one's decision. Kennedy . . . did not want
the church to be a mere moral echo of the state even though, as a
representative of the state, he may have felt shut up to a course of
action that gave him moral distress."[25]

It is precisely through the idea of national interest that moral principles enter most effectively into the formation of foreign policy. The
function of morality is not to supply directives for policy. It is to supply perspectives that clarify and civilize conceptions of national interest. Morality primarily resides in the content a nation puts into its idea
of national interest.

The moral content of national interest is determined by three
things: by national traditions, by political leadership and by public
opinion. The meaning of moral values in foreign policy lies not in
what a nation says but in what it does. Morality is basically a matter
of keeping faith with a nation's own best ideals. If a course in foreign
affairs involves behavior incompatible with the standards of the national community, either the nation will refuse after a time to follow
the policy, or else it must forsake its standards. A democracy is in bad
trouble when it keeps two sets of books—when it uses one scale of
values for its internal polity and uses another in foreign affairs. The
consequent moral schizophrenia is bound to convulse the homeland.
This happened to France during the Algerian War. It happened to
the United States during the Vietnam War.

Nor was this the first time the moral critique caused Americans to think harder about the meaning of national interest. "The United States will conquer Mexico," Emerson wrote in 1846, "but it will be as the man swallows the arsenic, which brings him down in turn. Mexico will poison us."[26] "My patriotism," William Graham Sumner wrote during the Spanish-American War, "is of the kind which is outraged by the notion that the United States was never a great nation until in a petty three months' campaign it knocked to pieces a poor, decrepit, bankrupt old state like Spain. To hold such an opinion as that is to abandon all American standards . . . and to go over to the standards of which Spain is a representative." He called his essay "The Conquest of the United States by Spain."[27] Watching the American subjugation of the Philippines, Mark Twain explained sardonically to the person sitting in darkness, "We have been treacherous; but that was only in order that real good might come out of apparent evil. . . . We have debauched America's honor and blackened her face before the world; but each detail was for the best." Let us wave the flag, Mark Twain said, but "with the white stripes painted black and the stars replaced by the skull and crossbones."[28]

Morality in foreign policy, in short, consists not in preaching one's values to lesser breeds but in living up to them oneself. The moral force of any foreign policy derives from the moral vitality of the national community, and the test of that vitality lies in the character of policies at home. The American leaders who had the greatest impact on the world in the twentieth century—Wilson, Franklin Roosevelt, Kennedy—exerted their influence because, in the world's view, their record at home had earned them the right to speak of justice and freedom abroad. Their professions before mankind, the abstractions to which they harnessed American policy, expressed visible realities of their domestic performance. Wilson's New Freedom validated his Fourteen Points, as FDR's New Deal validated his Four Freedoms. So ideals themselves, when verified by performance, become instruments of national power and therefore an essential component of national interest.

Moral language is nevertheless something the prudent statesman uses warily. And the statesman who talks in moral terms had better be sure that national performance does not refute his words. Policy that invokes abroad principles the government ignores in its dealings with its own people is the diplomacy of Pecksniff. Foreign policy has its moral meaning as a projection of what a nation is at home.

VII

There are certain international questions with so clear-cut a moral character that moral judgment must guide political judgment—slavery, genocide, torture, atrocities, racial justice, human rights. Some of these questions are already defined in international documents. Others define themselves when the consequences of decision transcend the interests of individual nations and threaten the very future of humanity.

The supreme case is nuclear war. This essay began with Robert Kennedy's terrifying question. The question has never been answered. Perhaps it is unanswerable. Unilateral renunciation of nuclear weapons is an escape from the question, raising moral and practical questions fully as awful as those it purports to solve. Deterrence through the matching of nuclear arsenals is a practical answer so long as it preserves the nuclear peace. But it is a perilous answer. When the guardians of the arsenals foster the delusion that nuclear weapons are usable and nuclear wars winnable, deterrence heads straight toward Armageddon. Should 'existential deterrence' break down, we are in a darkness, analytically as well as literally; for no one can foresee the character of nuclear war. Perhaps the vision of Nuclear Winter, falling impartially on aggressor and victim alike, will be the ultimate deterrent.

On lesser issues, two standards serve to mediate the tension between moral and political judgment. The first standard is prudence, the quality implied by Weber's ethic of responsibility. When is a nation justified in using force beyond its frontiers or in providing armed support of or opposition to revolutions in other countries? Plainly such questions cannot be answered by a priori moral principle, only by case-by-case assessment of the consequences of alternative courses. Burke long ago pointed out the difference between the statesman and the moralist: "The latter has only a general view of society; the former, the statesman, has a number of circumstances to combine with those general ideas, and to take into his consideration. Circumstances are infinite, are infinitely combined, are variable and transient. . . . A statesman, never losing sight of principles, is to be guided by circumstances."[29]

So Daniel Webster, considering the Greek War of Independence in the 1820s, condemned intervention by the Holy Alliance, which had moved in to crush the rebellion, but did not propose to act against it. The danger to America, Webster explained, was remote, and remoteness, while it could not change principle, could affect policy. Intervention by the Holy Alliance in Greece was one question; intervention in South America would be quite another question. The principle remains the same, but "our duty to ourselves, our policy, and wisdom might indicate very different courses as fit to be pursued by us in the two cases."[30]

Prudence implies the old theological principle of proportionality — the principle that means must bear a rational relationship to ends. American intervention in Vietnam lost its last claim to legitimacy when the means employed and the destruction wrought grew out of any rational relationship to the interests threatened and the objectives sought. In fact, the interventionist policy lacked legitimacy from the start. No administration asked in any searching way what danger to national security, what involvement of national interest, could justify the commitment of American troops to what became the longest war in American history, the systematic deception by American leaders of the American people and of themselves, the death of thousands of Americans and of hundreds of thousands of Vietnamese, Laotians and Cambodians. Prudence vanished in Vietnam before strategic misconceptions and illusions of moral obligation.

VIII

The second standard mediating between moral and political judgment is law. International law, as noted earlier, is patchy and limited. There is no world legislature to enact it, no world court of universal jurisdiction to interpret it, no world police to enforce it. Yet international law is not negligible, and the steady extension of its reach is a necessary condition of lasting peace. For most of their history, Americans regarded the establishment of neutral standards of international behavior — freedom of the seas or whatever — as a good thing for the United States. In the old days realists even used to deride American statesmen for investing excessive faith in legal formulas.

In recent years American commitment to a world of law has been in decline. One factor sapping the old faith has been the increasing weight placed on the Central Intelligence Agency as an instrument of foreign policy. All powers of course have espionage services. Spies routinely break the law and, when caught, accept the consequences. Rival services may even develop a reciprocal ethic of their own, as intricately imagined by John le Carré in his tales of MI-6 and the KGB. But, except in wartime, most intelligence services concentrate on the collection and analysis of intelligence. The CIA's great innovation has been to concentrate in peacetime on 'covert action' — that is, the use of clandestine means to change policies and regimes in other countries. Instead of contenting itself with finding out what is happening, the CIA surpasses other intelligence services in trying to make things happen.[31]

Espionage is in a sense 'normal,' with an accepted if illegal status in interstate relations. Covert action carries a far more drastic threat to treaty obligations and to interstate comity. But successive American administrations have ignored the implications of CIA covert action for a world of law. The vice chairman of the Senate Select Committee on Intelligence, Senator Daniel Patrick Moynihan of New York, observed in 1983 that, although covert operations were almost in their nature violative of treaty law, "in six and more years of seemingly interminable closed hearings and briefings, I do not ever recall hearing a discussion of legal obligations of any kind."[32]

The erosion of American concern about a world of law intensified after 1980. A renascent CIA launched a secret (or not so secret) war against Nicaragua, doing so in defiance of the Neutrality Act of 1794, which makes it a crime to subsidize or prepare an armed expedition against a country at peace with the United States; in defiance of congressional prohibitions of attempts to overthrow the Nicaraguan regime; in defiance of nonintervention pledges repeatedly made to the Organization of American States ever since the Montevideo conference of 1933, when the United States first subscribed to the declaration that "no state has the right to intervene in the internal or external affairs of another"; in defiance of the United Nations Charter. After Nicaragua appealed to the World Court, the Reagan administration rejected the Court's jurisdiction in Central America for the next two years, doing so in defiance of the 1946 agreement in which the United States pledged six months' notice of any such termination. Subsequently the administration, repudiating the policy of forty years, withdrew from the compulsory jurisdiction of the World Court.

In 1983 Reagan despatched an expeditionary force against the island of Grenada, an action undertaken without warning, without congressional authorization, and in violation of the charters of the United Nations and the Organization of American States. The pretext—the rescue of American citizens—had ample standing under international law; but the real and unconcealed purpose was to destroy an obnoxious regime. The legal fig leaves failed to impress the British Prime Minister or the UN General Assembly. The fact that the people of Grenada and of neighboring islands applauded the invasion affected the politics of the action but did not alter the principle.

It is ironic that Americans remember 7 December 1941 as the date that will live in infamy. But Japan, in carrying out its surprise attack on Pearl Harbor, was at least picking on someone its own size. In October 1962, when the Joint Chiefs of Staff advocated a surprise attack to take out the nuclear missiles in Cuba, Robert Kennedy successfully opposed the idea as a "Pearl Harbor in reverse." "For 175 years," he told the group advising the President, "we had not been that kind of a nation. A sneak attack was not in our traditions. . . . We were fighting for something more than just survival . . . all our heritage and our ideals would be repugnant to such a sneak military attack."[33] The popularity of Reagan's sneak attacks on Grenada and Libya showed how far we have progressed since 1962.

Unquestionably there are occasions when nations, their security mortally endangered, are justified in acting beyond the law: *salus populi suprema lex est.* But such occasions are rare. Grenada was not one of them. To override international law casually, on the basis of ideological obsessions and hypothetical fears, would appear to abandon American standards and to go over to the standards of which the Soviet Union is the representative. "If you are going to pronounce a new law that, wherever communism reigns against the will of the people, even though it has happened internally there, the United States shall enter," said Mrs. Thatcher, "then we are going to have really terrible wars in the world." Most Americans, I judge, dismissed such thoughts as tiresome legal quibbles. A *Wall Street Journal* editorial approvingly quoted a dinner party remark: "We are only going to be able to talk sensibly about Grenada if anyone here who is an international lawyer agrees to keep his mouth shut." "What is missing from this," Senator Moynihan commented, "is the sense we once had that it is in our *interest* to advance the cause of law in world affairs."[34]

In 1983 Reagan explicitly affirmed "the right of a country when it believes its interests are best served to practice covert activity." In 1985 he added a novel principle: "Support for freedom fighters is self-defense, and totally consistent with the OAS and UN Charters." "Freedom fighters" is Reagan's term for guerrillas on our side, and he applied his principle to "every continent, from Afghanistan to Nicaragua."[35] The Soviet Union operates on the same principle, only its preferred term is "wars of national liberation." Each superpower in effect thus proclaims its right to act as a law unto itself in world affairs. But is the United States wise to abandon neutral standards of international behavior? Does our interest lie in imitating the Soviet model, or does it lie in opposing the Soviet model with the idea of a world of law?

To deny that the United States has a fundamental interest in the operation of law in international affairs is to embark on a course that, in harder cases than Grenada (i.e., more American casualties), Congress and public opinion will likely not sustain. "A policy is bound to fail which deliberately violates our pledges and our principles, our treaties and our laws," Walter Lippmann wrote after the Bay of Pigs.

". . . The American conscience is a reality. It will make hesitant and ineffectual, even if it does not prevent, an un-American policy."[36]

IX

Moral values do have a fundamental role in the conduct of foreign affairs. But, save in extreme cases, that role is surely not to provide abstract and universal principles for foreign policy decisions. It is rather to illuminate and control conceptions of national interest. The righteousness of those who freely apply their personal moral criteria to the complexities of international politics degenerates all too easily into absolutism and fanaticism. The assumption that other nations have legitimate traditions, interests, values, and rights of their own is the beginning of a true morality of states. The quest for values common to all states and the embodiment of these values in international covenants and institutions is the way to establish a moral basis for international politics.

This will not happen for a long, long time. The issues sundering our world are too deep for quick resolution. But national interest, informed by prudence, by law, by scrupulous respect for the equal interests of other nations and above all by rigorous fidelity to one's own national sense of honor and decency, seems more likely than the trumpeting of moral absolutes to bring about restraint, justice and peace among nations.

FIVE

Human Rights
and the American Tradition

———◆———

L ITTLE HAS EXCITED MORE hope, puzzlement and cynicism around the world in recent years than the emergence of
human rights as an international cause. Critics have had an easy time
exposing ambiguity, selectivity and contradiction in the human rights
campaign. Yet, for all its incoherence, the campaign has firmly inscribed human rights on the world's agenda and on the world's conscience—a very remarkable achievement after dark centuries that casually accepted man's inhumanity to man; all the more remarkable
for taking place in one of the most inhumane centuries of all. But
one wonders how much further can the human rights campaign go
along present lines. At what point will its contradictions begin to betray its intentions? Wherein lies its future?

I

Human rights—roughly the idea that all individuals everywhere are
entitled to life, liberty and the pursuit of happiness on this earth—is
a modern proposition. Orators like to trace this idea to religious
sources, especially to the so-called Judeo-Christian tradition. In fact
the great religious ages were notable for their indifference to human
rights in the contemporary sense—not only for their acquiescence in
poverty, inequality and oppression, but for their enthusiastic justification of slavery, persecution, torture and genocide.
  Christianity assigned to human misery an honored and indispensable role in the drama of salvation. The trials visited on mankind in
this world were conceived as ordained by the Almighty in order to

test sinful mortals. From the religious perspective, nothing that took place on earth mattered in comparison to what must take place hereafter. The world was but an inn at which humans spent a night on their voyage to eternity, so what difference could it make if the food was poor or the innkeeper a brute? Till the end of the eighteenth century, torture was normal investigative procedure in the Catholic church as well as in most European states.[1]

No doubt the idea of natural rights has classical antecedents, among, for example, the Stoics. But humanitarianism—the notion that natural rights have immediate, concrete and universal application—is a product of the last four centuries. Tocqueville persuasively attributed the humanitarian ethic to the rise of the idea of equality. In aristocratic societies, he wrote, those in the upper caste hardly believed that their inferiors "belong to the same race." When medieval chroniclers "relate the tragic end of a noble, their grief flows apace; whereas they tell you at a breath and without wincing of massacres and tortures inflicted on the common sort of people." Tocqueville recalled the "cruel jocularity" with which the delightful Madame de Sévigné, one of the most civilized women of the seventeenth century, described the breaking on a wheel of an itinerant fiddler "for getting up a dance and stealing some stamped paper." It would be wrong, Tocqueville observed, to suppose that Madame de Sévigné was inhuman or sadistic. Rather, she "had no clear notion of suffering in anyone who was not a person of quality."

Once people began seeing each other as equals, however, there arose a new mood of "general compassion." And, where inequality survived, as it did in the American south, so did inhumanity. "The same man who is full of humanity toward his fellow creatures when they are at the same time his equals," Tocqueville observed of the slaveholder, "becomes insensible to their afflictions as soon as the equality ceases. His mildness should therefore be attributed to the equality of status rather than to civilization and education."*

Equality thus bred "sympathy," which Dr. Johnson defined as "the consciousness that we have the same nature with the sufferer, that we

---

*Alexis de Tocqueville, *Democracy in America*, II, Third Book, ch. i. With her usual acuteness, Harriet Beecher Stowe in *Uncle Tom's Cabin* repeatedly noted the relationship between equality and humanitarianism. Thus St. Clair on his father: "*Among his equals*, never was a man more just and generous; but he considered the Negro . . . as an intermediate link between man and animals, and graded all his ideas of justice and generosity on this hypothesis" (ch. xix). Marie St. Clair: "Mammy couldn't have the feelings that I should. It's a different thing altogether" (ch. xvi). The lady on the steamboat: "We can't reason from our feelings to those of this class of persons" (ch. xii). In an early use of the phrase, Mrs. Stowe has St. Clair condemn slavery as a "bold and palpable infringement of human rights" (ch. xix).

are in danger of the same distresses."[2] This was a novel thought, and the cult of sympathy made it increasingly difficult to dismiss the less fortunate as creatures of some other race. The upper caste and the churches began at last to attend to the condition of the enslaved, the poor and the mad. It was the age of equality that saw the decline of religious persecution, the abolition of torture and of public executions, the emancipation of the slaves.

Since religion had traditionally ordained hierarchy and inequality, and since it had traditionally disdained earthly happiness, early human rights formulations, as with Voltaire and later in the French Revolution, had a markedly anti-religious cast. Only later, as religion itself succumbed to the humanitarian ethic and began to see the Kingdom of God as attainable within history, could the claim be made that the Judeo-Christian tradition commanded the pursuit of happiness in this world. The basic human rights documents—the American Declaration of Independence and the French Declaration of the Rights of Man—were written by political, not by religious, leaders. The revival of religious absolutism in the twentieth century, whether in ecclesiastical or secular form, brought with it a revival of torture and of other monstrous violations of human rights.

II

The United States was founded on the proclamation of "unalienable" rights, and human rights ever since have had a peculiar resonance in the American mind. Nor was the application of this idea to foreign policy an innovation of recent times. Americans have agreed since 1776 that the United States must be the beacon of human rights to an unregenerate world. The question has always been how America is to execute this mission. The early view was that America would redeem the world not by intervention but by example.

John Quincy Adams thus presented the American choice in his famous Fourth of July address in 1821. "Wherever the standard of freedom and independence has been or shall be unfurled," Adams said, .

there will her heart, her benedictions and her prayers be. But she goes not abroad, in search of monsters to destroy. She is the well-wisher to the freedom and independence of all. She is the champion and vindicator only of her own. She will commend the general cause by the countenance of her voice, and the benignant sympathy of her example. She well knows that by once enlisting under other banners than her own, were they even the banners of foreign independence, she would involve herself beyond the power of extrication, in all the wars of interest and intrigue, of individual avarice, envy, and ambition, which assume the colors and usurp the standard of freedom. The fundamental maxims of her policy would insensibly change from *liberty* to *force*. . . . She might become the dictatress of the world. She would no longer be the ruler of her own spirit.[3]

In 1847 Albert Gallatin, the last survivor among the great statesmen of the early republic, renewed the point. "Your mission," he reminded his countrymen, "was to be a model for all other governments and for all other less-favored nations . . . to apply all your faculties to the gradual improvement of your own institutions and social state, and *by your example* to exert a moral influence most beneficial to mankind" (emphasis added).[4]

Then in December 1849 Senator Lewis Cass of Michigan, the Democratic presidential candidate in 1848 and later Buchanan's Secretary of State, introduced a resolution instructing the Foreign Relations Committee to inquire into the "expediency" of suspending diplomatic relations with Austria. Cass intended this as the national response to the bloody suppression by Austrian and Russian troops of the Hungarian revolution of 1848—"atrocious acts of despotism," Cass said, "by which human liberty and life have been sacrificed."

Louis Kossuth, the president of the short-lived Hungarian republic, soon reproached Americans for talking endlessly about their mission of liberty while declining "to take any active part in the regulation of the condition of the outward world." Yet, if the American destiny was what "you all believe it to be," Kossuth told audiences on his American tour, "then, indeed, that destiny can never be fulfilled by acting the part of passive spectators and by this very passivity granting a charter to ambitious czars to dispose of the condition of the world." Americans, Kossuth said, trusted too much to the power of example. "I have never yet heard of a despot who had yielded to the moral influence of liberty."[5]

Cass's resolution and Kossuth's challenge confronted the republic with the question of how it was to fulfill the mission of human rights. John Parker Hale, a Free Soil Democrat from New Hampshire, opened the debate. "Aching and throbbing hearts," he said ironically, "[had] been waiting, and watching, and agonizing for just such a day as that when the Government shall . . . express its sympathies for the millions who are under the heel of power." But, if the Hungarian repression were indeed a moral question, Hale thought, the resolution should speak not of the "expediency" of suspending relations with Austria but the "duty." Cass, however, had assured the Senate that American trade with Austria was negligible, thus making it "quite clear to the country that they can let off a good deal of indignation, and that it will cost them but very little." Was this the way to treat a moral question? Imagine the American minister in Turkey, where Kossuth had now fled, trying to cheer the Hungarian refugees by telling them "that the Senate of the great American Republic are inquiring, this very day, how much it will cost to utter a little indignation in their behalf?"

The future historian, Hale said, might start off his chapter about the year 1850:

At the commencement of this year, the American Senate, the highest legislative body of the world, the wisest, greatest, and most magnanimous people that ever lived or ever will live, forgetting and neglecting the trifling local affairs which concerned their own limits, constituted themselves into a high court, and proceeded to try the nations of the earth for "atrocious acts of despotism."

What Cass proposed, Hale continued, was "that we erect ourselves into a high court of indignation! We are to arraign at our bar the nations of the earth, and they are to pass in trial before us, and we are to pass judgment upon them." An excellent principle—but why stop with Austria?

Hale hoped that the future historian would write that the United States proceeded "to try, not some few second-rate Powers with but little commerce, and whom it would cost but little to deal with, but that they took the empire of Russia first, and tried her." After all, Russian arms had overcome Kossuth. "I will not consent to sit in judgment upon Austria, until we have passed judgment upon some of these larger criminals. I am not willing that our action should be like that of small nets which catch the small fishes but let the great ones go." I want to try the czar of Russia, Hale said, not alone for what he did to Hungary but "for what he had done long ago in sending those unfortunate exiles to Siberian snows. . . . When we have done this, we shall show that we are governed by no pusillanimous motives in expressing our indignation against a weaker Power."

And "when we have tried Russia," Hale continued, "let us not stop there. I think we ought to arraign . . . England for the manner in which she tried Smith O'Brien and the Irish patriots. . . . I want to go to India, and to try England for the oppressions, the cruelties, and the wars that she waged there." If the principle was good, it should be applied universally. "After we have got through with Russia and England, I want . . . France to be placed at the bar . . . I want to go to Algiers and to inquire what France has done there. . . . Then, sir, while the court is in session . . . I want to try Spain. . . . Let us show that we are in earnest, and not merely showing off our indignation where there is no power of resentment, and where it will not be likely to cost us anything."

And, after we have passed judgment on the nations of Christendom and "they lie writhing in an agony of mortification at our feet," then let us "go from these high places down before the bar, and plead ourselves." For in "the capital of the Model Republic . . . within sight of the flag of freedom that floats over our heads . . . men are to be bought, and women are to be bought, and kept at twenty-five cents per day, until ready to be transported to some other market." The principle of the Cass resolution—"that liberty is [man's] God-given right, and the oppression that takes it from him by man is a wrong"— ought to begin at home.

Henry Clay, then in the twilight of his career, brought another perspective to the debate. He was struck by the "incongruity" between Cass's premises and his remedy. Cass had discoursed about the "enormities of Austrian despotism," but his conclusion was only to recall "a little chargé d'affaires that we happen to have at Vienna. Why, the natural conclusion would be to declare war immediately against Austria." But was it really sensible to close the door of intercourse with Austria? Why not send a distinguished American to Vienna to plead quietly on behalf of the Hungarians? And why not "bring forward some original plan for affording succor and relief to the exiles of Hungary?"

In any event, Clay said, the Cass resolution asks us to judge foreign nations "as their conduct may be found to correspond with our notion and judgment of what is right and proper in the administration of human affairs." It assumes "the right of interference in the internal affairs of foreign nations. . . . But where is to be the limit?" You may say to Spain that unless it abolishes the Inquisition, to Turkey that unless it abolishes polygamy, the United States will cease all intercourse with you. "Where, again I ask, are we to stop? Why should we not interfere in behalf of suffering Ireland? Why not interfere in behalf of suffering humanity wherever we may find it?" Let the Senate reflect, Clay warned, that in going down this road, we may "open a new field of collision, terminating perhaps in war, and exposing ourselves to the reaction of foreign Powers, who, when they see us assuming to judge of their conduct, will undertake in their turn to judge of our conduct."[6]

III

This ancient debate serves as a reminder of what small progress America has made since the Thirty-first Congress in deciding how best to promote human rights in the world. Cass's resolution expressed the profound and admirably uncontrollable American impulse to exhibit sympathy for victims of despotism in other lands. The response by Hale and Clay conveyed doubts that still persist: Is the point of foreign policy to discharge moral indignation or to produce real changes in a real world? May quiet diplomacy not be more effective than public denunciation? Must not the United States, when it invokes human rights, apply the principle across the board and not just to small and weak countries? May not intervention on behalf of human rights jeopardize other national interests and increase the danger of war? By what authority do we interfere in the internal affairs of foreign countries? Should all nations be expected to embrace the American conception of human rights? Does not the habit of passing judgment on foreign states nourish national self-righteousness? Should not a human rights crusade begin at home?

Cass's resolution failed. Yet the questions raised by his appeal nagged the national conscience. After the Civil War President Grant observed in his first annual message that while Americans sympathized "with all people struggling for liberty . . . it is due to our honor that we should abstain from enforcing our views upon unwilling nations and from taking an interested part, without *invitation,* in the quarrels . . . between governments and their subjects."[7] Nonetheless, both Congress and the executive thereafter condemned assaults on human rights abroad—the persecution of Jews in Russia, Eastern Europe and the Levant; the massacre of Armenians in Turkey; the oppression of the Irish; "the cruel treatment of State prisoners in Siberia."[8] Justification presumably lay in the doctrine of humanitarian intervention.* "Although we . . . as a rule scrupulously abstain from interfering, directly or indirectly, in the public affairs" of the Austro-

---

*Grotius and many subsequent authorities defended the legality of such intervention, even in the form of invasion and war. E. M. Borchard thus defined the doctrine in 1915: "When . . . 'human' rights are habitually violated, one or more states may intervene in the name of the society of nations and may take measures to substitute at least temporarily, if not permanently, its own sovereignty for that of the state thus controlled." E. M. Borchard, *The Diplomatic Protection of Citizens Abroad* (New York, 1915), 14. Other authorities have been skeptical of the doctrine. A. Rougier concluded after systematic inquiry into "*la théorie de l'intervention d'humanité*" that it was "neither possible to separate the humanitarian from the political grounds of intervention nor to assure the complete disinterestedness of the intervening States. . . . Barbarous acts are committed by the thousands every day in some corner of the globe which no State dreams of stopping because no State has an interest in stopping them." See the discussion in L. B. Sohn and Thomas Buergenthal, *International Protection of Human Rights* (Charlottesville, 1973), ch. 3.

Hungarian Empire, Secretary of State Hamilton Fish informed the American minister in Vienna in 1872, the persecution of Jews in Moldavia and Wallachia was so "inhuman" as to impart to the situation "a cosmopolitan character, in the redress of which all countries, governments, and creeds are alike interested."[9] Twenty years later Secretary of State James G. Blaine told the Russian Minister of Foreign Affairs that, while the American government "does not assume to dictate the internal policy of other nations . . . nevertheless, the mutual duties of nations require that each should use its power with a due regard for the result which its exercise produces on the rest of the world."*

The pressures of conscience, reinforced by ethnic lobbies fearful for relatives in the homeland, injected human rights into foreign affairs so regularly in these years that Theodore Roosevelt in 1904 felt impelled to issue a warning. No shrinking violet when it came to the assertion of American power in the world, TR nonetheless cautioned Congress:

Ordinarily it is very much wiser and more useful for us to concern ourselves with striving for our own moral and material betterment here at home than to concern ourselves with trying to better the condition of things in other nations. We have plenty of sins of our own to war against, and under ordinary circumstances we can do more for the general uplifting of humanity by striving with heart and soul to put a stop to civic corruption, to brutal lawlessness and violent race prejudices here at home than by passing resolutions about wrongdoing elsewhere.†

Despite TR's effort to recall his countrymen to the older tradition of doing good by example rather than by interference, the conviction grew in the bloody twentieth century that crimes against humanity indeed had "a cosmopolitan character" and were humanity's business. Wilsonianism gave this view general blessing, though Wilson cast the issue in terms of national self-determination. Meanwhile the conception of an international interest in *individual* rights was evolving. The eighth Conference of American States (1938) produced resolutions in "defense of human rights." Franklin Roosevelt's Four Freedoms (1941) applied to people, not to nations, and embraced not only free-

---

*John Bassett Moore, *A Digest of International Law* (Washington, 1906), 354–356. The "result" that disturbed Blaine was the discharge into the United States of large numbers of destitute Jews from Russia.

†Theodore Roosevelt, fourth annual message, 6 December 1904. Roosevelt went on to acknowledge it as "inevitable" that the nation "should desire eagerly to give expression to its horror on an occasion like the massacre of the Jews in Kishenef" and conceded that "in extreme cases action may be justifiable." The form of action, however, must depend "upon the degree of the atrocity and upon our power to remedy it."

dom of speech and worship but freedom from want ("economic understandings which will secure to every nation a healthy peacetime life for its inhabitants") and freedom from fear (that is, of military aggression). FDR's third freedom, supplemented by his Economic Bill of Rights (1944), soon flowered into the idea of social and economic rights to be sought along with traditional "Bill of Rights" rights. The "Declaration by United Nations" (1942) called for "complete victory" in order, among other things, "to preserve human rights"; and Articles 55 and 56 of the UN Charter (1945) pledged member nations to joint and separate action to promote "human rights."

IV

The idea of human rights, like nearly everything else, was soon caught up in the Cold War. The democratic states assailed the communist world for its abuse of civil and political rights; the communist world assailed the democratic states for their neglect of social and economic rights. Human rights began to emerge as a theme in American foreign policy in this context; thus Kennedy in his inaugural address spoke of a new generation of Americans "unwilling to witness or permit the slow undoing of those human rights to which this nation has always been committed." Human rights were also seen as an object of détente; thus Kennedy asked at American University in 1963: "Is not peace, in the last analysis, basically a matter of human rights?" "Since human rights are indivisible," Kennedy told the United Nations two months before Dallas, "this body cannot stand aside when those rights are abused and neglected by any member state." [10]

Vietnam interrupted Washington's embrace of human rights as a major theme of foreign policy. It was not an altogether credible issue for a state engaged in indiscriminate slaughter; and it lay dormant in Washington even after American forces left Vietnam. Henry Kissinger's diplomacy made a virtue of the de-ideologization of foreign relations. A policy aiming at the manipulation of the balance of power doubtless contained an inner bias in favor of governments that could deliver their nations without having to worry about political opposition or a free press. In any event, the United States in these years accepted without visible disgust despotic governments of both right (Greece, Portugal, Brazil, Chile) and left (Russia, China, Romania, Yugoslavia).

What forced the human rights issue on the world in the 1970s was the courage of the dissenters in the Soviet Union. Sakharov, Solzhenitsyn, the Medvedevs, and the rest of those intrepid men posed the challenge to the democratic conscience that Kossuth and the heroes of 1848 had posed a century earlier. The initial response to this challenge came not at all from Washington but from the governments of Western Europe, especially Britain and France, and resulted in the agreement at Helsinki in 1975 by which the west ratified Europe's postwar frontiers in exchange for the Soviet pledge to increase the flow of people and ideas across the Iron Curtain—the pledge embodied in the celebrated Basket Three of the Helsinki Final Act. In 1975 and 1976 many Americans denounced Helsinki—among them, Jimmy Carter.

But the dominance of *Realpolitik* in the Kissinger years frustrated Americans in the Wilsonian tradition who felt that foreign policy should be founded on ideals. It frustrated equally those in the school of Franklin Roosevelt who did not doubt that foreign policy must be founded on national interest but considered ideals an indispensable constituent of American power. Official indifference to the Soviet dissidents, symbolized by President Ford's refusal in 1975 to receive Solzhenitsyn, seemed to reveal a moral vacuum at the center of American foreign policy.

Congress thereupon undertook to force the human rights issue on the executive. It used its legislative power to forbid or restrict economic or military aid to countries that engaged "in a consistent pattern of gross violations of internationally recognized human rights."[11] It required the State Department to submit annual reports on the state of human rights in more than a hundred countries. In the case of the Soviet Union, the Jackson-Vanik amendment demanded relaxation of Soviet emigration restrictions as a condition for export credits and most-favored-nation trade status.

Congressional concern soon affected Foggy Bottom. "If the Department did not place itself ahead of the curve on this issue," Deputy Secretary of State Robert Ingersoll warned Secretary Kissinger in 1974, "Congress would take the matter out of the Department's hands." In 1975 the Department established an Office of Humanitarian Affairs. But the Secretary doubted that human rights had a serious place in foreign policy. Informed that the American Ambassador to Chile had raised human rights issues with the military dictatorship, he said, "Tell Popper to cut out the political science lectures."[12] In so far as human rights were a proper object of policy, the Secretary was sure that quiet diplomacy, not public pressure and punitive action, was the way to promote them—a view that received a measure of vindication when Jewish migration from the Soviet Union sharply declined after the passage of the Jackson-Vanik amendment. Congressional concern continued to rise nevertheless. Eventually it affected the Secretary himself. In 1976 Kissinger pronounced human rights "centrally important . . . one of the most compelling issues of our time."[13]

V

By 1977 the world was well prepared for new human rights initiatives. The new American President, in a notable display of leadership, now seized the human rights standard and brandished it as if it had been American property all along.

It is not altogether clear how Jimmy Carter personally came to human rights. The phrase does not appear in the chapter on foreign policy in his memoir *Why Not the Best?* (1975). Nor was the issue prominent in his presidential campaign. On occasion, indeed, he seemed to be moving in the opposite direction. He criticized not only the Helsinki Agreement but the whole philosophy of intervention. "Our people have now learned," he told the Foreign Policy Association in June 1976, "the folly of our trying to inject our power into the internal affairs of other nations." At the same time, he had a general feeling, as he wrote in *Why Not the Best?*, that "our government's foreign policy has not exemplified any commitment to moral principles," that foreign policy must rest on the same moral standards "which are characteristic of the individual citizens"* and that "there is only one nation in the world which is capable of true leadership among the community of nations, and that is the United States."[14] In September 1976 Senator Henry Jackson of Washington persuaded him to adopt human rights as a major theme in his campaign.

One can surmise that Carter, seeking to give American foreign policy a moral content it had lacked in the Nixon years, arrived at human rights as the perfect unifying principle. This principle tapped the most acute contemporary concerns as well as the finest American traditions. It promised to restore America's international moral position, so sadly eroded by Vietnam, Watergate, support of dictatorships, CIA assassination plots, and so on. It promised also to restore a domestic consensus behind foreign policy. The doctrine gratified both cold

---

*This was an odd proposition to come from a man who had announced himself a disciple of Reinhold Niebuhr. In the first sentence of *Moral Man and Immoral Society*, Niebuhr wrote: "The thesis to be elaborated in these pages is that a sharp distinction must be drawn between the moral and social behavior of individuals and of social groups, national, racial, and economic; and that this distinction justifies and necessitates policies which a purely individualistic ethic must always find embarrassing." *Moral Man and Immoral Society* (New York, 1932), 11.

warriors, who wanted to indict the communist world, and idealists, who saw human rights as the only basis for lasting peace. Hence the striking words of the inaugural address: "Because we are free we can never be indifferent to the fate of freedom elsewhere. . . . Our commitment to human rights must be absolute." (Carter also said that the United States had a special obligation "to take on those moral duties which, when assumed, seem invariably to be in our own best interests." The irony appears to have been unconscious.)

The campaign was launched with appropriate pyrotechnics—a presidential letter to Sakharov; a White House meeting with Vladimir Bukovsky; brave declarations of human rights principles. But it soon ran into trouble. The idea, critics were quick to point out, had not been "thought through." Perhaps this was just as well. Had the new President confided the idea to the State Department for analysis, there very likely would have been no human rights campaign at all. Confronted by new departures, bureaucracies customarily feel that risks outweigh opportunities. Sometimes changes can be wrought in government only when a President, by publicly committing the government to a new course, forces the bureaucracy to devise new policies. Truman's Point Four, Kennedy's Alliance for Progress, and Reagan's Star Wars are other examples.

"I did not fully grasp all the ramifications of our new policy," Carter later admitted.[15] The failure to think the initiative through led him to make the promotion of human rights sound a little too easy. He would have been wiser to admit the difficulties of converting principle into policy. "When I began to speak out for human rights," David Owen, then British Foreign Secretary, remarked, ". . . I warned that there was a price to pay, and that the price was a little inconsistency from time to time. If I had to make that comment again, I would no longer say a *little* inconsistency, I would say a *very great deal* of inconsistency."[16] The questions that John P. Hale and Henry Clay had raised long before against Lewis Cass returned to bedevil the Carter administration.

In 1977, Secretary of State Cyrus Vance made a valiant and judicious essay at definition. He distinguished three categories of human rights: the right to be free from government violation of the integrity of the person (an adaptation of FDR's freedom from fear); the right to the fulfillment of vital needs as for food, shelter, health care and education (freedom from want); and the right to civil and political liberties (FDR's other two freedoms). In pursuing these rights, Vance warned, we must recognize "the limits of our power and of our wisdom," avoid "a rigid, hubristic attempt to impose our values on others" and reject the illusion that "a call to the banner of human rights will bring sudden transformations in authoritarian societies. We have embarked on a long journey." But Vance did not really try to deduce a policy from the principle, saying enigmatically that "there may be disagreement on the priorities these rights deserve."[17]

Disagreement on the priorities was indeed unceasing. Diplomats objected when the human rights campaign threatened arms control negotiations or political relationships. Admirals and generals objected when it imperiled military bases and alliances. Treasury officials estimated that foreign policy restrictions cost the economy up to $10 billion a year, thereby increasing the trade deficit.[18] Businessmen objected when the campaign hurt exports. Carter himself, the presumed number one human rights crusader, was soon found visiting authoritarian nations, selling them arms and saluting their leaders. His human rights policy, it appeared, was compatible with effusive support for the Shah of Iran, with an egregious letter of commendation to Somoza in Nicaragua, with the possible recognition of Vietnam and Cuba. Washington was fearless in denouncing abuses in countries like Cambodia, Paraguay and Uganda, where the United States had negligible strategic and economic interests; a good deal less fearless toward South Korea, Saudi Arabia, Yugoslavia and most of black Africa; circumspect about the Soviet Union; totally silent about China.

By mid-1978 Solzhenitsyn could speak sarcastically of bureaucrats who exploded in "anger and inflexibility . . . when dealing with weak governments and weak countries" but became "tongue-tied and paralyzed when they deal with powerful governments."[19]

VI

The campaign—it could hardly be termed a policy—raised other problems. There was the question of its impact on the Soviet Union. "What we are now facing," Georgi Arbatov, the Kremlin's house Americanologist, told an English interviewer in November 1978, "is a consistent effort of interference in the internal affairs of the Soviet Union and an attempt to inflict harm on some of our institutions. It is waged in a way that would have produced a serious uproar in the United States if we'd done what you've done toward us."[20] This was, of course, a ridiculous complaint from the representative of a country that for more than half a century had consistently tried to interfere in American internal affairs and to inflict harm on American institutions (and especially ridiculous in view of the fact, well known to Arbatov, that such interference had long since produced "a serious uproar" in the United States). Still, if Americans recalled their own resentment of Soviet subversion, they might understand Soviet resentment of the human rights campaign. Nor could anyone doubt that the campaign, pursued *à outrance*, would strike at the very foundation of the Soviet order.

Soviet resentment, for some mysterious reason, astonished Carter himself; he spoke in June 1977 of the "surprising adverse reaction in the Soviet Union to our stand on human rights."[21] But he accepted it as a fact of life and moderated his campaign, thereby disappointing Americans who had seen the campaign primarily as a means of reviving the Cold War. The deterioration of Soviet-American relations in 1977 meanwhile alarmed those who believed that the ultimate human right was the right to be alive and that the prevention of nuclear war was the condition for the promotion of all other human rights. Carter's campaign, French President Giscard d'Estaing observed, "has compromised the process of détente."[22]

There was the question, too, of the impact on the United States. America was once again erecting itself into a "high court of indignation." But was not public preachment more likely to anger governments violating human rights than to reform them? In any event, who was America to sit in judgment upon the world? A born-again President might have remembered Matthew 7: 2–3: "And why beholdest thou the mote that is in thy brother's eye, but considerest not the beam that is in thine own eye?" As John P. Hale had reminded the Senate in 1850 of the slave markets in the District of Columbia, so latter-day critics asked whether the United States ought not, before setting forth to reform the world, secure human rights for its own black, red and brown citizens. How could the government condemn the Soviet Union for violating Helsinki's Basket Three while it denied visas to left-wing trade unionists and intellectuals? How dared it lecture Fidel Castro about human rights after having spent a number of years trying to murder him?

An even more difficult question was involved — Henry Clay's question about the presumption of the United States in supposing all nations morally bound to accept the American notion of what was "right and proper" in human affairs. Was it reasonable, asked the Iranian Ambassador to the United Nations, "to expect from developing countries in Asia, Africa and Latin America to apply overnight your high standards when most of them are still grappling with problems of food, education, health, employment, etc.?"[23] Was not the whole concept of political and civil rights ethnocentric and culture-bound and therefore the American determination to cram it down the throats of the world an adventure in cultural imperialism? "Those Americans who profess to know with such certainty what other people want and what is good for them in the way of political institutions," wrote George Kennan, "would do well to ask themselves whether they are not actually attempting to impose their own values, traditions, and habits of thought on peoples for whom these things have no validity and no usefulness."[24]

Observers commented on the "holier than thou" attitude of the Washington human rights bureaucracy—a condescension toward lesser breeds summed up in the odious remark an unnamed official made to Elizabeth Drew of *The New Yorker:* "I think that the mulish world has noticed the two-by-four."[25] Little has done more harm to human affairs than illusions on the part of leaders and of nations of their superior righteousness. What Hawthorne said about John Bull in the nineteenth century many were saying about Uncle Sam in the late twentieth: "Nobody is so humane . . . when his benevolent propensities are to be gratified by finding fault with his neighbor."[26] The human rights campaign led even pro-American Europeans to worry about rekindled messianism across the Atlantic—"the newest version," Ferdinand Mount wrote in England, "of the American mission to improve the world."[27] Countess Marion Dönhoff of West Germany observed that "foreign policy based on moral values, as espoused by Wilson and Dulles, did not make the world noticeably more moral. On the contrary it led to dead ends and catastrophes."[28]

VII

In short order the human rights campaign was haled before a high court of indignation of its own, and readily convicted of hypocrisy, double standards, undermining détente, undermining stalwart anti-communist allies, cultural imperialism, racism, messianism and so on. It is little wonder that the initiative, buffeted by intractable circumstance, by plausible criticism and by quarrels among its original supporters over its emphases, came to seem selective, unpredictable and riddled with contradiction.

The criticism was plausible. It may also have been excessive. Patricia Derian, Assistant Secretary of State for Human Rights and Humanitarian Affairs, made a persuasive defense:

We candidly recognize that diversity of cultures and interests and different stages of economic and political maturity make it essential to treat each country on the merits of its own situation. It would be impossible to pursue our human rights objectives in precisely the same way for all countries, and silly to try.[29]

In fact the double standard is inherent in the problem—not only because nations are in varying stages of maturity but, more crucially, because the promotion of human rights cannot in any case be the exclusive goal of foreign policy. Human rights constitute only one of a number of national interests and not the overriding interest to which all else is to be subordinated.

A nation's supreme interest is self-preservation. When national security and the promotion of human rights come into genuine conflict, national security must prevail (which is not at all to accept the national security bureaucracy as the infallible judge of national security). Because, in the nature of foreign policy, human rights can only be one of several competing interests, principle must be tempered by prudence. In short, a state cannot apply the human rights standard consistently. This does not mean, however, that the standard should be abandoned.

Most of the malign effects of the human rights campaign of the late 1970s were considerably exaggerated. Though the campaign vastly annoyed the Soviet Union, it was not decisive in Soviet thinking about détente. Nor could American concern about human rights be blamed for the overthrow of the Shah and of Somoza. Actually, as noted, both despots received accolades as well as rebukes from the Carter administration. Both would have been overthrown had Washington never uttered a word about human rights. The impact on the United States was exaggerated too. In practice, the human rights campaign turned out to be considerably less than a crusade, and American messianism remained well under control.

Nor is it by any means certain that concern for human rights is a form of cultural imperialism. If the assertion that such rights are universal, and not merely the local prejudice of Caucasian societies bordering the North Atlantic, implies racial arrogance, the limitation of these rights implies that nonwhite peoples are incapable of appreciating due process, personal liberty and self-government—racial arrogance as well. History certainly suggests that democracy has worked best in the North Atlantic orbit, but democratic aspiration cannot be so easily confined.

"Human rights," a distinguished Filipino admonished Americans in 1978 with understandable irritation, "are not a western discovery"[30]—a proposition vindicated by the Philippine people in 1986. Even in China Peking wall posters proclaimed in 1978, "We cannot tolerate that human rights and democracy are only slogans of the western bourgeoisie, and [that] the eastern proletariat only needs dictatorship."[31] Another poster: "As Chinese citizens, we think that truth is universal and that the soul of mankind, human rights, is not limited by national boundaries or geography."[32] In 1984 the Chinese Writers' Association, to tumultuous applause, called on the Communist party to reject ideological restrictions on artistic freedom.[33]

Perhaps human rights are less culture-bound than some Americans, in an excess either of humility or vanity, like to believe. In the end, the answer to the question whether the concern for political and civil rights is local or universal depends on one's view of humanity. Over the long run, this historian finds it hard to believe that the instinct for political and civil freedom is confined to the happy few in the North Atlantic littoral.

VIII

The Carter administration, by establishing the Bureau of Human Rights in the State Department, institutionalized the role of human rights in American foreign policy. Foreign assistance took account of human rights in cases where strategic considerations were not deemed overriding. Countries violating human rights were denied aid or permitted it only under severe restrictions: Cuba, Vietnam, Cambodia, Chile, Argentina, Uganda, Mozambique, Ethiopia, Paraguay and others. American embassies became human rights watch offices. Nor was it always a policy of public preachment. When Kim Dae Jung, the opposition leader in South Korea, was sentenced to death in 1980, Carter privately informed the South Korean government that an execution would cause a serious breach in relations. The South Korean President indicated that, if American intercession were not made public, Kim Dae Jung would be spared, and so he was.

The Carter campaign altered the international atmosphere. The campaign was especially effective in Latin America. When Carter visited Argentina and Brazil four years after his defeat for reelection, leaders in politics, journalism and academia thanked him for the lives he saved. Around the world the human rights initiative gave new heart to brave men and women. It brought about the release of political prisoners in Indonesia, South Korea, Syria, the Philippines, even behind the Iron Curtain. By exerting pressure, however unevenly, for human rights, the American government for a moment helped restore the broken link between the United States and ordinary people around the planet.

When Carter mentioned his intervention on behalf of Kim Dae Jung to Ronald Reagan after the 1980 election, the President-elect, as Carter remembered it, confined his comment to expressing "with some enthusiasm his envy of the authority that Korean President

Park Chung Hee had exercised during a time of campus unrest, when he had closed the universities and drafted the demonstrators."[34] This reaction foretold the fate of human rights in the next administration.

The new President accepted the argument that the Carter campaign had undermined non-democratic but 'friendly' leaders, like the Shah and Somoza, that it had brought anti-American regimes to power in Iran and Nicaragua, and that, by harassing friends without harming enemies, it had damaged America throughout the world. Reagan chose not to dismantle the human rights apparatus but instead to turn it initially against Marxist-Leninist states.

The Reaganites began by applying to human rights the notorious distinction between 'totalitarianism' and 'authoritarianism.' According to that distinction, a familiar one to political scientists, a totalitarian regime crushes all autonomous institutions in its drive to seize the human soul, while an authoritarian regime, despotic in character but limited in reach, leaves the soul alone, tolerating institutions that give the individual a measure of shelter from the state. Reaganites added a corollary. The transformation of totalitarian regimes in a democratic direction was deemed a phenomenon unknown to history, but authoritarian regimes, it was held, readily evolved into democracies. The further assumption was that Marxist dictatorships were totalitarian, while anti-Marxist dictatorships were authoritarian and hence less noxious.

The totalitarianism-authoritarianism distinction, valid in theory, crumbled in application. For pure totalitarianism has proved hard to achieve and impossible to sustain. Totalitarian states begin as messianic regimes dedicated to the transformation of human nature. But in time the messianic frenzy dissipates, old habits and patterns reemerge, the monolithic commitment breaks down, and the regimes dwindle into tyrannies run by opportunists and cynics. If 'pluralism'—the existence of autonomous institutions—is proof of authoritarianism, then Marxist states in Eastern Europe, Poland and Hungary, for example, are plainly authoritarian and not totalitarian. So for that matter was Sandinista Nicaragua in its early years. If state torture and murder are proof of totalitarianism, then Pinochet's Chile, pre-Alfonsín Argentina and the Shah's Iran were more totalitarian than Poland or Nicaragua. The near half century of Somoza tyranny suggested, moreover, that the translation of authoritarianism into democracy was neither quick nor certain. And there is the anomaly of China—surely a totalitarian regime, yet spared obloquy for compelling geopolitical reasons.

IX

The distinction between totalitarianism and authoritarianism did not in fact coincide, as the Reagan ideologues had expected, with the distinction between pro-Soviet and anti-Soviet states. It therefore failed to provide the anticipated justification for a double standard. The Reagan administration developed in practice a double standard anyway—for pro-Soviet dictatorships, pitiless censure; for anti-Soviet dictatorships, 'constructive engagement,' a term invented for South Africa but a policy extended to right-wing authoritarian regimes across the board. Constructive engagement meant the use of quiet diplomacy, friendly admonition, economic and military support, a general atmosphere of tea and sympathy, to persuade governments like those of South Africa, Chile, the Philippines, Haiti, El Salvador, to change their repressive ways.

Thus the Reagan administration, reversing Carter's policy, voted for Inter-American Development Bank loans to Pinochet's Chile. Vice President Bush declared that he loved Marcos of the Philippines for his "adherence to democratic principles," and Reagan himself said that the choice lay between Marcos or "a large Communist movement to take over the Philippines."[35] Authoritarian leaders naturally interpreted such tender treatment as a license to commit further repression. The democratic opposition in their countries felt themselves betrayed by the United States. Marxist revolutionaries gained new popularity and legitimacy. Far from minding this polarization of their people, leaders like Pinochet and Marcos expected that polarization would leave the United States no alternative but to back their regimes.

The ultimate justification for the Reagan approach was that it is necessary to be realistic about friends and enemies in a dangerous world. But the approach did not turn out to be defensible even as *Realpolitik*. Though the Reagan policy professed to regard authoritarian regimes as transient, in practice it assumed their permanence. The policy was to propitiate the authoritarians in power rather than the democrats who might succeed them. The Carter policy, on the other hand, really regarded authoritarianism as transient and therefore had fewer inhibitions about snubbing despots and helping their democratic opponents. When authoritarian regimes disappeared in Brazil, Argentina and Uruguay, the new democratic leadership remembered the Carter administration with gratitude and harbored friendly feelings toward the United States.

The Carter policy unquestionably strengthened America's geopolitical position in the longer run. The Reagan policy of supporting right-wing dictatorships was the contrary of realism, as the Reagan administration itself was eventually forced to recognize in the Philippines and Haiti. In abandoning Marcos and Duvalier, Reagan replicated the policy for which he had roundly denounced Carter in the cases of the Shah and Somoza. But it proved impossible to prop up the unproppable. An uncontrollable surge of internal protest against crooked authoritarian leaders left Reagan no more choice in 1986 than Carter had had in 1979. The momentum of events soon forced Reagan to jettison the talk about authoritarianism and totalitarianism and to announce that "the American people believe in human rights and oppose tyranny in whatever form, whether of the left or the right." Going even farther than Carter, Reagan now called for "an active diplomacy backed by American economic and military power" in support of a worldwide "market-oriented . . . democratic revolution."[36]

The earlier Reagan policy had been a great boon to Moscow. The American embrace of unpopular despots alienated democratic allies and strengthened Marxist revolutionaries. Moreover, the grand philosophical distinction between the Soviet Union and the United States lies precisely in the field of human rights. The commitment to individual dignity and freedom is the abiding source of American appeal to the world. Sakharov—what better witness?—affirms that the Soviet Union is the "crux" of the totalitarian threat but adds that "the global character" of the American human rights campaign "is particularly important, that is, the attempt to apply the same legal and moral criteria to human rights violations to every country in the world—to Latin America, Africa, Asia, the socialist countries, and to one's own country."[37] Why should the United States cultivate its own gang of squalid tyrants, betray its historic commitment to human rights and throw away its greatest comparative advantage in the struggle with the Soviet Union?

X

The contrasting experiences of Carter and Reagan illustrate the limitations of government as a unilateral agency for the promotion of human rights. The more zealously the United States pressed human rights under Carter, the more it seemed a high court of indignation. The more zealously the United States used human rights as a Cold War club in the first Reagan phase, the more it provoked worldwide cynicism. The more, as in the second Reagan phase, the United States invoked human rights to promote market-oriented revolution, especially when it employed such dubious agents as ex-Somocistas in Nicaragua, the more it aroused worldwide fears of an American capitalist crusade. Future administrations might well ponder the point made by American statesmen from John Quincy Adams to Theodore Roosevelt that, save in extreme cases, we can probably do more for human rights by example at home than by intervention abroad.

One state cannot do a great deal to reform another. Most states are hard enough put to reform themselves. When states agitate about human rights in other states, their motives are always suspect. The "moral duties" thus assumed by governments seem "invariably," in Carter's unfortunate but accurate phrase, to be in their own "best interests." Politicization is not necessarily the best destiny for human rights.

"Governments cannot by their nature *consistently* put human rights first," Ferdinand Mount has well said. "People can."[38] It is often the duty of diplomats to maintain correct relations with cruel as well as with civilized governments. It is equally the duty of citizens to speak mind and conscience against cruelty without the inhibitions imposed by diplomacy. It can therefore be said that the moral obligations of human rights rest more strongly on non-governmental than on governmental bodies.

Amnesty International, the International League for Human Rights, the International Commission of Jurists, Helsinki Watch, America's Watch and similar organizations have done magnificent work. But the promotion of human rights should not be confined to human rights organizations. Churches, universities, trade unions, business groups, all have a role to play. A special obligation rests, I think, on professional associations.

Many political prisoners are professionals themselves. When they are arrested, sent to labor camps or insane asylums, tortured, murdered, their professional colleagues around the world have the obligation to rally to their defense. So the National Academy of Sciences spoke out for Sakharov, Shcharansky and other Soviet scientists; so the American Psychiatric Association protested the arrest of Alexander Podrabinek after the publication of his book on the confinement of Soviet dissenters to insane asylums; so the World Psychiatric Association condemned the political misuse of psychiatry in the Soviet Union and elsewhere; so PEN, the Authors League and the Association of American Publishers have protested the suppression of cultural freedom.

It is singular that American scientists, psychiatrists and publishers have been so much more sensitive to human rights issues than American political scientists and historians. The American Political Science

Association, after piously declining to meet in Chicago because Illinois had not ratified the Equal Rights Amendment, could find no human rights obstacle to participating in the 1979 meeting of the International Political Science Association in Moscow. The American Historical Association watched the persecution of Soviet historians— Andrej Amalrik, Medvedev, Solzhenitsyn (whose *Gulag Archipelago* is a historical work), Valentyn Moroz—in silence and held regular meetings with Soviet historians approved by the regime. Not till 1985, after years of internecine argument, did the American Historical Association agree to protest human rights violations involving historians in their civic as well as in their professional capacities.

The argument against protests is that they antagonize orthodox Soviet scholars without helping the dissenters. Yet experience has shown that it is precisely the spotlight of international concern that exerts a restraining effect on arbitrary government. "The most frightening thing that can happen to a person," Mihajlo Mihajlov, the dissident Yugoslav writer, has noted, "is to be forgotten in prison."[39] Amalrik has testified that it plays "a very important part in terms of moral support, to know that one is known and well-known. . . . The Soviet authorities do react quite sensitively to western public opinion."[40] "It must be understood," Solzhenitsyn himself has said, "that the East is not at all indifferent to protests from Western society. On the contrary it mortally fears them—and only them."[41] E. P. Thompson, the historian of the English working class, commented: "Solzhenitsyn has asked us to shout once more. And we must, urgently, meet his request. . . . We must make it clear again, without equivocation, that we uphold the right of Soviet citizens to think, communicate, and act as free, self-activating people; and that we utterly despise the clumsy police patrols of Soviet intellectual and social life."[42] Nor should professional protest confine itself to the abuse of human rights in the communist world. Since professional associations need not respect geopolitical considerations, they can speak without constraint about the persecution of their colleagues in all countries, including those allied to the United States.

XI

People can and must put human rights first, whatever states may do. But in the end human rights must find their sanctions in laws and institutions. Given the limitations on the role of national states, the long-term hope lies in international organization. In 1948 the UN General Assembly adopted the Universal Declaration of Human Rights. This lengthy document covered both "civil and political rights" and "economic, social and cultural rights," the second category designed to gratify states that denied their subjects the first. The Declaration was followed by a series of subsidiary UN conventions, including two Covenants on Civil and Political Rights and on Economic, Social and Cultural Rights adopted in 1966 and entering into force for the signatory states in 1976.

For all the resounding declarations and covenants, the UN was for a long time a bitter disappointment in the struggle for human rights. It was hard to count on serious action from an international body in which two-thirds of the member governments freely violated the human rights of their own citizens. The General Assembly's interest in human rights was generally exhausted by fulminations against South Africa, Chile and Israel. There were no resolutions against the *gulags*. Even such appalling regimes as Pol Pot's in Cambodia and Idi Amin's (and thereafter Obote's) in Uganda escaped rebuke. In fact the murderous Pol Pot regime, expelled from Cambodia itself but retaining Cambodia's UN seat with the support of the American government (first Carter, then Reagan), had the insolence in 1980 to sign the Covenant on Civil and Political Rights.

Not until the 1980s did the UN Commission on Human Rights begin to emerge from years of shameful desuetude. Moving beyond the familiar General Assembly targets, the Commission in 1985 submitted a scathing report on torture, mutilations and other atrocities perpetrated during the Soviet occupation of Afghanistan. A separate Human Rights Committee set up by the states adhering to the Political and Civil Rights Covenant enlarged UN concern. The UN agencies now investigate complaints, collect and release information, harass governments and publicize standards.[43] They are at last developing institutional independence and momentum. Support mounts for the creation of a UN High Commissioner for Human Rights. The UN effort, moreover, has had a multiplier effect. The Universal Declaration had inspired more than twenty human rights treaties as well as the establishment of regional human rights institutions. Nineteen states have consented to the jurisdiction of the European Court of Human Rights, and its decisions are legally binding. The Inter-American Commission on Human Rights does useful work in exposing abuses in the western hemisphere.

The UN declarations have abolished the old theory that human rights are exclusively matters of domestic jurisdiction. International law, once deemed to apply only to states, applies today in this field, in principle at least, to individuals as well. Of course the principle is trampled on by leaders who feel they must persecute their subjects in order to preserve themselves. UN agencies lack enforcement power. Their practical impact thus far has been limited. Still, as people around the world shout and shout once more, international institutions begin to respond. International standards define the world's goals and have their gradual effect on national governments anxious for international respectability.

It is unrealistic to expect that we will soon, or ever, have a world in which human rights will be universally assured. FDR's Four Freedoms expressed a generous aspiration, not, despite his occasional words to the contrary, an attainable objective. The instinct for domination is deeply imbedded in human institutions and in human nature. Yet the Four Freedoms crystallized what has come to seem in the years since a rising conviction of plain people around the planet. The long, stumbling march toward human freedom has resumed in our own time. The struggle may never make human rights forever secure. But at least it will make tyranny insecure for a while to come. The issue of human rights, as finally propounded in the twentieth century, will not be easily deleted from the agenda for the twenty-first century.

SIX

The Solzhenitsyn Challenge

———◆·◆———

The concern in the west over the place of human rights and moral standards in the conduct of foreign policy is in part a response, at once marveling and guilty, to the valor of dissidents in the Soviet Union. Among these heroes of our time, two stand out—because they are men of outstanding accomplishment, one in science, the other in literature; and because they embody sharply contrasting versions of the moral issue in the Cold War. Andrei D. Sakharov represents the democratic faith in reason, free inquiry and self-government. Alexander Solzhenitsyn represents something very different—a faith, almost medieval in character and intensity, in an organic society founded on authority, hierarchy and religion. The two men express the historic split in the Russian tradition between the Westernists and the conservative Slavophiles. On 8 June 1978 Solzhenitsyn, expelled from Russia and now in reluctant exile in Vermont, delivered a strong and somber address at the Harvard Commencement.

Wherefore is all this evil come upon us? Is it not because we have forsaken the Lord? . . . Do not our follies and iniquities testify against us? Have we not, especially in our Seaports, gone much too far into the pride and luxuries of life? Is it not a fact open to common observation, that profaneness, intemperance, unchastity, the love of pleasure, fraud, avarice, and other vices, are increasing among us from year to year?
SAMUEL LANGDON, President of Harvard, 1775

THE VOICE that echoed in Harvard Yard in 1978 would not have surprised the first several generations of Harvard men. For Alexander Solzhenitsyn renewed an ancient if, in those precincts, forgotten tradition of apocalyptic prophecy. In Harvard's first century, the jeremiad—the lamentation over the weakness of man and the degeneration of society, the summons to humiliation and repentance—was the supreme theme of the preachers of New England. That was long, long ago; but at the 1978 Harvard Commencement Solzhenitsyn, not only sounding but looking like a figure from the Old Testament, preached an impassioned sermon in the old style, warning America of the progress of evil and the imminence of judgment, urging Americans to repent their sins, forsake their idols and prostrate themselves before the "Supreme Complete Deity."

I

Few men living have as clearly earned the right to assume the prophetic stance. Solzhenitsyn is a man of exemplary nobility and extreme bravery. A powerful novelist and an indispensable historian, he is an artist and moralist who has taken unto himself the suffering of his countrymen and has magnificently indicted a monstrous system in the name of the Soviet people and of Russian history. When Solzhenitsyn speaks, the world has a duty to listen. But it must listen with care, understanding that prophets are not infallible and that prophecy has its own fantasies.

Solzhenitsyn's Harvard speech, like much prophetic utterance, lacked a clear line of argument. Casual readers seized upon his more sensational judgments, such as his assertion that "a decline in courage" is "the most striking feature which an outside observer notices in the West." This decline is "particularly noticeable among the ruling groups and the intellectual elite." It has produced a foreign policy founded on "weakness and cowardice." The American refusal to win the war in Vietnam, Solzhenitsyn declares, is a grievous and perhaps decisive example of the "loss of willpower in the West."

He finds the United States equally a failure as a national community. "Destructive and irresponsible freedom" has resulted, Solzhenitsyn tells us, in an "abyss of human decadence," marked by the "revolting invasion of publicity, by TV stupor, and by intolerable music," by violence, crime and pornography. The proliferation of laws in American society has become a shoddy substitute for self-discipline.

Most dangerous of all, in his view, is freedom of the press. The mass media are corrupt and licentious, unwilling to confess or correct error, inundating the people with an "excessive burdening flow of information" and "superficial and misleading judgments." Yet "the press has become the greatest power within the western countries."

"By what law has it been elected," Solzhenitsyn asks, "and to whom is it responsible?"

It is easy but pointless to note that Solzhenitsyn sounds rather like General LeMay on Vietnam, like Jerry Falwell on pornography and like Spiro T. Agnew on the press. These and other items in his bill strike responsive chords in many American breasts. But his specific charges cannot be divorced from his cosmic philosophy. The Harvard jeremiad rests on a drastic view of modern history.

The west went wrong, Solzhenitsyn believes, with the Renaissance and the Enlightenment. "We turned our backs upon the Spirit and embraced all that is material with excessive and unwarranted zeal." Communism is an abomination, but so is capitalism. Commercial interest tends to "suffocate" spiritual life. Or, as he put it in 1973, "no incentive to self-limitation ever existed in bourgeois economics. . . . It was as a reply to the shamelessness of unlimited money-grubbing that socialism in all its forms developed." For all their differences, communism and capitalism are equally the results of "the logic of materialistic development."

Just as Solzhenitsyn's conservative admirers will reject his views on capitalism, so his liberal admirers will reject his views on democracy— views his great fellow dissident, Andrei Sakharov, characterized in 1975 as "untrue and disturbing." Sakharov, for example, wants to liberalize and democratize the Soviet Union. He calls for a multiparty system and for the establishment of civil liberties. Little could be more remote from Solzhenitsyn's intentions. In 1975 he dismissed the Sakharov program as one more example of Russia's "traditional passive imitation of the West."

"A society in which political parties are active," he said, "never rises in the moral scale. . . . Are there no *extraparty* or *nonparty* paths of national development?" As for civil liberty, "the West," he wrote in 1969, "has supped more than its fill of every kind of freedom, including intellectual freedom. And has this saved it? We see it today crawling on hands and knees, its will paralyzed." (This was five years before the Kremlin expelled him. His Harvard testimony therefore recorded not what he discovered after he came west but what he believed long before he went west.)

To regard freedom "as the object of our existence," he said in 1973, "is nonsense. . . . There is, therefore, a miscalculation in the urgent pursuit of political freedom as the first and main thing." He finds it equally nonsensical to regard earthly happiness as the object of existence. At Harvard he expressly condemned the proposition that "man lives to be free and to pursue happiness. (See, for example, the American Declaration of Independence.)"

II

In short, Solzhenitsyn has no belief in what he called at Harvard "the way of Western pluralistic democracy." People lived for centuries without democracy, he wrote in 1973, "and were not always worse off." Russia under authoritarian rule "did not experience episodes of self-destruction like those of the 20th century, and for 10 centuries millions of our peasant forebears died feeling that their lives had not been too unbearable." In "patriarchal" societies people "even experienced that 'happiness' we are forever hearing about." Moreover, they preserved the health of the nation—"a level of moral health incomparably higher than that expressed today in simian radio music, pop songs and insulting advertisements."

As against the moral chaos of democracy, Solzhenitsyn argues the virtues of "subordination to authority." His objection to the Soviet system, he has explained, is "not because it is undemocratic, authoritarian, based on physical constraint—a man can live in such conditions without harm to his spiritual essence." His objection is that "over and above its physical constraints, it demands of us total surrender of our souls." Authoritarian regimes "*as such* are not frightening—only those which are answerable to no one and nothing." The autocrats of religious ages "felt themselves responsible before God. . . . The autocrats of our own time are dangerous precisely because it is difficult to find higher values which would bind them."

Solzhenitsyn's ideal has nothing to do with liberal democracy. If asked whether he saw the west "as a model to my country, frankly I would have to answer negatively." His model is a Christian authoritarianism governed by God-fearing despots without benefit of politics, parties, undue intellectual freedom or undue concern for popular happiness. Repression, indeed, is good for the soul. "The need to struggle against our surroundings," he wrote in 1973, "rewards our efforts with greater inner success."

Even today the Soviet Union, he assures us, provides a healthier moral environment than the United States. "Through intense suffering our country has now achieved a spiritual development of such intensity," he said at Harvard, "that the Western system in its present state of spiritual exhaustion does not look attractive." The superior moral weight and complexity of life in the Soviet Union produce "stronger, deeper and more interesting characters than those generated by standardized Western well-being." Where the Declaration of Independence talked about life, liberty and the pursuit of happiness, Solzhenitsyn's essential thesis is strength through suffering.

For Solzhenitsyn, with his organic view of society, the nation even more than the individual is the crucial moral unit. Nations too can partake of the mystique of suffering. They "are very vital formations, susceptible to all moral feelings, including—however painful a step it may be—repentance." In his fascinating essay "Repentance and Self-Limitation in the Life of Nations," published in 1975, Solzhenitsyn argued that repentance could lead nations to the possibility of self-limitation. "Such a change will not be easy for the free economy of the West. It is a revolutionary demolition and total reconstruction of all our ideas and aims. . . . We must abjure the plague of expansion beyond our borders, the continuous scramble after new markets and sources of raw material, increases in our industrial territory or the volume of production, the whole insane pursuit of wealth, fame and change."

All this, he said, is catastrophically wrong. "Let us give up trying to restore order overseas, keep our grabbing imperial hands off neighbors who want to live their own lives. . . . We must stop running out into the street to join every brawl and instead retire virtuously into our own homes so long as we are in such a state of disorder and confusion." The nation must concentrate on *inner* tasks: on healing its soul, educating its children, putting its own house in order. "Should we be struggling for warm seas far away, or ensuring that warmth rather than enmity flows between our citizens?"

These eloquent words might have come from speeches by George Kennan or George McGovern. Yet, when Americans repenting the excesses of Vietnam called for a policy of self-limitation, Solzhenitsyn, instead of rejoicing in them as converts, denounced them as cowards. Can he really believe that bombing the Vietnamese back to the Stone Age would have been a proof of courage and virtue?

III

Still, prophets are not always consistent. Probably, as a fervent Russian nationalist, he is more concerned with the salvation of Russia than of America. He should not be so disdainful of Americans, who want to save their own souls. Or perhaps his is the understandable frustration of the messenger who tries to tell the west about the true nature of Soviet tyranny and encounters only complacency and indifference.

Before the Second World War, Arthur Koestler wrote with comparable frustration about the inability of the victims of Nazism to make the British believe Hitler's terror. Later Koestler decided that what the English lacked was not courage but imagination. No doubt it was this very lack of imagination that made Britain stand alone against Hitler after the fall of France. Maybe Solzhenitsyn understands the United States as little as Koestler understood Britain in 1939.

In any event, Solzhenitsyn at Harvard was offering a grand vision of the nature and destiny of man. Regeneration can come, for nations as well as for individuals, only through confession of sin and acknowledgment of the sovereignty of the Almighty. This vision would have been familiar to the Puritan divines who preached in Harvard Yard three centuries ago. It includes the premonitions of Armageddon, the final struggle with Satan. "The forces of Evil have begun their decisive offensive," Solzhenitsyn cried at Harvard. "You can feel their pressure." It partakes of the millennial dream as set forth in the books of Daniel and Revelation. "If the world has not come to its end, it has approached a major turn in history . . . it will exact from us a spiritual upsurge."

This is a searching vision. The challenge to American smugness and hedonism, to the mediocrity of our mass culture, to the decline of self-discipline and civic spirit, is bracing and valuable. To this extent Solzhenitsyn shares common ground with our Puritan ancestors. But Solzhenitsyn's faith is suffused, in addition, by the otherworldly mysticism of the Russian Church—a mysticism that reflected the political absolutism of Russian society. By Russian religious standards, earthly happiness is nothing compared to the divine judgment.

The Puritan tradition was more empirical. Even the New England ministry had to temper its conviction of divine sovereignty with concession to the rough democracy of a nonprescriptive society, where men made their way in life through their own labor. In the eighteenth century Calvinism absorbed John Locke and laid the philosophical basis for the American experiment in democracy.

This is why the two traditions diverged—why the Solzhenitsyn vision, with its fear of human freedom, its indifference to human happiness, its contempt for democracy, its faith in the authoritarian state, is so alien to the great tradition of the west. The greatest American theologian of our time, Reinhold Niebuhr, demolished years ago the mystical illusion that nations have souls like individuals. Nor would he for a moment accept the authoritarian pretense that rulers, when avowing religious faith, are thereby rendered more immune than the rest of us to the corruptions of power. "The worst corruption," said Niebuhr, "is a corrupt religion."

At Harvard Solzhenitsyn remarked that the west "never understood" Russia. One may respond that Solzhenitsyn has never understood America. He arrived complete with preconceptions about American decadence and cowardice and evidently nothing he has found in the mass media has disabused him. But, as Archibald MacLeish has well said, "What he knows of the Republic he knows not from human witnesses but from television programs, which present their depressing parody of American life to him as they present it also to us, but with this difference—that we know the parody for what it is."

He comes, moreover, as a messenger of God. "Truth eludes us," he said at Harvard, "if we do not concentrate with total attention on its pursuit." He has concentrated with total attention and does not doubt that the truth is his. But the notion of absolute truth is hard for Americans to take. If absolute truth exists, it is certainly not confided intact to frail and sinful mortals. As Jefferson said in his first inaugural: "Sometimes it is said that man cannot be trusted with the government of himself. Can he, then be trusted with the government of others? Or have we found angels in the form of kings to govern him? Let history answer this question." History has answered this question with terrible certitude in the twentieth century. "The unfortunate thing," Pascal said long before, "is that he who would act the angel acts the brute."

If prophecy is one Christian virtue, humility is another. Knowing the crimes committed in the name of a single Truth, Americans prefer to keep their ears open to a multitude of competing lower-case truths. Ours has been a nation of skepticism, experiment, accommodation, self-criticism, piecemeal but constant reform—a collection of traits repugnant to the authoritarian and messianic personality, but perhaps not too bad for all that.

Americans were deemed as sinful in the seventeenth century as Solzhenitsyn deems them in the twentieth century. The Day of Judgment was quite as near and remote then as now. We welcome his presence and honor his witness; but he must understand the irrelevance of his grand vision to a democratic society. Emerson, once again, said it best:

> *I like the church, I like a cowl,*
> *I love a prophet of the soul;*
> *And on my heart monastic aisles*
> *Fall like sweet strains or pensive smiles;*
> *Yet not for all his faith can see*
> *Would I that cowled churchman be.*

SEVEN

America and Empire

———◆·◆———

FOR NINE CENTURIES after the First Crusade, western civilization was engaged in the adventure of entering and altering
nonwestern societies. During eight of those nine centuries aggression
went on without benefit of theory. The great wave of European expansion took place in the sixteenth, seventeenth and eighteenth centuries. It provoked no systematic analysis of causes. Explorers, *con-
quistadores*, friars and settlers were doing what came naturally—
claiming land, seeking gold, saving souls, establishing colonies. 'Imperialism' did not even exist as a word until the nineteenth century,
and its first application in English was not to overseas expansion at
all but to the pretensions of Emperor Napoleon III.[1] As late as 1874,
when Bagehot wrote "Why an English Liberal May Look Without Disapproval on the Progress of Imperialism in France," he referred to
France's internal polity, not to its external policy.[2] The contemporary
meaning of imperialism as the domination of distant peoples finally
appeared toward the end of the nineteenth century in the wake of a
new wave of territorial acquisition by western states. Only since then,
in this ninth and last century of western expansion, has a literature
emerged to analyze the phenomenon of empire.

I. *Imperialism: The Classic Theories*

I

The literature of imperialism arose when the democratization of foreign policy gave politicians the need, and intellectuals the opportu-

nity, to offer electorates reasons to advocate or oppose expansion. That literature is copious, discordant, confusing and largely polemical. As early as 1919, Joseph A. Schumpeter could write, "The word 'imperialism' has been abused to the point where it threatens to lose all meaning."[3] The abuse, if possible, is worse today. Still one can divide the classical theories of imperialism into four broad categories: apologias; economic interpretations; sociological interpretations; and geopolitical interpretations.

The essence of apologia is the claim of a civilizing mission. European imperialists portrayed themselves as bearers of the white man's burden, carrying western culture, technology and religion to the benighted peoples of the world. They enlightened the backward, developed the undeveloped and protected the powerless—women, children, slaves. They eradicated polygamy and suttee, abolished the slave trade, introduced due process and schools, railways, sanitation, hospitals.

In later times such explanations were dismissed as self-serving and hypocritical. Unquestionably they often cloaked ugly intentions. Yet the *mission civilatrice* was not a total fiction. It sent thousands of westerners to the ends of the world in the hope of doing good, from missionaries and administrators in earlier times to the Peace Corps today. The civilizing mission received its ironic vindication when the colonies in the twentieth century invoked western morality to overthrow western domination. The revolt against colonialism was carried out in the name of independence, nationalism and democracy—alien values instilled by European masters. "You taught me language," said Caliban; "and my profit on't / Is I know how to curse."

Winston Churchill, exasperated by American notions of an irrepressible conflict between imperialism and democracy, once told Franklin Roosevelt, without undue exaggeration, "British imperialism has spread and is spreading democracy more widely than any other system of government since the beginning of time."[4] An independent India, though Churchill had done his best to prevent it, illustrates his point. It has been said that the British Empire was destroyed by the London School of Economics and Sandhurst—two British institutions that taught a generation of Asians and Africans to think and act for themselves.

Karl Marx, of all people, had his own powerful version of the *mission civilatrice*. The oriental world, in Marx's view, was mired in the past. Stagnant and unchanging, Asia lacked the internal stimulus required to set the dialectic of history in motion. External stimulus was essential. This, as Marx saw it, was the function of the western intrusion. European imperialism, by shattering regressive social and religious structures, became the necessary condition of Asian revolution. "England has to fulfill a double mission in India," Marx wrote, "one destructive, the other regenerating—the annihilation of the old Asiatic society, and the laying of the material foundations of Western Society in Asia." While denouncing "swinish" British plunder and atrocity, Marx commended the British for bringing in the railroad, the telegraph and the free press and for training native military and administrative elites on the western model. The question, he said, was whether mankind could "fulfil its destiny without a fundamental revolution in the social state of Asia? If not, whatever may have been the crimes of England she was the unconscious tool of history in bringing about that revolution."[5]

Marx defended the United States in the Mexican War, asking sarcastically whether "it was such a misfortune that glorious California has been wrenched from the lazy Mexicans who did not know what to do with it." Engels said that "in the interest of its own development Mexico should be placed under the tutelage of the United States." He called the French conquest of Algeria "an important and fortunate fact for the progress of civilization," and pronounced Canada "ripe for annexation. . . . The economic necessity of an infusion of Yankee blood will have its way." Come the European revolution, Engels wrote in 1882, "the countries inhabited by a native population . . . must be taken over for the time being by the [European] proletariat."[6]

II

Some apologists for imperialism, while happy to proclaim the benefits to the benighted, were more impressed by the benefits to themselves. "The act is virtuous," observed the young Winston Churchill, "the exercise invigorating, and the result often extremely profitable."[7] Greed was always more potent than uplift in inducing the European diaspora. And what in earlier centuries was the rapacity of individual adventurers seeking spices, gold and furs began in the late nineteenth century to be accounted as a blessing for the nation as a whole.

The economic interpretation was invented by the defenders of imperialism, not by its critics. It was first put in analytic form by the American financial journalist Charles A. Conant. In an 1898 article entitled "The Economic Basis of Imperialism" Conant argued that oversaving—i.e., an excess of capital—was the great cause of economic distress and social tension in industrial nations. The "system of abstinence from consumption for the sake of saving" had produced "a glut of goods which has destroyed profits, bankrupted great corporations, and ruined investors." Developed countries required "an outlet for their surplus savings, if the entire fabric of the present economic order is not to be shaken by a social revolution." Doubting that new demand could be created at home to absorb the capital surplus, Conant found the solution in investing capital in the development of Asia and Africa. Oversaving, he noted, was thus far a European phenomenon; the United States was still a net importer of capital. But the United States could not afford to lag behind while European nations were dividing up the undeveloped world, or nothing would be left when America's time came.[8]

The argument that expansion was an economic necessity was seized upon with alacrity by imperialist politicians. Joseph Chamberlain in Britain, Jules Ferry in France, Henry Cabot Lodge in the United States, hoped thereby to overcome business opposition to colonial ventures they wished to undertake for the power and prestige of the state. It was seized upon with equal alacrity by critics of imperialism, especially the radical economist J. A. Hobson in Great Britain. In *Imperialism,* his telling book of 1902, Hobson carefully explained imperialism as the search for capital outlets while at the same time condemning it as unnecessary. The true remedy for oversaving, he said, lay in the expansion of domestic demand through redistribution of purchasing power.

For Hobson, imperialism was simply a policy that ignorant capitalist governments chose to pursue. Enlightened governments were free to pursue other policies. Nevertheless Hobson's argument had great impact on Marxists, above all on Lenin, who, using Hobson's data, claimed imperialism not as an option for capitalism but as an ineluctable necessity when capitalism reached its monopoly phase. The inherent inability of monopoly capitalism to invest the capital surplus at home, Lenin said, forced capitalist nations into the undeveloped world in a desperate effort to avert the final crisis of the system.

Lenin's *Imperialism: The Highest State of Capitalism* (1917) established the 'Marxist' theory of imperialism, though his analysis bore little relation to anything Marx himself had written on the subject. The hard-hitting pamphlet responded both to the end-of-an-era mood that accompanied the First World War and to the organizational needs of the class struggle. The Leninist theory quickly became not only gospel for revolutionaries but a serious hypothesis for journalists and even scholars.

The economic interpretation in a broad sense illuminates many aspects of the imperial enterprise. But Lenin's version, with its single-minded emphasis on the export of capital, raises obvious objections.

If imperialism is the monopoly stage of capitalism, how to account for the fact that the great burst of empire-building took place in the earliest years of capitalism, when there were no internal monopolies, no capital surplus and no pressure of accumulation on the rate of profit? How to account for the fact that the two greatest imperial powers, Britain and France, lacked monopolistic economic structures even in the later years? If monopoly capital requires colonies for investment and markets, how to account for the fact that capitalist states in Lenin's chosen period expanded into areas—tropical Africa, Polynesia—where prospects for investment and markets were limited? for the fact that investment by rich countries was greater in other rich countries than in colonies? that trade was greater with other rich countries? If excess of capital is what drives nations to imperialism, how to account for the expansion of capital-poor countries like Portugal, Russia and the United States in the nineteenth century, Italy and Japan in the 1930s? If capitalism without colonial empire is doomed, how to account for capitalism's extraordinary revival in the age of decolonization?

Lenin failed to demonstrate any consistent correlation between capital investment and colonialism with regard either to historic epoch or to geographical area. His assumption—that the 'monopoly capitalism' of the turn of the century was capitalism in extremis—proved hopelessly wrong. Far from a system at the end of its tether, capitalism in 1900 was poised on the brink of a century of spectacular growth, most of it taking place during the dissolution, not the conquest, of empire. For all its seductiveness as propaganda, Lenin's *Imperialism* fizzles as serious explanation.

III

As a political weapon, however, the economic interpretation remained potent. Lenin himself had insisted that imperialism required "colonial possession,"[9] but when formal colonialism crumbled away after the Second World War, Marxists sought refuge in the concept of 'neo-colonialism.' This concept implied that political independence made no difference so long as poor countries were integrated into the capitalist world market. *Dependencia* theory, originating in Latin America and elaborated in Arab countries, became the popular reformulation of the Leninist interpretation for the post-colonial world.

Dependency theory argues that the world market both creates and perpetuates underdevelopment—a condition distinguished from the precapitalist state of 'undevelopment.' In the dependency model the 'core'—the industrialized world—automatically drains off any surplus from the 'periphery,' thereby dooming the periphery to permanent poverty. "Economic development and underdevelopment," in the words of Andre Gunder Frank, a leading dependency theorist, "are the opposite faces of the same coin."[10] The implication is that, if it had not been for the world market, the poor countries would long since have developed themselves.

Dependency theory claims Marxist legitimacy on the basis of Marx's scattered references to the world market and of his endorsement of Henry C. Carey's argument that England "is trying to turn every country into a mere agricultural nation, whose manufacturer is to be England."[11] In fact, dependency theory turns Marx on his head. For Marx blamed underdevelopment on the self-perpetuated stagnation of poor societies and looked to the world market precisely as the means of salvation. Capitalism, Marx believed, meant exploitation; but it also meant the stimulus and the capital essential for economic growth. Visiting Canada, Engels wrote, "Here one sees how necessary the feverish speculative spirit of the Americans is for the rapid development of a new country."[12]

Marx and Engels, as so often, proved more correct than the Marxists. The world market, through trade and through investment, has been in fact the great engine of Third World development. In South Asia, Gunnar Myrdal noted in 1968, "The countries with the highest income per person, Ceylon and Malaya, have the highest ratio of foreign trade, while India and Pakistan, the poorest countries, have the lowest."[13] "In Indo-America," said Haya de la Torre, founder of the radical APRA party in Peru, ". . . foreign capital has done everything; without it, there would be no mechanized agriculture, no industry, no cultural development, no working class."[14]

Nor in the longer run has colonialism held back development. "Would India, Pakistan, or Bangladesh be more developed had the British never come?" asks John Kenneth Galbraith. "Or Indonesia had the Dutch never been there? or North Africa without the French?" As the radical economist Joan Robinson once put it, "The misery of being exploited by capitalists is nothing compared to the misery of not being exploited at all."[15] Or, she might have added, to the misery of being exploited by native tyrants from Genghis Khan to Bokassa and Idi Amin.

The most backward countries today are generally those least integrated into the world market. Conor Cruise O'Brien called western imperialism "one of the greatest and most dangerous forces in the world" in 1971; but, reconsidering Africa in 1985, he reported that "all the (relatively) successful states have been capitalist. 'African socialism' has no success stories to tell."[16] Far from deploring foreign trade and investment, poor countries more commonly object that rich countries do not buy enough from them or invest enough in them. Nor is it only the non-socialist Third World that seeks access to the world market. Communist countries are just as eager for foreign trade and investment: look at Eastern Europe, or at Fidel Castro, who for years has tried to persuade the United States to lift its trade embargo. "Large-scale investments and technical aid," wrote Frantz Fanon, the ideologue of Third World revolution, "must be given to under-developed regions. The fate of the world depends on the answer that is given to this question."[17]

The Soviet Union itself has never doubted that foreign investment would promote Soviet economic growth. The 1920 decree on concessions, as described by E. H. Carr, asserted that "recovery of the Russian economy could be 'increased many times over' by bringing in foreign firms or institutions 'for the exploitation and development of the natural riches of Russia.'"[18] That is why Armand Hammer, Bernard Baruch and Averell Harriman were invited to Russia in the 1920s. And there are few more ardent champions of the world market today (1986) than Deng Xiaoping, the leader of Communist China. The Chinese people always suffered, Deng said, when their government closed the door to the world, as the Ming dynasty had done in the fourteenth century and as Mao Tse-tung did during the Cultural Revolution. "No country can now develop by closing the door," Deng continued. ". . . We say that China will continue to draw on foreign capital and practice an open policy for a long time to come."*

The notion that, left to themselves, the poor countries would be well on the road to modernization betrays a most shallow understanding of the nature of mass poverty. The sources of poverty lie far deeper than the accusatory polemic of dependency theory dare acknowledge. The very conception of material progress was imported from, even imposed by, the west. Marx showed long ago how Asian religion, culture and caste conspire against development. Myrdal has exposed the internal obstacles to growth in poor countries and the extreme difficulty of overcoming the social inertia caused by "the vicious circle of cumulative interrelation and causation."[19] "The tendency of the poor country," writes Galbraith, "is to an equilibrium of poverty."[20]

*New York Times, 2 January 1985. Hu Yaobang, the general secretary of the Chinese Communist party, soon added that the People's Republic had "wasted twenty years" in its struggle for modernization because of the "radical leftist nonsense" of Mao. *New York Times*, 21 February 1985.

The concept of 'neo-colonialism' turns out on examination to be nothing more than a dramatic, or melodramatic, label for the unequal economic relationship between rich and poor nations. Of course political independence makes a difference. Independent countries are free to reclaim profits and nationalize industries—if they have the will to do so. Gunboats are no longer employed to chastise unruly poor nations. Covert action, though still on occasion (Guatemala, 1954) an effective instrument of capitalist domination, excites increasing disapproval in the metropole. Possession of vital raw materials, which once placed poor nations at the mercy of the west, now has the potentiality, as recurrent oil crises have shown, of placing the west at the mercy of poor nations. In raw materials, the terms of trade have been turning steadily against the industrialized world. Far from retarding industrialization in poor countries, the world market is today despoiling the west of its heavy industry and transferring it to the Third World. The west cannot even collect Third World debts without threatening the stability of their own banking systems.

Dependency theory caters to the political and psychological needs of Third World nationalists. It also caters to the psychological needs of those in the west who, contemplating appalling Third World poverty, are consumed by guilt. To see poverty in poor nations as the consequence of exploitation by rich nations, Galbraith has ironically commented, becomes "a test of political detachment for the scholar from the affluent world."[21] But for all its current vogue, dependency theory is even feebler than Lenin's doctrine as serious explanation. In the end Marx was surely right in predicting that imperialism would help the undeveloped world economically more than hurt it.

Did imperialism pay the imperialists? The effort to construct a balance sheet encounters insuperable difficulties of calculation. Some individuals and corporations did very well out of imperialism. Governments, on the other hand, spent more in colonies on administration, infrastructure, defense and social improvement than they received in return. As time passed, the cost-benefit ratio clearly turned against the metropolis. "It is an odd, though widespread, delusion," the radical historian A. J. P. Taylor has said, "that colonies keep the capitalist system going. On the contrary they have nearly been its ruin." Of course, he said, they brought untold wealth to a few scoundrels, and they were a useful dumping ground for public school men who would otherwise have been nuisances at home. "But tot up the national balance sheet of any imperial country over the last 50 years, and you will find the community is staggeringly out of pocket." If the Communists have their way "and the colonial revolt becomes universal, capitalism will be on its feet more firmly than ever."[22]

IV

The manifold difficulties with the economic interpretation provoked alternative hypotheses. In 1919 Joseph A. Schumpeter, though himself an economist, presented a fruitful analysis of "The Sociology of Imperialisms." Schumpeter shifted the discussion, to adapt Bert Hoselitz's phrase, from what imperialism was to who the imperialists were and what drove them to the far corners of the earth.

Rejecting the equation between capitalism and imperialism, Schumpeter explained imperialism as the survival within bourgeois society of a precapitalist warrior mentality, devoted, as in classical empires, to expansion for the sake of expanding, war for the sake of fighting, dominion for the sake of ruling. The imperialists were men who, because they inherited a code of physical risk and valor, could not find a solid footing in the new commercial society. James Mill, the historian of British India, described empire as "a vast system of outdoor relief for the upper classes."[23] Empire renewed the legitimacy and extended the contract of the aristocracy in a bourgeois age.

The great instrument of imperialism, Schumpeter added, was the institutionalization of the warrior mentality in the "war machine," the professional military caste. "Created by wars that required it, the machine now created the wars it required." The rationalistic and prudential climate of capitalism, Schumpeter supposed, would in time eradicate the anachronism of the warrior class, "though every warlike involvement, no matter how non-imperialist in character, tends to revive it."[24]

Where Lenin saw imperialism as the response to dislocations in the capital market and Schumpeter saw it as a response to dislocations in the social structure, the geopolitical school attributed imperialism to dislocations in the balance of power. For there had been empires and colonies long before there was capitalism; and history suggests that nations as well as individuals are animated by Hobbes's "perpetual and restless desire of power." The desire of power is an independent motive, not the function of internal economic arrangements. Or so it has seemed to political scientists like Hans Morgenthau and Arnold Wolfers, to historians like William L. Langer, A. J. P. Taylor, D. K. Fieldhouse and David Landes and to sociologists like Max Weber.

The first duty of the state, in the geopolitical view, is self-preservation. It seeks to protect its citizens and its borders against enemies. It aspires to control strategic points that an enemy might turn against it. It works to enhance its own prestige and glory. If it falls behind other nations in the pursuit of international status, its own influence will wane. Power remains the decisive motive—balances of power, disparities of power, vacuums of power, illusions of power.

The geopolitical interpretation gives ample play to economic factors. But it distinguishes the economic necessities of the state from the profit interests of private owners. Whatever the system of ownership or ideology, the state, in its quest for national power, requires wealth, trade, raw materials—not because these things enrich private corporations but because they strengthen the state itself. Max Weber proposed the "mental experiment" of imagining capitalist as socialist states. The situation, he said, would hardly change fundamentally. Socialist states are just as eager for access to raw materials and markets, just as likely to use force to gain that access, just as disposed "to squeeze tribute out of the weaker communities," just as inclined to imperialism.[25]

From the geopolitical perspective, the renewal of imperialism in the late nineteenth century had little to do with the capitalist search for markets or investment outlets. It represented rather, in a period when the alliance system had produced stalemate in Europe, the projection of European state rivalries into the undeveloped world. Colonies, as the historian D. K. Fieldhouse put it, were "assets in the struggle for power and status."[26] Nations seized territory not for its economic value but in order to deny it to rivals. It was largely, in Langer's phrase, "preclusive imperialism." The pressure behind it came from military and official classes. "Business interests may have an interest in the acquisition of territory, or they may not," as Langer wrote. "But military and official classes almost always have."[27]

Where the Leninist has the state adopting imperialist policies at the bidding of capitalist interests, the geopolitician finds many more instances of capitalist interests entering economically unpropitious areas at the bidding of the state. "By no means has trade always pointed the way for political expansion," Weber wrote. "The causal nexus has very often been the reverse."[28] "So far from commercial expansion requiring the extension of territorial claims," the historians of the British in tropical Africa have written, "it was the extension of territorial claims which in time required commercial expansion."[29] Lord Cromer promoted British investments in Egypt, but he did so, A. J. P. Taylor noted, "to strengthen British political control, and not the other way round." Similarly "French financiers were forced to invest in Morocco, much against their will, in order to prepare the way for French political control. They knew they would lose their money; and they did. But Morocco became a French protectorate."[30] Far from trade and investment commanding the flag, the flag more often commanded trade and investment.

The classical theories arising to explain imperialism thus traced the expansion of Europe respectively to the selfless service of mankind, to the needs of the European economy, to the frustrations of European society and to the power requirements of the European state.

II.   *The American Experience*

I

The classical theories of imperialism arose to account for the European invasion of the undeveloped world. The next question is the extent to which any or all of these theories explain the foreign policy of the United States.

The United States has been an expansionist country. In the two centuries since the adoption of the Constitution the national area has more than quadrupled. The drive across the continent does not call for complicated analysis. An energetic, acquisitive people were propelled by their traits and their technologies to push restlessly into contiguous western spaces sparsely inhabited by wandering aborigines. This was a primal instinct. Bishop Berkeley's course of empire took its way westward; Thoreau walked eastward by force but westward walked free; Horace Greeley instructed the young man to go west; Huck Finn lit out for the territory. Politicians, publicists and professors invented reasons afterward.

In a masterful book half a century ago, *Manifest Destiny*, Albert K. Weinberg sardonically exposed the long parade of ex post facto justifications—natural right, geographic predestination, natural growth, political gravitation, and so on through the dusty years to "world leadership."[31] But these were rationalizations of the day, not causes in the sense required by historians. And, if the drive across the continent was more or less self-explanatory, the further drive into southern and western seas raised questions and demanded answers.

Americans, as Tocqueville noted, tend to deal in extremely large and vague ideas or extremely minute and clear ones. In accounting for expansion over water, historians until rather recently found no middle ground of analytic theory between hortatory generalities, like Manifest Destiny, and ad hoc, case-by-case explanations. This is why James A. Field, Jr., could call his witty essay on the subject "American Imperialism: The Worst Chapter in Almost Any Book."[32]

Over the last generation, however, a sort of analytic theory has emerged, even if it does not necessarily invalidate the title of Professor Field's essay. The premise is that Americans, even before independence, had more than a primal instinct for expansion: they had a coherent vision of empire. By 1783 Washington called the infant republic a "rising Empire." "Extend the sphere," Madison urged in the 10th *Federalist;* in the 14th, he spoke of the "extended republic" as "one great, respectable, and flourishing empire." However much Hamilton and Jefferson, John Quincy Adams and Jackson, disagreed on other matters, they agreed on expansion. "Conceived as an empire," wrote R. W. Van Alstyne, the United States was "by its very essence an expanding imperial power."[33]

Professor Van Alstyne, though he allowed for economic motives, saw American imperialism as the predictable behavior of an ambitious and dynamic national state. In recent years the so-called Open Door interpretation of expansion has given American empire a specifically economic explanation. William Appleman Williams, the godfather of this interpretation, is one of the few contemporary American historians who can be said to have founded a school. Both his own impassioned writings and the multiplying books of his disciples had for a season extensive influence on the way younger historians thought about American foreign policy.

The Open Door, of course, refers to the policy, announced at the end of the nineteenth century by Secretary of State John Hay, of safeguarding "for the world the principle of equal and impartial trade." By reasonable extension, the doctrine implies the determination to open the door for American trade and capital around the planet. This determination, according to the Open Door school, springs from structural necessities of the economic system. "The capitalist political economy," Williams says, "is inherently imperialist."[34] American foreign policy has been governed by "the firm conviction, even dogmatic belief, that America's *domestic* well-being depends upon such sustained, ever-increasing overseas economic expansion."[35] Capitalism is forever driven to conquer new worlds in order to escape the threat of fundamental change in American society.

Though the Open Door thesis bears a superficial resemblance to the Leninist theory, its supporters seem generally innocent of the European debate over the nature of imperialism. The Open Door school is a home-grown product in the intellectual tradition, though without the panache, of Charles A. Beard.* Because the United States remained a capital-importing nation until the First World War, the

---

* The school derives especially from Beard's *The Open Door at Home* (New York, 1934).

Open Door thesis could hardly blame American imperialism, in the manner of Lenin, on surplus capital in search of foreign investment outlets. The thesis turns rather, for most of American history, on surplus production in search of foreign markets.

In his earlier writings Williams found the expansionist motive in the industrial surplus. The imperialist outbreak at the turn of the century, he argued in *The Tragedy of American Diplomacy,* was forced by manufacturers seeking foreign markets in a time of depression. Later, in *The Roots of the Modern American Empire,* he traced the expansionist compulsion back to the agricultural surplus in the earlier nineteenth century. By midcentury American commercial agriculture had become habituated to overseas sales. Depression in the early 1870s intensified the need for markets abroad. The export boom later in that decade confirmed the agrarian faith in overseas solutions. Agricultural pressure, Williams contends, led to the redefinition of the American marketplace as the world marketplace and to the consequent redirection of American foreign policy. Finally, in the 1890s, a new depression along with the closing of the frontier not only remobilized the farmers but alarmed urban businessmen facing their own surplus problems; facing also economic contradictions and class tensions that threatened social upheaval.

The result was national consensus on the expansion of the marketplace, by peaceful means if possible, by military means if necessary; by territorial acquisition for a season, by economic penetration over the longer run. "The control of policy making by the industrialists and financiers," as Walter LaFeber put it in his influential book *The New Empire,*[36] resulted in the creation of an informal American empire in which the United States, after a brief colonial fling, used its economic might to secure hegemony without the embarrassment of traditional colonialism.

The expansionist compulsion, so deeply rooted in the economic structure, committed all American administrations in the twentieth century to the promotion of empire. Nations seeking to defend themselves against American economic aggression were defined as dangers to American freedom. Hence the war with Spain; hence the First and Second World Wars; hence the Cold War; hence the war in Vietnam. The drive to conquer the markets of the world, according to the Open Door thesis, explains everything in American foreign policy.

II

Historians have long recognized the crucial role that exports played in stimulating American economic development. The Founding Fathers, it is true, initially regarded foreign trade as a threat to the

American experiment. "Commerce produces money, money Luxury and all three are incompatible with Republicanism," said John Adams. Jefferson on occasion wished the Atlantic were "an ocean of fire between the new and old world." But Americans, Adams noted with regret, were "as aquatic as the Tortoises," and "the love of Commerce with its conveniences and pleasures" was an addiction "as unalterable as their Natures."[37] As the love of commerce grew, it hastened the transition from republicanism to laissez-faire liberalism and the adoption of what A. O. Hirschman calls the "doux-commerce thesis."[38]

Commerce, it was contended, enlarges the mind, softens manners, confers reciprocal benefits, reduces prejudice and diffuses enlightenment. If world trade were relieved of its shackles, Jefferson said as Secretary of State, "the greatest mass possible would then be produced of those things which contribute to human life and human happiness."[39] Trade was the carrier of civilization. "The historian," said Emerson, "will see that trade was the principle of Liberty; that trade planted America and destroyed Feudalism; that it makes peace and keeps peace, and it will abolish slavery."[40] "Under the beneficent sway of the Genius of Commerce," thought Melville's Redburn as he gazed on the docks of Liverpool, "all climes and countries embrace; and yard-arm touches yard-arm in brotherly love."[41]

The Genius of Commerce joined comparative advantage to idealistic hope, and its spirit pervaded the diplomacy of the early republic. The "great rule" in regard to foreign nations, said Washington in his Farewell Address, "is, in extending our commercial relations to have with them as little *political* connection as possible." The rule was so faithfully followed that by 1826 Theodore Lyman, Jr., wrote in *The Diplomacy of the United States*, the first manual on the subject, "Our diplomacy may be termed, altogether, of a commercial character." Intending to enlarge economic and minimize political ties, the American government preferred to send consuls rather than ministers to foreign lands. Jefferson fought the Barbary pirates to protect American shipping, bought the Louisiana Territory to gain the port of New Orleans and was the one American President, James A. Field, Jr., reminded us in *America and the Mediterranean World, 1776–1882*, to spend more money on the Navy than on the Army. "The American ship of state remained a merchantman," Field wrote of this period, "the need for commercial links and for the earnings of the merchant marine remained undiminished, and the forty-five years that followed the Treaty of Ghent [which ended the War of 1812] witnessed the great age of American shipping."[42]

These years also witnessed the great age of Manifest Destiny. The

United States annexed Texas, California and Oregon. The Mexican War generated the movement to seize "all Mexico." The refusal of Spain to sell Cuba led American diplomats in Europe to draft the Ostend Manifesto proposing its conquest by force. The Young America movement combined liberating fervor in the spirit of the Revolutions of 1848 with demands for freedom of commerce, foreign markets and southward expansion. North American adventurers—the notorious *Filibusteros*—invaded Cuba, Nicaragua, Honduras, Ecuador and several Mexican states.[43]

Now the striking thing is that this zeal for foreign trade and for territorial expansion predated the general agricultural surplus (cotton always excepted; but the great cotton market was in Britain) and long predated the industrial surplus. Moreover, when the United States moved into the era of surplus after the Civil War, the passion to promote trade and exports subsided, instead of intensifying as it should have done according to the Open Door thesis.

The consular service declined. "The whole of South America," a congressman who had himself served as consul in Brazil complained in 1874, "is without a consular clerk."[44] The merchant marine collapsed. The tonnage of United States shipping in foreign trade was actually smaller in the McKinley administration than it had been in the second administration of Jefferson. "We have almost entirely lost our Eastern trade," said a commander of the European squadron, "and American vessels are as rare as black swans."[45] As sail gave way to steam, the great American Navy fell into desuetude. "We have nothing which deserves to be called a Navy," said Secretary of the Navy William C. Whitney in 1885.[46] The Navy's operating range shrank; and, when new steel ships were commissioned, they were assigned, not to the Pacific or Asiatic Squadron, as Open Door logic should have dictated, but to the North Atlantic Squadron.[47] In short, contrary to the Open Door thesis, the era of surplus was accompanied not by an elaboration but by a marked neglect of the instrumentalities of commercial conquest.

III

Why did the passion for foreign markets decline at just the time the United States was entering the era of surplus? The answer lies in the expansion of the home market. Capital earned in the export sector had by the 1840s begun to propel the United States into self-sustaining economic growth. The shift from agriculture to industry reduced the dependence of the American economy on the world market. Foreign trade declined as a proportion of the gross national product, to 10 percent by 1850, to 6 percent by 1860. The home market, properly cultivated, appeared capable of indefinite enlargement. The protective tariff was the home market's guarantee. The protective tariff was also a major obstacle to American penetration of foreign markets.

The tariff is an issue as slighted by historians today as it was exaggerated by politicians at the time. It deserves attention. Henry C. Carey, who made the intellectual case for protection, rejected free trade as a racket by which Great Britain, the premier manufacturing power, dominated and exploited the rest of the world. Free trade, Carey contended, would retard American industrial development and leave the republic in colonial bondage. Only when protection had won the United States industrial independence would free and equal commerce be possible.

The growth of manufacturing after the Civil War persuaded some people that industrial independence was secure and that America could now compete in the world market. Those most eager for foreign markets were most determined on tariff reduction. "All who desire to see the products of American skill and ingenuity in every market of the world, with a resulting restoration of American commerce," Grover Cleveland told Congress in his 1888 State of the Union message, must join in lowering the tariff. "We have got to let prices down," Henry Adams told Secretary of State John Hay, "if we are to get markets."[48]

Of all the Secretaries of the Treasury Henry Adams had seen, he considered Hugh McCulloch, who served Andrew Johnson, "the best" and fondly recalled in the *Education* the hopeful days after the Civil War when McCulloch was "surrounded by all the active and intelligent young men in the country."[49] "The tariff," McCulloch wrote in 1888, "is gradually shutting up foreign markets against our manufactured goods." Except for Great Britain, European nations "are following our example, and, in self-defence, are adopting a protective policy. . . . What the great productive interests of the United States now need is, not protective duties, but *markets*." Tariff reduction, McCulloch said, was essential "to open foreign markets to our various manufactured goods and our agricultural productions. Without these markets our great industrial interests can never be permanently prosperous."[50]

Hugh McCulloch and Friedrich Engels probably agreed on very little, but they agreed on this. "Protective tariff in the form given it by McKinley," Engels wrote after the enactment in 1890 of the McKinley Tariff, "has become an intolerable fetter." High tariffs had "to a large extent excluded American industry from the world market, at a time when the home market has already been suffering from a glut. . . . America can only escape from its permanent industrial crisis, brought about by the protective tariff, if it enters the world market, and to do that it has to liberate itself from the protective tariff. . . . If America introduces free trade, it will beat England on the world market in ten years' time."[51]

According to the Open Door thesis, the search for foreign markets was the dominating motive in American foreign policy. This search required the lowering of tariff barriers. In fact, tariff reduction got nowhere. Protectionists like William D. "Pig Iron" Kelley of Pennsylvania scorned the "preposterous assertions" of "school-men and the organs of these foreign commercial agents that [we] are suffering from 'over-production.'" Henry George thought the argument "preposterous when there is actual want among large classes."[52] "The time is long past," said Senator Justin S. Morrill, "when nations can be enormously enriched by any excessive profits upon foreign trade. . . . National wealth must now and hereafter be mainly created by labor at home; and the home market is the only one of value over which any nation now has absolute control."[53] The Republican platform of 1896, adopted in the midst of depression, proclaimed Republican allegiance to the home market and to "the policy of protection as the bulwark of American industrial independence and the foundation of American development and prosperity." Tariff rates mounted steadily from the Morrill Act in 1861 to the Smoot-Hawley Act in 1930.

If the conquest of foreign markets was, as the Open Door school claims, the dominating motive, the protective tariff could not have survived. But protectionism had the solid support of the business community and the approval of most farmers. Its grip on Congress and the country demonstrates how limited the concern for foreign markets in fact was. As a proportion of the gross national product, exports were 6.2 percent in 1869–1873 and 5.8 percent in 1907–1911; the highest percentage reached in these years was 8.2 in the agricultural boom years of 1877–1881.[54] Foreign markets, in short, had a low priority in the American business consciousness.

Confronted by depression in the 1890s, the leaders of the steel industry, for example, turned not to foreign markets but to rationalization of the home market as the means of preserving profits. They set up gentlemen's agreements, pools and holding companies to control production and prices. High costs in any case made American steel non-competitive in the international market, nor could American producers easily adapt to foreign requirements. The Carnegie

Company contemplated a London sales office in 1896 but abandoned the idea as soon as recovery began.[55] "It is amazing to me," said Woodrow Wilson, ". . . that the businessmen of America have concerned themselves so little with the commerce of the world, as distinguished from the commerce of America."[56]

IV

The transformation of America during the First World War from a debtor to a creditor nation made protection more than ever the mortal enemy of foreign markets. For if other countries could not earn dollars in the American market, how could they pay for American goods? Yet the business community and the Republican party, oblivious to the behavior demanded of them by the Open Door school, responded by establishing the highest tariff rates up to that point in American history in 1922 and still higher rates in 1930. By 1932 exports fell to 2.8 percent of the gross national product.

When the Roosevelt administration came in the next year, Cordell Hull, a champion of the doux-commerce thesis, became Secretary of State. "To me," Hull wrote, "unhampered trade dovetailed with peace; high tariffs, trade barriers, and unfair economic competition, with war."[57] In this spirit, the Roosevelt administration proposed to lower rates through reciprocal trade agreements as a means of gaining access to foreign markets. The business community, instead of welcoming the bill, opposed it. "This proposal," declared Senator Arthur H. Vandenberg, a conservative leader, "is Fascist in its philosophy, Fascist in its objective." In the House, only two Republicans voted for the bill; only three in the Senate.[58]

From the time of takeoff, American economic growth has been based on the home market. When the home market collapsed in the Great Depression, Keynes came to the rescue and showed how deficit spending could restore domestic demand. After the Second World War capitalists continued to oppose the liberalization of trade. In 1947 Truman tried to get the Senate to ratify the charter of the International Trade Organization. In a speech at Baylor University he used the most honeyed free enterprise rhetoric to persuade businessmen of the virtues of an open trading world. This speech has been quoted (and flagrantly misquoted)* as evidence of capitalist control

---

*Noam Chomsky in *American Power and the New Mandarins* (New York, 1969) twice claimed that Truman had said : "All freedom is dependent on freedom of enterprise. . . . The whole world should adopt the American system. . . . The American system can survive in America only if it becomes a world system." Stephen E. Ambrose in *Rise to Globalism: American Foreign Policy Since 1938* (Baltimore, 1971), 19, claimed that

of policy-making. In fact, though Truman's free enterprise blandishments seduced Open Door historians in later years, they failed to seduce the business community at the time. Because of business opposition, the Senate refused to ratify the charter, and the ITO never came into existence.

In the half century after 1920, omitting the years of the Second World War, exports exceeded 6 percent of the gross national product in only two years (1921 and 1947) and went overwhelmingly, not to the underdeveloped world, but to other developed countries. As late as 1970, exports and imports together amounted to only 8.5 percent of the gross national product. One is familiar with the counterargument that the margin, however small, may be vital; that iron constitutes only .0004 percent of the human body but is essential to the functioning of the organism, and so on. But even Open Door theorists who advance the physiological analogy agree that it is "somewhat far-fetched" applied to the economy.[59]

Not until the 1980s did foreign trade assume real importance for the modern American economy, accounting for nearly 20 percent of the gross national product. The merchandise trade deficit—the gap between imports and exports—was the highest in American history. Now, if ever, foreign markets were essential. Now, if ever, foreign market imperialism ought to dominate American foreign policy. Foreign policy did indeed take an aggressive form, but foreign markets hardly seemed the object: the vast markets of Nicaragua? For remedy Americans, as through their history, looked homeward and called for higher tariffs against imports. The Reagan administration meanwhile revived the home market through a $200 billion budgetary deficit.

From Hamilton and Clay to the present, most business leaders and their political allies have remained stalwart in their conviction that economic salvation lies not in foreign markets but in the home market.

V

Open Door historians are scholars possessed by dogma. The all-powerful role of overseas markets in determining American foreign policy is their article of faith. Dogma sweeps the home market and the protective tariff out of their line of vision. It leaves no doubt in their minds about, in LaFeber's words, "the control of policy-making

---

Truman said: "The whole world should adopt the American system. The American system can survive only if it becomes a world system." Truman said nothing of the sort, at Baylor or elsewhere. The quotation is fabricated. Accuracy is not an Open Door school strong point.

by the industrialists and financiers." They are not discouraged by absence of documentation proving that industrialists and financiers controlled specific decisions. If evidence is lacking, it is, William Appleman Williams said, because policy-makers "had internalized, and had come to *believe,* the theory, the necessity, and the morality of open-door expansion. Hence they seldom thought it necessary to explain or defend the approach."[60] In short, the less evidence, the better.

Historians do not ordinarily go for the argument *ex silentio.* In their anxiety to satisfy their colleagues, Open Door historians are led by their dogma, I am sure unconsciously, to distort evidence in order to bolster their thesis. They make much play, for example, with the use of the word "empire" by the Founding Fathers as proof of the incurable American disease of expansionism. Thus Van Alstyne cited Washington's "rising Empire" to show that the United States was by its essence an expanding imperial power. Thus from Madison's "Extend the sphere" and "one great, respectable and flourishing empire" Williams deduced that Madison "clearly understood that foreign markets were part of the sphere that had to be enlarged to insure the continuation of republican institutions and of prosperity."[61]

All this may or may not have been so; but the evidence adduced proves nothing of the sort. The case turns on the meaning of the word "empire" in the 1780s. If one consults a contemporaneous dictionary—say the first edition of the *Encyclopaedia Britannica,* published in 1771—one finds "empire" defined as "a large extent of land, under the jurisdiction or government of an emperor." "Emperor" is defined as "a title of honour among the ancient Romans . . . now made to signify a sovereign prince, or supreme ruler of an empire." The first European example mentioned is Charlemagne, of whom the *Encyclopaedia Britannica* says, "It is to be observed that there was not a foot of land or territory annexed to the emperor's title."[62]

Or, if one consults the standard modern work on the subject, Richard Koebner's *Empire,* one finds that the Latin word *imperium* meant command, rule, sovereignty, the exercise of authority, and that in the eighteenth century the word "empire" by no means implied territorial expansion. As the British historian E. A. Freeman wrote in 1885, "It is only in quite later times within my own memory, that the word 'empire' has come into common use as a set term for something beyond the kingdom."[63] In any case, an examination of the context in which Washington used the phrase makes it clear that by "rising Empire" he meant no more than a new nation securing its national sovereignty. As for Madison's supposedly damning words, A. K. Wein-

berg was indisputably correct when he wrote in *Manifest Destiny* that
Madison referred "not to expansion but only to the amalgamation of
the thirteen States."[64]

The Open Door school's exploitation of the word empire can only
be described as an unscrupulous philological excursion. It is unhap-
pily characteristic of the way Open Door historians press recalcitrant
evidence into the service of dogma. Again and again in *The Roots of
the Modern American Empire* Williams overstated and manipulated his
case in order to insert foreign market preoccupations where they existed feebly or not at all. Thus he wrote that Grant in his annual message of 5 December 1870 "first reiterated his argument that Santo
Domingo should be annexed because of its value as a market for farm
surpluses."[65] But the first argument advanced in Grant's message for
the annexation of what he called "San Domingo" was the preclusive
argument: that, if the United States did not act, Europeans would.
Grant mentioned the strategic argument and the raw materials argument before he got to the market argument, and even here his
concern was as much with industrial as with agricultural products.

In 1895 a boundary dispute between Venezuela and British Guiana
led Grover Cleveland to send a bellicose message to Congress. This
message, according to Williams, was a "well-nigh definitive application of the marketplace conception of the world."[66] Actually the message said nothing at all about markets—how in the world could the
Venezuela border dispute affect either American or British access to
Latin American markets?—and rested on the determination to keep
British political and military presence, not British exports or investment, out of the hemisphere. As Henry Cabot Lodge stated the issue,
"If Great Britain can extend her territory in South America without
remonstrance from us, every other European power can do the same
and in a short time you will see South America parcelled out as Africa
has been." With great powers to the south, "we should be forced to
become at once a nation with a powerful army and navy with difficulties and dangers surrounding us." "The United States," said Theodore Roosevelt, "cannot tolerate the aggrandizement of a European
power on American soil." Williams's claim that Cleveland was acting
on behalf of American business interests ignores Cleveland's own
sharp testimony to the contrary. "Those among us who most loudly
reprehended and bewailed our vigorous assertion of the Monroe
Doctrine," Cleveland later wrote, "were the timid ones who feared
personal financial loss, or those engaged in speculation and stock-
gambling."[67] Or as Lodge commented at the time: "Outside of the
moneyed interests in New York and Boston, the American people,

like Congress and the press, are solidly behind the President in defense of the Monroe Doctrine."[68]

Similarly Williams tried to force the Populist party of the 1890s into the foreign markets straitjacket. Several hundred pages of *The Roots of the Modern American Empire* argued that American agriculturalists in the nineteenth century thought of little else but foreign markets. Then the People's party arose in 1892 as the national culmination of a generation of agrarian discontent. Nearly thirteen hundred Populist delegates adopted a platform at Omaha—a document of 2500 words into which the embattled farmers poured all their grievances and nostrums. Yet not a resolution, not a plank, not a word about foreign markets! Only a historian blinded by dogma could fail to regard this omission as worthy of note. That the omission was hardly accidental is suggested by the fact that the Populists did not mention foreign markets in their platforms of 1896, 1900, 1904 and 1908.

VI

Such instances of historical malpractice can be multiplied to wearying length.[69] The foreign markets obsession leads Open Door historians to hear music when there is no one there. It leads them also, when foreign markets are sung, to parade every reference as the true revelation of motive and to dismiss noneconomic reasons as deception and rationalization.

And it fills their texts with implicit moral undertones. Open Door historians write as if every expression of a desire to sell domestic products in foreign lands is evidence of original sin. Students who read their tracts come away with the idea that anyone who seeks foreign markets is by definition an imperialist. Obviously, as American protectionists pointed out in the nineteenth century, there are inequities in terms of trade between manufacturing and extractive countries. But in the end is the Open Door—the principle of nondiscrimination in trading—really so wicked? Even unequal trade is often better than no trade at all. Does the Open Door lead implacably to hegemony? Deng Xiaoping evidently does not think so. If foreign markets, multilateral commercial relations and so on are so sinister, what sort of trading pattern would Open Door historians approve? Bilateralism? Managed trade? Barter? Autarky? While condemning multilateralism, they remain notably silent about alternatives short of the abolition of capitalism. Beard at least advocated an Open Door at home.

Dogma leaves them no doubt, however, that the American Open Door policy is responsible for most of the troubles of the world. Open

Door historians suffer as much as zealots of the right from what D. W. Brogan called the "illusion of American omnipotence."[70] They see the world beyond America as passive and powerless, its destiny determined by decisions made in Washington. "One searches in vain," writes N. Gordon Levin, a scholar who defected from the Open Door school, ". . . for any real effort to describe and understand the motivations or behavior of the leaders of any of the major states with whom America has dealt. Other nations and critical world events seem to exist . . . as a shadowy backdrop against which the inscrutable teleology of the expansive American Open Door works out its inevitable course."[71]

This provincialism is expressed in the school's incuriosity about the experience of other nations. Open Door historians never ask themselves why, if the capitalist economy is inherently imperialistic, European and Asian capitalism in recent times refuses empire and still prospers. The provincialism is expressed too, very damagingly, in disdain for non-American sources. Williams rarely cites a foreign book or archive. Of the 1700 footnotes in *The Roots of the Modern American Empire,* only 22 referred to non-American books, periodicals or articles (apart from ritual citations of Locke, Quesnay, Adam Smith and Alfred Marshall). In one footnote Williams spoke of "my own research in the relevant European sources, greatly aided by German and French colleagues"[72]; but his list of manuscript collections consulted did not include a single European depository. Of the 557 footnotes in LaFeber's *Inevitable Revolutions: The United States in Central America,* only 7 were to works in Spanish. Carl P. Parrini's *Heir to Empire: United States Economic Diplomacy, 1916–1923* attempted to tell the story of American economic relations during and immediately after the First World War without consulting British, French and German archives or even biographies of Lloyd George, Clemenceau or any other European leader. As Akira Iriye has written of the typical historian of American empire, "No other nation's historian could so complacently write of his country's imperialism without reference to its interaction with other powers."[73]

It is difficult to understand why any thesis so intellectually parochial, so thinly documented and so poorly argued as the Open Door interpretation should have cast a spell on a generation of American historians. Part of the answer lies in understandable revulsion against follies and crimes of American foreign policy in the Vietnam years. Part too lies in the heads-I-win-tails-you-lose character of the thesis itself.

The philosopher Karl Popper was once shocked to discover that

Marxists and psychoanalysts "were able to interpret any conceivable event as a verification of their theories." This led him to propose a test of the scientific character of a hypothesis: "What conceivable facts would I accept as refutations, or falsifications, of my theory?"[74] What conceivable facts, one must ask, would Open Door historians accept as a refutation of the Open Door thesis? If statesmen mention the Open Door, that proves the thesis; if they fail to mention the Open Door, that proves they have "internalized" the thesis. If statesmen defend corporate interests, that proves the thesis; if they fail to defend corporate interests, that proves their devilish cunning in sacrificing short-term to long-term corporate interests. If they enter an area that has economic value, that proves the thesis; if the area has no economic value, like Vietnam, that proves the need to defend their control of the world market as a whole. In Williams's *Roots of the Modern American Empire* every policy and its opposite turn out to prove the national dedication to the conquest of foreign markets: high tariffs as well as low tariffs (page 247); gold as well as silver (199, 361–365); low railroad rates and high (309); prosperity as well as depression (208); peace as well as war (215, 410); anti-annexation just as much as pro-annexation (263, 440). Talk about "internalization"!

The Open Door thesis is evidently not falsifiable. Because it explains everything, it explains very little. It is not a testable historical hypothesis at all. It is a theological dogma.

VII

Yet who can doubt that there is an American empire?—an 'informal' empire, not colonial in polity, but still richly equipped with imperial paraphernalia: troops, ships, planes, bases, proconsuls, local collaborators, all spread wide around the luckless planet. If the Open Door thesis does not account for this empire, what does?

An alternative hypothesis is that the American empire was produced not by the economic system demanding expansion in order to survive but by the political state demanding expansion in order to feel safe; not by the quest for material prosperity but by the quest for physical security; not by businessmen and farmers seeking private profit but by politicians and military men seeking national power; not by a *Weltanschauung* peculiar to American capitalism but by *raisons d'état* common to all nations.

This hypothesis assumes that the pursuit of national security is an independent variable, not reducible to economic motives. Proponents of the economic interpretation generally reject this assumption, at least when they write about the United States. (They regularly claim national security as an independent motive for the Soviet Union.) For they are primarily concerned with getting rid of capitalism. To acknowledge the autonomy of geopolitical motives would undermine the theory that capitalism is the root of all evil. It would admit the possibility that non-capitalist states may have imperialist propensities. Still if what the Soviet Union did in Eastern Europe, above all in Hungary in 1956 and Czechoslovakia in 1968, is not imperialism, then the term has little meaning; if it is imperialism, then we must dismiss the notion that imperialism is unique to capitalism or that the abolition of capitalism would abolish imperialism.

The politics of the Open Door school will not permit it to acknowledge that national security supplies independent reasons for American foreign policy decisions. Williams, for example, finds it "extremely difficult" to identify any cases where American leaders "could fairly be said to be acting on a strategic motive."[75] "Blaine and Harrison," he writes in a characteristic passage in *Roots,* "did not want power for its own sake. . . . They sought it in order to act upon a broad policy of overseas economic expansion that they considered necessary and desirable for the entire political economy, as well as for specific interests within it."[76]

But political and military leaders very often want power for its own sake—for the sake, that is, of the interest and security of the state. Trade is part of the system of power, so they promote trade. They see trade, however, as the handmaiden to power; as a means to a national and public end, not as an end in itself. Strategic and economic motives, however much intertwined in practice, are analytically distinguishable. "External interests," as Admiral Mahan said, "cannot be confined to those of commerce."[77] Even the Marxist economist Thomas Weisskopf, while suspecting that national security is often invoked to justify imperialist policies motivated by other concerns, finds "no reason to doubt that a modern nation state does have an interest in national security that can independently motivate imperialist activity." He adds that "the national security interest is one that would not seem to be dependent in any significant sense on whether a society is capitalist or socialist."[78]

Imperial initiatives in American history have come in the main from politicians, military men and publicists, not from the business community. The historic springs of American expansion were twofold—the disparity of power between white and red Americans; and the determination of white Americans to protect national power against European rivals, first in North America and later in the seas beyond. Economic advantage was secondary. American expansion was essentially the product of what Langer called "preclusive imperialism." The Louisiana Purchase eliminated the French on the North American continent. The annexation of Florida eliminated the Spanish. The Monroe Doctrine warned European powers not to meddle in the western hemisphere. The annexation of Texas and of Oregon snuffed out British intrigue in North America. The war of 1846 eliminated Mexican obstacles to the transcontinental drift.

The foreign markets interpretation of post–Civil War expansion is ludicrous. The consequential foreign market, then and thereafter, lay in Europe, not in the undeveloped areas coveted by political and military men in the decades after Appomattox. The markets of Alaska? of Santo Domingo? of the Danish West Indies? of Samoa? of Puerto Rico? of Guam? of Midway? The Open Door historians must be kidding.

Consider, for example, the case of Samoa. According to Williams, American farmers wanted to open the Samoan market for the wheat and flour surpluses of the Pacific coast. Also, quoted with apparent approval from a man who ran a shipping line to Samoa, Samoa was "vital" to the control of "the whole commerce of the Pacific." [79] The British diplomatic historian Paul M. Kennedy, drawing on German, British and American archives ignored by Williams, presented a very different picture. The competition for Samoa, he showed in his authoritative work *The Samoan Tangle: A Study in Anglo-German-American Relations, 1878–1900*, [80] resulted not from economic factors but from a great-power political fracas in which colonies were assets in the struggle for status. Kennedy found little evidence of American concern for Samoa except for brief moments of naval encounter in 1889 and 1899. A look at the map dispels any idea that the Samoan islands controlled the commerce of the Pacific. The notion that poverty-stricken Samoans had the money to buy American wheat and flour, even if it were part of their diet, is absurd; and copra, the one commodity they could offer in exchange, had no market in the United States. Britain lost interest in Samoa once it decided that the islands had no strategic value. Germany cared most, but not for economic reasons. German trade with Samoa was and remained insignificant. The German government wanted a colonial success to appease its conservative nationalists at home.

Preclusive imperialism, here and elsewhere, was the motive. Writing in 1895, Henry Cabot Lodge, a proud American imperialist, saw England "reaching out for every island in the Pacific." Had it not been for the German interest, he said, we would have abandoned Samoa to England, and he feared that weak American policy "can result only in throwing the Hawaiian people into the arms of England." Lodge summed up the rationale of preclusive imperialism with perfect clarity. "The great nations," he said, "are rapidly absorbing for their future expansion and their present defence all the waste places of the earth. . . . As one of the great nations of the world, the United States must not fall out of the line of march."[81] In short, America must meet the competition. "If we shrink from the hard contests where men must win at the hazard of their lives and at the risk of all they hold dear," said Theodore Roosevelt, "then the bolder and stronger peoples will pass us by, and will win for themselves the domination of the world."[82]

Williams wrote of Roosevelt and Lodge that, while they had no personal economic stakes in imperialism, "economics was nevertheless at the center of their thinking about foreign policy."[83] How insulted Roosevelt and Lodge would have been by such a thought! TR looked with contempt on "the typical big moneyed men of my country. I do not regard them as furnishing sound opinion as regards either foreign or domestic policies."[84] He saw the world in terms of the balance of power. He did not give the time of day to foreign markets. Lodge talked more about foreign markets, but even Lodge condemned both "the doctrine that there is no higher aim or purpose for men or for nations than to buy and sell, to trade jack-knives and make everything cheap" and the people "who think the price of calico more important than a nation's honor, the duties on pig iron of more moment than the advance of a race."[85]

Howard K. Beale, whom the Open Door school can hardly dismiss as a conservative historian, has written the most comprehensive and careful account of TR and foreign affairs. As Beale correctly puts it, "The Roosevelt-Lodge expansionists who took the American people into an imperialist struggle for world power were not primarily concerned with American economic interests around the world. The primary concern of Roosevelt and his fellow-expansionists was power and prestige and the naval strength that would bring power and prestige. They gloried in the thought of American greatness and power that their expansionist policies would create."[86]

VIII

The Open Door policy itself, ironically enough, refutes the obsession of the Open Door school with the alleged search for foreign markets.

When the scramble for the waste places of the earth resumed after 1880, American imperialists felt that a role in Asia was essential if the United States was not to fall out of the line of march. But, apart from missionaries, the United States had limited interests and influence in China—far less than Britain, Russia, Japan or Germany. John Hay's Open Door notes were a gesture against the dismemberment of the Chinese Empire, a plea for equal treatment of Americans and a hopeful signal to the world that the United States was now a great power too. The notes were not enforced, nor indeed enforceable; nor did they imply imperialistic designs on China; nor did Chinese at the time think they did. "Because China's power . . . is insufficient to hold back the advance of Japan and Russia," wrote Hsi-liang, governor-general of Manchuria, "we must depend on the United States and Britain and on the policies of the open door and of the balance of power to save ourselves from oblivion."[87]

American business showed little interest in the China market. Lord Charles Beresford, a British enthusiast for that market, wrote after an American tour in 1899, "I could discover no desire on the part of the commercial communities in the United States to engage in any practical effort for preserving what to them might become in the future a trade, the extent of which no mortal can conjecture."[88] Another enthusiast, the former American minister to China Charles Denby, lamented more broadly that the American business community did not seem to "feel the necessity of cultivating foreign markets."[89] When the Taft administration sought to increase American political influence in China by promoting American participation in investment consortiums, American financiers, with better investment opportunities elsewhere, balked at going along.

In the main, the government did little to facilitate business penetration of the China market. "Efforts to assert American power for the benefit of American businessmen," writes Marilyn Blatt Young, "were, in contrast to European countries, noticeable by their absence."[90] The State Department intervened more often on behalf of American missionaries than of American businessmen. But it displayed no great concern about China at all. In 1900 only one member of the legation staff in Peking spoke Chinese as against six Chinese speakers in both the British and French legations.[91] In 1905 the consul general reported the United States had the most underfunded consular office in Shanghai except for Portugal.[92]

Americans had dreamed about the China market at least since the start of the nineteenth century. The imperialists of the 1890s encouraged this dream. But when Roosevelt and Lodge mentioned foreign markets, as Howard K. Beale points out, "it was because economic advantages won converts to imperialist policies or enhanced the prestige of the country. . . . When therefore they came to sell expansion to the American people they gladly talked up its economic profitableness."[93] Doubtless they thought too that markets were bound to develop in the long run and that, if Americans were in a position to exploit them, it would enhance national power. They certainly did not see the China market (or the markets of Samoa, Hawaii, Central America and the West Indies) as immediate remedies for the contradictions of capitalism. Nor, judging by their indifference to the China market, did American capitalists. The notion that the search for the China market was a mainspring of American foreign policy perishes under examination, like the China market itself.

Because the American interest in China at the turn of the century was one of international prestige rather than of direct strategic or economic concern, American policy was relatively passive. In Latin America, however, the United States perceived both strategic and economic interests and acted on them. American policy in the hemisphere is supposed to offer the classic example of 'dollar diplomacy,' and it is true that, especially in Central America and in the Caribbean, corporate interests have shaped United States policy a great deal of the time. Yet even in Latin America the search for markets does not emerge as the supreme determinant.

The Monroe Doctrine established the framework for United States policy. The Doctrine was aimed at European political encroachment in the hemisphere, not at European economic penetration. For a century after 1823, Great Britain had far more trade and investment in South America than the United States. This did not worry the United States. Economics mattered far less than geopolitics. Lodge identified the real worry when he charged that Britain had "studded the West Indies with strong places which are a standing menace to our Atlantic seaboard."[94] Germany was now increasing its activity in the hemisphere and joined Britain in a blockade of Venezuela in 1902. Conditions of chronic instability in the Caribbean countries led to the non-payment of European debts and created pretexts for European intervention. The building of the Panama Canal increased U.S. strategic stakes in Central America.

The result was a United States policy designed to eliminate pretexts for European intervention. As Dana G. Munro shows conclusively in *Intervention and Dollar Diplomacy in the Caribbean, 1900–1921*, the State Department took the initiative in persuading a reluctant banking and business community to go into the Caribbean; and State's object was not to make money for American bankers but to drive out European bankers. In Munro's words, "The purpose of dollar diplomacy was to promote the political objectives of the United States, not to benefit private financial interests."[95]

This policy succeeded in replacing European by North American financial influence. When the First World War knocked out the German threat, strategic urgencies subsided. After 1920 the United States entered the private-interest phase of its political cycle. In the absence of overriding geopolitical claims, the corporate presence took control of policy.

Then, in the 1930s, the political cycle went into the public-purpose phase. Germany reappeared as an international menace. When the pursuit of profits for United States corporations now threatened strategic and political interests, geopolitics won out, as in the case of the nationalization of oil in Mexico. The oil companies, said a State Department memorandum in 1939, must not be permitted "to jeopardize our entire Good Neighbor policy through obstinacy and shortsightedness. Our national interests as a whole far outweigh those of the petroleum companies." President Eduardo Santos of Colombia called the Good Neighbor policy "so effective that where previously American companies were accustomed to threaten the government [of Colombia] by saying an appeal would be made to Washington, the picture was reversed, and it now was the government who made or threatened to make the appeals to Washington."[96]

Geopolitical and corporate interests have struggled ever since for control of Latin American policy. In the private-interest 1950s, the Eisenhower CIA threw out a radical government in Guatemala at the behest of the United Fruit Company.[97] Kennedy's Alliance for Progress in the public-purpose 1960s was disliked by both North American corporations and Latin American oligarchs. Fidel Castro considered the Alliance "a very intelligent strategy" doomed to failure. "The trusts see that their interests are being a little compromised ... the Pentagon thinks the strategic bases are in danger; the powerful oligarchies in all the Latin American countries alert their American friends; they sabotage the new policy; and in short, Kennedy has everyone against him."[98]

That security may outweigh economic interests does not ensure wiser policy. Since the Second World War the Pentagon has been busy negotiating bilateral defense arrangements, despatching arms and military missions, training Latin Americans in the black arts of counterinsurgency, stimulating militarist appetites and developing back-channel relations with Latin American colonels. Cold War ideology, by finding global stakes in Latin American civil wars, inflates geopolitical concerns. In the name of anticommunism Latin graduates of U.S. Army schools overthrow democratic regimes, torture revolutionaries and establish dictatorships. The special interests of the United States military establishment have corrupted hemisphere policy in recent times quite as much as the special interests of United States business corrupted hemisphere policy in the 1920s. But it is a different brand of corruption directed toward different ends.

IX

The foreign markets explanation of United States policy reaches its heights of provincialism, and of absurdity, when it deals with the Second World War. According to Williams, "the leaders of Germany, Japan, and Italy were working with the most powerful weapon available—the determination, born equally of desperation and hope, of large numbers of people to improve, radically and immediately, the substance and tone of their daily lives." Franklin Roosevelt, pursuing "traditional policies of economic and ideological empire," portrayed Germany, Italy and Japan "as dangers to the well-being of the United States. This happened before those countries launched military attacks into or against areas that the United States considered important to its economic system. It occurred instead as those nations began to compete vigorously with American entrepreneurs in Latin America and Asia. . . . American leaders began to go to war against the Axis in the Western Hemisphere."[99]

The Open Door thesis has no place for the balance of power as a factor in foreign policy. The thesis omits the possibility that, in Jefferson's old proposition, it might not be in the interest of the United States to see the whole force of Europe wielded by a single hand. In its ethnocentric preoccupation with America as the only actor on the world scene, the thesis ignores the expansionist drives of Nazism, Fascism and Japanese militarism and reduces Hitler, Mussolini and the Japanese imperialists to hapless victims of the American drive for foreign markets.

Moreover, if the Open Door interpretation were correct, the United States would surely have supported Japan, not China, in the Far East in the years before the war. American exports to Japan in the 1930s exceeded its exports to all of South America and far exceeded those to China; indeed Japan provided the third largest market for the American surplus, surpassed only by Great Britain and Canada.[100] If foreign markets were the determinant of policy, there would have been no Pearl Harbor, except on the metahistorical theory that hard-headed capitalists preferred a nebulous China market on the bush to a profitable Japanese market in the hand.

If doubts remain that the pursuit of national power is an independent variable, let us return to Max Weber's "mental experiment." The Open Door school assumes that, had the United States not been a capitalist country, it would not have engaged in the quest for empire. Let us imagine that the United States had always been a communist country, like the USSR. The Union of American Socialist Republics would presumably not have required an Open Door for American trade and investment. But how different would the diplomatic history of the UASR have been? Would a communist United States have declined to expand westward across the continent? Would it have refrained from murdering Indians, dispossessing Mexicans and expelling Britishers, Frenchmen and Spaniards along the way? Would it have refused the Monroe Doctrine and permitted Britain, France, Spain, Russia, Germany, to enlarge territorial control in the western hemisphere? Would it have been less interested than a capitalist America in dominating Central America and the Caribbean? Would it have been indifferent to the balance of power in Europe and East Asia? Would it have stood idly by while a hostile power from another continent placed nuclear missiles in Cuba? Does not expansionism derive therefore from the characteristics of a great power rather than from the characteristics of an economy?

Fidel Castro does not share the illusion of the Open Door school that all would be different if only the United States abolished capitalism. "Even if the United States became socialist," he observes, "we would have to be armed and keep our guard up, so nobody would be tempted to intimidate us, just in case there were to be a cultural revolution or some such thing in that neighboring socialist state."[101]

Raisons d'état, not the dynamics of capitalism, created the American thrust for world influence. A Soviet America would have behaved the same way, no doubt with greater ruthlessness. Political and strategic motives, national power and national security, have a life and force of their own, independent of systems of ideology and ownership. There are other things in life besides foreign markets. One looks forward to the Open Door school's explanation of the latest display of the American expansionist compulsion—that is, the voyage into outer space, motivated, no doubt, by the determination to stake out the American title to those vast new markets in the solar system.

X

Still has not the United States, for whatever reason, been a constantly expanding nation? Has not this expansion been based, as the Open Door school claims, on an eager national consensus? Have not the American people been from the start hell bent on empire?

Well, yes and no. Leaders of the early republic would have been astonished to discover that by the twentieth century the constitutional writ ran westward from the Atlantic to the Pacific. Jefferson expected white settlers to spread across the continent but never supposed that the Stars and Stripes would accompany them. "Whether we remain in one confederacy," he wrote after acquiring the Louisiana Territory, "or form into Atlantic and Mississippi confederations, I believe not very important." While the Americans had embarked on the project of embracing half a continent in one republican system, they were so little confident of success, Henry Adams commented, that even Jefferson "thought the solitary American experiment of political confederation 'not very important' beyond the Alleghanies."[102] Later Jefferson decided that the United States might extend as far as the Rockies. Along the Pacific would arise "a great, free and independent empire," populated by white Americans "unconnected with us but by the ties of blood and interest, and employing like us the rights of self-government."[103]

Even Thomas Hart Benton of Missouri, for all his flamboyant vision of expansion, proposed in 1825 to draw "the Western limits of the republic" along the ridge of the Rocky Mountains and to erect a statue of the fabled god Terminus on the highest peak. On the Pacific coast, "the new Government should separate from the mother Empire as the child separates from the parent."[104] Twenty years later Daniel Webster still anticipated an independent "Pacific republic" on the west coast.[105] John C. Calhoun disagreed, however, remarking presciently to John Quincy Adams "that the passion for aggandizement was the law paramount of man in society, and that there was no example in history of the disruption of a nation from itself by voluntary separation."[106]

On the other hand, Jefferson and J. Q. Adams would have probably been even more astonished to discover how little the United States had expanded to the south and to the north. Jefferson thought Cuba "the most interesting addition which could ever be made to our system of States" and told John C. Calhoun in 1820 that the United States "ought, at the first possible opportunity, to take Cuba."[107] Adams considered the annexation of Cuba "indispensable to the continuance and integrity of the Union itself" and thought Cuba would inexorably fall to the United States by the law of political gravitation.[108] So did W. H. Seward and many other nineteenth-century expansionists.

As for Canada, Adams held "our proper domain to be the continent of North America."[109] Charles Sumner was sure that the law of gravitation would bring in Canada. "That the whole continent of North America and all its adjacent islands," said Henry Adams in

1869, "must at last fall under the control of the United States is a conviction absolutely ingrained in our people."[110] "Long ere the second centennial arrives," Walt Whitman wrote in *Democratic Vistas* (1871), "there will be some forty to fifty great States, among them Canada and Cuba." Engels thought the annexation of Canada inevitable in 1888. As late as 1895, Henry Cabot Lodge declared, "From the Rio Grande to the Arctic Ocean there should be but one flag and one country."[111]

These things, so authoritatively predicted, never came to pass. We have not annexed Cuba or Canada. There is no likelihood that we ever will. The record hardly sustains the thesis of a people red hot for empire. From the Louisiana Purchase on, territorial acquisition has always met opposition. Texas waited outside the Union for a decade as an independent republic and then entered only through sleight of hand, John Tyler procuring admission by joint resolution after the Senate had rejected a treaty of annexation. The movement during the Mexican War to take "all Mexico" failed. Polk even feared that Congress would turn against the war and that he would lose New Mexico and California.[112] The Ostend Manifesto was disclaimed, and the filibusters of the 1850s were repudiated.

After the Civil War Seward's ambitious expansionist program got nowhere, except for the flyspeck of Midway and for Alaska, which Russia wanted to get rid of and which Congress reluctantly accepted after members were bribed, perhaps by the Russian minister. The Senate rejected the Hawaiian reciprocity treaty, the purchase of the Virgin Islands from Denmark, the annexation of Santo Domingo and the annexation of Samoa. We did not reduce the tariff nor restore the merchant marine nor reinvigorate the consular service. It took half a century of argument before we annexed Hawaii, and this might not have taken place had it not been for the war with Spain. Even with that war we still did not annex Cuba. We did annex the Philippines but set them free forty years later. And by 1960 Alaska and Hawaii were states, not colonies.

For all the Open Door school's talk about the national consensus, the imperial dream has encountered consistent indifference and recurrent resistance through most of American history. Imperialism was never a broadly based mass movement. There were spasms of jingoistic outrage, as over the sinking of the *Maine,* but no sustained demand for empire. Americans, wrote Bryce in 1888, "have none of the earth-hunger which burns in the great nations of Europe. . . . The general feeling of the nation is strongly against a forward policy."[113] At the height of American territorial imperialism, Americans never developed a colonial outlook in the British or French fashion. The United States established no colonial office. It trained no administrators to man the outposts of empire. It had no upper class with younger sons who needed outdoor relief. As for the age of 'neo-colonialism,' informal empire is even less capable than empire of evoking a mass movement. Multinational corporations do not inspire Mafeking nights. Whoever produced the American empire, it was not a broad populace electrified by the imperial idea.

Imperialism in the United States has always been the creed of a minority—which is why its history has largely been one of frustration. Let us then ask the Schumpeterian question: who were the American imperialists? The answer is appropriately Schumpeterian: they were mostly men extruded in one way or another from the mainstream of American life.

The filibusters of the 1850s were displaced men—adventurers, desperadoes, disappointed gold-seekers, ex-soldiers who could not settle down in civilian life, seamen who had tired of the discipline of the forecastle, losers at home seeking wealth and glory in undeveloped countries. Conrad distilled the type in his description of the Eldorado Exploring Expedition in *Heart of Darkness*—"reckless without hardihood, greedy without audacity, and cruel without courage." They had no theory but smash and grab.

The imperialists of the 1890s were men of a very different type, but they were displaced too. They did have a theory, but their theory ran against the grain of the prevailing culture. As historians, Roosevelt, Lodge, Brooks Adams, Mahan, had celebrated the old Federalist vision of a heroic America. As aristocrats and warriors, they hoped to redeem the odious plutocratic society by giving it a martial purpose. In Schumpeter's terms, these neo-Federalists represented an atavistic revival of an obsolete warrior class. Their fin de siècle imperialism was a flash in the pan. Even Roosevelt and Lodge would have liked at the moment of acquisition to trade the Philippines to Britain for Canada. "Public opinion," said Roosevelt in 1901, "is dull on the question of China." By 1907 even he decided that "from a military standpoint the Philippines form our heel of Achilles."[114]

Schumpeter supposed that the United States as a pure bourgeois society, uncontaminated by feudal reminiscences, would exhibit the weakest imperial tendencies among the great powers. In 1919 he cited the continuing independence of Canada and Mexico, the revulsion against Theodore Roosevelt's imperialism, the prospective independence of the Philippines, to prove his case.[115] In the short run, he was right. The imperialism of the neo-Federalist elite could not last because it lacked an institutional base in American society.

XI

But in his American predictions Schumpeter did not allow for an essential part of his own theory—that warlike involvements revive the warrior mentality. Half a century after the neo-Federalists, two world wars had created a great military establishment, and the Cold War made it permanent. The institutional base the neo-Federalists lacked came into powerful existence.

Of course a number of separate factors joined to produce the American empire in the years after the Second World War. These factors will be discussed in essays that follow. The initiating motive, I believe, was preclusive action—the protection of national security and the advancement of national power against real or fancied communist enemies. A hard precipitating factor, encouraging the militarization of policy and remedy and giving the empire much of its proconsular paraphernalia, has been the emergence of a new class of professional warriors. Schumpeter's portrait of the military imperialism of ancient Rome has disquieting contemporary resonance. He spoke of

that policy which pretends to aspire to peace but unerringly generates war, the policy of continual preparation for war, the policy of meddlesome interventionism. There was no corner of the known world where some interest was not alleged to be in danger or under actual attack. If the interests were not Roman, they were those of Rome's allies; and if Rome had no allies, then allies would be invented. When it was utterly impossible to contrive such an interest—why, then it was the national honor that had been insulted. The fight was always invested with an aura of legality. Rome was always being attacked by evil-minded neighbors, always fighting for a breathing space. The whole world was pervaded by a host of enemies.[116]

The active carriers of American imperialism have not been Lenin's villains, bankers and monopolists seeking capital outlets, nor the Open Door school's villains, exporters seeking foreign markets. The active carriers have been politicians, diplomats and military leaders. Consider the case of Vietnam. Was the clamor of American capitalists for foreign markets responsible for the Americanization of the war? Obviously the United States expended more money destroying Vietnam than it could have hoped to get back in a century of imperial exploitation. At every stage in the descent into the quagmire the military played a dominant role. First, they defined the Vietnam problem as a military problem, requiring a military solution. Then, at each point along the ghastly way, the generals promised that more military escalation would bring the victory so long sought and so steadily denied. The Pentagon not only succeeded in casting the problem in military terms; it cherished the war for its own institutional reasons. Vietnam became an invaluable testing ground for new weapons and tactics as well as an indispensable place for on-the-job training and for promotion. "Civilians can scarcely understand," General Shoup, the admirable former commandant of the Marine Corps, wrote, ". . . that many ambitious professionals truly yearn for wars and the opportunities for glory and distinction afforded only in combat." All the services, General Shoup said, wanted part of the action in Vietnam and competed for "the opportunity to practice their trade."

The problem is not that of Eisenhower's "military-industrial complex." That phrase implies that the military obediently execute the bidding of business leaders. But the military are not the agents of the capitalists. They are a powerful force in their own right. Often the policies they have urged, as in the later stages of the Indochina War, were opposed by preponderant forces in the business community. They are driven by institutional self-interest to demand more men, more money, more weapons systems, more military involvement in policy and often (though not always) more military solutions. And they play on powerful sentiments of virility and patriotism. Tocqueville foresaw the problem long ago when he wrote his great chapter "Why Democratic Nations Naturally Desire Peace, and Democratic Armies, War." "The army, taken collectively," Tocqueville said, "eventually forms a small nation by itself, where the mind is less enlarged and habits are more rude than in the nation at large. . . . A restless and turbulent spirit is an evil inherent in the very constitution of democratic armies and beyond hope of cure."

The warriors are not wicked men. They are honorable men, professionals doing a professional job and making exactly the arguments that the nature of their responsibility requires. It is foolish to blame them for the advice they give. Blame rests on the civilian government that takes their advice. Their importunities are especially effective in amorphous situations and with irresolute masters. "The remedy for the vices of the army," said Tocqueville, "is not to be found in the army itself, but in the country. . . . Teach the citizens to be educated, orderly, firm, and free and the soldiers will be disciplined and obedient." [117]

The incessant pressure of the professional military in an age of incessant crisis is a major cause of the imperial drift. This confirms the view that imperialism is not rooted in a particular economic structure or system of ownership. Every great power, whatever its ideology, has its warrior caste. Marxist states are most vulnerable of all to militarism. Measured by force-ratio—the number of full-time military

personnel for every thousand in the population—the 32 Marxist regimes around the world in 1985 had an average ratio of 13.3 as
against a 6.1 average for 109 non-Marxist regimes. When nations
went Marxist, the average rise in force-ratio was 282 percent.[118] "The
increasing predominance of the military in political life," Milovan Djilas has observed, "represents a trend no communist country is likely
to avoid."[119] The Soviet warrior caste, operating in the same way as
the American warrior caste, both operating much as Schumpeter described the warriors of ancient Rome, is a crucial influence on Soviet
policy.

It is the dynamics not of capitalism but of power that produces
empire. Imperialism is what happens when a strong state encounters
a weak state, a soft frontier or a vacuum of power and uses its superior strength to dominate other peoples for its own purposes. Motives, rationales and mechanisms vary according to the culture and
technology of the epoch. Religion may be the motive in one age and
the rationale in another; so too with politics; so too with economics.
The war machine is the most constant and indispensable of imperial
mechanisms. But it is always inequality of power that is the primary
condition and ultimate source of imperialism.

III.   *The Missing Dimension*

I

The classical theories of imperialism have in common a focus on the
imperial nation, the western, white, industrialized nation, and—
whether to praise, explain or condemn—on its peculiar drives,
needs, problems. However much classical theorists disagreed on
other points, they agreed in seeing the indigenous peoples, the 'natives,' as passive and inert, waiting for the west to strike off their
chains and summon them into history.

It is easy to see how this theory of native quiescence arose. After
all, one native society after another had fallen before a handful of
western invaders and had thereafter accepted the rule of a handful
of western administrators. The fate of the natives under imperialism
might be deplorable, but their existence need not form part of the
theory. The native was the invisible man in the classical interpretations. Marx's chapter in *Capital* on "The Modern Theory of Colonialism" dealt exclusively with white settlers; that colonies had indigenous inhabitants did not interest him. Lenin's imperialism paid
hardly more attention to the subject peoples. Geopoliticians saw im-

perialism as the mere reflection of European power struggles. The *mission civilatrice* took the imperialized a little into account, but chiefly to tell them how lucky they were.

It was only when the undeveloped world bestirred itself after the Second World War that the subject peoples began to edge into the analytical picture. The conviction of their impotence survived, however, from the Eurocentric phase of imperialism theory. The *dependencia* school adapted Marxism to explain how the western market doomed poor nations to permanent poverty. The idea of 'cultural imperialism' arose to explain how western culture doomed them to permanent spiritual emasculation.

Cultural imperialism was well defined in 1982 by Jack Lang, the French minister of culture, as "imperialism that no longer grabs territory . . . but grabs consciousness, ways of thinking, ways of living."[120] The notion was not new, but heretofore it had been mainly employed by Europeans against the United States (as in Georges Duhamel's book of 1931, *America the Menace*). It acquired new cogency from the viewpoint of the Third World, applying, for example, as African intellectuals quickly reminded M. Lang, to the French cultural conquest in Africa.

Cultural aggression had not always accompanied political and economic aggression. Colonial administrators and imperial apologists often sought to protect the native culture, including even the traditional religion, against westernization. Kipling told a Protestant minister how "cruel" he found it that white men should confound their fellow creatures with "a code of ethics foreign to the climate and instinct of those races whose most cherished customs they outrage and whose gods they insult."[121] The proponents of 'indirect rule' in Britain and of 'association' in France believed in disturbing native political and religious institutions only to the extent necessary to facilitate administration or plunder. Some westerners genuinely respected the inherent worth of the native culture. Others were racists who believed the natives genetically incapable of rising to the standards of western civilization. Ironically, it was the missionaries who, in order to prove the native's spiritual equality, were most prepared to destroy his cultural identity.

Political and economic imperialism was limited and utilitarian. It assumed little more than that one state was stronger than another. It did not covet the mind and soul of native societies. Cultural imperialism maintained that one set of values was better than another. This was far more demoralizing. "The king of Spain," said Fidel Castro, "would send a letter every once in a while and it was published in some gazette; but these people try to speak on radio, television, the cinema, twenty-four hours a day; they sell us thousands of alienating films, programs, and serials. Their invasion of every man's soul, man's mind is incredible . . . one that Spain never attempted and with an influence that Spain never had."[122]

As nationalism began to awaken the non-western world, the rising bitterness came in the end more from cultural than from political or economic wounds. "The most humiliating kind of defeat," Jean-François Revel points out, "is a cultural defeat. It is the only defeat that one can never forget, because it cannot be blamed on bad luck, or on the barbarism of the enemy. It entails not only acknowledgment of one's own weakness, but also the humiliation of having to save oneself by taking lessons from the conqueror—whom one must simultaneously hate and imitate."[123]

The most benign and selfless of the western intruders—missionaries, doctors, educators, social reformers—sometimes roused the most resentment. Enlightened colonial administrations prided themselves, for example, on the liberation of women. But to Frantz Fanon, a black born in Martinique, trained in psychiatry in France and transformed into a revolutionary in Algeria, the French determination to free Algerian women from the veil appeared an attempt to make them "an ally in the work of cultural destruction." French officials, committed "to bring about disintegration, at whatever cost, of forms of existence likely to evoke national reality," were cleverly striking at the weakest, that is the least defensible, links in the native culture. Every veil that fell from a woman's face, Fanon wrote, demonstrated that "Algeria was beginning to deny herself and was accepting the rape of the colonizer."[124] The argument applies equally to the abolition of infanticide and child marriage, of suttee in India or of footbinding in China.

Western medicine was another instrument to subvert native folkways. The doctor, said Fanon, was "a link in the colonialist network . . . a spokesman for the occupying power." Education represented a still more deadly assault. The Christian assertion of the universal dignity of man was a special act of aggression, for individualism was a western heresy, and, when natives threw off colonial bonds, Fanon said, "the idea of a society of individuals . . . is the first to disappear." "The enterprise of deculturation," Fanon declared, was fundamental to imperialist control. Colonialism, not satisfied with mere political and economic domination, sought to empty the native's brain of all form and content, to discredit his language, his diet, his sexual behavior, his ways of sitting down, of resting, of laughing, of enjoying himself, to divest him of his history and his selfhood. At every point, Fanon insisted, it was necessary to reject European values, to insult them and vomit them up, "even if these values objectively be worth choosing." [125]

Fanon saw himself as a 'native.' But he was also a Freudian, a Marxist, an existentialist and a nationalist, in short, a product of western culture. His eloquent writings marvelously illuminate springs of antiwestern hatred. But they fall into the old Eurocentric trap of exaggerating the powerlessness of the native before the aggressor. Only violence, Fanon argued, could awaken the native from his immobility. Postwar developments, however, were already putting in doubt the assumption that subject peoples were no more than passive victims.

II

History, like many other things, is a reflection of power relations. So long as the Third World was relatively powerless, westerners, whether pro- or anti-empire, found it easy to exclude the native as a factor in the equation of imperialism. The years after the Second World War saw a dramatic shift in the balance of power. Transplantation to the Third World of western principles of nationalism and self-determination brought the colonial system to an end. The use of western principles to challenge western dominion intensified the bad conscience of the west. Guilt made it impossible to exploit nonwhite peoples with the old careless arrogance and encouraged the illusion of (in Bertrand Russell's phrase) "the superior virtue of the oppressed." At the same time, the Third World's control of raw materials deemed vital to western economies—one of the things that led the west into empire—now supplied new leverage against the west.

The shift in the balance of power speeded the shift in analytical perspective. As the racial revolution in the United States forced American historians to recognize strength, cunning and capacity for manipulation and resistance among southern slaves, so the anticolonial revolution forced theorists of imperialism to recognize that the natives in the Third World were not just victims but actors as well. It compelled new attentions to the inner character of poor countries. As the new social history writes 'from the bottom up' instead of 'from the top down,' so new interpretations of imperialism portray the western impact on the Third World no longer 'from the outside in' but 'from the inside out.'

It was true enough that native societies had often crumbled before the onslaught of a few white men. But, on examination of their inner character, it did not seem obvious that this happened because these societies were passive and inert or had a 'dependency complex' or

lacked power of resistance or even because the invaders had the
Maxim gun and the natives not. Native societies were in fact not so
homogeneous as they might seem looking from the outside in. Many
were periodically convulsed by quarrels within the ruling elite or by
attacks from hostile tribes without. The enemies of the Aztecs, as Cor-
tez discovered when he invaded Mexico, saw it to their advantage to
help the invader. Europeans in Africa had no trouble in picking up
African allies. Apolo Kagwa, the chief minister of Buganda, had his
own reasons for helping the British conquer the rest of Uganda.[126]
The western assault was most successful when it touched nerves of
discontent in the native culture. Western control depended everywhere on native collaboration. That is why so few westerners were
required.

In the last generation, British historians of imperialism, led by
Ronald Robinson and D. K. Fieldhouse, have moved the native society into the center of the picture.[127] They see imperialism as a response to indigenous political crisis in the periphery and imperial
rule as impossible without indigenous collaboration. This view may
underestimate the extent to which great-power competition stimulated the late-nineteenth-century effort to carve up what remained of
the undeveloped world. But it convincingly shows that imperialism
involved complex western interaction with native societies acting on
interests, motives and perplexities of their own.

In short, as western imperialists were using native societies for their
purposes, so groups in native societies were using the west for *their*
purposes. The collaborators constituted the notorious *comprador* class
that facilitated colonial control in exchange for a share of the profits.
In due course this class sent sons and (sometimes) daughters to be
educated in the west. The younger generation often returned with
nationalism and other dangerous thoughts. To maintain their mediating position, collaborators had to give ground to nationalists or
else lose their touch with the native constituency and thereby their
usefulness to the colonial master. The better educated they became,
the more they resented white domination. As the world spun on, collaboration began to metamorphose into anti-colonialism. The emergence of a nationalist elite brought about the crisis of imperialism.
"When the colonial rulers had run out of indigenous collaborators,"
as Robinson puts it, "they either chose to leave or were compelled
to go."[128]

III

Who whom? asked Lenin in a famous question. It is not so clear as it
used to be that imperialism is always a case of great powers exploiting

undeveloped countries. The experience of the United States shows how undeveloped countries seek, often with success, to exploit great powers. During the Mexican War, the radical Puro party favored annexation by the United States in order to foster republican institutions in Mexico.[129] In 1848, the state of Yucatan offered to surrender its sovereignty if the United States would intervene to protect the whites against the Indians. The filibuster William Walker was invited into Nicaragua by a faction in a local civil war. The government of Santo Domingo applied to join the American Union in the hope of saving itself from overthrow. Central American governments requested admission to the Union, and Central American diplomats called on the United States to serve as "the natural protector" of Central America against Mexico.[130] Anti-Spanish Cubans started pleading for admission to the American Union as early as 1822. During the Grito de Yara rebellion against Spain in 1868–1869, the revolutionaries meeting at Guanaro called for annexation by the United States.[131] The Chinese Empire, as part of its old policy of frontier defense, did its best to lure America into Manchuria. "Where will you then find a place for your surplus product and capital?" asked one Chinese official. ". . . 'New China' is the place."[132]

American Presidents in the nineteenth century were (Grant excepted) skeptical enough to resist such blandishments. They were well aware of the limits of American power. As power has grown, however, skepticism has languished. The euphoria of the Second World War began the imperial process. The United States started its disastrous involvement in Iran not because of the pressure of the oil companies but because the Shah wanted the Americans to offset the older imperialists, the British and the Russians. The Cold War added political and strategic urgencies to the expansion of American influence. Illusions of omnipotence, joined to ideological obsessions and personal naiveté, have made recent Presidents especially vulnerable to exploitation by Third World leaders.

These leaders, adept at the tricks of survival, are often proficient confidence men. If they are on the left, they extract dollars from Washington by threatening to turn to Moscow, as they extract roubles from Moscow by threatening to turn to Washington. If they are on the right, they invoke the menace of communist takeover to preserve their own control. By the 1980s Nicaraguan guerrillas, hoping to recover position and property they had enjoyed under the Somoza tyranny, had only to strike the proper anti-communist chords for President Reagan to pronounce them the moral equals of the Founding Fathers.

Who whom? The idea that the supplier of arms can control the recipient, that the imperial patron can control the Third World client, is an abiding American delusion—a delusion that has mysteriously survived bitter experience to the contrary in China in the 1940s and in Vietnam in the 1960s. Once the patron pledges himself to the achievement of the client's goals, his own leverage shrinks. The patron has now renounced the ultimate sanction—the withdrawal of support from the client.

Once promised American backing, the client finds no reason to make concessions to local groups demanding democratic change and a share in the political process. Instead he calls them Marxists and, with tacit American acquiescence, cracks down on them. Because the client has contempt for a patron so easily bamboozled and because the client cannot afford to appear an American puppet, he will assert his independence by resisting American proposals that he sees, probably correctly, as fatal to his privilege and power. The military shield becomes a blank check. The patron ends up the prisoner of the client. What an empire!

The worse part of the American 'empire' of the 1980s is the product of incorrigible American gullibility and vanity, so easily played upon by Third World con men. The better part is quite as much the product of the desire of other nations for protection as of the desire of the United States for domination. NATO, for example, serves the interests of its European members as much as, if not more than, it serves the interests of the United States. The far-flung chain of American troops and bases around the globe largely exists not against the will but with the grateful consent of the host countries. If this is empire, it is, in Geir Lundestad's phrase, "empire by invitation."[133]

And, in the end, what kind of empire is it? From the viewpoint of the great empires of history, the Roman Empire, the Napoleonic Empire, even the British Empire, the American empire of the 1980s is no empire at all. The old empires controlled their subjects. The American empire controls very little. It cannot even control regimes most dependent on its support—Israel, El Salvador, Honduras, the Philippines. It cannot control its closest neighbors—Canada and Mexico. Perhaps it controls Grenada. But, though it exerts influence in Britain, Japan, France, Italy, Australia, New Zealand, it can hardly be said to control them, as the British Empire controlled its colonies in the nineteenth century, or as the Soviet Union controls the countries of Eastern Europe. For all the supposed American domination of poor countries via the world marketplace, the American empire exercises little political control in the Third World, as repeatedly demonstrated by the votes in the United Nations General Assembly. It can best be described as a quasi-empire.

Americans yearn for an international environment favorable to democratic values and institutions. They really do not—always excepting the imperialist minority—think this environment can be created by main force. Inhibited by democratic ideals and by abiding popular distaste for empire, America has been a fitful and unenthusiastic dreamer of imperial dreams. War, not economics, forced Americans into their quasi-empire. International crisis nourishes the war machine and gives official and military classes pretexts to flourish ideology and to enlarge hegemony.

A dangerous world demands military strength. It does not demand the militarization of the national life. "Militarism," said Woodrow Wilson, "does not consist in the existence of any army. . . . Militarism is a spirit. It is a system. It is a purpose. The purpose of militarism is to use armies for aggression."[134] The demilitarization of national policy is the best safeguard against American imperialism.

In its ninth century the era of western expansion around the planet has at last encountered the fabled god Terminus. In the new world of raging nationalisms, the prospects for extended empires, whether American or Soviet or Chinese, are bleak. Yet imperialism—the instinct of strong states to dominate weak states—will continue until the anarchy of nation-states yields to the ultimate imperialism of a single world empire and until the "perpetual and restless desire of power" vanishes from the heart of man. Imperial adventures will find new forms in new eras, meet obstacles, succeed for a season, founder in time and leave benefit as well as havoc in their trail. One sees no end to imperialism, for history will always deposit humanity somewhere short of the millennium.

EIGHT

Why the Cold War?

———————◆◆———————

THE PROBLEM OF American imperialism leads directly into the controversy over the origins of the Cold War. For the great Cold War between communism and democracy has produced a lesser cold war among historians. The Open Door school argues that the American drive for empire caused the Cold War. The geopolitical school argues that the Cold War caused the American drive for empire. At times the scholarly battlefield has seemed almost as angry as the great Cold War itself. Still, as the smoke of historiographical battle drifts away, a pattern of development may perhaps be discerned.

In the agitated days of the early Cold War, the perceptive British historian Sir Herbert Butterfield gave a lecture at Notre Dame entitled "The Tragic Element in Modern International Conflict." The historiography of international conflict, Butterfield said, went characteristically through two phases. In the first or Heroic phase, historians portray a struggle of right with wrong, of good men resisting bad. "In the midst of the battle, while we are in a fighting mood, we see only the sins of the enemy." Then, as time passes and emotions subside, historians enter the Academic phase, when they seek to be "careful" with the other party, to understand their motives through "internal sympathetic infiltration" and to define the structural dilemmas that so often underlie great conflicts between masses of human beings. The "higher historiography" moves on from melodrama to tragedy. "In historical perspective we learn to be a little more sorry for both parties than they knew how to be for one another."[1]

Butterfield's air of superiority toward the conflict between the Soviet Union and the West pained some of the embattled historians of the time (this writer included). But his lecture has turned out to be a pretty good forecast of Cold War historiography. The picture of the Cold War as melodrama, after holding sway among historians for a generation, has begun to give way to more analytical and tragic views. (When I wrote in the first of the following essays that the Cold War had to be seen as tragedy, I had quite forgotten Butterfield's Notre Dame lecture. Very likely he had planted the idea in my unconscious.) Actually some quite early works—notably W. H. McNeill's remarkable *America, Britain and Russia,* written for Chatham House in 1953—attained a high degree of objectivity. But most Cold War history, especially in the United States, remained in the Heroic mode. This mode took two forms: the orthodox in the 1940s and 1950s, with the Russians as the bad guys; and the revisionist in the 1960s, with the Americans as the bad guys.

Cold War studies may at last be entering the Academic phase. John Lewis Gaddis, a notably dispassionate Cold War scholar, perceived in 1983 an "emerging postrevisionist synthesis."[2] Still history rarely reaches final verdicts. Book reviewers who apply the adjective "definitive" to historical works misunderstand the historian's enterprise. On all important issues, disagreement abides—and enriches. "Any one thesis or presentation may in itself be unacceptable," remarked Pieter Geyl, the great Dutch historian, in *Napoleon: For and Against,* his study of conflicting interpretations of Napoleon, "and yet, when it has been jettisoned, there remains something of value." As Geyl beautifully puts it, "History is indeed an argument without end."[3]

Two essays follow. "Origins of the Cold War" was published in *Foreign Affairs* in October 1967. It is reprinted here without alteration as an illustration of the state of the art twenty years ago. "The Cold War Revisited" is an amended version of a piece originally published in the *New York Review of Books* of 25 October 1979.

I. *Origins of the Cold War*

The Cold War in its original form was a presumably mortal antagonism, arising in the wake of the Second World War, between two rigidly hostile blocs, one led by the Soviet Union, the other by the United States. For nearly two somber and dangerous decades this antagonism dominated the fears of mankind; it may even, on occasion, have come close to blowing up the planet. In recent years, however, the once implacable struggle has lost its familiar clarity of outline. With the passing of old issues and the emergence of new conflicts and contestants, there is a natural tendency, especially on the part of the generation which grew up during the Cold War, to take a fresh look at the causes of the great contention between Russia and America.

Some exercises in reappraisal have merely elaborated the orthodoxies promulgated in Washington or Moscow during the boom years of the Cold War. But others, especially in the United States (there are no signs, alas, of this in the Soviet Union), represent what American historians call "revisionism"—that is, a readiness to challenge official explanations. No one should be surprised by this phenomenon. Every war in American history has been followed in due course by skeptical reassessments of supposedly sacred assumptions. So the War of 1812, fought at the time for the freedom of the seas, was in later years ascribed to the expansionist ambitions of congressional war hawks; so the Mexican War became a slaveholders' conspiracy. So the Civil War has been pronounced a "needless war," and Lincoln has even been accused of maneuvering the rebel attack on Fort Sumter. So too the Spanish-American War and the First and Second World Wars have, each in its turn, undergone revisionist critiques. It is not to be supposed that the Cold War would remain exempt.

In the case of the Cold War, special factors reinforce the predictable historiographical rhythm. The outburst of polycentrism in the communist empire has made people wonder whether communism was ever so monolithic as official theories of the Cold War supposed. A generation with no vivid memories of Stalinism may see the Russia of the forties in the image of the relatively mild, seedy and irresolute Russia of the sixties. And for this same generation the American course of widening the war in Viet Nam—which, even non-revisionists can easily regard as folly—has unquestionably stirred doubts about the wisdom of American foreign policy in the sixties that younger historians may have begun to read back into the forties.

It is useful to remember that, on the whole, past exercises in revisionism have failed to stick. Few historians today believe that the war hawks caused the War of 1812 or the slaveholders the Mexican War, or that the Civil War was needless, or that the House of Morgan brought America into the First World War or that Franklin Roosevelt schemed to produce the attack on Pearl Harbor. But this does not mean that one should deplore the rise of Cold War revisionism.* For revisionism is an essential part of the process by which history, through the posing of new problems and the investigation of new possibilities, enlarges its perspectives and enriches its insights.

* As this writer somewhat intemperately did in a letter to *The New York Review of Books*, 20 October 1966.

More than this, in the present context, revisionism expresses a deep, legitimate and tragic apprehension. As the Cold War has begun to lose its purity of definition, as the moral absolutes of the fifties become the moralistic clichés of the sixties, some have begun to ask whether the appalling risks which humanity ran during the Cold War were, after all, necessary and inevitable; whether more restrained and rational policies might not have guided the energies of man from the perils of conflict into the potentialities of collaboration. The fact that such questions are in their nature unanswerable does not mean that it is not right and useful to raise them. Nor does it mean that our sons and daughters are not entitled to an accounting from the generation of Russians and Americans who produced the Cold War.

I

The orthodox American view, as originally set forth by the American government and as reaffirmed until recently by most American scholars, has been that the Cold War was the brave and essential response of free men to communist aggression. Some have gone back well before the Second World War to lay open the sources of Russian expansionism. Geopoliticians traced the Cold War to imperial Russian strategic ambitions which in the nineteenth century led to the Crimean War, to Russian penetration of the Balkans and the Middle East and to Russian pressure on Britain's "lifeline" to India. Ideologists traced it to the Communist Manifesto of 1848 ("the violent overthrow of the bourgeoisie lays the foundation for the sway of the proletariat"). Thoughtful observers (a phrase meant to exclude those who speak in Dullese about the unlimited evil of godless, atheistic, militant communism) concluded that classical Russian imperialism and Pan-Slavism, compounded after 1917 by Leninist messianism, confronted the west at the end of the Second World War with an inexorable drive for domination.[4]

The revisionist thesis is very different.* In its extreme form, it is that, after the death of Franklin Roosevelt and the end of the Second

---

*The fullest statement of this case is to be found in D. F. Fleming's voluminous *The Cold War and Its Origins* (New York, 1961). For a shorter version of this argument, see David Horowitz, *The Free World Colossus* (New York, 1965); the most subtle and ingenious statements come in W. A. Williams's *The Tragedy of American Diplomacy* (rev. ed.; New York, 1962) and in Gar Alperowitz's *Atomic Diplomacy: Hiroshima and Potsdam* (New York, 1965) and in subsequent articles and reviews by Mr. Alperowitz in *The New York Review of Books*. The fact that in some aspects the revisionist thesis parallels the official Soviet argument must not, of course, prevent consideration of the case on its merits, nor raise questions about the motives of the writers, all of whom, so far as I know, are independent-minded scholars.

World War, the United States deliberately abandoned the wartime policy of collaboration and, exhilarated by the possession of the atomic bomb, undertook a course of aggression of its own designed to expel all Russian influence from Eastern Europe and to establish democratic-capitalist states on the very border of the Soviet Union. As the revisionists see it, this radically new American policy—or rather this resumption by Truman of the pre-Roosevelt policy of insensate anti-communism—left Moscow no alternative but to take measures in defense of its own borders. The result was the Cold War.

These two views, of course, could not be more starkly contrasting. It is therefore not unreasonable to look again at the half-dozen critical years between 22 June 1941, when Hitler attacked Russia, and 2 July 1947, when the Russians walked out of the Marshall Plan meeting in Paris. Several things should be borne in mind as this reexamination is made. For one thing, we have thought a great deal more in recent years, in part because of writers like Roberta Wohlstetter and T. C. Schelling, about the problems of communication in diplomacy—the signals which one nation, by word or by deed, gives, inadvertently or intentionally, to another. Any honest reappraisal of the origins of the Cold War requires the imaginative leap—which should in any case be as instinctive for the historian as it is prudent for the

---

I might further add that all these books, in spite of their ostentatious display of scholarly apparatus, must be used with caution. Professor Fleming, for example, relies heavily on newspaper articles and even columnists. While Mr. Alperowitz bases his case on official documents or authoritative reminiscences, he sometimes twists his material in a most unscholarly way. For example, in describing Ambassador Harriman's talk with President Truman on April 20, 1945, Mr. Alperowitz writes, "He argued that a reconsideration of Roosevelt's policy was necessary" (p. 22, repeated on p. 24). The citation is to pp. 70–72 in President Truman's *Years of Decision*. What President Truman reported Harriman as saying was the exact opposite: "Before leaving, Harriman took me aside and said, 'Frankly, one of the reasons that made me rush back to Washington was the fear that you did not understand, as I had seen Roosevelt understand, that Stalin is breaking his agreements.'" Similarly, in an appendix (p. 271) Mr. Alperowitz writes that the Hopkins and Davies missions of May 1945 "were opposed by the 'firm' advisers." Actually the Hopkins mission was proposed by Harriman and Charles E. Bohlen, who Mr. Alperowitz elsewhere suggests were the firmest of the firm—and was proposed by them precisely to impress on Stalin the continuity of American policy from Roosevelt to Truman. While the idea that Truman reversed Roosevelt's policy is tempting dramatically, it is a myth. See, for example, the testimony of Anna Rosenberg Hoffman, who lunched with Roosevelt on March 24, 1945, the last day he spent in Washington. After luncheon, Roosevelt was handed a cable. "He read it and became quite angry. He banged his fists on the arms of his wheelchair and said, 'Averell is right; we can't do business with Stalin. He has broken every one of the promises he made at Yalta.' He was very upset and continued in the same vein on the subject."

statesman—into the adversary's viewpoint. We must strive to see how, given Soviet perspectives, the Russians might conceivably have misread our signals, as we must reconsider how intelligently we read theirs.

For another, the historian must not overindulge the man of power in the illusion cherished by those in office that high position carries with it the easy ability to shape history. Violating the statesman's creed, Lincoln once blurted out the truth in his letter of 1864 to A. G. Hodges: "I claim not to have controlled events, but confess plainly that events have controlled me." He was not asserting Tolstoyan fatalism but rather suggesting how greatly events limit the capacity of the statesman to bend history to his will. The physical course of the Second World War—the military operations undertaken, the position of the respective armies at the war's end, the momentum generated by victory and the vacuums created by defeat—all these determined the future as much as the character of individual leaders and the substance of national ideology and purpose.

Nor can the historian forget the conditions under which decisions are made, especially in a time like the Second World War. These were tired, overworked, aging men: in 1945, Churchill was 71 years old, Stalin had governed his country for 17 exacting years, Roosevelt his for 12 years nearly as exacting. During the war, moreover, the importunities of military operations had shoved postwar questions to the margins of their minds. All—even Stalin, behind his screen of ideology—had become addicts of improvisation, relying on authority and virtuosity to conceal the fact that they were constantly surprised by developments. Like Eliza, they leaped from one cake of ice to the next in the effort to reach the other side of the river. None showed great tactical consistency, or cared much about it; all employed a certain ambiguity to preserve their power to decide big issues; and it is hard to know how to interpret anything any one of them said on any specific occasion. This was partly because, like all princes, they designed their expressions to have particular effects on particular audiences; partly because the entirely genuine intellectual difficulty of the questions they faced made a degree of vacillation and mind-changing eminently reasonable. If historians cannot solve their problems in retrospect, who are they to blame Roosevelt, Stalin and Churchill for not having solved them at the time?

II

Peacemaking after the Second World War was not so much a tapestry as it was a hopelessly raveled and knotted mess of yarn. Yet, for purposes of clarity, it is essential to follow certain threads. One theme indispensable to an understanding of the Cold War is the contrast between two clashing views of world order: the "universalist" view, by which all nations shared a common interest in all the affairs of the world, and the "sphere-of-influence" view, by which each great power would be assured by the other great powers of an acknowledged predominance in its own area of special interest. The universalist view assumed that national security would be guaranteed by an international organization. The sphere-of-interest view assumed that national security would be guaranteed by the balance of power. While in practice these views have by no means been incompatible (indeed, our shaky peace has been based on a combination of the two), in the abstract they involved sharp contradictions.

The tradition of American thought in these matters was universalist—i.e. Wilsonian. Roosevelt had been a member of Wilson's subcabinet; in 1920, as candidate for Vice President, he had campaigned for the League of Nations. It is true that, within Roosevelt's infinitely complex mind, Wilsonianism warred with the perception of vital strategic interests he had imbibed from Mahan. Moreover, his temperamental inclination to settle things with fellow princes around the conference table led him to regard the Big Three—or Four—as trustees for the rest of the world. On occasion, as this narrative will show, he was beguiled into flirtation with the sphere-of-influence heresy. But in principle he believed in joint action and remained a Wilsonian. His hope for Yalta, as he told the Congress on his return, was that it would "spell the end of the system of unilateral action, the exclusive alliances, the spheres of influence, the balances of power, and all the other expedients that have been tried for centuries—and have always failed."

Whenever Roosevelt backslid, he had at his side that Wilsonian fundamentalist, Secretary of State Cordell Hull, to recall him to the pure faith. After his visit to Moscow in 1943, Hull characteristically said that, with the Declaration of Four Nations on General Security (in which America, Russia, Britain and China pledged "united action . . . for the organization and maintenance of peace and security"), "there will no longer be need for spheres of influence, for alliances, for balance of power, or any other of the special arrangements through which, in the unhappy past, the nations strove to safeguard their security or to promote their interests."

Remembering the corruption of the Wilsonian vision by the secret treaties of the First World War, Hull was determined to prevent any sphere-of-influence nonsense after the Second World War. He therefore fought all proposals to settle border questions while the war was still on and, excluded as he largely was from wartime diplomacy, poured his not inconsiderable moral energy and frustration into the promulgation of virtuous and spacious general principles.

In adopting the universalist view, Roosevelt and Hull were not indulging personal hobbies. Sumner Welles, Adolf Berle, Averell Harriman, Charles Bohlen—all, if with a variety of nuances, opposed the sphere-of-influence approach. And here the State Department was expressing what seems clearly to have been the predominant mood of the American people, so long mistrustful of European power politics. The Republicans shared the true faith. John Foster Dulles argued that the great threat to peace after the war would lie in the revival of sphere-of-influence thinking. The United States, he said, must not permit Britain and Russia to revert to these bad old ways; it must therefore insist on American participation in all policy decisions for all territories in the world. Dulles wrote pessimistically in January 1945, "The three great powers which at Moscow agreed upon the 'closest cooperation' about European questions have shifted to a practice of separate, regional responsibility."

It is true that critics, and even friends, of the United States sometimes noted a discrepancy between the American passion for universalism when it applied to territory far from American shores and the preeminence the United States accorded its own interests nearer home. Churchill, seeking Washington's blessing for a sphere-of-influence initiative in Eastern Europe, could not forbear reminding the Americans, "We follow the lead of the United States in South America"; nor did any universalist of record propose the abolition of the Monroe Doctrine. But a convenient myopia prevented such inconsistencies from qualifying the ardency of the universalist faith.

There seem only to have been three officials in the United States Government who dissented. One was the Secretary of War, Henry L. Stimson, a classical balance-of-power man, who in 1944 opposed the creation of a vacuum in Central Europe by the pastoralization of Germany and in 1945 urged "the settlement of all territorial acquisitions in the shape of defense posts which each of these four powers may deem to be necessary for their own safety" in advance of any effort to establish a peacetime United Nations. Stimson considered the claim of Russia to a preferred position in Eastern Europe as not unreasonable: as he told President Truman, "he thought the Russians perhaps were being more realistic than we were in regard to their own security." Such a position for Russia seemed to him comparable to the preferred American position in Latin America; he even spoke of "our respective orbits." Stimson was therefore skeptical of what he regarded as the prevailing tendency "to hang on to exaggerated views of the Monroe Doctrine and at the same time butt into every question that comes up in Central Europe." Acceptance of spheres of influence seemed to him the way to avoid "a head-on collision."

A second official opponent of universalism was George Kennan, an eloquent advocate from the American Embassy in Moscow of "a prompt and clear recognition of the division of Europe into spheres of influence and of a policy based on the fact of such division." Kennan argued that nothing we could do would possibly alter the course of events in Eastern Europe; that we were deceiving ourselves by supposing that these countries had any future but Russian domination; that we should therefore relinquish Eastern Europe to the Soviet Union and avoid anything which would make things easier for the Russians by giving them economic assistance or by sharing moral responsibility for their actions.

A third voice within the government against universalism was (at least after the war) Henry A. Wallace. As Secretary of Commerce, he stated the sphere-of-influence case with trenchancy in the famous Madison Square Garden speech of September 1946 which led to his dismissal by President Truman:

On our part, we should recognize that we have no more business in the *political* affairs of Eastern Europe than Russia has in the *political* affairs of Latin America, Western Europe, and the United States. . . . Whether we like it or not, the Russians will try to socialize their sphere of influence just as we try to democratize our sphere of influence. . . . The Russians have no more business stirring up native Communists to political activity in Western Europe, Latin America, and the United States than we have in interfering with the politics of Eastern Europe and Russia.

Stimson, Kennan and Wallace seem to have been alone in the government, however, in taking these views. They were very much minority voices. Meanwhile universalism, rooted in the American legal and moral tradition, overwhelmingly backed by contemporary opinion, received successive enshrinements in the Atlantic Charter of 1941, in the Declaration of the United Nations in 1942 and in the Moscow Declaration of 1943.

III

The Kremlin, on the other hand, thought *only* of spheres of interest; above all, the Russians were determined to protect their frontiers, and especially their border to the west, crossed so often and so bloodily in the dark course of their history. These western frontiers lacked natural means of defense—no great oceans, rugged mountains, steaming swamps or impenetrable jungles. The history of Russia had been the history of invasion, the last of which was by now horribly killing up to twenty million of its people. The protocol of Russia therefore meant the enlargement of the area of Russian influence. Kennan himself wrote (in May 1944), "Behind Russia's stubborn expansion lies only the age-old sense of insecurity of a sedentary people reared on an exposed plain in the neighborhood of fierce nomadic peoples," and he called this "urge" a "permanent feature of Russian psychology."

In earlier times the "urge" had produced the tsarist search for buffer states and maritime outlets. In 1939 the Soviet-Nazi pact and its secret protocol had enabled Russia to begin to satisfy in the Baltic states, Karelian Finland and Poland, part of what it conceived as its security requirements in Eastern Europe. But the "urge" persisted, causing the friction between Russia and Germany in 1940 as each jostled for position in the area which separated them. Later it led to Molotov's new demands on Hitler in November 1940—a free hand in Finland, Soviet predominance in Romania and Bulgaria, bases in the Dardanelles—the demands which convinced Hitler that he had no choice but to attack Russia. Now Stalin hoped to gain from the West what Hitler, a closer neighbor, had not dared yield him.

It is true that, so long as Russian survival appeared to require a second front to relieve the Nazi pressure, Moscow's demand for Eastern Europe was a little muffled. Thus the Soviet government adhered to the Atlantic Charter (though with a significant if obscure reservation about adapting its principles to "the circumstances, needs, and historic peculiarities of particular countries"). Thus it also adhered to the Moscow Declaration of 1943, and Molotov then, with his easy mendacity, even denied that Russia had any desire to divide Europe into spheres of influence. But this was guff, which the Russians were perfectly willing to ladle out if it would keep the Americans, and especially Secretary Hull (who made a strong personal impression at the Moscow conference) happy. "A declaration," as Stalin once observed to Eden, "I regard as algebra, but an agreement as practical arithmetic. I do not wish to decry algebra, but I prefer practical arithmetic."

The more consistent Russian purpose was revealed when Stalin offered the British a straight sphere-of-influence deal at the end of 1941. Britain, he suggested, should recognize the Russian absorption of the Baltic states, part of Finland, eastern Poland and Bessarabia; in return, Russia would support any special British need for bases or security arrangements in Western Europe. There was nothing specifically communist about these ambitions. If Stalin achieved them, he would be fulfilling an age-old dream of the tsars. The British reaction was mixed. "Soviet policy is amoral," as Anthony Eden noted at the time; "United States policy is exaggeratedly moral, at least where non-American interests are concerned." If Roosevelt was a universalist with occasional leanings toward spheres of influence and Stalin was a sphere-of-influence man with occasional gestures toward universalism, Churchill seemed evenly poised between the familiar realism of the balance of power, which he had so long recorded as an historian and manipulated as a statesman, and the hope that there must be some better way of doing things. His 1943 proposal of a world organization divided into regional councils represented an effort to blend universalist and sphere-of-interest conceptions. His initial rejection of Stalin's proposal in December 1941 as "directly contrary to the first, second and third articles of the Atlantic Charter" thus did not spring entirely from a desire to propitiate the United States. On the other hand, he had himself already reinterpreted the Atlantic Charter as applying only to Europe (and thus not to the British Empire), and he was, above all, an empiricist who never believed in sacrificing reality on the altar of doctrine.

So in April 1942 he wrote Roosevelt that "the increasing gravity of the war" had led him to feel that the Charter "ought not to be construed so as to deny Russia the frontiers she occupied when Germany attacked her." Hull, however, remained fiercely hostile to the inclusion of territorial provisions in the Anglo-Russian treaty; the American position, Eden noted, "chilled me with Wilsonian memories." Though Stalin complained that it looked "as if the Atlantic Charter was directed against the U.S.S.R.," it was the Russian season of military adversity in the spring of 1942, and he dropped his demands.

He did not, however, change his intentions. A year later Ambassador Standley could cable Washington from Moscow: "In 1918 Western Europe attempted to set up a *cordon sanitaire* to protect it from the influence of bolshevism. Might not now the Kremlin envisage the formation of a belt of pro-Soviet states to protect it from the influences of the West?" It well might; and that purpose became increasingly clear as the war approached its end. Indeed, it derived sustenance from Western policy in the first area of liberation.

The unconditional surrender of Italy in July 1943 created the first major test of the Western devotion to universalism. America and Britain, having won the Italian war, handled the capitulation, keeping Moscow informed at a distance. Stalin complained:

The United States and Great Britain made agreements but the Soviet Union received information about the results . . . just as a passive third observer. I have to tell you that it is impossible to tolerate the situation any longer. I propose that the [tripartite military-political commission] be established and that Sicily be assigned . . . as its place of residence.

Roosevelt, who had no intention of sharing the control of Italy with the Russians, suavely replied with the suggestion that Stalin send an officer "to General Eisenhower's headquarters in connection with the commission." Unimpressed, Stalin continued to press for a tripartite body; but his Western allies were adamant in keeping the Soviet Union off the Control Commission for Italy, and the Russians in the end had to be satisfied with a seat, along with minor Allied states, on a meaningless Inter-Allied Advisory Council. Their acquiescence in this was doubtless not unconnected with a desire to establish precedents for Eastern Europe.

Teheran in December 1943 marked the high point of three-power collaboration. Still, when Churchill asked about Russian territorial interests, Stalin replied a little ominously, "There is no need to speak at the present time about any Soviet desires, but when the time comes we will speak." In the next weeks, there were increasing indications of a Soviet determination to deal unilaterally with Eastern Europe — so much so that in early February 1944 Hull cabled Harriman in Moscow:

Matters are rapidly approaching the point where the Soviet Government will have to choose between the development and extension of the foundation of international cooperation as the guiding principle of the postwar world as against the continuance of a unilateral and arbitrary method of dealing with its special problems even though these problems are admittedly of more direct interest to the Soviet Union than to other great powers.

As against this approach, however, Churchill, more tolerant of sphere-of-influence deviations, soon proposed that, with the impending liberation of the Balkans, Russia should run things in Romania and Britain in Greece. Hull strongly opposed this suggestion but made the mistake of leaving Washington for a few days; and Roosevelt, momentarily free from his Wilsonian conscience, yielded to Churchill's plea for a three-months' trial. Hull resumed the fight on his return, and Churchill postponed the matter.

The Red Army continued its advance into Eastern Europe. In August the Polish Home Army, urged on by Polish-language broadcasts from Moscow, rose up against the Nazis in Warsaw. For 63 terrible days, the Poles fought valiantly on, while the Red Army halted on the banks of the Vistula a few miles away, and in Moscow Stalin for more than half this time declined to cooperate with the Western effort to drop supplies to the Warsaw Resistance. It appeared a calculated Soviet decision to let the Nazis slaughter the anti-Soviet Polish underground; and, indeed, the result was to destroy any substantial alternative to a Soviet solution in Poland. The agony of Warsaw caused the most deep and genuine moral shock in Britain and America and provoked dark forebodings about Soviet postwar purposes.

Again history enjoins the imaginative leap in order to see things for a moment from Moscow's viewpoint. The Polish question, Churchill would say at Yalta, was for Britain a question of honor. "It is not only a question of honor for Russia," Stalin replied, "but one of life and death. . . . Throughout history Poland had been the corridor for attack on Russia." A top postwar priority for any Russian regime must be to close that corridor. The Home Army was led by anti-communists. It clearly hoped by its action to forestall the Soviet occupation of Warsaw and, in Russian eyes, to prepare the way for an anti-Russian Poland. In addition, the uprising from a strictly operational viewpoint was premature. The Russians, it is evident in retrospect, had real military problems at the Vistula. The Soviet attempt in September to send Polish units from the Red Army across the river to join forces with the Home Army was a disaster. Heavy German shelling thereafter prevented the ferrying of tanks necessary for an assault on the German position. The Red Army itself did not take Warsaw for another three months. None the less, Stalin's indifference to the human tragedy, his effort to blackmail the London Poles during the ordeal, his sanctimonious opposition during five precious weeks to aerial resupply, the invariable coldness of his explanations ("the Soviet command has come to the conclusion that it must dissociate itself from the Warsaw adventure") and the obvious political benefit to the Soviet Union from the destruction of the Home Army—all these had the effect of suddenly dropping the mask of wartime comradeship and displaying to the West the hard face of Soviet policy. In now pursuing what he grimly regarded as the minimal requirements for the postwar security of his country, Stalin was inadvertently showing the irreconcilability of both his means and his ends with the Anglo-American conception of the peace.

Meanwhile Eastern Europe presented the Alliance with still another crisis that same September. Bulgaria, which was not at war with

Russia, decided to surrender to the Western Allies while it still could; and the English and Americans at Cairo began to discuss armistice terms with Bulgarian envoys. Moscow, challenged by what it plainly saw as a Western intrusion into its own zone of vital interest, promptly declared war on Bulgaria, took over the surrender negotiations and, invoking the Italian precedent, denied its Western Allies any role in the Bulgarian Control Commission. In a long and thoughtful cable, Ambassador Harriman meditated on the problems of communication with the Soviet Union. "Words," he reflected, "have a different connotation to the Soviets than they have to us. When they speak of insisting on 'friendly governments' in their neighboring countries, they have in mind something quite different from what we would mean." The Russians, he surmised, really believed that Washington accepted "their position that although they would keep us informed they had the right to settle their problems with their western neighbors unilaterally." But the Soviet position was still in flux: "the Soviet Government is not one mind." The problem, as Harriman had earlier told Harry Hopkins, was "to strengthen the hands of those around Stalin who want to play the game along our lines." The way to do this, he now told Hull, was to

be understanding of their sensitivity, meet them much more than half way, encourage them and support them wherever we can, and yet oppose them promptly with the greatest of firmness where we see them going wrong. . . . The only way we can eventually come to an understanding with the Soviet Union on the question of non-interference in the internal affairs of other countries is for us to take a definite interest in the solution of the problems of each individual country as they arise.

As against Harriman's sophisticated universalist strategy, however, Churchill, increasingly fearful of the consequences of unrestrained competition in Eastern Europe, decided in early October to carry his sphere-of-influence proposal directly to Moscow. Roosevelt was at first content to have Churchill speak for him too and even prepared a cable to that effect. But Hopkins, a more rigorous universalist, took it upon himself to stop the cable and warn Roosevelt of its possible implications. Eventually Roosevelt sent a message to Harriman in Moscow emphasizing that he expected to "retain complete freedom of action after this conference is over." It was now that Churchill quickly proposed—and Stalin as quickly accepted—the celebrated division of southeastern Europe: ending (after further haggling between Eden and Molotov) with 90 percent Soviet predominance in Romania, 80 percent in Bulgaria and Hungary, fifty-fifty in Yugoslavia, 90 percent British predominance in Greece.

Churchill in discussing this with Harriman used the phrase "spheres of influence." But he insisted that these were only "immediate wartime arrangements" and received a highly general blessing from Roosevelt. Yet, whatever Churchill intended, there is reason to believe that Stalin construed the percentages as an agreement, not a declaration; as practical arithmetic, not algebra. For Stalin, it should be understood, the sphere-of-influence idea did not mean that he would abandon all efforts to spread communism in some other nation's sphere; it did mean that, if he tried this and the other side cracked down, he could not feel he had serious cause for complaint. As Kennan wrote to Harriman at the end of 1944:

As far as border states are concerned the Soviet government has never ceased to think in terms of spheres of interest. They expect us to support them in whatever action they wish to take in those regions, regardless of whether that action seems to us or to the rest of the world to be right or wrong. . . . I have no doubt that this position is honestly maintained on their part, and that they would be equally prepared to reserve moral judgment on any actions which we might wish to carry out, i.e., in the Caribbean area.

In any case, the matter was already under test a good deal closer to Moscow than the Caribbean. The communist-dominated resistance movement in Greece was in open revolt against the effort of the Papandreou government to disarm and disband the guerrillas (the same Papandreou whom the Greek colonels have recently arrested on the claim that he is a tool of the communists). Churchill now called in British Army units to crush the insurrection. This action produced a storm of criticism in his own country and in the United States; the American Government even publicly dissociated itself from the intervention, thereby emphasizing its detachment from the sphere-of-influence deal. But Stalin, Churchill later claimed, "adhered strictly and faithfully to our agreement of October, and during all the long weeks of fighting the Communists in the streets of Athens not one word of reproach came from *Pravda* or *Izvestia*," though there is no evidence that he tried to call off the Greek communists. Still, when the communist rebellion later broke out again in Greece, Stalin told Kardelj and Djilas of Yugoslavia in 1948, "The uprising in Greece must be stopped, and as quickly as possible."

No one, of course, can know what really was in the minds of the Russian leaders. The Kremlin archives are locked; of the primary actors, only Molotov survives, and he has not yet indicated any desire to collaborate with the Columbia Oral History Project. We do know that Stalin did not wholly surrender to sentimental illusion about his new friends. In June 1944, on the night before the landings in Normandy, he told Djilas that the English "find nothing sweeter than to trick their allies. . . . And Churchill? Churchill is the kind who, if you don't watch him, will slip a kopeck out of your pocket. Yes, a kopeck out of your pocket! . . . Roosevelt is not like that. He dips in his hand only for bigger coins." But whatever his views of his colleagues it is not unreasonable to suppose that Stalin would have been satisfied at the end of the war to secure what Kennan has called "a protective glacis along Russia's western border," and that, in exchange for a free hand in Eastern Europe, he was prepared to give the British and Americans equally free hands in their zones of vital interest, including in nations as close to Russia as Greece (for the British) and, very probably—or at least so the Yugoslavs believe—China (for the United States). In other words, his initial objectives were very probably not world conquest but Russian security.

IV

It is now pertinent to inquire why the United States rejected the idea of stabilizing the world by division into spheres of influence and insisted on an East European strategy. One should warn against rushing to the conclusion that it was all a row between hard-nosed, balance-of-power realists and starry-eyed Wilsonians. Roosevelt, Hopkins, Welles, Harriman, Bohlen, Berle, Dulles and other universalists were tough and serious men. Why then did they rebuff the sphere-of-influence solution?

The first reason is that they regarded this solution as containing within itself the seeds of a third world war. The balance-of-power idea seemed inherently unstable. It had always broken down in the past. It held out to each power the permanent temptation to try to alter the balance in its own favor, and it built this temptation into the international order. It would turn the great powers of 1945 away from the objective of concerting common policies toward competition for postwar advantage. As Hopkins told Molotov at Teheran, "The President feels it essential to world peace that Russia, Great Britain and the United States work out this control question in a manner which will not start each of the three powers arming against the others." "The greatest likelihood of eventual conflict," said the Joint Chiefs of Staff in 1944 (the only conflict which the J.C.S., in its wisdom, could then glimpse "in the foreseeable future" was between Britain and Russia), ". . . would seem to grow out of either nation initiating attempts to build up its strength, by seeking to attach to herself parts of Europe to the disadvantage and possible danger of her potential adversary." The Americans were perfectly ready to acknowledge that

Russia was entitled to convincing assurance of her national security—but not this way. "I could sympathize fully with Stalin's desire to protect his western borders from future attack," as Hull put it. "But I felt that this security could best be obtained through a strong postwar peace organization."

Hull's remark suggests the second objection: that the sphere-of-influence approach would, in the words of the State Department in 1945, "militate against the establishment and effective functioning of a broader system of general security in which all countries will have their part." The United Nations, in short, was seen as the alternative to the balance of power. Nor did the universalists see any necessary incompatibility between the Russian desire for "friendly governments" on its frontier and the American desire for self-determination in Eastern Europe. Before Yalta the State Department judged the general mood of Europe as "to the left and strongly in favor of far-reaching economic and social reforms, but not, however, in favor of a left-wing totalitarian regime to achieve these reforms." Governments in Eastern Europe could be sufficiently to the left "to allay Soviet suspicions" but sufficiently representative "of the center and *petit bourgeois* elements" not to seem a prelude to communist dictatorship. The American criteria were therefore that the government "should be dedicated to the preservation of civil liberties" and "should favor social and economic reforms." A string of New Deal states—of Finlands and Czechoslovakias—seemed a reasonable compromise solution.

Third, the universalists feared that the sphere-of-interest approach would be what Hull termed "a haven for the isolationists," who would advocate America's participation in Western Hemisphere affairs on condition that it did not participate in European or Asian affairs. Hull also feared that spheres of interest would lead to "closed trade areas or discriminatory systems" and thus defeat his cherished dream of a low-tariff, freely trading world.

Fourth, the sphere-of-interest solution meant the betrayal of the principles for which the Second World War was being fought—the Atlantic Charter, the Four Freedoms, the Declaration of the United Nations. Poland summed up the problem. Britain, having gone to war to defend the independence of Poland from the Germans, could not easily conclude the war by surrendering the independence of Poland to the Russians. Thus, as Hopkins told Stalin after Roosevelt's death in 1945, Poland had "become the symbol of our ability to work out problems with the Soviet Union." Nor could American liberals in general watch with equanimity while the police state spread into countries which, if they had mostly not been real democracies, had mostly not been tyrannies either. The execution in 1943 of Ehrlich and Alter, the Polish socialist trade union leaders, excited deep concern. "I have particularly in mind," Harriman cabled in 1944, "objection to the institution of secret police who may become involved in the persecution of persons of truly democratic convictions who may not be willing to conform to Soviet methods."

Fifth, the sphere-of-influence solution would create difficult domestic problems in American politics. Roosevelt was aware of the six million or more Polish votes in the 1944 election; even more acutely, he was aware of the broader and deeper attack which would follow if, after going to war to stop the Nazi conquest of Europe, he permitted the war to end with the communist conquest of Eastern Europe. As Archibald MacLeish, then Assistant Secretary of State for Public Affairs, warned in January 1945, "The wave of disillusionment which has distressed us in the last several weeks will be increased if the impression is permitted to get abroad that potentially totalitarian provisional governments are to be set up without adequate safeguards as to the holding of free elections and the realization of the principles of the Atlantic Charter." Roosevelt believed that no administration could survive which did not try everything short of war to save Eastern Europe, and he was the supreme American politician of the century.

Sixth, if the Russians were allowed to overrun Eastern Europe without argument, would that satisfy them? Even Kennan, in a dispatch of May 1944, admitted that the "urge" had dreadful potentialities: "If initially successful, will it know where to stop? Will it not be inexorably carried forward, by its very nature, in a struggle to reach the whole—to attain complete mastery of the shores of the Atlantic and the Pacific?" His own answer was that there were inherent limits to the Russian capacity to expand—"that Russia will not have an easy time in maintaining the power which it has seized over other people in Eastern and Central Europe unless it receives both moral and material assistance from the West." Subsequent developments have vindicated Kennan's argument. By the late forties, Yugoslavia and Albania, the two East European states farthest from the Soviet Union and the two in which communism was imposed from within rather than from without, had declared their independence of Moscow. But, given Russia's success in maintaining centralized control over the international communist movement for a quarter of a century, who in 1944 could have had much confidence in the idea of communist revolts against Moscow?

Most of those involved therefore rejected Kennan's answer and stayed with his question. If the West turned its back on Eastern Europe, the higher probability, in their view, was that the Russians would use their security zone, not just for defensive purposes, but as a springboard from which to mount an attack on Western Europe, now shattered by war, a vacuum of power awaiting its master. "If the policy is accepted that the Soviet Union has a right to penetrate her immediate neighbors for security," Harriman said in 1944, "penetration of the next immediate neighbors becomes at a certain time equally logical." If a row with Russia were inevitable, every consideration of prudence dictated that it should take place in Eastern rather than Western Europe.

Thus idealism and realism joined in opposition to the sphere-of-influence solution. The consequence was a determination to assert an American interest in the postwar destiny of all nations, including those of Eastern Europe. In the message which Roosevelt and Hopkins drafted after Hopkins had stopped Roosevelt's initial cable authorizing Churchill to speak for the United States at the Moscow meeting of October 1944, Roosevelt now said, "There is in this global war literally no question, either military or political, in which the United States is not interested." After Roosevelt's death Hopkins repeated the point to Stalin: "The cardinal basis of President Roosevelt's policy which the American people had fully supported had been the concept that the interests of the U.S. were worldwide and not confined to North and South America and the Pacific Ocean."

V

For better or worse, this was the American position. It is now necessary to attempt the imaginative leap and consider the impact of this position on the leaders of the Soviet Union who, also for better or for worse, had reached the bitter conclusion that the survival of their country depended on their unchallenged control of the corridors through which enemies had so often invaded their homeland. They could claim to have been keeping their own side of the sphere-of-influence bargain. Of course, they were working to capture the resistance movements of Western Europe; indeed, with the appointment of Oumansky as Ambassador to Mexico they were even beginning to enlarge underground operations in the western hemisphere. But, from their viewpoint, if the West permitted this, the more fools they; and, if the West stopped it, it was within their right to do so. In overt political matters the Russians were scrupulously playing the game. They had watched in silence while the British shot down Communists in Greece. In Yugoslavia Stalin was urging Tito (as Djilas later revealed) to keep King Peter. They had not only acknowledged Western preeminence in Italy but had recognized the Badoglio regime; the Italian Communists had even voted (against the Socialists and the Liberals) for the renewal of the Lateran Pacts.

They would not regard anti-communist action in a Western zone as a *casus belli;* and they expected reciprocal license to assert their own authority in the East. But the principle of self-determination was carrying the United States into a deeper entanglement in Eastern Europe than the Soviet Union claimed as a right (whatever it was doing underground) in the affairs of Italy, Greece or China. When the Russians now exercised in Eastern Europe the same brutal control they were prepared to have Washington exercise in the American sphere of influence, the American protests, given the paranoia produced alike by Russian history and Leninist ideology, no doubt seemed not only an act of hypocrisy but a threat to security. To the Russians, a stroll into the neighborhood easily became a plot to burn down the house: when, for example, damaged American planes made emergency landings in Poland and Hungary, Moscow took this as attempts to organize the local resistance. It is not unusual to suspect one's adversary of doing what one is already doing oneself. At the same time, the cruelty with which the Russians executed their idea of spheres of influence—in a sense, perhaps, an unwitting cruelty, since Stalin treated the East Europeans no worse than he had treated the Russians in the thirties—discouraged the West from accepting the equation (for example, Italy = Romania) which seemed so self-evident to the Kremlin.

So Moscow very probably, and not unnaturally, perceived the emphasis on self-determination as a systematic and deliberate pressure on Russia's western frontiers. Moreover, the restoration of capitalism to countries freed at frightful cost by the Red Army no doubt struck the Russians as the betrayal of the principles for which *they* were fighting. "That they, the victors," Isaac Deutscher has suggested, "should now preserve an order from which they had experienced nothing but hostility, and could expect nothing but hostility . . . would have been the most miserable anti-climax to their great 'war of liberation.'" By 1944 Poland was the critical issue; Harriman later said that "under instructions from President Roosevelt, I talked about Poland with Stalin more frequently than any other subject." While the West saw the point of Stalin's demand for a "friendly government" in Warsaw, the American insistence on the sovereign virtues of free elections (ironically in the spirit of the 1917 Bolshevik decree of peace, which

affirmed "the right" of a nation "to decide the forms of its state existence by a free vote, taken after the complete evacuation of the in-
corporating or, generally, of the stronger nation") created an insoluble problem in those countries, like Poland (and Romania) where free
elections would almost certainly produce anti-Soviet governments.

The Russians thus may well have estimated the Western pressures
as calculated to encourage their enemies in Eastern Europe and to
defeat their own minimum objective of a protective glacis. Everything
still hung, however, on the course of military operations. The wartime
collaboration had been created by one thing, and one thing alone:
the threat of Nazi victory. So long as this threat was real, so was the
collaboration. In late December 1944, von Rundstedt launched his
counter-offensive in the Ardennes. A few weeks later, when Roosevelt, Churchill and Stalin gathered in the Crimea, it was in the shadow
of this last considerable explosion of German power. The meeting at
Yalta was still dominated by the mood of war.

Yalta remains something of an historical perplexity—less, from the
perspective of 1967, because of a mythical American deference to the
sphere-of-influence thesis than because of the documentable Russian
deference to the universalist thesis. Why should Stalin in 1945 have
accepted the Declaration on Liberated Europe and an agreement on
Poland pledging that "the three governments will jointly" act to assure "free elections of governments responsive to the will of the
people"? There are several probable answers: that the war was not
over and the Russians still wanted the Americans to intensify their
military effort in the West; that one clause in the Declaration prem-
ised action on "the opinion of the three governments" and thus implied a Soviet veto, though the Polish agreement was more definite;
most of all that the universalist algebra of the Declaration was plainly
in Stalin's mind to be construed in terms of the practical arithmetic
of his sphere-of-influence agreement with Churchill the previous October. Stalin's assurance to Churchill at Yalta that a proposed Russian
amendment to the Declaration would not apply to Greece makes it
clear that Roosevelt's pieties did not, in Stalin's mind, nullify Churchill's percentages. He could well have been strengthened in this supposition by the fact that *after* Yalta, Churchill himself repeatedly reasserted the terms of the October agreement as if he regarded it,
despite Yalta, as controlling.

Harriman still had the feeling before Yalta that the Kremlin had
"two approaches to their postwar policies" and that Stalin himself was
"of two minds." One approach emphasized the internal reconstruction and development of Russia; the other its external expansion. But

in the meantime the fact which dominated all political decisions—
that is, the war against Germany—was moving into its final phase. In
the weeks after Yalta, the military situation changed with great rapid-
ity. As the Nazi threat declined, so too did the need for cooperation.
The Soviet Union, feeling itself menaced by the American idea of
self-determination and the borderlands diplomacy to which it was
leading, skeptical whether the United Nations would protect its frontiers as reliably as its own domination in Eastern Europe, began to
fulfill its security requirements unilaterally.

In March Stalin expressed his evaluation of the United Nations by
rejecting Roosevelt's plea that Molotov come to the San Francisco conference, if only for the opening sessions. In the next weeks the Russians emphatically and crudely worked their will in Eastern Europe,
above all in the test country of Poland. They were ignoring the Declaration on Liberated Europe, ignoring the Atlantic Charter, self-
determination, human freedom and everything else the Americans
considered essential for a stable peace. "We must clearly recognize,"
Harriman wired Washington a few days before Roosevelt's death,
"that the Soviet program is the establishment of totalitarianism, ending personal liberty and democracy as we know and respect it."

At the same time, the Russians also began to mobilize communist
resources in the United States itself to block American universalism.
In April 1945 Jacques Duclos, who had been the Comintern official
responsible for the Western communist parties, launched in *Cahiers
du Communisme* an uncompromising attack on the policy of the American Communist Party. Duclos sharply condemned the revisionism of
Earl Browder, the American Communist leader, as "expressed in the
concept of a long-term class peace in the United States, of the possibility of the suppression of the class struggle in the postwar period
and of establishment of harmony between labor and capital." Browder was specifically rebuked for favoring the "self-determination" of
Europe "west of the Soviet Union" on a bourgeois-democratic basis.
The excommunication of Browderism was plainly the Politburo's considered reaction to the impending defeat of Germany; it was a signal
to the communist parties of the West that they should recover their
identity; it was Moscow's alert to communists everywhere that they
should prepare for new policies in the postwar world.

The Duclos piece obviously could not have been planned and written much later than the Yalta conference—that is, well before a number of events which revisionists now cite in order to demonstrate
American responsibility for the Cold War: before Allen Dulles, for
example, began to negotiate the surrender of the German armies in

Italy (the episode which provoked Stalin to charge Roosevelt with seeking a separate peace and provoked Roosevelt to denounce the "vile misrepresentations" of Stalin's informants); well before Roosevelt died; many months before the testing of the atomic bomb; even more months before Truman ordered that the bomb be dropped on Japan. William Z. Foster, who soon replaced Browder as the leader of the American Communist Party and embodied the new Moscow line, later boasted of having said in January 1944, "A post-war Roosevelt administration would continue to be, as it is now, an imperialist government." With ancient suspicions revived by the American insistence on universalism, this was no doubt the conclusion which the Russians were reaching at the same time. The Soviet canonization of Roosevelt (like their present-day canonization of Kennedy) took place after the American President's death.

The atmosphere of mutual suspicion was beginning to rise. In January 1945 Molotov formally proposed that the United States grant Russia a $6 billion credit for postwar reconstruction. With characteristic tact he explained that he was doing this as a favor to save America from a postwar depression. The proposal seems to have been diffidently made and diffidently received. Roosevelt requested that the matter "not be pressed further" on the American side until he had a chance to talk with Stalin; but the Russians did not follow it up either at Yalta in February (save for a single glancing reference) or during the Stalin-Hopkins talks in May or at Potsdam. Finally the proposal was renewed in the very different political atmosphere of August. This time Washington inexplicably mislaid the request during the transfer of the records of the Foreign Economic Administration to the State Department. It did not turn up again until March 1946. Of course this was impossible for the Russians to believe; it is hard enough even for those acquainted with the capacity of the American government for incompetence to believe; and it only strengthened Soviet suspicions of American purposes.

The American credit was one conceivable form of Western contribution to Russian reconstruction. Another was lend-lease, and the possibility of reconstruction aid under the lend-lease protocol had already been discussed in 1944. But in May 1945 Russia, like Britain, suffered from Truman's abrupt termination of lend-lease shipments—"unfortunate and even brutal," Stalin told Hopkins, adding that, if it was "designed as pressure on the Russians in order to soften them up, then it was a fundamental mistake." A third form was German reparations. Here Stalin in demanding $10 billion in reparations for the Soviet Union made his strongest fight at Yalta. Roosevelt, while agreeing essentially with Churchill's opposition, tried to postpone the matter by accepting the Soviet figure as a "basis for discussion"—a formula which led to future misunderstanding. In short, the Russian hope for major Western assistance in postwar reconstruction foundered on three events which the Kremlin could well have interpreted respectively as deliberate sabotage (the loan request), blackmail (lend-lease cancellation) and pro-Germanism (reparations).

Actually the American attempt to settle the fourth lend-lease protocol was generous and the Russians for their own reasons declined to come to an agreement. It is not clear, though, that satisfying Moscow on any of these financial scores would have made much essential difference. It might have persuaded some doves in the Kremlin that the U.S. government was genuinely friendly; it might have persuaded some hawks that the American anxiety for Soviet friendship was such that Moscow could do as it wished without inviting challenge from the United States. It would, in short, merely have reinforced both sides of the Kremlin debate; it would hardly have reversed deeper tendencies toward the deterioration of political relationships. Economic deals were surely subordinate to the quality of mutual political confidence; and here, in the months after Yalta, the decay was steady.

The Cold War had now begun. It was the product not of a decision but of a dilemma. Each side felt compelled to adopt policies which the other could not but regard as a threat to the principles of the peace. Each then felt compelled to undertake defensive measures. Thus the Russians saw no choice but to consolidate their security in Eastern Europe. The Americans, regarding Eastern Europe as the first step toward Western Europe, responded by asserting their interest in the zone the Russians deemed vital to their security. The Russians concluded that the West was resuming its old course of capitalist encirclement; that it was purposefully laying the foundation for anti-Soviet regimes in the area defined by the blood of centuries as crucial to Russian survival. Each side believed with passion that future international stability depended on the success of its own conception of world order. Each side, in pursuing its own clearly indicated and deeply cherished principles, was only confirming the fear of the other that it was bent on aggression.

Very soon the process began to acquire a cumulative momentum. The impending collapse of Germany thus provoked new troubles: the Russians, for example, sincerely feared that the West was planning a separate surrender of the German armies in Italy in a way which would release troops for Hitler's eastern front, as they subsequently feared that the Nazis might succeed in surrendering Berlin to the West. This was the context in which the atomic bomb now appeared. Though the revisionist argument that Truman dropped the bomb less to defeat Japan than to intimidate Russia is not convincing, this thought unquestionably appealed to some in Washington as at least an advantageous side-effect of Hiroshima.

So the machinery of suspicion and counter-suspicion, action and counter-action, was set in motion. But, given relations among traditional national states, there was still no reason, even with all the post-war jostling, why this should not have remained a manageable situation. What made it unmanageable, what caused the rapid escalation of the Cold War and in another two years completed the division of Europe, was a set of considerations which this account has thus far excluded.

VI

Up to this point, the discussion has considered the schism within the wartime coalition as if it were entirely the result of disagreements among national states. Assuming this framework, there was unquestionably a failure of communication between America and Russia, a misperception of signals and, as time went on, a mounting tendency to ascribe ominous motives to the other side. It seems hard, for example, to deny that American postwar policy created genuine difficulties for the Russians and even assumed a threatening aspect for them. All this the revisionists have rightly and usefully emphasized.

But the great omission of the revisionists—and also the fundamental explanation of the speed with which the Cold War escalated—lies precisely in the fact that the Soviet Union was *not* a traditional national state.* This is where the "mirror image," invoked by some psychologists, falls down. For the Soviet Union was a phenomenon very different from America or Britain: it was a totalitarian state, endowed with an all-explanatory, all-consuming ideology, committed to the infallibility of government and party, still in a somewhat messianic mood, equating dissent with treason, and ruled by a dictator who, for all his quite extraordinary abilities, had his paranoid moments.

Marxism-Leninism gave the Russian leaders a view of the world

* This is the classical revisionist fallacy—the assumption of the rationality, or at least of the traditionalism, of states where ideology and social organization have created a different range of motives. So the Second World War revisionists omit the totalitarian dynamism of Nazism and the fanaticism of Hitler, as the Civil War revisionists omit the fact that the slavery system was producing a doctrinaire closed society in the American South. For a consideration of some of these issues, see "The Causes of the Civil War: A Note on Historical Sentimentalism" in my *The Politics of Hope* (Boston, 1963).

according to which all societies were inexorably destined to proceed along appointed roads by appointed stages until they achieved the classless nirvana. Moreover, given the resistance of the capitalists to this development, the existence of any non-communist state was *by definition* a threat to the Soviet Union. "As long as capitalism and socialism exist," Lenin wrote, "we cannot live in peace: in the end, one or the other will triumph—a funeral dirge will be sung either over the Soviet Republic or over world capitalism."

Stalin and his associates, whatever Roosevelt or Truman did or failed to do, were bound to regard the United States as the enemy, not because of this deed or that, but because of the primordial fact that America was the leading capitalist power and thus, by Leninist syllogism, unappeasably hostile, driven by the logic of its system to oppose, encircle and destroy Soviet Russia. Nothing the United States could have done in 1944–45 would have abolished this mistrust, required and sanctified as it was by Marxist gospel—nothing short of the conversion of the United States into a Stalinist despotism; and even this would not have sufficed, as the experience of Yugoslavia and China soon showed, unless it were accompanied by total subservience to Moscow. So long as the United States remained a capitalist democracy, no American policy, given Moscow's theology, could hope to win basic Soviet confidence, and every American action was poisoned from the source. So long as the Soviet Union remained a messianic state, ideology compelled a steady expansion of communist power.

It is easy, of course, to exaggerate the capacity of ideology to control events. The tension of acting according to revolutionary abstractions is too much for most nations to sustain over a long period: that is why Mao Tse-tung launched his Cultural Revolution, hoping thereby to create a permanent revolutionary mood and save Chinese communism from the degeneration which, in his view, has overtaken Russian communism. Still, as any revolution grows older, normal human and social motives will increasingly reassert themselves. In due course, we can be sure, Leninism will be about as effective in governing the daily lives of Russians as Christianity is in governing the daily lives of Americans. Like the Ten Commandments and the Sermon on the Mount, the Leninist verities will increasingly become platitudes for ritual observance, not guides to secular decision. There can be no worse fallacy (even if respectable people practiced it diligently for a season in the United States) than that of drawing from a nation's ideology permanent conclusions about its behavior.

A temporary recession of ideology was already taking place during the Second World War when Stalin, to rally his people against the invader, had to replace the appeal of Marxism by that of nationalism. ("We are under no illusions that they are fighting for us," Stalin once said to Harriman. "They are fighting for Mother Russia.") But this was still taking place within the strictest limitations. The Soviet Union remained as much a police state as ever; the regime was as infallible as ever; foreigners and their ideas were as suspect as ever. "Never, except possibly during my later experience as ambassador in Moscow," Kennan has written, "did the insistence of the Soviet authorities on isolation of the diplomatic corps weigh more heavily on me . . . than in these first weeks following my return to Russia in the final months of the war. . . . [We were] treated as though we were the bearers of some species of the plague"—which, of course, from the Soviet viewpoint, they were: the plague of skepticism.

Paradoxically, of the forces capable of bringing about a modification of ideology, the most practical and effective was the Soviet dictatorship itself. If Stalin was an ideologist, he was also a pragmatist. If he saw everything through the lenses of Marxism-Leninism, he also, as the infallible expositor of the faith, could reinterpret Marxism-Leninism to justify anything he wanted to do at any given moment. No doubt Roosevelt's ignorance of Marxism-Leninism was inexcusable and led to grievous miscalculations. But Roosevelt's efforts to work on and through Stalin were not so hopelessly naive as it used to be fashionable to think. With the extraordinary instinct of a great political leader, Roosevelt intuitively understood that Stalin was the *only* lever available to the West against the Leninist ideology and the Soviet system. If Stalin could be reached, then alone was there a chance of getting the Russians to act contrary to the prescriptions of their faith. The best evidence is that Roosevelt retained a certain capacity to influence Stalin to the end; the nominal Soviet acquiescence in American universalism as late as Yalta was perhaps an indication of that. It is in this way that the death of Roosevelt was crucial—not in the vulgar sense that his policy was then reversed by his successor, which did not happen, but in the sense that no other American could hope to have the restraining impact on Stalin which Roosevelt might for a while have had.

Stalin alone could have made any difference. Yet Stalin, in spite of the impression of sobriety and realism he made on Westerners who saw him during the Second World War, was plainly a man of deep and morbid obsessions and compulsions. When he was still a young man, Lenin had criticized his rude and arbitrary ways. A reasonably authoritative observer (N. S. Khrushchev) later commented, "These negative characteristics of his developed steadily and during the last

years acquired an absolutely insufferable character." His paranoia,
probably set off by the suicide of his wife in 1932, led to the terrible
purges of the mid-thirties and the wanton murder of thousands of
his Bolshevik comrades. "Everywhere and in everything," Khrushchev says of this period, "he saw 'enemies,' 'double-dealers' and
'spies.'" The crisis of war evidently steadied him in some way, though
Khrushchev speaks of his "nervousness and hysteria . . . even after
the war began." The madness, so rigidly controlled for a time, burst
out with new and shocking intensity in the postwar years. "After the
war," Khrushchev testifies,

the situation became even more complicated. Stalin became even more capri-
cious, irritable and brutal; in particular, his suspicion grew. His persecution
mania reached unbelievable dimensions. . . . He decided everything, without
any consideration for anyone or anything.

  Stalin's wilfulness showed itself . . . also in the international relations of the
Soviet Union. . . . He had completely lost a sense of reality; he demonstrated
his suspicion and haughtiness not only in relation to individuals in the USSR,
but in relation to whole parties and nations.

A revisionist fallacy has been to treat Stalin as just another Realpolitik
statesman, as Second World War revisionists see Hitler as just another
Stresemann or Bismarck. But the record makes it clear that in the
end nothing could satisfy Stalin's paranoia. His own associates failed.
Why does anyone suppose that any conceivable American policy
would have succeeded?

  An analysis of the origins of the Cold War which leaves out these
factors—the intransigence of Leninist ideology, the sinister dynamics
of a totalitarian society and the madness of Stalin—is obviously incomplete. It was these factors which made it hard for the West to
accept the thesis that Russia was moved only by a desire to protect its
security and would be satisfied by the control of Eastern Europe; it
was these factors which charged the debate between universalism and
spheres of influence with apocalyptic potentiality.

  Leninism and totalitarianism created a structure of thought and
behavior which made postwar collaboration between Russia and
America—in any normal sense of civilized intercourse between national states—inherently impossible. The Soviet dictatorship of 1945
simply could not have survived such a collaboration. Indeed, nearly
a quarter-century later, the Soviet regime, though it has moved a
good distance, could still hardly survive it without risking the release
inside Russia of energies profoundly opposed to communist despotism. As for Stalin, he may have represented the only force in 1945

capable of overcoming Stalinism, but the very traits which enabled him to win absolute power expressed terrifying instabilities of mind and temperament and hardly offered a solid foundation for a peaceful world.

VII

The difference between America and Russia in 1945 was that some Americans fundamentally believed that, over a long run, a modus vivendi with Russia was possible; while the Russians, so far as one can tell, believed in no more than a short-run modus vivendi with the United States.

Harriman and Kennan took the lead in warning Washington about the difficulties of short-run dealings with the Soviet Union. But both argued that, if the United States developed a rational policy and stuck to it, there would be, after long and rough passages, the prospect of eventual clearing. "I am, as you know," Harriman cabled Washington in early April, "a most earnest advocate of the closest possible understanding with the Soviet Union so that what I am saying relates only to how best to attain such understanding." Kennan has similarly made it clear that the function of his containment policy was "to tide us over a difficult time and bring us to the point where we could discuss effectively with the Russians the dangers and drawbacks this status quo involved, and to arrange with them for its peaceful replacement by a better and sounder one." The subsequent careers of both men attest to the honesty of these statements.

There is no corresponding evidence on the Russian side that anyone seriously sought a modus vivendi in these terms. Stalin's choice was whether his long-term ideological and national interests would be better served by a short-run truce with the West or by an immediate resumption of pressure. In October 1945 Stalin indicated to Harriman at Sochi that he planned to adopt the second course—that the Soviet Union was going isolationist. No doubt the succession of problems with the United States contributed to this decision, but the basic causes most probably lay elsewhere: in the developing situations in Eastern Europe, in Western Europe and in the United States.

In Eastern Europe, Stalin was still for a moment experimenting with techniques of control. But he must have begun to conclude that he had underestimated the hostility of the people to Russian dominion. The Hungarian elections in November would finally convince him that the Yalta formula was a road to anti-Soviet governments. At the same time, he was feeling more strongly than ever a sense of his opportunities in Western Europe. The other half of the Continent lay

unexpectedly before him, politically demoralized, economically prostrate, militarily defenseless. The hunting would be better and safer
than he had anticipated. As for the United States, the alacrity of postwar demobilization must have recalled Roosevelt's offhand remark at
Yalta that "two years would be the limit" for keeping American troops
in Europe. And, despite Dr. Eugene Varga's doubts about the imminence of American economic breakdown, Marxist theology assured
Stalin that the United States was heading into a bitter postwar depression and would be consumed with its own problems. If the condition
of Eastern Europe made unilateral action seem essential in the interests of Russian security, the condition of Western Europe and the
United States offered new temptations for communist expansion.
The Cold War was now in full swing.

It still had its year of modulations and accommodations. Secretary
Byrnes conducted his long and fruitless campaign to persuade the
Russians that America only sought governments in Eastern Europe
"both friendly to the Soviet Union and representative of all the democratic elements of the country." Crises were surmounted in Trieste
and Iran. Secretary Marshall evidently did not give up hope of a modus vivendi until the Moscow conference of foreign secretaries of
March 1947. Even then, the Soviet Union was invited to participate
in the Marshall Plan.

The point of no return came on 2 July 1947, when Molotov, after
bringing 89 technical specialists with him to Paris and evincing initial
interest in the project for European reconstruction, received the hot
flash from the Kremlin, denounced the whole idea and walked out
of the conference. For the next fifteen years the Cold War raged unabated, passing out of historical ambiguity into the realm of good
versus evil and breeding on both sides simplifications, stereotypes and
self-serving absolutes, often couched in interchangeable phrases.
Under the pressure even America, for a deplorable decade, forsook
its pragmatic and pluralist traditions, posed as God's appointed messenger to ignorant and sinful man and followed the Soviet example
in looking to a world remade in its own image.

In retrospect, if it is impossible to see the Cold War as a case of
American aggression and Russian response, it is also hard to see it as
a pure case of Russian aggression and American response. "In what
is truly tragic," wrote Hegel, "there must be valid moral powers on
both the sides which come into collision. . . . Both suffer loss and yet
both are mutually justified." In this sense, the Cold War had its tragic
elements. The question remains whether it was an instance of Greek
tragedy—as Auden has called it, "the tragedy of necessity," where the

feeling aroused in the spectator is "What a pity it had to be this way"—or of Christian tragedy, "the tragedy of possibility," where the feeling aroused is "What a pity it was this way when it might have been otherwise."

Once something has happened, the historian is tempted to assume that it had to happen; but this may often be a highly unphilosophical assumption. The Cold War could have been avoided only if the Soviet Union had not been possessed by convictions both of the infallibility of the communist word and of the inevitability of a communist world. These convictions transformed an impasse between national states into a religious war, a tragedy of possibility into one of necessity. One might wish that America had preserved the poise and proportion of the first years of the Cold War and had not in time succumbed to its own forms of self-righteousness. But the most rational of American policies could hardly have averted the Cold War. Only today, as Russia begins to recede from its messianic mission and to accept, in practice if not yet in principle, the permanence of the world of diversity, only now can the hope flicker that this long, dreary, costly contest may at last be taking on forms less dramatic, less obsessive and less dangerous to the future of mankind.

II. *The Cold War Revisited: 1986*

During the 1960s, the simplifications of the early Cold War appeared to be yielding to more complex conceptions; melodrama to tragedy. "No government or social system is so evil," President Kennedy had said at American University in 1963, "that its people must be condemned as lacking in virtue," and he called on Americans as well as Russians to reexamine attitudes toward the Cold War "for our attitude is as essential as theirs." Who would have supposed that exactly twenty years later another American President would brand the Soviet Union "the focus of evil in the modern world" and call on Americans to "oppose it with all our might"? In the age of Ronald Reagan, the official American version of the Cold War regressed, past Richard Nixon and Henry Kissinger and détente, past Kennedy and the "world of diversity," back to the holy war of John Foster Dulles.

I

The Reagan version has not produced a new scholarly orthodoxy in support of its dogmas. Nor has it ended the scholarly drift toward Professor Gaddis's post-revisionist synthesis. But, by reviving forebodings about the motives of United States policy, it has awakened a new audience for the revisionist critique.

The Cold War, in the perspective of the Open Door school, was simply the most recent episode in the long, predictable line of international conflicts created by the imperialist compulsion of American capitalism. Driven by the insatiable requirements of an economic system that has to expand in order to survive, Washington, according to the revisionist tale, embarked after the Second World War on a course of world economic domination. Demanding an open door for American trade and investment around the planet, the United States sought to "integrate" the rest of the world into the American economic system. The Soviet Union was the great barrier in the American path. American leaders thereupon portrayed that weak and battered country as a military and ideological threat in order to justify their policy of removing all obstacles to the American conquest of world markets. Franklin Roosevelt bequeathed Harry Truman and his associates, in the words of William Appleman Williams, "little, if anything, beyond the traditional outlook of open-door expansion. They proceeded rapidly and with a minimum of debate to translate that conception of America and the world into a series of actions and policies which closed the door to any result but the cold war."[5]

This course was not simply a mistaken choice by one or another American President. It was a structural imperative to which American leaders had no choice but to respond. "The commitment to the global Open Door," Williams wrote, "was as much a part of Roosevelt's refusal to make firm agreements with Stalin in 1941–42 and 1944 as it was of Truman's call in 1945 for the internationalization of the Danube and the Open Door in Manchuria."[6] So the United States forced the Cold War on a hapless Soviet Union and an innocent world.

Because the Cold War broke out in Eastern Europe, this region is a particular object of revisionist attention. According to Williams, American capitalism well before the Second World War had "penetrated the economies" of Poland, Bulgaria, Romania, Yugoslavia and Albania, acquiring "significant interests in eastern Europe throughout the 1920s." When these countries dared resist American economic hegemony during those years, "businessmen turned to Washington for help. . . . The first official move usually was a note to the country in question, reminding it of the principle and practice of the Open Door Policy. If that hint proved insufficient, American leaders resorted to economic pressure directly, by withholding approval of projected loans or similar projects; or indirectly, by threatening, subtly or blatantly, to break diplomatic relations."[7]

Needless to say, Williams supplied no instances of American cancellation of loans or of threats, subtle or blatant, to break diplomatic relations. His picture of "significant" American business interests in Eastern Europe between the wars can be described most charitably as fantasy. Eastern Europe before the Second World War received only about 2 percent of American exports.[8] In the words of the Soviet historian K. P. Voshenkov, "The economic interests of the U.S. in the Danubian area were both during and after the [First World] War quite negligible. The U.S. export and import trade with the Danubian countries between the wars was almost nil."[9] Far from being "significant," American economic interests were so insignificant that American capitalists watched the Nazi takeover of the area with total indifference.

Nevertheless, Williams described United States policy after the Second World War as one of "reasserting" American influence in Eastern Europe while "pushing the Russians back to their traditional borders," a policy prescribed by "the traditional outlook of the open door and the specific desire to keep the Soviets from establishing any long-range influence in eastern Europe."[10] The "main" effort of the Truman administration, a revisionist ally, Barton J. Bernstein, added, was "to pry the Eastern bloc away from the Soviets" in the conviction that "the closing of this sector of the world economy . . . endangered the American system."[11] Such American meddling in Eastern Europe, revisionists continued, was naturally seen in Moscow as a threat to Soviet security. The result was to goad the Soviet Union into defensive countermeasures that the United States then cited as evidence of aggressive purposes.

II

More serious scholars have questioned whether the United States pursued a coherent anti-Soviet policy in Eastern Europe and whether indeed the United States had an East European policy at all. Lynn Etheridge Davis discussed the period 1941–1945 in *The Cold War Begins: Soviet-American Conflict over Eastern Europe* (1974). Professor Davis found no evidence for the Open Door thesis. "The United States never sought to prevent the establishment of Soviet economic predominance in Eastern Europe and defined no vital economic interests in this part of the world." But, while the American government saw no American interests in Eastern Europe, it was unwilling for global as well as domestic reasons to acknowledge a breach in the Atlantic Charter. So it kept on proclaiming its lofty principles. At the same time, it systematically rejected anti-Soviet initiatives proposed by its men in the field and took "minimal action" to discourage Soviet violations of inter-Allied understandings.

The State Department rejected pleas from General Cortland Schuyler, the American representative on the Romanian Control Commission, that the United States withdraw economic assistance from Russia in order to bring about Soviet compliance with the Yalta agreement on Eastern Europe. It ignored urgent requests from Maynard Barnes, the American representative in Bulgaria, that Washington take action to obtain international supervision of the Bulgarian elections. When Averell Harriman, the ambassador to the Soviet Union, said that, if America and Britain were unwilling to intervene in favor of such elections, then Washington should inform the American people of the character of the communist dictatorship in Bulgaria, the State Department declined even to do that. When Barnes instructed the American representative on the Control Commission to ask for the postponement of the elections until assurances could be given that they would be free, the Department countermanded his action. And when Barnes's unauthorized initiative succeeded and the elections were postponed, Washington rejected recommendations by Barnes and the British government that the western allies should follow up this success with firm action to achieve a revision of the electoral law. "No one in the State Department argued that the United States should learn from the success of Barnes's initiatives in Bulgaria and undertake more active protests against Soviet actions throughout Eastern Europe."[12]

The result of maximalist rhetoric and minimalist action was the worst of both worlds: Soviet suspicions inflamed and Soviet ambitions unchecked. Professor Davis's incisive critique of American nonplanning in Eastern Europe—left in the hands of the European Division of the State Department since no one higher up considered Eastern Europe sufficiently important—is generally persuasive. But each of the choices Washington failed to make—on the one hand, explicit abandonment of Eastern Europe; on the other, concrete opposition to Soviet actions—had weighty disadvantages. Was it after all a real choice?

A book by a young Norwegian historian carried the story forward to 1947. Geir Lundestad discussed the Cold War with the happy detachment of a Scandinavian born in 1945. *The American Non-Policy Towards Eastern Europe, 1943–1947: Universalism in an Area Not of Essential Interest to the United States* (1978) is solidly researched, well organized, and clearly if repetitiously written.

Lundestad's findings paralleled those of Davis. Washington, he wrote, contemplated Eastern Europe in its general postwar spirit of "universalism"—a term he intelligently redefined as the effort by the United States, having secured its own sphere of influence in the western hemisphere, to discourage the establishment of equivalent spheres of influence by other powers. But Washington made no serious attempt to apply universalist policies to Eastern Europe—because Soviet interests in the area were primary and self-evident, because American interests were meager and vague, because Washington's means of enforcement were limited almost to the point of nonexistence, and, most important, because Washington found it useful to make a practical retreat in Eastern Europe in order to limit Soviet influence in areas of greater consequence to the United States, above all in Japan.

The problem was more difficult because many, perhaps most, East Europeans preferred democracy to communism. In the election in Hungary in November 1945, the Communists polled 17 percent of the vote as against 57 percent for the Smallholders. "There is little reason to doubt," Lundestad wrote, "that Mikolajczyk in Poland, Maniu in Rumania, and probably also Petkov in Bulgaria would have piled up percentages in any free elections on a scale comparable to what the Smallholders achieved in Hungary."

Despite the moral claims and political possibilities created by this preference for democracy, a recognition of the limits of American power and the desire for a free hand in Japan led to concessions that, Lundestad observed, "actively furthered the Soviet domination over Eastern Europe." For all his "outward bluster," Truman consented to do what Roosevelt had declined to do—to increase the percentage of Stalin's Poles in the Polish Provisional government and thereby "to reduce U.S. demands as to what constituted an acceptable government in Poland, the crucial country in the region." Byrnes's peace treaties with the other countries confirmed Soviet ascendancy; Moscow in exchange abandoned Japan. At the same time, Washington's refusal to renounce universalist declarations only increased Soviet-American tension. "The United States never resolved the basic dilemma between universalism and the many modifying elements" and "never developed a clear-cut policy towards Eastern Europe"—a point Lundestad demonstrated by a detailed country-by-country analysis of what the United States actually did.

As for the alleged American obsession with the Open Door, Lundestad's country-by-country examination showed that the American objection was not to "domestic economic radicalism"—planning, nationalization, expropriation—but to "Soviet economic domination" and hence was political rather than commercial in its motive. And though Lundestad felt that the revisionists had usefully "pierced the screen of official and self-serving proclamations," he rejected their "two major assumptions"—that the United States was definitely superior in strength to the Soviet Union and that the Truman administration was determined to remove Soviet domination over Eastern Europe. The trouble with these assumptions, Lundestad sensibly remarked, is that

they are not consistent with one of the few absolutely certain facts we have on this controversial period, viz. final Soviet control over Eastern Europe. How could the Soviet Union have come to exert complete domination there if the United States, clearly the strongest power in the world, was "aggressively" intent on playing the predominant role in the region?[13]

The United States did not in fact try to push the Russians back to their traditional borders. On the contrary, it recognized the inevitability of Soviet predominance in Eastern Europe and accepted the Soviet desire for "friendly governments" on its western frontiers. "Far from opposing," as Secretary of State James F. Byrnes said in October 1945, "we have sympathized with . . . the effort of the Soviet Union to draw into closer and more friendly association with her central and eastern European neighbors. We are fully aware of her special security interests in these countries."[14] Charles E. Bohlen, the State Department's resident Soviet expert, distinguished between "open" and "exclusive" spheres of influence. It was "legitimate" for the Soviet Union to expect East European countries to follow its lead in foreign policy, as, Bohlen observed, Latin American countries followed the lead of the United States. But attempts to dictate their internal life were "illegitimate." The hope, Bohlen said, was that the Soviet Union would treat Eastern Europe as it was treating Finland.[15]

The notion of the Finlandization of Eastern Europe soon perished. Stalin moved for his own reasons to consolidate Soviet control. He did not, Harriman thinks, sign the Yalta Declaration on Liberated Europe with the intention of breaking the pledge of free elections. Stalin saw little risk in this pledge, Harriman surmises, because he had been misinformed about the popularity of East European Communist parties and expected they would win. In the months after Yalta he discovered that much of Eastern Europe viewed Soviet troops as invaders, not as liberators. After the miserable Communist showing in the Hungarian election, he very likely decided that he had to secure the Soviet frontiers by unilateral action.[16] The hardening of western policy no doubt contributed to this decision.

Even then Stalin did not, as revisionist mythology suggests, seal off this sector of the world economy. Far from regarding the Open Door as a threat to Eastern Europe, the Kremlin protested bitterly when the United States itself began closing the door and cutting off trade.[17] And, when the United States on occasion sought to use economic pressures in connection with loans, reparations and trade, it did so primarily to attain political objectives—free elections, human rights—not to promote American trade and investment. Revisionists particularly condemn the United States for failing to offer the Soviet Union a postwar reconstruction loan. Of course, an American loan, had it been offered, would have been equal grist to the revisionist mill. Thus the revisionist Gabriel Kolko condemned the $10 billion loan proposal drawn up by Henry Morgenthau, Jr., and Harry D. White of the Treasury as an insidious attempt to integrate the Soviet Union "into the capitalist world economy on a basis which economists have dubbed as neo-colonialism."[18] The Open Door thesis, in short, is like Lorenzo Dow's definition of Calvinism: you will be damned if you don't, and you will be damned if you do.

III

The application of the Open Door thesis to Eastern Europe collapses when placed against the facts of American policy, or non-policy. And the thesis in broader application faces equally decisive objections. Its basic assumption is that American capitalists insisting on the conquest of foreign markets—an insistence intensified by the fear of postwar depression—dictated the decisions that caused the Cold War. Research, however, fails to reveal the hand of private capitalists in these decisions. It fails even to reveal great capitalist concern about foreign markets. Gunnar Myrdal, after talking with American business and government leaders in 1943 and 1944, reported that "foreign trade is no longer considered an important lever for keeping up employment in American postwar industry." The Committee for Economic Development, a group of progressive businessmen, said in 1945 that the "level of employment in the United States is not primarily dependent on international trade."[19]

The record shows, not business insistence on the Open Door, but business resistance to Truman's program of trade liberalization. Revisionists make much of the free enterprise blandishments Truman used in 1947 in his effort to sell the International Trade Organization to American business. They do not note that business opposition, led by the National Association of Manufacturers and the United States Chamber of Commerce, killed the ITO.[20] The political hero of businessmen in these years, Senator Robert A. Taft of Ohio, continually called the home market the key to American prosperity, denounced "the Hull-Clayton theory of free trade" (Will Clayton was Undersecretary of State for Economic Affairs and the great champion of the ITO) and proclaimed himself "strongly opposed to committing ourselves to any overall global plan to make up some theoretical deficiency in exports."[21]

The administration mounted carefully designed campaigns to win business acceptance for the containment policy. The wooing persuaded some capitalists. Others, like Joseph P. Kennedy, refused to go along. "From the start I had no patience with a policy—what has become known as the 'Truman Doctrine'—" Kennedy said in 1950, "that, without due regard to our resources—human and material— would make commitments abroad that we could not fulfill. . . . What business is it of ours to support French colonial policy in Indo-China or to achieve Mr. Syngman Rhee's concepts of democracy in Korea?"[22]

Within the government the talk was of geopolitical, not economic, goals. George Kennan's famous "long telegram" of February 1946 devoted 120 out of 8000 words to a perfunctory paragraph on economic issues. Revisionists call the celebrated National Security Council paper of 1950, NSC-68, "a classic expression of late 20th-century American imperialism" (William Appleman Williams).[23] But NSC-68 says nothing about an Open Door for American capitalism. Nor was the theme repressed in order to deceive the public; for NSC-68 was highly secret, not declassified for another quarter century.

The failure of evidence does not, however, discourage Open Door historians. I have noted Williams's bizarre claim that the very absence of documentation is itself proof that the imperialist compulsion dominated American leaders. To fortify their case, revisionists emphasize the capitalistic backgrounds of people involved in making policy. A key revisionist villain, for example, is Harriman, a railroad magnate, an international banker and an authentic capitalist with a world outlook. "Harriman's natural antagonism to the Soviets," according to Williams, "was reinforced by his vigorous belief in the necessity of open-door expansion, a belief that may have been heightened even more by an unhappy experience with the Russians in the 1920s, when his attempt to control a sizable segment of the world's manganese market by developing Russian supplies ended in mutual dissatisfaction."[24]

The Harriman case provides a reasonable test of revisionist method. Harriman's own despatches and memoirs are notable for their indifference to questions of trade and investment. And Harriman himself, without altering his 1945 views about Soviet communism (incompatible with democracy) or about the necessity to live peacefully in the same world with Russia (imperative), has been through the years a leading advocate of negotiation and détente. The Soviet government hardly shares the revisionist belief in Harriman's villainy. In 1985 it conferred on him the Order of the Patriotic War, First Degree, "for his profound personal contribution to the establishment and consolidation of Soviet-American cooperation in the years of the Great Patriotic War and on the occasion of the 40th Anniversary of the Victory." In presenting the award, Ambassador A. F. Dobrynin said that Harriman "had spared no effort to lay a firm foundation for Soviet-American political, economic, and military cooperation."[25] Valentin Berezhkov, the Soviet diplomat and journalist who interpreted for Molotov with Hitler and for Stalin with Roosevelt and Churchill, remembered Harriman in his memoirs as "a consistent advocate of peaceful Soviet-American dialogue."[26] Even the Soviet historians N. V. Sivachev and N. N. Yakovlev in their propagandist tract *Russia and the United States* describe Harriman as a "statesman . . . whose standing in the Soviet Union has *always* been high" (emphasis added).[27] The revisionist tactic of substituting biography for evidence is not persuasive.

Beyond its methodological infirmities, the Open Door interpretation is logically vulnerable as well. Why, for example, should Roosevelt and Truman, both engaged in bitter struggles with the business community at home and both persuaded of the folly and greed of business leaders, have allowed those same business leaders to dictate their policies abroad? No doubt Roosevelt and Truman believed in a freely trading world, if this is such a heinous offense, but most American businessmen, then and now, are protectionists, not free traders.

Even more vulnerable is the revisionist assumption that the quest for a liberalized commercial policy led ineluctably to a policy of confrontation with the Soviet Union. For world trade expansion obviously does not, as revisionists claim, oblige Marxist states to assume subordinate roles in an American economic empire. American trade with Russia, Eastern Europe and China disproves every day the myth that capitalism requires an economically integrated world. Indeed communist countries want *more*, not less, western trade and investment and complain over impediments imposed by western Cold Warriors.

More than that, some of the most ardent proponents of trade expansion in the 1940s argued that accommodation with Russia, not confrontation, was the surest road to markets for American goods. From Eric Johnston, Donald Nelson and Joseph E. Davies on the right to Earl Browder on the left, these Americans saw rapprochement as the only means of assuring access to the Soviet market. "It is a fact, whether we like it or not," Browder put it, "that the American economy requires expanded foreign markets in order to live, and that there is not the slightest chance of organizing such markets except through a durable peace guaranteed by Soviet-American cooperation."[28] Such calls for cooperation did indeed expose Browder himself to brutal harassment and obloquy. His persecutors, however, were not American capitalists but his former brethren in the CPUSA.

Revisionists often cite the Bretton Woods agreement as a first step in the master plan of American capitalism to take over the world economy. Yet the architect of Bretton Woods was Harry D. White, who, whatever his precise relationship to communism (and this was overstated in the McCarthy days), can hardly be described as an agent of American capitalism or as an enemy of the Soviet Union.

Henry A. Wallace, the leading political opponent of the Truman containment policy, the apostle of conciliation and a revisionist hero, was himself a fervent champion of the Open Door. "We cannot permit the door to be closed against our trade in Eastern Europe," he said in the very speech that led to his dismissal from the Truman administration, "any more than we can in China."[29] Later he attacked the Truman Doctrine on the ground that it threatened "the open door to trade and invest with safety. . . . Under the Truman Doctrine Anglo-American business operations in Eastern Europe will never be safe." Under a policy of accommodation, however, "there can be a great expansion of business and markets for the benefit of the United States, Britain, and Russia."[30]

Insofar as the Open Door affected American policy at all, it obviously did not lead implacably to the Cold War. It is necessary to introduce other factors to explain why some devotees of the Open Door favored accommodation and others favored containment.

IV

The irreducible factor accounting for American involvement in the Cold War was undoubtedly the venerable Jeffersonian concern about the balance of power. Whenever the whole force of Europe was wielded by a single hand, Jefferson had suggested, America was in danger. This was a geopolitical concern. It had nothing to do with capitalism. It would have been quite as acute if the United States had been, like the Soviet Union, a Marxist-Leninist state. Common allegiance to communist principles never prevented *raisons d'état* from producing a Cold War between communist Russia and communist China.

Franklin Roosevelt had learned geopolitics from his cousin Theodore and from Admiral Mahan long before he learned idealism from Woodrow Wilson. The balance of power always shaped his thought on foreign policy. It seems improbable that he suddenly forgot about it during the Second World War and naively set out to charm Stalin into postwar amity. Roosevelt's determination to concentrate on Stalin was based on an astute insight. For Stalin was not necessarily the helpless prisoner of ideology. He saw himself less the disciple of Marx and Lenin than their fellow prophet. He had already rewritten Russian history, and he had the power to rewrite communist doctrine. Indeed, *only* Stalin could revise the doctrine, and the doctrine unrevised condemned the Soviet Union and the United States to permanent enmity.

Recent scholarship casts doubt on the notion that Roosevelt's wartime policy was to subordinate the balance of power to military victory. Revisionists even darkly cite his decision to deny Russia information about the atomic bomb as evidence of a belief "that the bomb could be used effectively to secure postwar goals."[31] Non-revisionists portray a generally undeceived leader struggling manfully to reconcile international geopolitical inevitabilities, such as Soviet predominance in Eastern Europe, with domestic political myths, such as the wickedness of spheres of influence. "Mindful that any emphasis on . . . *Realpolitik* might weaken American public resolve to play an enduring role in world affairs," Robert A. Dallek wrote in his admirable study *Franklin D. Roosevelt and American Foreign Policy* (1979), "Roosevelt made these actions the hidden side of his diplomacy." Roosevelt's "complicated strategy" by the time of Yalta, Dallek contended, was to withhold the atomic secret until the Russians demonstrated a capacity for postwar cooperation, to get Stalin to move slowly in taking over Eastern Europe, to bargain about the Far East, and to bring both the Soviet Union and the United States into a new world organization that could fix up the details later. He was in effect offering Stalin a series of tests. "Had he lived, Roosevelt would probably have moved more quickly than Truman to confront the Russians."[32] The trouble, as Daniel Yergin put it in *Shattered Peace* (1977), was "the considerable gap between Roosevelt's *foreign* foreign policy and his *domestic* foreign policy";[33] and, of course, his failure to live long enough to bring the two together.

Professor Gaddis in his able studies *The United States and the Origins of the Cold War, 1941–1947* (1972) and *Strategies of Containment* (1982)

similarly portrayed Roosevelt as a President seeking within limits imposed by American public opinion to keep the Soviet Union in the
war and thereafter to contain the Soviet Union by integrating it, not
into an international economic market, but into an international political order. "There are grounds for thinking," Gaddis concluded,
"that Roosevelt might not have continued his open-handed approach
once the war had ended: his quiet incorporation of counter-weights
and linkages into his strategy suggests just that possibility. One is left
. . . with the surface impression of casual, even frivolous, superficiality, and yet with the growing realization that darker, more cynical, but
more perceptive instincts lay not far beneath."[34]

The issue was always the balance of power, not the Open Door. The
reason why some Americans favored accommodation and others containment was that they disagreed over the nature of the threat the
Soviet Union posed to the balance of power. Yergin tried to explain
this disagreement by inventing a distinction between what he calls the
"Riga" and the "Yalta" axioms. He supposed that one school of American policy-makers, guided by foreign service officers like George F.
Kennan and Charles E. Bohlen who had studied the Soviet Union
from the Riga listening post in the years before American recognition, saw a revolutionary state committed by Leninist ideology to
world conquest. The Yalta school, on the other hand, saw just another
traditional great power.

Yergin's *Shattered Peace* excited attention for its wide-ranging research, its lucid and lively exposition, its instinct for bureaucratic politics, its eye for personalities as well as for issues and also for the
beyond-the-old-battle tone of its judgments. Reviewers accustomed to
the Cold War debate found *Shattered Peace* hard to deal with. The
traditionalist Herbert Meyer condemned it in *Fortune* as a "dangerously specious" revisionist essay likely to produce "a dangerous
change in the way Americans think about the U.S.-Soviet rivalry,"
while the revisionist Carolyn Eisenberg condemned it in *Diplomatic
History* as a dangerously specious traditionalist attempt to co-opt and
emasculate revisionism by leaving out its essence—the capitalist drive
for world economic hegemony.[35]

Despite many excellences, *Shattered Peace* had visible defects. As
Daniel Harrington later showed, neither Kennan nor Bohlen, the alleged apostles of the Riga outlook, subscribed to the so-called Riga
axioms. Kennan's argument was that ideology was the instrument of
Soviet power, not vice versa, and that the "basic motive" behind Soviet
expansion lay in the desire to guarantee "the internal security of the
regime itself." Bohlen similarly saw ideology as a means, not an end,

"essential for the maintenance of the Communist Party and the Soviet system."[36]

NSC-68 may have embodied the Riga axioms, but both Kennan and Bohlen disagreed with NSC-68. In 1949 James V. Forrestal, Secretary of Defense, asked the National Security Council to prepare the paper that eventually became the basis for NSC-68. The draft called on the United States to "develop a level of military readiness adequate as a basis for immediate military commitments and for rapid mobilization should war prove unavoidable." Kennan rejected the draft because of "its assumption that a war with Russia was necessary"; he preferred the State Department's assumption that some "modus vivendi" was possible. "On seeing the final document," Kennan wrote, "I think it dangerous to give State Department approval to it, and feel that we must make an issue of it in the NSC." Bohlen said, "We must not be stampeded into unwise and hysterical action because of a 'war scare' or other type of crisis deliberately stimulated."[37]

"It is central to my argument," Yergin wrote, "that diplomacy *did* matter." That was the point that Kennan and Bohlen had made to the NSC. But Yergin did not tell what he thinks diplomacy might have done, referring instead to Adam Ulam in *The Rivals* as "one of the few writers to emphasize the possible utility of diplomacy in the postwar years."[38] Surely he misread Ulam, for *The Rivals* argued not that diplomacy could have averted the Cold War but that *tougher* western diplomacy—i.e., fighting the Cold War earlier—might have held the Russians back.[39]

Both Kennan and Bohlen, contrary to Yergin, were alert to opportunities for diplomacy. The reign of the Riga axioms came with John Foster Dulles in the 1950s when Kennan and Bohlen were excluded from influence. Nor do other American policy-makers of the early Cold War—Harriman, Byrnes, Marshall—fit into Yergin's scheme. Truman himself tried in 1946 to promote a coalition between the Nationalists and Communists in China and, after the Communist victory in 1949, moved toward the recognition of the new regime.[40] As for the Soviet Union, Truman said as late as 1948, "I like old Joe," and proposed to send Chief Justice Vinson on a mission to Moscow.

The true disagreement lay between those who saw the Soviet Union as essentially a political threat and those who saw it as essentially a military threat. The military establishment itself—Schumpeter's warrior caste—played a significant role in the debate. The armed services, anxious to retain roles and budgets acquired during the war, sought justifications by uncovering a new enemy.[41] The Department of Defense was established in 1947, and Secretary of Defense Forrestal became the forceful proponent of a hard line toward the Soviet Union. But Truman, despite the revisionist myth of his aggressive policy, kept the military establishment under tight control. He brought national defense spending down from $81.5 billion in 1945 to $13 billion in 1947 and, over military protests, kept it at that level till the Korean War. By 1949 the Army was down to ten active divisions. In the same year he dismissed Forrestal and brought in a more compliant Secretary of Defense. He declined to approve NSC-68 until the North Koreans invaded South Korea. Only with the Korean War did those who saw the Soviet threat as primarily military begin to redefine and intensify the Cold War.

V

Which theory of the Soviet Union was right? Were its aims limited or global? Were its means political or military? The revisionist theme with the most impact on Cold War analysis has been the insistence on looking at the postwar world through Soviet eyes. The revisionists themselves have not seriously pursued this theme, since their own eyes remain firmly fixed on the United States. They issue general statements—"the sources of Russian conduct are the drives to conquer poverty and achieve basic security" (Williams)[42]—but do not dig deeply into Soviet evidence. I do not know of any Soviet specialists who are revisionists.

Still the revisionists have an important point. For the Soviet Union had suffered greater losses in the Second World War than any other nation. After the war its consuming motives might well have been to reconstruct its devastated economic life, to seal off the historic invasion routes from the west, and to prevent any revival of German aggression. It is ironic that Open Door historians, who scornfully reject national security as an independent motive for the United States, should claim it for the Soviet Union. But then, according to the Open Door thesis, imperialism is unique to capitalism, and the Soviet Union is therefore by definition immune to the imperialist taint. Nor did revisionists invent the idea that the Soviet Union had legitimate security interests. Soviet experts in the State Department like Bohlen and Kennan had said this in the 1940s; so, as noted, had Secretary Byrnes. Still early historians of the Cold War did not fully absorb the point, and on this question the revisionist critique has prevailed. Post-revisionist historiography accepts that the Soviet Union acted less out of some master plan for world domination and more for local and defensive reasons than the official west admitted or, probably, understood at the time.

But what in fact did the Soviet leaders think? Of course Soviet archives remain sacrosanct; Soviet leaders do not speak to oral historians; and Soviet contemporary history is for the most part worthless. Consider the Sivachev-Yakovlev *Russia and the United States,* a peculiar entry by the University of Chicago Press in its otherwise estimable series "The United States in the World: Foreign Perspectives."

Sivachev and Yakovlev gave the Open Door historians a benign pat on the head: "the 'revisionists,' somewhat tardily, have agreed with Soviet historians regarding who bears the responsibility for the cold war." But even the revisionists had not gone far enough to satisfy the Soviet historians, who presented a benevolent and infallible Soviet Union, incapable of offense, miscalculation or error, patiently seeking peace against all manner of western provocation. Excerpts convey the flavor:

In spite of all this, the Soviet Union continued efforts directed toward reducing international tension, and sought ways to normalize relations with the United States. . . .

As far as the USSR was concerned, there was no necessity for any reappraisal of values, for the Soviet government continued, as before, to adhere to the principles of peaceful coexistence. . . .

The cold war had not achieved the goals on which those who initiated it in the West had been counting. . . .

The notion of "two superpowers" is alien to Soviet foreign policy in principle; our diplomacy works in the interests of universal peace and international security. . . .

Therefore Moscow has been so serious and tireless in promoting the course of peaceful coexistence, slowing down the arms race, and disarmament.[43]

This is history not just as melodrama but as dime novel melodrama. There are, alas, no revisionists in the Soviet Union.

Since Soviet historians can't or won't do a competent job on Soviet policy, western historians have to do what they can with what evidence they can disinter. We have had a very few revealing glimpses behind Kremlin gates—Khrushchev's memoirs, for example, and Djilas's *Conversations with Stalin.* Joseph Starobin in *American Communism in Crisis, 1943–1957* and Philip J. Jaffe in *The Rise and Fall of American Communism* supplied informed accounts of the view from Twelfth Street CP headquarters. There are several able books on the French and Italian Communist parties. Eugenio Reale's *Avec Jacques Duclos . . . à la réunion constitutive du Kominform* gave an invaluable inside picture of the crucial Cominform meeting in September 1947 in Poland. Soviet memoirs and the Soviet press when carefully decoded, the

writings of defectors, commentary from West European Marxists—
this rather considerable body of secondary evidence, if no substitute
for the Kremlin documents, still provides the basis for reasoned and
reasonable conjecture. As Vojtech Mastny pointed out in *Russia's Road
to the Cold War,* the student of Soviet policies is not notably worse off
than historians of the ancient world who also must form judgments
from fragmentary evidence.

Drawing on German, Czech, Polish, Yugoslavian, Hungarian and
Romanian as well as Russian sources, Mastny sought to work out the
theory of the postwar world that inspired Soviet actions during and
immediately after the Second World War. He dismissed the idea of a
Soviet master plan: "Stalin's goals should be considered as evolving
rather than as a design firmly fixed and single-mindedly pursued."
He was unimpressed too by the notion of Stalin's total control in the
USSR. "Behind the formidable façade of Stalinism there loomed
inefficiency, opportunism, and drift." And he accepted the view of
relative Soviet weakness. "As an art of compensating for the deficiency of power, diplomacy loomed large in the Russian conduct of
the war."

Mastny's Stalin was secure but not all-powerful at home, cautious
and opportunistic abroad, mistrustful of left-wing partisan movements in Europe, ineradicably hostile to the Western allies, determined to defend Soviet security. A more effective diplomat than Roosevelt and Churchill, Stalin "had by the fall of 1944 secured Russia's
supremacy in all the countries he regarded as vital for its security,
and beyond." But in Mastny's view, the ease with which this was accomplished stimulated Stalin to inflate Soviet security requirements.
"His craving for security was limitless."[44]

A key Mastny witness was Maxim Litvinov, Commissar of Foreign
Affairs from 1930 to 1939, spokesman at the League of Nations, ambassador to Washington from 1941 to 1943. As early as October 1944,
Litvinov warned the journalist Edgar Snow that trouble was brewing:
"Diplomacy might have been able to do something to avoid it if we
had made our purposes clear to the British and if we had made clear
the limits of our needs, but now it is too late, suspicions are rife on
both sides." When Snow came again to Moscow in June 1945, Litvinov
asked, "Why did you Americans wait till now to begin opposing us in
the Balkans and Eastern Europe? . . . *You should have done this three
years ago.* Now it's too late and your complaints only arouse suspicion
here" (emphasis added). In November 1945 Harriman asked Litvinov
what could be done to reverse the trend toward confrontation. Litvinov replied bleakly, "Nothing." Asked the same question by Richard

C. Hottelet of CBS in June 1946, Litvinov said, "If the West acceded to the current Soviet demands it would be faced, after a more or less short time, with the next series of demands."* No Soviet diplomat was better known to the west than Litvinov. If this was his informed view of Soviet policy, American policy-makers cannot be blamed for accepting it. Nor can historians easily claim that Litvinov was saying such things to serve the interests of an expansionist capitalism.

Mastny himself endorsed the Litvinov thesis. "Russia's striving for power and influence far in excess of its reasonable security requirements was the primary source of conflict, and the Western failure to resist it early enough an important secondary one." Stalin, he added, "might have acted with more restraint if . . . the Western powers had taken a firm and unequivocal stand early enough."[45] But would earlier western firmness have discouraged or would it have intensified the Soviet determination to grab, as Litvinov put it to Alexander Werth, "all they could while the going was good?"[46] No one can answer this question with any confidence.

Mastny overlooks, moreover, the constraints on western policy. Until Germany was beaten, the American and British governments could not risk demands that might have driven Stalin to make a separate peace with Hitler. Until Japan was beaten, they would have found it impossible to justify a new conflict in Europe. After V-J day, the western governments remained for a season the prisoner of their own wartime propaganda about the noble Soviet ally. Their peoples, desperately weary of war, demanding the swift demobilization of the armed forces, would have required compelling evidence before they could rouse themselves to face a new international crisis. Had their leaders seemed to prejudge Soviet purposes, domestic resistance to a firm policy, considerable enough in any event, would have been overwhelming, and the revisionist case would be far more persuasive today. The experiment in postwar collaboration had to be seen to fail before counteraction was politically acceptable.

The question remains of the primary motives behind Stalin's policy. For the Soviet course may have been dictated less by revolutionary ideology or by traditional *Realpolitik* than by the requirements of a ruling class determined to hold on to its power. This was the explanation generally favored by Kennan and Bohlen. It was also Earl Browder's conclusion. "Stalin needed the Cold War," he told an interviewer in 1973, ". . . to keep up the sharp international tensions by

*Litvinov made similar comments to Alexander Werth and Cyrus Sulzberger. Mastny has assembled the Litvinov dossier in his article "The Cassandra in the Foreign Commissariat," *Foreign Affairs*, January 1976. Revisionists ignore Litvinov's testimony.

which he alone could maintain such a regime in Russia. Stalin had to pick a quarrel with the United States, the leading capitalist country. And I was the victim of it."[47]

The thesis that Soviet policy was determined by the interests of the Soviet ruling class received Marxist elaboration in the long book by Fernando Claudin, *The Communist Movement from Comintern to Cominform.* Claudin joined the Spanish Communist party in the 1930s. Santiago Carrillo purged him in 1965, along with Jorge Semprun, who wrote the screenplays for *La Guerre est finie* and *Z.* Semprun gave his own highly personal account of these matters in *The Autobiography of Frederico Sanchez.* Claudin's book supplied theoretical and historical underpinnings.

In Claudin's view Stalin's dissolution of the Comintern in 1943, far from being a trick to gull the west, or even to expedite victory over Hitler, was "the necessary condition for the division of the world between the Stalinist state and its capitalist allies." Stalin's objective was "a durable compromise with American imperialism which would allow joint control of the world." His foreign policy, after all, "could be no more than the reflection of his domestic policy," and he was "pursuing the aims of the bureaucratic class which had replaced the revolutionary October proletariat in the leadership of the Soviet state." He could not afford a revolutionary policy because he dared "not encourage in other countries the freedom and democracy . . . denied to the workers of the USSR." His goal was to build power on the prostrate body of Lenin's world revolution.

Like the revisionists Claudin saw the American goal as the removal of barriers to the expansion of world capitalism. Unlike them, he did not believe that this goal made the Cold War inevitable.

Roosevelt and his colleagues included in this vision collaboration with the Soviet Union; in their view American industry's contribution to the reconstruction of the USSR would have advantages for both countries and would be reflected in the political education of the Soviet regime. As a result of this beneficial support, "socialism in one country" would become able to fit smoothly into the Roosevelt world.

The Americans, moreover, counted on Stalin to save Western Europe and China from proletarian revolution. Stalin "faithfully" cooperated with that objective. These factors "forced Washington into a policy of conciliation towards Moscow, in spite of the instinctive anti-Communism of Truman and his team."

Why then the Cold War? The answer, Claudin suggested, lay in the obscurity and instability of the power balance. The first upsetting factor was the American monopoly of the atomic bomb. Having gained the bomb, Claudin said, "American imperialism finally turned the corner toward world dominion," not, however, in order to destroy the Soviet Union but in order to facilitate "the policy of 'containment' under the protection of the atomic umbrella." American policy, while pursuing consolidation in its own sphere, was nonetheless "dominated by the need to avoid at all costs a direct armed confrontation with the military power of the Soviet bloc." Stalin responded with a consolidationist policy of his own, expecting that his hard line would "impose on the White House a worldwide arrangement on the basis of an allocation of 'spheres of influence' which would satisfy Soviet interests." But "no compromise was possible as long as the two parties had not reached a realistic, and therefore similar, appraisal of the relation of forces."

According to Claudin the Cold War

was a sort of exploration or sounding carried out to gain a more exact knowledge of the forces and dispositions of the enemy. . . . The two most serious "soundings" carried out during the "cold war," those which gave the world the impression of being on the brink of a major conflict, were the Berlin crisis and the Korean war. In fact, both cases showed the firm determination of the two super-powers to maintain the positions they had won during the Second World War and to make no attempt to modify them by war against each other.

In 1949 the Soviet Union achieved its own bomb, and by 1951–1952 "the two super-powers began to get a clear idea of each other's strength and intentions and of the new balance which had been established in the world." The Cold War thereafter began to give way to "peaceful coexistence." Though Claudin's argument bristled with Marxist trimmings, it turned in essence on the old question of the balance of power. Stalin, Roosevelt and Churchill, he wrote, "had only one true God between them—*raison d'état*." In the end, this was Claudin's true God too, and *Realpolitik* rather than Marxism accounted for the force of his analysis.[48]

VI

Cold War revisionism has been a peculiarly American enterprise. There are few British or French or German revisionists. Writing from American records for an American audience rendered both guilty and cynical about American foreign policy by the Vietnam War, the revisionists were as ethnocentric as the Free World crusaders they opposed. Revisionists and crusaders ended as mirror images of each other. One believed in the capitalist master plan, the other in the Soviet master plan. Both vastly overrated the ability of the United States to control events in other countries. Both reduced the far-flung and multifarious Cold War spectacular to a two-character closet drama: the United States versus the Soviet Union. Both viewpoints had scant relation to the real world. The debate between them was largely an exercise in irrelevance. The judgment of the British diplomatic historian D. C. Watt is not excessive: "American historiography of the Cold War tells us very little of the Cold War, much of American intellectual history in the 1960s and 1970s."[49]

The urgent need for Cold War historiography in the United States is to get off the American base, to add more actors to the drama and to broaden research and analytical perspectives. It is essential, for example, to recognize, as the revisionists decline to do, that Western Europe had its entirely independent reasons to resist the Stalinization of the continent. These were not capitalist reasons but democratic reasons.

Most West European nations after the war had Socialist governments. Even West Germany had a strong Socialist party. Socialists like Attlee and Bevin in Britain, Blum, Ramadier and Moch in France, Spaak in Belgium, Schumacher, Reuter and Brandt in West Germany, could not have cared less about finding outlets for American trade and investment. But they cared passionately about the future of democratic socialism, and they watched with personal, there-but-for-the-grace-of-God concern the extermination of the non-communist left (and soon of the national Communist left) in Eastern Europe. In 1951 Denis Healey of the British Labour party edited *The Curtain Falls*, a volume of reports on the fate of East European Socialists. Aneurin Bevan, leader of the Labour party's left wing, wrote the foreword. "The Communist party," Bevan said, "is the sworn and inveterate enemy of the Socialist and Democratic parties. When it associates with them it does so as a preliminary to destroying them." The revisionist obsession with the imperial drives of American capitalism quite fails to account for the reaction of the European non-communist left to the imperial drives of Stalinism.

Nor were these Socialists bribed or bullied by Washington into anti-Soviet policies. On the contrary: many regarded Washington's response to the Soviet challenge as disquietingly tentative and slow. "We have heard of American 'aggression,'" Sir Herbert Butterfield himself wrote in 1969, "and a new generation often does not know (and does not credit the fact when informed) that Western Europe once wondered whether the United States could ever be awakened to the danger from Russia."[50] British Foreign Office papers recently opened under the thirty-year rule document Butterfield's point.

Far from seeing Truman as an anti-Soviet zealot hustling the world into the Cold War, the Foreign Office saw him until 1947 as an irresolute leader wobbled by the delusion that the United States could serve as honest broker between Britain and Russia. Sir Orme Sargent, soon to be permanent undersecretary, defined American policy six weeks after Truman took over (and after Truman's notorious spat with Molotov) as one of being "tough to both the Soviet Union and Great Britain until both became reasonable and cooperative."[51] In July 1945, after Truman, according to revisionist myth, was well launched on the Cold War, a Foreign Office paper lamented that the United States saw itself as "mediator" between Britain and Russia and that it seemed "very anxious" not to offend the latter.[52]

Byrnes as Secretary of State roused particular mistrust. The Foreign Office called him "the slippery Mr. Byrnes" and compared him to Neville Chamberlain.[53] As late as January 1946 Ernest Bevin, the British Foreign Secretary, still believed that Byrnes's aim was a settlement that "would allow the Americans to withdraw from Europe and in effect leave the British to get on with the Russians as best they could."[54] As for Byrnes, he and Truman had found Bevin's anti-Soviet presentation at Potsdam "so aggressive that both the President and I wondered how we would get along with this new Foreign Minister."[55] Twenty-five years later, the distinguished historian Sir John Wheeler-Bennett in his massive account (with Anthony Nicholls) of the beginnings of the Cold War could still describe Byrnes's policy with evident feeling as "whole-hearted appeasement of Moscow."[56]

The British picture of American policy in the early Truman years could hardly be more different from the revisionist legend of a truculent American administration forcing an anti-Soviet showdown on innocent Europeans. The Foreign Office estimates were based in great part on despatches from the British Embassy in Washington. Six months into Truman's presidency, Ambassador Halifax reported, "To serious observers it seems pitifully obvious that the man at the helm is no longer the master of the ship." At the start of the Iranian crisis of 1945–1946, Halifax complained that the American government was persisting in its "stubborn determination to rationalise Soviet actions whenever possible and thereby to reduce the prevailing fear of the Russians in the hope of realising the American dream of one world." Even after Churchill went to Fulton: "Profound as the uneasiness is about Soviet policies, there is still [in the American government] a strong underlying anxiety if possible to find a way of cooperation with the Russians."[57]

According to the revisionists, the American government invented a phony Soviet threat in order to frighten war-weary Americans into an anti-Soviet crusade. This was hardly the way it seemed to British diplomats in Washington at the time. It was not the American government, Ambassador Inverchapel told London in 1946, but the mass of ordinary people who became angry over Soviet actions and then turned the Truman administration around. "The driving force," a colleague reported, "has come not from the top but from below. Events and public opinion have forced the obviously uncertain and reluctant administration into affording to the world at least some measure of the leadership which the United States ought to be providing."[58]

In April 1946 Christopher Warner, chief of the Russian section of the Foreign Office, was dubious "how far the United States Government would be likely to take part in the general, world-wide anti-Communist campaign." As late as January 1947 the Foreign Office was still dubious. A "stock-taking" memorandum on east-west relations, while noting that the "mediation" phase "is apparently over for the present," continued to see the American commitment to the Cold War as "precarious." The Americans, the paper continued, "are a mercurial people, unduly swayed by sentiment and prejudice rather than by reason or even by consideration of their own long term interests. Their Government is handicapped by an archaic Constitution, sometimes to the point of impotence, and their policy is to an exceptional degree at the mercy both of electoral changes and of violent economic fluctuations, such as might at any moment bring about a neutralisation of their influence in the world."[59]

The Truman Doctrine in March 1947 was momentarily reassuring; the Marshall Plan in June even more so. But even in late 1947 the Foreign Office doubted that Washington would provide anything beyond economic assistance. Bevin thought in December that the United States was far from ready to commit itself to the defense of Western Europe. "Our task was to save Western civilization," Bevin told Georges Bidault, the French Foreign Minister. ". . . America must now face the situation. If we and the French played our part it would not be good enough for the Americans to expect us to take action while they themselves were not ready to take any risk until a much later stage. They had to be persuaded that we were all in this together as allies."[60]

The studied purpose of British policy from 1945 to 1948 was to maneuver what they saw as a reluctant and uncertain United States into a forward role in the Cold War. As one British official condescendingly noted in 1945, Britain "shall have to suffer from American arrogance and suspicious inexperience as the price of their participation in world affairs. We must resist the inclination to annoyance and in the light of our greater experience try to guide them on sound lines without appearing to patronize." Stalin proved a stalwart British ally in this effort. "Russian intransigence is being a real help in the U.S.," another official wrote. ". . . I would not be sorry to see that intransigence last a little longer!"[61] Bevin reminded Bidault at the end of 1947 that "America would never agree to military alliances or treaties. [But] there were ways and means of bringing the American Chiefs of Staff to work with us. One had to build up their confidence and not rush matters." The trick, Bevin said, was to get the United States to do the right thing in Europe "while letting the Americans say and think that it was they who were acting."[62] Attlee himself later remarked that it was not "until the Berlin airlift [in the summer of 1948] that American public opinion wakened up to the facts."[63]

The British documents rather undermine the revisionist theory of an American government hell-bent after the war on making the world safe for American capitalism. In time British persuasion—or rather the persuasion of events—prevailed, and the United States took command of the democratic camp in the Cold War. The British, in the style of a junior partner, soon objected to that too, as the Americans, in their own style, the bit between their teeth, pushed the Cold War to extremes the British did not want to follow. But that is another story.

The European perspective compels revaluation of America's part in the Cold War. British and French reactions support the view that geopolitical and not free enterprise considerations—the balance of power and not the expansion of capitalism—rallied the western democracies. For its part, the Soviet Union had its own interests and apprehensions. The Cold War soon became an intricate, interlocking reciprocal process, involving authentic differences in principle, real and supposed clashes of interest and a wide range of misunderstanding, misperception and demagoguery. Each camp persevered in corroborating the fears of the other. Together they marched in fatal lockstep to the brink of the abyss.

The more one broods about the Cold War, the more irrelevant the assessment of blame seems. The Second World War had left the international order in acute derangement. With the Axis states vanquished, the European allies exhausted, the colonial empires in tumult and dissolution, great gaping holes appeared in the structure of world power. The war had left only two states—America and Soviet Russia—with the political, ideological and military dynamism to flow into these vacuums. The two states were constructed, moreover, on opposite and antagonistic ideas. Neither knew with any precision what the other was up to. Decisions were made in a darkness. "It is very difficult to remember," as Maitland once said, "that events now in the past were once far in the future." No one should be surprised at what ensued. The real surprise would have been if there had been no Cold War.

PART III

NINE

Affirmative Government and the American Economy

G OVERNMENT IS NOT the solution to our problem," Ronald Reagan said in his first inaugural address. "Government is the problem." With these words and with the policies that followed, President Reagan renewed one of the earliest debates in the American republic. When younger and perhaps wiser, Reagan had cast his first four presidential votes for Franklin D. Roosevelt; and it seems ironic that he should have dedicated his own Presidency to a counterrevolution against Roosevelt's New Deal. But then the history of affirmative government in the United States is a tale replete with ironies.

I

The cherished national myth ascribes the economic development of the United States to the operations of unfettered individual enterprise, as if the mighty economy of the twentieth century had sprung by immaculate conception from the loins of Adam Smith. *The Wealth of Nations* and the Declaration of Independence were indeed both products of that *annus mirabilis* 1776—a coincidence that has encouraged the notion that the stars of laissez-faire and of the American republic rose in unison and shone forth jointly upon a fortunate world. Yet, while private initiative has unquestionably been the mainspring of American economic growth, the story is a good deal more complicated. In fact, the economic ideas in the minds of the American revolutionaries were to a large extent precisely those that Smith wrote his great work to refute.

The characteristic economic philosophy in Western Europe in the eighteenth century was mercantilism. Mercantilism was essentially the use of state action by predominantly agricultural countries to transform themselves into commercial and industrial states. The great mercantilist planner was Colbert, under whose direction France took the lead in national economic development. In time, the new business class entrenched by mercantilism began to find mercantilist constraints irksome and, in consequence, mercantilist economics fallacious. It was to Colbert that the exasperated French merchant addressed the famous plea: "Laissez-nous faire."

The American colonies had long been accustomed to government intervention in economic affairs. In the seventeenth century such intervention was essential to survival in a society of limited resources. In the eighteenth century colonial resentment of British mercantilist restrictions led on to the American Revolution; but independence tempted the revolutionaries in part because it promised them the opportunity of establishing a mercantilist regime of their own. Interventionist habits were reinforced by the political philosophy of civic republicanism with its subordination of individual interests to the public good. Republicanism preferred virtue to commerce, commonwealth to wealth, and feared that uncurbed self-interest would bring social decay.

The Wealth of Nations was not published in the United States until 1789. Though read and admired, it did not at once persuade. "In the United States," E. A. J. Johnson, the most careful student of economic policy in the early republic, has written, ". . . it is difficult to find any thoroughgoing, eighteenth-century proponents of *laissez-faire,* and even harder to find much explicit evidence of legislative acceptance of a theory of economic freedom." In his first annual message, Washington recommended a national policy of advancing "agriculture, commerce, and manufactures by all proper means." The early Congresses assumed that the national authority ought to help any interest significant enough to deserve national attention. All sides invoked the "fostering hand of government." Disagreement arose over priorities, not over principles.[1]

Two visions then competed for the economic future. One, associated with Hamilton, saw America as a dynamic capitalist republic, mobilizing law, technology and corporate organization to promote economic development. For the Hamiltonians, the national government was the grand instrument by which to transform a pastoral economy into a booming industrial nation.

Dismissing the "reveries" of Adam Smith, Hamilton invoked the example of "the great Colbert" as showing the way to national power.[2]

He believed more than Colbert in individual acquisition as a motive but had little confidence in self-interest as the organizing principle of society. The notion that the economy could regulate itself Hamilton called a "wild speculative paradox." The "spirit of enterprise," he wrote in the 7th *Federalist,* when "unbridled," leads to "outrages, and these to reprisals and wars." Americans, as his *Report on Manufactures* summed up his view, had "a certain fermentation of mind, a certain activity of speculation and enterprise which if properly directed may be made subservient to useful purposes; but which if left entirely to itself, may be attended with pernicious effects."[3] His great program of the 1790s called on the state to steer wealth to those who would employ it under public guidance to stimulate national productive energies.

The competing vision, associated with Jefferson, saw America as a paradise of small farms, a rural arcadia with every freeholder secure under his own vine and fig tree. This was by no means a static conception. Farmers and planters were units in a widening market. They had a growing interest in the export trade and in the development of western lands. Though Jefferson remained in a general way the champion of the agricultural way of life, he was too astute a statesman, especially when in power, to be doctrinaire in his defense of the agrarian economy. He welcomed commerce; he was fascinated by technology; in time he regarded manufacturing as inevitable. He was never, however, reconciled to banking and stockjobbing. This was his abiding difference with the Hamiltonians.

Not all Jeffersonians were originally disposed to question national authority. Before the framers gathered in Philadelphia, Madison tried to persuade George Washington that the central government must have the power to veto state legislation *"in all cases whatsoever."* Otherwise the states would "harass each other with rival and spiteful measures dictated by mistaken views of interest" and would permit "the aggressions of interested majorities on the rights of minorities and of individuals."[4] Enough states rallied in the convention to beat back Madison's proposal. Subsequently Hamilton's policies as Secretary of the Treasury persuaded the Jeffersonians that capitalists were better placed than agriculturists to dominate the central government and that they would use devices like tariffs and paper money to transfer capital from the agricultural sector to finance and industry.

The Jeffersonians thereafter sought refuge in state and local government. "Were we directed from Washington when to sow, & when to reap, we should soon want bread," Jefferson said, and pronounced *The Wealth of Nations* "the best book extant" on political economy.[5] John Taylor of Caroline, the most assiduous Jeffersonian theorist, dreamed of a "natural" economic order in which the producer (i.e., planter and farmer), undisturbed by the state, could enjoy the full fruits of his labor. That government was best, the Jeffersonians concluded, which governed least.

Yet they readily qualified the pure faith in the name of what Madison, fending off Adam Smith's free trade doctrines, called "national prudence."[6] Even Taylor of Caroline favored government intervention on behalf of agriculture. Jefferson, for all his rhetoric, did little to alter the frame of government he inherited from the Federalists. In his first annual message, after endorsing individual enterprise in principle, he added that government should provide agriculture, industry and trade "protection from casual embarrassments" and invited Congress to speak up when these "pillars of our prosperity . . . should appear to need any aid." In his second term he repeatedly urged (as in his last annual message) that surplus federal revenues be applied to "the improvement of roads, canals, rivers, education, and other great foundations of prosperity and union under the powers which Congress may already possess or such amendment of the Constitution as may be approved by the States."

Albert Gallatin, Jefferson's Secretary of the Treasury, drew up a detailed ten-year plan for the construction of roads and waterways, asking Congress to pledge an annual $2 million of the surplus for this purpose over the next decade. The future of the transportation net, Gallatin emphasized, could not "be left to individual exertion" because of the scarcity of capital and of the extent of territory compared with population; "the General Government alone can remove these obstacles."[7] As the pioneer economic historian G. S. Callender later wrote, "Before any European government had projected a comprehensive system of State canals and roads, President Jefferson had called the attention of Congress to such a policy."[8]

In the states, government intervention was routine. As Johnson portrays the situation after independence: "A weird tangle of state law circumscribed and limited entrepreneurial freedom. A maze of inspection laws governed the quality of goods offered for sale, and sometimes the prices at which they could be sold. Nor does the annual crop of state laws regulating enterprise show any signs of abating in the 1790s; if anything, the legislative harvest increases."[9]

The ease with which the Jeffersonians adopted and extended the Hamiltonian system demonstrated the broad national belief in government intervention. Jeffersonian doubts concerned constitutionality, which they proposed to repair by amendment, and not economic principle. The Founding Fathers, in short, had no doctrinal commitment to the unregulated marketplace. They were not proponents of laissez-faire. Their legacy was rather that blend of public and private initiative known in our own day as the mixed economy.

The disagreement between Hamiltonians and Jeffersonians followed less from conflicts of principle than from differences in constituency. Hamilton represented merchants, bankers and manufacturers; Jefferson, planters and farmers. Each believed in a republic founded on private property, but Hamilton thought private property in danger of subversion from below by debtors, Jefferson from above by bankers. Each accepted the legitimacy of government intervention; but, where Hamilton used the activist state to help the rich and well-born, Jefferson sought to limit the power of the state to harm the agricultural interest. Each expounded a philosophy of government in language that exaggerated practical differences. The competing rationales—the purposeful state versus the uncontrolled market—foretold debates of the future. Meanwhile capitalist expansion roared ahead, fueled by both public and private energies. Ironically Hamilton furnished capitalist expansion with its immediate program, Jefferson with its eventual ideology.

II

The affirmative state emerged in America as an agency of economic development. In 1816 President Madison signed bills chartering the Second Bank of the United States and imposing a protective tariff. The Gallatin program, deferred when the War of 1812 used up the budgetary surplus, was now urged by John C. Calhoun, first in Congress, later as Secretary of War. The General Survey Act of 1824 instructed President Monroe to report on road and canal routes of national significance. The project of national economic expansion, based on internal improvements, tariff protection, the Bank and land legislation, soon acquired a name—the American System. Henry Clay was its most eloquent spokesman, and John Quincy Adams its most far-seeing advocate.

"The great object of the institution of civil government," Adams said in his first message to Congress, "is the improvement of the condition of those who are parties to the social compact, and no government, in whatever form constituted, can accomplish the lawful end of its institution but in proportion as it improves the condition of those over whom it is established." Adams proposed that the national government organize a system of transportation, public works and industrial development, along with a national university and a national observatory. For government to refrain from "promoting the improvement of agriculture, commerce, and manufactures, the cultivation and encouragement of the mechanic and of the elegant arts, the advancement of literature, and the progress of the sciences . . . would be treachery to the most sacred of trusts."

State governments were even more active in promoting economic development, as G. S. Callender demonstrated at the start of the twentieth century. His findings made little dent, however, on the free enterprise myth. After the Second World War, the new interest in Third World development led the economist Carter Goodrich to re-open the question of American economic growth, and the Committee on Research in Economic History sponsored studies of state economic policy. Monographs on Massachusetts, Pennsylvania, Georgia, New York, Virginia, Michigan, Missouri and Ohio have revised historical understanding of the role of government in the early republic.

The transition from an agricultural to an industrial society re-quired a vast expansion of infrastructure—roads, canals, bridges, harbors, railroads. The need for such expansion came in the United States at a time when there was a shortage of private domestic capital and a reluctance to use this capital on risky undertakings. Turnpikes and canals were not always built to connect thriving communities; they were often built to penetrate the wilderness in the hope of cre-ating thriving communities in the uncertain future. "In a new coun-try," said Henry Clay, "the conditions of society may be ripe for public works long before there is, in the hands of individuals, the necessary accumulation of capital to effect them."[10] Foreign capital supplied some of the developmental needs (not to mention the debt American development owed to foreign crafts, technologies, workers, entrepre-neurs and inventors migrating across the Atlantic). But government on all levels—local, state and national—was an indispensable source of capital. Where in Great Britain most canals and all railroads were built by private capital, in the United States, by Goodrich's estimates, government was responsible for 70 percent of the investment in ca-nals and probably 30 percent of the investment in railroads.[11] In the southern states public authorities furnished nearly three quarters of the capital for railroads.[12]

Nor was capital scarcity the only reason for the public role. Con-sider some statements from the 1820s. "Too great a national interest is at stake," said the New York Canal Commissioners in rejecting the idea of private ownership for the Erie Canal. ". . . Such large expend-itures can be more economically made under public authority than by the care and vigilance of any company." "It does not consist with the dignity, the interest, or the convenience of the State," the Ohio Canal Commissioners declared of the state's canals, "that a private company of citizens or foreigners (as may happen) should have the management and control of them. . . . As a public work, the public convenience is the paramount object; and a private company will look only to the best means for increasing their profits."[13] "The important interests of the people," said Governor Levi Lincoln of Massachusetts, "can only be preserved, and the honour and prosperity of the State promoted, by a system of Governmental enterprise."[14]

The Erie Canal was built, owned and operated by the state of New York. It was brilliantly successful as a stimulus to development, and the revenues accumulated in the Canal Fund provided public assistance to a diversity of private undertakings. The state-owned Western & Atlantic Railroad in Georgia similarly opened southern routes between the seaboard and the west. There were other examples of projects directly operated by the states, but more common were systems of mixed enterprise. Here the corporation became the chosen instrument by which the commonwealth guided, promoted and supervised economic growth.

III

Early American corporations were quasi-public agencies, chartered individually by statute. They were granted franchises, bounties, bond guarantees, rights of way, immunities and other exclusive privileges to enable them to serve specified public needs.

In many cases state governments bought shares in corporations and installed their representatives on boards of directors. The state of Pennsylvania owned stocks in over 150 such mixed corporations — banks, turnpike and canal companies, railroads. In Virginia the state government subscribed three fifths of the equity capital in the state's railroad companies, loaned them $4 million by 1861, guaranteed their bonds and oversaw their finances. "Virginia directors dominated the board rooms of a majority of the carriers within her limits," the historian of southern railroads had written. ". . . Railroading was no free enterprise in Virginia in 1861. It was not even private."[15]

In the first forty years of the nineteenth century, while the national government was paying off its debt, the states created a debt of more than $200 million — "a larger debt," wrote Callender, "than the federal government had ever owed, and the first large funded debt created by the government of any country for purely industrial purposes."[16]

Even when the state government was not a partner, corporations were considered public in nature, and legislatures subjected them to detailed regulation. Corporate charters controlled the size and authority of boards and directors, established standards for capital structure and stock ownership and gave the legislature powers of amendment and revocation. "Bank charters specified maximum interest rates," wrote the economic historian Stuart Bruchey, "dividends were controlled by law, and public utilities were subjected to rate regulation."[17] In addition to charter restrictions, a variety of laws regulated subsequent performance—licensing systems, inspection systems, regulation of hours, working conditions and child labor, trackage specifications for railroads, specie-paper ratios for banks and so on. "Far from being limited," Louis Hartz wrote of state policy in Pennsylvania, "the objectives of the state in the economic field were usually so broad that they were beyond its administrative power to achieve."[18]

As striking as the extent of government intervention was the absence of opposition on grounds of economic theory. When interventionist policies were attacked, they were opposed as inexpedient or impractical, not as violations of immutable economic law. Businessmen welcomed government favor. Charters, it is true, contained restrictions as well as privileges, but in practice restrictions were often evaded while privileges were always enjoyed. Abbott Lawrence, the Massachusetts millowner, expressed a general sentiment when he dismissed laissez-faire as "a transcendental philosophy, which is not likely to be adopted by any government on the face of the globe."[19]

The closest approach to laissez-faire dogma came from those radical Jacksonians—"locofocos"—who assailed corporations as monopolies receiving exclusive and therefore anti-democratic privileges. The anti-monopoly movement derived less, however, from the economics of Adam Smith than from the republican philosophy of the Revolution. The banner under which Jacksonians marched against the system of special charters was inscribed not Laissez-nous Faire but Equal Rights. Among Locofoco publicists William Leggett was the most eloquent in opposing the Second Bank of the United States, the paper-money system and corporate monopoly. These evils had arisen, Leggett wrote, because the power of the state was "always" exercised "for the exclusive benefit of wealth. It was never wielded on behalf of the community." Whenever the state interferes, "it will always be found to be in favor of wealth. These immunities are never bestowed on the poor. . . . Thus it will be seen that the sole reliance of the laboring classes . . . is the great principle of *equal rights*." Where laissez-faire zealots denounced trade unions for violating the principle of free competition, Leggett defended unionism as "the great instrument of the rights of the poor."[20]

The radical democrats were hostile to government favoritism, not to government intervention per se. In Massachusetts the historians

Oscar and Mary Handlin found no "tendency to transpose objections against privilege into objections against government regulation. In the United States the people who favored reform were not held back by a fear of the state; the people were the state."[21] In Pennsylvania Louis Hartz found anticharter and state-ownership doctrines fused in "a single politico-economic position—pro-state, anti-corporate. . . . The anti-charter theory was contending for state entrepreneurship on a scale greater than any dared in the subsequent history of the state."[22]

In place of the system of special charters the Locofocos called for general incorporation laws—"rigid and unwelcome rules," one historian has described them, "written by men who wanted to restrict corporate power and growth."[23] "Those who despaired of abolishing the corporation," observed the Handlins, "hoped to render it innocuous by eliminating the last vestige of state favoritism."[24] Businessmen continued for another generation to prefer special charters with special privileges.

Because capitalists regarded public initiative as helpful in raising capital, protecting industry and promoting development, the business community favored interventionist government in the interest of business enterprise. Because the opponents of business rule feared that such intervention was, in the words of John Taylor of Caroline, but "a slow and legal" means "by which the rich plunder the poor,"[25] they favored the negative state. The history of economic policy in the next century was the history of the gradual exchange of these positions.

IV

In the meantime, the national economy forged its own way, and economic change began to undermine the established premises of politics. The United States in the 1830s and 1840s entered the period of takeoff into self-sustaining growth. When the private sector began to generate its own capital, the need for public capital declined. The task now, moreover, was less the provision of infrastructure than the stimulation of production and innovation. Here private enterprise came into its own.

The surge of the private sector increased the number of corporations and soon began to change the nature of the corporate institution. As corporations multiplied, whether ordained by special charter or by general law, the capacity of the state to use them for public ends progressively weakened. A distinction emerged between public and private corporations. The profit-making corporation lost its original character as a public instrumentality and in due course claimed exemption from detailed public regulation—exemption later transformed into immunity by judicial decree. Private corporate law, which had started as a means of subjecting business to public purpose, became a means of vindicating corporate independence.[26] Thus—another irony—the corporation, which came into use in America as the agent of the state, ended as the stronghold of business freedom from the state.

The rise of the private corporation was matched by the decline of governmental enterprise. State and sectional rivalries had prevented the Gallatin-Adams vision of internal improvements from crystallizing in a comprehensive national plan. Then in 1830 Jackson vetoed a bill calling on the national government to buy stock in a company building a local road in Kentucky. In this veto of the Maysville road, Jackson condemned public subscription to the stock of private corporations as "artful expedients to shift upon the Government the losses of unsuccessful private speculation."[27] Van Buren, who wrote the veto message, supposed they were combatting the policy of "private gains to a busy few."[28] The same reasons, in short, that led the busy few to seek public intervention led the Jacksonians to oppose it. Jacksonian opposition, as Carter Goodrich has said, "was based on a desire to keep business out of government . . . rather than a desire to keep government out of business."[29]

The system of public improvement envisaged by Gallatin and Adams was now dead. "With this system in ten years from this day," Adams lamented in 1837, "the surface of the whole Union would have been checkered over with railroads and canals. It may still be done half a century later and with the limping gait of State legislature and private adventure. I would have done it in the administration of the affairs of the nation. . . . I fell and with me fell, I fear never to rise again, the system of internal improvement by means of national energies."[30]

Jackson's strictures on the mixing of public and private money soon affected policy in the states. The Panic of 1837, moreover, damaged state credit and forced a few states to default on interest payments. Some state projects were too ambitious for the rudimentary administrative skills of the day. Some were discredited by waste and graft. A good many lost money. There arose what Goodrich has called "the revulsion against internal improvements."[31] State constitutions began to prohibit loans to private companies. Pressure developed to sell state holdings to private investors. "No government," said a select committee of the Virginia House of Delegates in 1860, "can manage public improvements with the same prudence, foresight and economy that characterizes those of private enterprise."[32]

The availability of private capital, the emergence of the private corporation and the new disrepute of public enterprise were transforming the conditions that had encouraged businessmen to seek government intervention. At the same time, the activist politics of the age of Jackson shocked them into a new mistrust of the state. "A good deal of positive government," wrote John L. O'Sullivan, the editor of the *Democratic Review,* "may be yet wanted to undo the manifold mischiefs of past misgovernment."[33] As Paul K. Conkin, the historian of early American economic thought, observed of Condy Raguet, the Jacksonian economist, "Despite his belief in laissez-faire, Raguet . . . ended up recommending an array of new state regulations to control such ungainly creations as chartered banks."[34] Businessmen were angered by the Jacksonian penchant for economic regulation and for administrative experiment. They were angered by Jackson's aggressive conception of presidential power. They were angered most of all by his aggressive employment of that power, in the words of his veto of the recharter of the Second Bank of the United States, against "the rich and powerful" and on behalf of "the humble members of society—the farmers, mechanics, and laborers."[35]

V

Jackson's economic views were simplistic, but the political philosophy behind them was not. He was contending that the democratic state had to be more powerful than any private concentration of wealth if a free republic were to be preserved. His administration demonstrated that popular government could turn from the servant into at least the rival, if not the master, of business.

Confidence in government was a Jacksonian addition to the democratic creed. "Free government," Jefferson had written in the Kentucky Resolutions of 1798, "is founded in jealousy and not in confidence." But time—and the exercise of power—weakened Jeffersonian mistrust of the state. Where the Jeffersonians supposed that government would inevitably abuse power, Jackson in his Farewell Address relegated such abuse to the category of "extreme cases, which we have no reason to apprehend in a Government where the power is in the hands of a patriotic people."

Negative government had served popular interests so long as the wide distribution of property in a predominantly agricultural society gave each freeholder a sufficiency with which to protect himself. But the rise of industry and the corporation was creating a new role for government as an instrument of the general welfare. Chief Justice Roger B. Taney, whom Jackson appointed to succeed John Marshall, expressed the emerging view when he wrote in the Charles River

Bridge case, "The object and end of all government is to promote the happiness and prosperity of the community . . . and it can never be assumed, that the government intended to diminish its power of accomplishing the end for which it was created."[36]

The changing attitude toward government even affected the supreme prophet of self-reliance. "The state is our neighbors," Emerson wrote in his journal; "our neighbors are the state. It is folly to treat the state as if it were some individual arbitrarily willing this and so. . . . I confess I lose all respect for this tedious denouncing of the state by idlers who rot in indolence, selfishness, & envy in the chimney corner."[37] In his lecture "The Young American" Emerson praised trade for its contribution to the emancipation of man; but trade, he added, "must give way to somewhat broader and better, whose signs are already dawning in the sky." The cry for reform, Emerson thought, stemmed from the feeling that "the true offices of the State, the State had let fall to the ground"; that government had overlooked its "main duties . . . the duty to instruct the ignorant, to supply the poor with work," to mediate "between want and supply." The Young American, by embracing and elevating government, could lead the nation "into a new and more excellent social state than history has recorded."[38]

Laissez-faire, said George Bancroft, the Jacksonian historian, might be a good rule in international trade, but "its abandonment of labor to the unmitigated effects of personal competition can never be accepted as the rule for the dealings of man to man. . . . The good time is coming, when humanity will recognize all members of its family as alike entitled to its care; when the heartless jargon of overproduction in the midst of want will end in a better science of distribution."[39] So the Jacksonian mood departed from the Jeffersonian verities. As the unscrupulous but intelligent Jacksonian Benjamin F. Butler observed of the Jackson administration, "I early had sense enough to see that it conflicted, in a very considerable degree, with the teachings of Jefferson." He drew the logical conclusion. "As to the powers and duties of the government of the United States, I am a Hamiltonian Federalist. As to the rights and privileges of the citizens, I am a Jeffersonian Democrat."[40]

VI

Under Old Hickory's flashing eye, businessmen began to retreat from the Hamiltonian conception of publicly guided private enterprise and to discover belated charm in the Jeffersonian proposition that government was best which governed least.

Laissez-faire liberalism now displaced what remained of mercantilism in the business community and of civic republicanism in the general society. In so doing, it gave new moral status to self-interest. Republicans had regarded self-interest as an incitement to socially ruinous passions; salvation lay in the capacity to transcend private interest for the sake of the commonwealth. Laissez-faire liberals valued self-interest precisely as the means of taming destructive passions. They believed with Montesquieu in the "douceur" of commerce and its tendency to soften and refine the manners of men. They believed with Mandeville that private vices yielded public benefits, with Adam Smith that the economy was best confided to the invisible hand and with Dr. Johnson that there were few ways in which men could be more innocently employed than in getting money. In this new light self-interest appeared not as a threat to the moral order but as its guarantee.[41]

Perceptions were still confused. As George Combe of Edinburgh reported after his American visit in the 1830s, political economy "is very little studied in the United States. As a branch of general education, it is nearly unknown. . . . The Union may be regarded as a vast field for the cultivation of the science of political economy *by experiment.*"[42] Nearly everyone entertained an indiscriminate mixture of economic ideas, drawn from both mercantilist and laissez-faire sources.

The analyst who came nearest in midcentury to ordering this mixture was Henry Charles Carey. Carey, an admirer both of Colbert and of Adam Smith, believed that the elements of the capitalist order—rent, profits and wages—made not for struggle and antagonism but for association and harmony. Initially a free trader, he later decided that Great Britain was propagating the free trade gospel in order to preserve its industrial monopoly and to prevent the rise of industry in other countries. He also decided that Ricardo and the Manchester school, with their iron law of wages and related pessimistic doctrines, were setting class against class and promoting industrial warfare. The protective tariff, Carey soon argued, was the means by which American harmonies could be saved from British corruption. Like Hamilton and Colbert, Carey called for "the application of intelligence to the coordination of the movements of the various members of the societary body."[43] His effort was to reconcile Hamilton and Adam Smith—to provide enough scope for government intervention to vindicate the protective tariff but not enough to hamper capitalist accumulation.

Carey, said Karl Marx, was "the only original economist the North

Americans have." Carey and Marx read and quoted each other, and
Marx devoted attention in *Capital* and elsewhere to disposing of Carey's case for the inherent harmonies of capitalism. Carey succumbed
to this illusion, Marx explained, because he came from a country
where "bourgeois society did not develop on a feudal basis, but has
been itself the starting point" and where the productive forces of the
old world had the huge natural territory of a new world to exploit.
In such propitious circumstances "the contradictions in bourgeois society seem to be merely transitory." Carey's error, Marx said, lay in
"taking the 'undeveloped' conditions of the United States for 'normal
conditions.'" America was simply not yet mature enough economically to have a class struggle. In advocating high tariffs to build manufacturing, Marx added, Carey was trying "to prevent the process of
separation [of capital and labor] by that very system of protection
which accelerates it."[44]

Marx had a point. In Carey's scheme, association was the key to
harmony, and the aim of coordination was to remove obstacles to association; in particular, to set free the corporation, which Carey saw
as the providential agency of economic progress. The autonomous
corporation became the operative center of Carey's economics: anything that strengthened the corporation, from the high tariff to limited liability, was good; anything that weakened it, from trade unions
to factory legislation, was bad. All power to the corporation might, as
Marx predicted, promote class tension rather than class harmony.
Still Carey's liberation of the corporation from the state and his assim-
ilation of the protective tariff to free enterprise smoothed the passage
of the business community from mercantilism to laissez-faire.

The process was now well under way by which the defenders of
corporate enterprise turned to Jeffersonian means to secure Hamiltonian ends, while the opponents of corporate ascendancy were turning to Hamiltonian means to secure Jeffersonian ends. The ironies
reminded Abraham Lincoln of two drunks who "engaged in a fight
with their great-coats on, which fight, after a long and rather harmless contest, ended in each having fought himself *out* of his own coat
and *into* that of the other. If the two leading parties of this day are
really identical with the two in the days of Jefferson and Adams, they
have performed the same feat as the two drunken men."[45]

VII

The victory of laissez-faire came after the Civil War. The war itself
stimulated industrial development both through direct government
demand and through the capital reserves created out of greenbacks

and war profits. At the same time, the war eliminated the main forces opposing corporate domination of the economy: the slaveholding aristocracy of the South, the foundation of whose power was destroyed, and the Jackson–Van Buren "radical democracy" of the North, whose energies, diverted for a generation to the crusade against the slave power, could not now regroup to cope with the new power of business. When the nation returned to the problems that had preoccupied the 1830s, the continuity of reform had been broken.

The result was to enable the business community, entering an epoch of robust economic growth, to make sure that this growth took place on its own terms. Those terms were tariff protection, 'sound' money and a ban on all forms of unsolicited government intervention, from regulation to taxation. This meant a repudiation of Hamiltonian notions about the economic leadership of the state. The corporation and the entrepreneur became the sacrosanct agencies of economic action.

The ideological need now was to move even beyond Henry C. Carey in making America safe for private enterprise. In this venture, publicists drew on elements in the native tradition. Jeffersonian formulations in particular lent themselves to the spreading faith in the virtues of individual self-interest and a self-regulated economy. More formulations came from Britain. The creed of Manchester was reinforced by the gospel of Darwin. Both laissez-faire economics and Darwinian evolution encouraged the conclusion that the survival of the fittest through free competition in the marketplace was necessary to the progress of civilization.

"So far as there can be said to be any theory on the subject in a land which gets on without theories," Bryce wrote in *The American Commonwealth* in 1888, "*laissez aller* is the orthodox and accepted doctrine in the sphere both of Federal and of State legislation."[46] The Supreme Court, Justice Holmes acidly observed, behaved as if the Fourteenth Amendment enacted Herbert Spencer's *Social Statics*.[47] Justices like David Brewer struck down social legislation in the sacred name of laissez-faire—a protean word that, as one historian has commented, "had different overtones for William Leggett, whose advocacy of the doctrine in the age of Jackson attacked class privilege and concentrated corporate power, than it had for David Brewer who applied the doctrine in the age of McKinley to defend class privilege and concentrated corporate power."[48]

These years entrenched the laissez-faire myth of American economic development. As G. S. Callender wrote in 1902, prefacing his own detailed demonstration to the contrary, everyone regarded

America as "the land of private enterprise *par excellence;* the place where 'State interference' has played the smallest part, and individual enterprise has been given the largest scope, in industrial affairs; and it is commonly assumed that this was always so."[49]

The exaltation of laissez-faire into a quasi-official creed was a conjuror's trick. Most of the worshippers at the shrine of undefiled private enterprise found the new cult entirely compatible with government assistance to business. The protective tariff flourished. The courts favored capitalists over trade unions, creditors over debtors, railroads over farmers and consumers. The "era of national subsidy," in Carter Goodrich's phrase, reached its height after the Civil War. The great change from antebellum projects of internal improvement lay in the denial to government of any role in construction or operation. The American version of laissez-faire meant aid from the state without interference by the state.

This interpretation exasperated rigorous laissez-faire advocates. William Graham Sumner argued that the system of tariffs and subsidies created a dangerous precedent. "*Protectionism,*" wrote Sumner, "*is socialism*. . . . If employers may demand that 'the State' shall guarantee them profits, why may not the employees demand that 'the State' shall guarantee them wages? . . . The argument that 'the State' must do something for me because my business does not pay, is a very far-reaching one. If it is good for pig iron and woolens, it is good for all the things to which the socialists apply it."[50]

Logic had no effect. Misery, however, was beginning to make a difference in the increasingly urban and industrial economy. Depression had been a recurrent American phenomenon, always producing appeals for government action. "*Distress,*" wrote Senator Thomas Hart Benton of the first national depression in 1819, was "the universal cry of the people; *relief,* the universal demand thundered at the doors of all legislatures, State and federal."[51] But in an age when most could survive on the produce of their own farms, the cry could be ignored. Political leaders regarded depression as a natural calamity beyond human control. In 1819, even John Quincy Adams, the apostle of the affirmative state, saw "no remedy but time and patience." Conditions, he wrote in his diary, "must work out their own termination. Government can do nothing, at least nothing by any measure yet proposed, but transfer discontents, and propitiate one class of people by disgusting another. . . . The healers and destroyers, Time and Chance, must bring the catastrophe or the cure."[52]

It was more doctrinally consistent for a President of the Jeffersonian school, Martin Van Buren, to invoke Time and Chance when

depression came again in 1837. Van Buren was enough of an interventionist to impose by executive order a ten-hour day for federal
public workers; but, confronted by depression, he told Congress that
"all communities are apt to look to government for too much" and
doubted that "any specific plan . . . interfering with the ordinary operations of foreign and domestic commerce" was constitutional.[53] The
next depression in 1857 found James Buchanan in the White House.
In his usual style Buchanan threw up his hands, declaring that "the
Federal Government can not do much to provide against the recurrence of existing evils."[54]

Depression struck again in 1873. For a moment President Grant
had heretical impulses. "We had somewhat of a struggle," James A.
Garfield wrote, "to keep him from drifting into that foolish notion
that it was necessary to make large appropriations on public works to
give employment to laborers. But the Secretary of the Treasury and
I united our forces in dissuading him from the scheme, insisting that
the true remedy . . . was economy and retrenchment."[55] Depression
lingered on in the countryside through the eighties and convulsed
the economy as a whole once more in 1893. In the face of spreading
unemployment, President Cleveland adhered to the Garfield line,
righteously condemning the "popular disposition to expect from the
operation of the Government especial and direct individual advantages. . . . While the people should patriotically and cheerfully support their Government its functions do not include the support of the
people."[56]

VIII

This was Jeffersonianism with a vengeance. But many Americans
were coming to regard the hallowed dogmas of an agrarian past as
irrelevant, even dangerous, in the commercial and industrial republic. Industrialization had heaped up wealth in great private agglom-
erations. It had created a propertyless and dependent laboring class.
Were workers not entitled to as much protection as the manufacturers of pig iron and woolens?

The giant corporations threatened to put democracy itself at risk.
Henry Adams posed the crucial issue as early as 1870. The Erie Railroad, he wrote, had "proved itself able to override and trample on
law, custom, decency, and every restraint known to society, without
scruple, and as yet without check. The belief is common in America
that the day is at hand when corporations far greater than Erie . . .
will ultimately succeed in directing government itself." Pessimistic as
usual, Adams returned a despairing answer. "Under the American

form of society no authority exists capable of effective resistance. The national government, in order to deal with the corporation, must assume powers refused to it by its fundamental law—and even then is exposed to the chance of forming an absolute government which sooner or later is likely to fall into the hands it is struggling to escape, and thus destroy the limits of its power only in order to make corruption omnipotent."[57]

Limited government, Adams thought, was powerless against the new industrial energies. While congressional reformers rejoiced at carrying a small reduction in the pig iron tariff, they created a new Pacific railway—"an imperishable corporation with its own territory, an empire within a republic, more powerful than a sovereign State, and inconsistent with the purity of Republican institutions or with the safety of any government, whether democratic or autocratic. While one monopoly is attacked, two are created. . . . The people require it, and even if the people were opposed, yet with the prodigious development of corporate and private wealth resistance must be in vain."[58]

Despite Adams's defeatism, resistance to corporate supremacy was under way. People in the Jacksonian tradition began to feel that Jeffersonian antistatism was serving the capitalism it had been designed to restrain. Laissez-faire, once the guarantee of equal opportunity, seemed increasingly the bulwark of inequality and exploitation. The state, which the Jeffersonians had condemned as the source of privilege, seemed increasingly the means of deliverance for the underprivileged. The old Jacksonian constituency finally accepted that Hamiltonian means might now be essential to attain Jeffersonian ends. "We believe," the Populists said in their 1892 platform, "that the powers of government—in other words, of the people—should be expanded . . . to the end that oppression, injustice and poverty shall eventually cease in the land."

Federal legislation—the Interstate Commerce Act in 1887, the Sherman Antitrust Act in 1890—already reflected this acceptance. Nor, despite its Spencerian proclivities, did the Supreme Court greatly object. "Our statute book," Henry Cabot Lodge, the biographer of Alexander Hamilton, told the Senate in 1894, "is filled with provisions which utterly disregard the let-alone theory of government." Lodge added that "it did not at all follow because the meddling tyranny of a personal monarchy was bad that the limited and intelligent intervention of every other kind of government must be bad too."[59]

State governments were even more active in passing regulatory and social legislation. State boards, bureaus and commissions were established to improve standards of work, health and welfare for individuals cast adrift in the industrial society, thereby laying the foundations, as the British historian W. R. Brock has pointed out, for the twentieth-century welfare state.[60] In legislative interference, Bryce noted at the time, Americans were going further than the English Parliament. This was especially true, he added ironically, in the west "which plumes itself on being pre-eminently the land of freedom, enterprise, and self-help." Americans, Bryce concluded, while conceiving themselves as dedicated to laissez-faire in theory and as the most self-reliant of peoples in practice, were carrying "the action of the State into ever-widening fields. Economic theory did not stop them. . . . The government is now their creature, their instrument— why should they fear to use it?"[61]

As corporate power grew and as local authority proved ineffectual in dealing with interstate activity, the inevitable response was increased federal intervention. In the first decade of the twentieth century, the neo-Hamiltonian President Theodore Roosevelt renewed the contention that corporate power posed a threat to democracy itself. "Only the National Government," TR said, could exercise the "needed control" over the industrial order. "This does not represent centralization. It represents merely the acknowledgment of the patent fact that centralization has already come in business. If this irresponsible outside power is to be controlled in the interest of the general public, it can be controlled in only one way—by giving adequate power of control to the one sovereignty capable of exercising such power—the National Government."[62]

In this spirit, TR was the first President to take action against depression. During the banking panic of 1907, the national government provided aid to the banks, enlarged the currency and reduced interest rates. Roosevelt was prepared to go farther. "Every man holds his property," he said in 1910, "subject to the general right of the community to regulate it to whatever degree the public welfare may require it."[63] Progressivism was now firmly set on a Hamiltonian course. As TR's friend Henry L. Stimson put it, instead of regarding the state as a potential tyrant, "as Jefferson did, we now look to executive action to protect the individual citizen against the oppression of this unofficial power of business."[64] Young militants like Walter Lippmann and Charles Beard detected dangerous Jeffersonian proclivities in Woodrow Wilson, but even Wilson said in 1912, "I feel confident that if Jefferson were living in our day he would see what we see. . . . Without the watchful interference, the resolute interference of the government, there can be no fair play between individuals and such powerful institutions as the trusts."[65]

In the meantime, Herbert Croly perfected the exchange of great-coats in that supreme vindication of the interventionist state *The Promise of American Life*. The Jeffersonian illusion, Croly argued, was that "a combination of self-interest and the natural goodness of human nature" would automatically fulfill the promise of American life. But history had shown that the individual pursuing his private purposes was hardly the "inevitable public benefactor" assumed by traditional American interpretations of democracy. The Jeffersonian order was "a system of unrestricted individual aggrandizement and collective irresponsibility." In the new economic order, unless changes were made, the promise of American life, far from being automatically fulfilled, would be automatically stifled. Croly called for a revival of the Hamiltonian policy of making "the central government the effective promoter of a wholesome and many-sided national development." This would require, he said, "active interference with the natural course of American economic and political business and its regulation and guidance in the national direction." Hamilton's failure, Croly added, had been his distrust of democracy, but in Theodore Roosevelt's program, which Croly dubbed the New Nationalism, he saw a movement to "emancipate American democracy from its Jeffersonian bondage" and to "give a democratic meaning and purpose to the Hamiltonian tradition and method."[66]

The case for affirmative government as an instrument of greater democracy thus received elaborate statement before the First World War. War itself appeared to validate the idea. For, with the nation's survival on the line, no one in his senses proposed to rely on laissez-faire and the free market. Government mobilized industry, regulated the production and consumption of food, tried to regulate private investment and took over the railroads, the telegraph and the telephone. Franklin Roosevelt and many who came with him to Washington in 1933 received their baptism in national economic management during the First World War.

IX

But the myth that America was built by unfettered private enterprise endured. The myth both flattered the vanity and served the interests of business leaders. It remained the cornerstone of the business creed and the abiding theme of corporate thought and publicity. The twenties saw a revival of the myth and a reversion to faith in the self-regulating economy.

Calvin Coolidge expressed the faith in its fundamentalist form. The more sophisticated Herbert Hoover had an ardor for economic coordination through private trade associations that recalled Henry

Charles Carey on the harmony of interests. But the free market soon led the nation into the worst of all American depressions, and arguments about the role of government burst out once more. With unemployment rising toward a quarter of the labor force, Hoover rejected measures of public intervention on behalf of those who sought work and could not find it. Bankers qualified for federal largesse, but not the unemployed. "The sole function of government," Hoover said in the fall of 1931, "is to bring about a condition of affairs favorable to the beneficial development of private enterprise."[67]

That same year Franklin Roosevelt as governor of New York advanced an opposing view: "I assert," he told the New York legislature, "that modern society, acting through its Government, owes the definite obligation to prevent the starvation or the dire want of any of its fellow men and women who try to maintain themselves but cannot." Laissez-faire in the face of human suffering, he said the next year, "requires not only greater stoicism, but greater faith in immutable economic law and less faith in the ability of man to control what he has created than I, for one, have."[68]

As against the idea of the self-regulating economy Roosevelt posed the idea of the "concert of interests." "I am not speaking of an economic life completely planned and regimented," he explained in 1932. "I am speaking of the necessity, however, in those imperative interferences with the economic life of the Nation that there be a real community of interest, not only among the sections of this great country, but among its economic units." He emphasized that the public interest must predominate. "To do otherwise is to go from group to group in the country, promising temporary and oftentimes inexpedient things. . . . Each unit of it must think of itself as a part of a greater whole; one piece in a large design."[69]

The New Deal was a return to the early traditions of blending public and private purpose in what George Combe had called "the cultivation of the science of political economy *by experiment.*" By a concert of interests Roosevelt meant government collaboration with industry and agriculture to arrest deflation and to restore employment and income. The centerpieces of the First New Deal—the National Industrial Recovery Act and the Agricultural Adjustment Act—were the first peacetime experiments in national economic planning since the abortive American System a century earlier. NRA tried to regulate too much and disappeared, unlamented, in a couple of years. AAA turned out to be considerably more successful.

The free market had left American agriculture a periodic disaster area. Productivity had grown at less than 1 percent a year in the first three decades of the twentieth century. The boom of the 1920s had skipped the farmers. Life on the countryside was hazardous and grim. With the New Deal and after, however, no sector of the economy received more systematic federal attention than agriculture; none more subsidy for research and development, more technical assistance, more public investment in education, in electrification and in infrastructure, more price stabilization, more export promotion, more credit and mortgage relief. Under public ministration, agricultural productivity increased 5 percent annually—more than three times as fast as productivity among non-farm businesses. In 1930 25 percent of the population lived on more than 6 million farms. By the 1980s farmers were 3 percent of the population living on 2.4 million farms, and the farmer of 1985 was thirteen times more productive than the farmer of 1930. As federal programs expanded, they involved excessive outlays, excessive rewards to big producers and excessive surpluses; but these were remediable faults. The trouble that hit farmers in the 1980s resulted mainly from the loss of foreign markets because of the overvalued dollar and of subsidized foreign competition—trouble compounded by debt imprudently incurred during the export boom of the 1970s. But, measured by gains in efficiency and productivity, government intervention in agriculture had been a dazzling success.

Nor did Roosevelt regard affirmative government simply as a temporary expedient in the face of emergency. In 1944 he set forth his agenda for the future in what he called an Economic Bill of Rights—the right to a job, the right to wages that assure food and clothing and recreation, the rights to a home, medical care, education, the right to protection against the economic distress of unemployment, sickness and old age. These were rights to be secured through public action. "The liberal party," FDR had written, "is a party which believes that, as new conditions and problems arise beyond the power of men and women to meet as individuals, it becomes the duty of the Government itself to find new remedies with which to meet them. The liberal party insists that the Government has the definite duty to meet new social problems with new social controls—to insure to the average person the right to his own economic and political life, liberty, and the pursuit of happiness." The conservative party, Roosevelt added, believes that "individual initiative and private philanthropy can take care of all situations."[70]

Truman, Kennedy and Johnson after the war shared Roosevelt's faith in "the ability of man to control what he has created." Rejecting the idea of the national government as "an intruder, an adversary," Kennedy in 1963 called it "the people of fifty states joining in a national effort" and sought to show in detail how much worse off the

American people would be "without the National Government."[71] But the popular mood changed, as the popular mood invariably does. Another Democratic President proclaimed in 1978: "Government cannot solve our problems. It can't set our goals. It cannot define our vision. Government cannot eliminate poverty, or provide a bountiful economy, or reduce inflation or save our cities."[72] These words, not likely to have been uttered by Franklin Roosevelt or by Truman, Kennedy or Johnson, expressed Jimmy Carter's eccentric effort to carry the Democratic party back to Grover Cleveland.

President Reagan thereafter devoted himself to the easier task of carrying the Republican party back to Calvin Coolidge. "Government is not the solution to our problem. Government is the problem"— and, once government is 'off our backs,' our problems will solve themselves. By 1982, the year of FDR's centennial, a national administration, unfurling the old standard of laissez-faire, had dedicated itself to denouncing Roosevelt's faith and dismembering his works.

The Reagan attack on affirmative government was the sharpest and shrewdest mounted in the twentieth century. Like his conservative predecessors, Reagan aimed to shrink the role of government. Unlike the others, he discovered a way to do it. His innovation was to use tax reduction and defense spending to create a vast budgetary deficit and then to use the deficit as a pretext for a permanent reduction in the functions of the national government. To this he added the gospel of 'privatization' in the sense employed by economists, not sociologists— the auctioning off to the highest private bidder of government agencies and assets; the policy, as defined by Harold Macmillan, of selling the family silver. (The American Civil Liberties Union at once put in a bid for the Department of Justice.)

And so the debate, as old as American history, continues. The alternation between affirmative and negative government corresponds to the alternation between the private-interest and public-purpose phases of the political cycle. The irony is that private interest invoked affirmative government in the early republic—and that the transformations since the days of Jefferson have led public purpose to invoke affirmative government in the twentieth century. The Jeffersonian constituency in the end rejected the Jeffersonian creed, as the Hamiltonian constituency rejected the Hamiltonian creed.

X

It is now necessary to extract from the historical recital the general factors responsible both for affirmative government and for the recurrent revolt against it.

The Jeffersonian preference for negative government was based on the assumption that the national authority was too remote from the people and that this very remoteness facilitated its capture by self-seeking business interests. The roots of free government, it was held, were in the community. Decentralization and localism were the safe-guards of popular democracy.

Such propositions were plausible enough in a society of agricultural freeholders. But, as the economy diversified and classes solidified, localism played a different role. It turned into the means by which the strongest local interests, whether planters, ranchers, merchants, bankers, industrialists, consolidated private power and escaped public control. In time it appeared an illusion to say that, because local government was closest to the people, it was therefore most responsive to the people. Local government became the government of the locally powerful. The way the locally powerless found to vindicate their human and constitutional rights was through appeal to the national authority.

Historically it has not been local government that has served as the protector of the powerless in the United States; it has been the national government. As Madison had predicted to George Washington, national authority was essential to counter the aggressions of local majorities on the rights of minorities and individuals. The national government has affirmed the Bill of Rights against local vigilantism and has preserved natural resources against local greed. It has civilized industry, secured the rights of labor organization, improved income for the farmer and provided a decent living for the old. Above all, the national government has vindicated racial justice against local bigotry. Had the state rights creed prevailed, there would still be slavery in the United States.

Only national policies, Americans decided in the twentieth century, could be relied on to humanize the industrial order. Voluntarism— leaving things to individual choice—helped the unscrupulous at the expense of the responsible. Communities enforcing decencies of corporate behavior were penalized. Without national standards, as Madison foresaw, states harassed each other with spiteful measures dictated by mistaken views of interest. They engaged in a debasing competition to attract business by promising lower labor costs through poor wages, worse working conditions and no unions. When each state pursued "a system of commercial policy peculiar to itself," the 7th *Federalist* predicted long ago, the result would be to set state against state and rend the fabric of the union.

So the first reason for the growth of affirmative government was the national determination to assure wider humanity and opportunity in a complex, competitive and, on occasion, callous society. The second reason was the point made so effectively by Jackson and the Roosevelts: that democracy would not endure if private concentrations of wealth were permitted to become more powerful than the democratic state. Ultimate power has to reside somewhere in a democratic polity. If that power is not exerted by the public government, then national policy is seized by self-serving private interests. Government off the back of business means business on the back of government. The attack on federal authority is conducted in the name of state and local rights but the beneficiary is corporate power. As Theodore Roosevelt said, "The effective fight against adequate Government control and supervision of individual, and especially of corporate, wealth engaged in interstate business is chiefly done under cover; and especially under the cover of an appeal to State's rights."[73]

The third reason is that affirmative government has been deemed necessary to deal with the chronic difficulties of a free economic order. Boom and bust, inflation and depression, are national problems. They are not amenable to local remedies. Before the New Deal, the free market produced depressions in the United States about every twenty years: 1819, 1837, 1857, 1873, 1893, 1907, 1929. The Great Depression, with the watching specters of communism and fascism abroad, gave the American democracy such a scare that policymakers resolved to ensure against future collapse. The New Deal equipped the economy with built-in stabilizers in the determination to make it depression-proof. The effort was relatively successful — as demonstrated by the fact that, for the first time in its history, the nation has gone for more than forty years without a major depression. The recession of 1982–1983, the worst since the 1930s, was contained by the stabilizers affirmative government had installed in the economy.

Making the economy depression-proof also made it inflation-prone; for putting the economy through the wringer had been the traditional means of squeezing inflation out of the system. As depression had been the inherent vulnerability of the pre–New Deal economy, inflation became the inherent vulnerability of the post–New Deal economy. The free market was no more successful in avoiding inflation than it had once been in avoiding depression. In the 1970s it produced the most sustained peacetime inflation in American history — an inflation slowed only by recession, thereby placing the brunt of the war against inflation on the poor and unemployed, those least able to bear it. If there are self-correcting mechanisms in the market, they exact severe economic, social and political costs.

The question of political costs leads to the fourth reason for the growth of affirmative government: the desire to protect democracy against revolution. Marx predicted that the capitalist system would be destroyed by its own contradictions. Capitalism has not triumphed over the dismal prophecy by fidelity to laissez-faire and *sauve qui peut*. It has survived because it has been obliged to heed the mordant question Joseph Chamberlain posed in England in 1885: "What ransom will property pay for the security it enjoys?" It has survived because, however grudgingly, it has followed the counsel of George Bancroft and conceded that all members of its family are alike entitled to its care. It has survived because democracy has summoned government to humanize the industrial order, to mitigate the impact of unrestrained competition, to combine individual opportunity with social responsibility. Capitalism has survived because of the long campaign, mounted by social liberalism in the teeth of capitalist resistance, to reduce the suffering, and thereby the resentment and revolutionary passions, of those to whom accidents of birth or fortune deny an equal chance in life.

What Marx failed to foresee was precisely the ability of the democratic state to nurture this sense of social responsibility. Those who would now have government abandon social responsibility in the name of unbridled individualism are doing Marx's work for him—and, it may be, more effectively than the wretched host of Communist parties has done. The policy in the 1980s of cutting taxes for the rich and social programs for the poor increased the number of poor people in America by more than six million. After five years of Reagan, more than one out of every five Americans under the age of eighteen were living in poverty. "We have become the first society in history," Senator Moynihan reminds us, "in which children are the poorest group in the population."[74] One result was the revival of political divisions along class and income lines in magnitudes unknown in the United States since the Great Depression.[75]

The Reagan policies brought real suffering to people living on the edge of subsistence. There may be an argument for purification through suffering. There is something distasteful, however, when one class calls for purification through the suffering of another class. Social responsibility is indispensable to the preservation of a free political order. As Orestes A. Brownson, the Jacksonian radical turned Catholic conservative, wrote more than a century ago in *The American Republic*, "The men of wealth, the business men, manufacturers and merchants, bankers and brokers, are the men who exert the worst influence on government in every country. . . . They act on the beautiful maxim, 'Let the government take care of the rich, and the rich will take care of the poor,' instead of the far safer maxim, 'Let government take care of the weak, the strong can take care of themselves.'"[76]

Social conscience has been the salvation of free society; and the final reason for affirmative government is that it preserves the moral basis of social order. Nothing worried Tocqueville more than the debasing consequences when social order relied on the principle of self-interest single-mindedly pursued. He counted on religion to supply the means of constraint. Adam Smith too had assumed that self-interest would operate in a moral context; *The Wealth of Nations* rested on *The Theory of Moral Sentiments*. But, with the fading of religion and the erection of self-interest as a supreme principle, the market system began to erode its own moral foundations. As Fred Hirsch has argued in our own time, the cult of self-interest, by discrediting longer and larger views, has drained the market system of its supporting morality.[77] Tocqueville had written presciently long before, "Governments must apply themselves to restore to men that love of the future with which religion and the state of society no longer inspire them."[78]

XI

If the citizenry has steadily approved a larger role for government and if affirmative government has on balance served the republic well, why the periodic revulsion against it?

The underlying cause is that elemental human experience in which enthusiasm gives way to fatigue and disenchantment—the experience that characterizes the ebb and flow of the political cycle. There are more specific reasons in the case of affirmative government. The national government, like all tools, is liable to misuse and to abuse. Centralization is not a sovereign remedy. The fewer responsibilities loaded on the national authority, the better it will be able to discharge those it cannot escape. The more responsibilities that can be discharged by the market or by local or voluntary initiative, the better. The national government should intervene only when local and private efforts manifestly fail to promote the general welfare. Sometimes government intervenes too much. Its regulations become pointlessly intrusive. Its programs fail. After a time exasperations accumulate and produce indictments.

The early 1980s were a time of indictment. Government intervention, it was said, abridges individual scope and freedom. It destroys self-reliance and stifles enterprise. It is inefficient, wasteful and corrupt. It erects an arbitrary and obnoxious bureaucracy. It creates worse problems than those it tries to solve. Overload leads on to ungovernability. The state is, beyond police functions, a burden and a menace. Such thoughts formed the background of Reaganism. And the Reagan counterrevolution may well turn out to be a bracing time for the American government, usefully purging the national system of assorted encrustations, excesses and vested interests.

However, an emetic is not necessarily a cure. And it is important to keep the problem in proportion. The national government, it is often said, is a behemoth, swallowing up the money, rights and liberties of the people. It is true that the federal debt is staggering. But it is also true that the greatest proportion of this debt arises from payments for war—past, present and future.

Nor for that matter has the federal establishment been growing so implacably as many Americans seem to believe. The number of civilian federal workers has not even kept pace with population growth. In 1949, the federal civilian establishment consisted of 2.1 million people. Thirty-five years later, while the country had grown by 90 million, the federal force had grown only by 800,000. Some 13.9 out of every 1000 Americans worked for the federal government in 1949; 12.3 in 1984. In short, the percentage of the population working for the federal government has actually declined over the last generation. Moreover, more than a third of the federal civilian work force—over a million of them—were in national defense, and another 660,000 delivered the mail. Together, defense and the postal service accounted in 1984 for 60 percent of federal employment.

Or take even the federal budget. In 1954 it represented 19.4 percent of the gross national product; thirty years later it represented 22.9 percent—an increase but hardly the hemorrhage of federal spending we have heard so much about. As for taxes, federal budget receipts amounted to a little more than 18 percent of GNP both in 1960 and in 1984. These spending and taxing ratios are lower in relation to GNP than those in the democratic states of Western Europe.

Why then the widespread idea about the remorseless growth of government? It is partly that in the 1960s the national government assumed new and intrusive functions: affirmative action in civil rights; environmental protection; safety and health in the workplace; community organization; legal aid to the poor. Moreover, this enlargement of the federal regulatory role was accompanied by marked growth in the size of government on all levels. The spectacular expansion, however, took place in state and local government. While the federal force grew by 27 percent in the thirty years after 1950, the state and local government force grew by 212 percent. In 1950 twice as many people worked for state and local as for federal government; thirty years later, it was four times as many. In 1960 federal purchases of goods and services exceeded those of state and local governments combined; in 1980, state and local government purchases had become twice as great.

President Reagan's New Federalism, along with the national fiscal paralysis produced by his budget deficits, has caused still greater acceleration in the growth of state and local bureaucracies. State governments have risen manfully to the challenge. But, even with recent notable improvement in state administrative skills, it is far from clear and more incorruptible than the federal government. It remains as generally true today as it was when Tocqueville visited America in 1832 that, as he then wrote, "the business of the Union is incomparably better conducted than that of any individual state."* As for bureaucracy, duplication and waste, will there be more or less of it if a single federal agency is replaced by fifty separate state agencies?

Even if the size of the federal government has not increased over the last generation, the federal presence has certainly expanded. This expansion is felt to have stifled economic growth by imposing burdensome regulations and taxes on private enterprise. Statistics show, however, that the post–New Deal economy has been astonishingly healthy and productive despite regulations and taxes, indeed that the gross domestic product actually grew at its highest rate since 1945 in the 1960s—the decade in which the alleged burdens were most aggressively enlarged. The 4.2 percent real growth rate in the affirmative-government sixties was more than twice the less than 2 percent in the first six years of the negative-government 1980s.

It is further charged that affirmative government has malign moral consequences. Public solicitude, it is said, corrupts the poor, depriving them of that economic insecurity the well-off hold to be the essential stimulus to achievement. Security, in this view, saps initiative and self-reliance and promotes dependency. "In order to succeed," George Gilder, the right-wing publicist, has written, "the poor need most of all the spur of their poverty."[79] Yet the argument that economic security saps initiative is one the well-off apply to the poor rather more than to themselves. If the rich really believed in the salubrious effects of economic insecurity, they would favor a 100 percent inheritance tax so that their own children would not be denied this great moral benefit. Instead, the Reagan tax law cut federal inheritance taxes in half. By the Reaganite creed, the poor need the spur

---

*Tocqueville continued: "The conduct of the Federal government is more fair and temperate than that of the states; it has more prudence and discretion, its projects are more durable and more skillfully combined, its measures are executed with more vigor and consistence." *Democracy in America,* I, ch. viii.

of poverty in order to succeed, and the rich the spur of wealth.

When the rich do not oppose affirmative government as a threat to the morals of the poor, then they oppose it as a menace to the liberties of the people, rushing the republic down the road to serfdom. But the record shows that the growth of national authority, far from diminishing the individual, has given a majority of Americans more personal dignity and liberty than they ever had before. The individual freedoms destroyed by the increase in national authority have been in the main the freedom to deny black Americans their elementary rights as citizens, the freedom to work little children in mills and immigrants in sweatshops, the freedom to pay starvation wages and enforce barbarous working hours and permit squalid working conditions, the freedom to deceive in the sale of goods and securities, the freedom to loot national resources and pollute the environment—all freedoms that, one supposes, a civilized country can readily do without.

Oddly enough—another irony in our story—the agencies of big government that genuinely threaten individual liberty, like the FBI and the CIA, are customarily applauded by the very people who most zealously denounce affirmative policies on behalf of the powerless and the dispossessed. As in the case of the national debt, it is not the welfare state but the warfare state that has produced the arrogant bureaucracies and victimized citizenry so bewailed by enemies of social programs. Moreover, the conspicuous popular pressures against individual liberty—censorship, book banning, loyalty oaths, control of sexual choices—come from the right. Where liberalism wants to regulate corporations and liberate individuals, conservatism, it would appear, wants to liberate corporations and regulate individuals.

History hardly validates the claim that social programs set a nation on the road to totalitarianism. Forty years ago Thurman Arnold scoffed at "the absurd idea that dictatorships are the result of a long series of small seizures of power on the part of the central government." The exact opposite, he pointed out, was true: "every dictatorship which we know flowed into power like air into a vacuum because the central government, in the face of a real difficulty, declined to exercise authority."[80] Or, as Franklin Roosevelt observed, "History proves that dictatorships do not grow out of strong and successful governments, but out of weak and helpless ones."[81]

XII

The rhythm of the political cycle predicts the replacement in due course of private interest by public purpose as the pervading national orientation. Many doubt that such problems as the decay of infra-structure, the decline of heavy industry, the crisis of the cities, the growth of the underclass, a generation of young people reared in poverty, unprecedented trade deficits, the flight of jobs to the Third World, can be safely confided to a deregulated marketplace domi-nated by great corporations. If the unfettered market is structurally incapable of solving such problems, affirmative government becomes a functional necessity in the years ahead.

Nor is popular resistance to affirmative government as profound as conservatives think. It is true that when pollsters ask large, spacious questions—Do you think government has become too much involved in your lives? Do you think government should stop regulating busi-ness?—a sizable majority says yes. But when asked specific ques-tions—Do you favor social security? unemployment compensation? Medicare? health and safety standards in factories? environmental protection? government guarantee of jobs for everyone seeking em-ployment? price and wage controls when inflation threatens?—a siz-able majority approves the intervention of the state.

All this expresses a disjunction in the American mind. Twenty years ago the public opinion specialists Lloyd A. Free and Hadley Cantril drew a distinction between the ideological and operational spectrums in the realm of political belief. The ideological spectrum referred to abstract ideas people hold about government; the operational spec-trum to their attitudes toward concrete programs affecting daily lives. Free and Cantril reported in 1967 that, while 16 percent came out as liberals on the ideological spectrum, 65 percent came out as liberals on the operational spectrum—a discrepancy "so marked as to be al-most schizoid."[82] Later polls do not display Americans as measurably less schizoid on the subject of government today.

But, when the national mood begins to change, will affirmative gov-ernment be prepared to meet the challenge? Contemporary liberal-ism, I read, is devoid of new ideas. It presents no coherent alterna-tive. It is in a state of political demoralization and intellectual bank-ruptcy.

"Once the New Deal reforms had become so much a part of the landscape that even the Republicans would be hard put to dislodge them," a commentator observed after the Republican landslide, "it was increasingly difficult to conceive of them as live political issues. Yet the liberal leaders realized this all too rarely and consequently expended their energy summoning the American people to ancient crusades." The Democratic party, this commentator continued, "can-not hope to win again until it solves . . . the problem of the younger voter," and it cannot do this merely "by reaffirming the programs or reiterating the issues which were vital in the 1930s." It is hardly surprising that young voters went Republican. They "turned to the party which held out glittering possibilities of tax reduction and the abolition of government controls; new wealth and new business opportunities."[83] Actually I am quoting from a piece I wrote two months after the election of 1952—another illustration of the cyclical effect in American politics—and I am therefore not unsympathetic to the call for 'rethinking' and for 'new ideas' after the election of 1980.

"Over the past decade," Mayor Edward Koch of New York City told the Democratic National Strategy Council in 1981, "the national Democratic party has lost the sense of where it came from, what its purpose should be and what the reality facing America is all about."[84] This thought was uttered in Reagan's first year. The moment evidently impended for a new liberal revelation. Rethinkers rapidly appeared, carrying a banner with a strange device: neo-liberalism. Brooding over Reagan's success, they concluded that he knew a secret they did not know. The Reagan secret, they decided, was that Americans were fed up with government, with bureaucracy, with regulation, with taxing and spending for churlish and ungrateful minorities; fed up with those who derided the ancient verities—business, family, the military, patriotism, religion; fed up with babying the Russians and lagging in the arms race. The time had come for new ideas. "We no longer automatically favor unions and big government or oppose the military and big business," Charles Peters of the *Washington Monthly* proclaimed in his Neo-Liberal Manifesto. ". . . Our hero is the risk-taking entrepreneur."[85]

Where liberals saw government as, historically and potentially, an indispensable instrument of the general welfare, neo-liberals saw government as a mélange of bureaucratic fiefs wasting the people's money and shackling the heroic entrepreneur. The New Deal impulse had gone sour, neo-liberals argued, because its ultimate effect was to legitimize group demands on government. "Interest-group liberalism" surrendered control over public policy to organized private constituencies, defined the public interest as the total of group claims and left an economy strangled by ever-increasing group entitlements.

There is some justice in this bill; also some confusion. Consider, for example, the call for new ideas. New ideas are rarities anywhere—above all in politics, where ideas have to be reduced to a low order of familiarity before they can hope for mass acceptance. Reaganism itself consisted of a systematic resurrection of very old ideas. Even the New Deal, the classic American example of new ideas in public policy, combined social insurance ideas derived from pre–First World War Britain and Germany, national planning ideas derived from Wilson's War Mobilization Board of 1917–1918 and agricultural, public power and conservation ideas worked out by dissenters from the orthodoxy of the 1920s. The compensatory fiscal policy of the Second New Deal was an authentic new idea in the 1930s, but it stood almost alone in novelty.

Neo-liberalism made useful points in its critique of vested interests, of bureaucratic follies, of clamant constituencies, of the no-growth economic philosophy, of the mandate millstone, of credentialism. None of these points, however, was at odds with the older liberalism. The New Deal, as conceived by Franklin Roosevelt, stood precisely for the supremacy of the general welfare—the "concert of interests"—over sectional and factional interests. And no 'traditional' liberal believes that the problems of the 1980s and 1990s will yield to the remedies of the 1930s or even less to the obsessions of the 1960s. While the spirit of FDR remains a resource, the New Deal remedies were designed for a different age.

Moreover, real difficulties have arisen in the entitlement society. There is simply not enough money around to guarantee everybody a rich, full life from womb to tomb. Even Keynesians admit apprehension about ever-escalating government deficits. But precisely because of their historic concern for the weak, Democrats are in a better political position than Republicans to deal with entitlements—just as Republicans, the professionally anti-communist party, were in a better political position to embrace Red China. A party devoted to social programs can cap them more persuasively than a party owned by the rich and the Pentagon. Against interest-group liberalism, Democrats must affirm, in the spirit of FDR, that the public interest is something greater than an aggregation of private claims. People will accept painful policies so long as they perceive them to be fair.

Nor, it must be added, does the older liberalism reject the entrepreneur and the market. It has no wish to move to a command economy. Many socialists and even a few Communists have come to recognize the immense advantages of the price system. But liberals do not see the contemporary market as the infinitely sensitive, frictionless, impartial, self-equilibrating mechanism imagined by conservatives. In the liberal view, market power reflects the distribution of power within society, and industrial concentration has long since filled the market with inequities and rigidities. Businessmen dislike competition and spend much of their time trying to escape it. Trade unions and social legislation are responsible for additional rigidities.

In vital sectors prices are set by administrative decision, not by the law of supply and demand. Realistic analysis of market power leaves liberals skeptical of the idea of a neutral, self-regulating economy.

In short, the older liberalism does not believe that the distinctive problems of the years ahead will solve themselves; or that they will be solved by the policy of all power to the risk-taking entrepreneurs. The liberal believes that the mitigation of these problems will require a renewal of affirmative government to redress the market's distortions and compensate for its failures—but affirmative government chastened and reformed, one must hope, by stringent review of the excesses and errors of the last half century.

Although neo-liberal rhetoric disparages government, neo-liberal practice can discover no alternative. Thus Mayor Koch in his 1981 speech, after lamenting that the Democrats had become "the party of government for government's sake," added without break of stride, once he got down to particulars: "The federal government has an obligation to provide shelter. . . . Washington has an obligation to help local governments rebuild their deteriorating physical plants. . . . The federal government has an obligation to insure employment. . . . Washington cannot abandon assistance to mass transit" and so on, for seven claims on affirmative government. "The national government," said Gary Hart, the neo-liberal favorite in the 1984 Democratic primaries, "must serve as the ultimate guarantor of social justice and equal opportunity."[86]

Or take the canonical document itself, Peters's Neo-Liberal Manifesto. After explaining the obsolescence of New Deal liberalism and the need for bold new ideas, Peters wrote—I am not kidding—"Consider my own latest cause: Bring back the W.P.A.—bring it back to rebuild the nation's infrastructure, to give people jobs, to give the poor money to spend." On this point Peters is right: the principle of government as the employer of last resort is one aspect of the New Deal well worth revival. For the New Deal did not believe in welfare (or 'relief,' as it was then called) as a solution. It believed in jobs and, when necessary, in public employment. The Democratic party would do well to dispel the current impression that it is the party of welfare and to recover its old identity as the party of jobs.

Under examination, neo-liberalism comes out less as a fundamental reformulation than as a ginger exercise. If neo-liberals accept, as they do in practice, the need for affirmative government, and if liberals accept, as they do, the need to revaluate programs and institutions in the light of half a century's experience, this factitious division in the liberal community can be readily overcome.

The Democratic party will doubtless remain programmatically incoherent through Reagan's second term. This confusion will not necessarily foretell the future. The notion that the opposition party is morally obliged to present a coherent alternative is against the genius of American politics. Major parties have never been disciplined and programmatic. The American political style is not close-order drill but guerrilla warfare. In 1931–1932, confronted by the worst economic collapse in American history, Democrats seemed if possible even more confused than they are half a century later. They united in denouncing Herbert Hoover but in little else. Some harried Hoover from the right; even more harried him from the left; a good many, including Governor Roosevelt of New York, harried him from right and left simultaneously. Nothing emerged from the clamor in the shape of a coherent alternative. Yet that did not prevent the Democrats from winning the 1932 election nor prevent Roosevelt once in the White House from launching the New Deal. Disarray in opposition may signify a healthy ferment that assures a vigorous President an arsenal of policy choices. A thousand Democratic flowers will bloom in the last years of Reagan; and why not?

XIII

What form will affirmative government take after the next spin of the wheel? In the past, public-purpose administrations have intervened in the economy to restore freedom of markets—the Jackson-Wilson aspiration—and they have intervened to institutionalize a concert of interests—the TR-FDR aspiration. The direction intervention takes depends on the margin for maneuver.

Eighteenth-century America was a land of limited capital, and economic policy saw no alternative but to harness public and private energies. Then for a heady time in the late nineteenth and early twentieth centuries America seemed a land of unlimited possibility. In these years, national policies emerged from conflict—North against South, the cities against the countryside, the working class against the capitalists, old Americans against new immigrants, white against black, the individual against the state. The style worked well enough when space and time conferred on America the luxury of large economic margins.

But when, as during the two world wars and the Great Depression, margins contracted, there was no fooling around with the allocation of resources through an unregulated marketplace. Then post–Second World War expansion renewed the mirage of a bottomless cornucopia and revived the free market ideology in pristine glory. By the 1980s, however, even as the laissez-faire faith reached a new zenith, the United States finds itself dependent, as it has not been for a long time, on the global economy—for capital, for trade, for raw materials, for energy. The American competitive position is in decline. Trade deficits have never been greater. Margins for error are contracting again.

So too are available remedies. Inflation and unemployment remain major domestic problems. Reagan's policy had been to combat inflation by recession (1981–1983) and then to combat recession in classic Keynesian style by running the largest peacetime budgetary deficits in American history (1984–1986). The deficit, as intended, denies government easy resort to social spending. It also denies government easy resort to fiscal stimulus at the next economic downturn. The fiscal medicine is less effective as the deficit grows. As with drugs, when you increase the dose too much it becomes lethal. Keynesianism is a conservative policy because it leaves the structure of private economic decision intact. It arose during the Second New Deal precisely as an alternative to the national planning of the First New Deal. With fiscal stimulus eliminated, the only recourse in the next economic crisis will be national planning. Reaganomics may end as the prelude to the planned economy. Another irony.

"America," Woodrow Wilson wrote a century ago, "is now sauntering through her resources and through the mazes of her politics with easy nonchalance; but presently there will come a time when she will be surprised to find herself grown old,—a country crowded, strained, perplexed,—when she will be obliged . . . to pull herself together, adopt a new regimen of life, husband her resources, concentrate her strength, steady her methods, sober her views, restrict her vagaries, trust her best, not her average, members. That will be the time of change."[87]

The time foreseen by Wilson may soon be upon us. The logic of an age that presses on the limits of resources is not competition but coordination, based on working partnership among government, business and labor and directed toward economic growth. The essence of the process must be consultation and negotiation, not edict or decree. If there is to be a binding common purpose to protect the general interest against the scramble of organized private interests, government, as the unit most directly accountable to the people, must always be the senior partner.

The idea of a public-private partnership in managing the economy does not win applause in all quarters. The right denounces it as statism, the left as corporatism. Perhaps Henry Adams was correct in thinking that affirmative government must fall sooner or later into the hands it is struggling to escape. Yet in view of the inequities produced by the unregulated market and the horrors produced by total state ownership, what alternative for those who cherish democracy is there to trying out forms of government-business-labor coordination in a free economy?

Such coordination has its eminent antecedents in the American past. Indeed it calls for the restoration of the spirit in which the republic was founded, the spirit of commonwealth, of the public good, of the general welfare. The tradition of affirmative government is quite as authentically American, quite as deeply ingrained in our national history, quite as strongly identified with our greatest statesmen, quite as expressive of American ideas and character, as the competing tradition of self-interest and scrambling private enterprise.

One must add, though this is doubtless personal prejudice, that undertakings which rely on social cooperation rather than individual greed, which call on people to work together rather than to do the other fellow in, may be somewhat more elevating for the nation than the dog-eat-dog, devil-take-the-hindmost ethic of self-interest. It would still appear that affirmative government offers the best chance in this horrid world of strengthening our democracy, preserving our institutions and enlarging the liberties of our people.

TEN

The Short Happy Life
of American Political Parties

———◆———

WHAT HAS HAPPENED to the American as political animal? In the nineteenth century visiting Europeans were awed by the popular obsession with politics. Tocqueville in the 1830s thought politics "the only pleasure an American knows."[1] Bryce half a century later found parties "organized far more elaborately in the United States than anywhere else in the world."[2] Voting statistics justified transatlantic awe. In no presidential election between the Civil War and the end of the century did the American turnout—the proportion of eligible voters actually voting—fall below 70 percent. In 1876 it reached nearly 82 percent.

But in no presidential election since 1968 has the American turnout exceeded 55 percent. In 1984, only 52.9 percent voted. In the meantime, turnout in the once awed European democracies is over 75 percent in Great Britain and France, over 80 percent in West Germany, the Low Countries and Scandinavia, over 90 percent in Italy. The United States ranks twentieth among twenty-one democracies in turnout as a percentage of the voting-age population (only Switzerland is worse).[3] Fifty million additional Americans would have had to vote in 1984 to bring turnout back to nineteenth-century levels.

I

Why have Americans stopped voting? The dutiful citizens of a century ago did not rush to the polls out of uncontrollable excitement over the choices before them. The dreary procession of presidential candidates in these high turnout years moved Bryce to write the famous chapter in *The American Commonwealth* on "Why Great Men Are Not Chosen President," nor did the major parties disagree much on issues.

Changes in the composition of the electorate doubtless contributed to the decline in turnout. The pool of eligible voters was enlarged in 1920 by the Nineteenth Amendment (women), in 1965 by the Voting Rights Act (blacks) and in 1971 by the Twenty-sixth Amendment (eighteen-year-olds). The newly enfranchised tend, for an interval at least, to vote less frequently than adult white males inured to the process. Each enlargement reduced the ratio of turnout. Still, the voting pool was steadily enlarged in the nineteenth century by an influx of immigrants far less habituated to the idea of voting than native-born women, blacks or eighteen-year-olds, and white male immigrants were rather promptly incorporated into the political system.

The agency that seized and indoctrinated the immigrant was the political party. In the twentieth century the party has proved notably less successful in mobilizing women, blacks, the young and even adult white males. The conspicuous difference between the 1880s and the 1980s lies in the decay of the party as the organizing unit of American politics.*

II

Parties have always represented the great anomaly of the American political order. The Founding Fathers were reared in an anti-party tradition. The eighteenth century had little use for parties. In France Rousseau condemned those "intriguing groups and partial associations" which, by nourishing special interests, obscured the general will.[4] For Britain party was "faction"—a selfish and irresponsible clique—and "the influence of faction," as Hume wrote, "is directly contrary to that of laws. Factions subvert government, render laws impotent, and beget the fiercest animosities among men of the same nation, who ought to give mutual assistance and protection to each other."[5] Parties were particularly at war with the philosophy, strong in colonial America, of civic republicanism and its emphasis on a public good beyond the sum of individual and group interests.

---

*Some political scientists argue that the basic cause of low American turnout is the registration requirement. Unlike most other democracies, the burden of registration in the United States rests on the individual citizen. Polls, however, find little evidence that the simplification of registration and voting procedures would increase turnout dramatically; see, for example, the ABC News poll reported by Adam Clymer, *New York Times,* 25 September 1983. In any event, strong parties would register as well as vote their adherents.

The American experience exemplified the anti-party philosophy. It was one of self-government without parties. There were no parties in the colonial assemblies or in the Continental Congress or under the Articles of Confederation. The Constitution made no provision for parties. "Such an addiction," Jefferson wrote of party spirit in 1789, "is the last degradation of a free and moral agent. If I could not go to heaven but with a party, I would not go there at all."[6] The republic began under non-party government; and in his Farewell Address the first President issued a "most solemn" warning "against the baneful effects of the spirit of party." That malign spirit, Washington emphasized, "is seen in its greatest rankness" in popular governments "and is truly their worst enemy."

Yet, as Washington spoke, parties were beginning to crystallize around him. Condemned by the Founding Fathers, unknown to the Constitution, they imperiously forced themselves into political life in the early years of the republic. Their extraconstitutional presence rapidly acquired a quasi-constitutional legitimacy. Even Jefferson decided in another decade that he would be willing to go with the right party, if not to heaven, at least to the White House. By the time the first President who was born an American citizen took his oath of office, parties had become, it seemed, the indispensable means of American self-government. (It was fitting that this President, Martin Van Buren, was both the creative architect and the classic philosopher of the role of party in the American democracy.)

This extraconstitutional revolution took place because parties met urgent social and political needs. In the dialect of the sociologists, parties were functional. They contributed in a variety of ingenious ways to the stability of the system.

American parties originated in the diversity of circumstance and aspiration in the new nation. Madison in the 10th *Federalist,* after the customary denunciation of "the mischiefs of faction," went on to observe that the most common source of faction was "the various and unequal distribution of property" and, more surprisingly, to acknowledge that "the regulation of these various and interfering interests . . . involves the spirit of party and faction in the necessary and ordinary operations of the government." The very expanse of the new nation now offered hope, Madison thought, of controlling the baneful effects of party by diluting the influence of the interfering interests.*

---

*It was in this connection, and not at all in connection (as Open Door historians unscrupulously pretend) with foreign affairs, that Madison wrote, "Extend the sphere,"

The expanse of the new nation gave parties another function. The thirteen colonies that had joined precariously to overthrow British rule were divided by local loyalties, by discrepant principles, by diverging folkways, by imperfect communications. Yet they were pledged to establish an American Union—and to do so over nearly a million square miles of territory. The parties as national associations were a force, soon a potent force, against provincialism and separatism. At the same time, they strengthened the fabric of unity by legitimizing the idea of political opposition—a startling development for a world in which that idea had little legitimacy (it has little enough for most of the world today). In 1800–1801 the American parties showed they could solve the most tense of all problems in new nations—the transfer of power from a governing party to its opponents.

"The party system of Government," Franklin D. Roosevelt once said, "is one of the greatest methods of unification and of teaching people to think in common terms."[7] When by the middle of the nineteenth century the growing tensions between North and South split most national institutions, even the churches, party organization, as that brilliant early analyst of American politics, Henry Jones Ford, observed, was "the last bond of union to give way."[8]

III

Parties performed an equally vital function within the national government itself by supplying the means of overcoming one of the paradoxes of the Constitution. The doctrine of the separation of powers, literally construed, warred against the principle of concerted action that is the essence of effective government. The need to make the new Constitution work demanded a mechanism that could coordinate the executive and legislative branches. The party now furnished the connective tissue essential to unity of administration.

The party found other functions in a polity groping to give substance to the implications of democracy. As vehicles for ideas, parties furthered the nation's political education, both defining national purposes and formulating national policies. As instruments of compromise, they encouraged, within the parties as well as between them, the containment and mediation of national quarrels. As agencies of

---

which he followed at once with "and you take in a greater variety of parties and interests; you make it less probable that a majority of the whole will have a common motive to invade the rights of other citizens; or if such a common motive exists, it will be more difficult for all who feel it to discover their own strength, and to act in unison with each other."

representation, they gave salient interests a voice in national decisions and thus a stake in the national political order. As agencies of recruitment, they brought ambitious men into public service and leadership. As agencies of popular mobilization, they drew ordinary people into political participation. As agencies of social escalation, they opened paths of upward mobility to vigorous newcomers debarred by class or ethnic prejudice from more conventional avenues to status. As agencies of 'Americanization,' they received immigrants from abroad, tending (to quote Henry Jones Ford again) "to fuse them into one mass of citizenship, pervaded by a common order of ideas and sentiments, and actuated by the same class of motives."[9] Thoreau cared little enough for politics, but he saw the point: "Politics is, as it were, the gizzard of society, full of grit and gravel, and the two political parties are its two opposite halves, which grind on each other,"[10] digesting and absorbing national differences.

On the local level the party, while generally organized for self-advancement and self-enrichment, prevailed because it also met community needs. Without mistaking the party boss for a sort of early social worker, one may still agree that city machines, with their patronage jobs, food baskets, Thanksgiving turkeys, friendly precinct captains, gave people lost in a frightening economic world a rare feeling of human contact. "There's got to be in every ward," Martin Lomasny of Boston told Lincoln Steffens, "somebody that any bloke can come to—no matter what he's done—and get help. Help, you understand, none of your law and your justice, but help." The machines, said Steffens, "provided help and counsel and a hiding-place in emergencies for friendless men, women and children who were in dire need, who were in guilty need, with the mob of justice after them."[11]

In an age lacking developed forms of popular amusement, political parties were even an essential source of diversion and fun. "To take a hand in the regulation of society and to discuss it," as Tocqueville noted, "is his biggest concern and, so to speak, the only pleasure an American knows. . . . Even the women frequently attend public meetings and listen to political harangues as a recreation from their household labors. Debating clubs are, to a certain extent, a substitute for theatrical entertainments."[12]

IV

In view of the manifold functions served, it is no surprise that American parties so quickly planted their roots deep into the political culture. The immediate post–Civil War years were, I suppose, the golden age of political parties. Party regularity was higher, party loyalty deeper and party stability greater than at any other time in American history. Bryce, writing in 1888, described American parties as marked by "a sort of military discipline."[13]

Independent voting was scorned, even when, as in 1884, it was urged by the most high-minded spokesmen of the genteel tradition. The young Theodore Roosevelt privately detested James G. Blaine, the Republican nominee, but stuck by the party and denounced his Mugwump friends as suffering "from a species of moral myopia, complicated with intellectual strabismus."[14] "A good party," said the ordinarily sardonic Thomas B. Reed, the despotic Speaker of the House, "is better than the best man that ever lived."[15] Or, in the sonorous language of Senator Ratcliffe in Henry Adams's *Democracy* (1880): "Believing as I do that great results can only be accomplished by great parties, I have uniformly yielded my own personal opinions where they have failed to obtain general assent."[16]

How remote this all sounds! The contrast between the 1880s and the 1980s could hardly be more spectacular. A century after the golden age, all the gauges that measure party efficacy register trouble. Not only has turnout alarmingly declined, but the straight party ticket has become a thing of the past. In 1900 only 4 percent of congressional districts voted one party for Presidents and another for the House of Representatives; in 1984 44 percent of congressional districts split their tickets. In their advertising, candidates minimize when they do not conceal their party affiliations. Voters who designate themselves "independents" in public opinion polls now make up a third of the electorate. The party of nonvoters is almost as large. The classic political machine has generally disappeared, even in Chicago. By every test party loyalty in the old style is nearing extinction. Recent presidential elections have been marked by the rise of personalist political movements—George Wallace in 1968, Eugene McCarthy in 1976, John Anderson in 1980. All these developments are symptoms of a party order in a state of dissolution. The most astute of contemporary political analysts, Samuel Lubell, wrote in 1970 of "the war of the voters against the party system."[17] What in the world has happened?

V

It is currently fashionable to explain recent party decline by citing allegedly novel and untoward developments assailing the system from without—the rise of single-issue movements, the power of lobbies, the fragmentation of Congress.

The historian may find such explanations unsatisfactory. Single-issue movements are hardly the horrifying novelty that our contemporaries, intimidated by the feminists, the environmentalists, the right-to-lifers, the Moral Majority, the anti–gun-controllers, the homosexuals and so on, suppose them to be. What, after all, was Madison writing about in November 1787 when he defined "a faction" as "a number of citizens . . . united and actuated by some common impulse of passion, or of interest"? [18]

The mischiefs of faction have been an abiding theme in American history. Single-issue movements have flickered through the political scene from 1787 to the present, dedicated to the extirpation of Freemasonry, abolition of slavery, discrimination against immigrants, issuance of greenbacks or (one of the most alarmingly successful of all) prohibition of drink. American democracy has taken these movements in stride. When the Native American or Know-Nothing party was at its height, Horace Greeley predicted that it was destined "to run its course, and vanish as suddenly as it appeared. . . . It would seem as devoid of the elements of persistence as an anti-cholera or an anti-potato-rot party would be." [19] The Know-Nothing party, it should be noted, won far more legislative seats than any single-issue movement of our own day has done. It vanished as Greeley predicted.

The same historical discount must be applied to the menace of lobbies. The United States has had lobbies as long as it has had Congresses. And lobbies were never more powerful than in the golden age of parties. Those who suppose lobbies to be some fearful invention of the late twentieth century should read *The Gilded Age* (1873), by Mark Twain and Charles Dudley Warner, or meditate the gaudy career of Sam Ward (1814–1884), the King of the Lobby. What the late twentieth century has raised to new levels of effectiveness is the public-interest lobby. This development somewhat offsets the less benign manipulations of special-interest lobbies. Common Cause and Ralph Nader become the antidote that Colonel Sellers and Sam Ward never had.

Nor is the fragmentation of Congress all that unprecedented. Political commentators write as if present indiscipline represents a lamentable lapse from better times when legislators unquestioningly obeyed their whips. But when were those better times? Even Franklin Roosevelt, in the epoch of 'rubber stamp' Congresses, had to fight hard for every New Deal bill after the Hundred Days. Congresses controlled by his own party defeated some of FDR's most cherished initiatives, such as discretionary neutrality legislation and the Supreme Court plan.

Nor was legislative indiscipline new in the days of FDR. Woodrow Wilson, writing during the golden age of party regularity, called his book *Congressional Government.* But Wilson did not portray a well-ordered Congress. "Outside of Congress," he observed in 1885, "the organization of the national parties is exceedingly well-defined and tangible . . . but within Congress it is obscure and intangible. Our parties marshal their adherents with the strictest possible discipline for the purpose of carrying elections, but their discipline is very slack and indefinite in dealing with legislation. . . . There are in Congress no authoritative leaders who are the recognized spokesmen of their parties. Power is nowhere concentrated; it is rather deliberately and of set policy scattered amongst many small chiefs."[20]

Legislative indiscipline is inherent in the American Constitution. The separation of powers denies the executive branch any organic means of controlling the legislative majority. Federalism turns national parties into loose coalitions of state parties. Between the commands of the Constitution and the sprawl of the country, strict party discipline has always been alien to Congress. Tocqueville made the point a century and a half ago. In the American democracy, he wrote, "Parties are impatient of control and are never manageable except in moments of great public danger"—and he knew the United States in an age of presidential domination as overweening as in the age of FDR. Tocqueville correctly traced this unmanageability to the dependence of the legislator on his constituents. "A representative," he wrote, "is never sure of his supporters, and, if they foresake him, he is left without a resource." Consequently legislators "think more of their constituents than of their party. . . . But what ought to be said to gratify constituents is not always what ought to be said to serve the party to which representatives profess to belong."[21]

The observation that a legislator's loyalty runs more to his constituents than to his party remains true today; but it is hardly a new truth. And is legislative indiscipline altogether a bad thing? Is the republic better off when legislators give unquestioning obedience to whips? "Reader, suppose you were an idiot," Mark Twain wrote. "And suppose you were a member of Congress. But I repeat myself."[22] Congressional fragmentation in recent times springs in part from the fact that Congress today probably has fewer idiots and more educated and independent-minded legislators than the nation has enjoyed since the early republic. The price democracy pays for independent-minded legislators is precisely their determination to make up their own minds.

Single-issue movements, lobbies, legislative fragmentation: these are the standard and abiding conditions of American politics. They are conditions with which the parties have cheerfully coexisted since the start of the republic. The causes of party decline must be sought elsewhere.

VI

Living as we do amidst the ruins of the traditional party system, we see a great yearning for the golden age of party supremacy. But let us not overdo the historic glory of American political parties. "America has had great parties, but has them no longer," Tocqueville wrote as early as 1835. By this he meant that parties of principle had already given way to parties of ambition and interest.[23]

Far from taking principled positions, our major parties have been at one time or another on all sides of major issues. "Each in turn," wrote Henry Adams, "belied its own principles according as each was in power or in opposition."[24] The Federalists were the party of secession (at the Hartford Convention) as well as of national government; the Democrats have been the party of state rights as well as of centralization; the Republicans, the party of centralization as well as of state rights. "American parties," my father once observed, "have been symbolized by such animals as the elephant and the donkey, but not by the leopard, which never changes its spots." Only minor parties have indulged the luxury of consistency "with the result that they have nearly always stayed minor."[25]

The late nineteenth century was a golden age for the party as an institution. It was not a golden age for Presidents or for public policy or for politics as a profession. The worship of party swallowed up the purposes that had initially called the party into being. Originating as a means to other ends, the party fatally became an end in itself.

As party became king, the quality of men entering public life declined. Not a single notable President led the nation in the forty years between Lincoln and the first Roosevelt; and Lincoln was a minority President and Roosevelt an accident. Politics fell into disrepute. Young Henry Adams, returning from London after the Civil War, "noticed with horror that the grossest satires on the American Senator and politician never failed to excite the laughter and applause of every audience. Rich and poor joined in throwing contempt on their own representatives."[26] The sympathetic Bryce reached the melancholy conclusion that "the ordinary American voter does not object to mediocrity" and that party professionals, "usually commonplace men," positively preferred the mediocre to the brilliant candidate.[27] When politicians were not mediocrities, they were all too often thieves. "It could probably be shown by facts and figures," wrote Mark Twain, "that there is no distinctly native criminal class except Congress."[28]

We are currently admonished to recall the blessings of boss rule. Contemplating the invasion of the parties by amateurs and zealots streaming up through primaries and caucuses, journalists and political scientists insist how much better things were in the good old days when a few bosses retired to the smoke-filled room and came out with a strong candidate and a balanced ticket. Yet bosses rarely proposed candidates they could not control. The typical candidate to emerge from the smoke-filled room was, of course, Warren G. Harding. The effective Presidents of the twentieth century all won nomination over the prostrate bodies of party bosses. New ideas gain access to politics through hard-to-control reformers like Theodore Roosevelt, Woodrow Wilson, Franklin Roosevelt, John Kennedy and, in his peculiar way, Ronald Reagan. These men were leaders who took their parties away from the bosses and remolded them in their own images. Bosses are responsive to local interest and local boodle; reformers, to national concerns and national aspirations. Boss rule was no blessing.

Moreover, as party loyalty, regularity and discipline solidified, so did the determination of parties to evade pressing issues. The major parties in the golden age scored badly in responding to popular urgencies. The result was increasingly angry resort to third parties (the Greenback party in 1880, the Anti-Monopoly party in 1884, the Labor party in 1888, the Populist party in 1892) and to non-party movements. All pressed issues the major parties ignored—issues the major parties grudgingly coopted (as the Democrats did in 1896) only when necessary to assure their own survival.

The cult of party stifled the art of politics. Walt Whitman, the old Locofoco editor, retained after the Civil War the Jacksonian faith in politics as the method of democracy. In *Democratic Vistas,* he condemned "the fashion among dilletants and fops . . . to decry the whole formulation of the active politics of America, as beyond redemption, and to be carefully kept away from." He urged young men "to enter more strongly yet into politics. . . . Always inform yourself; always do the best you can; always vote." But he added with emphasis: "These savage, wolfish parties alarm me. . . . It behooves you to convey yourself implicitly to no party, nor submit blindly to their dictators, but steadily hold yourself judge and master over all of them."

Party supremacy, in short, bred political frustration. Whitman looked for the redemption of politics to "the floating, uncommitted electors, farmers, clerks, mechanics, the masters of parties—watching aloof, inclining victory this side or that side—such are the ones most needed, present and future."[29] With his usual expansive prescience, Whitman prophesied the steady drift of voters from parties that has characterized the evolution of American politics over the last century.

VII

The parties were their own gravediggers. They were also the victims of changes in the political environment. For the modern history of political parties has been the story of the steady loss of the functions that gave parties their classical role.

The rise of a civil service based on merit largely dried up the reservoir of patronage. The decline (until recently) of mass immigration deprived the city machine of its historic clientele. Social workers and the welfare state took over the work of parties in ministering to the poor and helpless. A more diversified society opened new avenues of upward mobility. The rise of the mass media reduced the centrality of parties as the instrument of national unification. The development of mass entertainment gave people more agreeable diversions than listening to political harangues. The better educated, college-bred, post–GI Bill of Rights, suburban electorate felt no inclination to defer to political bosses. And parties in recent times have conspicuously failed to recognize urgent popular concerns. So many influential movements of our own age have developed outside the party process. Civil rights, women's liberation, the environmental movement, the antinuclear movement, the Moral Majority—all surged up from the grass roots to impose themselves on American politics.

The decomposition of parties has been under way a long time. The Progressive period at the start of the twentieth century mounted a purposeful assault on the party. Herbert Croly, the great Progressive theorist, considered "the overthrow of the two-party system indispensable to the success of progressive democracy," at least in the long run, and hoped to establish forms of direct democracy.[30] This particular assault languished rather quickly.

But erosion continued. "The last twenty years," Calvin Coolidge wrote in 1929, "have witnessed a decline in party spirit and a distinct weakening in party loyalty."[31] The twentieth century had no shrewder politician than the second Roosevelt. FDR was without nineteenth-century illusions about the sanctity of party. A Democrat, he cast his first presidential vote for a Republican, appointed two Republicans to his cabinet when elected President himself (and two more in the shadow of war), and a few months before his death was exploring the possibility of a political alliance with the very man the Republicans had run against him four years earlier. "People tell me that I hold to party ties less tenaciously than most of my predecessors in the Presidency," he told a Jackson Day dinner in 1940. ". . . I must admit the soft impeachment." Parties, FDR added,

are good instruments for the purpose of presenting and explaining issues, of drumming up interest in elections, and, incidentally, of improving the breed of candidates for public office.

But the future lies with those wise political leaders who realize that the great public is interested more in Government than in politics. . . . The growing independence of voters, after all, has been proven by the votes in every Presidential election since my childhood—and the tendency, frankly, is on the increase.[32]

The tendency that FDR discerned greatly intensified in the next forty years and has landed the parties in the condition of desuetude we gloomily acknowledge today.

It was this situation that produced the zeal some years ago for party reform. That reform movement has been much misunderstood. It is currently fashionable to ascribe the contemporary party crisis to changes in party rules. But the reform movement of the 1960s, unlike the Progressive movement at the turn of the century, was designed not to overthrow but to save the party system. The theory of the reforms was to tame the new social energies and incorporate them into the party process. In particular, it was to do for women, non-whites and the young what nineteenth-century parties had done for immigrants. Nor can one reasonably argue that the enlargement of citizen participation is such a bad thing in a democracy.

Some of the reforms—the modernization of procedures, for example, the new strength and autonomy conferred on the national committee, and the larger representation of women and of minorities—probably gave parties a somewhat longer life expectancy. Other new rules carelessly or deliberately ignored the interests of party as institutions—for example, in denying preference to party officials and elected representatives. Most of these lapses were subsequently corrected. In any event, the idea that rule changes caused the party crisis, and that repealing those changes will cure it, is akin to the delusion of Rostand's Chantecler that his cock-a-doodle-do made the sun rise. Party reform was not a cause of but a response to organic maladies.

Another blow to the parties came when reforms designed to control the role of money in elections had unexpected consequences in reducing the party's command of campaign finance. The Federal Election Campaign Act of 1974 provided for public funding of presidential elections. It also imposed limits both on political contributions and political spending. In limiting contributions to candidates, the law permitted larger contributions by non-party political action committees (PACs) than by individuals.

The advantage thus conferred on PACs was greatly increased two years later when the Supreme Court in *Buckley v. Valeo* knocked out the spending ceilings in congressional campaigns, doing so on the bizarre ground that political spending was equivalent to speech and therefore protected by the First Amendment. The Court evidently had no doubt that money talks. This ill-considered decision not only stimulated the formation of PACs as well as the appetite of candidates but also sanctioned, even in publicly financed presidential campaigns, "independent expenditures" by PACs—that is, political spending not coordinated with the favored candidate and his campaign. No aggregate limit, moreover, was placed on the amount of money PACs could receive and disburse. With a freer hand to play, PACs lured an increasing share of political money from the parties. By the mid-1980s PACs had increased sevenfold in number since 1974 (from 600 to more than 4000); the money they spent increased tenfold. PAC contributions accounted for 13 percent of congressional campaign funds in 1974; 41 percent in 1984.[33] Because PACs often represented corporate and other particular interests, their expanding role threatened further distortions and corruptions in the democratic process.

VIII

Parties are in trouble, in short, because they failed to meet national needs in their season of supremacy and because they thereafter lost one after another of their historic functions. And today a fundamental transformation in the political environment is further undermining the already shaky structure of American politics. Two modern electronic devices—television and the computerized public opinion poll—are having a devastating and conceivably fatal impact on the party system.

Television has not had all the malign consequences for the political process that some commentators expected. It was predicted, for example, that television would breed candidates endowed with histrionic skills, photogenic profiles and ingratiating personalities. Ronald Reagan is cited as the inevitable product of the television age. But Reagan, one surmises, would have been equally successful in the age of radio, like Franklin D. Roosevelt, or in the age of newsreels, like Warren G. Harding, or in the age of steel engravings and the penny press, like Franklin Pierce. Presidential candidates in the television era—Johnson, Nixon, Humphrey, McGovern, Ford, Carter, Mondale—hardly constitute a parade of bathing beauties calculated to excite Atlantic City. Highly photogenic aspirants, like John Lindsay and John Connally, men qualified by experience and intelligence as well, got nowhere in their presidential quests.

It was feared too that Presidents, with their ready command of television opportunities and ready access to polling data, would use the electronic techniques to enhance the Imperial Presidency. Yet during most of the television era the Presidency has been in an embattled and beleaguered condition. It was feared that the rich men who owned the networks would use the medium to buttress privilege. Yet television has given dissenters and agitators, from the National Organization of Women to the Moral Majority, unprecedented opportunities to influence opinion. While politicians try to use television to manipulate the public, the public is using television to manipulate the politicians.

And television enables voters to know their leaders far better than they did when newspapers were the primary source of political information. Television is more pitiless than the press because the moving image is more revealing than the printed word. In earlier times, as that old political stager Harold Macmillan has recalled, "the public character of any leading politician seldom bore any close relationship to his true nature. It was largely represented or distorted by party bias, by rumor, and above all by the Press. . . . The radio, and especially the television, allow the mass of the public to hear, see and judge for themselves. Indeed, with all its faults—its triviality and superficiality—this medium can be very penetrating."[34] This capacity for demystification—who can forget Nixon's darting, shifty eyes on the tiny screen?—is one reason why television has not filled all the dark expectations pundits had about it.

In some respects television may well have strengthened the checks and balances in the political order. And television, it must be remembered, is a case of multiple personality—one part snapshots of reality, one part commercial manipulation, one part dream factory. Even as collective fantasy television introduces people to new thoughts, habits and possibilities. Very likely, on balance, television shakes people up more than it settles them down, encourages equality more than it does hierarchy and thereby is generally diversifying and liberating in its social effect.

IX

On the other hand, television has dismally reduced both the intellectual content of campaigns and the attention span of political audiences. In the nineteenth century political speeches generally lasted for two or three hours and dealt with issues in systematic and exhaustive fashion. Voters drove wagons for miles to hear Daniel Webster and Henry Clay, William Jennings Bryan and Fighting Bob La Follette, and felt cheated if the famous orator did not give them their money's worth. Then radio came along and cut the length of political speeches first to an hour, soon to thirty minutes. It was still possible to develop substantive arguments even in half an hour. But television appeared, and the political talk shrank to fifteen minutes.

In recent years the fifteen-minute talk has given way to the commercial spot. Advertising agencies sell candidates in sixty seconds with all the cynical skill and contrivance they previously devoted to selling mouthwash and detergents. "The idea that you can merchandise candidates for high office like breakfast cereal," Adlai Stevenson said in 1952, "is the ultimate indignity to the democratic process."[35] Stevenson did not foresee that by the 1980s even the spot might begin to give way to the political rock video, replacing all pretense of argument by a dreamlike flow of music and image.

Television, moreover, is the major cause of the appallingly high costs of modern campaigns. Presidential candidates devote more than half their federal campaign funds to television. In contests for lesser offices, where no public funds are available, the cost is even greater. The result is increasingly to limit politics to candidates who have money of their own or who take money from political action committees: in either case, a bad outcome for democracy.

Television is here to stay. But some of the accompanying abuses are not beyond remedy. America is almost alone among the Atlantic democracies in declining to provide political parties free prime time on television during elections. Were the United States to follow the civilized example, it could do much both to bring inordinate campaign costs under control and to revitalize the political parties. The airwaves after all belong to the people. Private operators use them only under public license. The Communications Act of 1934 empowered the Federal Communications Commission to grant licenses to serve the "public convenience, interest, or necessity." A television channel is immensely lucrative. The television barons are not owners of private property with which they can do anything they want. They are trustees of public property obligated to prove their continuing right to the public trust. If anything is central to the public interest, it is to use the airwaves to improve the process by which a people chooses its rulers.

When political parties receive free time, the purchase of additional political time should be prohibited, and the use of free time in less than five-minute segments should also be prohibited. Even advertising men feel that the spot mania has gone too far. "The time has come," the chairman of Foote Cone & Belding has said, "to stop trivializing the electoral process by equating a candidate and a public office with an antiperspirant and an armpit. It is time to stop selling television spots to political candidates."[36]

X

Legislative action can moderate both the financial costs and the intellectual trivialization imposed by television on politics. It is much more difficult, however, to moderate the impact of television and the computer on the structure of the party system.

The old system had three tiers: the politician at one end; the voter at the other; and the party in between. The party's indispensable function was to negotiate between the politician and the voters, interpreting each to the other and providing the links that held the political process together. The electronic revolution has substantially abolished this mediatorial role. It has thereby undermined the traditional party structure.

Television presents the politician directly to the voter, who judges candidates far more on what the box shows him than on what the party tells him. Computerized polls present the voter directly to the politician, who judges the electorate far more on what the polls show him than on what the party tells him. The prime party function that A. Lawrence Lowell classically described as "brokerage"[37] has disappeared in the electronic age. The political organization is left to wither on the vine.

The party has lost control of the lines of information and communication. It has also lost control of the selection of top candidates. This loss is often blamed on the proliferation of presidential primaries. But primaries have been around since the start of the century. It took television to transform them into the ruling force they are today. Television gives candidates the means of appealing to the electorate over the head of the party organization. It also gives voters a sense of entitlement in the political process. Ordinary citizens now nominate presidential candidates long before the professional politicians gather at the quadrennial conventions. The cherished American political drama of the 'dark horse' conjured out of the smoke-filled room has gone, never to return. Presidential conventions, once forums of decision, become in the electronic age ceremonies of ratification. The last year in which a convention required more than one ballot to choose the presidential candidate was 1952, more than a generation ago.

The party, in addition, is losing its control of campaigns. Television and the computer have produced a new class of electronic political specialists. Assembled in election-management firms, working indifferently for one party or the other, media mercenaries usurp the role once played by the party organization. Computers organize mailings and telephone banks. Campaigns abandon the traditional paraphernalia of mass democracy—volunteers, rallies, torchlight processions, leaflets, posters, billboards, bumper stickers. Politics, once labor-intensive, becomes capital-intensive. With elections dominated by signals from the computer and by the insensate pursuit of television opportunities, the voters' new sense of entitlement becomes vicarious. Personal participation ebbs away. Television makes spectators of us all.

Beyond these specific effects, the very atmosphere generated by television is antipathetic to parties. For obvious technical reasons, television focuses on personality, not on organization; on immediate events, not on historical tendencies. The more it monopolizes the presentation of political reality to the electorate, the less will voters conceive of politics in terms of parties. Television, as Austin Ranney points out, is "by its very nature an antiparty medium."[38]

XI

The electronic age threatens the withering away of the traditional political party. Can the party system be saved?

Political scientists propose structural remedies: formal party membership; midterm party conferences; local party caucuses; binding party discipline and accountability; in short, the revitalization of the party through stronger rules and regulations. I must confess skepticism. The effort is to call the old parties from the vasty deep. It is not likely that they will come when we do call for them, even with the incantations of rules and regulations. Proposals to centralize the parties run against the historical grain of American politics as well as against the centrifugal impact of the electronic age. Actually some of the much-abused reforms have already given the parties new institutional and financial strength as national organizations. Yet, for all this, the party continues to decay as a force in politics. Carried too far—the midterm party conference, for example—efforts to discipline the party only speed up the process of dissolution.

Obviously we must avoid weakening the party system further. Such schemes as the direct election of Presidents, a national primary, a national initiative and referendum, might well administer the coup de grace. Even if the quadrennial conventions are not likely to recover the power to nominate, they provide the party an invaluable opportunity to come together after divisive contests for the nomination. As fraternal gatherings, the conventions introduce activists across the country to each other, foster the exchange of ideas, promote discussion and accommodation, produce a common platform, renew the party's sense of national identity. The allocation of a share of public funds and the provision of free television time to national committees during elections would be modestly useful in propping up the parties. But, in an age when the political culture is turning away from parties, structural remedies will have limited effect. The attempt to shore up structure in the face of loss of function is artificial and futile.

The party is simply no longer indispensable as an agency of mass mobilization; or as an agency of information and communication; or as an agency of brokerage; or as an agency of welfare and acculturation; or even as a manager of campaigns. Parties no longer serve as the gizzard of our politics. They no longer supply the links between government and the people. They no longer give jobs to the unemployed and soup to the poor. What use are they?

Yet the alternative to the party system would be a slow, agonized, turbulent descent into an era of what Walter Dean Burnham calls "politics without parties." This is the politics foreshadowed by independent voting, ticket-splitting, non-voting, running without party identification, professional campaign management, the substitution of television for organization, the rise of personalist movements—by the spreading war of the voters against the party system.

Of course "politics without parties" is the way America began.[39] But even in the simpler eighteenth century parties were required to make the Constitution work. One shudders at the consequence for the republic of "politics without parties" in the late twentieth century. The crumbling away of the historic parties would leave political power concentrated in the leaders of personalist movements, in the interest groups that finance them and in the executive bureaucracy, which will supply the major element of stability in an ever more unstable environment.

Political adventurers might roam the countryside, like Chinese warlords, building personal armies equipped with electronic technologies, conducting hostilities against some rival warlords, forming alliances with others, and, if they win elections, striving to govern through ad hoc coalitions. The rest of the voters might not even have the limited entry into and leverage on the process that the party system, for all its manifold defects, has made possible. Accountability would fade away. Without the stabilizing influence of parties, American politics would grow angrier, wilder and more irresponsible.

XII

How to avert this fate? If present tendencies continue, parties will soon have little more to do than collect money, certify platforms and provide labels for the organization of elections and legislatures. What other functions are left in the electronic age?

We might begin by recalling what politics is about. We are often told that politics is about power, and that is, of course, true. More recently, it is said that politics in the age of the mass media is about image; there is something in that too. But in a democracy politics is about something more than the struggle for power or the manipulation of image. It is about the search for remedy. In a country where citizens choose their own leaders, the leaders must justify themselves by their effectiveness in meeting the problems of their time. No amount of power and publicity will avail if, at the end of the day, policies are not seen to work. A major source of the anxiety and frustration that darken the climate of democratic politics is surely the gnawing fear that our masters are intellectually baffled by and analytically impotent before the long-term crises of our age—that they know neither causes nor cures and are desperately improvising on the edge of catastrophe.

"In a country so full of change and movement as America," Bryce wrote a century ago, "new questions are always coming up, and must be answered. New troubles surround a government, and a way must be found to escape from them; new diseases attack the nation, and have to be cured. The duty of a great party is . . . to find answers and remedies."[40]

Bryce was right; and one way by which these decrepit organizations may acquire a new lease on life would be to revive the parties as incubators of remedies. One wishes that the intellectual energy expended in recent years on procedural reform had been devoted instead to the substance of our problems. Nor are substantive problems going to be solved by large committees with two representatives from every state, Puerto Rico and the District of Columbia. Ideas are produced by individuals working in solitude. They are refined and extended by informal discussions with other individuals. They are disseminated when political leaders, conscious both of the world's problems and their own ignorance, reach out for counsel. The incubation of remedy depends, not on techniques of party organization, but on the intelligence and resourcefulness of people outside the organization and on the receptivity and seriousness of individual politicians, who will then use the parties as vehicles for ideas.

The second hope for party restoration follows in sequence. It lies in the election of competent Presidents who will thereafter act to revitalize their party in the interest of their own more effective command of the political process. The future of the party may well depend on Presidents who, in order to put new programs into effect, invoke the party to overcome the separation of powers in Washington and to organize mass support in the country. A strong President needs a strongish party in order to govern effectively. The serious remaining function for the party is as an instrument of leadership.

It is not necessary to forecast precise institutional changes. One imagines that party names will survive while party structures modulate to fill new needs. The power of American democracy lies in its capacity for adaptation. Democracy has flourished in a succession of social contexts, from the rural rides of the eighteenth century to the urban jungles of today. Every innovation in modes of communication has added to the need for readjustment. Democracy along the way has absorbed the penny press, the telegraph, the movie and the radio. It will doubtless find ways of turning television and the microchip to its purposes.

Electronic techniques may subvert the present but they do not determine the future. In a despotic state, they become weapons of manipulation and controls. In a democracy, the electronic age remains open. The new media have the capacity to strengthen hierarchy or to strengthen equality; to centralize or to decentralize political power; to concentrate or to diffuse power over information; to increase anomie or to increase participation; to invade or to intensify privacy; to clarify the political process or to distort it; to reinforce representative democracy or to undermine it. These choices remain within democracy's power to make. So far the electronic age has not notably weakened the democratic commitment to individual freedom and the constitutional state, nor the American capacity for administrative innovation.

The national penchant for experiment, subdued in the 1980s, will burst out again at the next turn of the cycle. "The sum of political life," Henry Adams wrote, "was, or should have been, the attainment of a working political system. Society needed to reach it. If moral standards broke down, and machinery stopped working, new morals and machinery of some sort had to be invented."[41] This is still the problem for American statecraft a century after—to reinvent the morals, mechanisms and ideas demanded by the harsh challenges of the waning years of the twentieth century. One thing is clear: we will not attain a working political system simply by fiddling with party rules and structure, nor by trying to reclaim a vanished past through act of will. We will attain it only by remembering that politics in the end is the art of solving substantive problems.

ELEVEN

After the Imperial Presidency

———◆·◆———

SOME YEARS AGO I was responsible for unleashing a phrase on the language—"the Imperial Presidency." This is the title of a book written in the latter days, hectic and ominous, of the Presidency of Richard M. Nixon. The book argues that the Constitution intends a strong Presidency within an equally strong system of accountability. The title refers to the condition that ensues when the constitutional balance between presidential power and presidential accountability is upset in favor of presidential power.

The perennial threat to the constitutional balance, I suggested, comes in the field of foreign policy. Confronted by presidential initiatives at home, Congress and the courts—the countervailing branches of government under the constitutional separation of powers—have ample confidence in their own information and judgment. They do not lightly surrender power to the executive. In domestic policy, the republic is all Missouri: it has to be shown. But confronted by presidential initiatives abroad, Congress and the courts, along with the press and the citizenry too, generally lack confidence in their own information and judgment. In foreign policy the inclination is to let the Presidency have the responsibility—and the power.

"It is chiefly in its foreign relations," as Tocqueville noted long ago, "that the executive power of a nation finds occasion to exert its skill and its strength. If the existence of the American Union were perpetually threatened, if its chief interests were in daily connection with those of other powerful nations, the executive would assume an increased importance." But the nation that Tocqueville visited in the

1830s subsisted in happy isolation from world power conflicts. So, he wrote, "the President of the United States possesses almost royal prerogatives which he has no opportunity of exercising."[1] In modern times, international crisis, real, contrived or imagined, has given Presidents the opportunity to exercise these almost royal prerogatives. Hence the Imperial Presidency.

I

Presidential aggrandizement under the spur of international crisis was visible from the start. "Perhaps it is a universal truth," Madison wrote Jefferson during the administration of John Adams, "that the loss of liberty at home is to be charged to provisions against danger, real or pretended, from abroad."[2]

Foreign perplexities tempted, sometimes forced, even the earliest Presidents to evade constitutional limitations. As Professor A. D. Sofaer (later a federal judge, still later legal adviser for Ronald Reagan's State Department) showed in his magistral work *War, Foreign Affairs and Constitutional Power: The Origins,* Jefferson himself, the apostle of strict construction, sent a naval squadron to the Mediterranean under secret orders to fight the Barbary pirates, applied for congressional sanction six months later and then misled Congress as to the nature of the orders. He unilaterally authorized the seizure of armed vessels in waters extending to the Gulf Stream, engaged in rearmament without congressional appropriations, developed "a system of secrecy largely immune from legislative check" and invoked the Lockean doctrine of emergency prerogative to justify presidential action beyond congressional authorization. The broad discretionary powers Madison as President obtained from Congress led on to the War of 1812. Long before there was a Central Intelligence Agency, Madison sent Joel R. Poinsett as a secret agent to Latin America and winked at his clandestine revolutionary adventures in Argentina and Chile; Madison's Secretary of State removed Poinsett's despatches from State Department files lest Congress request them. The Madison and Monroe administrations used covert action to facilitate the annexation of Florida.[3]

When perplexities exploded into war, the flow of power to the executive accelerated. During the Mexican War, John C. Calhoun warned Congress that, with foreign conquest, "this Union would become imperial. . . . All the added power and added patronage which conquest will create, will pass to the Executive. In the end you put in the hands of the Executive the power of conquering you."[4] "We elect a king every four years," Secretary of State William H. Seward told

Louis Jennings of *The Times* (London) during the Civil War, "and give him absolute power within certain limits, which after all he can interpret for himself."[5] Abraham Lincoln, as Bryce wrote twenty years later, "wielded more authority than any single Englishman has done since Oliver Cromwell."[6]

Peace brought a reaction against executive excess. Jennings observed three years after Appomattox that no American statesman would now defend the Seward theory of an elective kingship. The nation entered the period famously characterized by Woodrow Wilson as one of "congressional government." Congressional encroachment into foreign affairs drove Henry Adams to the conclusion that the Secretary of State existed only to recognize "obligations which Congress repudiates whenever it can."[7] But the flow to the Presidency resumed once the Spanish-American War brought the United States back into the great world. In his preface to the fifteenth edition in 1901, the author of *Congressional Government* himself called attention to "the greatly increased power . . . given the President by the plunge into international politics." When foreign policy becomes a nation's dominant concern, Wilson said, the executive "must of necessity be its guide: must utter every initial judgment, take every first step of action, supply the information upon which it is to act, suggest and in large measure control its conduct."[8]

Disenchantment with the First World War restored congressional activism in foreign affairs. In the 1930s, Franklin Roosevelt, a mighty domestic President, could not prevent Congress from enacting a rigid neutrality law that put American foreign policy in a straitjacket while Hitler ran amok in Europe. Since Pearl Harbor, however, Americans have lived under a conviction of international crisis, sustained, chronic and often intense. We are at last in the age foreseen by Tocqueville: American interests are in daily connection with those of other powerful nations, the republic itself seems perpetually threatened and Presidents freely exercise their almost royal prerogatives.

The most palpable index of executive aggrandizement is the transfer of the power to go to war from Congress, where the Constitution expressly lodged it, to the Presidency. In June 1940, when the last prime minister of the Third Republic in France pleaded for American aid against Hitler's *Blitzkrieg*, Franklin Roosevelt, after saying that the United States would continue supplies so long as the French continued resistance, took care to add: "These statements carry with them no implication of military commitments. Only the Congress can make such commitments."[9] In 1941 Roosevelt sent naval forces into an undeclared war in the North Atlantic. He did so in a penumbra of consent generated by the congressional enactment of Lend-Lease: if it was national policy to give goods to Britain, it was inferentially national policy to make sure they got there. But Roosevelt relied on a murky proclamation of "unlimited national emergency" and on the public response to Nazi aggression to justify his forward policy. He did not claim inherent power as President or as Commander-in-Chief to send the Navy into combat without congressional authorization.

Nine years later, after North Korea invaded South Korea in June 1950, Harry Truman committed American forces to the war on his own authority. When Senator Robert A. Taft proposed a joint resolution sanctioning military intervention, Truman was persuaded by Dean Acheson, his Secretary of State and an eminent lawyer, that congressional approval was unnecessary. This idea of inherent presidential power to send troops into combat was unwisely defended at the time by some historians, including this one. In its acquiescence, Congress surrendered the war-making power to the executive and has never reclaimed it since.

The Imperial Presidency reached its culmination under Nixon. "I felt," Nixon wrote in his memoirs, "that we were at a historical turning point. My reading of history taught me that when all the leadership institutions of a nation become paralyzed by self-doubt and second thoughts, that nation cannot long survive unless those institutions are either reformed, replaced, or circumvented. In my second term I was prepared to adopt whichever of these three methods—or whichever combination of them—was necessary."[10]

Historically Congress had maintained the rough balance of the Constitution because it retained three vital powers: the war-making power; the power of the purse; and the power of oversight and investigation. By 1950 it had relinquished the war-making power. Johnson fought in Vietnam and Nixon in Cambodia without the explicit congressional authorization required by the Constitution. In 1969–1974 the Nixon administration tried systematically and, until Watergate, successfully to nullify the other two powers: countering the power of the purse by the doctrine of unlimited impoundment of appropriated funds; countering the power of oversight and investigation by the doctrine of unreviewable executive privilege and the extension of the presidential secrecy system. Had Nixon succeeded in imposing these doctrines on top of his amplified claims for the presidential war-making power, he would have effectively ended Congress as a serious partner in the constitutional order.

His further contribution to the Imperial Presidency was to take emergency powers the Presidency had accumulated in order to save the republic from foreign adversaries and to turn these powers against his political opponents—"enemies," he called them—at home. Invoking "national security" as an all-purpose justification for presidential criminality, he set up a secret White House posse to burgle offices, forge historical documents and wiretap officials, embassies, newspapermen and "enemies." The Presidency was above the law, and national crisis justified extreme methods.

Whether a conscious or unconscious revolutionary, Nixon was carrying the Imperial Presidency toward its ultimate form in the plebiscitary Presidency—with the President accountable to the voters only once every four years, shielded by his quadrennial mandate from congressional and public interference between elections, empowered by his mandate to make war or to make peace, to spend or to impound, to give out information or to hold it back, to pursue and punish the opposition, all in the name of a majority whose choice must prevail till it makes another choice four years later.* It was Seward's old dream of an elective kingship. It was hardly what the Founding Fathers had in mind.

Events frustrated Nixon's revolution. The press and the courts exposed his methods as furtive and lawless. Congress, at last bestirring itself, acted to save the Constitution. The House of Representatives prepared articles of impeachment, charging Nixon, in words too soon forgotten, with acting "in a manner contrary to his trust as President and subversive of constitutional government, to the great prejudice of the cause of law and justice and to the manifest injury of the people of the United States."

Nixon resigned to avoid impeachment and jail. Subsequently, I might add, he became my neighbor over the back fence in New York City. I had been on Nixon's Enemies List; and, when his Secret Service agents, their salaries paid by me and other taxpayers, tried to stop my children from their time-honored habit of climbing on the fence, it seemed to be carrying harassment a little far. Since then Nixon has made with astonishing dexterity the transition from disgraced politician to respected elder statesman. One thinks of William Cullen Bryant's obituary comment on Nicholas Biddle, the president of the Second Bank of the United States. Biddle, Bryant wrote, "passed the last of his days in elegant retirement, which, if justice had taken place, would have been spent in the penitentiary."[11]

*The term 'plebiscitary Presidency' as used here and in *The Imperial Presidency* (Boston, 1973, 254, 264) has a different meaning from its use by Theodore Lowi, for whom the plebiscitary Presidency is already here; see *The Personal President* (Ithaca, 1985).

II

Nixon's attempt to institutionalize the Imperial Presidency failed. By the 1970s, Vietnam had shattered public trust of the Presidency in foreign affairs, Watergate in domestic affairs. A pervasive cynicism spread about Presidents. In 1959, when pollsters asked which knew best, the President or Congress, 61 percent of respondents had voted for the President, only 17 percent for Congress. A comparable question in 1977 almost reversed the proportions, favoring Congress by 58 to 26 percent.[12]

Congress, seized by a temporary passion to prevent future Vietnams and Watergates, enacted laws designed to reclaim lost powers, to dismantle the executive secrecy system and to ensure future presidential accountability. The War Powers Resolution of 1973 was meant to restrain the presidential inclination to go to war. A variety of laws limited presidential resort to paramilitary and covert action. Congress set up select committees to monitor the Central Intelligence Agency. It gave the Freedom of Information Act new vitality. It imposed its own priorities—human rights and nuclear nonproliferation, for example—on the executive foreign policy. The Congressional Budget Act of 1974 restricted presidential impoundment. The National Emergencies Act of 1976 terminated existing presidential emergency authority and established congressional review for future national-emergency declarations. Legislative vetoes and reporting requirements curtailed presidential freedom of action in a diversity of fields.

A few scholars had feared during the Watergate crisis that too zealous an investigation might cripple the presidential office. Some formed a committee in defense of the Presidency, its eminent members claiming that their interest lay in the preservation not of Richard Nixon but of an office indispensable to the republic. The Luce Professor of Jurisprudence at the Yale Law School actually argued that, if Nixon turned over his White House tapes to Congress and the courts, it would raise the "danger of degrading or even destroying the Presidency" and constitute a betrayal of his "successors for all time to come."[13]

After Congress began its mild post-Watergate effort to restore the constitutional balance, scholarly pessimism intensified. Some saw the once mighty Presidency tied down, like Gulliver, by a web of debilitating statutory restraints. A theory arose about the fragility of the American Presidency. Not only Congress but history itself seemed, as political scientists saw it, to be conspiring against Presidents. The job was overwhelmed by insuperable problems—inflation, energy short-ages, urban decay, the nuclear arms race, the Communists. The na-tional consensus on which Presidents had relied since the war for domestic as well as foreign policy was disintegrating. The party sys-tem, which had long supplied the connective sinews of government, was in decay. Lobbies were importunate. Single-issue fanaticisms were distorting the political process.

Presidents, it was added, had compounded their problems by per-sonifying the government in themselves, promising miracles they could not work and exciting hopes they could not fulfill. "The presi-dent," said Theodore Lowi, "is the Wizard of Oz."[14] The inevitable gap between popular expectation and presidential delivery guaran-teed both presidential failure and popular resentment. Vice Presi-dent Walter Mondale, defending Jimmy Carter in 1979, cited an ob-servation John Steinbeck had made in the previous decade in defense of Lyndon Johnson: "We give the President more work than a man can do, more responsibility than a man should take, more pressure than a man can bear. . . . We wear him out, use him up, eat him up. . . . He is ours and we exercise the right to destroy him."[15]

The Presidency appeared in rout. Vietnam drove Johnson from the White House. Nixon drove himself. Nixon's successors—the hapless Gerald Ford and the hapless Jimmy Carter—proved incapable of mastering the discordant frustrations of the day. Failure, it seemed, had passed the point of coincidence. These recent Presidents, a vet-eran political reporter noted in a book on the Presidency, came from a variety of political backgrounds and from all sections of the coun-try; they ran the spectrum in personal temperament and social phi-losophy. "Their combined experience suggests that the chronic fail-ings of the presidency" sprang not from personal characteristics but from "the political and governing system to which presidents must respond."[16] "When five consecutive men . . . all fail to operate an of-fice, when their tasks seem to get progressively more and more diffi-cult with the passing of time," wrote an intelligent English journalist in his own book on the subject, "then the fault can hardly be in the individuals. It must be in the institution."[17]

"Never has so powerful a leader," the English commentator added, "been so impotent to do what he wants to do, what he is pledged to do, what he is expected to do."[18] Columnists wrote of "the Presidency in decline." Scholars mobilized their colleagues to join in producing books under such titles as *The Tethered Presidency, The Post-Imperial Pres-idency, The Impossible Presidency.* Pundits confidently predicted an age of one-term Presidents. The impression arose at the end of the 1970s

of a beleaguered and pathetic fellow sitting forlornly in the Oval Office, assailed by unprecedentedly intractable problems, paralyzed by
the constitutional separation of powers, hemmed in by congressional
and bureaucratic constraints, pushed one way and another by exigent
interest groups, seduced, betrayed and abandoned by the mass media. "Presidential government is an illusion," proclaimed one political
scientist in 1980, "—an illusion that misleads presidents no less than
the media and the American public, an illusion that often brings
about the destruction of the very men who hold the office. Presidential government is the idea that the president, backed by the people,
is or can be in charge of governing the country. . . . Far from being
in charge or running the government, the president must struggle
even to comprehend what is going on."[19] In 1980 ex-President Ford
said to general applause, "We have not an imperial presidency but an
imperiled presidency."[20]

III

There is a sense in which the Presidency has always been weak. The
President's power over policy is great; for the power to set the nation's
course derives from the constitutional prerogatives of the office. But
the President's power over execution is incomplete; for the power to
manage the vast, whirring machinery of government derives from
individual skills as persuader, bargainer and leader. Even Franklin D.
Roosevelt, who possessed all those skills to a high degree, had his
problems. "Half a President's suggestions, which theoretically carry
the weight of orders," one of his assistants, Jonathan Daniels, later
recalled, "can be safely forgotten by a Cabinet member."[21] "He'll sit
here," Harry Truman said in contemplation of Eisenhower, "and he'll
say, 'Do this! Do that!' *And nothing will happen.*" Even when the Imperial Presidency culminated in Nixon, the President lived in a state
of chronic and profane frustration, unable to command Congress,
the judiciary, the press, the universities, unable even to get the FBI,
the CIA and the Internal Revenue Service to do his bidding. This, I
take it, was Richard Neustadt's point when he said that the underlying
theme of his brilliant book of 1960, *Presidential Power,* was presidential
weakness.[22]

But presidential power is more than Neustadt's "power to persuade"; and the exercise of administrative authority is only part of
the President's task. Neustadt's illuminating concern was with the way
Presidents defend themselves against choices pressed by others with
interests of their own. The capacity for presidential self-defense is a
personal variable. But the constitutional and institutional strengths

of the Presidency endure. I cannot confess to a moment's worry during the lamentations of the 1970s about the fragility of the office. Whatever political scientists, lawyers and journalists may think, historians know that the American Presidency is indestructible.

This is partly so for functional reasons. A governing process based on the separation of powers among three supposedly equal and coordinate branches has an inherent tendency toward stalemate and inertia. One of the three branches must take the initiative if the system is to move. The executive branch alone is structurally capable of taking that initiative. The Founding Fathers intended that it should do so. "Energy in the Executive," said Hamilton in the 70th *Federalist,* "is a leading character in the definition of good government."

Moreover, the growth of presidential initiative resulted not from presidential capacity for power but from the necessities of governing an increasingly complex society. As a tiny agricultural country, straggling along the Atlantic seaboard, turned into a mighty continental, industrial and finally world power, the problems assailing the national polity increased vastly in size, number and urgency. Most of these problems could not be tackled without vigorous executive leadership. Through American history, a robust Presidency kept the system in motion. The President remains, as Woodrow Wilson said, "the only national voice," the Presidency "the vital place of action in the system."[23]

A further reason for the indestructibility of the Presidency lies in the psychology of mass democracy. Once again Tocqueville provides the text. "Our contemporaries," he wrote, "are constantly excited by two conflicting passions: they wanted to be led, and they wish to remain free. . . . By this system the people shake off their state of dependency just long enough to select their master and then relapse into it again."[24] Americans have always had considerable ambivalence about the Presidency. One year they denounce presidential power. The next they demand presidential leadership. While they are quite capable of cursing out Presidents, they also have a profound longing to believe in and admire them.

The political irritations assailing the Presidency in the 1970s were hardly unprecedented. Belligerent Congresses, greedy lobbies, wild-eyed single-issue movements—all were old hat in American history. They were no more the cause of the plight of the Presidency than they were of the decay of the party system. Most preposterous of all is the theory that the Presidency did itself in when recent Presidents started personalizing the office, appealing over the heads of Congress to the people and arousing expectations beyond hope of fulfillment.

Radio and especially television, it is suggested, are responsible for the corruption of what had presumably been up till a few years before an impersonal, modest, well-behaved office. Personalization, the plebiscitary stance and presidentially induced mass expectations, we are told, began with John Kennedy or, at the earliest, with Franklin Roosevelt.

This notion springs from a curiously foreshortened view of American history. In fact, the Presidency has been a personalized office from the start, both for political reasons—the interests of the President—and for psychological reasons—the emotional needs of the people. The office would not even have taken the form it did "had not," as one member of the Constitutional Convention wrote, "many members cast their eyes toward General Washington as President; and shaped their ideas of the Powers to be given the President, by their opinions of his Virtue."[25] Washington exploited his advantage and helped create his own myth. The admiring Garry Wills (better as scholar than as journalist) portrays him as "constantly testing public opinion and tailoring his measures to suit it"; and the even more admiring Douglas Southall Freeman found him on occasion "too much the self-conscious national hero." The Father of his Country did not need television in order to personify the nation in the Presidency. Parson Weems (Wills praises his "cinematic vigor") was sufficient.[26]

When Andrew Jackson made his "grand triumphal tour" of the northeastern states in the late spring of 1833, it was "an emotional debauch," as Jackson's most recent biographer describes it; a continuous experience of cheering crowds, booming cannon, popular frenzy. "I have witnessed enthusiasms before," the Hero of New Orleans wrote his son after two days in New York, "but never before have I witnessed such a scene of personal regard as I have today, and ever since I left Washington. I have bowed to upwards of two hundred thousand people to day."[27] Every commanding President in the nineteenth century was guilty of personalizing the office and appealing over the heads of Congress to the people, from Old Hickory through Father Abraham to Teddy Roosevelt at the turn of the century, with his bully pulpit and his highly publicized personality and family.

Nor was the backlash against Presidents an innovation of the 1960s. Dickens anticipated Steinbeck by more than a century. "You no sooner set up an idol firmly," he observed of the American people in 1842, "than you are sure to pull it down and dash it into fragments. . . . Any man who attains a high place among you, from the President downwards, may date his downfall from that moment."[28]

Nor is the expectations gap, so widely invoked to explain the troubles of the contemporary Presidency, a novel phenomenon. The Presidency by its very existence excites expectations. It has always been a target of popular hope and supplication. "I am applied to almost daily," Polk wrote in 1846. ". . . The idea seems to prevail with many persons that the President is from his position compelled to contribute to every loafer who applies."[29] When a friend said to Lincoln that he must get tired of shaking hands, Lincoln supposedly replied that "the tug of the hand was much easier to bear than that upon the heartstrings for all manner of favors beyond his power to grant." Benjamin Harrison, who reported this remark, added that letters imploring help "come from every part of the land, and relate to every possible subject. . . . Many people greatly enlarge the powers of the President, and invoke his interference and protection in all their troubles."[30]

William Howard Taft can hardly be accused of seeking to personalize the office or to rouse excessive expectations. But, long before FDR, JFK or television, Taft wrote of the President that "the whole government is so identified in the minds of the people with his personality, that they make him responsible for all the sins of omission and of commission of society at large." Taft complained bitterly of those who "visit the President with responsibility for everything that is done and that is not done," adding that "the President cannot make clouds to rain, he cannot make the corn to grow, he cannot make business to be good."[31] Gabriel has always hovered over the White House.

The expectations-gap thesis rests on the assumption that voters really believe campaign promises and are consequently overcome with astonishment and anger when those promises are not thereafter fulfilled. It assumes, in other words, that the electorate is a pack of fools. But voters are on the whole as intelligent as you or I. They do not take it literally when presidential candidates say they will make the clouds rain, abolish poverty and usher in utopia. They regard campaign oratory as campaign oratory—that is, not as a solemn covenant with the people but as a clue to the candidate's values, priorities and character. They are not greatly bothered by 'overpromising.' They understand with Emerson that "nothing great was ever achieved without enthusiasm."*

The situation today is far from one of voters deluded by excessive

---

*In "Circles." Giscard d'Estaing, when President of France, observed sensibly, "A word about optimism. I have to inspire people. . . . It would be quite inconceivable to ask someone to make an effort and then tell him that this effort would be of no avail. . . . Mine is, therefore, not the optimism of illusion but rather the optimism of proposal, which is inherent in the nature of my office." *Paris Match,* 14 September 1979.

expectations. It is, on the contrary, one of voters depressed by ab-sence of expectation. Too many think it makes little difference who is President. They doubt that any President can do what he promises. This is another reason for the steady decline in turnout.

As for the idea that overwhelming historical forces conspire against the contemporary Presidency, obviously the substantive problems of the 1970s and 1980s were not easy. But do we really face tougher problems than our forefathers did? Tougher problems than independence? slavery? the Civil War? the Great Depression? the Second World War? The substantive problems confronting contemporary Presidents are, nuclear weapons aside, relatively manageable com-pared to those that confronted Washington or Lincoln or Franklin Roosevelt. Let us avoid the fallacy of self-pity that leads every gen-eration to suppose that it is peculiarly persecuted by history. Histori-cal forces have always conspired against the Presidency. The Presi-dency has survived.

IV

The indestructibility of the Presidency was demonstrated in the very years when political scientists were pronouncing presidential govern-ment as illusion. After Nixon resigned, everyone expected a shift in the balance of the system. Congress would now come into its own. Its acquiescence and pusillanimity, which had contributed so much to the rise of the Imperial Presidency, would end. Having tasted power and recovered a sense of responsibility, Congress would resume the role of partnership in government the Founding Fathers had intended for it. The press, basking in worldwide congratulations over the intrepid-ity of its investigative reporting, would be more vigilant than ever as a check on an overweening executive. The voters, now so sadly aware of the infirmity of Presidents, would be less inclined to see the man in the White House as larger than life.

The new President, moreover, was more than any of his predeces-sors an accidental and therefore especially vulnerable President. He arrived in the White House not through the choice of the voters but through the operations of the Twenty-fifth Amendment. No one out-side of 120,000 people in the Fifth District of Michigan had ever voted for him for any federal office. The Presidency he had inherited was badly damaged by the revulsion against Nixon. Gerald Ford him-self was a modest, unassuming conservative politician, a loyal Capitol Hill man, without great appetite for adulation or power. Moreover, by pardoning Nixon, he dissipated in one stroke the confidence that had come to him on his succession and inflicted a wound on his own administration from which it never recovered. Nor did he succeed even in winning the clear backing of his own party—as shown by the challenge mounted against him by Ronald Reagan in 1976. And he became in these years the butt of nightclub comics across the country for his supposed dumbness and clumsiness. Vice President Nelson Rockefeller, it was said, was "a banana peel away from the Presidency."

Gerald Ford had every strike against him in the White House. Yet, for all his political and personal vulnerability, he retained a dominant role in the American polity. This was because the Presidency itself, as an office and institution, confers power on even a weak incumbent. It enabled Ford, for example, to institute a policy of government by veto. The loyal Capitol Hill man only a short time before, Ford vetoed seventy-two acts passed by Congress in a little over two years. It had taken the imperial Nixon nearly six years to veto forty-two bills. The mighty Lyndon Johnson vetoed only thirty in five years. More than four fifths of Ford's vetoes were sustained.

In foreign policy the resurgent Congress had its way on a number of specific points. Some of its actions—such as the restraint on CIA intervention in Angola and elsewhere, the insistence on human rights, the resistance to arms sales and to nuclear proliferation—were an improvement over what the executive branch would have done on its own. Others—such as the Jackson-Vanik amendment tying Soviet-American trade to the emigration of Russian Jews—were ill-considered initiatives produced by what one senator termed "domestic ethnic politics."[32] Ford complained, in the manner of Presidents, about "impermissible shackles" on his ability to conduct foreign relations.[33] One doubts that his foreign policy would have been greatly better unshackled.

Certainly the most publicized shackle of all turned out to be a toy handcuff. The War Powers Resolution, enacted over Nixon's veto in 1973, was acclaimed as a triumph of congressional self-assertion. If it was a triumph of anything, it was of symbol over substance. The Resolution began by yielding the President what he had heretofore lacked: statutory authority to begin wars without congressional consent. The Resolution's preamble laid down various standards, but the conference report said that the rest of the act was "not dependent" on the preamble, thereby leaving the standards as pious rhetoric rather than binding law. The Resolution went on to direct the President to terminate what the Senate-House conferees interestingly called "unauthorized use of the Armed Forces" within sixty days (in practice, ninety days, since the Resolution offered the President thirty additional days if he thought it necessary in the interests of disengagement) *unless* Congress explicitly provided otherwise. Congress, moreover, could order the withdrawal of American forces at any point by concurrent resolution, which is, of course, not subject to presidential veto.[34]

This proved from the start a richly ambiguous statute. Legislators argued whether it was an expansion or limitation of presidential warmaking power. Some liberals, looking at the early sections of the Resolution, denounced it as an unconstitutional delegation of the warmaking power to the executive. Senator Thomas Eagleton of Missouri called the Resolution "an undated, 90 day declaration of war."[35] Congressman John Culver of Iowa said it would give the President "a blank check to wage war anywhere in the world for any reason of his choosing for a period of 60 to 90 days."[36] Conservatives, looking at the later sections of the Resolution, denounced it as an intolerable restriction of presidential authority. Barry Goldwater called it "destructive of America's credibility in any future crisis."[37] Nixon in his veto message said ominously that, since his powers could be altered only by constitutional amendment, "any attempt to make such alterations by legislation alone is clearly without force"—a statement that, taken literally, appeared to serve notice that, because he personally found the law unconstitutional, he would not be bound by it.

Both sides exaggerated the significance of a pretentious and empty statute. Those who felt that it strengthened presidential war-making power probably had the better of the argument. Before the passage of the Resolution, unilateral presidential war was a matter of usurpation. Now, at least for the first ninety days, it was a matter of law. Practically speaking, the machinery of restraint was a hoax. Most wars are popular in their first ninety days. The President who orders military action can overwhelm Congress and public opinion with his own rendition of the facts and his own interpretation of the crisis. Given the President's ability to define the emergency, to control the flow of information and to appeal to the nation, it would require an unwontedly bold Congress to reject a presidential request for the continuation of hostilities or to recall the fighting forces over presidential opposition.

The War Powers Resolution in fact assumed that the President would make the vital decisions by himself. The efficacy of the statute depended altogether on the presence of a congressional will to bring fighting to an end. If such a will existed, Congress could gain the same result, as it had finally done in Indochina, by using the power of the purse to cut off appropriations. Without such a will, the Resolution was persiflage.

Post-Watergate congressional bravado had a way of sputtering out in the face of crisis. Eighteen months after the passage of the War Powers Resolution, Cambodia seized the American freighter *Mayaguez*. The supposedly helpless Gerald Ford ignored the Resolution, ordered American troops into combat and sent forty-one Marines to their death. It was Congress that turned out to be helpless, then and thereafter—in Iran, Grenada, Lebanon, Libya. When the Supreme Court in 1983 declared the legislative veto unconstitutional,[38] thereby destroying the congressional power to terminate hostilities through concurrent resolution, it killed an effort that had already perished through its own inanition.

A good deal of the much-vaunted congressional reclamation of power after Watergate similarly turned out to be make-believe. In the Congressional Budget Act of 1974 Congress planned to give itself a legislative budget process comparable to the one it had long before given the President in the Budget and Accounting Act of 1921. Some features of the Act, like the Congressional Budget Office and the control of impoundment, proved useful, though the 1983 Supreme Court decision invalidating the legislative veto probably invalidates the impoundment restrictions too. But the Act itself, as President Reagan demonstrated in 1981, failed in its purpose of assuring Congress a coordinate voice in determining budget priorities. What began as a statute designed by Congress to discipline itself and to retrieve power from the President ended, a careful student of the budget process has written, "as an instrument which enhanced the president's power and allowed him to discipline Congress."[39] By 1985, with the Gramm-Rudman Act, Congress handed over the impoundment authority laboriously reclaimed in 1974 and relinquished much of its constitutional power, bestowed on it by the Founding Fathers, to decide taxing and spending policy.

Nor had Congress in its post-Watergate righteousness taken effective action to restrain presidential abuse of executive privilege. The secrecy system, that bulwark of the Imperial Presidency, found new sustenance and support. When Frank Snepp, a former CIA officer, published *Decent Interval*, a book about the fall of Saigon, the Carter administration prosecuted and convicted him on the ground that he had violated his CIA contract by failing to submit his manuscript for clearance. No classified information was involved; no allegation was made of injury to national security; no one denied that Snepp's book was of value to the concerned citizen and the future historian. Congress rolled over and did nothing.

"The rise of presidential authority," as Henry Jones Ford wrote in his penetrating book of 1898, *The Rise and Growth of American Politics*, "cannot be accounted for by the intention of presidents: it is the product of political conditions which dominate all the departments of government, so that Congress itself shows an unconscious disposition to aggrandize the presidential office. The existence of a separate responsible authority to which questions of public policy may be resigned opens to Congress an easy way out of difficulty when the exercise of its own jurisdiction would be troublesome."[40] Ford was writing in the fading twilight of congressional government. His words became truer than ever in the high noon of presidential power. Watergate produced much huffing and puffing, but the White House was not blown in. Far from justifying fears or hopes about the resurgence of Congress, the post-Watergate tale illustrates once again the indestructibility of the Presidency.

V

"In analysing history," Emerson said, "do not be too profound, for often the causes are quite simple."[41] Journalists and political scientists, seeking to understand the troubles of the Presidency in the 1970s, rashly ignored Emerson's dictum. They advanced 'profound' explanations—unprecedentedly intractable problems, excessive personalization of the office, excessive expectations in the country, the constitutional separation of powers, the post-Watergate resurgence of Congress, the rise of single-issue movements, the power of lobbies; and they reached a 'profound' conclusion—that the fault lay not in the men who occupied the Presidency but in the institution itself and the system to which it responded.

   The conditions invoked as explanations were real enough, and they had acquired great salience in the 1970s. But they were far from new; they were indeed recurrent conditions of American politics, and less causes of the presidential dilemma than alibis for it. The commentators got their order wrong. They argued that these conditions accounted for the supposed failure of the Presidency. On closer examination, perhaps the failure of particular Presidents accounted for the salience of the conditions. The absence of effective presidential leadership created a vacuum in the center of the political system. It was this vacuum that Congress, lobbies and single-issue movements rushed to fill. The Presidency was in trouble not because of the fragility of the office or the unworkability of the system nor even because of restrictions imposed in the post-Watergate frenzy. It was in trouble because President Nixon had acted in a manner contrary to his trust as President and subversive of constitutional government, and because of the feebleness of the leadership Presidents Ford and Carter provided and of the remedies they proposed.

Whatever else may be said about Ronald Reagan, he quickly showed that the reports of the death of the Presidency were greatly exaggerated. By 1986 the lamentations of 1980 seemed overwrought and irrelevant. A comparison of Reagan with his immediate predecessor is instructive.

Reagan was obviously no student of public affairs. He did not work nearly so hard as Jimmy Carter nor know nearly so much. But he understood the Presidency as Carter never did. In particular, he understood that an effective President must meet two indispensable requirements. And he was right in supposing that, when a President meets these requirements, the fact that he does not command or even comprehend the details of policy need not be of major political consequence.

The first requirement is to point the republic in one or another direction. This can be done only if the man in the White House possesses, or is possessed by, a vision of the ideal America. The President, said Henry Adams, "resembles the commander of a ship at sea. He must have a helm to grasp, a course to steer, a port to seek."[42] After four years of the Carter Presidency, no one knew where Carter wished to steer the country. But no one could doubt that Reagan had a deeply felt and, indeed, explicitly ideological sense of his destination. No one could doubt either that his personal values dominated his administration or that his subordinates, far from manipulating him, labored to make administrative and policy sense out of his bundle of prejudices.

The second requirement is to explain to the electorate why the direction the President proposes is right for the nation. Reagan understood, as Carter never did, that politics is ultimately an educational process. Where Carter gave the impression of regarding presidential speeches as disagreeable duties, to be rushed through as perfunctorily as possible, Reagan knew that the speech is the vital weapon of presidential leadership. His best speeches had a structure and an argument. They were well written and superbly delivered. They were potent vehicles for the President's charm, histrionic skill and genius for simplification.

If the President can point the country and persuade the voters that it is the right direction in which to go, and if he can find reasonably competent subordinates to figure out the details, it does not matter so much politically that he himself hardly knows what is going on. Reagan's success proved that the Presidency, if you know how to work it, is not all that tough a job. He spent fewer hours at his desk and more on holiday than most readers of this book are accustomed to doing. Yet in short order he brilliantly dispelled the learned doubts of the late 1970s about the capacity of Presidents to govern and brilliantly restored national confidence in the workability of the office and the system. The foe of government ironically revived faith in government.

Reagan added to this a talent that was Eisenhower's signal strength—the ability to divorce himself from the actions and consequences of his own administration. He piled up the largest budgetary deficits in American peacetime history. Yet no one continued to denounce deficits with more impassioned eloquence and apparent sincerity. He sent Marines to Lebanon in 1983 and insisted that their continued presence was crucial to America's position in the world. When he withdrew them in 1984, the nation, instead of demanding an accounting for an indefensible fiasco, breathed a sigh of grateful relief. If Carter had been President, Congress and the press would have been merciless. But Carter, by priding himself on his mastery of detail, acquired a responsibility in the public mind that Reagan, by eschewing detail, adroitly escaped.

As John R. Sears, Reagan's first campaign manager in 1980, remarked, "He walks away from more political car crashes than anyone"[43]—walks away and never looks back. When pressed, Reagan genially blamed his troubles on someone else, with Congress usually the favored scapegoat. Voters forgave and forgot.

In the same way, Reagan was indulged in his manifold misstatement of facts and in his endless flow of fable and fantasy. He gave the Prime Minister of Israel and Simon Wiesenthal, the Nazi hunter, on separate occasions the clear impression that, as a Signal Corps photographer, he had personally filmed Nazi concentration camps toward the end of the war. Of course, he never left the United States during the Second World War.[44] Similarly he told an assembly of winners of the Congressional Medal of Honor about the posthumous award to a B-17 commander who chose to go down in his plane with a wounded soldier. Lars-Erik Nelson of the *New York Daily News* checked all 434 citations of the Medal of Honor winners in the Second World War and could not find the Reagan tale. Eventually Nelson established that the tale came from the April 1944 *Reader's Digest* and from a 1944 movie, *Wing and a Prayer*.[45] Such revelations fell with a dull thud. No one appeared to care about the President's affable fabrications.

Reagan was the President as master illusionist. Many Americans perceived him as the personification of patriotism, of 'standing tall' and rushing to the defense of the republic. If asked to compare Reagan with, say, George McGovern, they would of course name Reagan as the exemplary American patriot. Yet, when the nation was in its greatest danger, McGovern was a bomber pilot, flew thirty-five missions, twice brought in planes severely damaged by antiaircraft fire and won the Distinguished Flying Cross, while Reagan fought the Second World War on the film lots of Hollywood, sleeping in his own bed every night. (The Reaganites of the 1980s continued in this tradition. Many of the fire-eaters so prepared to risk the lives of younger Americans by pushing a hard line against Nicaragua and the Soviet Union — Richard Perle, John Lehman, Elliot Abrams, Newt Gingrich, Pat Buchanan, Richard Burt — had managed for one reason or another, when they were themselves of military age in the 1960s, not to fight in Vietnam.)*

Similarly Reagan made himself exceptional among American Presidents in the public zeal with which he advocated and exploited religion. Yet he rarely went to church himself. The proclaimed champion of the family, he was the only divorced man ever elected President, and his relations with some of his own children were strained. The proclaimed champion of traditional morality, he had spent more of his life in a long Hollywood career in friendly association with adulterers, alcoholics, homosexuals, with people who procured abortions and people who took drugs, than any previous President. The proclaimed champion of law, order and virtue, he headed an administration marked at home by the debasement of public ethics and abroad by a determination to make the United States a law unto itself in the world.

Reagan's triumph over anomaly, fantasy and failure was due in part to the serene and contagious optimism with which he walked away from car crashes. Like Franklin Roosevelt, the hero of his youth, he radiated a reassuring confidence that all contradictions would be dissolved and all difficulties overcome. In addition, he enjoyed that most useful of political blessings — luck. Optimism and luck, along with an instinct for the levers of presidential effectiveness and a gift for dodging accountability, carried him very far.

They may not carry him to the top of the presidential rankings. Franklin Roosevelt was a great President not alone because he possessed and communicated a vision of the ideal republic but even more because he had an inexhaustible, grasping curiosity about American life, a sympathy for the insulted and injured of society and a creative

---

*Jane Mayer, "Vietnam Service Isn't on the Resumes of Some Vocal, Middle-Aged Hawks," *Wall Street Journal*, 11 January 1985; Jack Newfield, "Reagan's War Hawks without Wings," *Village Voice*, 11 June 1985. Congressman Andrew Jacobs, a Democrat who had fought as a Marine in Korea, called these characters "War Wimps." A War Wimp is "one who is all too willing to send others to war, but never gets around to going to war himself."

delight in public policy. Reagan's objectives—to repudiate public purpose and to enthrone private interest—did not call for much curiosity, sympathy or creativity; and, enviably secure in his ideological certitudes, he remained impervious to everything that conflicted with his preconceptions. While he showed considerable skill in using the presidential office to achieve the ends, his place in history will depend on whether posterity will judge his ends beneficial to the nation.

Still Reagan's record showed how far competence in the use of executive resources can go in revitalizing an office over which last rites had been recently pronounced. It is a salutary reminder of the indestructibility of the American Presidency.

VI

Is it also a portent of the revival of the Imperial Presidency? The critical tests of the Imperial Presidency are threefold: the war-making power; the secrecy system; and the employment against the American people of emergency authority acquired for use against foreign enemies.

In 1973, when I wrote *The Imperial Presidency* and when Congress debated the War Powers Resolution, rhetoric about the war-making power considerably outran knowledge about the way that power had been exercised in American history. The State Department used to vindicate the presidential prerogative in committing troops to combat by putting out lists of the 80 or 125 or 150 times Presidents had done so without congressional authorization; the number escalated like Joe McCarthy's estimate of the number of Communists in the State Department. Senator Goldwater once announced the score as "at least 197 foreign military hostilities," of which 192 were "undeclared wars." He added, a little anticlimactically, "Nearly half involved actual fighting."*

No one, however, really knew the facts till Judge Sofaer ascertained the circumstances in which fighting took place on unilateral presidential initiative and published the results of his research in 1976. Sofaer showed that unauthorized presidential adventurism thrived in the early republic. Whether the pattern thus revealed legalized unilateral war-making by modern Presidents is a separate question. Sofaer's surmise is that the early Presidents deliberately selected venturesome

---

*Barry M. Goldwater, "The President's Ability to Protect America's Freedoms—The Warmaking Power," *Arizona State University Law Journal*, 1971, no. 3, 423–424. Goldwater thereby claimed a war every eleven months or so throughout American history—an insatiable bellicosity that might astound, and would certainly gratify, our Marxist critics.

agents, deliberately kept their missions secret, deliberately gave them vague instructions, deliberately failed either to approve or to disapprove their constitutionally questionable plans and deliberately denied Congress and the public the information to determine whether aggressive acts were authorized—all because they wanted their men in the field to do things that they knew lay beyond the constitutional right of Presidents to command. "At no time," Sofaer writes of the classical period, "did the executive claim 'inherent' power to initiate military actions."[46]

The vital difference between the early republic and the Imperial Presidency resides not in what Presidents did but in what Presidents believed they had the inherent right to do. Early Presidents, even while they circumvented the Constitution, had a cautious and vigilant concern for consent in a practical if not a formal sense. They had legislative majorities; they obtained broad delegations of authority; Congress approved their objectives and chose to let them take the lead; they acted in secret only when they had some assurance of support and sympathy if they were found out; and, even when they occasionally withheld essential information, they willingly shared much more than their twentieth-century successors, including such choice items as the instructions given envoys despatched on overseas negotiations. And, when Presidents initiated military action in the nineteenth century, it was typically against brigands, pirates, revolutionaries and other non-governmental groups; not, as in the twentieth century, against sovereign states.

In the late twentieth century Presidents made sweeping claims of inherent power, neglected the collection of consent, withheld information *ad libitum* and went to war against sovereign states. In so doing, they departed from the principles, if less from the practice, of the early republic. Reagan warmly embraced latter-day theories of inherent presidential power, including the inflation of the title Commander-in-Chief into a source of extra constitutional authority.* He launched sneak attacks without congressional authorization against Grenada and Libya. He brought the CIA back from its season of disgrace, made it once again the President's private army and sent it off, without congressional approval, to overthrow the government of Nicaragua. In the use of the war-making power, Reagan was a stout defender of the "almost royal" prerogatives.

---

*Hamilton in the 69th *Federalist* emphasized that the President's designation as Commander-in-Chief amounted "to nothing more than the supreme command and direction of the military and naval forces ... while that of the British king extends to the *declaring* of war and to the *raising* and *regulating* of fleets and armies,—all which, by the Constitution under consideration, would appertain to the legislature."

VII

Reagan, moreover, devoted particular energy to reversing the post-Watergate movement to open up government and to rebuilding that fortress of the Imperial Presidency, the secrecy system. In his Executive Order 12356 of 2 April 1982 he discarded the Carter doctrine that the case for secrecy had to be weighed against the "public interest in disclosure." The Reagan order also discarded the standard that required a finding of "identifiable" potential damage to national security before documents can be classified. It eliminated the automatic declassification of government records. It even provided for the reclosing of records already declassified. The message to the bureaucracy was unmistakable: when in doubt, classify. The State Department, for example, after declassifying a minimum of 30 million pages a year in 1973–1981, declassified less than 13 million pages in both 1983 and 1984; the percentage of documents censored after review for declassification increased from 10 percent in 1983 to 75 percent in 1984.[47]

On 11 March 1983, Reagan promulgated National Security Decision Directive 84. This one required all officials with security clearances to sign agreements promising not to disclose classified information. It required them, if called upon, to take lie detector tests, with "adverse consequences" in event of refusal—even though evidence from such tests is too unreliable for admission to federal courts. And, most astonishing of all, it required those with access to "sensitive compartmented intelligence"—i.e., the 120,000 officials who see secret intelligence reports—to submit all their writings to prepublication censorship for the rest of their lives.

Congressional protest caused Reagan to suspend the provision for prepublication review. But a General Accounting Office report in June 1984 showed, in the words of Congressman Jack Brooks of Texas, that the alleged suspension "has, in reality, suspended very little of this administration's censorship and polygraph policies."[48] Over 100,000 government officials, including the Secretary of State and the Attorney General, had signed agreements accepting some form of lifetime prepublication review, and the lie detector program was continuing unabated. On 1 November 1985 a new Reagan national security directive applied the lie detector to "all individuals with access to United States Government sensitive compartmentalized information."

The Reagan administration reasserted claims to unconditional executive privilege. The Freedom of Information Act was subjected to administrative restriction and sabotage. The press was forbidden to cover the invasion of Grenada. In the case of Samuel Loring Morison, the administration moved to convert the Espionage Act of 1917 into an Official Secrets Act by successfully prosecuting a government employee for the delivery of classified photographs, not to a foreign power, but to *Jane's Defence Weekly,* a respected journal published in London; not for espionage but for leaking to the press. The administration has even floated the idea of an American Official Secrets Act on the British model. One wonders what dire crisis justifies so improbable a repudiation of the American libertarian tradition. The republic faced the gravest perils of its history—the Civil War, two world wars—without an Official Secrets Act. What mightier emergency demands an intensification of executive secrecy today?

No one questions the state's right to keep certain things secret— weapons technology and deployment, intelligence methods and sources, diplomatic negotiations in progress, military contingency plans and the like. But the target of the Reagan program was not the disclosure of information to enemy governments; it was the disclosure of information to the American Congress, press and people.

All Presidents are exasperated by leaks. They are really not, however, against leaks in principle. The selective leak is a familiar tool of government. What enrages Presidents are the leaks they do not ordain themselves—leaks that embarrass, expose or undermine their policies, which is to say leaks that stimulate and fortify national debate.

Presidents like to claim that such leaks do ineffable harm to national security. What they mostly mean is that leaks do harm to the political interests of the administration. The harm to national security through leaks is always exaggerated. We have had leaks from the start of the republic—from the day in 1795 when Senator Mason of Virginia enraged President Washington by giving the secret text of Jay's Treaty to the *Philadelphia Aurora,* or the day in 1844 when Senator Tappan of Ohio enraged President Tyler by giving the secret text of the treaty annexing Texas to the *New York Evening Post.* No one has ever demonstrated that these leaks, or the publication of the Pentagon Papers either, harmed national security. No one can doubt that the disclosures benefited the democratic process.

Presidents are not infallible. Bureaucrats brandishing Top Secret stamps are even less infallible. The prime historic function of the secrecy system has not been to protect national security. In this respect, it has done rather badly. As the system expands, too much paper is classified (19.6 million "classification decisions" in 1984, an increase of 60 percent over 1973), too many people get security clearances (4.2 million), and too many spies slip through the net. The real function

of the secrecy system is to protect the executive branch from accountability for its incompetence and its venality, its errors and on occasion
its crimes.* The secrecy system, moreover, emboldens government to
undertake rash and mindless adventures. "Though secrecy in diplomacy is occasionally unavoidable," wrote Lord Bryce, himself a distinguished diplomat, "it has its perils. . . . Publicity may cause some
losses, but may avert some misfortunes."[49] Conceivably the United
States might have been spared one or two disasters—the Bay of Pigs,
for example—had recent history been marked by more rather than
fewer leaks.

Nicholas P. Trist once expostulated to Andrew Jackson about Old
Hickory's indifference to the fact that an unreliable servant had access
to his official papers. "They are welcome, sir," Jackson replied, "to
anything they can get out of my papers. . . . Let them make the most
of it. Our government, sir, is founded upon the intelligence of the
people; it has no other basis; upon their capacity to arrive at right
conclusions in regard to measures and in regard to men." Trist, who
was a professional diplomat, observed that this was all very well if the
people had access to the whole truth; but what about partial disclosures and selective quotations? "Well, if they can't know all," said Jackson, "let them know as much as they can. The more they know of
matters the better."[50]

This is the tradition that the secrecy system seeks to abolish. "Executive secrecy," John Taylor of Caroline, the philosopher of Jeffersonianism, wrote in 1814, "is one of the monarchical customs, plau-
sibly defended, and certainly fatal to republican government. . . .
How can national self government exist without a knowledge of national affairs? or how can legislatures be wise or independent, who
legislate in the dark upon the recommendation of one man?"[51]

The secrecy system and the presidential claim to inherent war-

---

*A recent illustration is the censorship by the Central Intelligence Agency of a book by
its former director Admiral Stansfield Turner. "Having been responsible for protecting
the nation's intelligence secrets for four years," Turner writes in his foreword, "I am
well aware what the release of some kinds of information could mean to our national
security." Yet the Reagan CIA demanded more than a hundred deletions, ranging,
Turner says, "from borderline issues to the ridiculous." They did this, Turner believes,
"because they were upset with the book's highly critical view of the Reagan administration's mishandling of our intelligence activities." *Secrecy and Democracy: The CIA in Transition* (Boston, 1985), xi. See also the *Preliminary Joint Staff Study on the Protection of National Secrets,* prepared for the House Subcommittee on Civil and Constitutional Rights
of the Judiciary Committee and for the Subcommittee on Civil Service of the Post Office
and Civil Service Committee, 25 October 1985; William McGowan, "Why We Can't
Catch Spies," *Washington Monthly,* July–August 1985; and George Lardner, Jr., "When
in Doubt, Classify," *Washington Post,* weekly ed., 14 May 1985.

making power are potent weapons of the Imperial Presidency. Reagan used them to fend off Congress and the press and to strengthen his unilateral control of foreign policy. He has not, however, brought the Imperial Presidency into the final stage—the policy of condemning opponents of the President as traitors to the republic. He seemed in his relaxed way to regard opposition as a part of democracy. One doubts that he had an Enemies List. There has been no McCarthyism in his administration. Thus far he has been more concerned with denying information than with destroying critics. The Imperial Presidency flourishes but is not yet (1986) in full bloom.

VIII

The debate over the Imperial Presidency raised doubts about the adequacy of the constitutional system—doubts persisting in influential quarters even after Reagan demonstrated that the Presidency still worked.

Watergate had produced in the early 1970s a cry for basic constitutional change. If the United States, reformers thought, only had the equivalent of the parliamentary question hour, the Nixon cover-up could not have been sustained, and, if it only had the equivalent of a parliamentary vote of confidence, the Nixon Presidency could have been terminated without the trauma of impeachment. At a conference on the Presidency in 1973, eminent foreigners—Gunnar Myrdal of Sweden and Lord Ritchie-Calder of Great Britain—impressed their audience by insisting "that Watergate simply couldn't happen in their countries—or rather that, if something like it did happen, the party in power would be out of office within a matter of hours."[52]

Under this benign light, parliament seemed an idyllic spot where legislators reveled in the power to oversee, interrogate and dismiss the executive. In the presidential model, the executive is protected by the separation of powers; in the parliamentary model, the executive is drawn from the legislative majority and presumably obedient to it. Would not constitutional revision along parliamentary lines supply the perfect antidote to the Imperial Presidency? In 1974 the political scientist Charles M. Hardin offered an elaborate parliamentary blueprint in his book *Presidential Power and Accountability: Toward a New Constitution.* In the same period Richard Lee Strout (TRB of the *New Republic*) argued the advantages of the British and Canadian systems in sprightly columns. Members of Congress advanced less sweeping proposals designed to appropriate two of the more beguiling features of the parliamentary model—the question period and the vote of confidence—and insert them into the presidential system.

Then, at the end of the 1970s, the frustrations of the Carter Presidency set off a new cry for constitutional reform. This time, however, the parliamentary model fascinated for opposite reasons—not as a means of restraining executive abuse but as a means of restoring executive authority. For in the parliamentary system the executive can count on the automatic enactment of his program, and the electorate knows where to fix accountability for the result. Lloyd N. Cutler, who as Carter's White House counsel had seen plenty of frustration at first hand, published an influential article in 1980, arguing that the constitutional diffusion of power made the national government incoherent and irresponsible and proposing reforms designed to move the political order in a parliamentary direction.[53]

Cutler then joined with Douglas Dillon, a distinguished public servant in the Eisenhower and Kennedy administrations, to set up a Committee on the Constitutional System. In the call for the Committee, Dillon wrote that the "question transcending all immediate issues is whether we can continue to afford the luxury of the separation of power" and whether we should not contemplate "a change to some form of parliamentary government that would eliminate or sharply reduce the present division of authority between the executive and legislative arms."[54] The Committee's Basic Problem Statement provided a powerful summary:

The checks and balances inspired by the experience of the Eighteenth Century have led repeatedly, in the Twentieth Century, to governmental stalemate and deadlock, to an incapacity to make quick and sharp decisions in the face of urgent problems. Rash and impulsive governmental actions have been deterred, and that is a benefit. But it is a benefit often gained at the cost of inability to act at all, or at least to act in a timely and decisive manner. When, after arduous delays, policies are produced, they are liable to be a contradictory hodge-podge that neither the President nor the legislators fully support. No one accepts responsibility, and the people have difficulty holding anyone accountable. The President blames the Congress, members of Congress blame the President and one another, and amid the recriminations people lose confidence in government altogether.[55]

The problem of bringing effective government out of a mandated separation of powers was not of course new. In the early republic, as Henry Jones Ford pointed out, rule by the gentry was relied on to maintain the unity of government. When the age of deference passed, political parties arose to supply the connections.[56] Intermittently commentators sought more formal ties between the two separated branches. In the 1830s Justice Story proposed that cabinet members go on to the floor of Congress to answer questions and participate in debate. Half a century later Senator George Pendleton, supported by James G. Blaine and (when he was in the House) James A. Garfield, revived the proposal. Professor Woodrow Wilson, another supporter, added that cabinet members should be chosen from the ranks of the legislative majority. Still later President Taft suggested that cabinet members be given access to the floor.

In 1945 Thomas K. Finletter, a liberal Democrat and afterward Truman's Secretary of the Air Force, published a closely reasoned book called *Can Representative Government Do the Job?* Seeking a middle ground between the separation-of-powers and parliamentary models, Finletter offered a joint executive-legislative cabinet as the keystone of a system in which the President could, if faced by legislative stalemate, dissolve Congress and call for new elections. *Can Representative Government Do the Job?* remains the most interesting book on the subject of American constitutional reform, and Finletter's emphasis on the power of dissolution was a striking and original contribution.*

Contemporary constitutional reformers thus have a certain amount of American history to draw upon. Lloyd Cutler's 1980 program proposed to bring about a quasi-parliamentary regime by providing that the President and Congress (both houses) be elected for simultaneous six-year terms and by empowering both the President and Congress to break stalemates by dissolving the government and calling for new elections.

Such a program, however, confronted the problem emphasized by that able and irrepressible reformer James MacGregor Burns in *The Power to Lead* in 1984: that constitutional reform, which Burns thought highly desirable along Finletter-Hardin-Cutler lines, can work only on the foundation of a revitalized party system. For the parliamentary model assumes centralized, disciplined and ideology-driven parties. Apart from the danger that excessively ideological parties might split the nation irremediably, as they did in 1860, history shows that American parties have always resisted centralization

---

*Senator J. W. Fulbright embodied the Finletter plan in a constitutional amendment introduced in the Eightieth Congress. The amendment provided that the President by executive order or Congress by concurrent resolution might at any time dissolve both the Presidency and Congress. In such event, a general election would be held in which the President, Senate and House would be elected for six years or until their terms were ended by a new executive order or concurrent resolution. The purposes of the amendment, as described by Finletter, were "(1) to give to Congress the ultimate power of dismissing the executive and thus to free Congress of the need to defeat the executive from time to time in order to assert its authority; and (2) to give the President the power to refer an issue on which he was defeated by the Congress to the people for their decision." T. K. Finletter, "The United States Government and the Future," *Parliamentary Affairs*, Winter 1949, 258.

and discipline. They are loose coalitions, open at the joints, filled with internal argument, held together by broad biases and historic memories. When Hardin, for example, proposed to veto the nomination of "persistent mavericks" for Congress and to punish legislators who made "a career of independence,"* he underlined the practical irrelevance of his plan. The systematic exclusion from Congress of all dissent save that of the official opposition is unimaginable in the American political culture. Rigid discipline, the prohibition of free voting, the persecution of mavericks, the abolition of primaries—all such things are against the genius of American politics, and never more so than in the electronic age.

The decisive fact is that Americans have come to *want* divided government. For half the time since the Second World War, control of the White House has rested in one party and control of one or both houses of Congress in the other party. What Samuel Lubell calls "the deliberate and widespread use of both parties," balancing one off against the other, began in the Eisenhower years.[57] It became thereafter a purposeful technique of self-defense against the Imperial Presidency. A Harris poll, taken shortly before Reagan's triumphant reelection in 1984, showed voters preferring by 54 to 39 percent that he not win both houses of Congress[58]—a preference quickly verified in the election.

At a time when political parties can hardly keep afloat in the turbulent sea of voter independence, the idea of making them more cohesive and commanding than ever before in American history is an exercise in fantasy. If a crisis of governmental impotence should arise in the future, a President is not likely to ask the Congress to move toward parliamentary government through the laborious process of constitutional amendment. He is more likely to say, as Franklin Roosevelt said in his first inaugural, "I shall ask the Congress for the one remaining instrument to meet the crisis—broad Executive power to wage a war against the emergency."

IX

Even if a conversion to parliamentarianism were possible, there is little reason to suppose it would be desirable. The American admiration for the parliamentary model springs from romantic misconceptions about the British system.

*C. M. Hardin, *Presidential Power and Accountability* (Chicago, 1974), 185. I should add that, though this book's essential argument seems to me to lie in the domain of political fantasy, there are many shrewd insights into the American political order along the way.

Our constitutional reformers yearned after the parliamentary model, as noted, for two contradictory reasons: the post-Watergate reformers because they believed it would assure legislative supremacy; and the post-Carter reformers because they believed it would assure executive supremacy. The second group understood the parliamentary system better. While the parliamentary model formally assumes legislative omnipotence, in practice it produces an almost unassailable dominance of the executive over the legislature.

The British Prime Minister thus appoints people to office without parliamentary confirmation, makes foreign policy without parliamentary participation, declares war without parliamentary authorization, concludes treaties without parliamentary ratification, sets the budget without parliamentary consultation, withholds information without parliamentary recourse and essentially inherits the prerogatives that once belonged to absolute monarchy. As Lloyd George said in 1931, "Parliament has really no control over the Executive; it is a pure fiction."[59] This is the continuing refrain of British politics. "The government controls Parliament," Lord Hailsham said in 1976, "and not Parliament the government. . . . We live under an elective dictatorship, absolute in theory, if hitherto thought tolerable in practice."[60] "Parliament," said Dr. David Owen, the leader of the Social Democrats, in 1985, "is the pawn of the Executive."[61] Nor in the British system does a Supreme Court exist to check executive abuse.

The alleged check on prime ministerial discretion is cabinet government—the theory of collective responsibility for government decisions. "You, Mr. President," Churchill said to Roosevelt during the Second World War, "are concerned to what extent you can act without the approval of Congress. You don't worry about your Cabinet. On the other hand, I never worry about Parliament, but I continuously have to consult and have the support of my Cabinet."[62] No doubt in the age of Bagehot and possibly even in the age of Churchill cabinet government was a reality. But collective decision-making has notably declined in modern times. Many vital decisions—Chamberlain at Munich, Attlee and the building of the British nuclear capacity, Eden and the Suez war—were taken by the Prime Minister and a small inner group. Cabinet government has given way to prime ministerial government.*

---

*See R. H. S. Crossman's introduction to Walter Bagehot, *The English Constitution* (London, Fontana paperback, 1963) and his Godkin Lectures, *The Myths of Cabinet Government* (Cambridge, Mass., 1972). Crossman's diaries and those of Barbara Castle provide ample evidence that cabinet government, in the sense of the collective making of decisions, has indeed become a myth.

American parliamentarists cite dissolution following the loss of a vote of confidence as the legislature's check on prime ministerial discretion. But in practice, the threat of dissolution hands the Prime Minister one more means of whipping recalcitrant MPs into line— lest they be forced to risk their seats in a general election. The vote of confidence is so drastic a resort that it is rarely employed. Losing a vote of confidence has not overthrown a British government for more than half a century, and in that case (1924) it was a minority Labour government dependent on Liberal support. The last time the loss of a vote of confidence overthrew a government commanding majority support in the House of Commons was a century ago, in 1885. Nor does defeat of a government bill automatically count as a vote of confidence. In the 1970s, British governments suffered a series of defeats without being forced to dissolve Parliament and call a new general election.[63] No doubt the possibility of a no-confidence vote has brought about changes in Prime Ministers, as after Narvik in 1940 and Suez in 1956. But this was done by reshuffling people inside the government, not by going to the electorate and getting a fresh mandate.

In the American system, the dissolution capability would give legislators the power, which they lack under the impeachment clause, to dismiss Presidents on grounds of disagreement over policy. Is this such a good idea? One has only to reflect what might have happened, for example, when John Adams resisted the congressional passion for war with France in 1798 or when Harry Truman faced down an explosion of congressional wrath after firing Douglas MacArthur in 1950. Yet in retrospect those two doughty Presidents never had finer hours. Nor, as Allan Sindler has pointed out, would a brisk no-confidence dismissal of Nixon have been nearly so satisfactory a resolution of the Watergate mess as the "thoroughness, deliberateness, gravity and nonpartisanship of the impeachment inquiry."[64]

It is conceivable that an incident like Watergate might have forced out a British Prime Minister through behind-the-scenes sleight of hand. But that does not mean that Parliament and the electorate would know what had been going on. "Don't think a Watergate couldn't happen here," Woodrow Wyatt, a former member of Parliament and a continuing political commentator, has written. "You just wouldn't hear about it."[65] Nixon might even have escaped unscathed. "If only Mr. Nixon had the blessing of the British system," according to Edward Pearce, the political correspondent of the *London Daily Telegraph*, ". . . Woodward and Bernstein would have been drowned in the usual channels, a D-Notice would have been erected over their evidence, and a properly briefed judge, a figure of outstanding integrity, would have found the essential parts of the tapes to be either not relevant or prejudicial to the national security. The British system of protecting the authorities is almost part of the constitution."[66]

The question period is another device much fancied by American parliamentarists. The notion of compelling executive officials to defend policies in face-to-face confrontation has initial appeal as a way to demystify the Presidency. But the device is less fancied by those who use it every week. "What most questions usually reveal," wrote R. H. S. Crossman, "is the capacity of a Minister to evade an issue."[67] Lord Hailsham spoke of "the twice-weekly exhibition of schoolboy humour in the House of Commons,"[68] *The Economist* of "an undergraduate pastiche of a White House press conference."[69] Woodrow Wyatt called question time a "useless privilege," a "charade," a "fake instrument of democracy," "a Punch and Judy show"; "when a Minister has something to hide, Question Time has little hope of dragging it into the open."[70] It works no better in Canada. "Anyone who has participated in question period," wrote Professor James Gillies, a former MP, "knows its main purposes are to embarrass the government, to amuse the tourists and TV audiences, and to make life easier for reporters. It is a totally ineffective way to elicit significant information."[71]

Given congressional obsequiousness toward Presidents, one doubts whether a presidential question time would help in the United States. Newspapermen at press conferences are less obsequious, but they rarely elicit significant information. As for cabinet members, they are subject to far more sustained and searching interrogation before congressional committees than they would ever receive in a general question hour.

X

The irony is that British reformers are as dissatisfied with the fusion of powers as American reformers are with the separation of powers.* And for many British reformers the model is—the American Congress. One reformer calls Congress "the quintessential legislature. As the grand inquest of the nation it functions on a grand scale. From

---

*Canadian reformers register similar complaints. A recent study reports the "growing misgivings about Parliament's capacity to exact accountability from the government and to provide a credible vehicle for the efficient development of policies and legislation." Thomas D'Aquino, G. B. Doern and Cassandra Blair, *Parliamentary Democracy in Canada: Issues for Reform* (Toronto, 1983), xi.

the points of view of expertise, political clout, facilities, interest articulation and constituency service, it is in a class by itself."[72]

British reformers want to set Parliament free. They want to increase legislative initiative, legislative scrutiny and executive accountability. They want a Bill of Rights. They want fixed terms for Parliament. (A former Prime Minister spoke to me with envy about the American system of midterm elections. "The only means we have between general elections of bringing public opinion to bear on national policies," he said, "is through by-elections, and this depends on a sufficiency of MPs resigning or dying. Luck has been with Mrs. Thatcher, and she has had far less than the average number of by-elections. How much better to give the whole country a chance to express itself every two years!") They want back bench independence. They want to select parliamentary candidates through primaries. They want the topmost civil service posts to be filled by political appointment. They want to abolish the Official Secrets Act and to enact a Freedom of Information Act. They finally (in 1979) forced the government to accept a system of watchdog committees overseeing major departments, and they want now to increase committee staffs and to gain authority to review pending legislation. They want a select committee to monitor the intelligence services. They want control over government spending through a national audit office solely responsible to Parliament, like the General Accounting Office in Washington. They want, in short, to limit power, in Lord Hailsham's words, "both by law and by a system of checks and balances."[73]

While American parliamentarists envy the centralized and disciplined parties of Britain and Canada, British and Canadian reformers think that centralization and discipline have reduced individual legislators to nonentities. The ordinary back-bencher, observes Woodrow Wyatt, "may be the greatest orator since Demosthenes, the finest administrator since Pericles, the shrewdest judge of men since Napoleon. It will be all to no avail."[74] The situation is no better in Canada. "Cicero and Demosthenes together could not change a vote in the Canadian parliament," writes Professor Gillies. ". . . Few [speeches] are even listened to."[75]

Nothing is more damaging to Parliament, British reformers argue, than the fusion of powers. Confining the selection of ministers to MPs narrows the pool of talent available for governing. It bases appointment on a superficial test—facility in debate—rather than on a serious test—ability in policy and administration. It creates "a conspiracy of common interest" (Wyatt) to keep the executive strong and the legislature weak, for two thirds of the House of Commons either have been or aspire to be ministers and find it personally advantageous to exalt the executive. "The presence of the Prime Minister, Ministers and the machinery of party discipline in the House of Commons results in its members being prisoners in their own House."[76]

Recent British developments—the spread of 'cross-voting' (that is, voting against measures advanced by one's own party); the establishment of watchdog committees; the demand to initiate legislation; the defiance of the Official Secrets Act by whistle-blowing civil servants and their vindication in the courts[77]—all represent movement in the American direction. In Great Britain as in the United States party dealignment increases in the electronic age.[78]

Where American constitutional reformers yearn after Parliament, the British reform agenda adopts essential features of the American system. Each country tends to play the defects of its own system against the charms of the one across the seas. 'Play' is the word, because constitutional blueprinting is in the end a game. Constitutions, whether written or unwritten, must express deeply imbedded values, habits and folkways of a nation. They cannot be revised mechanically.

XI

The argument thus far has been about the structure of government. But are the difficulties encountered these days in governing really the consequences of defects in structure? After all, the United States has had the separation of powers from the beginning of the republic. The existence of an independent Congress and of an independent Supreme Court has not prevented competent Presidents from acting with decision and despatch.

In practice the separation of powers is a rather flexible and accommodating doctrine. The Founding Fathers were intensely practical men determined to charter a republic that would work and last in a dangerous world. They recognized, as the Supreme Court itself has said, that a "hermetic sealing off of the three branches of Government from one another would preclude the establishment of a Nation capable of governing itself effectively."[79] The system devised at Philadelphia in 1787 did not separate the powers of government into three watertight compartments. The Philadelphia system, as Richard Neustadt has notably said, was rather one of "separated institutions *sharing* powers."[80] Justice Robert H. Jackson provided the classic statement in the steel seizure case: "While the Constitution diffuses power the better to secure liberty, it also contemplates that the practice will integrate the dispersed powers into a workable government. It enjoins upon its branches separateness but interdependence, autonomy but reciprocity."[81]

The independence of Congress and the courts did not disable Jefferson or Andrew Jackson or Lincoln or Wilson or the two Roosevelts. Of course they all complained on occasion. Theodore Roosevelt once clenched his fist and said to the young Franklin Roosevelt, "Sometimes I wish I could be President and Congress too." FDR added thirty years later, "I suppose if the truth were told, he is not the only President that has had that idea."[82] But they all persevered, and mostly succeeded where they deserved to succeed. The most powerful plea this century for strong national authority—Herbert Croly's *The Promise of American Life*—did not see the separation of powers as an obstacle to effective government. Frank J. Goodnow's *Social Reform and the Constitution,* another classic of the Progressive era, worried far more about federalism, the division of power between national and state governments, as a bar to reform than about the division of power within the national government.

Why are things worse now? It cannot be because of the separation of powers itself; this has been a constant through American history. It cannot be because contemporary problems are worse; this, as noted, is hardly the case. The real difference is that the Presidents who operated the system successfully in the past knew what they thought should be done—and were able to persuade Congress and the nation to give their ideas a try. The problem today is not at all that our leaders know what to do and are prevented from doing it by structural gridlock in the system. The problem is that they know not what to do.

Efficient enactment of a poor program is a dubious triumph. A system in which a rubber stamp legislature delivers whatever the executive requests is only as good as the executive and his requests. If the United States had had a parliamentary system in 1937, Congress would have given Franklin Roosevelt his court-packing plan. If it had had a parliamentary system in the 1980s, Congress would have illegalized abortion and legalized school prayer.

A century ago Bryce in *The American Commonwealth* reported the English view that the separation of powers made it almost impossible for the American polity to settle major national issues. He also reported the rejoinder by American political leaders. Congress, they told Bryce, had forborne to settle such issues not because of defects in structure,

but because the division of opinion in the country regarding them has been faithfully reflected in Congress. The majority has not been strong enough to get its way; and this has happened, not only because abundant opportunities for resistance arise from the methods of doing business, but still more because no distinct impulse or mandate towards any particular settlement of these questions has been received from the country. It is not for Congress to go faster than the people. When the country knows and speaks its mind, Congress will not fail to act.[83]

When the country is not sure what ought to be done, it may be that the delay, debate and further consideration enjoined by the separation of powers are not a bad idea. What is the virtue of acting with decision and despatch if you don't know what you are doing? And, when our leadership is sure what to do, it must begin by educating Congress and public opinion—and that is not a bad idea either. A competent President with a sensible policy or even (as in the case of the Reagan tax bill of 1981) a less than sensible policy has the resources under the present Constitution to get his way.

The separation of powers is most deplored in the field of foreign policy. Yet here it is the indispensable engine of consent, and consent is never more indispensable than on questions of peace and war. Congressional criticism alerts a President to flaws in his policies. Congressional support strengthens his hand and increases his authority. After Vietnam, an intelligent President would surely wish to secure congressional consent to any course on foreign affairs carrying the risk of war.

Both Ford and Carter complained about the Clark amendment of 1976, prohibiting military or paramilitary operations in Angola without express congressional authorization. Had there been no Clark amendment, either President might have sent the CIA or even the Marines into the Angolan civil war. Apart from the question whether armed intervention in Angola made any sense, it obviously could not have been sustained without a clear and formal expression of congressional support. Presidents should regard the requirement of congressional collaboration in foreign policy not as a burden from which to be delivered but as an opportunity to be embraced in order to give policy a solid basis in consent. "No foreign policy will stick," Averell Harriman has wisely said, "unless the American people are behind it. And unless Congress understands it the American people aren't going to understand it."[84]

The separation of powers has caused its share of problems. But in the main it has worked well enough. It has ensured discussion when no consensus exists for action, and it has permitted action when a majority is convinced that the action is right. In short, if the executive has a persuasive remedy, you don't need fundamental constitutional change. If the executive remedy is not persuasive, you don't want fundamental constitutional change.

XII

But what about limited constitutional change to improve specific aspects of a less than perfect document? Despairing of root-and-branch transformation, reformers propose a series of discrete amendments: a single six-year presidential term; a presidential item veto; the direct election of the President by popular vote.

The idea of a single six-year term has been around for a long time. The perennial argument for this amendment is that the quest for reelection, in the words of a bipartisan group of former cabinet members in 1985, lies "at the heart of our inability to manage complex, long-term national problems."[85] The prospect of a second term, it is claimed, stains Presidents with partisanship. It makes the nation suspect their motives and tempts them to issue easy promises and to postpone hard decisions. A single six-year term would liberate Presidents from the low business of politics. Instead of urging measures designed to secure their reelection, they would gain the freedom, the time and the public trust to enable them to do only what is best for the country.

The argument has surface plausibility. As Andrew Jackson put it, single-term Presidents would approach their responsibilities "uncommitted to any other course than the strict line of constitutional duty"[86]—a thought that did not, however, keep Jackson himself from running for a second term. The Confederate Constitution provided for a single six-year term. Among later Presidents, Andrew Johnson, Rutherford B. Hayes, Benjamin Harrison, William Howard Taft and, in our own time, Dwight Eisenhower, Lyndon Johnson and Jimmy Carter have endorsed the amendment. So have high-minded people ranging along the political spectrum from William E. Simon through Milton Eisenhower to Harold J. Laski.

The argument, however superficially enticing, is profoundly antidemocratic in its implications. It assumes that Presidents know better than anyone else what is best for the country and that the people are so wrong-headed and ignorant that Presidents should be encouraged to disregard their wishes. It assumes that, the less responsive a President is to popular desires and needs, the better President he will be. It assumes that the democratic process itself is the obstacle to wise decisions.

The theory of American democracy is quite the opposite. It is that the give-and-take of the democratic process is the best guarantee of wise decisions. It is that the President's duty is not to ignore and override popular concerns but to acknowledge and heed them. It is that the President's accountability to the popular will is the best means of ensuring that he will do a decent job.

The Founding Fathers dismissed the single-term idea. The proposal, Hamilton told the Constitutional Convention, would make the President "a Monster elected for seven years, and ineligible afterwards; having great powers . . . & continually tempted by this constitutional disqualification to abuse them." The one-term limitation, said Gouverneur Morris, would "destroy the great motive to good behavior," which is the President's hope of reelection; "it was saying to him, make hay while the sun shines." A President, added Oliver Ellsworth of Connecticut, "should be reelected if his conduct proved himself worthy of it. And he will be more likely to render himself, worthy of it if he be rewardable with it."[87] Reeligibility, Hamilton explained in the 72nd *Federalist*, was essential to give the President "the inclination and the resolution to act his part well" and to give the people "time and leisure to observe the tendency of his measures." The Founders had rejected the single term precisely because it would diminish "the inducements to good behavior."

The opposing argument is that a ban on reelection, by emancipating Presidents from partisanship, would inspire the nation to follow the President as a man above politics. This argument finds no historical sustenance. The second-term records of Presidents elected under the anti-third-term Twenty-second Amendment (Eisenhower, Nixon, Reagan) show that ineligibility for reelection purifies neither their own performance nor the national attitude toward them. And while the quest for reelection may on occasion cause Presidents to defer hard decisions — for example, Kennedy's refusal to pull out of Vietnam till after the 1964 election — it more often has a salutary impact in increasing sensitivity to public needs and hopes. "A President immunized from political considerations," Clark Clifford told the Senate Judiciary Committee in 1971, "is a President who need not listen to the people, respond to majority sentiment, or pay attention to views that may be diverse, intense and perhaps at variance with his own. . . . Concern for one's own political future can be a powerful stimulus to responsible and responsive performance in office."[88]

The nation saw the tempering effect of the desire for reelection on President Reagan in 1984. He dropped his earlier talk about the "evil empire," announced a heretofore concealed passion for arms control, slowed down the movement toward intervention in Central America, affirmed his loyalty to social security and the safety net and in other ways moderated his ideological positions. A single six-year term would have given hard Reaganite dogma full and uninhibited sway.

The ban on reelection has other perverse consequences. Forbidding a President to run again, Gouverneur Morris said, is "as much as to say that we should give him the benefit of experience, and then deprive ourselves of the use of it."[89] George Washington stoutly opposed the idea. "I can see no propriety," he wrote the year after the adoption of the Constitution, "in precluding ourselves from the service of any man, who on some great emergency shall be deemed universally most capable of serving the public."[90] Hamilton believed that such a ban might imperil the nation's very "political existence."[91]

Jefferson, after initially favoring a single seven-year term, thought more carefully and changed his mind. Seven years, he concluded, were "too long [for a President] to be irremovable"; "service for eight years with a power to remove at the end of the first four" was the way to do it.[92] Woodrow Wilson agreed, observing that a six-year term is too long for a poor President and too short for a good one and that the decision belongs to the people. "By seeking to determine by fixed constitutional provision what the people . . . are perfectly competent to determine by themselves," Wilson wrote in 1913, "we cast a doubt upon the whole theory of popular government."[93]

A single six-year term would release Presidents from the test of submitting their records to the voters. It would enshrine the 'President knows best' myth that has already got us into sufficient trouble as a nation. It would be a mighty blow against presidential accountability. It would be a mighty reinforcement of the Imperial Presidency. It would be an impeachment of the democratic process itself. The Founding Fathers were everlastingly right when they turned down this well-intentioned but ill-considered proposal two centuries ago.

If popular government is about anything, it is about the unfettered right of the voters to choose their leaders. This was certainly the way the Founders saw it. The wisdom of the Founders was rejected in 1947 when a conservative Congress carried out an act of retrospective vengeance against Franklin D. Roosevelt and perpetrated the Twenty-second Amendment. There is much to be said for the two-term principle as a tradition. In normal times two terms are enough. Third terms should be reserved for the most compelling and exceptional circumstances. The two-term tradition effectively deterred Presidents from seeking to continue in office for no better reason than the delights of power. The only time the tradition was breached was in precisely the kind of national crisis foreseen by Washington and Hamilton. But there is nothing to be said for setting the two-term tradition in constitutional concrete and thereby denying the people the right to elect the person deemed most capable of serving the public in great emergencies.

If the Twenty-second Amendment was intended as an obstacle to presidential aggrandizement, the subsequent growth of the Imperial Presidency showed how ineffective it was. In the meantime, unlike all other constitutional amendments save the Eighteenth, it has narrowed rather than enlarged the power of the people. The Eighteenth Amendment was, thank heavens, repealed. Despite my belief that the practical argument against a President serving more than two terms has great force, I think that the Twenty-second Amendment should be repealed too. Surely the object of the amending process must be to expand and not to shrink the scope of democratic choice in the national polity.

XIII

"The President," the Constitution reads (Article I, Section 7), "may approve any appropriation and disapprove any other appropriation in the same bill. In such case he shall, on signing the bill, designate the appropriations disapproved; and shall return a copy of such appropriations, with his objections, to the House in which the bill shall have originated."

Actually I am quoting the *Confederate* Constitution. But the idea of an 'item' or 'selective' veto—now mysteriously and redundantly known as a 'line-item' veto—has enchanted Presidents ever since Appomattox. Ulysses S. Grant, to whom the Confederates surrendered on the battlefield, surrendered himself thereafter to the Confederate theory of the veto; indeed, he proposed to extend its reach beyond appropriations to all congressional statutes. In recent times Franklin D. Roosevelt, Dwight D. Eisenhower and Ronald Reagan have all requested an item veto for appropriations bills. Forty-three state governors had the limited item veto in the mid-1980s.

The late-nineteenth-century argument for the item veto, as advanced especially by Rutherford B. Hayes, was as a presidential defense against 'riders' tacked on to appropriations bills—that is, against objectionable amendments that Presidents could not reject without rejecting the entire bill. The twentieth century added a new argument—that the item veto would enable the executive to check extravagant legislative appropriations. This argument had particular appeal in the era of Reagan's massive budget deficits. Forty-seven senators sponsored an item-veto bill in 1985, and, according to the Gallup poll, two thirds of the electorate favored it. Armed with the item veto, the argument ran, Presidents would put on their green eyeshades, edit social and pork barrel legislation and strike out all manner of wasteful projects.

The argument that the item veto would bring about a material reduction in government spending proved on examination less than convincing. More than 85 percent of the Reagan deficit was caused by defense, untouchable by presidential decree, and by entitlements, debt service and tax giveaways, immune to the item veto since they do not require appropriation lines. The remaining 15 percent of the budget offered meager opportunities for savings. "Approval of a line item veto," Reagan's own Council of Economic Advisers declared in its annual report in February 1985, "may not have a substantial effect on total federal expenditures," pointing out that per capita spending in the seven states without the item veto was actually lower than in the forty-three states enjoying the supposed blessing. Moreover, Reagan already enjoyed a de facto item veto in the rescission authority granted Presidents by the Budget Act of 1974—the power not to spend appropriated funds if Congress approves within forty-five days. In 1981 Congress accepted nearly 90 percent of the $16 billion in rescissions requested by Reagan. But, since rescission leaves the decision to a simple congressional majority, the executive prefers the item veto, which would require a two-thirds vote to override. In any event, the item veto campaign of the mid-1980s was largely a function of Reagan's presence in the White House. Few advocates would have been enthusiastic if a different President were set to wield it against the defense budget.

The item veto raises deeper problems. It would empower the President to dictate spending priorities, giving him the unlimited impoundment authority supposedly withheld by the Budget Act of 1974. An unscrupulous President could use his life-or-death power over specific projects to blackmail legislators by threatening to kill their pet projects unless they supported unrelated administration measures. The item veto would significantly alter the historic balance between the executive and legislative branches.

At the same time, it would invite congressional irresponsibility. Legislators would be inclined to propitiate importunate lobbies and authorize more spending than ever, trusting to the President to defend the budget. The item veto, moreover, would imperil the complex of compromises that give stability to congressional action, for no legislator could be sure that a deal with a colleague would survive once the bill reached the White House. The subversion of congressional deals by item veto would raise questions of double-cross and undermine confidence in the legislative leadership of the President's own party.

With the item veto, said Senator Mark Hatfield, a Republican, "we will be giving up one of our most important powers—'the power of the purse.'"[94] A conservative congressman warned his ideological comrades, "Powers delegated to the presidency to be dispensed according to the wisdom and conscience of a Ronald Reagan will remain in place for a time, certain to come, when a Democrat again ascends to that increasingly lofty presidential throne. . . . The acquiescence to the imperial presidency for the immediate short-term gain threatens the foundation of our form of government."[95]

A conservative President who became an even more conservative Chief Justice had summed up the case against the item veto long before. "If it is urged that the President should have the power to veto items in an appropriation bill to restrain Legislative extravagance," said William Howard Taft, "the answer is that this is not the best way." The item veto, Taft said, "would greatly enlarge the influence of the President, already large enough from patronage and party loyalty and other causes. I am inclined to think that it is better to trust to the action of the people in condemning the party which becomes responsible for such riders, than to give, in such a powerful instrument like this, a temptation to its sinister use by a President eager for continued political success."[96]

Failing an item veto, opponents of social spending seek a final solution in a constitutional amendment mandating a balanced budget. This idea violates Justice Holmes's dictum: "A Constitution is not intended to embody a particular economic theory."[97] If rigidly enforced, a balanced-budget amendment would make government impossible. Since government must somehow continue, such an amendment would simply challenge the President and Congress to discover creative ways of circumvention, substitution and evasion. The prohibition of deficits, like the prohibition of hard liquor, would end in bootlegging.

XIV

The Electoral College is the vermiform appendix in the American body politic. It was a last-minute addition to the Constitution. It installs a mystic agency between the electorate and the President. It systematically distorts the popular vote. It is impossible to explain to foreigners. Even Americans don't understand it.

When Jimmy Carter in 1977 proposed a constitutional amendment for the direct popular election of the President, he gave new impetus to a cause that goes back at least to Andrew Jackson. Carter offered only one reason for the abolition of the Electoral College, but it was a powerful one. The amendment, he said, would "ensure that the candidate chosen by the voters actually becomes President. Under the Electoral College, it is always possible that the winner of the popular vote will not be elected."[98] This had already happened, Carter said, in 1824, 1876 and 1888.

Jackson had expounded the deeper rationale a century and a half before. "To the people belongs the right of electing their Chief Magistrate," he told Congress in his first annual message. He mentioned the constitutional provisions for election by the Electoral College or, failing a majority there, by the House of Representatives. "Experience proves," he said, having in mind no doubt his own defeat in the House of Representatives in 1824 after leading in the popular vote, "that in proportion as agents to execute the will of the people are multiplied there is danger of their wishes being frustrated. . . . It is safer for them to express their own will. . . . A President elected by a minority can not enjoy the confidence necessary to the successful discharge of his duties."[99] The winner of the popular vote, in other words, has the strongest claim to democratic legitimacy.

This line of argument received added force when the Supreme Court in 1963 established the principle of one person, one vote in statewide elections. Under the Electoral College each state casts its total electoral vote for the winner even if the win is by a single vote. This procedure obviously tramples on the one person, one vote principle; as the Court itself noted, the conception of political equality embodied in the Electoral College "belongs to a bygone day."[100] And it does more than disenfranchise those who voted for the loser. The case, as Senator Thomas Hart Benton pointed out in 1824, is not just one "of votes lost, but of votes taken away, added to those of the majority, and given to a person to whom the minority is opposed."[101] In a fair system, surely every voter should have equal weight and every vote count as the voter intended.

By the 1970s many eminent leaders and organizations — Richard Nixon, Gerald Ford, Hubert Humphrey, Edward Kennedy, Henry Jackson, Howard Baker, Robert Dole; the American Bar Association, the League of Women Voters, the AFL/CIO, the Chamber of Commerce — joined Carter in advocating that the people vote directly for their candidates. Polls showed overwhelming public support for direct presidential elections. The favorite amendment, devised by that indefatigable constitutional reformer Senator Birch Bayh, provides that if no candidate receives more than 40 percent of the vote, the top two candidates would fight it out in a run-off election. This process, the argument goes, would meet the moral criteria of a democracy. It would ensure equal treatment of all votes. It would elect the people's choice. It would reduce the power of sectionalism in politics. It would reinvigorate party competition and combat voter apathy by giving parties an incentive to get out their vote in states in which they are hopeless minorities. The abolition of the Electoral College would also solve the problem of the 'faithless elector'—the person who is sent to the Electoral College to vote for one candidate and then votes for another. This has happened a few times in the past, could happen again and might change the result when the electoral vote is closely divided.*

All this sounds reasonable enough. But there are countervailing arguments. Let us put aside the problem of the faithless elector. That problem can be easily solved by abolishing the Electoral College while retaining the electoral vote and the unit rule. Let us put aside too the wearisome and inconclusive debate over who benefits from the Electoral College: large states or small states, whites or blacks, urban or rural interests. It was long supposed that the Electoral College gave special weight to large swing states and therefore benefited minorities holding the balance of power in such states. Computer analysis suggests that the Electoral College favors both the largest and the smallest states and disfavors medium-size states. Contrary to traditional belief, it may hurt black voters more than it helps them.[102] Such calculations, however, do not allow for changes wrought in voter dynamics by candidates, issues and external events.

But there are compelling reasons to believe that the abolition of state-by-state electoral votes would hasten the disintegration of the party system. Direct election with a run-off would give single-issue movements, major-party dissidents and free-lance media adventurers an unprecedented incentive to jump into presidential contests. Ecological parties, old folks' parties, women's parties, racial parties, right-to-life parties, Moral Majority parties, prohibitionist parties, homosexual rights parties—for that matter, communist or fascist parties—have a dim future in the Electoral College. Unless third parties have a solid geographical base, like the Populists of 1892 or the Dixiecrats of 1948, they cannot hope to win electoral votes. Millard Fillmore, the Know-Nothing candidate in 1856, received 21.6 percent of the popular vote and only 2 percent of the electoral vote. In 1912, when Theodore Roosevelt's Bull Moose candidacy turned the Republicans

---

*There is a myth, much cherished by non-historians, that the Founding Fathers intended the electors to be free agents. As Lucius Wilmerding, Jr., has pointed out, the preponderance of evidence is that the Founding Fathers fully expected the Electoral College to execute the popular will; see Wilmerding, *The Electoral College* (1958; Beacon paperback, 1964), 19–21, 171–174.

into a third party, William Howard Taft carried 23 percent of the popular vote and only 1.5 percent of the Electoral College. But under direct elections ideological parties and personalist movements could drain away enough popular votes, cumulating from state to state, to win the 20 percent necessary to force the presidential contest into a run-off. The encouragement of multiple parties would be a further blow to a party structure already gravely weakened by passage into the electronic age.

Moreover, these ad hoc political raids on the presidential process might well make run-offs the rule rather than the exception. It would also threaten to cloud the ultimate result with a stigma of deals and illegitimacy. For third parties would enter the contest not in order to win but in order to extract concessions from the run-off candidates in exchange for promises of support. In the House of Representatives run-off of 1824, Henry Clay gave his backing to J. Q. Adams and was thereafter pursued by charges of a "corrupt bargain." Direct elections would very likely usher in an age of corrupt bargains.

Direct elections would very probably lead in addition to a procession of Presidents who do not get anywhere near a majority of the popular vote. This probability is tacitly recognized by the run-off provision and the 40 percent cut-off. The prospect would be a succession of 41 percent Presidents or else a fatiguing succession of double national elections — in which case the final prize might sometimes go to the person who came in second in the first round. The result in either case would hardly strengthen the sense of legitimacy the presidential election is supposed to provide.

In short, an amendment designed to ensure that the popular-vote winner gains the Presidency may have the paradoxical effect of reducing the proportion of the popular vote required for victory. Far from relieving frustrations in the electorate, this result could weaken the presidential mandate, confirm the conviction that tricky politicians are manipulating the system and intensify mistrust of the political process.

Jimmy Carter's problem remains, however — the possibility that the winner of the popular vote will not be elected. In fact, of Carter's three popular-vote-loser Presidents — J. Q. Adams in 1824, Hayes in 1876, Benjamin Harrison in 1888 — the first two cases had nothing to do with the Electoral College. Eighteen twenty-four is no test since the present system did not exist. There were no parties, no popular vote in six states and no unit electoral vote in six others. In any event, it was the House of Representatives, not the Electoral College, that put Adams in over Jackson. In 1876 Samuel J. Tilden initially led in the Electoral College; it was a rigged electoral commission that put in Hayes.

This leaves only one occasion in American history where the Electoral College deprived the popular-vote winner of the Presidency. This was in the dead heat election of 1888 when neither candidate received a majority and the gap between them was 95,000 votes. Even here the claim was made, and was widely accepted at the time and by historians since, that over 300,000 black Republican voters in southern states were denied participation in the election.[103] But it is unprofitable to go behind official election figures, and 1888 may be granted as a case of Electoral College misfire.

One instance in two hundred years hardly seems enough to justify a drastic alteration of the system—especially if the proposed alteration is quite likely to produce second-choice Presidents itself. However, there is a simple and effective way to guard against the theoretical possibility that a candidate might come in first in the popular vote but second in the Electoral College. The answer is the National Bonus Plan proposed in 1978 by the Twentieth Century Fund Task Force on Reform of the Presidential Election Process.*

Under the National Bonus Plan, a national pool of 102 electoral votes—two for each state plus the District of Columbia—would be awarded to the winner of the popular vote. The national bonus would balance the existing federal bonus—the two electoral votes conferred by the Constitution on each state regardless of population. This reform would virtually guarantee that the popular-vote winner would also win a majority of electoral votes. At the same time, by retaining state electoral votes on a winner-take-all basis, the National Bonus Plan would preserve both the constitutional and the practical role of the states in the presidential election process, thereby contributing to the vitality of federalism. By discouraging the proliferation of presidential candidates, the Plan would protect the party system. By encouraging parties to maximize their vote in states they have no hope of winning, it would stimulate turnout, revitalize state parties and enhance voter equality. It would eliminate the faithless elector by abolishing the Electoral College and allocating electoral votes to the popular winner in each state and in the nation as a whole. The National Bonus Plan would, in short, combine the advantages of the historic system with the assurance that the popular-vote winner would also be

---

*See *Winner Take All: Report of the Twentieth Century Fund Task Force on Reform of the Presidential Election Process* (New York, 1978). I must declare an interest: I was a member of the Task Force, and I first proposed the bonus plan in "The Electoral College Conundrum," *Wall Street Journal*, 4 April 1977.

the electoral-vote winner. It represents a sensible and desirable project of constitutional reform.*

XV

I confess myself a conservative with regard to the Constitution. But one additional change tempts: the shortening of the interregnum between election and inauguration.

Just before the presidential election in 1916, Woodrow Wilson, anticipating possible defeat at the hands of Charles Evans Hughes, sent a letter to his Secretary of State. If Hughes won, Wilson wrote, "Four months would elapse before he could take charge of the affairs of the government, and during those four months I would be without such moral backing from our nation as would be necessary to steady and control our relations with other governments . . . and yet the accredited spokesman would be without legal authority to speak for the nation. Such a situation would be fraught with the gravest dangers." It would be his duty, Wilson continued, "to relieve the country of the perils of such a situation at once." He proposed therefore, in case of defeat, to appoint Hughes Secretary of State. Then he and the Vice President would resign "and thus open to Mr. Hughes the immediate succession to the presidency."[104]

Wilson won, but what he called "the extreme disadvantage of having to live for four months after a[n] election under a party whose guidance has been rejected at the polls" remains a perennial possibility. When, as in the early republic, it took days to ascertain election results and weeks for the winners to get to Washington, the four-month interregnum was defensible. But by the twentieth century communications had improved. Yet Presidents were inaugurated on the fourth of March until George W. Norris's Twentieth Amendment in 1933 cut the delay to ten weeks. The 'Lame Duck' Amendment aimed particularly at postelection congressional sessions in which de-

---

*In 1979 a majority report of the Senate Judiciary Committee advocating a direct popular election amendment dismissed the National Bonus Plan as "nothing more than a direct election achieved by a highly complicated mechanism." The Committee did this on the ground that under either system candidates would concentrate on winning the greatest number of popular votes nationwide. No doubt they would. But the national bonus amounts to only 16 percent of the total electoral vote. To get the further 35 percent required for a majority, candidates would have to carry particular states—a concern they would not have under direct elections. In this regard the National Bonus Plan respects and the direct election amendment overrides the federal character of American politics. Nor is the national bonus "a highly complicated mechanism." It is a device of elegant simplicity. See Senate Judiciary Committee, *Direct Popular Election of the President and Vice President of the United States: Report,* 96th Cong., 1st Sess. (1979), 40.

feated legislators still participated (as 158 did in the lame duck session beginning in December 1932). Ratified during the banking crisis of early 1933, the Twentieth Amendment also recognized Wilson's point that a protracted entr'acte causes problems when crisis calls for effective government.

In the years since the Twentieth Amendment, communications have improved still more. The republic has rushed into the age of jet planes, television and electronic tabulation of election results. The United States, moreover, has become a world power. Few features of the American political process dismay our allies (and doubtless delight our adversaries) more than the yawning gap between administrations—a time of inevitable drift, of incipient paralysis, in the operations of government. No other democracy subjects itself to such damaging delay before a new administration takes over.

In France the presidential transition in 1981 from Giscard d'Estaing to Mitterrand took eleven days. In Canada the new Prime Minister is sworn in within a fortnight after the election. In Great Britain, when one government gives way to another, the new Prime Minister moves into 10 Downing Street almost overnight. As R. H. S. Crossman described the 1970 transition from Harold Wilson to Edward Heath: "The change-over took place with the speed, completeness, and precision of a ceremonial exercise on the parade ground. . . . The only operation to which I can compare the Whitehall drill for a change in Government is the hospital drill for removing a corpse from the ward and replacing it with a new patient."[105] In Washington, however, the corpse lies in state for two and a half months while the successors quarrel over the inheritance.

Two factors, it is true, simplify transitions in a parliamentary regime. One is the limited number of jobs open to political appointment. The other is the requirement (in most cases) that the cabinet be chosen from the parliament and the consequent prior existence of a shadow government. Still Wilson's "extreme disadvantage" may be even more extreme in an age of chronic international crisis. The time has come to consider reducing the interregnum again. Under an amendment introduced in the mid-1980s by Senators Claiborne Pell and Charles Mathias, the President and the Vice President would be inaugurated on 20 November instead of on 20 January. The newly elected Congress would set to work on 15 November instead of on 3 January.

The possibility of a swifter transition deserves exploration for other reasons, among them the noxious consequences of the Presidential Transition Act of 1963. That act was designed to institutionalize the change from one administration to the next. In practice, it has transformed that process into a bureaucratic monstrosity. In the old days transition was handled by a modest presidential staff with expenses met by the national committee of the victorious party. When Kennedy succeeded Eisenhower in 1960–1961, the change was accomplished with a minimum of fuss and on a shoestring. Clark Clifford and a small group dealt with the outgoing administration. Sargent Shriver and another small group organized a talent hunt. A few select (and unpaid) task forces prepared recommendations on critical issues. The enterprise was carried out with speed and efficiency—and cost the taxpayer nothing.

When Reagan succeeded Carter in 1980–1981, the transition staff consisted of 1500 people and occupied a ten-story federal office building. The Presidential Transition Act gave the newcomers $2 million, and another million or so was raised privately. Transition teams barged around Washington, promoting themselves for jobs, sideswiping rivals, paying off old scores, making self-serving leaks to the press and turning out reports that few people ever had time to read. The Transition Act inflates and complicates what has hitherto been a manageable process, wastes the taxpayers' money and, by cutting the party out of the process, diminishes its role still further. For nearly two centuries American Presidents contrived to succeed each other without making an elaborate production of it. The case seems strong for a repeal of the Presidential Transition Act.

Shortening the interregnum would eliminate this bureaucratic orgy. It would relieve Washington of the spectral presence of a slowly vanishing administration. It would minimize the dangerous policy void that paralyzes domestic decisions and invites trouble in world affairs. It would end lame duck sessions of Congress, supposedly eliminated by the Twentieth Amendment but creeping back in abbreviated form; there were nine such sessions between 1933 and 1980. It would end the last-minute rush of departing administrations to expend funds, make contracts and appoint judges. It would also—and this is a significant technical point—enable the new President to submit his own budget instead of struggling over a budget drawn up for the record by his departing predecessor. And it would give new significance to the civil service in providing continuity during the transition.

It may be that the November inauguration proposed in the Pell-Mathias amendment is a little soon. The President-elect needs time to rest up after the campaign. Passions need time to cool; wounds, time to heal. The top three hundred appointments need time for consideration and clearance. The first of December might be a better date. Some object that even this interval would not give the new person time to figure out policies and key appointments. But, if the President-elect has not thought hard about these matters before his election, he (she) has no business being President. Compelling candidates to assemble plans and teams in advance of the polling would be entirely beneficial. With commercial television spots driving out the policy speeches of better days, a listing of people under consideration for the key jobs would do something to restore substance to campaigns and to offer the electorate evidence on which to base their votes.*

The Pell-Mathias approach would reduce the postelection interlude of national impotence. It would enforce on presidential candidates the discipline of advance planning and remind them at an early point that winning the election is only the prelude to governing.

XVI

Another proposal, much discussed in recent years, is that the republic make better use of its ex-Presidents. As I write, three ex-Presidents live among us. At other times — in that dangerous year when the Civil War broke out, for example — five ex-Presidents were alive and reasonably active. Indeed, in nearly two centuries, there have been only four brief interludes, adding up to about sixty months, when the United States lacked a living ex-President.

What unique wisdom ex-Presidents must possess! Only thirty-nine men have served as President, and the office is sui generis. "Even after passing through the Presidential office, it still remains a great mystery," wrote Calvin Coolidge, a man not ordinarily given to poetic fancy. ". . . Like the glory of a morning sunrise, it can only be experienced — it cannot be told."[106] Secular life has no equivalent for what these thirty-nine men learned, no substitute for the ultimate responsibility concentrated in the Oval Office. Yet when this rare education is completed, the President's time is up, and the nation abruptly turns him out to pasture. "The United States has had six presidents and eight secretaries of state since 1960," laments one writer, "but this priceless talent pool is treated by America's throwaway society like any

* For a discussion of the issues involved, see Senate Judiciary Committee, Subcommittee on the Constitution, *Commencement of Terms of Office of the President and Members of Congress: Hearing*, 98th Cong., 2d Sess., 24 April 1984. The testimony in favor of the Pell-Mathias approach by John W. Macy, Jr., the former chairman of the Civil Service Commission, indicates that this experienced public servant does not see the appointments problem as a serious obstacle to the shortening of the interregnum.

other disposable commodity."[107] Is this not a grave loss to the republic? Cannot some way be found to organize their hard-bought knowledge and draw on it through dark days to come?

For a long time Americans did not think so. In 1891 Grover Cleveland observed ironically that the people had no idea what to do with ex-Presidents: "Of course the subject would be relieved of all uncertainty and embarrassment if every President would die at the end of his term." Some citizens "think we should interfere in every political contest. . . . Others still regard it as simply dreadful for us to do these things. . . . Not a few appear to think we should simply exist and be blind, deaf and dumb the remainder of our days."[108] William Howard Taft, another ironist, thought the best solution might be "a dose of chloroform . . . and the reduction of the flesh of the thus quietly departed to ashes in a funeral pyre."[109] Millard Fillmore long before had pleaded in vain for a presidential pension. Many men, he said, "give up a lucrative profession" for the White House. (The President was then paid $25,000 a year.) "It is a national disgrace that our Presidents, having occupied the highest position in the country should be cast adrift, and, perhaps, be compelled to keep a corner grocery for subsistence."[110]

But cast adrift ex-Presidents were "wandering among the people like discontented ghosts," as Hamilton predicted in the 72nd *Federalist*. They themselves were uncertain what their role should be. Monroe thought ex-Presidents should abstain from politics, reserving themselves for emergencies "in which the opinion of those who have had long experience may be useful."[111] Monroe's successor, J. Q. Adams, pointed out that the two-term tradition meant that "ex-Presidents will survive for many years the termination of their offices";[112] and he was not inclined to take the veil for the rest of his life. Adams went on to serve nine embattled terms in the House of Representatives. Van Buren, Fillmore, Cleveland and the first Roosevelt all ran for President again after a period of retirement. John Tyler was elected to the Confederate House of Representatives, dying before he took his seat. Andrew Johnson became a senator. Several ex-Presidents wrote books. None became a grocer.

Harry Truman was the first ex-President to agitate seriously about the fate of what he insisted on calling the "former President." (An otherwise sensible man, Truman perceived a mighty distinction between "ex-President," a usage he abhorred, and "former President," which he declared was alone correct—a metaphysical subtlety invisible to grammarians. If "ex-President" was acceptable to such punctilious fellows as J. Q. Adams and Benjamin Harrison, the author of

Views of an Ex-President, there seems no reason for the rest of us to renounce it.) When Truman retired in 1953 to Independence, Missouri, one of the first things he thought about, he later wrote, was the question of "how the unique experience and special knowledge that a former President acquires could be put to some use to serve the country. . . . We ought not waste all these assets." He envied the British and their Privy Council, where former Prime Ministers and cabinet members are available to advise the government in office. If the United States could not establish an equivalent council of state, then why should not ex-Presidents be designated Free Members of the Congress, entitled to sit in either House and take part in debate though not to vote? [113]

The second Charles Francis Adams had proposed in 1906 that ex-Presidents be made Senators at Large. At least twenty-five bills to this effect have been introduced in Congress since the Second World War. In 1963 the Bureau of the Budget saw problems in having senators "who would be accountable to no one and who would represent no one," whose views might be "decades behind those of the American consensus or who would be both talkative and senile." [114] The proposal also raised constitutional questions, and the Senate that year decided instead to permit ex-Presidents to address the Senate on their own initiative. Truman and Ford have been the only ex-Presidents thus far to avail themselves of this opportunity. Despite the unique wisdom supposedly confided to ex-Presidents, no one remembers what either of them said.

In the meantime, Congress through the Presidential Libraries Act of 1955 and the Former Presidents Act of 1958 in effect established what John W. Chambers II, the authority on the subject, has called "a quasi-public office, the office of the former president." [115] The theory was that public provender would enable ex-Presidents to live out their lives in dignified retirement, sparing them from the pressure to demean themselves and the office by cashing in on their Presidencies. The result of this institutionalization of the ex-Presidency is that ex-Presidents by the mid-1980s were endowed by the taxpayers with annual pensions of $83,000, office space in federal buildings, free personal staff, free mailing privileges, free telephone privileges, free health care at military hospitals, free subscriptions to newspapers and magazines, travel allowances, Secret Service protection, classified foreign policy briefings, a residence for their Washington visits and the maintenance of libraries for their papers. This largesse did not visibly reduce the determination of the beneficiaries to cash in on their Presidencies. The ex-President who used to live over my back fence was given in those years to upbraiding the American people as unduly "coddled, pampered, truckled to."[116] My impression, from glances out the window, is that exceedingly few Americans are nearly so coddled, pampered and truckled to as ex-Presidents, even the one who resigned the office in order to escape impeachment.

In 1955 Congress had appropriated $64,000 to maintain presidential libraries. Thirty years later the annual bill for ex-Presidents was nearly $30 million. It cost more each year to take care of ex-Presidents than to run the White House for the incumbent President. Pampering eventually reached the point where it caused serious discomfort in Congress. One senator spoke darkly of the Imperial Ex-Presidency.[117] Congressional reformers proposed to set limits on ex-presidential expenditures and to prohibit federal employees from helping an ex-President to make money or to engage in partisan activities. These are sound proposals.

Some reformers wanted to go farther and replace the presidential library system by a central depository for presidential papers. Though library maintenance accounts for over half the ex-presidential bill, this proposal seems to me far less sound. The dispersion of presidential libraries around the country has been a stimulus to scholarship, enabling many more students to work in modern political history than would be the case if they had to make expensive trips to Washington. The management of documents by specialists is of inestimable benefit to scholars. And there is value to studying Presidents in their native habitats—Franklin Roosevelt in the Hudson Valley, Kennedy by Massachusetts Bay, Johnson in Texas, Ford in Michigan, Carter in Georgia, Reagan in California.

Institutionalization of the ex-Presidency, if it could be restrained from fiscal improvidence, confers a few benefits. It speeds the opening of presidential papers and changes their legal status. Papers once were private property of Presidents to open, close or burn as they wished; now they belong to the people. But institutionalization does not solve the problem of tapping the accumulated sagacity of these few men with the singular advantage of presidential experience.

Still one wonders whether the Founding Fathers might not have had a point in casting ex-Presidents adrift. For is it correct to suppose that ex-Presidents are automatically blessed with superior wisdom, especially on questions that have emerged since their own days in office? Patriarchy works in traditional societies, where problems remain much the same from one generation to the next. But, with the acceleration of change in modern times, patriarchs swiftly become obsolescent.

Ex-Presidents, like other old folk, tend to live in the past, preoccupied with the issues, remedies and self-justifications of another time. Their excursions into the unfamiliar present—Tyler's chairmanship in 1861 of a peace conference designed to avert the Civil War, for example, or Hoover's impassioned isolationism in 1940—are often the height of irrelevance. Would the republic have benefited if Lincoln had been compelled by some mechanism of state to listen to the advice of the five living ex-Presidents—Buchanan, Pierce, Fillmore, Tyler, Van Buren? We are alert to superannuation in the private sector. When presidents retire from corporations or from universities, no one wants them hanging around and proffering advice. William Howard Taft proposed chloroforming ex-Presidents precisely in order to "enable the public to pass to new men and new measures."[118]

This is not to say that ex-Presidents should take vows of silence. When they think they have some profound revelation to utter, let them by all means utter it. When a successor calls on them for counsel or for service, let them by all means cooperate. But imposing ex-Presidents on the Senate as daily participants, or assembling them in a council of state, or otherwise giving their ruminations official status would be a superfluity. Why anyone should think it "necessary to add to the discussion in the Senate the lucubrations of ex-presidents," observed Taft, "I am at a loss to say."[119] No one has greater access than ex-Presidents to every forum; no one has greater opportunity to command every channel of public influence. They can write books and articles, deliver speeches, hold interviews, organize conferences, dispense wisdom on television, testify before congressional committees, address the Senate in formal session. The public cannot be said to be deprived of their most vagrant thoughts.

If the three ex-Presidents living in the mid-1980s were really all that wise, they would surely have been better Presidents when they had the chance. People who believe that ex-Presidents are a wasted national asset should turn their energies to repealing the Twenty-second Amendment, thereby permitting these great oracles to stay on as President. In the meantime, the rest of us must remember that ex-presidential musings must stand or fall on the merits of the argument, not on the sanctity of the source.

XVII

Nixon showed the abuses of the Presidency. Carter showed the vulnerabilities of the Presidency. Both abuse and vulnerability provoked structural panaceas. As our most thoughtful foreign visitors have pointed out, Americans attribute excessive importance to structure. "The student of institutions, as well as the lawyer," wrote Bryce, "is apt to overrate the effect of mechanical contrivances in politics." [120] Constitution-tinkering is a flight from the hard question, which is the search for remedy. Structure is an alibi for policy failure. Let us not be beguiled by constitutional reform from the real tasks of statecraft. In the end, politics is the high and serious art of solving substantive problems.

Constitutions and statutes succeed, moreover, only as they express the temper, circumstances, traditions, history—the mores—of a people. "Laws are always unstable," said Tocqueville, "unless they are founded upon the customs of a nation." [121] Changes uncongenial to the mores—the Eighteenth Amendment, for example, and the Volstead Act—will be ejected in time like artificial hearts. Enacted into law, such changes are easily revoked. Engraved in the Constitution, they are harder to efface. So long as they remain in the fundamental charter, they touch off the law of unintended consequences. People zealous to put right the abuse of the fleeting moment are as likely to deform as to reform the constitutional order. In his great opinion in the steel seizure case, Justice Jackson warned against the error "of confounding the permanent executive office with its temporary occupant. The tendency is strong to emphasize transient results . . . and lose sight of enduring consequences upon the balanced power structure of our Republic." [122] There is no fail-safe mechanism guaranteed either to contain or to restore presidential authority. The effort to devise such a mechanism may lead to forms of constitutional or statutory overkill damaging to other national interests, such as liberty. Digging in the foundations of the state, Burke said, is a dangerous adventure.

Except to repair past error, as by repealing the Eighteenth, Twenty-second and (to be argued in the next essay) Twenty-fifth Amendments, and except to modernize existing provisions, as by shortening the interregnum and adding the National Bonus Plan, I would leave the Constitution alone. As Lord Falkland used to say, "If it ain't broke, don't fix it."* The salvation of the Presidency lies in the realm of politics, not of constitutional reform.

Let us return to where we began: the Founding Fathers. They had two things in mind: fashioning a strong national government and holding that government within a strong system of accountability.

---

*I quote loosely. Falkland said, "When it is not necessary to change, it is necessary not to change."

The perennial problem is twofold: to preserve the Presidency as the robust office that, despite a bad apple or two, has served the republic nobly and to reinvigorate the system of accountability that checks the abuse of executive power. The challenge is to balance power and accountability without creating a government too strong, in Lincoln's words, for the liberties of the people or too weak to maintain its own existence.[123]

The Constitution gives competent Presidents the authority to govern and competent Congresses the authority to make them accountable. But the Constitution is not self-executing. It requires Presidents, Congresses and citizens who are responsive to constitutional standards. The hope lies in a campaign of national consciousness-raising. The object must be to raise the consciousness of Presidents, so that they will honor the system of accountability; to raise the consciousness of Congresses, so that they will discharge their constitutional responsibilities; and to raise the consciousness of citizens, so that, as they enter the voting booth, they will think about a candidate's openness, integrity and commitment to constitutional values as well as about his program and his charm.

Since Presidents and Congresses are chosen by the electorate, citizens bear a heavy responsibility. They must begin by abandoning the latter-day myth of the President as a man raised above the rest, not to be questioned except at risk of lèse-majesté. In 1937 Kingsley Martin, the English editor, wondering how the British throne had gained its sacrosanct character, wrote a book called *The Magic of Monarchy*. In the nineteenth century the crown had been freely criticized. As late as the 1870s Britain had a thriving republican movement. In the twentieth century British republicanism was extinct. Martin concluded that the magic of monarchy emerged with the British Empire when the Queen-Empress was systematically glorified as the symbol of imperial grandeur.

As in Britain, the notion of the Presidency as a sacrosanct institution is a comparatively recent development. Washington, Jackson and Lincoln stirred mass emotions, but they excited vituperation as well as worship. There were no nineteenth-century personality cults of Franklin Pierce, say, or Chester A. Arthur. As in Britain, the myth rose in unison with empire. The Imperial Presidency began with the first Roosevelt and was nourished by the second Roosevelt. It burst into full splendor in the days after the Second World War. "By the twentieth century," writes George Reedy, a former presidential press secretary, "the presidency had taken on all the regalia of monarchy except ermine robes, a scepter, and a crown."[124]

Presidential magic may well be more potent than the magic of monarchy. For the President is not just the supreme national symbol. He is also the supreme repository of public authority. As the incarnation of power as well as of myth, he appeals to prudential as well as to mystical motives. The word 'incarnation' has a religious flavor; perhaps rightly so in this context. Some people behave as if the presidential oath works a miraculous personality change, a kind of transubstantiation. So a run-of-the-mill politician, with whom one had exchanged drinks and jokes a few months before, is transformed by the anointment of the Oval Office into an awe-inspiring being.

Strong men wilt in the august presence. When Walter F. Mondale was Vice President, friends would ask him to take them to see the President, saying, "I'm going to tell him bluntly the mistakes he's making, and he's going to get it raw from me." But when Mondale led them into the Oval Office: "'Hello, Mr. President. How is Rosalynn and how is Amy? You're doing a wonderful job.' Hawks would become doves, conservatives would become liberals. I did not recognize half my friends when they got in there." [125]

Nixon used to talk a good deal about the importance of "respect for the Presidency"—a curious phrase to fall from the lips of a man who showed such systematic disrespect for the Presidency. Yet perhaps a little disrespect for the office might not be a bad idea on the part of everyone except the President himself. Little is more mischievous than the singular idea that the President has a sacred right to be protected from secular exposure and confrontation; little more damaging than the ghastly neoconservative theory that persons in authority must have respect, whether or not they have done anything to earn it. An American President is entitled to full courtesy, like every other citizen of the land, but only to the respect his words and actions earn him.

The President, after all, is simply a politician luckier than the rest—the one who made it, in Disraeli's phrase, to the top of the greasy pole. Shinnying up the pole does not transform him into a demigod and carry him out of our sight and jurisdiction. He can expect to stay on top only so long as he remains in close touch with the people below and operates within the disciplines of consent. "There is no worse heresy," said Lord Acton, "than that the office sanctifies the holder of it." [126]

It is not required to dig into the foundation of the state. If the political will exists in Congress and the citizenry, structural surgery is not necessary. If the will does not exist, structural surgery will make little difference. The secularization of the Presidency is indispensable for the reassertion of congressional and popular prerogative. And, from a President's viewpoint, consensus secured by consent rather than by command and coercion is far more likely both to supply a solid basis for executive policy and to keep the White House in touch with the reality principle.

XVIII

"Power," Henry Adams once said, "is poison. Its effect on Presidents had been always tragic."[127] But is this really so? I do not think that power per se removes a President from reality. The achievement of the great Presidents springs precisely from the fact that they had a deeper sense of reality than most of their contemporaries and penetrated to problems their fellow countrymen preferred to ignore.

Power isolates Presidents only to the extent they wish to be isolated. If they want to know what is going on, they have better facilities than anyone else in the country for finding out. Mediocre Presidents passively accept information percolating up through official channels. Great Presidents reach out for information not contaminated by self-serving bureaucratic processes. "Men moving only in an official circle," said Lincoln, "are apt to become merely official—not to say arbitrary—in their ideas." Lincoln valued his twice-a-week White House receptions, where ordinary citizens seized his elbow, offered recommendations and aired grievances. "I call these receptions my public-opinion baths . . . and, though they may not be pleasant in all particulars, the effect as a whole is renovating and invigorating to my perceptions of responsibility and duty. It would never do for a President to have guards with drawn sabres at his door, as if he fancied he were, or were trying to be, or were assuming to be, an emperor."[128]

The press conference is the contemporary equivalent of Lincoln's White House receptions, and the White House staff has become the guard with drawn sabres at the presidential door. "A president's most persistent problem in staying in touch with reality," George Reedy says, "lies in his staff."[129] As another ex–White House special assistant, I could not agree more. Nothing has carried recent Presidents away from the reality principle more than the remorseless expansion of the White House staff.

The Government Reorganization Act of 1939 created the modern White House staff. Franklin Roosevelt, the first beneficiary, kept his staff small enough so that he could deal personally with all his special assistants. His executive order setting up the staff specified that the special assistants should have "no authority over anyone in any department or agency" and should "in no event be interposed between

the President and the head of any department or agency."[130] FDR
served as his own chief of staff. So too did Truman, Kennedy and
Johnson. The quantum leap in the White House staff took place
under Nixon, thereby demonstrating the law propounded by Woodrow Wilson's biographer, Arthur Link: "The less secure a President
is, the larger staff he will want."* Nixon interposed his swollen White
House staff between himself and most of the cabinet and Congress,
and then interposed an inner circle of palace guards between himself
and most of his White House staff.

The concentration of power in the White House enfeebled the cabinet. Once a proud instrument of government containing strong leaders with positions and constituencies of their own, the cabinet under
Nixon and his successors became, with few exceptions, a collection of
faceless clerks. The concentration of power in the White House also
concealed much of the policy process behind the shield of executive
secrecy, because White House aides, unlike cabinet ministers, are not
ordinarily subject to the call of congressional committees.

Nixon's successors — Ford, Carter, Reagan — all entered office proclaiming their iron determination to combat bureaucracy. None significantly reduced the White House staff. A Carter special assistant
reported that many top assistants "don't see the President once a
week or speak to him in any substantive way once a month." Try to
communicate directly with the President, and irate colleagues accuse
you of "circumventing the system." "Feed your advice through the
system, and what may have begun as a bold initiative comes out the
other end as unrecognizable mush."[131] By the mid-1980s the President's wife had a larger staff than Roosevelt had when he was fighting
the Great Depression; the Vice President, a larger staff than Roosevelt had when he was fighting the Second World War.

Of course a President needs a White House staff. He needs eyes
and ears throughout his administration so that he can find out what
is going on, introduce a measure of coordination into public policy
and make the sprawling executive bureaucracy reasonably responsive
to presidential purpose. He needs a few special assistants — but he
does not need a sprawling bureaucracy of his own. A small staff,
keeping the President up to date on the government and the country,
reinforces the presidential link to reality. But the bloated staffs of
modern times withdraw the President from the real world.

* Arthur Link, "Enormous White House Staff Weakens the Presidency," *U.S. News &
World Report*, 15 August 1983. The number of full-time White House employees increased from 203 in Johnson's last year to 547 in 1971. Hugh Heclo, *Studying the Presidency*, a report to the Ford Foundation, 1977, 36. The number of senior presidential
aides increased proportionately.

Far from facilitating presidential control, enlarging his staff beyond a point quickly reached makes the President's problems worse. Consider the testimony of two men who witnessed the inordinate expansion from FDR's small, crack staff to the tumescent White House of modern days. "The larger such a staff gets," said Sam Rosenman, "the more clumsy and inefficient it becomes. It demands more and more time from the President, whereas a staff's basic function should be to leave him more, rather than less, time to concentrate on major policy decisions." Rosenman recalled that, when he served as Roosevelt's counsel in the war years, "I had no assistants at all. The man in that position today has at least four or five. I cannot imagine what they all do." Averell Harriman: "A large staff around a President can waste, rather than save, his time, and its simple existence can lessen, rather than increase, the hours he has for quiet thought and independent work." [132]

Moreover, by building a wall of separation between himself and the rest of the government, a President diminishes his direct influence and dilutes the impact of his personal leadership. The larger the staff grows, the more endless meetings the staff calls, the more useless paper the staff generates, the more the President will hunker up behind it; the less he will know what is going on. The staff becomes the shock absorber, shielding the President against the facts of life.

The White House staff should be the personal extension of the President—and stop there. A large praetorian bureaucracy, filled with ambitious, possessive, overprotective and often sycophantic people, makes work and makes trouble. It cuts off the nation from the President and the President from the nation. When Presidents find themselves in difficulties, they must sometimes feel, like Shakespeare's King John:

> *It is the curse of kings to be attended*
> *By slaves that take their humours for a warrant*
> *To break within the bloody house of life. . . .*
> *Hadst thou but shook thy head or made a pause*
> *When I spake darkly what I purposed,*
> *Or turn'd an eye of doubt upon my face,*
> *As bid me tell my tale in express words,*
> *Deep shame had struck me dumb, made me break off.* [133]

A President needs people around him who will, when necessary, turn eyes of doubt and shake their heads.

There is little more typically American than to despair of the republic. As early as 1802, Hamilton pronounced the Constitution a "frail and worthless fabric." [134] Seventy years later Henry Adams declared that "the system of 1789" had "broken down."[135] The dirges of our own day are hardly novel. Still the Constitution staggers along, and the republic with it. The political give-and-take invited by a flexible constitutional process offers Presidents ample opportunity to govern and Congress ample opportunity to restrain Presidents. Secularize the Presidency, elect Presidents who understand their business, cut the White House staff in half, revitalize the system of accountability—and forever seek serious solutions to substantive problems. Long live the republic.

But in the end it comes down to the people. Truman's famous sign—"The buck stops here"—tells only half the story. It is on the decision of the voter, not on the desk of the President, that the buck finally stops. "Toute nation," said de Maistre, "a le gouvernement qu'elle mérite." Let us conclude with the ever skeptical, ever hopeful poet of American democracy:

> *A great city is that which has the greatest men and women . . .*
> *Where the populace rise at once against the never-ending audacity*
>   *of elected persons,*
> *Where fierce men and women pour forth as the sea to the whistle of*
>   *death pours its weeping and unript waves,*
> *Where outside authority enters always after the precedence of inside*
>   *authority,*
> *Where the citizen is always the head and ideal, and President, Mayor,*
>   *Governor and what not, are agents for pay. . . .*
> *There the great city stands.*[136]

TWELVE

The Future of the Vice Presidency

———◆———

J OHN ADAMS, the first person to occupy the position, called the American Vice Presidency "the most insignificant office ever the invention of man contrived or his imagination conceived."[1] For a century and a half thereafter, neither Adams's successors nor the American people found much reason to revise this judgment. Mr. Dooley's account of the Republican convention's pursuit of a running mate for Theodore Roosevelt in 1904 summed up the older estimate of the office.

They offered it to me frind Joe Cannon, and th' language he used brought th' blush iv shame to th' cheeks iv a naygur dillygate fr'm Allybamy. They thried to hand it to Hinnery Cabin Lodge, an' he wept bitterly. They found a man fr'm Wisconsin, who was in dhrink, an' had almost nommynated him whin his wife came in an' dhragged him away fr'm timptation. . . . Why is it, I wondher, that ivrybody runs away fr'm a nommynation f'r vice-prisidint as if it was an indictment be th' gran' jury?[2]

Thomas R. Marshall, Woodrow Wilson's Vice President, used to tell the story of two brothers: one went to sea, the other was elected Vice President, nothing was heard of either again. In *Of Thee I Sing*, the hit musical of 1932, Vice President Alexander Throttlebottom was the forlorn little man whose name no one could remember, who received the nomination because straws were put in a hat and he lost and who dared not mention his new job lest his mother find out about it.

That was only half a century ago. It is all different now. No one runs away from the vice presidential nomination. Mothers are proud. Throttlebottom is extinct. Since 1941, four Vice Presidents (Truman, Johnson, Nixon, Ford) have become President. Three more (Wallace, Humphrey, Mondale) have run for President. Three others (Barkley, Rockefeller, Bush) have sought the presidential nomination; and the remaining postwar Vice President, Spiro T. Agnew, would no doubt have done so too had justice not caught up with him. Shunned for most of American history as a dead end, the Vice Presidency today is prized as the springboard into the White House. Why and how has this magical transformation taken place?

I

Why indeed is there an American Vice President at all? It is an unusual office. "There is no corresponding position," Theodore Roosevelt wrote in 1896, "in any constitutional government."* Most of us assume that the Founding Fathers invented the Vice Presidency in order to provide for the succession in case of the death or resignation of the President. In fact, the Founding Fathers had a different solution for the presidential succession and a different reason for the Vice Presidency.

The draft of 6 August 1787 from the Constitutional Convention's all-important Committee of Detail recommended that, in case of a vacancy in the Presidency, "the President of the Senate shall exercise those powers and duties, *until another President of the United States shall be chosen.*" Some members objected to the President of the Senate as the "provisional successor." Gouverneur Morris thought it should be the Chief Justice. Madison suggested that "the Executive powers during a vacancy" be administered by a Council of State. But agreement was general on Madison's idea of "a supply of the vacancy by an intermediate election of the President." Article II of the Constitution embodied this idea, providing that the person acting in place of a disabled or dead President shall act only "until the Disability be removed, or *a President shall be elected*" (emphasis added).[3] Careful study of the Convention records shows, in the words of Ruth Silva, a modern authority on the presidential succession, that the Founding Fathers never intended any officer "to become President by succession. If his exercise of the presidential power was founded on vacancy, he

---

*Theodore Roosevelt, "The Three Vice-Presidential Candidates," *Review of Reviews,* September 1896, 290. Only a very few more governments—Brazil, for example—have Vice Presidents today. Brazil would probably have been better off had the death of Tancredo Neves in 1985 been followed by a special election on the French model rather than by vice presidential succession on the American model.

was to act as President until a President should be supplied by special election."[4]

Meanwhile, a fortnight before the Convention adjourned, a new drafting committee went off for a weekend and returned with the Vice Presidency. The committee did not propose the office in order to provide for the succession. The succession was already provided for by the formula of an acting President followed by an intermediate election. The Vice Presidency emerged for quite other reasons. Hugh Williamson, a member of the new committee, frankly told the Convention that "such an office as vice-President was not wanted. He was introduced *only* for the sake of a valuable mode of election which required two to be chosen at the same time" (emphasis added)[5] in order to ensure the election of a *national* President.

For the United States had as yet little conviction of national identity. Loyalty ran to the states rather than to the country as a whole. If presidential electors could vote for only one candidate, local feeling would lead them to vote for the fellow from their own state. The new draft required them to vote for two persons "of whom one at least shall not be an inhabitant of the same State with themselves." By means of the double vote, localism could be overcome, and a President with broad appeal beyond his own state would emerge. "The second best man in this case," as Madison observed, "would probably be first, in fact"[6]—i.e., the favorite second choice would be the person commanding national confidence.

The double vote was additionally intended to defeat cabal and corruption in the selection process. Because each elector must vote for two persons without indicating a preference, "the precise operation of his vote," James Wilson observed, "is not known to himself at the time when he gives it." Conspiracy would therefore be "under the necessity of acting blindfold at the election" and would be "defeated by the joint and unforeseen effect of the whole."[7] Hamilton concluded in the 68th *Federalist* that the double vote made it a "moral certainty" that the Presidency would be filled "by characters preeminent for ability and virtue." Popularity and intrigue might enable a man to carry his own state; "but it will require other talents, and a different kind of merit, to establish him in the esteem and confidence of the whole Union."

Under the double vote, the person winning most votes became President, the runner-up Vice President. It was not logically essential that the runner-up be anything at all; and no doubt consideration of the succession played a larger part here than was reflected in the discussions at the Convention and the state ratifying conventions. For both President and Vice President would be voted on for the Presidency, and both presumably would be well qualified for the office. The primary point of the Vice Presidency, however, was not as a mode of succession but as an organic part, in Williamson's phrase, of the "valuable mode of election."

II

Even then the new office was not received with enthusiasm. Elbridge Gerry told the Convention that he was "ag.st having any vice President."[8] Gerry was the only member of the Convention ever to become Vice President. George Clinton, not a delegate, denounced the office from outside as dangerous and unnecessary. Clinton later served as Vice President under two Presidents. James Monroe told the Virginia ratifying convention that he saw no need for the office.[9] *The Federalist* tried to ignore the issue, devoting two quick paragraphs to it in the entire series of eighty-five papers. Noting that the Vice Presidency had been "objected to as superfluous, if not mischievous," Hamilton defended it in perfunctory fashion because the Vice President's casting vote could prevent deadlocks in the Senate and because the Vice President himself could be on occasion a "constitutional substitute" for the President. Privately he complained to James Wilson, "Every body is aware of that defect in the constitution which renders it possible that the man intended for Vice President may in fact turn up President."[10]

The double vote did produce two remarkable figures, Adams and Jefferson, as the first two Vice Presidents. But as an occupation for a grown man the Vice Presidency proved a disaster. "I am Vice-President," Adams told the Senate. "In this I am nothing, but I may be everything"—a concise statement of the paradox of the office. Jefferson called it "the only office in the world about which I am unable to decide whether I had rather have it or not have it."[11] Neither man tried to make anything of the job.

In the meantime, the rise of the party system, a development unanticipated in 1787, was placing the "valuable mode of election" under severe strain. In 1796, the Federalists gave their second ballots to Thomas Pinckney, who was manifestly not the second citizen of the country. Adams himself, the top Federalist candidate, would have preferred, if defeated, to lose to Jefferson rather than to his fellow Federalist.[12] In 1800 the Republicans gave the same number of electoral votes to Jefferson, their presidential choice, as they gave to Aaron Burr, a man of undoubted talents who, however, was trusted by no one in the long course of American history except for his daughter Theodosia and Gore Vidal. Burr was nearly chosen President, though the voters never intended him for the Presidency. The fear of comparable slip-ups in 1804 led to the adoption of the Twelfth Amendment, requiring the electoral college to vote separately for President and Vice President.

With the abolition of the "valuable mode of election," the Vice Presidency lost the function for which it had originally been designed. The office had been created for the loser in the presidential election; in other words, for a man of presidential quality. The rise of party tickets changed the situation, and the Twelfth Amendment formalized the change. The Vice Presidency, it was at once predicted, would cease to attract first-rate men. It would become only a bargaining counter in the presidential contest—"a bait to catch state gudgeons," in Gouverneur Morris's scornful phrase.[13]

Samuel White, a senator from Delaware, summed up with admirable prescience the consequences of the Twelfth Amendment: "Character, talents, virtue, and merit will not be sought after, in the candidate. The question will not be asked, is he capable? is he honest? But can he by his name, by his connexions, by his wealth, by his local situation, by his influence, or his intrigues, best promote the election of a President?" Roger Griswold of Connecticut said that the Vice Presidency would thereafter be "worse than useless." A number of political leaders, Republicans and Federalists—John Randolph of Roanoke; former Speaker of the House, now Senator Jonathan Dayton; Griswold; Samuel W. Dana—drew the logical conclusion. The Vice Presidency was an organic part of a particular mode of election. That mode of election was now terminated. Should not the Vice Presidency be terminated too? "The reasons of erecting the office," Dayton correctly said, "are frustrated by the amendment. . . . It will be preferable, therefore, to abolish the office."[14] Henry Adams tells us in his great history of these years that, "had the question risen as a new one, perhaps a majority might have favored abolition." But the discussion was hampered by instructions from state legislatures, and abolition failed by 19–12 in the Senate and 85–27 in the House. The Federalists thereafter, Adams wrote, were able to charge Jefferson and his party with "putting in the office of President, in case of vacancies, men whom no State and no elector intended for the post."[15]

The charge proved correct. The Twelfth Amendment sent the Vice Presidency into prompt decline. The first two Vice Presidents had moved on directly to the Presidency. After the Amendment the Vice Presidency became a resting place for mediocrities. Who can remember Burr's successors—George Clinton, Elbridge Gerry, Daniel D.

Tompkins? For a generation the Secretary of State became the stepping-stone to the Presidency; thereafter Presidents were elected from anywhere except the Vice Presidency. In the 180 years since the Twelfth Amendment only one Vice President—Martin Van Buren—has advanced directly to the Presidency by election.

More than half the Vice Presidents in the nineteenth century were actually *older* than their Presidents. William R. King, when nominated as Vice President with Franklin Pierce, was known to have a mortal disease and died six weeks after inauguration. Clinton, Gerry, Henry Wilson, Thomas A. Hendricks, and Garret A. Hobart also died in office. Apart from their families, few cared or even noticed. The Vice Presidency was nothing. "It is not a stepping stone to anything except oblivion," said Theodore Roosevelt when Boss Platt conned him into accepting the vice presidential nomination in 1900. "I fear my bolt is shot." Asked if he planned to attend McKinley's second inaugural, Platt replied with relish, "I am going to Washington to see Theodore take the veil."[16] Four years later the Democrats nominated Henry G. Davis, then eighty-one years old, for the Vice Presidency (the ticket lost). For thirty-eight years the republic has been without any Vice President at all. No catastrophe resulted.

III

In the meantime, however, the Vice Presidency edged its way into the presidential succession. When the Second Congress passed the Presidential Succession Act of 1792, it assumed that in case of a vacancy the Vice President would act as President for the remainder of the President's term. If the Vice President died too, Madison's idea of an "intermediate election" was to prevail. The President pro tempore of the Senate (or, if there were none, the Speaker of the House) would "act as President . . . until a President be elected," and a special election would be called the next November to choose a new President unless the double vacancy occurred in the last months of the presidential term.[17]

"It is unlikely," E. S. Corwin, that mordant annotator of the Constitution, has written, "that Congress ever passed a more ill-considered law."[18] This is harsh language. Corwin did not live long enough to see the Twenty-fifth Amendment. Still, the Act of 1792 unquestionably had its defects. Corwin was particularly upset because he regarded the intrusion of the legislative branch into the line of succession as a violation of the separation of powers. (Madison had made this point against the bill in Congress, but Madison was aggrieved because, had Hamilton not intrigued to shift the succession to Congress, Jefferson as Secretary of State would have been next in line. If Jefferson had been President pro tem of the Senate and Hamilton Secretary of State, would Madison have cared so much about the separation of powers?) In any case, the Madison-Corwin doubt had not impressed the Committee of Detail in the Constitutional Convention; and it may be considered to have been laid to rest by the long life of the Act of 1792 and by the reenactment of the principle of congressional succession in 1947.

There still remained, though, the more substantial objection that the qualifications for President pro tem and for Speaker are less stringent than for the White House. The congressional officers, for example, need not be natural-born citizens; the Speaker may be under thirty-five (as Henry Clay demonstrated in 1811); and, peculiarly, neither is required to be a member of the body over which he presides, which makes them less than perfect exemplifications of the elective principle. Still, in practice, the congressional officers have met the presidential qualifications most of the time. A graver objection was that they might be on occasion members of the opposite party; in 1792, however, Congress was not thinking in terms of the party system. A still graver objection was that there might be times when there would be neither a Vice President nor a President pro tem nor a Speaker.

The Twelfth Amendment came a dozen years after the Act of 1792. It was intended to make it impossible for persons who had not really been voted on for the Presidency, like Aaron Burr, nearly to become President. It had precisely the opposite effect.[19] After 1804 Vice Presidents were no longer voted on for the Presidency. But the retention of the office and the ambiguity of the Constitution enabled Vice Presidents to make themselves President.

The Founding Fathers assumed that, if a President died, the Vice President would inherit the powers and duties of the President but not the office itself; he would only be Acting President. Corwin judged it the clear expectation of the Framers that, if there were a vacancy in the Presidency, "the Vice-President should remain Vice-President, a stopgap, a locum tenens, whatever the occasion of his succession, and should become President only if and when he was elected as such."[20] A modern scholar, John D. Feerick, agrees that the men who signed the Constitution accepted the language limiting tenure ("until . . . a President shall be elected") "as applicable to all successors, including the Vice-President."* The Twelfth Amendment

---

*Feerick adds: "The debates at the Convention clearly show that the Vice-President was merely intended to discharge the powers and duties of the President temporarily. All of the drafts before the Committees of Detail and Style were explicit in this regard." Feerick, *From Failing Hands*, 50–51.

substantiates this surmise; for it provides that, if a presidential choice went to the House and could not be made before inauguration day, "the Vice-President shall *act* as President, as in the case of the death or other constitutional disability of the President" (emphasis added).

But the debate over the Twelfth Amendment showed incipient congressional confusion as to whether the Vice President, in the event of a vacancy in the Presidency, was only to exercise the powers and duties of the office or was to acquire the office as well, thereby becoming President in every sense of the term.[21] Then in 1841 William Henry Harrison died a month after his inauguration. At last there was brought to test, as John Quincy Adams said, "that provision of the Constitution which places in the Executive chair a man never thought of for it by anybody." Vice President John Tyler staged a constitutional coup by successfully insisting—"in direct violation," Adams testily noted, "both of the grammar and context of the Constitution"*—that, when a Vice President inherited the powers and duties of the presidential office, he inherited the office too and became, not Acting President but President in his own right. Harrison's cabinet registered objections, and there were unavailing protests from senators who thought that a man could gain the Presidency only by election.[22] But Tyler won his point, though the point did not gain explicit constitutional sanction until 125 years later in the Twenty-fifth Amendment.

The United States lived under the Succession Act of 1792 for ninety-four years. Since a double vacancy never occurred, the intermediate-election feature, evidently intended by the Founding Fathers as a routine part of the process, never came into play. But a problem emerged. In 1881 James A. Garfield, shot by an assassin, died at a time when there was neither a President pro tem of the Senate nor a Speaker of the House. If anything had simultaneously happened to his Vice President, Chester A. Arthur, the Presidency would have been in limbo. This was strangely also the case when Grover Cleveland's Vice President died four years later. Moreover, the Republicans were in control of the Senate in 1885, which meant that the President pro tem of the Senate, when chosen, would be of the opposite party from Cleveland as well as his statutory successor.

*J. Q. Adams, *Memoirs*, ed. C. F. Adams (Philadelphia, 1877), X, 457, 463–464. J. Q. Adams's great-great-grandson Thomas B. Adams has speculated that, if a special election had been held following Harrison's death, Henry Clay would probably have been the choice of the nation, in which case there might have been no President Polk, no Mexican War, and a different course of national development. See "On the Threshold of the White House," *Atlantic Monthly*, July 1974.

The cry for reform produced the Presidential Succession Act of 1886. The new law put the line of descent through the cabinet, thereby making succession automatic and preventing the mechanics of succession from transferring the Presidency from one party to another. Some members of Congress opposed this idea—among them Congressman William McKinley of Ohio—on the ground that it would contravene the elective principle by empowering a President to name his successor.[23] The 1886 law did not, however, eliminate the idea of intermediate elections. It provided that the cabinet successor should "act as President until the disability of the President or Vice-President is removed, or *a President shall be elected*" (emphasis added). "The powers and duties of the office of President," and apparently not the office itself, devolved upon the cabinet successor, and "it shall be the duty of the person upon whom said powers and duties shall devolve" to convene Congress within twenty days, presumably in order to provide for a special election.[24]

IV

In spite of Tyler's constitutional coup and the subsequent assassinations of Lincoln and Garfield, the Vice Presidency remained a dismal job. Except for Calhoun, who resigned out of frustration, and Van Buren, who went on to the Presidency, it attracted no major figures in the nineteenth century.

It was hardly a job at all. The Constitution's only assignment was that the Vice President "shall be President of the Senate, but shall have no Vote, unless they be equally divided." When there had been objection to this in the Convention, Roger Sherman remarked that, if the Vice President did not preside over the Senate, "he would be without employment."[25] The First Congress even wrangled over the question of paying the Vice President a salary. Some legislators thought he should only receive a per diem for those days when he actually presided over the Senate. Finally they voted him $5000 a year.

The Vice President's constitutional employment did not amount to much. Tie votes in the Senate were infrequent, and breaking a deadlock, as James G. Blaine dryly remarked, was "more apt to embarrass than to promote his political interests."[26] In the modern era, Vice Presidents spend as little time as possible presiding over the Senate. Early Vice Presidents filled their days reflecting on the iniquities of the national government. Jefferson wrote the Kentucky Resolutions as Vice President, Calhoun the South Carolina Exposition. Later Vice Presidents lacked this taste for political philosophy. Richard M. Johnson, who served under Van Buren, ran a tavern and kept a black mistress. Thomas R. Marshall and Alben W. Barkley made jokes. But most Vice Presidents lacked a taste for humor too.

The Vice Presidency seemed a job of spectacular and incurable frustration. Why did Presidents not give the Vice President serious work? For a long time they believed themselves constitutionally forbidden to do so. Washington did on occasion ask his Vice President to attend cabinet meetings; but Jefferson, as John Adams's Vice President, was quick to erect a wall of separation. "I consider my office," he wrote, "as constitutionally confined to legislative functions, and that I could not take any part whatever in executive consultations."[27] Most Presidents and Vice Presidents until our own day accepted the Jeffersonian doctrine. When William Howard Taft asked his Vice President, James S. Sherman, to serve as the administration's liaison with the House of Representatives, Sherman refused on the ground that "acting as messenger boy is not part of the duties of a Vice President."[28] Truman wrote in 1955 that the Vice President "is not an officer of the executive branch" and Eisenhower as late as 1963 that the Vice President "is not legally a part of the Executive branch and is not subject to direction by the President."[29]

Even if the Vice President were accounted part of the executive branch, constitutional obstacles remained. Any formal allocation of authority to the Vice President would conflict with the clause in the Constitution vesting the undivided "executive power" to the President. Political obstacles reinforced the constitutional bar. Until 1940, party conventions ordinarily imposed the vice presidential nominee on the presidential candidate, 'balancing the ticket' by picking someone from the defeated faction of the party. The Vice President, in Blaine's words, was "not unnaturally thrown into a sort of antagonism with the Administration" and often, he said, was the center of a coterie of malcontents, as the heir to the throne is apt to be in monarchies.[30]

Even when the two men began as political allies, psychological obstacles tended to separate them. Except for Jackson and Van Buren, no President and Vice President fully trusted each other from 1789 to 1977. Polk had amiable personal relations with George M. Dallas, McKinley with Garret Hobart and Truman with Barkley, but none of these Presidents gave their Vice Presidents a policy role in the administrations.

The psychological grounds for mistrust are self-evident and fundamental. "The only business of the vice-president," wrote the sardonic Thomas R. Marshall, "is to ring the White House bell every morning and ask what is the state of health of the president."[31] "It is princip'lly, Hinnissy, because iv th' vice-prisidint," explained Mr. Dooley,

that most iv our prisidints have enjoyed such rugged health. . . . Th' prisidint, afther sizin' up th' vice-prisidint, con-cludes that it wud be betther f'r th' counthry if he shud live yet awhile. "D'ye know," says th' prisidint to th' vice-prisidint, "ivry time I see you I feel tin years younger?" "Ye'er kind wurruds," says th' vice-prisidint, "brings tears to me eyes. My wife was sayin' on'y this mornin' how comfortable we are-re in our little flat." Some vice-prisidints have been so anxious f'r th' prisidint's safety that they've had to be warned off th' White House grounds.[32]

In short, the only serious thing the Vice President has to do is to wait around for the President to die. This is hardly the basis for cordial and enduring friendships. No one appreciates daily reminders of his own mortality. "Every time I came into John Kennedy's presence," said Lyndon Johnson, who experienced both ends of the relationship, "I felt like a goddamn raven, hovering over his shoulder."[33] Presidents resent the death's head at the feast. Vice Presidents equally resent the monarch who stuffs himself at the banquet table while they scramble for leavings. Elbridge Gerry worried in the Constitutional Convention about the "close intimacy" that he thought "must subsist between the President & vice-president." Gouverneur Morris responded acidly, "The vice president will then be the first heir apparent that ever loved his father."[34]

V

Modern Presidents characteristically start out with ritual pledges about the creative use they plan to make of their Vice Presidents. The pledges ordinarily pay out in tokens.

Historically the first token was to invite vice presidential participation in cabinet meetings. Theodore Roosevelt suggested this in 1896.* But when he became President himself after an exasperating interlude as Vice President, he did not give his own Vice President, Charles W. Fairbanks, a seat in the cabinet or anywhere else. Vice President Marshall presided at cabinet meetings when Wilson was at Versailles. But, since he regarded himself as a "member of the legislative branch," he questioned the propriety of doing so and carefully explained to the cabinet that he was acting "in obedience to a re-

---

*Roosevelt, "The Three Vice-Presidential Candidates," 291. TR also thought that the Vice President should be given a vote on ordinary occasions in the Senate and "perchance on occasions a voice in the debates."

quest" and "in an unofficial and informal way."[35] Harding was the first President to make his Vice President, Calvin Coolidge, a regular at cabinet meetings. Coolidge expected his own Vice President to follow this example; but Charles G. Dawes rejected entanglement with the executive as a "wrong principle" and in due course supported farm legislation from his office on Capitol Hill that his President opposed and eventually vetoed.[36]

As a vice presidential candidate in 1920, Franklin D. Roosevelt called the office a prime example of "industrial waste" and explained how to make something of it. A Vice President with an "intimate and sympathetic" connection with the President, FDR said, could serve as "a kind of super handy man" in the administration, helping especially to bring about government reorganization and to bridge the gap between Congress and the executive branch. A constitutional amendment would be required, he conceded, to give the Vice President serious authority; but, even without an amendment, there was much a Vice President could do.[37]

As President, however, the second Roosevelt was little more inclined than the first Roosevelt to follow the precepts he had laid down when he aspired only to the Vice Presidency. He did reinstate vice presidential attendance at cabinet meetings, and that became routine thereafter. But he showed no interest in sharing authority with any "super handy man" of his own. When William O. Douglas, who had been chairman of the Securities and Exchange Commission, suggested to FDR that the heads of independent agencies report to his Vice President, Henry Wallace, the President replied, "Would you like to see Henry Wallace instead of me? What would Henry know about all these matters?"[38] "You cannot, under the Constitution," FDR explained to a press conference in 1940, "set up a second President. . . . The Constitution states one man is responsible. Now that man can delegate, surely, but in the delegation he does not delegate away any part of . . . the ultimate responsibility that rests on him."[39]

Presidents will delegate power to men they can hire and fire. But they cannot fire Vice Presidents. This discourages Presidents from giving Vice Presidents jobs at which they may fail—or succeed too well. FDR came closest of any President to giving real power to his Vice President when he made Wallace chairman of the Board of Economic Warfare ten days after Pearl Harbor—the only big job ever handed a Vice President in the two hundred years of the American republic. The experiment only proved the embarrassment bound to arise when an agency chief who happens to be Vice President, and is therefore not dismissible from the administration, gets into fights with powerful cabinet members.

No subsequent President has gone so far as Roosevelt. Barkley was a ceremonial Vice President. Eisenhower did not much like his Vice President and, when asked to name major decisions in which Nixon had participated, responded, "If you give me a week, I might think of one."[40] Kennedy liked Johnson, thought "the poor guy's got the lousiest job in government"[41] and treated him with great personal consideration but gave him no power. "President Kennedy," as George Reedy, a Johnson special assistant, later said, "was rather generous to Vice-President Johnson. But that didn't mean that Vice-President Johnson appreciated it in the slightest."* As President, Johnson systematically tormented and humiliated his Vice President, Hubert Humphrey. He did not want any goddamn raven hovering over his shoulder.

Nixon, who had carved out a vice presidential role as political hit man of the Eisenhower administration, assigned as President the same delicate responsibility to Agnew, thereby making him, as Eugene McCarthy said, "Nixon's Nixon." But when asked whether he had told his Vice President about the plan for the diplomatic opening to China, Nixon, replying in what James J. Kilpatrick reported as an "incredulous" tone, said, "Agnew? Agnew? Of course not."[42] Jeb Stuart Magruder, of Nixon's White House, described Agnew as "frozen out by Nixon."[43]

Yet attendance at cabinet meetings proved an opening wedge. Despite presidential snubs, the Vice Presidency grew in importance during the postwar years. The decay of political parties permitted presidential candidates, within certain limits, to impose their vice presidential choices on the party conventions. This development increased presidential control of the once antagonistic relationship. In 1949 Truman got Congress to pass legislation making the Vice President a member of the National Security Council. The Vice President thereby received his first statutory sanction within the executive branch as well as exposure to, and potentially a voice in, foreign affairs.

Vice Presidents still operated out of their office in the Capitol—a chamber "so small," Tom Marshall had claimed in the Wilson years, "that to survive it is necessary to keep the door open in order to obtain the necessary cubic feet of air. When the vice-president is in the

---

*American Bar Association, Symposium on the Vice-Presidency, 3 December 1976, in *Fordham Law Review*, February 1977, 750. However, Bobby Baker, another Johnson intimate, quotes him as saying, "Jack Kennedy's as thoughtful and considerate of me at those meetings as he can be. But I know his snot-nosed brother's after my ass, and all those high-falutin' Harvards." Bobby Baker, *Wheeling and Dealing* (New York, 1978), 101.

room . . . guides go by with their guests, stop and point him out, as though he were a curiosity."[44] Then in 1961 Kennedy gave Johnson space in the building next to the White House. At the time this seemed a reasonable act of courtesy and of convenience. We did not consider the constitutional implication of moving the Vice Presidency from the Capitol to the Executive Office Building—that is, from the legislative to the executive.

Johnson had what seemed then an enormous vice presidential staff of twenty, but he still had to hire them on his Senate payroll or borrow them from executive agencies. After Johnson became President, Humphrey retained the executive suite but lived even more from hand to mouth. In 1969 Nixon, while keeping Agnew on a tight White House leash, nevertheless provided the Vice Presidency a line in the executive budget. The existence of the vice presidential budget encouraged Gerald Ford after Agnew's resignation in 1973 to extract pledges of more staff and independence from a now beleaguered Nixon. The Ford staff grew from seventeen to seventy by August 1974, and his combined executive and senatorial budget exceeded $1 million. Paul C. Light, an analyst of the "institutional Vice Presidency," writes that Ford created "the first self-contained Vice President's office."[45]

When Ford became President in 1974, Nelson Rockefeller bargained with him as Ford had previously bargained with Nixon. Brimming with self-confidence and big ideas, gratified by vague presidential promises, soon endowed with a staff of eighty-four, Rockefeller carried institutionalization still further. The Vice President gained a residence of his own, leaving well behind Mr. Dooley's comfortable little flat. Rockefeller even paid personally for the redesign of the vice presidential seal.

VI

The accession of Ford and Rockefeller meanwhile confronted the republic with an unprecedented situation. They were the first President and Vice President in American history who had come to office and power, not through election like all their predecessors, but through appointment. No American outside the Fifth District of Michigan had ever voted for the President for national office, and no American anywhere had ever voted for the Vice President for national office.

Nothing like this could have happened in the earlier history of the republic. A major premise of American politics had always been that the President was an elected, not an appointed, official. The Constitution expressly provided that the President and Vice President were to "be elected." The Founding Fathers believed that no one who had not been elected to the Presidency should serve as President any longer than necessary to organize a new presidential election. They unquestionably would have been appalled, having written the Constitution as they did, to discover that two centuries after the Declaration of Independence, neither the President nor the Vice President had ever faced a national election and that each owed his office, not to the voters, but to the gift of his direct predecessor.

How had a democratic republic come to this pass? The nation had lived under the Presidential Succession Act of 1886 for nearly sixty years when Truman, abruptly raised to the Presidency in 1945, faced the prospect of serving the balance of Roosevelt's term, nearly four years, without a Vice President. The law of 1886 put the Secretary of State next in line. "It now lies within my power," Truman declared with customary directness, "to nominate the person who would be my immediate successor in the event of my own death or inability to act. I do not believe that in a democracy this power should rest with the Chief Executive."[46]

Rejecting the principle of the law of 1886, Truman contended that the succession should go not through the cabinet but to an "elective officer"—that is, one who gained public office through election. So he called for a reversion to the principle of the Succession Act of 1792, though with the Speaker of the House first and the President pro tem of the Senate second. There were manifest defects in the scheme. Neither the Speaker nor the President pro tem, as we have seen, need be an elective officer. Both posts were in part the reward of seniority, which often meant long tenure in a safe and therefore unrepresentative district. James F. Byrnes, George C. Marshall and Dean Acheson, Truman's Secretaries of State, were far better equipped for the Presidency than Joseph Martin of Massachusetts, who, as Speaker of the House, became heir apparent under the Truman reform. In general, Secretaries of State have been more impressive figures than Speakers. Polk is the only Speaker to have made it to the White House.

Truman, however, saw this part of the scheme as provisional. Reaffirming the conviction of the Founding Fathers, he said, "No matter who succeeds to the Presidency after the death of the elected President and Vice President, it is my opinion that he should not serve longer than until the next Congressional election or until a special election called . . . to fill the unexpired term of the deceased President and Vice President."[47]

Truman's proposal that the intermediate election fill the unexpired term gave trouble to some constitutional scholars who read the language on the Presidency in Article II, Section 1, of the Constitution—"He shall hold his Office during the term of four Years"—as guaranteeing every new President four years in the White House. The Succession Act of 1792 did provide that the term following the special election should be for four years. The Act of 1886 was mute on the point, though the debate assumed a four-year term. It is far from self-evident, however, that the Constitution forbids elections to fill unexpired terms. There are such elections every day for senators and representatives, though they, no less than Presidents, serve for terms specified in the Constitution. The House Judiciary Committee, under the chairmanship of that rugged old Texas strict constructionist Hatton W. Sumners, went into this question at length in 1945 and found no constitutional problem in the case of the Presidency.

The Constitution, the House Judiciary Committee said, "does not provide that the term of each incumbent shall be 4 years, but that the President shall hold his office 'during the term of 4 years.' This language appears to have reference to a fixed quadrennial term, permitting the filling of an unexpired portion thereof by elections. The tradition of special elections for unexpired terms of other officers also supports the provision."[48] "During" often means "in the time of"; it does not necessarily mean "throughout the entire course of." Had the Constitution said *"for* a Term of four Years," this would clearly assure a four-year term to every new President. But the Constitution does not say this.

And if John Tyler was correct in saying that a Vice President became President, not just Acting President, and if it is correct to construe the Constitution as assuring every President a four-year term, then this reading must surely apply to Presidents who gain the office by inheritance quite as much as those who gain it by election. This would mean that, when a President dies, the Vice President who succeeds him is entitled to a four-year term of his own. Ben Butler made this point during the impeachment trial of Andrew Johnson. "Whose presidential term is the respondent now serving out?" he asked. "His own or Mr. Lincoln's? If his own, he is entitled to four years up to the anniversary of the murder, because each presidential term is four years by the Constitution."[49] But no one has ever argued, not even John Tyler, that a Vice President has any right to do more than serve out his President's unexpired term. On what principle, when there is no Vice President, should a specially elected "constitutional substitute" be in a more favored position?

The House unwisely dropped Truman's provision for special presidential elections, and the bill died in the Senate. The 1946 midterm election gave the Republicans control of the Congress. The Republican leadership, seizing the chance to make Joe Martin Truman's absolute and not provisional successor, revived the bill without the provision for intermediate elections. As finally enacted, the law thus departed critically from Truman's original intention. He signed it nevertheless in order to shift the succession back to elected officials.

In the next decade two things happened. The situation of 1947— a President of one party, a Speaker of the other party—became less uncommon. The Succession Act of 1947 therefore contained the threat in case of a double vacancy of the opposition taking over the White House without benefit of election. Then after Eisenhower's heart attack, ileitis and stroke in 1955–1957, the question of presidential disability came to the fore. In an exchange of letters with Nixon in 1958, Eisenhower said that, if he were incapacitated, the Vice President was authorized to serve as Acting President. Kennedy followed Eisenhower's precedent, and in 1965 Johnson recommended a constitutional amendment to resolve the problems both of presidential disability and of the presidential succession.

The result was the Twenty-fifth Amendment. Presidential disability was the primary concern of the drafters. Sections 3 and 4 of the Amendment established an exceedingly cumbersome but possibly defensible procedure for dealing with this problem. These sections do not define presidential disability. They delegate this decision to a single elected official, the Vice President, and the unelected cabinet members. Some critics feared that, in the words of Representative Henry Gonzalez, "the almost unchecked ease with which the President can be removed by either an unscrupulous or mistaken subordinate" would be a standing invitation to intrigue and conspiracy. "In a democracy such as ours," Gonzalez added, "the power to change the government is vested in the people. But . . . the 25th amendment removes the decisionmaking prerogative of the people. . . . The very person who has the most to gain by the removal of the President is the person who is vested with that decisionmaking power. . . . If you ask the fox what is best for the hen, the hen is likely to come up short."[50]

Congressman Gonzalez's concern may seem overwrought. Still, after Nixon and Agnew, who knows what sort of people are likely to be empowered by the Twenty-fifth Amendment? The republic, as the Supreme Court said many years ago in *ex parte Milligan*, has "no right to expect that it will always have wise and humane rulers, sincerely attached to the principles of the Constitution. Wicked men, ambitious of power, with hatred of liberty and contempt of law, may fill the place once occupied by Washington and Lincoln."[51] A serious Constitution is drawn for foul weather as well as for fair.

Still, Sections 3 and 4 of the Twenty-fifth Amendment have not created problems so far (1986). But Sections 1 and 2, though they attracted less interest at the time, caused trouble almost at once. Section 1 justified Tyler's claim that, when a President vanished, the Vice President became President in the full sense of the word. And the fatal Section 2, carelessly conceived in the high noon of the Imperial Presidency, empowered the President, when there was a vacancy in the second place, to nominate a Vice President who would take office upon confirmation by a majority of both houses of Congress.

Section 2 thus repudiated Truman's principle that in a democracy such power should not rest with the Chief Executive. If Truman applied this principle to himself, an elected Vice President, it should apply far more powerfully to a Chief Executive who had been an appointed Vice President and whose name had never gone before the national electorate. But the Twenty-fifth Amendment cavalierly tossed away Truman's old-fashioned scruple and sanctified the appointive principle at the highest level of the American government. It thereby created the monstrous possibility—within a decade a fact—that an appointed Vice President would himself become President and would then appoint his own Vice President.

There was opposition to this extraordinary departure from democratic principle. The Presidency, as Charles Mathias of Maryland observed in a brilliant dissent from the House report, would no longer be a purely elective office if the Amendment were adopted. The Constitutional Convention "would surely have rejected an appointed Vice President on grounds of principle alone." The Amendment, Mathias continued, was based not only on a false view of democracy but on a false view of human nature. It assumed

that a President will always be enlightened and disinterested in naming a Vice President. While this optimism reflects well on the 20th Century's opinion of itself in contrast to the pragmatic 18th century estimate of human frailty, it may not be a prudent basis for constitutional law.

Mathias dismissed the argument that Presidents picked their Vice Presidents anyway at the nominating convention. A candidate for the Presidency, bent on winning national approval, had to choose a running mate generally acceptable to the party and to the electorate. "The electability of the vice-presidential candidate is a form of accountability for the head of the ticket." Once elected, a President in appointing a Vice President could employ any criteria he personally preferred. Congressional confirmation would be "a mere formality in a period of national emotional stress." In addition, the choice by the presidential candidate of his running mate was merely the contemporary political custom. It had not always been the custom in the past and might not always be the custom in the future. Putting it into a constitutional amendment would transform a passing practice into a permanent principle.[52]

Nonetheless, Congress, with the support of the establishment press, the American Bar Association and, I am sorry to say, an assortment of scholars voted overwhelmingly to recommend the Twenty-fifth Amendment. Thirty-eight state legislatures voted ratification, and it sank into the Constitution in February 1967.

VII

Section 2 of the Twenty-fifth Amendment sprang into action sooner than anyone could have expected. Under that section, Nixon, after Agnew's resignation in 1973, named Ford as Vice President. (Suppose that Nixon himself had been forced to resign before Agnew's crimes had been uncovered. What kind of a Vice President would Agnew have picked? And, if justice managed thereafter to catch up with President Agnew, what kind of Vice President would Agnew's Vice President have selected as his own successor?) After Nixon's resignation, in 1974 Ford named Nelson Rockefeller as Vice President. "For the first time in the history of this great Nation," John Pastore of Rhode Island thereupon cried with pardonable senatorial hyperbole, "the President and Vice President will both be appointed—not elected by the people and not responsive to any mandate from the citizens. The Nation will no longer be democratically governed."[53]

The architects of the Twenty-fifth Amendment neither anticipated nor desired this particular result—a fact that casts the gravest doubt on the quality of their draftsmanship. The constitutional sanctification of a government headed by two persons receiving office and power by appointment rather than by election was inadvertent, not premeditated. But for anyone concerned with democratic principle the result raises the sternest difficulties. Not only is the conception of the President as an elected official breached; but the award to the President of the power to appoint his own successor in the case of a vice presidential vacancy grafts a quasi-dynastic feature on to the American democratic system. Like a king, the American President is now empowered to produce his own heir.

The congressional tests of the Amendment, moreover, exposed se-

rious contradictions in Section 2. According to the original understanding, as set forth in the legislative history, the election of the Vice
President by Congress was to take the place of election by the voters.
As Birch Bayh, the manager of the Twenty-fifth Amendment, otherwise an admirable senator, had put it, the role of Congress "in this
one, unique instance [is] that of surrogate electors. Congress is to represent the people of the country in a Congressional election of, and
not merely acquiescence in, the choice of a new Vice-President." In
other words, as Bayh said, the election of a Vice President was definitely not "just another traditional nomination to be handled in the
traditional way."[54] The theory that Congress was acting in lieu of the
electorate was expressed in the requirement that both houses — not
the Senate alone, as in the case of usual presidential appointments —
must give their consent to the election of a midterm Vice President.

One doubts that this original understanding was a good idea. The
Founding Fathers, after careful consideration, had rejected the proposal that Congress choose the Chief Executive. As Gouverneur Morris put it in the Convention, the President would be "the mere creature of the Legisl: if appointed & impeachable by that body."[55] The
Constitution even prohibited members of Congress from serving as
presidential electors. It brought Congress into the picture only in case
of a tie in the Electoral College. The Twenty-fifth Amendment greatly
enlarges the congressional role. It gives Congress in relatively common cases (almost a quarter of the time since the ratification of the
Twelfth Amendment) what the Founding Fathers resolved to deny it
except in the most extreme cases: control over the choice of a potential President. This control was cloaked in the affirmation that
congressional election was the replacement of popular election. And,
since Congress was supposed to act as the surrogate for the voters,
there is no escape from the conclusion that members of Congress
were commanded to apply to a person nominated for the Vice Presidency the same tests that the voters apply to candidates in a regular
election.

In practice, Congress failed to live up to its charge to serve as surrogate electors for the people. If it had supplied, as it was obligated
to supply, an equivalent of a popular election, Ford and Rockefeller
would not have been confirmed by the overwhelming margins they
received; for no popular election would have given them such extraordinary majorities. Many legislators voted to confirm the names
submitted to them by the President who would not have dreamed of
voting for the same candidates in a polling booth. Instead of applying
the standards plainly demanded by Section 2, Congress applied the

standards routinely used for routine presidential appointments. The original understanding, in short, was quickly forgotten. It was abandoned because it came into conflict with another and politically more compelling standard: that the process should produce a Vice President who would be acceptable to the President. As Bayh himself frankly confessed, "It was an irreconcilable difference between the person that Birch Bayh would vote for to be President and someone who could work with Gerald Ford or Richard Nixon."[56] The existence of this "irreconcilable difference" between the two standards expresses a fundamental and disqualifying infirmity in Section 2 of the Twenty-fifth Amendment.

The nomination of Rockefeller in 1974 exposed further defects in the new process. This time Congress did not cheer the nomination through at once. Before confirming Rockefeller by a large margin, it subjected him to a minute and demeaning inquisition. Yet who in their senses would argue that a Vice President designated in midterm should be subjected to more searching examination than presidential candidates ever undergo? Which office is more important: the Presidency or the Vice Presidency? The curious double standard enjoined by the Twenty-fifth Amendment leads logically to two opposite alternatives. Either Congress should do the same inquisitorial job on potential Presidents as well; or the idea of presidential appointment and congressional confirmation of midterm Vice Presidents should be abandoned.

Alas, for all its obscurantism and ambiguity, for all its thoughtless rejection of the commitment of the Framers to elected Presidents, the Twenty-fifth Amendment, that mindless by-product of the Imperial Presidency, is now inscribed in the Constitution. It gives a President— even an appointed President—new power to name his own heir. It gives a Vice President—even an appointed Vice President—new power to take over from a President presumed unable to discharge the duties of the office. And it produced on the eve of the bicentennial of American independence a President and Vice President who owed their high offices not to election by the voters but to the gift of their immediate predecessors.

VIII

By offering the Vice President plausible constitutional reasons to prepare himself for presidential disability, the Twenty-fifth Amendment contributed to the institutional Vice Presidency. But the transformation of what had been for 180 years an empty and laughable office had still deeper causes.

Institutionalization has plainly not taken place because of any increase in the Vice President's power. Indeed, none of the institutional Vice Presidents had nearly as great substantive responsibilities as those conferred by Roosevelt on Henry Wallace a generation earlier. No doubt a new sense of the frailty of Presidents—FDR's death in office, the attempted assassination of Truman, Eisenhower's sicknesses, the assassination of Kennedy, the resignation of Nixon—focused unprecedented public attention on the succession. Still, Lincoln, Garfield and McKinley had been assassinated and Wilson disabled without leading to an aggrandizement of the Vice Presidency.

The factors explaining the new Vice Presidency are the decline of the political party and the rise of the mass media. For the Vice Presidency is the only place except the Presidency itself that ensures its occupant automatic and comprehensive national exposure. The Vice President is forever on television, even if mostly shaking the hands of foreign dignitaries or attending their funerals. Name recognition gives him high ratings in the polls. In an age of weakened parties he becomes at once, as nineteenth-century Vice Presidents almost never did, a national political luminary. Spiro Who? turned into a household word within two years of his inauguration. No one would forget Alexander Throttlebottom's name today. And, once the Vice Presidency achieved star billing, the iron law of status escalation decrees that the Vice President must have the staff, the budget, the residence, the airplane and all the other perquisites appropriate to a star.

In short, institutionalization did not take place because new duties required new vice presidential machinery. Rather the contrary: new machinery produced the vice presidential search for new duties. Louis Sullivan said, "Form ever follows function." Perhaps that is, or should be, true of architecture. In the age of great organizations, however, function ever follows form.

Unrelated developments gave further momentum to the institutional Vice Presidency. In 1976 Jimmy Carter was elected President. A self-proclaimed outsider, ill informed on the wicked ways of Washington, he badly needed the expertise available from his running mate, Senator Walter F. Mondale. Mondale received an office near the President's in the West Wing of the White House, saw the secret papers, sat in on the meetings, influenced appointments and made himself an effective general adviser to the President. The Vice President and his staff were integrated more than ever before into the policy operations of the White House. Not since Jackson and Van Buren had a President and Vice President worked so closely together.

In 1981 Ronald Reagan, another outsider in similar need of Washington expertise, followed the Carter-Mondale model in giving access, status and Mondale's West Wing office to George Bush. By 1984 the Office of the Vice President had a budget of $2 million and a staff of seventy. It was the fifth largest unit in the Executive Office of the President and had become, in Paul Light's words, "a replica of the President's office, with a national security adviser, press secretary, domestic issues staff, scheduling team, advance, appointments, administration, chief of staff, and counsel's office."[57]

The institutional Vice Presidency has increased vice presidential recognition and comfort. It has not, however, assuaged the historic humiliations of the office. The ambitious and energetic Rockefeller should have understood what he was getting into. "I have known well all the Vice Presidents since Henry Wallace," he once said, "and . . . all of them were frustrated."[58] Embittering fights with Ford's White House staff and the derailing of his major initiatives, along with external political harassment, led Rockefeller to withdraw his name from consideration for renomination in less than a year after he was sworn in.

Mondale warmly appreciated Carter's determination to make him a full working partner. Some of his colleagues in the administration appreciated it less. The Attorney General, Griffin Bell, thought that moving Mondale into an independent "power center at the White House" was Carter's "crucial error."[59] And, even with its high degree of personal compatibility, the Carter-Mondale partnership was incomplete. When Mondale ran for President in 1984, he revealed a long list of issues on which he and Carter had disagreed: the Soviet grain embargo; the 1979 "crisis of confidence" speech and the ensuing cabinet purge; the "racetrack" basing system for MX missiles; the sale of F-15 fighters to Saudi Arabia; standby draft registration; the presidential seclusion during the Iranian hostage crisis.

Like Mondale, George Bush enjoyed a high degree of personal compatibility with his principal. As a good Yale team player, he transcended his early doubts about "voodoo economics" and became a valued member of the Reagan administration. Moreover, Reagan, by keeping the Vice President in the White House, made it difficult for future Presidents to return their Vice Presidents to the Executive Office Building (and impossible to exile them to the Hill).

Mondale and Bush were probably as happy in the job as any Vice President is likely to be. The fundamental dilemma of the office remains. Some constitutional obstacles have crumbled away. The Vice President is now accepted as an officer of the executive branch. Can his powers be increased? This is what Theodore and Franklin Roosevelt advocated when they thought they might be Vice Presidents, even if they dropped the idea once they became Presidents. But the Constitution still forbids the division of the executive power, as FDR had recognized when he judged a constitutional amendment necessary in 1920. "If the Congress were to enact or assign, on a legislative basis, certain responsibilities to the Vice President," Nelson Rockefeller correctly said in 1979, "whoever was President at that time should veto the legislation."[60]

Gerald Ford forgot the Constitution when he proposed to Ronald Reagan in 1980 that he would run for Vice President if Reagan agreed to yield some of his powers and made Ford a deputy President. "Take England," Ford said. "You have a queen who is the Head of State, and then you have the Prime Minister who's the Head of Government. What you can argue is that the President is the Head of State and the Vice President is the Head of Government and the operating officer in the organization."[61] You can argue that, but the argument plainly violates the basic charter of the republic.

And the psychological obstacles remain. Presidents who choose their own Vice Presidents, whether at the nominating convention or through the Twenty-fifth Amendment, may have kindlier feelings toward them (though not always) than when the choice was imposed by the convention. But Presidents must still spend time they could put to better use figuring out ways to keep the Vice President innocently occupied. "They seek to put him," as Tom Marshall said, "where he can do no harm."[62]

For a season Vice Presidents received portentous but powerless assignments as chairmen of interdepartmental committees, like the Aeronautics and Space Council or the Council on Indian Opportunity or the National Commission on Water Quality or the Task Force on Regulatory Relief. Some suggest that the Vice President take over the ceremonial side of the President's job. But Presidents perform few ceremonial functions they do not want to perform; and Vice Presidents would be acceptable substitutes only on the most footling occasions. Nor would an exclusively ceremonial role satisfy any but the most vacuous or aged Vice President. Getting Vice Presidents out of sight by sending them abroad is a solution much favored by recent Presidents. "I go to funerals," said Nelson Rockefeller when asked what he did as Ford's Vice President. "I go to earthquakes."[63]

The vice presidential office in recent years has become busy enough, measured by staff, budget, meetings, paper in and paper out. It is make-work. Despite institutionalization and those quadrennial presidential pledges, the Vice Presidency remains the "fifth wheel to a coach" (Senator Samuel White in 1803), "the fifth wheel in our government" (Albert J. Beveridge in 1909), "the spare tire on the automobile of government" (John N. Garner).[64] As Gertrude Stein said of Oakland, California, there is no there there.

IX

The single point of the Vice Presidency is to provide for the succession in case of the death, disability, resignation or removal of the President. There have been repeated attempts to give it other points. They have all failed. They are all bound to fail. The Vice Presidency cannot be made a working job. Invincible constitutional, political and psychological reasons doom it to impotence. No there can be permanently placed there.

The real question is why have a Vice President at all? "His importance," as Woodrow Wilson said, "consists in the fact that he may cease to be Vice-President."[65] The only conceivable argument for keeping the office is that it provides an automatic solution to the problem of succession. No doubt it does. But does it provide the *best* solution?

First in defense of the Vice Presidency is the mystical argument that the Vice President is the proper successor when a President vanishes in midcourse because, as Truman said and many have repeated, "There is no officer in our system of government, besides the President and Vice President, who has been elected by all the voters of the country."[66] Truman's proposition, advanced nine weeks after Roosevelt's death, was natural enough to a man concerned with legitimating his own recent succession to the Presidency. But insofar as it implied that the voters in some sense intended him or any other Vice President (since 1796) for the Presidency, it was an amiable myth. No one votes for a Vice President. He is part of a package deal, "a sort of appendage to the Presidency" (Truman's own phrase); not an independent choice.[67]

To this hazy theory of an electorally sanctified connection between the Vice Presidency and the succession there is added the conventional wisdom of political science departments (and of Vice Presidents) that the Vice Presidency is the best school for the Presidency. It is above all, we are told, a "learning office" where men educate themselves for the great responsibility that may one day be theirs. Even if the Vice President has nothing to do, he can—we are assured—watch what the President is doing and prepare himself to take over if calamity strikes. Thus Richard M. Nixon: "The Vice Presidency . . . is the only office which provides complete on-the-job training for the duties of the Presidency."[68]

This implies, one fears, an unduly romantic view of Presidents. Nixon himself made this perfectly clear as soon as he had a Vice President or two at his mercy. Presidents, whatever they may say, do not pick their running mates because they want to raise them up to be their successors. All Presidents see themselves, if not as immortal, at least as good for a couple of terms. They pick a running mate not because he is the second citizen of the republic and splendidly qualified to replace them in the White House but because of occult and very often mistaken calculations about the contribution he will make to their own victory at the polls. "Whether they should or not," Congressman James G. O'Hara of Michigan has realistically observed, "they will not, in the final analysis, choose their Vice-Presidential candidate to succeed them. They will choose them to help them succeed."[69]

These calculations, I say, are very often mistaken. It is an exceedingly rare case when the vice presidential candidate makes a difference. Very likely Johnson made a difference in Texas in 1960. But much more typical was the outcome in 1948. Earl Warren was the most popular governor California had had in a generation, but Truman carried California against the Dewey-Warren ticket. If vice presidential candidates make any difference at all, it is probably a negative difference. "The Vice President can't help you," said Nixon. "He can only hurt you." Polling analysis suggests that people tend to vote more against vice presidential candidates than for them.[70]

As for the idea, much discussed by sages of the press, of a "balanced ticket," this is a fraud on the public. It pretends that the Vice President's views will somehow "balance" the views of the President when all our history testifies that they have no impact at all on the President. Should the President die, however, then the difference in views could have a serious effect. Theodore Roosevelt, recalling what happened when Tyler succeeded Harrison and what might have happened had Grover Cleveland died and Vice President Adlai Stevenson taken over, observed, "It is an unhealthy thing to have the Vice-President and the President represented by principles so far apart that the succession of one to the place of the other means a change as radical as any possible party overturn."[71] In modern times, balance in the old political-ideological sense, placating an antagonistic faction in the party, has been replaced by regional, religious and (after 1984) gender balance, providing visual reassurance to key voting groups.

The new form of balance produces a higher degree of ideological compatibility. But it is still just as true that Presidents do not choose running mates primarily to become successors. "The selection of a Vice President," as Barry Goldwater said in 1972, "is to get more votes."[72] And, once in the White House, very few Presidents before 1977 did much to prepare their Vice Presidents for the succession. A Vice President can learn only as much as a President is willing to have him learn—which, given presidential resentment of vice presidential existence, is not ordinarily very much. Truman, recalling how little he had been told as Vice President, tried harder than most Presidents to clue in his second man. His conclusion about on-the-job training is not encouraging. "No Vice-President," he wrote three years after he left the White House, "is ever properly prepared to take over the presidency because of the nature of our presidential, or executive, office." It is "very difficult," Truman continued, for a President to take the Vice President "completely into his confidence." The President "by necessity" builds his own staff and makes his own decisions, and "the Vice-President remains an outsider."[73]

Moreover, seeing things as an ill-informed, impotent and often sullen outsider, the Vice President will very likely "learn" the wrong things. Lyndon Johnson thought Kennedy too cautious at the time of the Cuban missile crisis and in Vietnam. What Johnson "learned" as Vice President led him on to policies of overkill in the Dominican Republic and Indochina. In any case, does a successor's responsibility lie to his predecessor or to himself? "A Vice-President might make a poor President," said Tom Marshall, who had to reflect on this question in Wilson's season of disability, "but he would make a much poorer one if he attempted to subordinate his own mind and views to carry out the ideas of a dead man."[74]

A learning office? Under most Presidents, the Vice Presidency is much less a making than a maiming experience. Most Presidents, far from preparing their Vice Presidents for the succession, treat them in ways likely to erode their capacity to succeed. The result is not education but emasculation. McKinley, wrote Vice President Theodore Roosevelt, "does not intend that I shall have any influence of any kind, sort or description in the administration from the top to the bottom. This he has made evident again and again. . . . I have much less influence with the President now that I am Vice-President than I had even when I was governor."[75] Fortunately for TR, he only had to endure six months of frustration. When he acquired a Vice President of his own, he could not have been more destructive of poor Charley Fairbanks. He used to regale Washington with Finley Peter Dunne's crack after the President remarked he was going down in a submarine: "You really shouldn't do it—unless you take Fairbanks with you."[76] Tom Marshall, who at least extracted a good deal of shrewd humor out of his predicament, concluded that the Vice President "is like a man in a cataleptic state: he cannot speak; he cannot move; he suffers no pain; and yet he is perfectly conscious of everything that is going on about him."[77] Lyndon Johnson, when Vice President, once remarked to Franklin D. Roosevelt, Jr., "Your daddy never let his Vice Presidents put their heads above water."[78]

X

In recent years, as men of larger aspirations and capacities have responded to the actuarial attractions of the office, the damage to Vice Presidents has increased. The more gifted and ambitious the Vice President, the better qualified (at the start) for the Presidency, the longer he serves, the more acute his frustration—and the less his President is inclined to do to alleviate it. Everyone knows the humiliation that Eisenhower repeatedly visited on Nixon. Malcolm Moos, the political scientist, after watching that relationship as an Eisenhower special assistant, concluded that the office was "a kind of coffin."[79] Only a man who has the overpowering ego of a Lyndon Johnson and is treated by his President, as Johnson was, with relative consideration can survive the Vice Presidency; and even Johnson was a subdued and shrunken man by 1963. "It's like being naked in the middle of a blizzard with no one to even offer you a match to keep you warm—that's the vice presidency," said Hubert Humphrey in 1969, eight months after he had been released from confinement. "You are trapped, vulnerable and alone, and it does not matter who happens to be President."[80]

Few Vice Presidents can survive the systematic demoralization inflicted by the office without serious injury to themselves. Bill Moyers, who was with Lyndon Johnson both as Vice President and President, later remarked that the Vice Presidency "is a man eater. It destroys individuals. This country was very lucky that Harry Truman was the vice president for only a year [actually for thirteen weeks and five days]. When he became President, he still had so much left. If we had gotten Truman three years later, he would have been much different."[81] The rating of Presidents by historians and political scientists bears out this assertion. One scholar divided all Presidents following Jefferson into three groups: those who had never served as Vice President, those who had served as Vice President for less than two years and those who had served as Vice President for more than two years. The Presidents who had served as Vice President for more than two years had the worst ratings in all four standard polls.[82]

The latter-day insistence on ideological and temperamental compatibility of Vice Presidents with Presidents sounds as if it would help Vice Presidents. In fact, it hurts them still more. So long as nineteenth-century antagonism governed the relationship, Vice Presidents were free to disagree with Presidents. They could be their own men and guard their own integrity. Jefferson opposed Adams. Calhoun resigned in protest against Jackson. Garfield and Arthur, Cleveland and Stevenson, represented hostile wings of their parties. Even in the twentieth century, Fairbanks opposed Theodore Roosevelt's Square Deal; Dawes opposed Coolidge's farm policies; Garner turned on FDR's New Deal.

The notion that the Vice President must be the echo of the President is relatively new. It took quick root under the Imperial Presidency. "Anyone who thinks that the Vice President can take a position independent of the President," Hubert Humphrey said in 1969, ". . . simply has no knowledge of politics and government. You are his choice in a political marriage, and he expects your absolute loyalty."[83] The compatibility requirement, now enshrined in the Twenty-fifth Amendment, is no builder of character. It makes Vice Presidents the lackeys and messenger boys of Presidents and ensures the corruption of their independence and self-respect.

Hyperactive men like Johnson, Humphrey and Rockefeller went into psychic decline as Vice Presidents. Even more stoic types like Mondale and Bush recognize that they exist on presidential sufferance and must prove themselves every day by sedulous loyalty, deference, self-effacement and self-abasement. Success in the office depends precisely on the extent to which Vice Presidents cease to be their own men. The Vice President, in Hubert Humphrey's stark words, is "the creature of the President. . . . The President giveth the Vice President his powers and duties, and can and often does taketh away."[84]

The Vice Presidency does a poor job of preparing politicians to become Presidents. But it has recently begun to do an excellent job of preparing politicians to become presidential candidates. This development has nothing to do with the presidential qualifications a Vice President might have and everything to do with the publicity in which the office bathes him. Whether or not a Vice President is any good, the office now makes him a front-runner in the polls. At the same time the office makes it impossible to find out whether or not he is any good.

"The Vice President," Donald Graham has written, "is the one American politician who is not held responsible for what he says."[85]

If he makes a militarist or a pacifist or a zealot or a fool of himself, it is always supposed that he is doing so at the behest of his President. No doubt he is, which is one reason why, at the very time the office enhances his political availability, it depletes and despoils his substantive value. So while the Vice Presidency is coming to be the main avenue to the Presidency, it is, alas, an avenue that typically specializes in the delivery of damaged goods.

There is no escape, it seems to me, from the conclusion that the Vice Presidency is not only a pointless but even a dangerous office. A politician is nominated for Vice President for reasons unconnected with his presidential qualities and elected to the Vice Presidency as part of a tie-in sale. Once carried to the Vice Presidency not on his own but as second rider on the presidential horse, where is he? If he is a first-rate man, his nerve and confidence will be shaken, his talents wasted and soured, even as his publicity urges him on toward the ultimate office for which, the longer he serves in the second place, the less ready he may be. If he is not a first-rate man, he should not be in a position to inherit or claim the Presidency.

XI

Theodore Roosevelt, who served in both top offices, concluded that the Vice Presidency was "an utterly anomalous office (one which I think ought to be abolished)."[86] TR was surely right. But how else to deal with the presidential succession? Here it would not seem unreasonable to return once more to the Constitutional Convention. While the Founding Fathers did not suppose that their descendants would be governed forever by what commended itself to an agricultural society of four million souls, they had insights into the axioms of self-government that later generations have not conspicuously improved.

They believed that the President and Vice President of the United States must "be elected." This was a fundamental principle of their Constitution, as it is surely a fundamental principle of a democratic polity. That fundamental principle was repealed by the Twenty-fifth Amendment. This Amendment also repudiated President Truman's principle that the President should not have the power to appoint his own successor. These departures from democratic philosophy and practice have already exacted their price. In 1974 the Twenty-fifth Amendment gave us a President appointed by a man shortly thereafter forced to resign to escape impeachment for high crimes and misdemeanors; the new President, had he died in office, would have been succeeded by a man he alone had appointed. So long as Section

2 of the Twenty-fifth Amendment survives, this result, so antipathetic to democracy, can happen again.

The fix into which the Twenty-fifth Amendment placed American democracy was emphasized by a striking contrast with events in France in the same year that Ford appointed Rockefeller as his Vice President. General de Gaulle had designed a very powerful Presidency for himself; but even that towering leader had not claimed for Presidents of France the authority the Twenty-fifth Amendment bestowed, in special cases, on Presidents of the United States: that is, the power to nominate his own successor. Instead, Article 7 of the Constitution of the Fifth Republic said that in case of a vacancy in the Presidency a new presidential election must be held within thirty-five days. In the meantime, the functions of the President (save for the powers of calling a national referendum and of dissolving the National Assembly) are to be exercised by the President of the Senate. On 2 April 1974, President Pompidou died. On 5 May the French had their election, followed by a run-off on 19 May and the inauguration of the new President on 27 May. In less than two months, in short, France had a new President, freely chosen by the people and equipped by them with a fresh mandate. Which government was the more legitimate—the elected government of France after the death of Pompidou or the appointed government of the United States after the resignation of Nixon? Which political system, in this respect at least, was the more democratic? The signal difference between the French and American systems in dealing with a vacancy in the Presidency is obvious: *the rational French have no Vice President.*

The Vice Presidency as exalted by the Twenty-fifth Amendment has carried the American republic away from democratic standards. This departure is unwarranted, unnecessary, disturbing and alien to our constitutional traditions. It is also not beyond recall. It is plain what must be done. We must repeal Sections 1 and 2 (at least) of the Twenty-fifth Amendment and adopt a new amendment abolishing the Vice Presidency, an office that has become more superfluous and more mischievous than Hamilton could have supposed when he applied those adjectives to it in the 68th *Federalist*. We should then provide for presidential succession in the spirit of the Founding Fathers through a congressional statute reestablishing the principle of special presidential elections.

This principle, announced by Madison in the Constitutional Convention, authorized by the Constitution, invoked by the Second Congress in 1792 in case of a double vacancy, reaffirmed in this context by the Forty-eighth Congress in 1886, reaffirmed again by Truman in 1945 and by Eisenhower in 1965,* would, if the Vice Presidency were abolished, work fully as well for a single vacancy. More than this: it would repair the fatal errors of the Twelfth and Twenty-fifth Amendments and make it certain that the republic would never have to suffer, except as a *locum tenens*, a Chief Executive who, in the words of John Quincy Adams, was never thought of for that office by anybody.

The notion is occasionally advanced that intermediate elections would be unconstitutional. This can be ignored. Madison himself introduced language into the Constitution specifically to make such elections possible. The Second Congress, which contained men who had served five years before in the Constitutional Convention, authorized them by statute. Anything with such patriarchal blessing may be taken as safely constitutional.

Another objection to intermediate elections springs from a reverence for routine. The quadrennial rhythm, though not regarded as untouchable by the Founding Fathers, has evidently become sacrosanct for their descendants. Thus Lewis Powell (before, it must be said, his ascension to the Court, though he was still holding forth from a respectable eminence as president-elect of the American Bar Association) rejected the idea of intermediate elections as a "drastic departure from our historic system of quadrennial presidential elections."[87] In fact, as Walter Lippmann put it in 1946, the Founding Fathers "thought the country should never for more than a few months have a President who had not been elected. They did not believe, as we now assume, that there can never be a Presidential election except once every four years."[88]

There is also the objection, formulated by (among others) that thoughtful student of the Presidency, Clinton Rossiter, that "it would be simply too much turmoil and chaos and expense to have a special nationwide election."† But one wonders how carefully Professor Ros-

---

*Eisenhower proposed that in case of a double vacancy there should be a return to the 1886 law, but the cabinet successor would be an "acting President" and "unless the next regularly scheduled presidential election should occur in less than 18 months, the Congress should provide for a special election of a President and Vice President to serve out the presidential term." He seemed to believe this would require a constitutional amendment. See Eisenhower, *Waging Peace*, 648. It is also of interest that, when the Louis Harris survey put the question in 1973 whether it would be a good idea to have a special election for President in 1974, its respondents favored such an election by 50 to 36 percent. *Washington Post*, 7 January 1974.

†Professor Rossiter's reference, however, was to the proposal of a special election to choose a new Vice President. He might have thought differently if the purpose was to choose a new President. See Senate Judiciary Committee, *Selected Materials*, 136.

siter considered the proposition. This plainly was not the French experience with regard to the Presidency in 1974, nor indeed has it been the experience in parliamentary states where elections are held at unpredictable intervals. Are we to suppose that the French, for example, are so much more cool and imperturbable, so much more Anglo-Saxon, than the Americans?

It could of course be said that special elections in a time of national disarray might only deepen popular confusions. Would it have been a good idea to hold elections after the wartime death of Franklin Roosevelt, after the murder of John Kennedy, after a successful presidential impeachment? Hubert Humphrey made the point that special elections in wartime, for example, might cause dangerous delay and irrelevant bickering at a time when the nation could afford neither.[89] No doubt such elections would test the poise and stamina of American democracy. Yet what is the gain in undue protectiveness? The same argument can be made against holding presidential elections in wartime at all. The elections of 1864 and 1944 were held in the midst of the two greatest crises of our history. They caused much irrelevant bickering. Had Lincoln and Roosevelt lost, there would have been an embarrassing interlude of lame-duckery and interregnum. But the nation survived these elections without undue trauma. The elections held in the bitter depth of the Great Depression reestablished confidence and halted social disintegration. Democracy is a system for storm as well as for calm. Our institutions are not so fragile as to compel the abandonment of democratic principles in seasons of adversity.

Though a special election in an hour of stress might conceivably demoralize the country, it might equally help to resolve its confusions and restore its unity and nerve. At the very least it would reaffirm the principle of self-government and place in the White House a man chosen by the people to be their President. An appointed President serving without the moral authority of popular election might well in the age of the Imperial Presidency cause more trouble than the alleged instabilities caused by special elections.

The best argument for the Vice Presidency is simply that our citizens are used to it, foreign countries are used to it, and its existence guarantees stability, continuity and swift and undisputed succession. Legitimacy, in this view, is in the eye of the beholder, not of the philosopher, and the unquestioning acceptance of any Vice President, even with Twenty-fifth Amendment embellishments, legitimates the result, however repugnant the democratic theorist may find the process. This argument is not without power. It might even be persuasive if our Vice Presidents did better in the Presidency. Since the Vice Presidency, on the historical record, destroys more character and ability than it builds, let us stand with Theodore Roosevelt.

XII

If the principle is accepted—the principle that, if a President vanishes, it is better for the people to elect a new President than to endure a Vice President who was never voted on for the Presidency, who became Vice President for reasons other than his presidential qualifications, and who may very well have been badly damaged by his vice presidential experience—the problem is one of working out the mechanics of the intermediate election. This is not easy but far from impossible. The great problem is that there can be no gap, no chink, in the continuity of the Presidency. "The President under our system, like the king in a monarchy," said Martin Van Buren, "never dies."* It would require up to three months to set up a special election. In the meantime the show must go on. If the Vice Presidency were abolished, who would act as President until the people had a chance to speak?

The historical preference, except for 1886–1947, has been for the President pro tem of the Senate (Committee of Detail in the Constitutional Convention, Succession Act of 1792) or the Speaker of the House (Succession Act of 1947). But given the frequency with which in recent years one party has controlled Congress and the other the executive branch, this formula risks an unvoted change in party control of the White House and in the whole direction of government. Such a change would be a graver infringement of the democratic principle than the provisional service of an appointed officer as acting President. The confusion would be even greater in the event of temporary presidential disability, in which case the Presidency might shuttle back and forth between the two parties in a period of a few months.

Fidelity to the results of the last election and to the requirements of continuity in policy creates, it seems to me, an irresistible argument for returning the line of provisional descent to the executive branch. A convenient way would be simply to make the Secretary of State Acting President for ninety days. If the Secretary of State is foreign-born or under thirty-five or has some other disqualifying eccentricity,

---

*Martin Van Buren, *Inquiry into the Origin and Course of Political Parties in the United States* (New York, 1867), 290. Because this is so, that highly dramatic occasion, the taking of the presidential oath by the successor, is supererogatory.

then the Secretary of the Treasury could be the automatic successor, and so on down the 1886 list of succession.*

Then, within ninety days, let the people choose the person to serve out the unexpired term. If the vacancy occurs within 120 days of the midterm election, then the two elections should take place at the same time. If it occurs within 120 days of the quadrennial election, then let the Acting President serve out the term. The modalities can be resolved once the principle is established.

If it be said that ninety days is not time enough to organize an election, let us recall that the French allow themselves only thirty-five days, and who will say that the French are better organizers than the Americans? This would only be an election to fill out a term and thus would not require the elaborate foreplay of the quadrennial orgy. Let the national committees, which have become increasingly representative bodies under the new party rules, canvass opinion and make the nominations, as they would do if a candidate died in the midst of a campaign. The committees might well be augmented by adding the party's members in Congress and in state governorships. Candidates can be established with astonishing speed in the electronic age. Short campaigns, federally financed, would be a blessing, infinitely appreciated by the electorate. Perhaps their brevity and their economy might have a salutary impact on the quadrennial elections, which in recent years have stretched to intolerable length and swelled to intolerable expense.

In doing this, we would not be departing from the spirit and intent of the Founding Fathers. Quite the contrary: we would be reaffirming their view—and what view could be more sensible for a self-governing democracy?—that the Chief Magistrate of the United States must, except for the briefest periods, be a person elected to that office by the people. "We have only to operate the Constitution as the men who wrote it thought it should operate," Walter Lippmann wrote in arguing for intermediate elections in 1946. "If we are the prisoners of a rigid system today, the fault lies not in the Constitution but in our own habits which have only rather recently become so hard and so fixed."[90]

This is surely what a rational society would do—abolish the Vice

---

*I have not discussed the issue of presidential inability—an issue that may have received attention out of all proportion to its importance. In any case, the Vice President is not indispensable to a solution of the inability issue. The majority of the cabinet, when making its determination of presidential inability as authorized in the Twenty-fifth Amendment, could simply designate one of their own number to serve as Acting President until the inability is removed.

Presidency and, if a President disappears in the midst of his term, provide for the succession through a special election. Alas, given the complacency of custom, the vested interest in existing procedures and the tyranny of inertia, I don't suppose we will ever do it—at least until the time, bound to come, when the Twenty-fifth Amendment blows up in our faces and causes some new and shattering crisis.

THIRTEEN

Vicissitudes of Presidential Reputations

THE AIM OF HISTORY is to reconstruct the past according to its own pattern, not according to ours. All epochs, said Ranke, are equally close to God. But historians, try as they will to escape, remain prisoners of their own epoch. "No man," wrote Emerson, "can quite emancipate himself from his own age and country, or produce a model in which the education, the religion, the politics, usages, and arts of his time shall have no share. Though he were never so original, never so wilful and fantastic, he cannot wipe out of his work every trace of the thoughts midst which it grew."[1] The historian, like everyone else, is forever trapped in the egocentric predicament, and 'presentism' is his original sin. His professional obligation is to strive to transcend the present. He can never quite succeed. Every generation of historians has its distinctive worries about the present and, consequently, its distinctive demands on the past.

The result is incessant fluctuation in historical judgment. Reputations rise and fall like stocks on Wall Street, determined by supply and demand equations of a later age. The reputation of American Presidents is particularly dependent on the climate in which historians render their verdicts. Judgment is very often a function of the political cycle—that perennial alternation of private interest and public purpose which characterizes American political history. Presidential reputations decline as the opposing mood takes over, only to climb again when the original mood regains the ascendancy.

Nor does time necessarily stabilize historical judgment. "It is impossible," wrote Pieter Geyl in *Napoleon: For and Against*, "that two historians, especially two historians living in different periods, should see any historical personality in the same light. The greater the political importance of a historical character, the more impossible this is."[2] The dimensions of Washington, Jefferson, Jackson, continue to vary with the perspective of the historian. Lincoln remains the general exception, defying even the iconoclasm of Gore Vidal, though not the rancor of black nationalists.

So the reputations of the great progressive Presidents, Theodore Roosevelt and Woodrow Wilson, went into eclipse in the decade and a half after their deaths. Henry F. Pringle's brilliantly deflationary biography of 1931 crystallized—it seemed for good—the theory of TR as the adolescent at large in delicate affairs. The First World War revisionists crystallized—it seemed for good—the theory of Wilson as the Presbyterian fanatic who misled the country into war and then botched the peace. When I was an undergraduate in the 1930s, Roosevelt and Wilson were still near the nadir of their reputations. But reassessment, stimulated by the New Deal and soon by the Second World War, was already under way. Theodore Roosevelt and Woodrow Wilson stocks have long since recovered on the historical exchange.

The private-interest mood of the 1970s and 1980s has revised presidential reputations in similar fashion. In the soft focus of Reaganism, conservative Presidents—Eisenhower, Hoover, even Calvin Coolidge[3]—acquire a new glow, while a shadow falls over liberal Presidents—Johnson, Kennedy, Franklin Roosevelt. (Truman remains a curious exception, evidently because he is popularly remembered not as the champion of the Fair Deal but as the fellow from Missouri who told the Russians where to get off.)

Revisionism is an indispensable part of the historical enterprise. "The one duty we owe to history," said Oscar Wilde, "is to rewrite it."[4] But second opinions are not necessarily wiser than first. Time in due course revises the revisionists. There follow, as a preliminary contribution to the process, discussions of current revaluations of Hoover and Eisenhower and some notes on Kennedy. As Pieter Geyl said, history is indeed an argument without end.

I.   *Hoover*

For many years Hoover's standing was as low among historians as it had been among voters during the Great Depression. He was portrayed as the embodiment of the illusions and complacencies of the New Era, a cold, self-righteous President who misconceived the problems of his age and willfully sacrificed human beings on the altar of dogma. Historians saw a sharp historical break between the rigid private-enterprise ideologue in the depression White House and the humane pragmatist who gave America a New Deal after 1932.

Hoover's tiny corps of defenders enthusiastically agreed on the sharp break between Hoover and Roosevelt but pronounced Hoover right and Roosevelt wrong. Hoover himself drew the contrast between the principled champion of private enterprise and the demagogic statist in *The Challenge to Liberty* and his *Addresses on the American Road* in the 1930s as well as in his *Memoirs* (1951–1952). This was the contrast set forth in authorized accounts of his Presidency by his friends William Starr Myers and Walter H. Newton in *The Hoover Administration: A Documented Narrative* (1936) and by his Secretaries of the Interior and Agriculture Ray Lyman Wilbur and Arthur M. Hyde in *The Hoover Policies* (1937). It was still urged by younger members of the Hoover circle forty years later, as in the book by Edgar E. Robinson and Vaughn D. Bornet, *Herbert Hoover: President of the United States,* published by the Hoover Institution in 1975. By exalting Hoover as an unregenerate conservative these devotional writings only persuaded most historians that their low opinion of him was correct.

I

In recent times, however, Hoover has made an astonishing comeback. Far from having been the enemy of the New Deal, some scholars now contend, he was its true begetter. Far from having been a dour conservative, he was the leading progressive of his day. Far from having a mind frozen in the past, he was clairvoyant in his anticipations of the later twentieth century—a man who "understood the necessity of accepting the Future" (William Appleman Williams) and is "emerging as a major twentieth-century prophet" (Joan Hoff-Wilson).[5]

The work of rehabilitation has followed three divergent lines. One approach argues a continuity between the Hoover and Roosevelt administrations—a proposition expounded originally by Walter Lippman. "If there has been anything in the nature of a sharp break with the past," Lippmann wrote in 1935,

the break occurred not in March, 1933, when Mr. Roosevelt was inaugurated, but in the autumn of 1929 when, with the collapse of the post-war prosperity, President Hoover assumed the responsibility for recovery. . . . The policy initiated by President Hoover in the autumn of 1929 was something utterly unprecedented in American history. . . . He intervened at every point in the national economy where he felt that something needed to be done. For that reason, it may be said, I believe, that his historic position as a radical innovator has been greatly underestimated and that Mr. Roosevelt's pioneering has been greatly exaggerated. . . . All the main features of the Roosevelt program were anticipated by Mr. Hoover.[6]

A generation later some historians started to embrace Lippmann's position, as in Carl Degler's influential essay of 1963, "The Ordeal of Herbert Hoover." It was, Degler said, Hoover, not Roosevelt, who deserved credit for "breaking precedent to grapple directly with the Depression." Hoover's principles, according to Degler, "were distinctly and publicly progressive."[7]

A second approach accepts the traditional thesis of a sharp break between Hoover and Roosevelt but claims Hoover as the more progressive of the two. This approach has particularly attracted the antiliberal historians of what used to be called the New Left. The Hoover revival was slow to take hold here too. In his book of 1950, *American-Russian Relations, 1781–1947*, William Appleman Williams portrayed Hoover as one more miscreant in his rogues' gallery of American leaders charged with criminal attempts to increase American foreign trade. But by 1960, in *The Tragedy of American Diplomacy*, he discovered great virtue in Hoover as the advocate of cooperation at home and isolationism abroad. By 1976 rehabilitation was turning almost into sanctification. Hoover, Williams wrote in *America Confronts a Revolutionary World*, understood

> that the possessive individualism of the capitalist marketplace would give way to some other principle of organization and action. . . . His preference was to revive the concept and practice of active citizenship which would lead people to come together in cooperative ventures to build a better America.[8]

The third approach, deriving from the consensus school of American historians that mirrored the age of Eisenhower, dismisses the agitating political and ideological disagreements of the day as of minor historical consequence. The major force shaping twentieth-century America, in this view, was the development of organizational institutions and values. From this perspective, in the words of its ablest exponent, Ellis W. Hawley, Hoover appeared "a man engrossed in the problems of ordering and managing the forces of modernization, seeking solutions in associative, corporative, and partnership mechanisms, and working assiduously to develop a planning and welfare apparatus that would remain free of the evils inherent in statist or socialist prescriptions."[9]

These three themes, despite divergences and incompatibilities, mingle in the Hoover revival. In the 1970s the rehabilitation project entered the collective phase. A congress of Hoover scholars of diverse faiths gathered at Geneseo, New York, and produced in 1974 a valuable volume of essays, edited by Martin L. Fausold and George T.

Mazuzan, *The Hoover Presidency: A Reappraisal.* The 1975 biography by Joan Hoff-Wilson, *Herbert Hoover: Forgotten Progressive,* was warmly endorsed by William Appleman Williams and provided an intelligent and informative statement of the revisionist case. David Burner's urbane *Herbert Hoover: A Public Life* (1978) and Martin L. Fausold's more summary *The Presidency of Herbert C. Hoover* (1985) are able recent contributions.

II

Hoover and Roosevelt: continuity or discontinuity? The continuity argument assumes that Hoover was the first President to take national responsibility for the economy in face of depression, that he therefore made the radical departure from the past and that all Roosevelt did was to carry Hoover's programs a little farther.

But Albert U. Romasco has effectively demolished the thesis that Hoover's depression effort represented "unprecedented innovation when compared to the tradition of prior recession Presidents, who, in effect, waited passively for recovery." After close examination of the three major twentieth-century economic disruptions before 1929—the banking panic of 1907, the recession of 1914, and the depression of 1920–1921—Romasco showed that Theodore Roosevelt, Wilson and Harding had established precedents on which Hoover drew in 1929–1932. All had issued statements of exhortation and reassurance. TR had provided direct federal aid to the banks, expanded the currency and facilitated the reduction of interest rates; Wilson had intervened to put a floor under stock prices and to relieve pressure against the banking system; Harding had met depression by programs of agricultural credit, tariff protection, and tax reduction (the last, alas, not a precedent for Hoover). "The long-standing contention that no President, prior to Hoover, accepted federal responsibility for assuring the economic well-being of the nation," Romasco concluded, "needs to be considerably modified, if not abandoned altogether."[10]

Hoover, like his three storm-tossed predecessors, made efforts to counter the economic cyclone. He was not, like Andrew Mellon, his first Secretary of the Treasury, a proponent of laissez-faire. He was prepared to enlist government up to a point. But his gestures of economic stimulus, like public works, perished before his increasing obsession with balancing the budget. Critics pointed out in vain that cutting government spending would only reduce purchasing power and deepen the depression. "The absolute necessity of a balanced budget," Hoover said on 25 March 1932, was "the most essential factor to economic recovery" (5 May), "the imperative and immediate step" (13 May), "indispensable" (21 May), "the first necessity of the Nation" (11 August), "the foundation of all public and private financial stability" (11 August).[11]

In its other aspects the Hoover recovery program had a fundamental limiting principle—the principle of voluntarism. Hoover relied on the readiness of business leaders by their own free choice to forgo individual self-interest in the struggle for survival. The hortatory approach proved a dismal failure. Voluntarism did not arrest the economic decline. It did not feed the hungry; David Burner shows how, despite Hoover's complacent reassurances—"No one is actually starving"[12]—there were numerous deaths by starvation. (Burner and other recent biographers charitably forbear to quote the memorable comment from Hoover's own *Memoirs* about the unemployed who were reduced to selling apples on street corners: "Many persons left their jobs for the more profitable one of selling apples.")[13] Voluntarism did not protect wages or raise farm prices or reduce the burden of debt or stop short selling on Wall Street. And voluntarism penalized decent businessmen—those who kept wages up instead of cutting them, who provided good working conditions instead of sweatshops, who hired adults rather than children, who traded honestly rather than fraudulently on the stock exchange.

In one area Hoover was forced to recognize the limitations of voluntarism. In September 1931 he told Eugene Meyer, then chairman of the Federal Reserve Board, that cooperative action by the bankers could end the financial crisis. Meyer, who knew bankers, was skeptical. He urged instead a revival of the War Finance Corporation, which he had run during the First World War and which had played an active role in financing industry, agriculture and exports. Hoover resisted, seeing the specter of the all-powerful state. Only when the experiment in voluntarism had manifestly failed and the bankers themselves backed Meyer did Hoover accede to the creation of the Reconstruction Finance Corporation.

Hoover began with a severely restricted conception of the RFC. He saw it as a means of making government loans to financial institutions. As unemployment spread in 1932, Hoover agreed to permit RFC to make relief loans to states and cities—a policy he had previously opposed. But when John N. Garner, the conservative Democratic Speaker of the House, pushed through Congress a bill broadly enlarging RFC's loan-making authority, Hoover vetoed it. "Never before," he said, "has so dangerous a suggestion been seriously made to our country."[14] Later he accepted a modified version of the Garner bill, extending RFC's authority into relief and self-liquidating public works. But RFC, grudgingly accepted and grudgingly employed, was a reluctant breach in the voluntarist philosophy. Hoover used the new powers with the utmost conservatism, and his RFC had little impact on the depression.[15]

The democratic alternative to voluntarism is law. Hoover did not see law as the means by which a community establishes equitable standards. He saw law as an invitation to the demon state to regiment the economy and crush individual freedom. A sharp break with the past did in fact occur in March 1933. The essence of that break lay precisely in the change from voluntarism to law as the means of ordering the economy—and in the absence of inhibition thereafter in the use of authority conferred by law.

Again the RFC case is instructive. The Hoover theory had been to save the banks by lending them money. The new administration considered this exactly the wrong medicine: what the banks needed was not more indebtedness but more capital. The emergency banking legislation of the Hundred Days, drafted by restive subordinates in Hoover's Treasury Department, gave RFC authority to buy preferred stock in banks. In the next two years this program stabilized the banking system. In the meantime, RFC acquired authority to make direct loans to business. It soon became the largest single investor in the American economy. "No one in February, 1932, at which time this Corporation was set up," Jesse Jones, the head of RFC, said in 1935, "had the faintest idea as to the extent that it would be called upon to assist business."[16] The New Deal RFC was virtually a new agency. It became in essential respects the plan Hoover had so indignantly vetoed in 1932.

Hoover saw all this coming and hated it. He clearly perceived the import of Roosevelt's summons to national planning in the 1932 campaign. He was in dead earnest when he cried at Madison Square Garden on 31 October 1932:

This campaign is more than a contest between two men. It is more than a contest between two parties. It is a contest between two philosophies of government. . . . They are proposing changes and so-called new deals which would destroy the very foundations of our American system.

Or at least of *his* American system: the system based on the principle of voluntarism, by which it was left to each individual to choose whether or not he would perform his social duty.

Hoover never doubted that the break was very sharp indeed. "When the American people realize some ten years hence," he wrote in December 1933, "that it was on November 8, 1932, that they surrendered the freedom of mind and spirit for which their ancestors had fought and agonized for over 300 years, they will, I hope, recollect that I at least tried to save them."[17] He tirelessly condemned the mild interventionism of the New Deal as, variously, socialism or fascism. While his definition of the issue—liberty versus regimentation—may have been self-serving and while his judgment of the matter need not be decisive on historians, the issue between private voluntarism and public law was not a figment of his imagination.

The vanity of historians is to suppose that they understand better than the people who were there what the shouting was about. Those poor fellows in the past may have thought they were acting for one set of reasons; but we, so much wiser, *know* they were acting on quite other reasons. This reductionism denies historical figures the validity of their own perceptions and thereby diminishes their human dignity. When participants themselves explain in urgent words why they lived, fought and bled, is it not intellectual arrogance for historians to reject their testimony? Hoover's own view on the question whether or not he was the progenitor of the New Deal is entitled to more respect than it has latterly received.

III

Hoover: conservative or progressive? It was Hoover's panic over the demon state that led New Left historians in the 1960s to present him as the champion of participatory democracy against overweening bureaucracy. "His central commitments," writes William Appleman Williams, "were to self-determination and to cooperation with other equals as members of a community." "His faith," Williams says, was "in the dream of a cooperative American community."[18] Such romantic claims turned Hoover, as Joan Hoff-Wilson wrote (sympathetically) in 1979, into "the darling of the New Left."[19]

The notion of Hoover as a forerunner of Students for a Democratic Society is truly bizarre. The cooperation he believed in was the cooperation of self-governing business trade associations. His contemporaries saw him, not as the scourge of bureaucracy, but as the supreme bureaucrat, determined to rationalize capitalism by mobilizing the resources of private organization. His "guiding vision," Ellis Hawley writes, "seemed to be a structure of semi-formal guilds or estates, each represented in a larger economic community and each having positive social obligations." Hawley dismisses the Williams theory as a function of "the leftist search for weapons that could be used against liberal history."[20]

The challenge to liberty, in Hoover's philosophy, was the regulatory state (by which he did not mean J. Edgar Hoover, whom he admired to the end of his days). His guild capitalism by creating a self-regulating system would make affirmative government unnecessary. The logic pointed to business syndicalism, the replacement of public government by corporate government. Where Lenin had said "all power to the Soviets," Hoover (almost) said "all power to the trade associations." But he did not follow his logic to its conclusion, insisting that trade associations must not after all infringe on the sacred principle of free competition. Repeatedly, writes Hawley, when his guiding vision "collided with the desire to preserve traditional liberties and incentives, Hoover and his lieutenants drew back, insisting that it was vital to the 'American system' that market forces, individual opportunity, and existing political arrangements be retained."[21]

William Appleman Williams writes with awe of Hoover's "ruthless intellectual analysis."[22] In fact, Hoover was far from a consistent or rigorous thinker. His social pontifications were an unstable and contradictory jumble of individualist and corporate ideals. He never confronted the question, for example, where his feudalism of private interest groups would leave the "American individualism" about which he had written a homiletic tract in 1922. He lived by rhetoric, not by analysis, and he rarely thought anything through. When he tried, he wobbled from one side to the other. His prose, as Burner puts it, "blurs edges and unites opposites by proclamation."[23]

Burner's material even suggests a tension between the cooperationist mystique and authoritarian drives in Hoover's own personality— his "self-serving dogmatism," "his capacity for self-delusion."[24] "Applying principles he had learned in private business," Burner writes in connection with Belgian relief during the First World War, "Hoover believed in a simple administrative structure with ultimate authority in one man, himself." Woodrow Wilson said of him, "I have the feeling that he would rather see a good cause fail than succeed if he were not the head of it." "Hoover's conduct of the Food Administration," Burner himself says, "would sometimes suggest that his idea of cooperation was to have everybody get together and do just as he said."[25] Absolutely convinced of his own superior wisdom and rectitude, Hoover abhorred disagreement and resented the need to persuade others. The record hardly confirms the Williams fantasy of Hoover as the dreamer of the cooperative commonwealth.

IV

David Burner and Martin L. Fausold do not, like William Appleman Williams, see Hoover as the apostle of the cooperative commonwealth. But they insist that he was essentially a progressive.

Burner, for example, claims Hoover as "a reader of Thorstein

Veblen"[26] and invokes Veblen eight times, once every fifty or so pages, as if to give Hoover's intellectual ramblings a measure of progressivism-by-association. Williams picks up this assertion with alacrity, speaking of "the strong toddy provided [Hoover] by reading Veblen."[27] Even Fausold guardedly cites Veblen.[28] The only trouble with this engaging theory is that no one at any point has adduced any evidence that Hoover ever read a line of Veblen.

Veblen believed in government by a soviet of engineers; and a few engineers, like Morris Llewellyn Cooke and Howard Scott, the father of Technocracy, were influenced by him. Hoover, however, was rather less an engineer than a businessman; in his own life, he himself said, there had been a "vast preponderance of the commercial over the technical."[29] As for Veblen, the biographers ignore the single reference to him in the three volumes of Hoover's *Memoirs*. Here Hoover describes Rexford G. Tugwell as one "devoted to 'planned economy'" and "the intellectual heir of Thorstein Veblen."[30] Since Hoover loathed both Tugwell and the idea of a planned economy, this hardly constitutes a hearty endorsement of Veblen. If anything Hoover, like Jimmy Carter in a later day, stands as a refutation of Veblen's illusions about engineers.

The portrait of Hoover as progressive requires systematic sanitation of the record. Burner thus disputes the view that Hoover was reluctant to sign the Norris–La Guardia Act, which protected workers by outlawing yellow-dog contracts and by restricting labor injunctions. Fausold, however, points out that the White House sent the Republican House leader a secret list of objections to the bill and that Hoover's Attorney General recommended signing only on the ground that a veto would be so overwhelmingly overridden that the Supreme Court might thereafter construe the act with undue liberality.[31] George W. Norris, the co-author of the act, later said, "We never received any assistance of any kind from the Department of Justice in the Hoover administration. There was that impenetrable wall of opposition, an opposition not voiced, not out in the open, but under cover, silent and effective."[32]

Or consider the case of Mrs. Oscar de Priest, the wife of a black congressman, who posed an intense social problem when Mrs. Hoover decided to invite all the congressional ladies to a series of White House teas. Burner depicts the invitation as a deliberate use of the executive mansion by the Hoovers for "public demonstrations of their feelings" against racial bigotry.[33] Fausold is hardly less enthusiastic. Hoover was no racist. But neither biographer mentions the acidulous description of Hooverian vacillation and anguish provided by the

White House chief usher Irwin H. Hoover in his *Forty-two Years in the White House*. Four congressional tea parties were held without an invitation to Mrs. de Priest, Ike Hoover tells us, until the social secretary insisted that something had to be done. An extra party was arranged; the other guests were warned in advance of the ordeal that awaited them; Mrs. de Priest arrived, and "in a short while Mrs. Hoover retired from the room." Mrs. de Priest, the chief usher commented, "seemed the most composed one in the group."[34]

Hoover was in his way a reformer. He wanted to reorganize the government, strengthen the civil service, improve the prisons, help the Indians and so on. But was Hoover a progressive in the historic sense of seeking national control of big business and natural resources in the public interest? Burner describes Theodore Roosevelt as Hoover's hero.[35] Yet Hoover's guild capitalism was a far cry from Theodore Roosevelt's view that big government was the democratic response to big business. There were still Progressive Republicans of the TR school about in Hoover's day. Surely the conclusive test of Hoover's alleged progressivism is what the authentic Progressive Republicans thought of him and what he thought of them.

V

The two most significant and effective Progressives in Hoover's party were George W. Norris of Nebraska and Robert M. La Follette, Jr., of Wisconsin. Their testimony is vital to the problem of the progressive Hoover. Far from seeing Hoover as friend, partner or ally, Norris and La Follette detested Hoover, and he them. Norris was the father of the Tennessee Valley Authority, of rural electrification, of the Norris–La Guardia Act, of the Twentieth Amendment, of Nebraska's unicameral legislature. No senator ever accomplished more. He was also the hero of many lost battles. No one more steadfastly kept the progressive faith. Like nearly everyone else, Norris had begun by admiring the Hoover he encountered during the First World War. But the Secretary of Commerce disillusioned him. In 1928 Norris declined to support Hoover and endorsed Al Smith. "I knew where Mr. Hoover stood," Norris wrote in his autobiography. ". . . He was most backward and reactionary."[36]

For his part Hoover considered Norris a "collectivist" and one of the "masters of demagoguery" in the Senate. In his *Memoirs* the old Quaker repeated with unseemly relish a story he claimed William E. Borah had told him a quarter century before. Borah allegedly said that Norris was "a devoted socialist" and that "left-wing women furnished funds for his elections and for the maintenance of a publicity bureau in Washington which constantly eulogized him."[37] Richard W. Lowitt in his excellent three-volume life of Norris characterizes Hoover's rendition of Borah as "bitter and false." (Lowitt is very likely right. "Hoover could have a cavalier way with detail," Burner writes. ". . . Hoover's *Memoirs* have him born on the wrong day, his mother dying in the wrong year, his leaving Iowa in the wrong year, and his leaving the United States for Australia in the wrong year—the errors are legion.")[38] In 1930 Senator Simeon Fess, an Ohio conservative, chairman of the Republican National Committee and one of Hoover's few intimates in the Senate, allowed his assistant to enter another George W. Norris, a politically unknown grocer from Broken Bow, in the Republican primary in an effort to defeat Norris. Norris never doubted that the adventure of Grocer Norris had Hoover's sympathy.

Norris was further angered by Hoover's pompous veto of the Muscle Shoals bill as "the negation of the ideals upon which our civilization has been based";[39] the Muscle Shoals bill, of course, laid the basis for the TVA. Nor could Norris abide Hoover's highfalutin reasons for denying direct federal assistance to the unemployed. Hoover finally consented to government loans for seed and animal food but drew the line at people. "Blessed be those who starve while the asses and mules are fed," said Norris.[40] In February 1931 Norris listed eleven reasons why the Republicans should not renominate Hoover. In May 1932 he announced that he would support Roosevelt if the Democrats nominated him, and that in no circumstance would he support Hoover.

La Follette, thirty-four years younger than Norris, represented the younger generation of Progressive Republicans. In 1928 he backed Norris for the Republican nomination. The convention that chose Hoover, La Follette said, "was controlled by the great bankers and industrialists of the East," and he declined to endorse the Republican ticket. Once in the White House, Patrick J. Maney writes in his thorough *"Young Bob" La Follette,* Hoover "avoided any personal contact with the Wisconsin senator." Hoover's response to unemployment outraged La Follette. "His calloused indifference got under my skin," La Follette wrote his mother.

. . . I suppose people will think I have an obsession on Hoover but it does seem as though someone should keep after him and no one else in Washington appears to feel as keenly as I do about the shameful manner in which he has neglected his responsibilities in this economic crisis.[41]

In February 1931, William Allen White found "no hope of reconciliation . . . between the Norris–Borah–La Follette group and the White

House."[42] In 1932 La Follette, like Norris, endorsed Roosevelt.

Norris and La Follette, in short, opposed Hoover well before the depression, refused to back him for President in 1928, found their worst forebodings confirmed by his Presidency, and worked for his defeat in 1932. Hoover sought his congressional allies not among the Progressive Republicans but among the party's stand-patters and right-wingers. All this suggests how mindless the contention is that Hoover himself was a progressive.

The lives of Norris and La Follette changed dramatically once Roosevelt became President. "From a political outcast," Lowitt writes of Norris, "he quickly became a welcome visitor and intimate at the White House." "From the beginning," writes Maney, "Roosevelt went out of his way to cultivate La Follette's support and friendship."[43] Together the two progressives contributed to the transformation of the American polity, not toward the business syndicalism of which Hoover dreamed, but toward a system of democratic control based on law.

Plainly, if Herbert Hoover is now to go down in the textbooks as a Progressive Republican, some other term will have to be found for those known as Progressive Republicans at the time—men like Norris and La Follette, Gifford Pinchot and Fiorello H. La Guardia, Harold Ickes and Henry Wallace, Bronson Cutting and Donald Richberg, whom Hoover despised and who despised Hoover.

VI

Hoover revisionism fails under cross-examination to sustain its theories of Hoover as the father of the New Deal or as the prophet of the New Left or as the Progressive Republican. There remains the theory of Hoover the master modernizer with an uncanny insight into the organizational energies shaping modern society and an unexcelled determination to achieve a reconciliation between freedom and order, the leader who accepted the Future and is a major twentieth-century prophet.

"No other twentieth-century American statesman," writes Joan Hoff-Wilson, "has had his range of interests and breadth of understanding of domestic and foreign economic problems, or has developed such a consistent and comprehensive scientific, organizational approach for dealing with the political economy of the United States."[44] According to James Stuart Olson, had it not been for the depression Hoover "would have been one of America's great presidents; his sophisticated understanding of corporate, industrial, and bureaucratic realities would have permitted him to coordinate the economy and at the same time restrain the government bureaucracy."[45] According to the endlessly credulous William Appleman Williams, "Hoover knew modern American industrial society better than *any* other President." But during the Great Depression, Williams explains, he was "traumatized by the failure of the people to take charge of their immediate lives and then join together in cooperative action, and by his terrifying insight into what the future would be if the people continued to duck their obligation."[46]

No one can doubt that voluntary action would be the ideal way to meet our problems. Cooperation remains effective in small settings, where people work directly with each other. But voluntarism cannot control the great impersonal modern economy, where people no longer feel the obligations created by face-to-face relationships and where the selfish benefit by the restraint of the virtuous. In the great society special-interest groups will always follow their special interests. One wonders why a President who knew industrial society so well, who had such a sophisticated understanding of corporate realities, whose approach was so comprehensively scientific, was traumatized by the failure of voluntarism. How could he ever have expected voluntarism to work? Burner writes more realistically, "Few sentimental liberals could have had a more naive expectation about human conduct."[47]

One wonders even more at Williams's belief that people, by taking charge of their immediate lives and joining together in cooperative action, can solve such aggregate and structural problems as depression, unemployment, inflation, racial injustice; and at his conviction that a resort to what Karl Popper has called "piecemeal social engineering" in order to meet such problems has been so "terrifying" in its consequence. In fact, Hoover's social philosophy was not only, as noted, shallow and feeble, a collection of sententious and incoherent generalities, but it bore the most tenuous relation to the realities of modern industrial society and to the behavior of special interests in a system of private profit. His naiveté about business behavior was the triumph of ideology over experience. Even Ellis Hawley asks himself whether the managerial Hoover may not be "another myth created in response to changing political circumstances and the emergence of new political and social needs" and especially in support of "new efforts to realize managerial ideals through non-statist institutions."[48]

No one who plows through the private-enterprise banalities of the two volumes of the *State Papers* can possibly take seriously Hoover's reincarnation as the progressive leader or as the master modernizer or as the profound social analyst. Myths serve other purposes. During private-interest swings of the political cycle, people encourage them-

selves by mythologizing private-interest Presidents of the past. As for
the New Left, opposed on principle to piecemeal reform and resent-
ful of the New Deal, it finds in Hoover one more convenient stick
with which to beat liberalism.

And a public man, if he lives long enough, will be forgiven nearly
everything. Emotions fade. Blunders recede in memory. A halo of
venerable benignity descends on the most unlikely characters. We already see the process at work for Richard Nixon. Nixon, indeed, became one of the chums of Hoover's old age. In the early 1950s he
used to supply Hoover on request with lists of supposed Communists
in government. During the debates of 1960, however, Hoover felt that
Nixon spent too much time in proclaiming agreement with Kennedy.
"Kennedy's goals were evil," the unforgiving old man opined, because
the Democratic candidate wanted "socialism disguised as a welfare
state" and therefore simply "a new, New Deal."

"You will discover," Hoover wrote Nixon the next year, "that elder
statesmen are little regarded . . . until they are over 80 years of age—
and thus harmless."[49] If Hitler and Stalin were still alive, they might
be receiving pilgrims and scholars like the old Kaiser at Doorn. Hoover lived on for more than thirty years after he left the White House.
As Emerson should have said, every bore becomes a hero at last.

II. *Eisenhower*

Eisenhower never sank so low as Hoover in the esteem of historians,
but his comeback has been still more impressive. The fashion in the
1980s is to regard Hoover rather as Hoover himself regarded Prohibition—"a great social and economic experiment, noble in motive
and far-reaching in purpose."[50] He is seen as a deep social thinker
but as a failed statesman. Eisenhower, on the other hand, has come
with time to be seen as above all a successful statesman. The year after
he left office, historians and political scientists in my father's poll of
1962 rated him twenty-second among American Presidents. In a poll
taken by Steve Neal of the *Chicago Tribune* twenty years later, Eisenhower rose to ninth place. In Professor Robert K. Murray's poll the
next year he finished eleventh. (Hoover meanwhile, despite revisionist ardor, dropped from nineteenth in 1962 to twenty-first in 1982
and 1983 polls.)

There are obvious reasons for Eisenhower's upward mobility. At
the time the 1950s seemed an era of slumber and stagnation, the
bland leading the bland. After intervening years of schism and hysteria, the Eisenhower age appears in nostalgic retrospect a blessed

decade of peace and harmony. Moreover, the successive faults of Eisenhower's successors—Kennedy's activism, Johnson's obsessions, Nixon's crookedness, Ford's mediocrity, Carter's blah, Reagan's ideology—have given his virtues new value. Historians should not overlook the capacity of Presidents to do more for the reputations of their predecessors than for their own. The final impetus was provided by the swing of the political cycle back to the private-interest mood of Eisenhower's own Presidency.

I

The opening of the papers in the Eisenhower Library in Abilene, Kansas, has speeded the revaluation by placing his character in striking new light. When he was President, most Americans cherished him as the national hero reigning benignly in the White House, a wise, warm, avuncular man who grinned a lot and kept the country calm and safe. His critics, whom he routed in two presidential elections, saw him as an old duffer who neglected his job, tripped up in his syntax, read Westerns, played golf and bridge with millionaires and let strong associates run the country in his name, a "captive hero." Both views assumed his kindness of heart and benevolence of spirit.

The Eisenhower papers powerfully suggest that the pose of guileless affability was a deliberate put-on and that behind the masquerade an astute leader moved purposefully to achieve his objectives. Far from being an openhearted lover of mankind, Eisenhower now appears a wily fellow, calculating, crafty and unerringly self-protective. Far from being a political innocent, he was a politician of the first water, brilliantly exploiting the popular illusion that he was above politics. Far from being an amiable bumbler, he feigned his incoherence to conceal his purposes. Far from being passive and uninterested, he had large and vigorous concerns about public policy.

The man who emerges, for example, from *The Eisenhower Diaries*[51] is shrewd, confident and masterful. He is hard and cold in his judgment of his associates. Some entries reveal the famous Eisenhower temper. ("One thing that might help win this war is to get someone to shoot King," he wrote in 1942 about the imperious Chief of Naval Operations.)[52] Others betray, while denying, his ambition. Occasional passages of ponderous philosophizing read as if they had been carefully indited for posterity.

We thought at the time that he lacked political experience. How wrong we were! Politics has few tougher training schools than the United States Army. Eisenhower, who began as a protégé of General MacArthur and then rose to eminence as a protégé of MacArthur's detested rival, General Marshall, was obviously endowed with consummate political talent. His later skill as President in distancing himself from his unpopular party infuriated Republican professionals but testified to his dazzling instinct for survival.

We must assume now that, however muddled he often appeared, Eisenhower knew perfectly what he was up to most of the time—not least when he encouraged his fellow citizens to think of him as (Good Old) Ike. Once, when the State Department pleaded with him to say nothing in a press conference about the then explosive question of Quemoy and Matsu, the besieged islands off the coast of China, he told James Hagerty, his press secretary, "Don't worry, Jim, if that question comes up, I'll just confuse them."[53] He confused us all. As Richard Nixon put it, Eisenhower was "a far more complex and devious man than most people realized, and in the best sense of those words."[54]

Martin Van Buren, John Randolph of Roanoke once said, "rowed to his object with muffled oars."[55] Phrased less elegantly, this is Fred I. Greenstein's thesis in his influential study of Eisenhower's administrative techniques. Greenstein ascribes six "political strategies" to Eisenhower—"hidden-hand" leadership; "instrumental"—i.e., manipulative—use of language; refusal to engage in personalities; taking action nevertheless on the basis of private personality analysis; selective delegation; and building public support.[56] While the author concedes that these strategies were hardly exclusive to Eisenhower, the loving care with which they are described gives the impression of attributing uniquely to Eisenhower practices that are the stock in trade of political leaders. Thus: "Eisenhower ran organizations by deliberately making simultaneous use of both formal and informal organizations."[57] What President does not?

I do not think that Greenstein fully considers the implications of a "hidden-hand Presidency." For in a democracy, politics must be in the end an educational process, resting above all on persuasion and consent. The Presidency, in Franklin D. Roosevelt's words, is "preeminently a place of moral leadership."[58] The hidden-hand Presidency represents an abdication of the preeminent presidential role. The concept is even a little unjust to Eisenhower, who was not entirely averse to using the Presidency as a pulpit.

On the whole, however, as his political confidant Arthur Larson later wrote, "He simply did not believe that the President should exploit his influence as a dominant national figure to promote good causes that were not within his constitutional function as Chief Executive." In consequence, Larson regretfully continued, Eisenhower denied the country the "desperately needed . . . educational guidance and moral inspiration that a President with a deep personal commitment to the promotion of human rights could supply."[59] Larson was talking about civil rights. His point applies equally to civil liberties.

Racial justice and McCarthyism were the great moral issues of the Eisenhower years. Eisenhower evaded them both. This may be in part because of his severely constricted theory of the Presidency. But it was partly too because Eisenhower did not see them as compelling issues. He did not like to use law to enforce racial integration, and, while he disliked McCarthy's manners and methods, he basically agreed with his objectives. His failure, as his biographer Stephen E. Ambrose has said, "to speak out directly on McCarthy encouraged the witch-hunters, just as his failure to speak out directly on the *Brown v. Topeka* [school integration] decision encouraged the segregationists."[60] It can be added that Eisenhower's failure to speak out directly on the Pentagon, at least before his Farewell Address, encouraged the advocates of the arms race.

Yet, whatever his defects as a public leader, we may stipulate that behind the scene Eisenhower showed more energy, interest, purpose, cunning and command than many of us understood in the 1950s; that he was the dominant figure in his administration whenever he wanted to be (and he wanted to be more often than it seemed at the time); and that the very talent for self-protection that led him to hide behind his reputation for muddle and to shove associates into the line of fire obscured his considerable capacity for decision and control.

II

To what end was this political cunning devoted beyond survival? Though his brother Milton had worked in the Roosevelt administration, Eisenhower did not like FDR or the New Deal. Truman had offered to help him get the Democratic presidential nomination, but he chose to run as a Republican. The reason, he used to explain, was his desire to redress the balance in the political system—the balance between the executive and legislative branches and the balance between the federal government and the states, both presumably upset during the age of Roosevelt.

This desire was largely frustrated. Indeed, while Eisenhower generally respected the congressional prerogative, in one area he greatly increased the imbalance between the executive and legislative branches. The doctrine of "executive privilege," by which Presidents claim the right to withhold information from Congress, received both its name and its most sweeping execution during the Eisenhower years. From June 1955 to June 1960 Eisenhower officials refused information to Congress forty-four times—more times in five years than in the first hundred years of the republic. And in the most critical area where Presidents encroach on the constitutional authority of Congress—the war-making power—Eisenhower faithfully preserved the claims of the Imperial Presidency. He never renounced the idea, advanced by Truman when North Korea invaded South Korea, that the President had inherent authority to send troops into major combat without congressional authorization.

Nor was he more successful in redressing the imbalance between Washington and the states. His Commission on Intergovernmental Relations could find only two minor federal programs, costing $80 million, to recommend for transfer to the states. When Eisenhower departed in 1961, the size of the federal government was about what it had been when he was inaugurated in 1953—and the White House staff was a good deal larger.

So was the deficit. In 1959, despite his passion for balanced budgets, Eisenhower produced the largest peacetime deficit up to that time in American history. The favorite, and most prodigal, of his domestic programs was the Interstate Highway Act of 1956. In 1966, when he compiled an inventory of the twenty-three major accomplishments of his administration, he listed the "most ambitious road program by any nation in all history."[61] No administration was more responsive to the business community, but 'business confidence' turned out, as so often, to be irrelevant to economic health. The average annual rate of economic growth slowed from 4.3 percent in the last six Truman years to 2.5 percent in the Eisenhower years.

In domestic policy, historians may well regard Eisenhower's Supreme Court appointments as his most distinguished achievement. Four of his five choices—Earl Warren, John M. Harlan, William J. Brennan and Potter Stewart—were men of preeminent judicial quality. Eisenhower himself, however, thought little of the Warren Court. He later told Ambrose that his biggest mistake was "the appointment of that dumb son of a bitch Earl Warren."[62] Heaven alone knows what he thought about Brennan. The Court appointments did not make the list of major accomplishments. He did put down "First Civil Rights Law in 80 years." But the Civil Rights Act of 1957 was in fact pushed through his administration by the Attorney General, Herbert Brownell, without much presidential understanding or encouragement. He would never have sought broad civil rights legislation like the Kennedy-Johnson act of 1964, Larson has written, because he was "skeptical both of the objective itself and of the method of achieving it—that is, by legislative compulsion."[63]

Eisenhower's other domestic achievement was simply to acquiesce in, and thereby to legitimate, the changes Franklin Roosevelt had wrought in American society. He did little to tackle emerging problems of racial justice, of urban decay, of the environment, of resources and energy at a time when these problems were still relatively manageable. Like Washington and Jackson, he left behind a testament to the people in the form of a Farewell Address. Here he famously warned against "the acquisition of unwarranted influence . . . by the military-industrial complex." The admonition was prescient, but it was a thought inserted by his ghostwriter, the political scientist Malcolm Moos. It was not a theme of his Presidency nor an item on his list of accomplishments.

Eisenhower in fact had little spontaneous interest in domestic affairs. He did what duty required. He was, said Larson, "a man for whom the primacy of the problems of peace and war was instinctive, and for whom domestic political questions were an acquired taste."[64]

III

It is on his handling of the problems of peace and war that Eisenhower's enhanced reputation rests. Robert A. Divine conveniently sums up the case for "a badly underrated President" in his *Eisenhower and the Cold War* (1981):

For eight years he kept the United States at peace, adroitly avoiding military involvement in the crises of the 1950s. Six months after taking office, he brought the fighting in Korea to an end; in Indochina, he resisted intense pressure to avoid direct American military intervention; in Suez, he courageously aligned the United States against European imperialism while maintaining a staunch posture toward the Soviet Union. He earnestly sought a reduction in Cold War tensions.

Professor Divine draws a particular contrast with his predecessor, claiming that the demands of foreign policy outran Truman's ability and that the result was "overreaction and tragedy for the nation and the world."[65]

In fact, Eisenhower thought that Truman underreacted to the Soviet menace. "In the fiscal years, 1947, 1948, 1949, and 1950," Eisenhower wrote in his diary the day after his inauguration, "the defense fabric continued to shrink at an alarming extent—and this in spite of frequent . . . warnings that people like Jim Forrestal had been expressing time and time again." Forrestal had been Eisenhower's mentor regarding the "threat by the monolithic mass of communistic imperialism." When Forrestal killed himself in 1949, Eisenhower recalled their talks in 1945 about the Russians: "He insisted they hated us, which I had good reason to believe myself. I still do."[66] In May 1953 Eisenhower complained to the legislative leaders that Truman "had let our armed forces dwindle after World War II and had thus invited the attack on Korea."[67]

Revisionists exalt Eisenhower not only over his predecessor but over his successor as well, contrasting Eisenhower's conciliatoriness with Kennedy's alleged bellicosity. N. S. Khrushchev, who was perhaps in a better position to judge, offers a different assessment. "If I had to compare the two American presidents with whom I dealt— Eisenhower and Kennedy—" Khrushchev tells us in his memoirs, "the comparison would not be in favor of Eisenhower. . . . I had no cause for regret once Kennedy became President. It quickly became clear he understood better than Eisenhower that an improvement in relations was the only rational course. . . . He impressed me as a better statesman than Eisenhower."[68]

Winston Churchill stands high on the revisionist hit list of Cold War villains. But Churchill knew Eisenhower well and when he heard that Eisenhower had defeated Adlai Stevenson in 1952 told his wartime private secretary John Colville: "For your private ear, I am greatly disturbed. I think this makes war much more probable." After Stalin's death in March 1953, the new Soviet regime signaled in various ways, as in the Austrian treaty negotiations, interest in the relaxation of tensions. Churchill, now Prime Minister again, rightly or wrongly perceived a major change in Soviet policy. "A new hope," he wrote Eisenhower, "has been created in the unhappy, bewildered world." "If we fail to strive to seize this moment's precious chances," he wrote in a Top Secret minute, "the judgement of future ages would be harsh and just."[69] Churchill was now an old man (seventy-nine), but he had been around, and his thoughts deserved at least as much respect as those of John Foster Dulles. Eisenhower, who had decided that Churchill was gaga, took the Dulles line. Churchill, Colville noted in his diary, was "very disappointed in Eisenhower whom he thinks both weak and stupid."[70]

When Eisenhower and Churchill met in Bermuda in December 1953, Churchill argued that the policy of strength toward the Soviet Union should be combined with the hand of friendship. "Ike followed," Colville recorded, "with a short, very violent statement in the coarsest terms." As regards the Prime Minister's belief that there was a new look in Soviet policy, Eisenhower said, "Russia was a woman of the streets and whether her dress was new, or just the old one patched, it was certainly the same whore underneath. America intended to drive her off her present 'beat' into the back streets." Colville wrote: "I doubt if such language has ever before been heard at an international conference. Pained looks all round."[71]

Eisenhower fully accepted the premises of the Cold War. He appointed the high priest of the Cold War as his Secretary of State. He allowed Dulles to appease Joe McCarthy, to purge the Foreign Service, to construct a network of military pacts around the globe and to preach interminably about godless communism and going to the brink and massive retaliation. Lord Salisbury, the quintessential British Tory and a leading figure in the Churchill cabinet, found Eisenhower in 1953 "violently Russophobe, greatly more so than Dulles," and believed him "personally responsible for the policy of useless pinpricks and harassing tactics the U.S. is following against Russia in Europe and the Far East."[72]

Eisenhower's superiority to the other Cold War Presidents, revisionists argue, lay not in the premises of policy but in the "prudence" with which he conducted the struggle.[73] It is true that, as a former general, Eisenhower was uniquely equipped among recent Presidents to override the national security establishment. Convinced that excessive government spending and deficits would wreck the economy, he kept the defense budget under control. He knew too much about war to send regular troops into combat lightly, especially on unpromising Third World terrain. Perhaps for this as well as for budgetary reasons—nuclear weapons cost less than large conventional forces— he contrived a military posture that made it almost impossible for the United States to fight anything short of nuclear war.

The doctrine of massive retaliation left the United States the choice, when confronted by local aggression in a distant land, of dropping the bomb or doing nothing. Eisenhower's critics feared he would drop the bomb. Most of the time his preference was for doing nothing—not always a bad attitude in foreign affairs. When the Democrats took over in 1961, they briskly increased conventional forces. Their theory was that enlarging the capability to fight limited wars would reduce the risk of nuclear war. The result was the creation of forces that enabled and emboldened us to Americanize the war in Vietnam. Had the Eisenhower all-or-nothing strategy survived, we might have escaped that unmitigated disaster. Or we might have had something far worse.

Eisenhower's budgetary concerns—"a bigger bang for a buck"— and his skepticism about the regular Army and Navy also had their disadvantages. They led him to rely exceptionally, and dangerously, on unconventional forms of coercive power: upon the covert operations of the Central Intelligence Agency, and upon nuclear weapons.

IV

Professor Divine in his apologia declines to write about CIA covert action "because the evidence on Eisenhower's role is not yet available."[74] This is surprising from such a competent historian. *Eisenhower and the Cold War* was published five years after the many revealing volumes of the Church Committee inquiry had become available. Indeed, in the same year of *Eisenhower and the Cold War* two other books—*Ike's Spies* by Stephen E. Ambrose with R. H. Immerman and *The Declassified Eisenhower* by Blanche Wiesen Cook—submit an impressive amount of evidence about Eisenhower and the CIA. Moreover, the CIA is central to any work purporting to discuss Eisenhower and the Cold War.

Instead of sending regular forces into combat abroad, Eisenhower silently turned the CIA into the secret army of the executive branch. The CIA, as originally conceived in 1947, was supposed to concentrate on the collection and analysis of intelligence. Covert action began in 1948 under the Truman administration, and there was more of it than Truman later remembered (or knew about?). But it was mostly devoted to supporting friends—socialist and Christian trade unions, Italian Christian Democrats, anti-Stalinist intellectuals—rather than to subverting foes. As Kermit Roosevelt, the CIA operative in Iran, has written about his project of overthrowing the Mossadegh government, "We had, I felt sure, no chance to win approval from the outgoing administration of Truman and Acheson. The new Republicans, however, might be quite different."[75]

Indeed they were. Where Truman had seen Mossadegh as an honest if trying nationalist, Eisenhower saw him as a tool of Moscow. Eisenhower, as Anthony Eden, the British Foreign Minister, reported to Churchill, "seemed obsessed by the fear of a Communist Iran."[76] The new President promptly gave Kim Roosevelt the green light. In August 1953 the CIA overthrew Mossadegh and restored the Shah. (One result of this disruption of indigenous political evolution in Iran was to stir resentments that after festering a quarter century overthrew the Shah in 1979. By that time Washington would have been delighted if it could have had a Mossadegh rather than a Khomeini.)

His thorough and generally approving biographer Stephen E. Ambrose has noted Eisenhower's "penchant for seeing Communists wherever a social reform movement or a struggle for national liberation was under way."[77] He saw Communists next in the reformist Arbenz government in Guatemala. The domino theory was already forming itself in Eisenhower's mind. "My God," he told his cabinet, "just think what it would mean to us if Mexico went Communist!"[78] Exhilarated by success in Iran, the CIA overthrew the Arbenz regime in 1954.

Exhilarated once more, the CIA helped install supposedly pro-western governments in Egypt (1954) and Laos (1959), tried to overthrow the Indonesian government (1958) and organized the expedition of Cuban exiles against Castro (1960). In December 1955 Eisenhower specifically ordered the CIA to "develop underground resistance and facilitate covert and guerrilla preparations . . . to the extent practicable" in the Soviet Union, China and their satellites; and to "counter any threat of a party or individuals directly or indirectly responsive to Communist control to achieve dominant power in a free-world country."[79]

The CIA evidently construed the verb "counter" in drastic fashion. There are indications that CIA operatives in 1955 blew up the plane on which Chou En-lai was scheduled to fly to the Afro-Asian conference in Bandung, Indonesia.[80] There is no question about later CIA assassination attempts in the Eisenhower years against Castro and against the Congolese leader Patrice Lumumba. There is no evidence, however, that these operations were undertaken with Eisenhower's knowledge or approval. Given the strong evidence that the CIA so often acted on its own, one may well conclude that assassination was another of its private initiatives.

By 1956 the CIA was spending $800 million a year for covert action as against $82 million in 1952.[81] That same year Eisenhower created a President's Board of Consultants on Foreign Intelligence Activities. Its members were private citizens of unimpeachable respectability. (One was Joseph P. Kennedy, who remarked about the CIA after the Bay of Pigs, "I know that outfit, and I wouldn't pay them a hundred bucks a week.")[82] The Board promptly commissioned Robert A. Lovett and David Bruce to take a look at the CIA's covert action boom.

Lovett had been Secretary of Defense and Undersecretary of State. Bruce had run the Office of Strategic Services in the European Theater of Operations and was a distinguished diplomat. Their report was stern and devastating. Those who made the 1948 decision to start a program of covert action, Lovett and Bruce said, "could not possibly have foreseen the ramifications of the operations which have resulted from it." CIA agents were making mischief around the planet, and "no one, other than those in the CIA immediately concerned with their day to day operation, has any detailed knowledge what is going on." Should not someone in authority, Lovett and Bruce asked, be continuously calculating "the long-range wisdom of activities which have entailed our virtual abandonment of the international 'golden rule,' and which, if successful to the degree claimed for them, are responsible in a great measure for stirring up the turmoil and raising the doubts about us that exist in many countries of the world today?" If we continue on this course, they concluded, "Where will we be tomorrow?"[83]

Where indeed? The Board endorsed the report and warned Eisenhower in February 1957 that CIA covert action was "autonomous and free-wheeling" and that few projects received the formal approval of the 5412 Special Group, the National Security Council's review mechanism.[84] In 1958 the Board asked Eisenhower to reconsider "programs which find us involved covertly in the internal affairs of practically every country to which we have access."[85] Eisenhower paid no attention. In 1959 his own Special Assistant for National Security, Gordon Gray, told him that the 5412 Committee had little control over covert operations.[86] The Committee began to meet more regularly, but the CIA continued to keep it in the dark—on assassination plots, for example. In its last written report to Eisenhower (January 1961) the Board declared that CIA covert action was not worth the risk, money and manpower it involved and had detracted "substantially" from the execution of the CIA's "primary intelligence-gathering mission." The Board begged still one more time for "a total reassessment of our covert action policies."[87]

Though this material was published in 1978, it was ignored both by Divine and by Ambrose. Eisenhower revisionism generally obscures Eisenhower's decisive personal role in converting the CIA from an intelligence agency into an instrument for American intervention around the world. This was a sea change from Truman's CIA. As Lovett told the Bay of Pigs board of inquiry in 1961, "I have never felt that the Congress of the United States ever intended to give the United States Intelligence Agency authority to conduct operations all over the earth."[88]

Eisenhower did not bring this change about through inattention or inadvertence. The Second World War had persuaded him of the value of covert action, and CIA excesses during his Presidency did not shake his faith. He strongly opposed Senator Mike Mansfield's resolution calling for a joint congressional committee to oversee the CIA, telling one Republican congressman that "this kind of bill would be passed over my dead body."[89] In his conference with President-

elect Kennedy the day before the inauguration, Eisenhower observed
of the CIA's anti-Castro expedition, "It was the policy of this government to help such forces to the utmost" and urgently recommended
to Kennedy that "this effort be continued and accelerated."[90]

Eisenhower's faith in covert action produced mindless international
meddling that exacerbated the Cold War, angered American allies
and in later years rebounded fiercely against American interests.
Moreover, by nourishing and cherishing the CIA more than any President before Reagan had done, Eisenhower released a dangerous vi-
rus in American society and life.

V

We are sensitive these days about the limitless horror of nuclear war.
Revisionist historians condemn Truman for his allegedly unrepentant
decision to drop the bomb in 1945. In fact, Truman behaved like a
man much shaken by the decision. He had directed that the bomb be
used "so that military objectives . . . are the target and not women
and children," and he was considerably disturbed when he learned
that most of those killed at Hiroshima were civilians.[91]

The day after Nagasaki he ordered that further atomic bombing
be stopped. He told his cabinet, as Henry Wallace recorded in his
diary, that "the thought of wiping out another 100,000 people was
too horrible. He didn't like the idea of killing, as he said, 'all those
kids.'" After the cabinet meeting he remarked to Wallace that he had
had bad headaches every day. Four months later, when the question
came up at cabinet as to how many atomic bombs there were, Truman
said that he didn't really want to know.[92]

Nor did he press the production of bombs in the next years. The
best estimates of the number of bombs stockpiled in early 1948 range
from less than six to two dozen.[93] When the Secretary of the Army
proposed using the bomb to break the Soviet blockade of Berlin, Truman told him, "You have got to understand that this isn't a military
weapon. It is used to wipe out women and children and unarmed
people, and not for military use. So we have to treat this differently
from rifles and cannon and ordinary things like that."[94] At the worst
moment of the Korean War, when the Red Chinese were storming
down the Korean peninsula, Truman remarked in casual answer to a
press conference question that the United States would employ "every
weapon" to end the war. But in fact the Joint Chiefs of Staff (though,
as always, it had contingency plans) never recommended the use of
the bomb, and Truman, as Gregg Herken writes, "consistently refused to be stampeded by the bad news from Korea into a precipitous

decision on its use in the Far East." [95] Reflecting about Korea in 1954, Truman wrote in a private memorandum that, to be effective, the bomb would have had to be used against China. Distinguishing the Korean case from ending the war against Japan, he wrote, "I could not bring myself to order the slaughter of 25,000,000 noncombatants. . . . I know I was *right.*" [96]

Revisionist historians are similarly severe in condemning Kennedy for running the risk of nuclear war to get the Soviet missiles out of Cuba in 1962. They seem strangely unconcerned, however, that Eisenhower used the threat of nuclear war far more often than any other American President has done, before or since. Nuclear blackmail was indeed the almost inevitable consequence of the military posture dictated by "massive retaliation." It is said in his defense that Eisenhower used the threat in a context of American nuclear superiority that minimized the risk. But the same condition of nuclear superiority prevailed for, and must equally absolve, Truman and Kennedy.

Eisenhower began by invoking the nuclear threat to end the fighting in Korea. He let the Chinese know, he later told Lyndon Johnson, that "he would not feel constrained about crossing the Yalu, or using nuclear weapons." [97] Probably the effectiveness of this threat has been exaggerated. The Chinese had compelling reasons of their own to get out of the war. The decisive shift in their position away from the forced repatriation of prisoners of war took place, as McGeorge Bundy has pointed out, after the death of Stalin in March 1953— and before Eisenhower sent his signals to Peking. [98] In May 1953 General J. Lawton Collins, the Army Chief of Staff, declared himself "very skeptical about the value of using atomic weapons tactically in Korea." Eisenhower replied that "it might be cheaper, dollar-wise, to use atomic weapons in Korea than to continue to use conventional weapons." If the Chinese persisted, "it would be necessary to expand the war outside of Korea and . . . to use the atomic bomb." In December, Eisenhower said that, if the Chinese attacked again, "we should certainly respond by hitting them hard and wherever it would hurt most, including Peiping itself. This . . . would mean all-out war." A joint memorandum from the State Department and the Joint Chiefs of Staff called for the use of atomic weapons against military targets in Korea, Manchuria and China. [99]

The next crisis came in 1954 in Vietnam. In March, according to Divine, Eisenhower was "briefly tempted" by the idea of American intervention, refusing, as he put it, to "exclude the possibility of a single [air] strike, if it were almost certain this would produce decisive results. . . . Of course, if we did, we'd have to deny it forever." As envisaged by General Twining of the Air Force and Admiral Radford, the strike would involve three atomic bombs.[100] Opposition by Congress and by the British killed the idea. Whether this was Eisenhower's hope when he permitted Dulles to carry the air strike proposal to London remains obscure. It was at this time that he propounded what he called "the 'falling domino' principle . . . a beginning of a disintegration that would have the most profound influences," a disintegration that, he said, could lead to the loss of Indochina, then Burma, then Thailand, Malaya, Indonesia, then Japan, Formosa and the Philippines.[101] This theory of the future entrapped Eisenhower's successors in the quicksands of Vietnam. The dominos did indeed fall in Indochina, as we all know now. But, with communist China invading communist Vietnam because communist Vietnam had invaded communist Cambodia, the dominos fell against each other, not against the United States.

Whatever Eisenhower's intentions regarding Vietnam, he definitely endorsed in May 1954 the recommendation by the Joint Chiefs to use atomic bombs in case of Chinese intervention if Congress and allies agreed. "The concept" in the event of a large-scale Vietminh attack, Dulles said in October, "envisions a fight with nuclear weapons rather than the commitment of ground forces."[102]

Eisenhower tried nuclear blackmail again during the Quemoy-Matsu crisis of 1955. In March of that year Dulles publicly threatened the use of atomic weapons. Eisenhower added the next day in his press conference, "I see no reason why they shouldn't be used just exactly as you would use a bullet or anything else."[103] In the 1958 replay of the Quemoy-Matsu drama, Dulles said that American intervention would probably not be effective if limited to conventional weapons; "the risk of a more extensive use of nuclear weapons, and even of general war, would have to be accepted."[104] "There [is] no use of having stuff," Dulles remarked over the phone to General Twining, "and never being able to use it."[105]

"The beauty of Eisenhower's policy," Divine writes with regard to Quemoy and Matsu, "is that to this day no one can be sure whether or not . . . he would have used nuclear weapons."[106] Nuclear blackmail may strike some as the beauty part, though we did not used to think so when Khrushchev tried it. In Eisenhower's case it was associated with an extraordinary effort to establish the legitimacy of nuclear war. One restraint on the use of the bomb was the opposition of American allies and of world opinion. This resistance Eisenhower was determined to overcome. As Dulles told the National Security Council on

31 March 1953, while "in the present state of world opinion we could not use an A-bomb, we should make every effort now to dissipate this feeling." The minutes of the meeting add: "The President and Secretary Dulles were in complete agreement that somehow or other the tabu which surrounds the use of atomic weapons would have to be destroyed."[107]

Eisenhower's campaign to legitimate the bomb appalled America's British ally. In their Bermuda meeting Eisenhower sought Winston Churchill's support for nuclear war if the Korean truce broke down. Churchill sent Jock Colville to Eisenhower with a message of concern. According to Colville's notes on the meeting, Eisenhower said "that whereas Winston looked on the atomic bomb as something entirely new and terrible, he looked upon it as just the latest improvement in military weapons. He implied that there was no distinction between 'conventional weapons' and atomic weapons: all weapons in due course become conventional." Colville wrote later, "I could hardly believe my ears."[108] In his diaries Eisenhower portrays the Churchill of the 1950s as on the verge of senility.[109] The old man made a good deal of sense at Bermuda.

The British were no happier the next year when Eisenhower asked their support for intervention in Vietnam. Churchill, who had received a long letter from Eisenhower lecturing him about Munich and the dangers of appeasement, was unmoved. "What we were being asked to do," he said to his Foreign Secretary, "was to assist in misleading Congress into approving a military operation, which would in itself be ineffective, and might well bring the world to the verge of a major war." He told Admiral Radford that the British, having let India go, were not about to give their lives to keep Indochina for France. "I have known many reverses myself," he said. "I have not given in. I have suffered Singapore, Hong-Kong, Tobruk; the French will have Dien Bien Phu." The Indochina War, he said, could only be won by using "that horrible thing," the atomic bomb. Eisenhower was enraged.[110]

In December 1954 Eisenhower ordered the Atomic Energy Commission to relinquish control of nuclear weapons to the Department of Defense. At the same time, he ordered Defense to deploy overseas a large share of the nuclear arsenal—36 percent of the hydrogen bombs, 42 percent of the atomic bombs—many on the periphery of the Soviet Union.[111] The movement of American policy continued to disturb our British allies.

According to the official minutes, Lord Salisbury told the cabinet in this period, "Some believed that the greatest threat to world peace came from Russians. He [Salisbury] himself believed that the greater risk was that the United States might decide to bring the East-West issue to a head while they still had overwhelming superiority in atomic weapons."[112]

Nor were the British happier when Eisenhower argued in 1955 for nuclear weapons in defense of Quemoy and Matsu. The British Chiefs of Staff, according to Harold Macmillan, saw "no purpose in it" and rejected Eisenhower's contention "that the smaller explosions produced no fall-out. . . . Eden and I proposed a firm line in opposition to the American argument."* (Why, one must ask parenthetically, do Eisenhower revisionists write about his foreign policy almost exclusively from American sources?)

Eisenhower's persevering effort was to abolish the "firebreak" between conventional and nuclear weapons. Fortunately for the world, this effort failed. By 1964 nearly everyone agreed with Lyndon Johnson when he said, "Make no mistake. There is no such thing as a conventional nuclear weapon."[113]

VI

In his first years in the White House, Eisenhower regarded nuclear attack as a usable military option. He had no compunction about threatening such attack. He hoped to destroy the taboo preventing the use of nuclear weapons. But in fact he never used them. As Ambrose points out, "Five times in one year [1954] the experts advised the President to launch an atomic strike against China. Five times he said no."[114] His campaign to legitimate the bomb was happily only a passing phase.

As the Soviet Union increased its nuclear arsenal, Eisenhower came to believe more and more strongly in the horror of nuclear war. The outlook was ever closer, he said in 1956, "to destruction of the enemy and suicide for ourselves." When both sides recognized that "destruction will be reciprocal and complete, possibly we will have sense enough to meet at the conference table with the understanding that the era of armaments has ended and the human race must conform its actions to this truth or die."[115]

For all his early talk about the "same old whore," Eisenhower now

---

*Harold Macmillan, *Tides of Fortune, 1944–1954* (London, 1969), 571. Eisenhower's pose of innocent affability took in the British as well as many Americans. "Our difficulty," writes Macmillan, who had worked closely with Eisenhower in the Second World War and knew him well, "was that Eisenhower was completely under his [Dulles's] influence; except on very rare occasions of supreme importance it was no good appealing to the President over the head of the Secretary of State." *Tides of Fortune,* 634.

sought better relations with the Soviet Union. As Sherman Adams, Eisenhower's chief of staff on domestic matters, later observed, "The hard and uncompromising line that the United States government took toward Soviet Russia and Red China between 1953 and the early months of 1959 was more a Dulles line than an Eisenhower line."[116] But Dulles retained his uses for Eisenhower, both in frightening the Russians and in enabling the President to reserve for himself the role of man of peace.

In his later mood, Eisenhower strove, less anxiously than Churchill and later Macmillan but a good deal more anxiously than Dulles, to meet the Russians at the conference table. In 1953 at the United Nations he set forth his Atoms for Peace plan, by which the nuclear powers would contribute fissionable materials to an International Atomic Energy Agency to promote peaceful uses of atomic energy. This well-intentioned but feckless proposal assumed that atoms for peace could be segregated from atoms for war—an assumption abundantly refuted in later years and the cause of dangerous nuclear proliferation in our own time. In 1955 at the Geneva summit he came up with a better idea, the creative Open Skies plan. A system of continuous reciprocal monitoring, Eisenhower argued, would reduce fears of surprise attack. The Russians turned Open Skies down as an American espionage scheme. Open Skies was a good idea; it deserves revival. In his second term, against the opposition of many in his own administration, Eisenhower fitfully pursued the project of a nuclear test ban.

He resented the mounting pressure from the Democrats and from the Pentagon to accelerate the American nuclear build-up. The Pentagon did not impress him. He knew all the tricks, having employed them himself. He used to say that he "knew too much about the military to be fooled."[117] He refused to be panicked by perennial Pentagon alarms about how we were falling behind the Russians and dismissed the 'missile gap' of the late 1950s with richly justified skepticism.

Yet he weakly allowed the build-up to proceed. In 1959 he complained that the Pentagon, after agreeing a few years earlier that hitting seventy key targets would knock out the Soviet system, now insisted on hitting thousands of targets. The military, he said, were getting "themselves into an incredible position—of having enough to destroy every conceivable target all over the world, plus a threefold reserve." The radioactivity from atomic blasts at this level, he said, would destroy the United States too. The United States already had a stockpile of "five thousand or seven thousand weapons or whatnot."

Why did the Atomic Energy Commission and the Department of Defense want more? "But then," writes Ambrose, "he reluctantly gave way to the AEC and DOD demands."[118]

In 1960, when informed at a National Security Council meeting that the United States could produce almost 400 Minuteman missiles a year, Eisenhower with "obvious disgust" (according to his science adviser George Kistiakowsky) burst out, "Why don't we go completely crazy and plan on a force of 10,000?"[119] The nuclear arsenal had now grown to a level that the Eisenhower of 1954 had considered "fantastic," "crazy" and "unconscionable."[120] There were approximately 1000 nuclear warheads when Eisenhower entered the White House, 18,000 when he left.[121]

For all his concern about nuclear war, for all his skepticism about the Pentagon, for all the unique advantage he enjoyed as General of the Armies in commanding confidence on defense issues, he never seized control of the military-industrial complex. "Being only one person," he lamely explained, he had not felt he could oppose the "combined opinion of all his associates."[122] In the measured judgment of the Regius Professor of History at Oxford, the military historian Michael Howard, "The combination of his constant professions of devotion to disarmament and peace with his reluctance to take any of the harsh decisions required to achieve those professed objectives leaves an impression, if not of hypocrisy, then certainly of an ultimate lack of will which, again, denies him a place in the first rank of world statesmen."[123]

Though Eisenhower carefully avoided war himself, he was surprisingly bellicose in his advice to his successors. He told Kennedy before the inauguration not only to go full speed ahead on the exile invasion of Cuba but, if necessary, "to intervene unilaterally" in Laos. So bent was Eisenhower on American intervention in Laos that Kennedy persuaded Macmillan to explain to him in detail the folly of such an adventure.[124] When Vietnam became the issue in the mid-1960s, Eisenhower advised Lyndon Johnson to avoid gradualism, "go all out," declare war, seek victory, not negotiations, warn China and the Soviet Union, as Eisenhower himself had done over Korea, that the United States might feel compelled to use nuclear weapons to break the deadlock, and, if the Chinese actually came in, "to use at least tactical atomic weapons." The antiwar protest, Eisenhower declared, "verges on treason." When Johnson announced in 1968 that he was stopping most of the bombing of North Vietnam, Eisenhower, Ambrose writes, "was livid with anger, his remarks [to Ambrose] about Johnson's cutting and running unprintable."[125] Eisenhower was more a hawk than a prince of peace.

"It would perhaps have been better for him, as in the last century for Wellington and Grant," Sir John Colville concludes, "if he had rested on his military laurels." [126] Walter Lippmann remarked in 1964 that Eisenhower's was "one of the most falsely inflated reputations of my experience" [127]—and he was speaking before the inflation was under way. In later years the Eisenhower boom has gathered momentum in cyclical response to a need and a time.

In due course the pendulum will doubtless swing back toward the view of Eisenhower presented in the illuminating early memoirs by men close to him—Sherman Adams's *Firsthand Report* (1961), Emmet Hughes's *The Ordeal of Power* (1963), Arthur Larson's *Eisenhower: The President Nobody Knew* (1968). In these works of direct observation, Eisenhower emerges as a man of intelligence, force and restraint who did not always understand and control what was going on, was buffeted by events and was capable of misjudgment and error. I lunched with Emmet Hughes in 1981. "Eisenhower was much more of a President than you liberals thought at the time," he said. "But Eisenhower revisionism has gone too far. Take Fred Greenstein of Princeton, for example. He is a nice fellow. But his thesis these days—Eisenhower the activist President—is a lot of bullshit." [128]

Yet we were wrong to have underestimated Eisenhower's genius for self-presentation and self-preservation—the best evidence of which lies in his capacity to take in a generation of scholars.

III. *Kennedy*

It is with some diffidence that I append these notes on the Kennedy Presidency. He was my friend; I served in his White House; and I cannot claim detachment from the events and personalities of those years. I do suppose, though, that Kennedy's reputation is subject to the usual fluctuations and that new times will bring new perspectives. Viewing the age of Kennedy through the lenses of the age of Reagan is not likely to produce the final judgment, and it may be useful to examine clichés before they harden into verdicts. The following assessment is adapted from a piece written twenty years after Kennedy's murder.

HE GLITTERED when he lived, and the whole world grieved when he died. In the years since, his memory has undergone vicissitude. Grief nourishes myth. The slain hero, robbed of fulfillment by tragic fate, is the stuff of legend. But legend has a short run in modern times. "Every hero," as Emerson said, "becomes a bore at last." So in retrospect John F. Kennedy, the slain hero, the bonny prince, the king at the Round Table, the incarnation of youth and glamour and magic, is the object of disillusion and the target of attack.

I

The whole idea of Camelot excites derision. In fact, I am sure Kennedy would have derided it himself. No one at the time ever thought of his Washington as Camelot. It was a stricken Jacqueline Kennedy who first so portrayed it to Theodore H. White a week after Dallas. The Camelot idea was the initiation of the legend. It was not JFK's sort of thing. He was no romantic, but a realist and ironist.

All right, forget Camelot. How in his own terms does John Kennedy stack up as President? His reputation, revisionist scholars assure us, rests on style, not on substance. No doubt he had wit, charm and eloquence. But his soaring rhetoric roused expectations that politics could never realize; and, in any event, he cared less about passing legislation than about projecting his "image."

In domestic policy, revisionists continue, history will remember him as a minor President of inconsequential achievement. Basically a conservative, he feared to risk popularity in the cause of reform. His liberalism was expedient and contrived, designed to seduce, not to succeed. His New Frontier was feeble and inauthentic next to the Great Society of his volcanic successor: Kennedy promised, Johnson delivered. Even his leadership in the civil rights struggle was forced upon him by events.

If revisionism finds Kennedy hopelessly cautious in domestic policy, it finds him (or the predominant school does) hopelessly bellicose in the world. He was, we are told, a rigid and embattled cold warrior, the reckless high priest of a cult of toughness. Where his predecessor, General Eisenhower, was committed to peace, Kennedy was addicted to crisis. He was a mindless activist, a war lover, who found macho relish in danger and felt driven to prove manhood by confrontation. Loving crisis, he provoked the crises he loved without regard to the perils for humanity. He brought the world needlessly to the brink of nuclear holocaust over the Soviet missiles in Cuba, entangled us in the Vietnam morass, ordered the assassination of Castro and probably Diem too, and was, in the words of the British historian Eric Hobsbawm, the "most dangerous and megalomaniac" of Presidents.[129]

Thus the predominant school. A minority school, however, sees Kennedy as incorrigibly weak and vacillating in foreign affairs. The Bay of Pigs, said the peace-loving Eisenhower, should be called a "Profile in Timidity and Indecision." As for the Cuban missile crisis,

Kennedy, in Richard Nixon's judgment, "enabled the United States to pull defeat out of the jaws of victory."[130] Instead of eliminating Castro, Kennedy guaranteed his safety against invasion and even left a Soviet brigade behind in Cuba, to be rediscovered by Jimmy Carter in 1979. "So long as we had the thumbscrew on Khrushchev," said Dean Acheson, "we should have given it another turn every day. We were too eager to make an agreement with the Russians."[131]

Then there is the question of Kennedy's private life. We live in an age obsessed with sex. It titillates us to know that Jefferson, FDR, Eisenhower, Johnson, and Martin Luther King, Jr., had (or may have had) mistresses. This obsession has bred the *National Enquirer* school of biographers. People like Garry Wills, Ralph Martin, John Davis, Horowitz and Collier collect unsubstantiated and unattributed rumors, treat them as if they were undisputed facts, and use them as the basis for a highly speculative character analysis. Every claim by anyone to have slept with John Kennedy is taken as gospel, though if half the claims were true he would have had time for little else. One scholar even tastefully suggested that I write a sequel to *A Thousand Days* and title it *A Thousand Nights*. One recalls Dickens's comment to the Americans that anyone who attains a high place, from the President down, may anticipate his downfall, "for any printed lie that any notorious villain pens, although it militate directly against the character and conduct of a life, appeals at once to your distrust, and is believed."[132]

Still, the allegations have unquestionably contributed to the demolition of the Camelot myth — not that Camelot was a place known for marital fidelity. And Kennedy revisionism has kindled in some people a growing resentment, bordering on rage. Remembering their days of naive faith and ingenuous hope, they feel that they were manipulated, seduced, betrayed and abandoned. Did he fool us? Did we fool ourselves?

II

Kennedy's campaign appeal in 1960 was to get the country moving again. He meant this in a large sense, hoping to lead an intellectual breakaway from the complacency and stagnation of the Eisenhower years. He meant it too in a more immediate economic sense; for the Eisenhower years had seen limping growth and three recessions, the last of which had bequeathed the Kennedy administration 7 percent unemployment. Kennedy responded with a set of expansionist policies: numerical targets for employment and growth; the investment tax credit and the liberalization of tax depreciation guidelines;

worker training programs; and finally the proposal of general tax reduction, enacted in 1964. During the Kennedy years, economic growth averaged 5.6 percent, unemployment was brought down below 5 percent, and inflation was held at 1.3 percent.

Not a bad record; and the last item deserves particular notice. Inflation was not the issue in the early 1960s that it became later. Nonetheless it was a problem much on Kennedy's mind. He understood the vital relationship between inflation and productivity: increased productivity was the only way to absorb higher wages without driving up prices. The problem therefore was to keep wage increases within the limits of advances in productivity. To do this, Kennedy introduced his "wage-price guideposts" in 1962. United States Steel's insolent rejection of the guideposts led to the great steel battle late that year. When U.S. Steel raised its prices after the administration had persuaded the union to accept a noninflationary wage contract, Kennedy exploded in cold anger—"My father always told me that all businessmen were sons-of-bitches, but I never believed it till now"[133]—and forced the company to retract its action.

Kennedy's wage-price guideposts constituted a form of what we today call incomes policy. A basic dilemma of modern capitalism is the conundrum, thus far unanswered, of achieving full employment without inflation. Our recent Presidents—Ford, Carter, Reagan—have been able to figure out no way to slow inflation except by inducing mass unemployment, and no way thereafter to restimulate the economy without resurrecting inflation. The Reagan administration brought down inflation at the cost of nearly 11 percent unemployment. Recovery, given the present structure of the economy, will eventually produce new inflation. So in recent times we have been on a dismal roller coaster: resorting to recession to combat inflation, and then resorting to inflation to combat recession. This is a hell of a way to run a railroad. The only way to combine high employment and stable prices is through incomes policy—through devising an institutional means of relating wages, prices, and profits to productivity. Kennedy perceived this twenty years ago. We will have to recapture that perception if we are ever to get off the roller coaster and bring stability into our economic life.

Kennedy thus sought, with skill and success, to ensure his expansionist policies against inflationary aftereffects. At the same time, he recognized that general fiscal stimulus, while it would increase aggregate output and employment, would not reach into pockets of localized and "structural" poverty. Income tax reduction, for example, was of limited help for people too poor to pay income taxes. The plight of the demoralized and inarticulate poor greatly concerned him. He had seen them in the black valleys of West Virginia when he campaigned for the Democratic nomination in 1960. He began to attack the "culture of poverty" with the Area Redevelopment Act of 1961 and the Appalachia program; and in 1963 he decided that, if these forgotten Americans were to be helped, tax reduction required a counterpart in the form of a comprehensive assault on poverty. "First we'll get your tax cut," he told the chairman of the Council of Economic Advisers before his death, "and then we'll get my expenditure programs."[134] Lyndon Johnson's war on poverty was the fulfillment of Kennedy's purpose.

In economic management, Kennedy was a most effective President. But his ambition for larger social programs—Medicare, federal aid to education and to the cities, civil rights—was frustrated by his parliamentary situation. For he had been elected President in 1960 with a slim margin of 120,000 in the popular vote. Though his Congress in 1961 was nominally Democratic, he lacked a working majority in the House of Representatives. Like every Democratic President since Roosevelt after 1938, he faced a House controlled by a conservative coalition made up of Republicans and Southern Democrats. With much of his legislative program thus blocked, he devoted himself to laying the groundwork for future action by education and persuasion.

III

The issue of equal opportunity for nonwhite Americans posed particular problems. If anyone had asked Kennedy in 1960 how he really felt about civil rights, he might have answered something like this: "Yes, of course, we must achieve racial justice in this country, and we will; but it is an explosive question, so let us go about it prudently." Like most white politicians, he underestimated the moral passion behind the movement. The protests of the Freedom Riders on the eve of his departure for his 1961 meeting with Khrushchev unduly irritated him. He stalled on fulfilling his campaign promise to issue an executive order ending discrimination in housing financed by federal loans and guarantees; this was in part because he wanted Congress to create a new department of urban affairs, to which he planned to appoint Robert C. Weaver, a black economist, as secretary. (The House Rules Committee, disliking the prospect of the first black cabinet member in history, killed the proposal anyway—which indicates why Kennedy despaired of getting comprehensive civil rights legislation.) He appointed Southern judges who turned out in some cases to be bitter-end segregationists; this was in part because he wanted the Senate Judiciary Committee, then headed by Eastland of Mississippi, to clear the appointment of Thurgood Marshall to the federal circuit court. It was a time when advance seemed possible only by small tradeoffs.

But in the country a flame had been lit. Led by Martin Luther King, Jr., civil rights workers, white and black, were bravely challenging the white supremacists. James Meredith applied to the University of Mississippi, and the courts ordered his admission. Governor Ross Barnett responded that Mississippi would "not surrender to the evil and illegal forces of tyranny."[135] Kennedy, hoping to avoid violence, tried to work things out with Barnett. Negotiation was unavailing. An angry mob tried to prevent Meredith's enrollment. Kennedy sent in the Army to win the black man his constitutional rights. It was the beginning of a mighty change, in Mississippi and in the nation. In 1984, Barnett attended a memorial service for Medgar Evers, who as director of the Mississippi National Association for the Advancement of Colored People had encouraged Meredith's application and who had been murdered the next year. In 1985, Jim Eastland himself, a few months before his death, sent a contribution of $500 to the Mississippi NAACP.

The change received new impetus in 1963 when Bull Connor, the police commissioner of Birmingham, Alabama, loosed police dogs against a nonviolent march led by Martin Luther King. "You shouldn't all be totally harsh on Bull Connor," Kennedy later told the black leaders. They were stunned until he added: "After all, he has done more for civil rights than almost anybody else."[136] The shocking photographs of Bull Connor's dogs, teeth bared, lunging viciously at the marchers, transformed the national mood. Legislation now was not only necessary: it was possible. "I shall ask the Congress," Kennedy said, ". . . to make a commitment it has not fully made in this century to the proposition that race has no place in American life or law." It was, he said, "a moral issue"—an issue "as old as the scriptures" and "as clear as the American Constitution."[137] No President had ever spoken such words.

Kennedy was now fully committed. The political risks were acute; the fight drove him down in the polls from an overwhelming 76–13 approval in January 1963 to 59–28 in November. Opponents said that the civil rights movement was a communist conspiracy, that Martin Luther King was under communist control. Both John Kennedy and his brother, Attorney General Robert Kennedy, publicly went to bail for King. Privately they acceded to J. Edgar Hoover's demand that King be wiretapped, confident that this would disprove the allegations. Kennedy took King for a walk in the Rose Garden to warn him that he was under FBI surveillance. (King, noting the fact that Kennedy had first taken him into the garden, reflected, "I guess Hoover must be bugging him too.") King did not hold the wiretaps against Kennedy, and, despite a general policy of not endorsing political candidates, planned to endorse him for reelection in 1964.[138]

The civil rights bill was moving toward enactment when Kennedy was killed; so was the tax reduction bill. Grief speeded enactment; but as Mike Mansfield, the Senate Democratic leader, later said, "The assassination made no real difference. Adoption of the tax bill and the civil rights bill might have taken a little longer, but they would have been adopted."[139] What soon made a real difference was the 1964 presidential election, which gave the Democrats an extra thirty-seven seats in the House, nearly all from the North, and thereby made Lyndon Johnson the first Democratic President since FDR to have a working progressive majority in Congress.

Johnson was a man of formidable skills in dealing with Congress, and he used these skills brilliantly in the sessions of 1965–1966. Still, what was decisive was the congressional arithmetic. In 1965 and 1966 Johnson won passage of more progressive legislation than any President since FDR; but when he lost his working majority in the 1966 election, his Great Society petered out. Had Johnson been elected in 1960 with Kennedy as his Vice President, and had Johnson offered the Eighty-seventh Congress the program actually offered by Kennedy, he would have had no more success than Kennedy—perhaps less, because he was less effective as a national persuader. If Johnson had died in 1963 and Kennedy had beaten Goldwater in 1964, then Kennedy would have had those lovely extra votes in the House; and political pundits would no doubt have contrasted his cool and efficient management of Congress with the ham-handed efforts of his predecessor. Too much gets attributed to parliamentary sorcery that is really due to the political mathematics.

One other point might be noted, in view of the White House feuds and the money scandals that have disgraced so many recent Presidencies. Kennedy's White House staff was small, generally harmonious, and honest. So was his administration. Someone asked the columnist Jack Anderson, the Mormon Savonarola, which of the many Presidencies he had covered stands out as the cleanest. Anderson replied, "The John Kennedy Administration."[140]

IV

Looking back in the fall of 1963, Kennedy was unhappy that he had been able to devote so little time to domestic policy; that would be, he said, his priority in the second term. But foreign affairs had been exigent: "each day was a new crisis."[141] Two weeks before his inauguration, Khrushchev had given a notably truculent speech in Moscow, promising communist victory in the Third World through wars of national liberation while at the same time arguing the impossibility of nuclear war between the superpowers. We can see now that Khrushchev had a double purpose: he was trying to tell the Chinese Communists, then in a fiercely militant mood, that he favored world revolution and the Americans that he favored peaceful coexistence. Inevitably, Beijing and Washington each believed the part of the message intended for the other. Kennedy's inaugural response, with its extravagant rhetoric about paying any price, bearing any burden, meeting any hardship, supporting any friend, opposing any foe, in order to assure the success of liberty resounded at the time, but in retrospect it was an overreaction. The distinctive note of the inaugural expressed a different concern. "Let us never negotiate out of fear," Kennedy said, "but let us never fear to negotiate."

Still, during his first months in office, each day did seem to bring a new crisis: Laos, where Eisenhower told him that the United States should, if necessary, fight "unilaterally"; the exile invasion of Cuba, which Eisenhower recommended should "be continued and accelerated"; the Congo; the Soviet astronaut in space; the assassination of Trujillo; vigorous Soviet support of "national-liberation wars" in Algeria, Cuba and Vietnam; the Vienna meeting with Khrushchev and the Soviet effort to drive the allies out of West Berlin; Soviet resumption of nuclear testing. It was a grim year.

Before satellite reconnaissance conclusively disproved the myth of the missile gap, Kennedy set in motion a build-up of long-range nuclear missiles. The build-up had baleful consequences. It was more than American security demanded; it ended any hope of freezing the rival missile forces; and it sent the wrong message to Moscow, compelling Khrushchev to worry about his own missile gap. But, contrary to revisionist myth, Kennedy did not relish confrontation. "Prudence" was one of his favorite words. He well understood the limits of American power. When Barry Goldwater was crying "Why not victory?," Kennedy, in a speech nine months after the inaugural, reminded his countrymen "that the United States is neither omniscient nor omnipotent, that we are only 6 percent of the world's population, that we cannot impose our will upon the other 94 percent of mankind, that we cannot right every wrong or reverse each adversity, and that therefore there cannot be an American solution to every world problem."[142]

But there could not be a Soviet solution either. Lines had to be drawn and positions held. When Khrushchev refused a global standstill agreement at Vienna and threatened to disturb the international equilibrium by negotiating a separate treaty with East Germany, Kennedy forced him to retreat. And, if national-liberation wars were to be the great new Soviet weapon, ways had to be found to check such wars. This led Kennedy for a season into the fantasy of counterinsurgency—a mode of warfare for which Americans were ill adapted, which nourished an American belief in the capacity and right to intervene in foreign lands and which was both corrupting in method and futile in effect.

Cuba became a particular target for covert action—the Bay of Pigs and thereafter infiltration, arms drops, sabotage. All this gave special power to the CIA, which carried its dark deeds further, judging by available evidence, than Kennedy knew. The project to assassinate Fidel Castro originated in the Eisenhower administration (which recruited gangsters to do the dirty work). It continued through the Kennedy administration and two years into the Johnson administration. The argument is made that, because Kennedy was President, he *must* have known what the CIA was doing. The argument applies equally to Eisenhower and to Johnson. There is no evidence that any of the three Presidents authorized or knew about (except as something over and done with) the CIA's assassination policy.

In the Kennedy years, the CIA officers directing the assassination project did not even inform John McCone, whom Kennedy had appointed to succeed Allen Dulles as CIA director. If they ever told Kennedy, they would have had to add, "By the way, don't mention this to McCone; he doesn't know about it"—an implausible bureaucratic situation. In the autumn of 1963 Kennedy altered his Cuban policy and explored through emissaries a possible normalization of relations with Castro. Ambassador William Attwood was set to make a secret visit to Cuba. But the CIA kept determinedly and secretly on the assassination track. On 22 November 1963, a CIA officer provided a Cuban defector with murder weapons for use against Castro. Kennedy was in Dallas.

Vietnam presented the most troubling case of national-liberation war. Kennedy accepted the line drawn by the previous administration and on occasion even endorsed Eisenhower's domino theory. He increased the number of American military advisers to more than sixteen thousand, of whom seventy-three were killed in combat. But he steadily opposed Pentagon recommendations for the despatch of American military units, and steadily pressed the authoritarian Ngo

Dinh Diem to broaden his base through political and economic reform. Diem disdained such advice, and his brutal repressions led his
generals to plot his overthrow. A message from Washington, later
characterized by Kennedy as a "major mistake,"[143] informed the generals that the United States would recognize a successor regime. Nine
weeks later the generals deposed and—despite American plans to fly
him out of the country—murdered Diem.

Kennedy expressed his basic view in September 1963 when he said
of the people of South Vietnam, "It is their war. They are the ones
who have to win it or lose it."[144] He had watched the French Army
flounder in Vietnam a dozen years before and was sure that large-
scale American military intervention would only rally the forces of
nationalism against the invader. Among the revelations of the Pentagon Papers was Kennedy's plan for the complete withdrawal of
American advisers from Vietnam by 1965—a plan canceled by Johnson a few months after Dallas. Kennedy confided to Mike Mansfield
that his goal was total withdrawal; "but I can't do it until 1965—after
I'm reelected."[145] Otherwise the Republicans might beat him in 1964
over the "loss" of Indochina as they had beaten the Democrats in
1952 over the "loss" of China. Yet he never disclosed his intention lest
the prospect undermine the Saigon regime. Though he privately
thought the United States "overcommitted" in Southeast Asia, he permitted the commitment to grow.[146] It was the fatal error of his Presidency.

V

The search for military remedies in the Third World was a wretched
chapter in the history of American foreign policy. Nor have we yet
shaken off the delusion. Though he had his counterinsurgency binge,
Kennedy's long-term approach to the Third World was not to repress
symptoms but to cure maladies. "Those who make peaceful revolution impossible," he told the Latin American ambassadors in 1960,
"will make violent revolution inevitable."[147] His Alliance for Progress
was designed precisely to encourage peaceful change. Even Castro
called it "a good idea . . . a politically wise concept put forth to hold
back the time of revolution."[148] After Kennedy's death, his policy of
supporting reform governments in Latin America was abandoned.
Yet his Alliance is still a good idea, and we will have to return to something like it if we are ever to have a democratic hemisphere.

Kennedy saw nationalism as the most powerful political emotion of
the time. His abiding purpose was to adjust American policy to what
he called the "revolution of national independence" he saw going on
around the world. His vision was of a "world of diversity"—a world

of nations varied in institutions and ideologies "where, within a framework of international cooperation, every country can solve its own problems according to its own traditions and ideals." He summed up his policy in a deliberate revision of Wilson's famous line about making the world safe for democracy. "If we cannot now end our differences," he said, "at least we can help make the world safe for diversity."[149]

In the nuclear age, he saw no alternative to a policy of prudence. "Mankind must put an end to war," he told the United Nations in 1961, "or war will put an end to mankind." General and complete disarmament was "a practical matter of life and death."[150] When Khrushchev sneaked nuclear missiles into Cuba in 1962, Kennedy had no doubt that they would have to be removed. Revisionist critics call it a needless crisis and condemn Kennedy for not negotiating the missiles out by trading them for the American missiles in Turkey. It is clear now that this is exactly what he did. Had the missiles stayed, the sixties would have been the most dangerous of decades. And if the Kennedys had really been consumed by a mania to eliminate Castro, the missiles would have supplied the perfect pretext. Instead, Robert Kennedy led the fight against the surprise air attack, and John Kennedy made the decision against it.

Once the missiles were out, Kennedy forgot recrimination, forbade gloating, and moved purposefully toward a reduction of international acrimony. He worried, as he told me the morning after the crisis ended, that people would draw all the wrong conclusions; that they would suppose that in dealing with the Russians you had only to be tough and they would collapse. The missile crisis, he went on, had three distinctive features: we enjoyed local superiority; Soviet national security was not directly threatened; and the Russians lacked a case they could justify before the world. Things would be different, he said, when the Russians felt they were in the right, had local superiority and believed vital interests to be involved.[151]

His great concern, now more anguished than ever, was nuclear war. "I am haunted," he told a press conference in March 1963, "by the feeling that by 1970 . . . there may be ten nuclear powers instead of four, and by 1975, fifteen or twenty."[152] He got his timing wrong, but his point haunts us still. In his speech at American University in June he called on Americans as well as Russians to rethink the Cold War. Both sides, he said, were "caught up in a vicious and dangerous cycle in which suspicion on one side breeds suspicion on the other, and new weapons beget counterweapons." Khrushchev called it "the greatest speech by any American President since Roosevelt."[153] A generation later, alas, we are caught up in the same vicious cycle again.

Kennedy's first step in breaking out of the cycle was the limited test ban treaty. To get this treaty ratified, he had to persuade, or at least silence, the congressional hawks and the military. He did this partly by concessions to the military and partly by appeals to the country. He noted ironically that both he and Khrushchev were under pressure from hard-liners who interpreted every move toward détente as appeasement. "The hard-liners in the Soviet Union and the United States feed on each other."[154] Kennedy was a peacemaker, as Khrushchev acknowledged in his memoirs: "someone we could trust. . . . He showed great flexibility and, together we avoided disaster. . . . He showed real wisdom and statesmanship."[155]

Far from being a confrontationist, Kennedy was by temperament a conciliator. His greatest disappointment, he told Bobby in the fall of 1963, was that he had not been able to make more progress toward disarmament. He had proved his manhood in the PT boat in the Solomon Islands and felt no need to prove it vicariously by sending young men to kill and to die. He had the capacity to refuse escalation—as he did in the Bay of Pigs, in Laos, in the Berlin crisis of 1961, in the Cuban missile crisis, and as he surely would have done in Vietnam. He was always hopeful that differences could be rationally worked out, whether with Khrushchev or with Ross Barnett; force was the last resort, and only to be used with restraint and circumspection. He liked to quote a maxim of the British military strategist Liddell Hart: "Never corner an opponent, and always assist him to save his face. Put yourself in his shoes—so as to see things through his eyes. Avoid self-righteousness like the devil—nothing is so self-blinding."[156]

VI

His brief days in the White House were days of steady growth—growth in confidence, in understanding and in purpose. He made mistakes but candidly acknowledged them and always learned from them. He knew the world was changing, and he had the courage and resilience to adapt to change. It is impossible to predict what Presidents who died might have done had they lived; it is hard enough, heaven knows, to predict what living Presidents will do. Still, one can reasonably suppose that Kennedy, had he lived, would have reached his New Frontier in his second term with a strengthened mandate and a more cooperative Congress. If he had followed his own plan, he would have withdrawn American troops from Vietnam in 1965, instead of Americanizing the war that year as Johnson did. And had Kennedy lived, Khrushchev might well have stayed in power longer

(Castro later told an American reporter that he thought Kennedy had refrained from tightening the thumbscrew during the missile crisis "to save Khrushchev");[157] and the two men, who had stared down the nuclear abyss together in that tense October, might have taken the world a good deal farther along the road to disarmament and peace.

He never had the chance. But he had his impact. Did he fool us? I think not. The public man was no different from the private man. He had humor, incisive intelligence, courage—not just the courage of war but the quieter courage that enabled him to endure illness and agony without complaint; "at least one-half of the days that he spent on this earth," his brother Robert once recalled, "were days of intense physical pain."[158] He had confidence in human reason and hope for human nature. His commitment was to a sane, rational and civilized world, and he believed such a world attainable.

His contagious optimism gave his country hope that, with sufficient ingenuity, steadfastness and goodwill, we could meet our responsibilities. He was sure that there was a great reservoir of idealism, especially among the young, a selfless desire to help the poor and the powerless. He proposed to tap that idealism through undertakings like the Peace Corps abroad and a domestic peace corps (later realized in VISTA) at home. His directness and openness of mind, his faith in reasoned discussion, his ironic, often self-mocking wit and his generous vision of American possibility broke the crust that had settled over the country in the 1950s. His irreverence toward conventional ideas and institutions provoked a discharge of critical energy throughout American society. He came to be loved in the black community and was the first President since FDR with anything to say to the young. In other lands he was seen as a carrier of American idealism and a friend of humanity. For a moment he made politics seem in truth (in the phrase he cherished from John Buchan's *Pilgrim's Way*) "the greatest and most honorable adventure."

And yet the reaction against him was palpable a dozen years after his death. These notes themselves are defensive in tone. Still one recalls that Henry Pringle wrote his biography, a far more scholarly and consequential book than any of the anti-Kennedy tracts, exactly a dozen years after Theodore Roosevelt's death. One recalls that the Nye Committee found the basest motives in the American decision to enter the First World War exactly a dozen years after Woodrow Wilson's death. I may perhaps be permitted to recall the foreword for the first volume of *The Age of Roosevelt,* published exactly a dozen years after FDR's death. Noting the anti-Roosevelt predispositions of the time, I wrote, "We are always in a zone of imperfect visibility so far as the history just over our shoulder is concerned. It is as if we were in the hollow of the historical wave; not until we reach the crest of the next one can we look back and estimate properly what went on before."[159] What happened to Kennedy after his death was historiographically routine.

Our politics flows in cycles. In the 1980s private interest displaced public purpose as the animating national motive. The themes of the Kennedy Presidency seem exotic in the self-congratulatory America of Ronald Reagan. We hate being nagged to think about the humiliated and the dispossessed. We hate being reminded of nobler and more demanding days. We hate the idea that we should not ask what our country can do for us but what we can do for our country. Because we cannot bear the challenge that Kennedy embodied, we escape into cynicism and sniggering gossip, using his failings in order to excuse our own failures.

But complacency in the end is as tiresome as idealism. The present mood too will pass. Kennedy's commitment to politics as the greatest and most honorable adventure touched and formed a generation of young men and women in the 1960s. They were moved by his aspirations and shaped by his ideals. Their day is still to come. When it comes, and come it will, Kennedy, seen from the crest of the next wave, will, I believe, assume his true proportions as a humane and creative political leader.

FOURTEEN

Democracy and Leadership

———◆———

L EADERSHIP is really what makes the world go round. Love no
doubt smooths the passage; but love is a private transaction between consenting adults. Leadership—the capacity to inspire and
mobilize masses of people—is a public transaction with history. I borrow the title of this essay, a little warily, from Irving Babbitt, a shrewd
scholar of eccentrically conservative tendencies who deserves to be
better remembered than he is. In his book of 1924, *Democracy and
Leadership*, Babbitt argued that leaders, good or bad, there will always
be and that democracy becomes a menace to civilization when it seeks
to evade this truth. Numerical majorities are no substitute for leadership. Salvation lies in leaders who can reestablish the inner check
on unbridled human impulse: self-reform, not social reform. I do not
know why Babbitt's traditionalism has not been rediscovered in the
age of Reagan. Perhaps it is because Babbitt detested greedy capitalists as much as he did sentimental liberals. His diagnosis of the democratic malady smells of the library lamp rather than of the smoke-
filled room; and he could have learned much about the world of
power from Machiavelli, whom he both disliked and misunderstood.
Yet Babbitt was everlastingly right in his conviction that democracy
will stand or fall on the quality of its leadership.

I

Now the very concept of leadership implies the proposition that individuals make a difference to history. This proposition has never

been universally accepted. From classical times to the present, eminent thinkers have regarded individuals as no more than pawns of larger forces, whether the gods and goddesses of Mount Olympus or latter-day divinities of Race, Class, Nation, Progress, the Dialectic, the General Will, the Spirit of the Age, History itself. Against such mighty deities the individual is deemed impotent, his sense of freedom and significance mere vanity and delusion.

So runs the thesis of historical determinism. Tolstoy's great novel *War and Peace* offers a famous statement of the case. Why, Tolstoy asked, did masses of men in the Napoleonic wars, denying their human feelings and their common sense, move back and forth across Europe, slaughtering their fellows along the way? "The war," Tolstoy answered, "was bound to happen simply because it was bound to happen." All history determined it. As for leaders, they were in Tolstoy's view the most deluded figures of all. Great men "are but the labels that serve to give a name to an end and, like labels, they have the least possible connection with the event." The greater the leader, "the more conspicuous the inevitability and the predestination of every act he commits." The leader, said Tolstoy, is "the slave of history."[1]

Determinism takes many forms. Marxism is the determinism of class, Nazism the determinism of race; Spengler and Toynbee are determinists of growth and decay. There is even a determinism of the free market. But however much determinists differ in the explanation of causes, they unite in the conclusion that the individual will is irrelevant as a factor in history. Determinism, as William James put it, "professes that those parts of the universe already laid down absolutely appoint and decree what the other parts shall be. The future has no ambiguous possibilities hidden in its womb." History is fixed from eternity, an iron block in which there can be no equivocation or shadow of turning.[2]

Determinism may or may not be true, but it unquestionably violates our deepest human instincts. It abolishes the idea of human freedom by discrediting the presumption of choice that underlies every word we speak and every decision we make. It abolishes the idea of human responsibility by depriving the individual of accountability for his acts. No one can live consistently by any deterministic creed. The communist and fascist states prove this themselves by their extreme susceptibility to the cult of the great leader. If we were to take determinism seriously, as Isaiah Berlin wrote in his brilliant essay "Historical Inevitability," then the changes "in the whole of our language, our moral terminology, our attitudes toward one another, our views of history, of society, and of everything else will be too profound to be even adumbrated"; it would be like living in a world without time or with seventeen-dimensional space.[3]

Apply determinism to specific historical episodes, and the results are self-convicting. According to the hard determinist view, no individual makes a difference. As slaves of history, we are all interchangeable parts. If Napoleon had not led those armies across Europe, slaughtering as they went, someone else would have done so. James, rebutting Herbert Spencer's onslaught on the 'great man' theory of history, asked whether Spencer really believed "the convergence of sociological pressures to have so impinged on Stratford-upon-Avon about the 26th of April, 1564, that a W. Shakespeare, with all his mental peculiarities, had to be born there." And did Spencer believe "that if the aforesaid W. Shakespeare had died of cholera infantum, another mother at Stratford-upon-Avon would needs have engendered a duplicate copy of him, to restore the sociologic equilibrium?"[4] James was kidding the determinists, but he did not greatly exaggerate their position. "In default of a Napoleon," said Engels, "another would have filled his place, that is established by the fact that whenever a man was necessary, he has always been found."[5] Shakespeare too? The principle is the same.

In December 1931 a British politician crossing Park Avenue in New York City between Seventy-sixth and Seventy-seventh streets around ten-thirty at night looked in the wrong direction and was knocked down by an automobile—a moment, he later recalled, of a man aghast, a world aglare: "I do not understand why I was not broken like an eggshell or squashed like a gooseberry."[6] Fourteen months later an American politician, sitting in an open car in Miami, Florida, was fired on by an assassin; the man beside him was killed. Those who believe with Spencer and Engels that individuals make no difference because substitutes are "sure to be found" (Engels) might well ponder whether the next two decades would really have been the same had the automobile killed Winston Churchill in 1931 and the bullet killed Franklin Roosevelt in 1933. Would Neville Chamberlain or Lord Halifax have rallied Britain in 1940? Would John N. Garner have produced the New Deal and the Four Freedoms? Suppose, in addition, that Lenin had died of typhus in Siberia in 1895 and Hitler had been killed on the western front in 1916. What would the twentieth century have looked like now?

Leadership may alter history for better or for worse. Leaders have been responsible for the most horrible crimes and the most extravagant follies that have disgraced the human race. They also have been vital in urging humanity on toward individual freedom, social justice and religious and racial tolerance. For better or for worse, they make a difference. "The notion that a people can run itself and its affairs anonymously," said James, "is now well known to be the silliest of absurdities. Mankind does nothing save through initiatives on the part of inventors, great or small, and imitation by the rest of us—these are the sole factors in human progress. Individuals of genius show the way, and set the patterns, which common people then adopt and follow."[7]

James did not suppose that genius was omnipotent. There is a necessary equation between the person and the times. Not every man fits every hour. Genius may come too early or too late. In the tenth century John Stuart Mill would have died an unknown. The nineteenth century would have sent Peter the Hermit to a lunatic asylum. Cromwell and Napoleon needed their revolutions, Grant his Civil War. Genius must be adapted to "the receptivities of the moment."[8] Nor, James should have added, is all social change the work of individuals of genius. Modes of production, of distribution, of communication, set the scene and have their independent dynamism. Still, without leadership, there would be little movement in history.

II

What does leadership in fact do? How does it work in a democracy?

The purpose of democratic statecraft is, or should be, to find the means of ordered liberty in a world condemned to everlasting change. "He that will not apply new remedies," said Bacon, "must expect new evils; for time is the greatest innovator." Time's winged chariot has been rushing on faster than ever in the centuries since Bacon. The result is a perennial gap between inherited institutions and beliefs and an environment forever in motion. The mission of democratic statecraft is to keep institutions and values sufficiently abreast of the accelerating velocity of history to give society a chance of controlling the energies let loose by science and technology. Democratic leadership is the art of fostering and managing innovation in the service of a free community.

I do not suppose that creativity in statecraft is essentially different from creativity in other fields. Let me, for purposes of illustration, offer a list of qualities required for creative statecraft—a list borrowed from a famous commentator on the French Revolution. The first requirement on the list is Observation, "the ability to observe with accuracy things as they are in themselves," to know "whether the things depicted be actually present." Next, Reflection, which teaches "the value of actions, images, thoughts, and feelings; and assists the sensibility in perceiving their connection with each other." Then

Imagination, "to modify, to create, and to associate"; then Invention; and finally Judgment, "to decide how and where, and in what degree, each of these faculties ought to be exerted."

These qualities, raised to the highest level, make for genius, "the only proof [of which] is, the act of doing well what is worthy to be done, and what was never done before. . . . Genius is the introduction of a new element into the intellectual universe." Now the introduction of a new element into the intellectual universe is a dangerous venture. "Breaking the bonds of custom" provokes resistance. The innovator therefore has the additional task of "*creating* the taste by which he is to be enjoyed. . . . To create taste is to call forth and bestow power."[9]

The reader will have guessed that I am quoting, not at all from a discourse on statecraft, but from Wordsworth's Preface to the 1815 edition of his poems, where the onetime enthusiast for the French Revolution was considering "the powers requisite for the production of poetry." His analysis suggests that creativity in politics draws on similar powers and risks similar rebuffs.

Differences remain between the creative process in science and art and the creative process in statecraft. One is the question of timing. The scientist or artist, even though his impact ultimately depends on creating the taste by which he is enjoyed, still creates by himself, in his own time, subject to his own discipline. He makes his own choices, vibrates to his own iron string, marches to his own drummer.

Science and art cannot be hurried. Statecraft is always under the clock. The statesman is the victim of emergency, the prisoner of crisis, and, even in tranquil times, the servant of deadlines. He must often seize ideas before their time and use them without knowledge of consequences. He operates in "chronic obscurity"—the phrase General Marshall applied to battlefield decisions, where one never quite knew how many troops the enemy had or where they were; one hardly knew where one's own troops were. Worse, the statesman often confronts situations in which, if he waits too long to be absolutely sure about facts, he may lose the opportunity to control developments. "When the scope for action is greatest," Henry Kissinger has observed, "knowledge on which to base such action is limited or ambiguous. When knowledge becomes available, the ability to affect events is usually at a minimum. In 1936, no one could know whether Hitler was a misunderstood nationalist or a maniac. By the time certainty was achieved, it had to be paid for with millions of lives."[10] Tocqueville said it shorter: "A democracy can obtain truth only as the result of experience; and many nations may perish while they are awaiting the consequences of their errors."[11]

The statesman must accept not only deadlines but also an exigent

environment. He is forever coming to terms with others. Even totalitarianism involves jostling forces, argument and adjustment, if only
at the top. In a democratic polity the dialectic of compromise prevails
all the way down. While artists and scientists reject compromise,
march ahead on their own and bet on the consent of the future,
statesmen require consent *now* if they are to achieve anything at all.
Stendhal expected vindication in a century; Napoleon had to vindicate himself at once, or he was nothing. The artist, the scientist, have
time and space; the statesman has little enough of either.

Statecraft, rushed on by crisis, acting on incomplete knowledge,
under constant pressure to win consent, demands and develops qualities rather different from those nourished in creative solitude. Freud
rightly placed government along with education and psychoanalysis
in his list of the three "impossible" professions, those "in which one
can be sure beforehand of achieving unsatisfying results." [12]

III

In art and science, the innovator has only to persuade one person:
himself. Changing one's own mind has its share of tensions. In matters of belief, as William James said, we are all extreme conservatives
and surrender old opinions only under pressure. But innovation in
a democracy faces a still harder task: the innovator must persuade
others to change *their* minds. The resistance already overcome within
himself returns with redoubled obstinacy in the multitude. "The key
to all ages," said Emerson, "is — Imbecility; imbecility in the vast majority of men, at all times, and, even in heroes, in all but certain eminent moments, victims of gravity, custom, and fear." [13]

Change is threatening. Innovation may seem an assault on the
foundations of the universe. "The reformer," said Machiavelli, "has
enemies in all those who profit by the older order, and only lukewarm
defenders in all those who would profit by the new order; this luke-
warmness arising partly from fear of their adversaries . . . and partly
from the incredulity of mankind who do not believe in anything new
until they have had actual experience of it." [14]

Profiting by the old order takes far more serious forms than making money out of it. Vested interest is protean. It may be personal —
investing a mind and a career in a particular system of belief. It may
be institutional — ideas embodied in institutions become especially
hard to abandon. It may be social — investment in a system of belief
that protects the power of a group or class. In whatever form, vested
interest refuses lines of thought that are unsettling to the person, the
discipline, the institution or the existing power arrangements.

Schumpeter's discussion of economic entrepreneurship illuminates difficulties of political leadership as well. Every step against routine raises doubts. The individual who ignores established channels, Schumpeter noted, lacks persuasive data to justify defiance of the rules. Where precedent had provided authoritative guidance, now "the success of everything depends upon intuition, the capacity of seeing things in a way which afterwards proves to be true, even though it cannot be established at the moment, and of grasping the essential fact, discarding the unessential, even though one can give no account of the principles by which this is done."[15] Few are prepared to abandon cherished assumptions for admitted risks.

Schumpeter also emphasized the revenge taken by the social environment against those who wish to do something new. Any group resents heresy on the part of its members. "In matters economic this resistance manifests itself first of all in the groups threatened by the innovation, then in the difficulty in finding the necessary cooperation, finally in the difficulty of winning over consumers."[16] Substitute "political" for "economic" in the first clause of this quotation, and "voters" for "consumers" in the last, and the description works as well for creative thinking in social policy.

Consider, for example, the life history of Say's Law of Markets—the proposition that supply creates its own demand and that there can therefore be no general overproduction of goods or general underutilization of resources. Malthus thought it possible, despite Say, that effective demand could be deficient. But he failed to establish his case, and professional economists thereafter banished the question from the literature. The issue lived on, Keynes tells us, "furtively, below the surface, in the underworlds of Karl Marx, Silvio Gesell or Major Douglas."[17]

Yet deficiency in demand was analytically conceivable; and with the Great Depression few could deny the reality. Still the profession remained united in its condemnation of heresy. "Professional economists, after Malthus," as Keynes noted, "were apparently unmoved by the lack of correspondence between the results of their theory and the facts of observation;—a discrepancy which the ordinary man has not failed to observe, with the result of his growing unwillingness to accord to economists that measure of respect which he gives to other groups of scientists whose theoretical results are confirmed by observation."[18] So the ordinary citizen began to call for state intervention in the economy, while economists, committed to convenient verities, kept explaining the futility of government action till people stopped listening to them.

The challenge to Say's Law is only one notable instance in the intellectual history of economics where, in J. K. Galbraith's words, "economics has excluded socially inconvenient analyses, at least until some combination of pressure—the need for practical action, the social intuition of the nonprofessional, competent heresy within the profession—has upset the accepted view." And it is a "perilous matter," as Galbraith pointed out, to try and overturn cherished assumptions from within the discipline. "The jury, or most of it, is a party at interest. The fate of all who attacked Say before Keynes is a warning." The alternative—to force the issue on the discipline from without—has its perils too.[19]

The Faustian societies of the west live in perpetual anticipation of change. Still, while democratic nations affirm the inevitability of change, democracy also inculcates habits of mind that strengthen resistance to new ideas. This was not the view of democracy's early critics, who brooded over the alleged instability of the masses and feared that popular rule would succumb to vagrant gusts of untutored opinion. But sympathetic observers like Tocqueville worried about the longer term. "What struck me in the United States," he wrote, "was the difficulty of shaking the majority in an opinion once conceived." The threat to democracy, he thought, was not radicalism but stagnation.[20]

Bryce shared this concern. Public opinion, he wrote, made American leaders "less eager and strenuous in striking out ideas and plans of their own, less bold in propounding those plans, more sensitive to the reproach, even more feared in America than in England, of being a crochet-monger or a doctrinaire." Bryce hoped for "a succession of men like the prophets of Israel to rouse the people out of their self-complacency."[21] The hope was thin. Twenty years later, even after half a dozen years of spectacular muckraking ferment, Herbert Croly called on the social critic to "stab away at the gelatinous mass of popular indifference, sentimentality, and complacency, even though he seems quite unable to penetrate to the quick and draw blood."[22]

Given the power of gravity, custom and fear, the dead weight of inertia, of orthodoxy and of complacency, the tasks of persuading majorities to accept innovations remain forever formidable. What counts in the end is the subversion of old ideas by the changing environment. It is this that gives the democratic leader the opportunity to create the taste by which he is to be enjoyed.

IV

The vast pervasive resistance of the psyche and of society leads some to foresake incremental change in favor of the millennial hope, "a new heaven and a new earth," the Kingdom of God or the kingdom of the proletariat. The argument between step-by-step and all-at-once has raged for centuries. Karl Popper formulated it for the postwar generation in his distinction between "piecemeal engineering," practical expedients in the service of a broad social tendency, and "utopian engineering," the total transformation of society according to an ideological master plan.[23]

The millennial hope is the begetter of revolution. The use of violence to destroy an old order and install a new one may at times be the last resort for societies entrapped in hopeless logjams. But, save in extremis, violence is not a sensible way to transform society. The membranes of civilization are fragile. Ripped asunder, they are difficult to restore. "In a rebellion, as in a novel," said Tocqueville, "the most difficult part to invent is the end."[24] In the meantime, the sleep of reason produces monsters. Those who profess to execute the mandates of God or of History are menaces to humanity. The Almighty has His own purposes.

Still, the millennial dream has its role in the dialectic of democratic statecraft. For the revolutionary witness exposes the hypocrisies of the standing order and sharpens objections to it, while the revolutionary challenge undermines the obstacles of imbecility and vested interest. The threat of violence may smooth the way for persuasion. Even the most intractable conservative, his back against the wall, will accept reform as an alternative to revolution. "Since the times of Rameses," commented Henry Adams, "revolutions have raised more doubts than they solved, but they have sometimes the merit of changing one's point of view."[25]

Reform avoids the arrogance of revolution. "The piecemeal engineer," observed Popper, "knows, like Socrates, how little he knows."[26] The consent of the majority is essential if both the fabric of society and the freedom of the individual are to survive. To devise remedies that will both work and elicit consent is the task of democratic leadership. That task requires attention to concrete human needs rather than the abstractions of God or History. "What is a short time in the history of a people," Winston Churchill said,

is a long time in the life of a human being. To a serene Providence a couple of generations of trouble and distress may seem an insignificant thing—provided that during that time the community is moving in a direction of a good final result. Earthly Governments however are unable to approach questions from the same standpoint. Which brings me to the conclusion that the duty of governments is to be first of all practical. I am for makeshifts and expediency. I would like to make the people who live on this world at the same time as I do better fed and happier generally. If incidentally I benefit posterity—so much the better—but I would not sacrifice my own generation to a principle—however high or a truth however great.[27]

V

The concept of leadership has always given the American democracy a little trouble, though more in theory than in practice. Democratic doctrine, arising in protest against the divine right of kings, placed its emphasis on the omnicompetence of the people (or a majority thereof) and identified no special role for leaders. John Locke, contemplating the circumstances in which people might overthrow their government, saw revolution as the result not of purposeful individual initiative but of spontaneous popular combustion. "The people," he wrote, ". . . will be ready upon any occasion to ease themselves of a burden that sits heavy upon them. They will wish and seek for the opportunity, which in the change, weakness, and accidents of humane affairs, seldom delays long to offer itself."[28] Classical democratic theory followed Locke in minimizing the need for leadership.

Democratic philosophers resisted a theory of leadership on doctrinal grounds; for the proposition that some lead and others follow offends democratic conceptions of equality and majoritarianism. They resisted a theory of leadership on moral grounds; for making too much of leaders clashes with the democratic apprehension that power is poison. They resisted a theory of leadership on emotional grounds; for the populist strain in democracy nourishes an envy of superior persons. And they resisted it on political grounds; for attempts to rehabilitate the doctrine of leadership are often disguised attacks on democracy itself. Ideologists of leadership claim the supposed ignorance and fickleness of the people as a chief reason for submitting to leaders. Historically leadership theory is a weapon brandished by reactionaries and by revolutionaries against bourgeois democracy. Caesarism appears its logical outcome.

This long-standing democratic mistrust of theories of leadership survives in the recent vogue of the word 'elitism' as a term of abuse— another pernicious conceit for Irving Babbitt's collection. Of all the cants canted in this canting world, the cant about elitism is the most futile. Government throughout human history has always been government by minorities—that is, by elites. This statement is as true for democratic and communist states today as it was for medieval monarchies and primitive tribes. Masses of people are structurally incapable of direct self-government. They must delegate their power to agents. Who says organization says oligarchy. Historians hardly needed Pareto, Mosca and Michels to demonstrate this point. The serious question is not the existence of the ruling elites but their character.

Jefferson, whose democratic credentials need no defense, concisely defined the problem in an exchange with John Adams in 1813. "I agree with you," Jefferson wrote, "that there is a natural artistocracy among men. The grounds of this are virtue and talents. . . . There is also an artificial aristocracy founded on wealth and birth, without either virtue or talents; for with these it would belong to the first class. The natural aristocracy I consider as the most precious gift of nature for the instruction, the trusts, and government of society." That form of government is best, Jefferson continued, that prevents the ascendancy of artificial aristocrats and provides for the ascendancy of natural aristocrats, the elite of virtue and talent.[29]

The great foreign observers agreed that leadership was the key to democratic success. "That is the problem," Tocqueville told John Stuart Mill. "I am fully convinced that upon its solution depends the fate of the modern nations."[30] "Perhaps no form of government," said Bryce, "needs great leaders so much as democracy."[31]

The Founding Fathers recognized the historic significance of their experiment in self-government. They believed, as Hamilton wrote in the 1st *Federalist,* that history had reserved for Americans the opportunity to decide whether men could found government on reflection and choice or whether they were forever condemned to be ruled by accident and force. The democratic myth might assume the omnicompetence of majorities. But government by reflection and choice called in practice for a new style of leadership and a new quality of followership. It required leaders to be responsive both to constitutional standards and to popular needs. It required followers to be informed and critical participants in the labor of governing themselves.

In the 70th *Federalist* Hamilton cited as "not without its advocates" the theory that "a vigorous Executive is inconsistent with the genius of republican government." On the contrary, Hamilton insisted, executive energy was a leading character in the definition of good government—essential to the defense of the nation against foreign attacks, to the administration of law, to the protection of property, to the security of liberty against the assaults of ambition, of faction and of anarchy. But how to reconcile executive energy with republican liberty? The Constitution solved the problem, Hamilton said, by making the executive dependent through elections and accountable through Congress and public opinion. The yearning for Washington as the first President expressed the practical desire for leadership, and the experience of self-government thereafter proved its functional indispensability, if only to overcome the deadlock inherent in the separation of powers.

Leadership is indispensable even in a regime of consent. Emerson's observations on Napoleon apply as well to Jackson or Lincoln or Franklin Roosevelt. Most persons in power, said Emerson, are much to be pitied, for they know not what they should do. The weavers strike for bread, and the rulers meet them with bayonets. "But Napoleon understood his business. Here was a man who, in each moment and emergency, knew what to do next. . . . He knew what to do, and he flew to his mark."[32]

Understanding your business and acting within the disciplines of consent: the first imperatives for democratic leadership. A further requisite is vision: the ends for which power is sought. When leaders have as their goal the enhancement of personal authority or the protection of greed and privilege or the advancement of empire, they will do little for democracy. When their goal is the abolition of slavery, the enlargement of opportunity for the poor and powerless, the emancipation of women and of racial minorities, the defense of the rights of expression and opposition, they will very likely increase the sum of human liberty and happiness. "I do not believe," said Woodrow Wilson, "that any man can lead who does not act, whether it be consciously or unconsciously, under the impulse of a profound sympathy with those whom he leads—a sympathy which is insight—an insight which is of the heart rather than of the intellect."[33]

The American democracy has readily resorted in practice to the very leadership it had disclaimed in theory. An adequate democratic theory must recognize that democracy is not self-executing; that leadership is not the enemy of self-government but the means of making it work; that followers have their own stern obligation, which is to keep leaders within rigorous constitutional bounds; and that Caesarism is more often produced by the failure of feeble governments than by the success of energetic ones.

VI

Winning consent requires leaders who possess not only a personal vision but the capacity to communicate that vision to their age. In a democracy leadership is peculiarly dependent on language, and the language used by leaders determines the tone of politics. For language is the means by which politics deals with reality. Words may express reality or simplify it or sentimentalize it or distort it or reject it.

I have often quoted *The Federalist* in these pages. Those great papers were the product of the Enlightenment in America. The cooling breeze of reason tempered the hot work of composition and argument. The result was the language of the Founding Fathers—lucid, measured and felicitous prose, marked by Augustan virtues of harmony, balance and elegance. People not only wrote this noble language. They also read it. The essays in defense of the Constitution signed Publius appeared week after week in the New York press during the winter of 1787–1788; and the demand was so great that the first thirty-six *Federalist* papers were published in book form while the rest were still coming out in the press. One can only marvel at the sophistication of an audience that consumed and relished pieces so closely reasoned, so thoughtful and analytical. To compare *The Federalist Papers* with their equivalents in the press of our own day—say, with the contributions to the op-ed pages of our great newspapers— is to annotate the decay of political discourse in America.

"The use of words," Madison wrote in the 37th *Federalist*, "is to express ideas. Perspicuity, therefore, requires not only that the ideas should be distinctly formed, but that they should be expressed by words distinctly and exclusively appropriate to them." Madison was under no illusion that this condition of linguistic beatitude was easy to attain. "No language is so copious," he continued, "as to supply words and phrases for every complex idea, or so correct as not to include many equivocally denoting different ideas. . . . When the Almighty himself condescends to address mankind in their own language, his meaning, luminous as it must be, is rendered dim and doubtful by the cloudy medium through which it is communicated."

The Founding Fathers nevertheless thought the quest for precision was worth the effort. They had the advantage of living in an age when politicians could say in public more or less what they believed in private. If their view of human nature was realistic rather than sentimental, they were not obliged to pretend otherwise. *The Federalist* is a work notably free of false notes. It must not be supposed, however, that even this great generation was immune to temptation. When the Founding Fathers spoke of and to the largest interest in a primarily agricultural nation, they changed their tone and relaxed their standards. Those who lived on the soil, Jefferson could incontinently write, were "the chosen people of God . . . whose breasts He has made His peculiar deposit for substantial and genuine virtue."[34] Such lapses from realism defined one of the problems of American political discourse. For as society grew more diversified, new interests claimed their place in the sun; and each in time had to be flattered as the Jeffersonians had flattered the agriculturists. The desire for success at the polls thus cheapened the language of politics.

And politics was only an aspect of a deeper problem. Society was taking forms that warred against clarity of thought and integrity of language. "The corruption of man," said Emerson, "is followed by the corruption of language. When simplicity of character and the sovereignty of ideas is broken up by the prevalence of secondary desires, the desire of riches, of pleasure, of power, and of praise . . . words are perverted to stand for things which are not."[35]

"The prevalence of secondary desires," the desire of riches, pleasure, power and praise—this growing social complexity began to divert the function of words from expression to manipulation and gratification. No one observed the impact of a mobile and egalitarian society on language more acutely than Tocqueville. Democracy, he argued, encouraged a dangerous addiction to the inflated style. "An abstract term," Tocqueville wrote, "is like a box with a false bottom; you may put in what ideas you please, and take them out again without being observed."[36] Words divorced from objects became instruments less of communication than of deception. Unscrupulous orators stood abstractions on their head and transmuted them into their opposites, aiming to please one faction by the sound and the contending faction by the meaning. They did not always succeed. "The word *liberty* in the mouth of Webster," Emerson wrote with contempt after the Compromise of 1850, "sounds like the word *love* in the mouth of a courtezan."[37]

Other developments hastened the dissociation of words from reality. The rise of mass communications, the growth of large organizations and novel technologies, the invention of advertising and public relations, the professionalization of education—all contributed to linguistic pollution, upsetting the ecological balance between words and their environment. In our own time the purity of language is under unrelenting attack from every side—from professors as well as from politicians, from newspapermen as well as from advertising men, from men of the cloth as well as from men of the sword, and not least from those indulgent compilers of modern dictionaries who propound the suicidal thesis that all usages are equal and all correct.

A living language can never be stabilized, but a serious language can never cut words altogether adrift from meanings. The alchemy that changes words into their opposites has never had more adept practitioners than in the twentieth century. We used to object when Communists described dictatorships as "people's democracies" or

North Korean aggression as the act of a "peace-loving" nation. But we are no slouches ourselves in the art of verbal metamorphosis. There was often not much that was "free" about many of the states that made up what we used to call, sometimes with capital letters, the Free World. In the days of the Indochina War, Americans found themselves systematically staving off reality by allowing a horrid military-bureaucratic patois to protect our sensibilities from the ghastly things we were doing in Vietnam. The official patter about "attrition," "pacification," "defoliation," "body counts," "progressive squeeze-and-talk," sterilized the frightful reality of napalm and My Lai. Today we call Somocista thugs "freedom fighters" and the neutron bomb a "radiation enhancement device" and inaccurate bombing a "surgical strike."

Social fluidity, moral pretension, political and literary demagoguery, corporate and academic bureaucratization and a false conception of democracy are leading us into semantic chaos. But language colors the depths of our consciousness. It is the medium that dominates perceptions, organizes categories of thought, shapes ideas and incorporates a philosophy of existence. Every political movement generates its own language-field; every language-field legitimates one set of motives, values and ideals and banishes the rest. The language-field of the Founding Fathers directed the American consciousness toward one constellation of standards and purposes. The language-field of Vietnam tried to direct the national consciousness toward very different goals. Politics is in part a symbolic and therefore a linguistic phenomenon.

It is idle to expect perfection in political discourse. The winning of consent often requires the bringing together of disparate groups with diverging interests. This inescapably involves a certain oracularity of expression. De Gaulle in Algeria, when the *pieds-noirs* chanted that Algeria belonged to France, replied solemnly, "Je vous comprends, mes camarades"—hardly a forthright expression of his determination to set Algeria free. Besides, oracularity may often be justified since no one can be all that sure about the future. The Founding Fathers understood this, which is why the Constitution is in many respects a document of calculated omission and masterful ambiguity whose "real" meaning—that is, what it would mean in practice—only practice could disclose. Yet in a polity governed by reflection and choice, the responsibility of leaders is to define real choices and explain soberly why one course is to be preferred to another—and, doing so, to make language a means not of deception but of communication, not an enemy but a friend of the reality principle.

Vietnam and then Watergate left a good many Americans with a hatred of double-talk and a hunger for bluntness and candor. Consider the posthumous revival of Harry Truman, disdained when he was President but celebrated in retrospect as the paladin of plain speaking. In this season of semantic malnutrition, who is not grateful for a public voice that blurts out what the speaker honestly believes? This is true, to a point at least, even when the belief itself is repugnant. George Wallace won support even among blacks (though ambition finally made Wallace bland, and blandness did him in). "There is a certain satisfaction in coming down to the lowest ground of politics," said Emerson, "for we get rid of cant and hypocrisy."[38]

The best leadership in a democracy will get rid of cant and hypocrisy on the higher ground too. Down with banality and cliché, with slogan and stereotype! Let Republicans stop talking about "values" and Democrats stop talking about "compassion" and the American government stop calling mercenaries "freedom fighters" and stop counting right-wing despots as leaders of the "Free World." "Wise men pierce this rotten diction"—Emerson once more—"and fasten words again to visible things; so that picturesque language is at once a commanding certificate that he who employs it is a man in alliance with truth and God."[39]

VII

Some political philosophers assert that democracy—government by reflection and choice—presupposes the perfectibility of man. They are demonstrably wrong both in history and in logic. The Constitution, as Bryce said, was the work of men who believed in original sin. "If men were angels," said the 50th *Federalist*, "no government would be necessary." Belief in human perfectibility, by exaggerating human wisdom and minimizing the corruptions of power, can lead as logically to absolutism as to democracy. And, paradoxically, belief in ineradicable human depravity also justifies absolutism as the necessary means of restraining human wickedness.

Democracy, properly construed, assumes neither total perfectibility nor total depravity. It sees humans simultaneously as tainted by original sin and as capable of redemption. The democratic way by no means guarantees the triumph of virtue. *Vox populi* is definitely not *vox dei*. Still, the exercise of dissent and opposition tempers the delusions of power. Nor does democracy eliminate irrationality from politics. It may foster cant and demagoguery. But it also fosters the conviction that, as the greatest of democratic leaders put it, you cannot fool all of the people all of the time. Democracy rests solidly on the mixed view of human nature, on people as they are in all their frailty and their glory. "Man's capacity for justice," said Reinhold Niebuhr, "makes democracy possible, but man's inclination to injustice makes democracy necessary."[40]

Leaders have done vast harm to the world. They have also conferred vast benefit. But even 'good' leaders, 'democratic' leaders, must be regarded with mistrust. Leaders are not demigods. They put on their trousers one leg after another like ordinary mortals. No leader is infallible. Every leader needs to be reminded of this at regular intervals. Unquestioning submission corrupts leaders and demeans followers. Hero worship fortunately generates its own antidote, every hero becoming a bore at last. Irreverence irritates leaders but is their salvation.

Though leadership is a common agency of human servitude, it is at the same time the supreme proof of human freedom. Great leaders embolden the rest of us to rise to our highest potentialities, to be active, insistent and resolute in affirming our own sense of things. "In picking out from history our heroes," said William James, ". . . each one of us may best fortify and inspire what creative energy may lie in his own soul."[41] A great man is a voyage of discovery, an exhibition of new possibilities. "We feed on genius," said Emerson. ". . . Great men exist that there may be greater men."[42]

Leaders affirm free choice against the supposed inevitabilities of history. The first hero was Prometheus, who defied the gods, brought fire to mortals and asserted free will against divine determinism. Zeus punished Prometheus, chaining him to a rock where an eagle plucked away at his liver. Ever since, humankind, like Prometheus, has warred against historical inevitability. The fight against gravity, custom and fear is often thankless; and history in revenge often chains the hero to the rock and spurs on the relentless eagle. Yet, in the model of Prometheus, leaders prove the reality of choice by continuing to struggle against the gods. They justify their role insofar as they emancipate and empower their followers. The great leader, as Emerson said, abolishes himself.

Humanity has never needed great leadership more urgently than it does in the nuclear age. For the infinitely powerful engines humans have recently invented are moving beyond their strength and wisdom to control. And leadership has never more urgently needed the collaboration and criticism of an ardent and informed people. We can avert the impending catastrophe only when leaders listen to followers as carefully as followers listen to leaders—which is why democratic leadership holds out the best hope.

Instead of restraining power through the cultivation of wisdom, wrote Irving Babbitt in 1924, man "is reaching out almost automatically for more and more power. If he succeeds in releasing the stores of energy that are locked up in the atom—and this seems to be the most recent ambition of our physicists—the final exploit may be to blow himself off the planet."[43] This ambition of the physicists now achieved, human destiny remains only precariously within the hands of humanity.

NOTES

INDEX

Notes

———◆———

Foreword

1. Emerson, "Circles."
2. Henry Adams, "The Rule of Phase Applied to History" (1909), in *The Tendency of History* (New York, 1919), 167.
3. Henry Adams, *The Education of Henry Adams* (Boston, 1918), ch. iii, xxxiv.
4. William James, "Is Life Worth Living?" in *The Will to Believe and Other Essays in Popular Philosophy* (New York, 1897), 54.
5. Ibid., 53.
6. William James, *Pragmatism* (1907), Lecture Two.
7. W. C. Ford, ed., *A Cycle of Adams Letters, 1861–1865* (Boston, 1920), I, 135.

1. The Theory of America: Experiment or Destiny?

This essay is adapted from "America: Experiment or Destiny?" in the American Historical Review, *June 1977.*

1. Vine Deloria, Jr., "The North Americans," reprinted from *Crisis* in the *Congressional Record*, 94th Cong., 2d Sess. (1976), E2494–95 (daily ed.).
2. Harriet Beecher Stowe, *Oldtown Folks* (Boston, 1869), 368.
3. "Sinners in the Hands of an Angry God."
4. "New England's True Interest," in *The Puritans*, ed. Perry Miller and Thomas H. Johnson (1938; New York, Torchbook reprint, 1963), I, 244.
5. Miller and Johnson, *Puritans*, II, 82–83.
6. Leopold von Ranke, "On Progress in History," in von Ranke, *The Theory and Practice of History*, ed. G. G. Iggers and Konrad von Moltke (Indianapolis, 1973), 53.
7. Jaroslav Pelikan, "The Lessons of History," in *The Nature of a Humane Society*, ed. H. O. Hess (Philadelphia, 1977), 35.
8. Number 34.
9. Dana's article, "The Winter of Criticism," appeared in the *Monthly Anthology*

and Boston Review, October 1805, in *The Federalist Literary Mind,* ed. Lewis P. Simpson (Baton Rouge, 1962), 209, 230.

10. Lucien Price, ed., *Dialogues of Alfred North Whitehead* (Boston, 1954), 161, 203.

11. In W. O. Clough, ed., *Intellectual Origins of American National Thought* (1955; New York, Corinth reprint, 1961), 71.

12. "The Age of Tacitus," in the *Monthly Anthology,* July 1807, in Simpson, ed., *Federalist Literary Mind,* 50.

13. Polybius was "diligently read in America especially during the Revolutionary period." Meyer Reinhold, ed., *The Classick Pages: Classical Reading of Eighteenth-Century Americans* (University Park, Pa., 1975), 121. Also see Richard M. Gummere, *The American Colonial Mind and the Classical Tradition* (Cambridge, Mass., 1963), *passim.*

14. J. G. A. Pocock, *The Machiavellian Moment: Florentine Political Thought and the Atlantic Republican Tradition* (Princeton, 1975). The same point is made with less elaboration by Gordon S. Wood, *The Creation of the American Republic, 1776–1787* (Chapel Hill, 1969), and by Gerald Stourzh, *Alexander Hamilton and the Idea of Republican Government* (Stanford, 1970). Reinhold writes that Polybius was known in America partly through direct study of Book VI of his *History* and "partly as mediated through Machiavelli's *Discourses* and Montesquieu's *Laws*" (*Classick Pages,* 121). But for a necessary corrective, see John P. Diggins, *The Lost Soul of American Politics: Virtue, Self-Interest, and the Foundations of Liberalism* (New York, 1984).

15. Henry Maine, *Popular Government* (1885; Indianapolis, 1976), 201.

16. See Joseph Ellis, "Habits of Mind and an American Enlightenment," *American Quarterly,* Summer 1976, esp. 161.

17. Stourzh, *Alexander Hamilton,* 71, 98.

18. Adams to Rush, 27 September 1808 in *The Selected Writings of John and John Quincy Adams,* ed. Adrienne Koch and William Peden (New York, 1946), 149–150.

19. Thomas Jefferson, "Notes on Virginia," in *Writings,* ed. Merrill D. Peterson (Library of America, 1984), 289.

20. Kentucky Resolutions of 1798, IX.

21. Wirt to Benjamin Edwards, 22 December 1809, in *Memoirs of the Life of William Wirt,* ed. J. P. Kennedy (New York, 1849), I, 246–247.

22. *Second Treatise on Civil Government,* ch. ii, par. 49.

23. Antonelli Gerbi, *The Dispute of the New World: The History of a Polemic, 1750–1900* (Pittsburgh, 1973), 160–175.

24. Henry Steele Commager, *Jefferson, Nationalism, and the Enlightenment* (New York, 1975), 43.

25. Jefferson to Chastellux, 7 June 1785, in Jefferson, *Writings,* 800.

26. Henry Steele Commager and Elmo Giodanetti, *Was America a Mistake? The Eighteenth-Century Controversy* (New York, 1967), 126, 129, 138, 16.

27. Gerbi, *Dispute,* 240–242.

28. The 11th *Federalist.* In a footnote Hamilton cited de Pauw's *Recherches Philosophiques sur les Américains.*

29. John Adams, *Defence,* Preface.

30. The 6th *Federalist.*

31. James Bryce, *The American Commonwealth* (New York, 1888), I, 299.

32. Woodrow Wilson, *Constitutional Government in the United States* (New York, 1908), 44–45.

33. Henry Adams, "The Session 1869–1870," in *The Great Secession Winter of 1860–61 and Other Essays*, ed. G. E. Hochfield (New York, 1963), 193.

34. Diggins, *Lost Soul of American Politics*, 58.

35. J. D. Richardson, comp., *Messages and Papers of the Presidents* (Washington, 1909), I, 579; II, 262; III, 295–296, 303.

36. Ibid., III, 483–484; IV, 532–533, 632; V, 9.

37. Abraham Lincoln, *Collected Works*, ed. R. P. Basler (New Brunswick, N.J., 1953), I, 113–115; VII, 17.

38. John Dillenberger, ed., *John Calvin: Selections from His Writings* (New York, 1971), 350, 564.

39. Jonathan Edwards, *A History of the Work of Redemption*, Section III, i.

40. Sacvan Bercovitch, *The Puritan Origins of the American Self* (New Haven, 1975), 41–42, 54–55.

41. Miller and Johnson, *Puritans*, 1, 145, 152, 199.

42. *The Scarlet Letter*, ch. xxiii.

43. Jonathan Edwards, *Thoughts Concerning the Present Revival of Religion in New England*, Part 2, section ii.

44. This discussion draws heavily on the brilliant analysis in Bercovitch, *Puritan Origins*, 89–90, 100–104.

45. Charles Sumner, *Prophetic Voices Concerning America* (Boston, 1874), 54–55. The second Adams quotation is from Wood, *Creation of the American Republic*, 571.

46. E. L. Tuveson, *Redeemer Nation: The Idea of America's Millennial Role* (Chicago, 1968).

47. A. K. Weinberg, *Manifest Destiny* (1935; Quadrangle reprint, 1963), 40.

48. Bercovitch, *Puritan Origins*, 87–88.

49. Gilbert Chinard, *Thomas Jefferson: The Apostle of Americanism* (1929; Ann Arbor reprint, 1957), 428.

50. Commager, *Enlightenment*, 188.

51. *White-Jacket*, ch. 36.

52. H. Richard Niebuhr, *The Kingdom of God in America* (1935; Torchbook reprint, 1959), 157.

53. Josiah Strong, *The New Era* (New York, 1893), 71, 354.

54. From the *Chicago Standard*, 6 August 1898, in J. W. Pratt, *Expansionists of 1898* (1935; Quadrangle reprint, 1964), 293.

55. In Norman A. Graebner, ed., *Ideas and Diplomacy* (New York, 1964), 372–373.

56. Phrases from speeches in Omaha, Sioux Falls, San Francisco, San Diego, Cheyenne, in Wilson, *Messages and Papers*, ed. Albert Shaw (New York, 1924), 2: 815, 822, 969, 1025, 1086.

57. Lyndon B. Johnson, *Public Papers* (Washington, 1963), I (1965), 180.

58. Thanksgiving Day Proclamation, 1982. This is an old and often repeated Reagan sentiment; see, for example, the *New York Times*, 1 April 1976.

59. *White-Jacket*, ch. 36.

60. Quoted in R. W. B. Lewis, *The American Adam* (Chicago, 1955), 159.

61. Lincoln, Second Inaugural Address; Lincoln to Weed, 15 March 1865, in *Works*, VIII, 333.

62. *Democratic Vistas*, in *Complete Poetry and Collected Prose* (Library of America), 930.

63. "The Fortune of the Republic."

64. Henry Adams, *History of the United States During the Administrations of Thomas Jefferson and James Madison* (New York, 1889–1891), IV, 289.

65. Henry Adams, *Democracy* (1880), ch. 4.

66. "The Rule of Phase Applied to History," in Henry Adams, *The Tendency of History* (New York, 1919), 172.

67. Henry to Brooks Adams, 23 November 1900 and 7 May 1901 in *Henry Adams and His Friends: A Collection of His Unpublished Letters*, ed. H. D. Cater (Boston, 1947), 502, 508.

68. Henry Adams to H. O. Taylor, 22 November 1909; to C. M. Gaskell, 1 June 1914; and to Ferris Greenslet, after 22 December 1915 in *The Letters of Henry Adams, 1892–1918*, ed. W. C. Ford (Boston, 1938), 526, 625, 635; and *The Education of Henry Adams* (Boston, 1918), ch. xxxiv.

69. F. O. Matthiessen, *The James Family* (New York, 1961), 624–627, 631.

70. Reinhold Niebuhr, *Faith and History* (New York, 1949), 31.

71. Reinhold Niebuhr, *The Irony of American History* (New York, 1952), 4, 42, 69–70, 85, 173.

72. Franklin D. Roosevelt, *Public Papers . . . 1928–1932* (New York, 1938), 646.

73. John F. Kennedy, *Public Papers . . . 1961* (Washington, 1962), 19.

74. Speech at Springfield, Ill., 26 June 1857, in *Works*, II, 406.

75. Gunnar Myrdal, *An American Dilemma* (New York, 1944), 4.

76. Charles Dickens, *Martin Chuzzlewit*, ch. 34.

77. F. Scott Fitzgerald, *The Great Gatsby*, ch. 9.

2. The Cycles of American Politics

This essay includes short passages from "The Shape of National Politics to Come," privately printed (New York, 1959); "Is Liberalism Dead?" New York Times Magazine, 30 March 1980; "The New Conservatism: Will It Last?" Family Weekly, 10 January 1982; "One Last Chance for the Democrats," Playboy, November 1982.

1. Emerson, "The Conservative."

2. Henry Adams, *History of the United States of America During the Administrations of Thomas Jefferson and James Madison* (New York, 1889–1891), VI, 123.

3. Arthur M. Schlesinger, *Paths to the Present* (New York, 1949), 93.

4. Ibid., 96.

5. Ibid., 98.

6. Ibid., 97.

7. Emerson, "The Conservative."

8. A. O. Hirschman, *Shifting Involvements: Private Interest and Public Action* (Princeton, 1982), 3, 8.

9. Herbert McClosky and John Zaller, *The American Ethos: Public Attitudes Toward Capitalism and Democracy* (Cambridge, Mass., 1984), esp. 162, 291–292.

10. On this point I am persuaded by John P. Diggins's stimulating book *The Lost Soul of American Politics: Virtue, Self-Interest, and the Foundations of Liberalism* (New York, 1984).

11. Walter B. Cannon, *The Way of an Investigator* (New York, 1945), 115.

12. Adam Smith, *The Wealth of Nations* (Modern Library ed.), 324–325.

13. Hirschman, *Shifting Involvements*, 11.

14. Emerson, "Fate."

15. *The Education of Henry Adams* (Boston, 1918), ch. xxi.

16. Alexis de Tocqueville, *Democracy in America*, II, First Book, ch. xiii.

17. J. S. Mill, *A System of Logic*, Book VI, ch. x, § 3.

18. Ortega y Gasset, "The Concept of the Generation," *The Modern Theme* (New York, 1961), 14–15.

19. Ibid., 15; Karl Mannheim, "The Problem of Generations," in *Essays on the Sociology of Knowledge* (London, 1952), 290.

20. For a discussion of Ortega's periodicity, see Julian Marias, *Generations: A Historical Method* (University, Ala., 1967), ch. 3; cf. also Mannheim, *Essays,* 277; and A. B. Spitzer, "The Historical Problem of Generations," *American Historical Review,* December 1973.

21. R. G. Collingwood, *Essays in the Philosophy of History* (Austin, 1965), 75, 89.

22. Arthur M. Schlesinger, Jr., *The Crisis of the Old Order* (Boston, 1957), 366.

23. H. L. Mencken, "In Praise of Gamaliel," *Baltimore Sun,* 18 October 1920.

24. Samuel Hopkins Adams, *Incredible Era: The Life and Times of Warren Gamaliel Harding* (Boston, 1939), 117.

25. Walter Lippmann, "Today and Tomorrow," *New York Herald Tribune,* 5 January 1954.

26. Samuel Lubell, *The Future of American Politics* (New York, 1952), 200, 203.

27. Kevin Phillips, "Hubris on the Right," *New York Times Magazine,* 12 May 1985.

28. See D. M. Gordon, Richard Edwards and Michael Reich, *Segmented Work, Divided Workers: The Historical Transformation of Labor in the United States* (Cambridge, England, 1982). In 1984, Gordon lengthened the cycle to "more or less fifty years"; "The Pulse of Capitalism," *Atlantic Monthly,* September 1984.

29. Newt Gingrich, open letter to David Stockman, *Washington Post Weekly,* 26 November 1984.

30. Schlesinger, *Crisis of the Old Order,* 113–114.

31. "The Politics of Nostalgia," *Reporter,* 16 June 1955, reprinted in Arthur M. Schlesinger, Jr., *The Politics of Hope* (Boston, 1962), 72ff.

32. Tocqueville, *Democracy in America,* II, Second Book, ch. ii, iv.

33. Ibid., Third Book, ch. xvii; Second Book, ch. x.

34. William J. Broad, "Space Arms Scientists in U.S. Selling Rights to Discoveries," *New York Times,* 4 November 1985.

35. Theodore Roosevelt to Sir Edward Grey, 15 November 1913, in Roosevelt, *Works,* Memorial ed., xxiv, 409.

36. For an interesting discussion of contemporary fiction in terms of the polarity between private interest and public action, see Robert Dunn, "Fiction That Shrinks from Life," *New York Times Book Review,* 30 June 1985.

37. *Democracy in America,* II, Third Book, ch. xxi.

38. Ibid., Second Book, ch. xiv, iv.

39. Ibid., ch. iv.

40. Ibid., I, ch. xiv.

41. Ibid., II, Second Book, ch. xiv.

42. Frank L. Klingberg, "The Historical Alternation of Moods in American Foreign Policy," *World Politics,* January 1952, elaborated in "Cyclical Trends in American Foreign Policy Moods and Their Policy Implications," in *Challenges to America: U.S. Foreign Policy in the 1980s,* ed. C. W. Kegley, Jr., and P. J. McGowan (vol. 4, Sage International Yearbook of Foreign Policy Studies, 1979), and in *Cyclical Trends in American Foreign Policy Moods: The Unfolding of America's World Role* (Lanham, Md., 1983).

43. See "The Election and After," excerpts from a discussion among Edmund G. Brown, Jr., Walter Dean Burnham, Kevin Phillips and Arthur M. Schlesinger, Jr., *New York Review of Books,* 16 August 1984; Walter Dean Burnham, "American Politics in the 1980s," *Dissent,* Spring 1980, 159.

44. McClosky and Zaller, *American Ethos*, 292–302.

45. Emerson, "Politics," "The Conservative."

46. Emerson, "The Conservative."

3. Foreign Policy and the American Character

This is an adaptation of the Cyril Foster Lecture at Oxford University in 1983, published in Foreign Affairs, *Fall 1983.*

1. Henry James, *Letters*, ed. Percy Lubbock (New York, 1920), I, 13.

2. Alexis de Tocqueville, *Democracy in America*, II, First Book, ch. i.

3. Ibid., ch. xviii.

4. Washington to Henry Lawrens, 14 November 1778, in *Writings*, ed. J. C. Fitzpatrick (Washington, 1936), XIII, 256.

5. John Adams to James Warren, 20 March 1783, in James H. Hutson, "Intellectual Foundations of Early American Diplomacy," *Diplomatic History*, Winter 1977, 13.

6. Norman A. Graebner, ed., *Ideas and Diplomacy* (New York, 1964), 11–12.

7. Ibid., 93, 122–123.

8. Fourth of July Address, 1821.

9. Herbert Croly, *The Promise of American Life* (New York, 1909), 306.

10. Woodrow Wilson, *Messages and Papers*, ed. Albert Shaw (New York, 1924), II, 777.

11. Speech at Orlando, Fla., 8 March 1983.

12. Press conference, 29 January 1981.

13. *Wall Street Journal*, 3 June 1980.

14. Henry Kissinger, *White House Years* (Boston, 1979), 522.

15. *New York Times*, 30 December 1984.

16. Richard H. Rovere and Arthur M. Schlesinger, Jr., *The General and the President* (New York, 1951), 234.

17. Address to joint session of Congress, 27 April 1983.

18. Ibid.

19. Lord Salisbury to Lord Lytton, 15 June 1877.

20. Norman Cousins, *The Improbable Triumvirate* (New York, 1972), 114.

21. Address to the UN General Assembly, 25 September 1961.

22. Winston S. Churchill, *The Gathering Storm* (Boston, 1948), 320.

23. Robert S. McNamara and Hans A. Bethe, "Reducing the Risk of Nuclear War," *Atlantic Monthly*, July 1985, 50.

4. National Interests and Moral Absolutes

This essay has its origins in a Christian A. Herter Lecture at Johns Hopkins University, reprinted under the title (not of my choosing) "The Necessary Amorality of Foreign Affairs," Harper's, August 1971, and reprinted again in Ernest W. Lefever, ed., Ethics and World Politics: Four Perspectives (Baltimore, 1972). I reconsidered the question a dozen years later in a lecture before the Council on Religion and International Affairs, which was excerpted as "In the National Interest," Worldview, December 1984.

1. Robert F. Kennedy, *Thirteen Days: A Memoir of the Cuban Missile Crisis* (New York, 1971 ed.), 106.

2. *New York Times*, 8 October 1984.

3. George Kennan, "Foreign Policy and Christian Conscience," *Atlantic Monthly*,

May 1959. See also Kennan's more recent discussion, "Morality and Foreign Policy," *Foreign Affairs*, Winter 1985/86.

4. Address to Congress, 3 April 1917.

5. John Foster Dulles, *A Righteous Faith for a Just and Durable Peace* (New York, Federal Council of Churches, 1942), 10.

6. Alexander Hamilton, *Pacificus*, No. 4, 10 July 1793.

7. Reinhold Niebuhr, *Moral Man and Immoral Society* (New York, 1932), pp. xi, 258, 267.

8. Winston Churchill, *The Gathering Storm* (Boston, 1948), 320. The Sermon was the "last word" in a sense Churchill may not have intended; for it defined the moral life in the context, not of day-to-day living, but of an imminent Day of Judgment.

9. Max Weber, "Politics as a Vocation" in *From Max Weber: Essays in Sociology*, ed. H. H. Gerth and C. Wright Mills (New York, 1958), 120.

10. Henry Adams, *The Education of Henry Adams* (Boston, 1918), ch. xxii.

11. *New York Times*, 7 July 1965.

12. Herbert Butterfield, *History and Human Relations* (London, 1951), 109–110.

13. Quoted in Gordon A. Craig and Alexander L. George, *Force and Statecraft* (New York, 1983), 264.

14. [Finley Peter Dunne], *Mr. Dooley's Philosophy* (New York, 1900), 258.

15. Washington to John Bannister, 21 April 1778, in E. S. Morgan, *The Genius of George Washington* (New York, 1980), 50–54.

16. Speech of 27 July 1965.

17. Hamilton, *Pacificus*, No. 4.

18. G. M. Young, *Victorian England: Portrait of an Age* (Oxford, 1953 ed.), 103.

19. Adams, *Education*, ch. x.

20. Ibid., ch. xviii.

21. Ibid., ch. xxiv.

22. Alexis de Tocqueville, *Democracy in America*, I, ch. xiii.

23. A. J. P. Taylor, *Europe: Grandeur and Decline* (London, Penguin, 1967), 357.

24. Theodore Roosevelt, sixth annual message, 3 December 1906.

25. John C. Bennett, "Moral Tensions in International Affairs," in *Moral Dimensions in American Foreign Policy*, ed. K. W. Thompson (New Brunswick, N.J., 1984), 184.

26. Joel Porte, ed., *Emerson in His Journals* (Cambridge, Mass., 1982), 358.

27. William Graham Sumner, *The Conquest of the United States by Spain and Other Essays*, ed. Murray Polner (Chicago, n.d.), 173.

28. Mark Twain, "To the Person Sitting in Darkness," *North American Review*, February 1901.

29. Quoted in Colin Bingham, ed., *Men and Affairs* (Sydney, 1967), 69.

30. Daniel Webster, "The Revolution in Greece," in the House of Representatives, 19 January 1824.

31. On this point, see R. W. Johnson, "Making Things Happen," *London Review of Books*, 6–19 September 1984, and H. S. Ferns, "This Spy Business," *Encounter*, May 1985.

32. Daniel Patrick Moynihan, "The Role of Law in World Affairs," *Bulletin of the American Academy of Arts and Sciences*, November 1983.

33. Arthur M. Schlesinger, Jr., *Robert Kennedy and His Times* (Boston, 1978), 508–509.

34. Daniel Patrick Moynihan, *Loyalties* (New York, 1984), 94.

35. Ronald Reagan, press conference, 19 October 1983; State of the Union address, 6 February 1985.

36. Walter Lippmann, "Today and Tomorrow," *New York Herald Tribune,* 9 May 1961.

5. Human Rights and the American Tradition

Published in Foreign Affairs, *"America and the World: 1978," this essay has been revised and brought up to date.*

1. See Edward Peters, *Torture* (New York, 1985).

2. In an *Idler* essay, quoted by Irvin Ehrenpreis, "Human Wishes," *London Review of Books,* 20 December 1984.

3. John Quincy Adams, Fourth of July address, 1821.

4. Albert Gallatin, *Peace with Mexico* (New York, 1847), sect. vii.

5. Kossuth's speech at Concord, 11 May 1852, *Old South Leaflets,* No. 111, p. 15.

6. *Congressional Globe,* 31st Cong., 2d Sess., 7 January 1850, 113–116. For this and other references to Senate debates, I am indebted to Richard Baker and the Senate Historical Office.

7. Ulysses S. Grant, first annual message, 6 December 1869.

8. The quoted phrase is from a resolution referred to the Senate Foreign Relations Committee in 1891. See *Congressional Record,* 51st Cong., 2d Sess., 14 February 1891, 141.

9. John Bassett Moore, *A Digest of International Law* (Washington, 1906), VI, 360–361.

10. John F. Kennedy, *Public Papers . . . 1961* (Washington, 1962), 1; *Public Papers . . . 1963* (Washington, 1964), 232, 697.

11. Section 116(a) of the Foreign Assistance Act of 1961, as amended in 1974.

12. See the well-informed article by Patrick Breslin, "Human Rights: Rhetoric or Action?," *Washington Post,* 17 February 1977.

13. E. P. Spiro, "A Paradigm Shift in American Foreign Policy," *Worldview,* January–February 1977.

14. Jimmy Carter, *Why Not the Best?* (New York, 1976), 140–141.

15. Jimmy Carter, *Keeping Faith* (New York, 1982), 144.

16. David Owen, *Human Rights* (New York, 1978), 2.

17. Address at the University of Georgia Law School, 20 April 1977.

18. "Trying to Right the Balance," *Time,* 9 October 1978.

19. In his Harvard Commencement speech; *Harvard Gazette,* 8 June 1978.

20. Interview with Arbatov by Jonathan Power, *Observer* (London), 12 November 1978.

21. *New York Times,* 26 June 1977.

22. Interview with Valéry Giscard d'Estaing by Arnaud de Borchgrave, *Newsweek,* 25 July 1977.

23. Fereydoun Hoveyda, "Not All Clocks for Human Rights Are the Same," *New York Times,* 18 May 1977.

24. George F. Kennan, *The Cloud of Danger: Current Realities of American Foreign Policy* (Boston, 1977), 43.

25. Elizabeth Drew, "Human Rights," *New Yorker,* 18 July 1977.

26. Nathaniel Hawthorne, *Our Old Home* (1863), in *Works* (Riverside ed.), VII, 49.

27. Ferdinand Mount, "Human Rights," *Encounter,* December 1980.

28. Marion Dönhoff, "Weltpolitik mit Fanfarenstössen," *Die Zeit*, 4 March 1977.

29. Patricia Derian, "A Commitment Sustained," *Worldview*, July–August 1978.

30. Raul S. Manglapus, "Human Rights Are Not a Western Discovery," *Worldview*, October 1978.

31. Fox Butterfield, "Peking's Poster Warriors Are Not Just Paper Tigers," *New York Times*, 26 November 1978.

32. "Peking Wall Poster Plea to Carter," *New York Post*, 13 December 1978.

33. John F. Burns, "Writers' Congress in China Demands Artistic Freedom," *New York Times*, 1 January 1985.

34. Carter, *Keeping Faith*, 578.

35. In his second debate with Mondale, 21 October 1984.

36. Reagan, message to Congress, 14 March 1986.

37. A. D. Sakharov, "The Human Rights Movement in the USSR and Eastern Europe," *Trialogue*, Fall 1978.

38. Mount, "Human Rights."

39. Mihajlo Mihajlov, "Notes of a Survivor," *New Leader*, 31 July 1978.

40. "Dissent in Exile—Andrei Amalrik Talks to Michael Charlton," *Listener*, 14 October 1976.

41. Interview in *Le Monde*, reprinted in the *New York Review of Books*, 4 October 1973.

42. Letter in *The Times* (London), 13 September 1973.

43. For recent accounts, see Hurst Hannum, ed., *Guide to International Human Rights Practice* (Philadelphia, 1984), and David P. Forsythe, "The United Nations and Human Rights, 1945–1985," *Political Science Quarterly*, Summer 1985.

6. The Solzhenitsyn Challenge

This essay was published under the title "The Solzhenitsyn We Refuse to See" in the Washington Post, *25 June 1978, and was reprinted in Ronald Berman, ed.,* Solzhenitsyn at Harvard *(Washington, 1979).*

7. America and Empire

I have drawn on my essay "The Missionary Enterprise and Theories of Imperialism" in The Missionary Enterprise in China and America, *ed. John K. Fairbank (Cambridge, Mass., 1974); also my review of William Appleman Williams's* The Roots of the Modern American Empire *in* Partisan Review, *No. 4, 1970 (with a response by Williams and a rejoinder by me in* Partisan Review, *No. 1, 1971); also a letter to the* New York Review of Books, *20 March 1980.*

1. Richard Koebner and H. D. Schmidt, *Imperialism: The Story and Significance of a Political Word, 1840–1960* (Cambridge, England, 1964), ch. i.

2. In *Bagehot's Historical Essays*, ed. Norman St. John-Stevas (New York, 1966), 447–452.

3. Joseph A. Schumpeter, "The Sociology of Imperialisms," in *Imperialism and Social Classes* (New York, 1951), 5.

4. Churchill to Roosevelt, 21 May 1944, in *Churchill and Roosevelt: The Complete Correspondence*, ed. W. F. Kimball (Princeton, 1984), III, 140.

5. Karl Marx in *New York Tribune*, 25 June, 8 August 1853; Marx to Engels, 14 June 1853, in *Karl Marx on Colonialism and Modernization*, ed. Shlomo Avineri (Garden City, N.Y., 1968), 94, 132–133, 455.

6. Engels in *The Northern Star*, 22 January 1848, to Karl Kautsky, 12 September 1882, in Avineri, *Marx on Colonialism*, 47, 473; Marx in *Neue Rheinische Zeitung*,

14 February 1849, Engels in January 1848, Max Nomad, *Apostles of Revolution* (rev. ed., New York, 1961), 103; Engels to F. A. Sorge, Marx and Engels, *Letters to America 1848–1895*, ed. Alexander Trachtenberg (New York, 1953), 204.

7. Valerie Pakenham, *The Noonday Sun* (London, 1985), 10.

8. Charles A. Conant, "The Economic Basis of Imperialism," *North American Review*, September 1898, in Conant, *The United States in the Orient* (Boston, 1900), 3, 9, 29.

9. V. I. Lenin, *Imperialism: The Highest Stage of Capitalism* (New York, 1939), 82.

10. Andre Gunder Frank, *Capitalism and Underdevelopment in Latin America* (New York, 1967), 9.

11. Karl Marx, *Capital* (Modern Library ed.), 821.

12. Marx and Engels, *Letters to Americans*, 204.

13. Gunnar Myrdal, *Asian Drama: An Inquiry into the Poverty of Nations* (abr. ed., New York, 1971), 111–112.

14. APRA stands for Alianza Popular Revolucionaria Americana. The quotation is from an interview with Victor Alba, *New Leader*, 26 April 1954.

15. J. K. Galbraith, *The Nature of Mass Poverty* (Cambridge, Mass., 1979), 91. The Robinson quotation, which I take from Galbraith, is from Joan Robinson, *Economic Philosophy* (Garden City, N.Y., 1964), 45.

16. Cf. Conor Cruise O'Brien, "Contemporary Forms of Imperialism," in *Readings in U.S. Imperialism*, ed. K. T. Fann and D. C. Hodges (Boston, 1971), 7, with O'Brien, "The Fall of Africa," *New Republic*, 18 March 1985.

17. Frantz Fanon, *The Wretched of the Earth* (London, 1967), 83.

18. E. H. Carr, *The Bolshevik Revolution, 1917–1923* (London, 1961), III, 61, quoted by Tony Smith, *The Pattern of Imperialism* (Cambridge, England, 1981), 210.

19. Myrdal, *Asian Drama*, 109, 442–443.

20. Galbraith, *Nature of Mass Poverty*, 46.

21. Ibid., 89.

22. A. J. P. Taylor, "London Diary," *New Statesman*, 7 January 1956. See also his essay "Economic Imperialism" in *Englishmen and Others* (London, 1956), 76–80.

23. Quoted by W. L. Langer, "Farewell to Empire," *Foreign Affairs*, October 1962, 118.

24. Schumpeter, *Imperialism*, 18, 25, 65.

25. Max Weber, "Structures of Power," in *From Max Weber: Essays in Sociology*, ed. H. H. Gerth and C. Wright Mills (New York, 1946), 169.

26. D. K. Fieldhouse, "'Imperialism': An Historiographical Revision," *Economic History Review*, December 1961, 204.

27. W. L. Langer, "Farewell to Empire," *Foreign Affairs*, October 1962, 120; Langer, "A Critique of Imperialism," *Foreign Affairs*, October 1935, 113.

28. *From Max Weber*, 164.

29. Ronald Robinson, John Gallagher and Alice Denny, *Africa and the Victorians: The Climax of Imperialism* (London, 1968), 472.

30. A. J. P. Taylor, *Englishmen and Others*, 79.

31. A. K. Weinberg, *Manifest Destiny: A Study of Nationalist Expansionism in American History* (Baltimore, 1935).

32. *American Historical Review*, June 1978.

33. R. W. Van Alstyne, *The Rising American Empire* (New York, 1960), 1, 9.

34. Interview with W. A. Williams in Henry Abelove et al., eds., *Visions of History* (New York, 1984), 139.

35. William Appleman Williams, *The Tragedy of American Diplomacy* (2nd rev. and enlarged ed., New York, 1972), 15.

36. Walter LaFeber, *The New Empire* (Ithaca, 1963), 7.

37. Quoted by J. H. Hutson, "Intellectual Foundations of Early American Diplomacy," *Diplomatic History*, Winter 1977, 6, 8, 10.

38. A. O. Hirschman, "Rival Interpretations of Market Society," *Journal of Economic Literature*, December 1982, 1464.

39. Jefferson, "Report of the Secretary of State on the Privileges and Restrictions on the Commerce of the United States in Foreign Countries," 16 December 1793, in *The Record of American Diplomacy*, ed. R. J. Bartlett (New York, 1947), 74.

40. Emerson, "The Young American."

41. *Redburn*, ch. xxxiii.

42. James A. Field, Jr., *America and the Mediterranean World, 1776–1882* (Princeton, 1969), 26, 59, 137.

43. See Robert E. May, *The Southern Dream of Caribbean Empire, 1854–1861* (Baton Rouge, 1973), and Charles H. Brown, *Agents of Manifest Destiny: The Lives and Times of the Filibusters* (Chapel Hill, 1980).

44. Representative James Monroe of Ohio, quoted by Paul S. Holbo, "Economics, Emotion, and Expansion: An Emerging Foreign Policy," in *The Gilded Age*, ed. H. Wayne Morgan (2nd ed., Syracuse, 1970), 202.

45. Field, *America and the Mediterranean World*, 313, 374.

46. Holbo, "Economics, Emotion, and Expansionism," 212.

47. Field, "American Imperialism," *American Historical Review*, June 1978, 658, 667.

48. Adams to Hay, 2 November 1901, in *Letters of Henry Adams, 1892–1918*, ed. W. C. Ford (Boston, 1938), 358.

49. Henry Adams, *The Education of Henry Adams* (Boston, 1918), ch. xvi.

50. Hugh McCulloch, *Men and Measures of Half a Century* (New York, 1888), 508–512.

51. Engels, "Presidential Election in America," *Vorwärts*, 16 November 1892, in *Marx and Engels on the United States* (Moscow, 1979), 300–301.

52. Quoted by Holbo, "Economics, Emotion, and Expansion," 203–204.

53. Quoted by David M. Pletcher, "1861–1898: Economic Growth and Diplomatic Adjustment," in *Economics and World Power: An Assessment of American Diplomacy Since 1789*, ed. W. H. Becker and S. F. Wells, Jr. (New York, 1984), 126.

54. *Historical Statistics of the United States: Colonial Times to 1970* (Washington, 1975), II, 887.

55. W. H. Becker, "Foreign Markets for Iron and Steel, 1893–1913," *Pacific Historical Review*, May 1975.

56. Quoted by Lloyd C. Gardner, *A Covenant with Power: America and World Order from Wilson to Reagan* (New York, 1984), 6.

57. Cordell Hull, *Memoirs* (New York, 1948), I, 81.

58. Arthur M. Schlesinger, Jr., *The Coming of the New Deal* (Boston, 1958), 254.

59. Harry Magdoff, "Comments," in *Testing Theories of Economic Imperialism*, ed. S. J. Rosen and J. R. Kurth (Lexington, Mass., 1974), 84.

60. Williams, *Tragedy*, 206.

61. Williams, *Roots*, 8.

62. *Encyclopaedia Britannica; Or, A Dictionary of Arts and Sciences* (Edinburgh, 1771), II, 494.

63. Richard Koebner, *Empire* (Cambridge, England, 1961), 295.

64. Weinberg, *Manifest Destiny*, 103.

65. Williams, *Roots*, 146–147.

66. Ibid., 379.

67. Grover Cleveland, *Presidential Problems* (New York, 1904), 279–280.

68. Howard K. Beale, *Theodore Roosevelt and the Rise of America to World Power* (1956; Collier paperback, 1962), 59–60.

69. For an analysis of comparable forcing of evidence in LaFeber's *The New Empire*, see Paul S. Holbo, "A View of *The New Empire*," a paper delivered before the Organization of American Historians, 16 April 1971.

70. D. W. Brogan, *The American Character* (1956; Time Inc. paperback, 1962), 220.

71. N. Gordon Levin, "The Open Door Thesis Reconsidered," *Reviews in American History*, December 1974.

72. Williams, *Roots*, 483.

73. Akira Iriye, "Imperialism and Sincerity," *Reviews in American History*, March 1973, 124–125.

74. Karl Popper, *Unended Quest: An Intellectual Autobiography* (London, 1976), 41–42.

75. William Appleman Williams, "America II," *Partisan Review* #1 (1971), 73.

76. Williams, *Roots*, 32.

77. A. T. Mahan, "Naval Strategy, Compared and Contrasted with the Principles of Military Operations on Land," in *Mahan on Naval Warfare*, ed. Allan Westcott (Boston, 1918), 355.

78. Thomas E. Weisskopf, "Capitalism, Socialism, and the Sources of Imperialism," in *Testing Theories of Economic Imperialism*, ed. Rosen and Kurth, 59, 70.

79. Williams, *Roots*, 150, 326–327.

80. New York, 1974.

81. Henry Cabot Lodge, "Our Blundering Foreign Policy," *Forum*, March 1895, 9, 10, 17.

82. Beale, *Roosevelt*, 84.

83. Williams, "America II," 73.

84. Roosevelt to F. S. Oliver, 9 August 1906, in Theodore Roosevelt, *Letters*, ed. E. E. Morison (Cambridge, Mass., 1951–1954), V, 352.

85. Lodge, "Our Blundering Foreign Policy," 15.

86. Beale, *Roosevelt*, 50–51.

87. Michael H. Hunt, *Frontier Defense and the Open Door* (New Haven, 1973), 230.

88. Charles Beresford, *The Break-Up of China* (London, 1899), 443–444, quoted by Marilyn Blatt Young, "American Expansion, 1870–1900: The Far East," in *Towards a New Past: Dissenting Essays in American History*, ed. B. J. Bernstein (New York, 1968), 190.

89. Charles Denby, *China and Her People* (Boston, 1906), II, 38, quoted by Young, "American Expansion," 179.

90. Young, "American Expansion," 186.

91. Hunt, *Frontier Defense*, 67.

92. Paul A. Varg, "The Myth of the China Market, 1890–1914," *American Historical Review*, February 1968, 749.

93. Beale, *Roosevelt*, 50, 80.

94. Lodge, "Our Blundering Foreign Policy," 17.

95. D. G. Munro, *Intervention and Dollar Diplomacy in the Caribbean, 1900–1921* (Princeton, 1964), 163.

96. Bryce Wood, *The Making of the Good Neighbor Policy* (New York, 1961), 265, 300.

97. See Stephen C. Schlesinger and Stephen Kinzer, *Bitter Fruit: The Untold Story of the American Coup in Guatemala* (New York, 1982).

98. Frank Mankiewicz and Kirby Jones, *With Fidel* (Chicago, 1975), 200–202; Jean Daniel, "Unofficial Envoy," *New Republic,* 14 December 1963. See also Arthur M. Schlesinger, Jr., "The Alliance for Progress: A Retrospective," in *Latin America: The Search for a New International Role,* ed. R. G. Hellman and H. J. Rosenbaum (New York, 1975), 57–92.

99. Williams, *Tragedy,* 164, 165, 173, 190.

100. Myra Wilkins, "The Role of U.S. Business," in *Pearl Harbor as History: Japanese-American Relations 1931–1941,* ed. Dorothy Borg and Shumpei Okamoto (New York, 1973), 346, 350.

101. Fidel Castro, *There Must Be an Economic War of All the People,* speech of 28 December 1984 (Havana, 1965), 24.

102. Henry Adams, *History of the United States During the Administrations of Thomas Jefferson and James Madison* (New York, 1889), I, 73.

103. Van Alstyne, *Rising American Empire,* 93; Weinberg, *Manifest Destiny,* 103.

104. Frederick Merk, *Albert Gallatin and the Oregon Problem* (Cambridge, Mass., 1951), 13.

105. J. W. Pratt, "The Ideology of American Expansion," in *Essays in Honor of William E. Dodd,* ed. Avery Craven (Chicago, 1935), 338–339.

106. J. Q. Adams, *Memoirs,* ed. C. F. Adams (Philadelphia, 1874–1877), VI, 251.

107. Jefferson to Monroe, 24 October 1823, in Jefferson, *Writings,* ed. Merrill D. Peterson (Library of America, 1984), 1482; J. Q. Adams, *Memoirs,* VI, 70–74.

108. Weinberg, *Manifest Destiny,* 228–229.

109. Adams, *Memoirs,* IV, 438.

110. Henry Adams, "The Session," *North America Review,* April 1869, in *The Great Secession Winter of 1860–61 and Other Essays,* ed. George E. Hochfield (New York, 1958), 92.

111. Lodge, "Our Blundering Foreign Policy," 16.

112. James K. Polk, *Diary,* ed. M. M. Quaife (Chicago, 1910), III, 348.

113. James Bryce, *The American Commonwealth* (New York, 1888), I, 400–401.

114. Beale, *Roosevelt,* 138, 165, 389.

115. Schumpeter, *Imperialism,* 73.

116. Ibid., 51.

117. Alexis de Tocqueville, *Democracy in America,* II, Third Book, ch. xxii.

118. James L. Payne, "Marx's Heirs Belie the Pacifist Promise," *Wall Street Journal,* 5 April 1985.

119. Milovan Djilas, "The Militarization of the Soviet Bloc," *Wall Street Journal,* 30 May 1984.

120. Quoted by John Vinocur, *New York Times,* 9 January 1983.

121. Richard Faber, *The Vision and the Need: Late Victorian Imperialist Aims* (London, 1966), 106–107.

122. Fidel Castro, *To Pay Tribute to the Empire or to Pay Tribute to the Homeland,* dialogue with delegates to the Trade Union Conference of Latin American and Caribbean Workers, 18 July 1985 (Havana, 1985), 26–27.

123. Jean-François Revel, *Without Marx or Jesus* (Garden City, N.Y., 1971), 139.

124. Frantz Fanon, *A Dying Colonialism* (New York, 1967), 49, 37, 42.

125. Fanon, *Dying Colonialism*, 131; Fanon, *Wretched of the Earth*, 34, 36; Fanon, *Toward the African Revolution* (New York, 1967), 31, 38; *Dying Colonialism*, 62–63.

126. See Roland Oliver, "Initiatives and Resistance," *Times Literary Supplement*, 9 August 1985.

127. See especially Ronald Robinson, "Non-European Foundations of European Imperialism: Sketch for a Theory of Collaboration," in *Studies in the Theory of Imperialism*, ed. Roger Owen and Bob Sutcliffe (London, 1972), reprinted in *Imperialism: The Robinson and Gallagher Controversy*, ed. W. R. Louis (New York, 1976); and D. K. Fieldhouse, *Economics and Empire, 1830–1914* (London, 1973).

128. Louis, ed., *Imperialism*, 147.

129. P. F. Lambert, "The 'All-Mexico' Movement," in *The Mexican War: Changing Interpretations*, ed. O. B. Faulk and J. A. Stout, Jr. (Chicago, 1973), 171.

130. Walter LaFeber, *Inevitable Revolutions: The United States in Central America* (New York, 1983), 33.

131. Hugh Thomas, *Cuba; Or the Pursuit of Freedom* (London, 1971), 100, 208–217, 250.

132. Hunt, *Frontier Defense*, 246–249.

133. Geir Lundestad, "Empire by Invitation? The United States and Western Europe, 1945–1952," Society for the History of American Foreign Relations, *Newsletter*, September 1984.

134. Speech at West Point, 13 June 1916, Woodrow Wilson, *Public Papers*, ed. Ray Stannard Baker and W. E. Dodd (New York, 1925–1927), IV, 203.

8. Why the Cold War?

The first part appeared in Foreign Affairs, *October 1967, under the title "Origins of the Cold War." It has not been revised for this book. The second part is based on "The Cold War Revisited,"* New York Review of Books, *25 October 1979.*

1. "The Tragic Element in Modern International Conflict" was originally published in *Review of Politics*, April 1950, and can be found in Butterfield's *History and Human Relations* (London, 1951).

2. John Lewis Gaddis, "The Emerging Post-Revisionist Synthesis on the Origins of the Cold War," *Diplomatic History*, Summer 1983.

3. Pieter Geyl, *Napoleon: For and Against* (1949; Peregrine paperback, 1965), 18.

4. Every student of the Cold War must acknowledge his debt to W. H. McNeill's remarkable account, *America, Britain and Russia: Their Cooperation and Conflict, 1941–1946* (New York, 1953), and to the brilliant and indispensable series by Herbert Feis: *Churchill, Roosevelt, Stalin: The War They Waged and the Peace They Sought* (Princeton, 1957); *Between War and Peace: The Potsdam Conference* (Princeton, 1960); and *The Atomic Bomb and the End of World War II* (Princeton, 1966). Useful recent analyses include André Fontaine, *Histoire de la Guerre Froide* (2 v., Paris, 1965, 1967); N. A. Graebner, *Cold War Diplomacy, 1945–1960* (Princeton, 1962); L. J. Halle, *The Cold War as History* (London, 1967); M. F. Herz, *Beginnings of the Cold War* (Bloomington, Ind., 1966) and W. L. Neumann, *After Victory: Churchill, Roosevelt, Stalin and the Making of the Peace* (New York, 1967).

5. William Appleman Williams, *The Tragedy of American Diplomacy* (2nd rev. ed., New York, 1972), 229.

6. William Appleman Williams, "Demystifying Cold War Orthodoxy," *Science and Society*, Fall 1975, 349.

7. Williams, *Tragedy*, 159.

8. Geir Lundestad, *The American Non-Policy Toward Eastern Europe, 1943–1947: Universalism in an Area Not of Essential Interest to the United States* (Oslo, 1978), 61.

9. K. P. Voshenkov, *SSR v Bor'be Za Mir* (Moscow, 1975), 78, quoted by Svatava Rakova, "U.S. Central European Policy," *Historica XXII* (Prague, 1983), 145.

10. Williams, *Tragedy*, 231.

11. Barton J. Bernstein, "Walter Lippmann and the Early Cold War," in *Cold War Critics*, ed. T. G. Paterson (Chicago, 1971), 30, 45.

12. Lynn E. Davis, *The Cold War Begins: Soviet-American Conflict over Eastern Europe* (Princeton, 1974), 311, 389.

13. Lundestad, *American Non-Policy*, 40–41, 43, 317–18, 416, 419–420, 424, 429.

14. James F. Byrnes, "Neighboring Nations in One World," *Department of State Bulletin*, 4 November 1945.

15. Eduard Mark, "Charles E. Bohlen and the Acceptable Limits of Soviet Hegemony in Eastern Europe: A Memorandum of 18 October 1945," *Diplomatic History*, Spring 1979, 207–209; see also Mark, "American Policy toward Eastern Europe and the Origins of the Cold War, 1941–1946: An Alternative Interpretation," *Journal of American History*, September 1981.

16. W. A. Harriman and Elie Abel, *Special Envoy to Churchill and Stalin 1941–1946* (New York, 1975), 414, 315.

17. Mark, "American Policy," 331–332.

18. Gabriel Kolko, *The Politics of War: The World and United States Foreign Policy, 1943–1945* (New York, 1968), 338.

19. Alfred E. Eckes, Jr., "Open Door Expansionism Reconsidered: The World War II Experience," *Journal of American History*, March 1973, 912, 916–917.

20. Richard N. Gardner, *Sterling-Dollar Diplomacy: The Origins and the Prospects of the International Economic Order* (1956; expanded ed., New York, 1969), 375.

21. Henry W. Berger, "Senator Taft Dissents from Military Escalation," in Paterson, ed., *Cold War Critics*, 176, 181.

22. Joseph P. Kennedy, "An American Policy for Americans," before the Student Legal Forum, Charlottesville, Va., 12 December 1950.

23. William Appleman Williams, "Our Invested Interests," *Nation*, 7 May 1977.

24. Williams, *Tragedy*, 219–220.

25. "Remarks of Ambassador A. F. Dobrynin," *Congressional Record*, 19 June 1985 (daily ed.).

26. Valentin Berezhkov, *History in the Making: Memoirs of World War II Diplomacy* (Moscow, 1983), 308.

27. N. V. Sivachev and N. N. Yakovlev, *Russia and the United States* (Chicago, 1979), 259.

28. Earl Browder, *War or Peace with Russia* (New York, 1947), 104–105.

29. At Madison Square Garden, 12 September 1946.

30. Henry A. Wallace, *Toward World Peace* (New York, 1948), 67, 40–41.

31. Martin Sherwin, *A World Destroyed: The Atomic Bomb and the Grand Alliance* (New York, 1975), 6.

32. Robert A. Dallek, *Franklin D. Roosevelt and American Foreign Policy, 1932–1945* (New York, 1979), 534, 507. It is evident that since the 1967 essay I have modified my own view regarding the extent of Roosevelt's devotion to Wilsonianism.

33. Daniel Yergin, *Shattered Peace: The Origins of the Cold War and the National Security State* (Boston, 1977), 68.

34. John Lewis Gaddis, *Strategies of Containment: A Critical Appraisal of Postwar American National Security Policy* (New York, 1982), 13.

35. Herbert E. Meyer, "A Trendy Cold War Fairy Tale," *Fortune*, November 1977; Carolyn Eisenberg, "Reflections on a Toothless Revisionism," *Diplomatic History*, Summer 1978.

36. Daniel F. Harrington, "Kennan, Bohlen, and the Riga Axioms," *Diplomatic History*, Fall 1978, 426, 432, 434.

37. Bohlen and Kennan, Memoranda of 14 April 1949, minutes of meeting of 15 April 1949, in *Foreign Relations of the United States: 1949* (Washington, 1976), I, 271–283.

38. Yergin, *Shattered Peace*, 8, 413.

39. Adam Ulam, *The Rivals* (New York, 1971), 96–101.

40. See Nancy B. Tucker, *Patterns in the Dust* (New York, 1983).

41. See Michael S. Sherry, *Preparing for the Next Way: American Plans for Postwar Defense, 1941–45* (New Haven, 1977); Perry McCoy Smith, *The Air Force Plans for Peace, 1943–1945* (Baltimore, 1970); Vincent Davis, *Postwar Defense Policy and the U.S. Navy, 1943–1946* (Chapel Hill, 1966); and M. P. Leffler, "The American Conception of National Security and the Beginnings of the Cold War, 1945–48," *American Historical Review*, April 1984.

42. Williams, *Tragedy*, 283.

43. Sivachev and Yakovlev, *Russia and the United States*, 247, 240, 249, 255, 269.

44. Vojtech Mastny, *Russia's Road to the Cold War: Diplomacy, Warfare, and the Politics of Communism, 1941–1945* (New York, 1979), xiv–xviii, 224, 41.

45. Ibid., 283, 306.

46. Alexander Werth, *Russia at War, 1941–1945* (New York, 1964), 938.

47. Steven G. Neal, "A Comrade's Last Harrumph," *Philadelphia Inquirer*, 5 August 1973.

48. Fernando Claudin, *The Communist Movement from Comintern to Cominform* (London, 1975), 620, 388–389, 426–432, 576, 587–589, 32.

49. D. C. Watt, "Rethinking the Cold War," *Political Quarterly*, October–December 1978.

50. Herbert Butterfield, "Morality and an International Order," in *The Aberystwith Papers: International Politics, 1919–1969*, ed. Brian Porter (Oxford, 1972), 353–354.

51. Terry H. Anderson, *The United States, Great Britain and the Cold War, 1944–1947* (Columbia, Mo., 1981), 80.

52. Victor Rothwell, *Britain and the Cold War, 1941–1947* (London, 1982), 413.

53. Ibid., 241.

54. Alan Bullock, *Ernest Bevin: Foreign Secretary 1945–1951* (London, 1983), 216.

55. James F. Byrnes, *Speaking Frankly* (New York, 1947), 79.

56. John W. Wheeler-Bennett and Anthony Nicholls, *The Semblance of Peace: The Political Settlement After the Second World War* (London, 1972), 424.

57. Peter G. Boyle, "The British Foreign Office View of Soviet-American Relations, 1945–46," *Diplomatic History*, Summer 1979, 311, 313, 314.

58. Ibid., 311.

59. Rothwell, *Britain and the Cold War*, 259, 434.

60. Ibid., 411–442, 454–455.

61. Anderson, *The United States, Great Britain, and the Cold War*, 209, 211.

62. Rothwell, *Britain and the Cold War*, 454–455.

63. Robert G. Kaiser, *Cold Winter, Cold War* (New York, 1974), 177.

9. Affirmative Government and the American Economy

I have drawn passages from "Ideas and the Economic Process" in Seymour E. Harris,
American Economic History *(New York, 1961); "Ideas and Economic Development"*
in Paths of American Thought, *ed. Arthur M. Schlesinger, Jr., and Morton White*
(Boston, 1963); from a Tocqueville lecture given at Wake Forest University in 1982;
and "Neo-Conservatism and the Class Struggle," Wall Street Journal, *2 June 1981.*

1. E. A. J. Johnson, *The Foundations of American Economic Freedom: Government and Enterprise in the Age of Washington* (Minneapolis, 1973), 153, 200, 260, 312.
2. John C. Miller, *Alexander Hamilton: Portrait in Paradox* (New York, 1959), 293.
3. Joyce Appleby, *Capitalism and a New Social Order: The Republican Vision of the 1790s* (New York, 1984), 88; Jacob E. Cooke, ed., *The Reports of Alexander Hamilton* (New York, 1964), 166.
4. Madison to Washington, 16 April 1787, in *The Complete Madison: His Basic Writings,* ed. Saul K. Padover (New York, 1953), 185.
5. Jefferson to T. M. Randolph, 30 May 1790, Jefferson, *Writings* (Memorial ed.), VIII, 31; Jefferson, "Autobiography," in *Writings,* ed. Merrill Peterson (Library of America, 1984), 74.
6. Johnson, *Foundations,* 305.
7. Gallatin, "Report on Roads and Canals," in *The Government and the Economy: 1783–1861,* ed. Carter Goodrich (Indianapolis, 1967), 6–8.
8. G. S. Callender, "The Early Transportation and Banking Enterprises of the States in Relation to the Growth of Corporations," *Quarterly Journal of Economics,* November 1902, 112.
9. Johnson, *Foundations,* 305.
10. Callender, "Early Transportation and Banking Enterprises," 157.
11. Goodrich, ed., *Government and the Economy,* xvi, xxii.
12. Calculated by Milton Heath, Robert A. Lively, "The American System," *Business History Review,* March 1955, 86.
13. Callender, "Early Transportation and Banking Enterprises," 155–156.
14. Oscar and Mary F. Handlin, *Commonwealth, A Study of the Role of Government in the American Economy: Massachusetts, 1774–1861* (New York, 1947), 186.
15. R. C. Black III, *Railroads of the Confederacy* (Chapel Hill, 1952), 41–45.
16. Callender, "Early Transportation and Banking Enterprises," 114.
17. Stuart Bruchey, *The Roots of American Economic Growth* (New York, 1965), 131.
18. Louis Hartz, *Economic Policy and Democratic Thought: Pennsylvania, 1776–1960* (Cambridge, Mass., 1948), 292.
19. H. A. Hill, *Memoir of Abbott Lawrence* (Boston, 1883), 169.
20. William Leggett, "True Functions of Government," *New York Evening Post,* 21 November 1834 and "Associated Effort," *Post,* 10 December 1836, in *Social Theories of Jacksonian Democracy,* ed. Joseph L. Blau (New York, 1947), 77, 82.
21. Oscar and Mary Handlin, *Commonwealth,* 262.
22. Hartz, *Economic Policy,* 80–81, 140, 172, 175.
23. Lively, "American System," 91.
24. Oscar and Mary Handlin, *Commonwealth,* 233.
25. John Taylor of Caroline, *An Inquiry into the Principles and Policy of the Government of the United States* (New Haven, 1950), 259.
26. See J. Willard Hurst, *The Legitimacy of the Business Corporation in the Law of the United States, 1780–1970* (Charlottesville, 1970).
27. Jackson, Maysville Road Veto, 27 May 1830.

28. Martin Van Buren, *Autobiography* (Washington, 1919), 172.

29. Carter Goodrich, *Government Promotion of American Canals and Railroads, 1800–1890* (New York, 1960), 44.

30. J. Q. Adams to C. W. Upham, 2 February 1837, in Brooks Adams, "The Heritage of Henry Adams," introduction to Henry Adams, *The Degradation of the Democratic Dogma* (New York, 1919), 25.

31. Carter Goodrich, "The Revulsion against Internal Improvements," *Journal of Economic History*, November 1950.

32. Carter Goodrich, "The Virginia System of Mixed Enterprise," *Political Science Quarterly*, September 1949, 384.

33. John L. O'Sullivan, "Note," *Democratic Review*, May 1843, 583.

34. Paul K. Conkin, *Prophets of Prosperity: America's First Political Economists* (Bloomington, Ind., 1980), 220–221.

35. Jackson's Bank Veto, 10 July 1832.

36. *Charles River Bridge v. Warren Bridge*, 11 Peters 547.

37. Joel Porte, ed., *Emerson in His Journals* (Cambridge, Mass., 1982), 334.

38. Emerson, "The Young American."

39. George Bancroft, *The Necessity, the Reality, and the Promise of the Progress of the Human Race* (New York, 1854), 34.

40. Benjamin F. Butler, *Butler's Book* (Boston, 1892), 85.

41. A. O. Hirschman, *The Passions and the Interests: Political Arguments for Capitalism before Its Triumph* (Princeton, 1977); also Hirschman, "Rival Interpretations of Market Society: Civilizing, Destructive, or Feeble?" *Journal of Economic Literature*, December 1982.

42. George Combe, *Notes on the United States of North America, During a Phrenological Visit in 1838–9–40* (Philadelphia, 1841), I, 303.

43. Kate McKean, ed., *Carey's Manual of Social Science* (Philadelphia, 1864), 516.

44. Karl Marx, *Capital* (Modern Library), 616, 821; Marx, from *The Economic Manuscripts of 1857–59*, also Marx to Joseph Weydemeyer, 5 March 1852, Marx to Engels, 14 June 1853, *Marx and Engels on the United States* (Moscow, 1979), 64–67, 70–72.

45. Lincoln to H. L. Pierce and others, 6 April 1859, in *Abraham Lincoln: His Speeches and Writings*, ed. R. P. Basler (Cleveland, 1946), 488–489.

46. James Bryce, *The American Commonwealth* (London, 1888), II, 408.

47. *Lochner v. New York*, 198 U.S., 75.

48. Alan Jones, "Thomas M. Cooley and 'Laissez-Faire Constitutionalism': A Reconsideration," *Journal of American History*, March 1967, 752.

49. Callender, "Early Transportation and Banking Enterprises," 111.

50. W. G. Sumner, "Protectionism: the Ism which Teaches that Want Makes Wealth" (1883), in *Essays*, ed. A. G. Keller and M. R. Davie (New Haven, 1934), II, 485–486.

51. Thomas Hart Benton, *Thirty Years' View* (New York, 1854), I, 6.

52. J. Q. Adams, *Memoirs*, ed. C. F. Adams (Philadelphia, 1874–1877), IV, 375 (27 May 1819), V, 128–129 (22 May 1820).

53. Martin Van Buren, Message to Congress, 4 September 1837.

54. James Buchanan, Message to Congress, 8 December 1857.

55. Garfield to B. A. Hinsdale, 8 December 1874, in Leonard D. White, *The Republican Era: A Study in Administrative History, 1869–1901* (New York, 1958), 4.

56. Grover Cleveland, Second Inaugural Address, 4 March 1893.

57. Henry Adams, "The New York Gold Conspiracy," in Adams, *The Great Secession Winter of 1860–61 and Other Essays*, ed. George E. Hochfield (New York, 1958), 189.

58. Adams, "The Session, 1869–1870," in *Great Secession Winter*, 221.

59. John A. Garraty, *Henry Cabot Lodge* (New York, 1953), 138.

60. See W. R. Brock, *Investigation and Responsibility: Public Responsibility in the United States, 1865–1900* (Cambridge, England, 1985); also W. E. Nelson, *The Roots of American Bureaucracy, 1830–1900* (Cambridge, Mass., 1982).

61. Bryce, *American Commonwealth*, II, 408–411.

62. Theodore Roosevelt, Message to Congress, 8 December 1908.

63. Theodore Roosevelt, *The New Nationalism* (New York, 1910), 23–24.

64. In a speech in January 1911. Henry L. Stimson and McGeorge Bundy, *On Active Service in Peace and War* (New York, 1948), 60.

65. Woodrow Wilson, *The New Freedom* (Englewood Cliffs, N.J., 1961), 164.

66. Herbert Croly, *The Promise of American Life* (New York, 1909), 22, 50, 106, 39–40, 169–170.

67. Herbert Hoover, *State Papers and Other Public Writings*, ed. W. S. Myers (New York, 1934), II, 8–9.

68. Franklin D. Roosevelt, *Public Papers and Addresses . . . 1928–1932* (New York, 1938), 458, 643.

69. Franklin D. Roosevelt, *Public Papers . . . 1928–1932* (New York, 1938), 632, 782, 784.

70. Franklin D. Roosevelt, *Public Papers and Addresses . . . 1938* (New York, 1941), xxix–xxx.

71. John F. Kennedy, *Public Papers . . . 1963* (Washington, 1964), 411.

72. Jimmy Carter, State of the Union address, 19 January 1978.

73. Theodore Roosevelt, Message to Congress, 8 December 1908.

74. D. P. Moynihan, "How Has the United States Met Its Major Challenges Since 1945?" *Commentary*, November 1985.

75. Thomas B. Edsall, "Republican America," *New York Review of Books*, 24 April 1986.

76. Orestes A. Brownson, *The American Republic* (New York, 1866), 383.

77. Fred Hirsch, *Social Limits to Growth* (Cambridge, Mass., 1976), 11–12, 143.

78. Tocqueville, *Democracy in America*, II, Second Book, ch. xvii.

79. George Gilder, *Wealth and Poverty* (Bantam paperback, 1982), 144.

80. Thurman Arnold, "How They Are Voting," *New Republic*, 30 September 1936.

81. Franklin D. Roosevelt, Fireside Chat, 14 April 1938.

82. Lloyd A. Free and Hadley Cantril, *The Political Beliefs of Americans* (New Brunswick, N.J., 1967), 33.

83. Arthur M. Schlesinger, Jr., "Which Road for the Democrats?" *Reporter*, 20 January 1953. I am grateful to Jefferson Morley for reminding me of these sapient words in his piece "The Old Idea of 'New Ideas,'" *New Republic*, 27 May 1985.

84. *New York Times*, 21 October 1981.

85. Charles Peters, "A Neo-Liberal's Manifesto," *Washington Post*, 5 September 1982.

86. Gary Hart, *A New Democracy* (New York, 1983), 26.

87. Woodrow Wilson, "Bryce's *American Commonwealth*: A Review," *Political Science Quarterly*, March 1889.

10. The Short Happy Life of American Political Parties

This essay is based on "Can the System Be Saved?" Encounter, January 1983, revised as "The Crisis of the American Party System" in Political Parties and the Modern State, *ed. Richard L. McCormick (New Brunswick, N.J., 1984); and also on "Crisis of the Party System,"* Wall Street Journal, *10 May, 14 May 1979, and "Can the Party System Be Saved?" in* The American Constitutional System under Strong and Weak Parties, *ed. Patricia Bonomi, James MacGregor Burns and Austin Ranney (New York, 1981).*

1. Alexis de Tocqueville, *Democracy in America,* I, ch. xiv.
2. James Bryce, *The American Commonwealth* (New York, 1888), I, 5–6.
3. David Glass, Peverill Squire and Raymond Wolfinger, "Voter Turnout: An International Comparison," *Public Opinion,* December/January 1984.
4. Rousseau, *The Social Contract,* Book II, ch. iii.
5. Hume, "Of Parties in General," in *Essays: Moral, Political and Literary* (World's Classics, 1903), 55.
6. Jefferson to Francis Hopkinson, 13 March 1789, in *Thomas Jefferson* (Library of America, 1984), 941.
7. Franklin D. Roosevelt, *Public Papers and Addresses* (New York, 1938), I, 628.
8. Henry Jones Ford, *The Rise and Growth of American Politics* (New York, 1898), 203.
9. Ford, *Rise and Growth,* 306.
10. Thoreau, "Life Without Principle," *Miscellanies* (Boston, 1893), 286.
11. *The Autobiography of Lincoln Steffens* (New York, 1931), 618. The classic functional analysis of city machines is in Robert K. Merton's essay "Manifest and Latent Functions," in *On Theoretical Sociology* (New York, 1967), esp. 126–136.
12. Tocqueville, *Democracy in America,* I, ch. xiv.
13. Bryce, *The American Commonwealth,* II, 20.
14. Henry F. Pringle, *Theodore Roosevelt* (New York, 1931), 89.
15. William A. Robinson, *Thomas B. Reed Parliamentarian* (New York, 1930), 379.
16. Henry Adams, *Democracy* (1880), ch. 4.
17. Samuel Lubell, *The Hidden Crisis in American Politics* (New York, 1970), 49.
18. The 10th *Federalist.*
19. Edward M. Stanwood, *A History of the Presidency* (Boston, 1898), 260.
20. Woodrow Wilson, *Congressional Government* (Boston, 1885), 92, 98–99.
21. Tocqueville, *Democracy in America,* II, First Book, ch. xxi.
22. Janet Smith, ed., *Mark Twain on the Damned Human Race* (New York, 1962), 105.
23. Tocqueville, *Democracy in America,* I, ch. x.
24. Henry Adams, *The Great Secession Winter of 1860–61 and Other Essays,* ed. George E. Hochfield (New York, 1963), 279.
25. Arthur M. Schlesinger, *Paths to the Present* (New York, 1949), 95, 91.
26. Henry Adams, *The Education of Henry Adams* (Boston, 1918), ch. xviii.
27. Bryce, *American Commonwealth,* I, 75.
28. Smith, ed., *Mark Twain,* 105.
29. Whitman, *Democratic Vistas,* in *Complete Poetry and Collected Prose* (Library of America), 965–966.
30. Herbert Croly, *Progressive Democracy* (New York, 1914), 324, 349.
31. Calvin Coolidge, *Autobiography* (New York, 1929), 230.

32. Franklin D. Roosevelt, *Public Papers and Addresses . . . 1940* (New York, 1941), 28.

33. For a tempered discussion, see *What Price PACs? Report of the Twentieth Century Task Force on Political Action Committees* (New York, 1984); and the informative article by David Shribman and Brooks Jackson in the *Wall Street Journal,* 22 November 1985.

34. Harold Macmillan, *The Past Masters* (London, 1975), 107. See also the suggestive discussion in Joshua Meyrowitz, *No Sense of Place: The Impact of Electronic Media on Social Behavior* (New York, 1984), ch. 14.

35. Recalled by Clayton Fritchey in "Out, Damn Spots," Los Angeles Times Syndicate, 31 March 1976.

36. Quoted by Newton Minow in a speech to the Association of American Law Schools, 5 January 1985, reprinted in *Congressional Record* (daily ed.), 20 February 1985, E 492.

37. A. Lawrence Lowell, *Public Opinion and Popular Government* (New York, 1913), esp. ch. v.

38. Patricia Bonomi, James MacGregor Burns and Austin Ranney, eds., *The American Constitutional System under Strong and Weak Parties* (New York, 1981), 137.

39. For an intellectual history (and muted vindication) of the era of nonpartisan Presidents, see Ralph Ketcham, *Presidents above Party: The First American Presidency, 1789–1829* (Chapel Hill, 1984).

40. Bryce, *American Commonwealth,* I, 660.

41. Adams, *Education,* ch. xviii.

11. After the Imperial Presidency

I have drawn on the Epilogue added to the paperback edition of The Imperial Presidency *(New York: Popular Library, 1974) and on "Parliamentary Government,"* New Republic, *31 August 1974. I have also borrowed from pieces written through the years for the* Wall Street Journal, *especially "The Electoral College Conundrum" (4 April 1977), "Reforming the American Presidency" (7 April 1981), "Time for Constitutional Change?" (24 December 1982), "Making Reagan Accountable" (20 April 1984); and from "Why Ex-Presidents Should Stay That Way,"* Parade, *21 June 1981; "The Item Veto Is a Bad Idea,"* Chicago Tribune, *2 April 1984; "Against a One-Term, Six-Year President,"* New York Times, *10 January 1986.*

1. Alexis de Tocqueville, *Democracy in America,* I, ch. viii.

2. Madison to Jefferson, 13 May 1798, in *The Complete Madison: His Basic Writings,* ed. Saul K. Padover (New York, 1953), 258.

3. Abraham D. Sofaer, *War, Foreign Affairs and Constitutional Power: The Origins* (Cambridge, Mass., 1976), 225–227, 265, 377–379. Judge Sofaer's work is ably continued by Henry Bartholomew Cox, *War, Foreign Affairs and Constitutional Power, 1829–1901* (Cambridge, Mass., 1984).

4. Calhoun in the Senate, 4 January 1848, quoted in Frederick Merk, *Manifest Destiny and Mission in American History* (New York, 1963), 163.

5. Louis J. Jennings, *Eighty Years of Republican Government in the United States* (London, 1868), 36.

6. James Bryce, *The American Commonwealth* (1888), I, ch. vi.

7. Henry Adams, *The Education of Henry Adams* (Boston, 1918), ch. xxviii.

8. Woodrow Wilson, *Congressional Government* (15th ed.; Boston, 1901), xi–xii.

9. W. L. Langer and S. E. Gleason, *The Challenge to Isolation* (New York, 1952), 539.

10. Richard M. Nixon, *Memoirs* (New York, 1978), 763.

11. Quoted by Philip Hone, *Diary . . . 1828–1851,* ed. Allan Nevins (New York, 1927), II, 686–687.

12. Thomas E. Cronin, "A Resurgent Congress and the Imperial Presidency," *Political Science Quarterly,* Summer 1980, 210.

13. Charles L. Black, Jr., "Mr. Nixon, the Tapes and Common Sense," *New York Times,* 3 August 1973.

14. Theodore Lowi, *The Personal President* (Ithaca, 1985), 151.

15. T. D. Schellhardt, "Do We Expect Too Much?" *Wall Street Journal,* 10 July 1979.

16. Robert Shogan, *None of the Above* (New York, 1982), 3–4.

17. Godfrey Hodgson, *All Things to All Men: The False Promise of the Modern American Presidency* (1980; Touchstone paperback, 1981), 49.

18. Ibid., 13.

19. Hugh Heclo, "The Presidential Illusion," in *The Illusion of Presidential Government,* ed. Heclo and L. M. Salamon (Boulder, Colo., 1981), 1.

20. Gerald R. Ford, "Imperiled, Not Imperial," *Time,* 10 November 1980.

21. Jonathan Daniels, *Frontier on the Potomac* (New York, 1946), 31.

22. Richard Neustadt, *Presidential Power: The Politics of Leadership* (1960; rev. ed., New York, 1976), 77, i.

23. Woodrow Wilson, *Constitutional Government in the United States* (New York, 1908), 68, 73.

24. Tocqueville, *Democracy in America,* II, Fourth Book, ch. vi.

25. Pierce Butler of South Carolina; D. S. Freeman, *George Washington* (New York, 1954), VI, 117.

26. Garry Wills, *Cincinnatus: George Washington and the Enlightenment* (Garden City, N.Y., 1984), 47, 103; Freeman, *Washington,* VI, 86. Samuel Eliot Morison wrote of Washington: "No other subsequent President of the United States has lived in such a glare of publicity." *Oxford History of the American People* (New York, 1965), 318.

27. Robert Z. Remini, *Andrew Jackson and the Course of American Democracy, 1833–1845* (New York, 1984), ch. 5.

28. Charles Dickens, *American Notes,* ch. xviii.

29. James K. Polk, *Diary,* ed. M. M. Quaife (Chicago, 1910), II, 28.

30. Benjamin Harrison, *This Country of Ours* (New York, 1897), 163–164, 180.

31. William Howard Taft, *The Presidency* (New York, 1916), 47–48, 50.

32. Senator Robert Griffin of Michigan, quoted by James L. Sundquist, *The Decline and Resurgence of Congress* (Washington, 1981), 292.

33. *New York Times,* 2 September 1976.

34. The quoted observations are from the Conference Report, *Congressional Record,* 4 October 1973, H8657 (daily ed.), and "Statement of War Powers Conferees," 4 October 1973, mimeographed, 2.

35. Eagleton cogently developed this theme in his *War and Presidential Power: A Chronicle of Congressional Surrender* (New York, 1974).

36. *Congressional Record,* 7 November 1973, H9661 (daily ed.).

37. Letter in *Washington Post,* 6 December 1973.

38. *Immigration and Naturalization Service v. Chadha,* 103 S. Ct. 2764 (1983).

39. Howard E. Shuman, *Politics and the Budget: The Struggle Between the President and the Congress* (Englewood Cliffs, N.J., 1984), 246.

40. Henry Jones Ford, *The Rise and Growth of American Politics* (New York, 1898), 284.

41. E. W. Emerson and W. E. Forbes, eds., *Journals of Ralph Waldo Emerson* (Boston, 1909–1914), IV, 160.

42. Henry Adams, "The Session, 1869–1870," in *The Great Secession Winter of 1860–61 and Other Essays,* ed. G. E. Hochfield (New York, 1958), 197.

43. Quoted by David Broder, *Washington Post,* 9 February 1984.

44. Lou Cannon, "Dramatic Account of Film of Nazi Death Camps Questioned," *Washington Post,* 5 March 1984.

45. Lars-Erik Nelson in *New York Daily News,* 16, 28 December 1983, 11 January 1984.

46. Sofaer, *War, Foreign Affairs and Constitutional Power,* 377–379.

47. "Resolution on the 1984 Annual Report of the Information Security Oversight Office," adopted by the Council of the American Historical Association, 27 December 1985.

48. *Congressional Record,* 18 June 1984 (daily ed.), H 6021. The GAO report is published in the *Record,* 20 June, S 7694–7697.

49. James Bryce, *Modern Democracies* (New York, 1921), II, 371.

50. James Parton, *Life of Andrew Jackson* (Boston, 1860), III, 607.

51. John Taylor of Caroline, *An Inquiry into the Principles and Policy of the Government of the United States* (1814; New Haven, 1950), 194.

52. The conference was sponsored by the Center for the Study of Democratic Institutions and held in December 1973. The quotation is from a report on the conference by Mortimer J. Adler to Joseph Slater of the Aspen Institute, 23 December 1973.

53. Lloyd N. Cutler, "To Form a Government," *Foreign Affairs,* Fall 1980.

54. Douglas Dillon, "The Challenge of Modern Governance," in *Reforming American Government: The Bicentennial Papers of the Committee on the Constitutional System,* ed. D. L. Robinson (Boulder, Colo., 1985), 28–29.

55. "After Two Centuries: Our Eighteenth Century Constitution in Today's Complex World," Committee on the Constitutional System Basic Policy Statement, 1 February 1983, 3.

56. Ford, *Rise and Growth of American Politics,* 59, 215.

57. Samuel Lubell, *The Hidden Crisis in American Politics* (New York, 1970), 43.

58. Louis Harris, "Reagan Wins Reelection, Loses Bid for Republican Congress," *The Harris Survey,* 8 November 1984.

59. Don K. Price, "The Parliamentary and Presidential Systems," *Public Administration Review,* Autumn 1943, 320.

60. Lord Hailsham, "Elective Dictatorship," *Listener,* 21 October 1976.

61. David Owen, "An Agenda for the New Year," *Observer* (London), 6 January 1985.

62. As told by FDR to Benjamin V. Cohen; see Cohen's 23 May 1974 Royer Lecture at the University of California, "Presidential Responsibility and American Democracy," 13.

63. See Philip Norton, "'The Norton View,'" in *The Politics of Parliamentary Reform,* ed. David Judge (Cranbury, N.J., 1984), esp. 62–65; and Norton, *The Constitution in Flux* (Oxford, 1982).

64. Allan Sindler, "A Critique of the Reuss Proposal," in Robinson, ed., *Reforming American Government,* 324.

65. Woodrow Wyatt, *Turn Again, Westminster* (London, 1973). The quoted sentiment is from the author's inscription in my copy of the book.

66. Edward Pearce, "London Commentary," *Encounter,* September–October 1982, 36.

67. Crossman, *Myths of Cabinet Government,* 16.
68. Lord Hailsham, "Wilson the Conservative," *Listener,* 28 October 1976.
69. "House of Cards," *Economist,* 4 August 1984.
70. Wyatt, *Turn Again, Westminster,* 17, 28–31.
71. James Gillies, "The Parliamentary Imperative," *Saturday Night,* June 1984, 55.
72. Malcolm Shaw, "Reform of the American Congress," in Judge, ed., *Politics of Parliamentary Reform,* 129.
73. Hailsham, "Elective Dictatorship."
74. Wyatt, *Turn Again, Westminster,* 50.
75. Gillies, "Parliamentary Imperative," 55.
76. Wyatt, *Turn Again, Westminster,* 57.
77. See Clive Ponting, *The Right to Know: The Inside Story of the 'Belgrano' Affair* (London, 1985), and Tam Dalyell, "Ponting Bites Back," *London Review of Books,* 4 April 1985.
78. Cf. Samuel H. Beer, *Britain Against Itself: The Political Contradictions of Collectivism* (New York, 1982), 189–192.
79. *Buckley v. Valeo,* 424 U.S. 1, 121 (1976).
80. Neustadt, *Presidential Power,* 101.
81. *Youngstown Sheet & Tube Company v. Sawyer,* 343 U.S. 579, 635 (1952).
82. In Dallas, Tex., 12 June 1936; Franklin D. Roosevelt, *Public Papers . . . 1936* (New York, 1938), 215.
83. Bryce, *The American Commonwealth,* I, 147–148.
84. Harriman before the Subcommittee on Separation of Powers, Senate Judiciary Committee, *Executive Privilege: The Withholding of Information by the Executive,* 92d Cong., 1st Sess. (1971), 360.
85. Griffin Bell, Herbert Brownell, William Simon and Cyrus Vance (the national co-chairmen of the Committee for a Single Six-Year Presidential Term), "For a One-Term, Six-Year Presidency," *New York Times,* 31 December 1985.
86. Jackson, second annual message, 6 December 1830.
87. C. C. Tansill, ed., *Documents Illustrative of the Formation of the Union of the American States* (Washington, 1927), 675, 396, 444.
88. Senate Judiciary Committee, *Single Six-Year Term for President: Hearing,* 92d Cong., 1st Sess. (1971), 63.
89. Tansill, *Documents,* 447.
90. Washington to Lafayette, 28 April 1788, in Washington, *Writings,* ed. P. L. Ford (New York), 1891, XI, 257–258.
91. The 72nd *Federalist.*
92. Jefferson to John Taylor, 6 January 1805, in Jefferson, *Writings,* ed. Merrill D. Peterson (Library of America, 1984), 1153.
93. Wilson to A. Mitchell Palmer, 5 February 1913, *Single Six-Year Term,* 239–240. James L. Sundquist asks with regard to the fourteen Presidents who were rejected for reelection, by their party or by the electorate (the two Adamses, Van Buren, Tyler, Fillmore, Pierce, Andrew Johnson, Arthur, Cleveland, Benjamin Harrison, Taft, Hoover, Ford, Carter), "How many would have been effective leaders if their terms had continued for two more years?" Sundquist, *Constitutional Reform and Effective Government* (Washington, 1986), 129.
94. *Congressional Record,* 5 February 1985 (daily ed.), S 1004.
95. Mickey Edwards, "A Conservative's Case Against the Line Item Veto," *Washington Post,* 8 February 1984.

96. William Howard Taft, *Our Chief Magistrate and His Powers* (New York, 1916), 27–28.

97. *Lochner v. New York*, 198 U.S. 45, 75.

98. *New York Times*, 23 March 1977.

99. Andrew Jackson, first annual message, 8 December 1829.

100. *Gray v. Sanders*, 372 U.S. 368 (1963).

101. Neal R. Peirce, *The People's President: The Electoral College in American History and the Direct-Vote Alternative* (New York, 1968), 152.

102. J. H. Yunker and L. D. Longley, *The Electoral College: Its Biases Newly Measured for the 1960s and 1970s* (Beverly Hills, Calif., 1976), 37.

103. See the Library of Congress study by Joseph Gorman, "The Election of 1888"; *Congressional Record*, 13 June 1979, S 7604–7615 (daily ed.).

104. Wilson to Robert Lansing, 5 November 1916, *The Papers of Woodrow Wilson*, ed. Arthur Link, XXXVIII, 617–618. Colonel House had made this suggestion to Wilson a fortnight before (493).

105. Crossman, *Myths of Cabinet Government*, xv–xvi.

106. Calvin Coolidge, *Autobiography* (New York, 1929), 234, 194.

107. Lincoln P. Bloomfield, "What's Wrong with Transitions," *Foreign Policy*, Summer 1984, 35.

108. Grover Cleveland, address at Sandwich, Mass., 25 July 1891, *Letters and Addresses*, ed. A. E. Bergh (New York, 1909), 234.

109. Henry F. Pringle, *The Life and Times of William Howard Taft* (New York, 1939), II, 845.

110. Millard Fillmore, *Papers*, ed. F. H. Severance (Buffalo, 1907), II, 139, quoted in A. B. Tourtellot's valuable compendium, *The Presidents on the Presidency* (New York, 1964), 384.

111. James Monroe, *Writings*, ed. S. M. Hamilton (New York, 1898–1903), VII, 54, quoted in Tourtellot, *Presidents*, 378.

112. J. Q. Adams, *Memoirs*, ed. C. F. Adams (Philadelphia, 1874–1877), VIII, 245.

113. Harry S. Truman, *Mr. Citizen* (1960; Popular Library paperback, n.d.), 78–79, 85, 91.

114. Bureau of the Budget Staff Memorandum, "Utilization of Former Presidents," 3 April 1963, transmitted by William Carey to Lawrence O'Brien, 8 April 1963, John F. Kennedy Library.

115. John W. Chambers II, "Transformation of the Ex-Presidency," prospectus (1981), 2.

116. Richard M. Nixon, *The Real War* (New York, 1980), 243.

117. Senator William V. Roth, Jr., "Ex-presidential Perks Are Way out of Hand," *USA Today*, 28 March 1984.

118. Pringle, *Taft*, II, 845–846.

119. Ibid., 846.

120. Bryce, *American Commonwealth*, I, 349.

121. Tocqueville, *Democracy*, I, ch. xvi.

122. *Youngstown Sheet & Tube Co. v. Sawyer*, 343 U.S. 579, 634 (1952).

123. In his message to Congress, 4 July 1861.

124. George Reedy, *The Twilight of the Presidency* (New York, 1970), 9.

125. Walter F. Mondale, "The Institution of the Vice Presidency," lecture at the University of Minnesota, 18 February 1981, mimeograph, 3.

126. In his letter to Bishop Mandell Creighton, 5 April 1887.

127. Adams, *Education*, ch. xxviii.

128. Lincoln in conversation with Major Charles Halpine, reported in Halpine's *Baked Meats of the Funeral* and quoted in *The Face of Lincoln*, ed. James Mellon (New York, 1979).

129. Reedy, *Twilight*, 85.

130. Franklin D. Roosevelt, *Public Papers . . . 1939* (New York, 1941), 492.

131. Greg Schneiders, "Goodbye to All That," *Newsweek*, 24 September 1979.

132. Rosenman and Harriman in interviews with Emmet J. Hughes, *The Living Presidency* (New York, 1973), 348, 362.

133. *King John*, Act IV, scene ii.

134. Hamilton to Gouverneur Morris, 27 February 1802, Hamilton, *Works*, ed. H. C. Lodge (New York, 1904), VIII, 591.

135. Adams, *Education*, ch. xviii.

136. Whitman, "Song of the Broad-Axe," *Leaves of Grass*.

12. The Future of the Vice Presidency

This essay brings up to date an argument originally advanced in "Is the Vice Presidency Necessary?" Atlantic Monthly, May 1974, and in "On the Presidential Succession," Political Science Quarterly, Fall 1974 (reprinted as an appendix in the paperback edition of The Imperial Presidency*).*

1. John D. Feerick, *From Failing Hands: The Story of Presidential Succession* (New York, 1965), 66–67.

2. Finley Peter Dunne, *The World of Mr. Dooley*, ed. Louis Filler (New York, 1962), 50–51.

3. C. C. Tansill, ed., *Documents Illustrative of the Formation of the Union of the American States* (Washington, 1927), 479, 621, 680.

4. Ruth Silva, *Presidential Succession* (New York, 1968), 167–168.

5. Tansill, ed., *Documents*, 682.

6. Ibid., 679, 454.

7. James Wilson, *Works*, ed. R. G. McCloskey (Cambridge, Mass., 1957), I, 439.

8. Tansill, ed., *Documents*, 682.

9. Feerick, *From Failing Hands*, 52, 54.

10. Alexander Hamilton, *Papers*, ed. H. C. Syrett (New York, 1962), V, 248.

11. Feerick, *From Failing Hands*, 66–67, 63.

12. Lucius Wilmerding, Jr., *The Electoral College* (Beacon paperback, 1964), 33–34.

13. Michael Harwood, *In the Shadow of Presidents* (Philadelphia, 1966), 27.

14. Feerick, *From Failing Hands*, 73.

15. Henry Adams, *History of the United States during the Administrations of Jefferson and Madison* (New York, 1889), II, 133–134.

16. I. G. Williams, *The Rise of the Vice Presidency* (Washington, 1956), 81.

17. The text of the 1792 Act can be conveniently found in Edward Stanwood, *A History of the Presidency* (Boston, 1901), 36–38.

18. E. S. Corwin, ed., *The Constitution of the United States of America: Analysis and Interpretation* (Washington, 1953), 387.

19. As Lucius Wilmerding, Jr., pointed out in two penetrating essays on the Vice Presidency, "The Presidential Succession," *Atlantic Monthly*, May 1947, and "The Vice Presidency," *Political Science Quarterly*, March 1953.

20. E. S. Corwin, *The President: Office and Powers* (New York, 1957), 54.

21. Feerick, *From Failing Hands*, 74–75.

22. Ibid., 95, and S. W. Stathis, "John Tyler's Presidential Succession: A Reappraisal," *Prologue*, Winter 1976.

23. Feerick, *From Failing Hands*, 146.

24. For text, Stanwood, *History of the Presidency*, 451–452.

25. Tansill, ed., *Documents*, 682.

26. James G. Blaine, *Twenty Years of Congress* (Norwich, Conn., 1884–1886), II, 57.

27. Jefferson to Elbridge Gerry, 13 May 1797, Jefferson, *Writings*, ed. Merrill D. Peterson (Library of America, 1984), 1042.

28. Michael Harwood, *In the Shadow of Presidents* (Philadelphia, 1966), 153.

29. H. S. Truman, *Year of Decisions* (New York, 1955), 197; D. D. Eisenhower, *Waging Peace* (New York, 1963), 6.

30. Blaine, *Twenty Years*, II, 57.

31. T. R. Marshall, *Recollections* (Indianapolis, 1925), 368.

32. *World of Mr. Dooley*, 53.

33. Doris Kearns, *Lyndon Johnson and the American Dream* (New York, 1976), 164.

34. Tansill, ed., *Documents*, 682.

35. Williams, *Rise*, 109–110.

36. Ibid., 134, 138.

37. Franklin D. Roosevelt, "Can the Vice President Be Useful?" *Saturday Evening Post*, 16 October 1920.

38. W. O. Douglas, *Go East, Young Man* (New York, 1974), 310–311.

39. Franklin D. Roosevelt, *Public Papers . . . 1940* (New York, 1941), 623.

40. *New York Times*, 25 August 1960.

41. Paul B. Fay, Jr., *The Pleasure of His Company* (New York, 1966), 4.

42. *Washington Star-News*, 16 May 1974.

43. J. S. Magruder, *An American Life* (New York, 1974), 128.

44. Marshall, *Recollections*, 230.

45. Two recent books ably describe the transformation of the Vice Presidency: Joel K. Goldstein, *The Modern American Vice Presidency* (Princeton, 1982), and Paul C. Light, *Vice-Presidential Power* (Baltimore, 1984). The quotation is from Light, 71–72. Both books, however, suffer from the illusion that the institutional Vice Presidency is a triumph of substance when it seems more realistically a triumph of public relations.

46. H. S. Truman, Special Message to Congress on the Succession to the Presidency, 19 June 1945, *Public Papers . . . 1945* (Washington, 1961), 129.

47. Ibid., 130.

48. The report is reprinted in the *Congressional Record*, 26 June 1947, 7854–7855 (daily ed.).

49. D. M. DeWitt, *Impeachment and Trial of Andrew Johnson* (New York, 1903), 411.

50. The quotations are from Henry Gonzalez's statement in the *Texas Observer*, May 1965, and from his remarks in the House, 4 June 1985, *Congressional Record*, H 3802 (daily ed.).

51. *Ex Parte Milligan*, 4 Wall 2, 125 (1866).

52. Senate Judiciary Committee, *Selected Materials on the Twenty-Fifth Amendment*, 67–68.

53. *Congressional Record*, 15 November 1973, S 20429 (daily ed.).

54. Birch Bayh, opening statement, in Subcommittee on Constitutional Amendments, Senate Judiciary Committee, *Examination of the First Implementation of Section Two of the Twenty-Fifth Amendment: Hearing*, 94th Cong., 1st Sess. (1975),

19; Bayh, "Statement . . . before the Senate Committee of Rules and Administration Regarding the Nomination of the Hon. Gerald Ford as Vice-President of the United States" [November 1973].

55. Tansill, ed., *Documents,* 392.

56. *Examination of the First Implementation of Section Two,* 124.

57. Light, *Vice-Presidential Power,* 63.

58. Rockefeller to Richard M. Rosenbaum, 18 January 1979.

59. Griffin B. Bell, with R. J. Ostrow, *Taking Care of the Law* (New York, 1982), 23; see also *New York Times,* 7 April 1982.

60. Rockefeller to Rosenbaum, 18 January 1979.

61. Interview in *Newsweek,* 28 July 1980.

62. Marshall, *Recollections,* 16.

63. J. E. Persico, *The Imperial Rockefeller* (New York, 1982), 262.

64. White quoted in Wilmerding, "The Vice Presidency," 17; A. J. Beveridge, "The Fifth Wheel in our Government," *Century,* December 1909; Garner quoted in James MacGregor Burns, "A New Look at the Vice Presidency," *New York Times Magazine,* 9 October 1955.

65. Woodrow Wilson, *Congressional Government* (Boston, 1901), 240.

66. Truman, *Public Papers . . . 1945,* 129.

67. Truman, *Year of Decisions,* 53.

68. In his testimony in 1964, before the Senate Judiciary Committee, reprinted in Senate Judiciary Committee, *Selected Materials on the Twenty-fifth Amendment,* Senate Document 93-42, 93rd Cong., 1st Sess. (1973), 95.

69. James G. O'Hara, testimony before the Vice Presidential Selection Commission of the Democratic National Committee, 7 November 1973 (mimeo.), 10.

70. Danny M. Adkison, "The Electoral Significance of the Vice Presidency," *Presidential Studies Quarterly,* Summer 1982, 330–336. The Nixon quotation is on 332.

71. Roosevelt, "The Three Vice-Presidential Candidates," 292.

72. In CBS News Special Report "On Choosing a Vice President," quoted in Goldstein, *Modern American Vice Presidency,* 66.

73. Truman, *Year of Decisions,* 54.

74. Williams, *Rise,* 110.

75. Theodore Roosevelt, *Letters,* ed. E. E. Morison (Cambridge, Mass., 1951), III, 57.

76. Williams, *Rise,* 89.

77. Alben Barkley, *That Reminds Me* (New York, 1954), 221.

78. As told by FDR, Jr., to me; Arthur M. Schlesinger, Jr., *A Thousand Days* (Boston, 1965), 704.

79. *Minneapolis Tribune,* 2 June 1974.

80. *Time,* 14 November 1969.

81. As told to Jimmy Breslin in Breslin, "Police Riot," *New York* magazine, 16 September 1968.

82. Danny M. Adkison, "The Vice Presidency as Apprenticeship," *Presidential Studies Quarterly,* Spring 1983, 212–218. The four polls cited are the Schlesinger poll (1962), the Maranell-Dodder poll (1970), the United States Historical Society poll (1977), and the *Chicago Tribune* poll (1982).

83. *Time,* 14 November 1969.

84. *Congressional Record,* 21 December 1973, S 23756 (daily ed.).

85. Donald Graham, "The Vice Presidency: From Cigar Store Indian to Crown Prince," *Washington Monthly,* April 1974.

86. Roosevelt, *Letters,* III, 60.

87. Senate Judiciary Committee, *Selected Materials on the Twenty-fifth Amendment,* 124.

88. Walter Lippmann, "Wrong Answer, Right Question," *New York Herald Tribune,* 12 November 1946.

89. "On the Threshold of the White House," *Atlantic Monthly,* July 1974.

90. Lippmann, "Wrong Answer, Right Question."

13. Vicissitudes of Presidential Reputations

This essay draws on "Hoover Makes a Comeback," New York Review of Books, 8 March 1979; "The Ike Age Revisited," Reviews in American History, March 1983; and "What the Thousand Days Wrought," New Republic, 21 November 1983.

1. Emerson, "Art."

2. Pieter Geyl, *Napoleon: For and Against* (1949; Peregrine paperback, 1965), 15.

3. See the panegyric in Paul Johnson, *Modern Times* (New York, 1983), 219–222; and the book by Thomas B. Silver, *Coolidge and the Historians* (Durham, N.C., 1983).

4. "The Critic as Artist," in *The Artist as Critic: The Critical Writings of Oscar Wilde,* ed. Richard Ellman (New York, 1969), 359.

5. William Appleman Williams, *America Confronts a Revolutionary World: 1776–1976* (New York, 1976), 180; Joan Hoff-Wilson, *Herbert Hoover: Forgotten Progressive* (Boston, 1975), 275.

6. Walter Lippmann, *The New Imperative* (New York, 1935), 12–13, 20.

7. Carl Degler, "The Ordeal of Herbert Hoover," *Yale Review,* Summer 1963.

8. Williams, *America Confronts a Revolutionary World,* 159.

9. Ellis W. Hawley, "Herbert Hoover and Modern American History Fifty Years After," *Congressional Record* (daily ed.), 27 February 1980, S 1931. This was one in a long series of papers solicited by Senator Mark Hatfield of Oregon and published in the *Record* to celebrate the 50th anniversary of Hoover's inauguration as President.

10. Albert U. Romasco, "Herbert Hoover's Policies for Dealing with the Great Depression: The End of the Old Order or the Beginning of the New?" in *The Hoover Presidency,* ed. Martin L. Fausold and George T. Mazuzan (Albany, 1974), 69–86.

11. Arthur M. Schlesinger, Jr., *The Crisis of the Old Order* (Boston, 1957), 232.

12. David Burner, *Herbert Hoover: A Public Life* (New York, 1978), 268.

13. Herbert Hoover, *Memoirs, III: The Great Depression* (New York, 1952), 195.

14. Herbert Hoover, *State Papers* (New York, 1934), II, 228ff.

15. J. S. Olson, *Herbert Hoover and the Reconstruction Finance Corporation, 1931–1933* (Ames, Iowa, 1955), 77–88.

16. Arthur M. Schlesinger, Jr., *The Coming of the New Deal* (Boston, 1958), 431.

17. Hoover to Simeon D. Fess, 27 December 1933, in Richard Norton Smith, *An Uncommon Man: The Triumph of Herbert Hoover* (New York, 1984), 192–193.

18. Williams, *America Confronts a Revolutionary World,* 159; Williams, *Some Presidents from Wilson to Nixon* (New York, 1972), 39.

19. Joan Hoff-Wilson, "Herbert Hoover Reassessed," *Congressional Record* (daily ed.), 25 June 1979, S 8464.

20. Ellis W. Hawley, "Herbert Hoover and American Corporatism, 1929–1933," in

The Hoover Presidency, ed. Fausold and Mazuzan, 104; Hawley, "Hoover and Modern American History," S 1931.

21. Hawley, "Hoover and American Corporatism," 104.

22. Williams, *Some Presidents*, 39.

23. Burner, *Hoover*, 141.

24. Ibid., 59, 249. Joan Hoff-Wilson used the second phrase twice in *Herbert Hoover: Forgotten Progressive* (Boston, 1975), 15, 166.

25. Burner, *Hoover*, 79, 110–111, 151.

26. Ibid., 63.

27. In his review of Burner, *New Republic*, 10 March 1979.

28. Martin L. Fausold, *The Presidency of Herbert C. Hoover* (Lawrence, Kans., 1985), 7.

29. Burner, *Hoover*, 141.

30. Hoover, *Memoirs*, III, 234.

31. Fausold, *Hoover*, 123.

32. George W. Norris, *Fighting Liberal: The Autobiography of George W. Norris* (New York, 1945), 314–315.

33. Burner, *Hoover*, 215.

34. I. H. Hoover, *Forty-Two Years in the White House* (Boston, 1934), 301–303. Nor does Donald J. Lisio cite Ike Hoover's testimony in his able study *Hoover, Blacks, and Lily-Whites* (Chapel Hill, 1985).

35. Burner, *Hoover*, 70.

36. Norris, *Fighting Liberal*, 287.

37. Hoover, *Memoirs, II: The Cabinet and the Presidency, 1920–1933* (New York, 1952), 197–198; *Memoirs*, III, 234, 329.

38. Burner, *Hoover*, 58.

39. Hoover, *State Papers*, I, 527.

40. Burner, *Hoover*, 264.

41. Patrick J. Maney, *"Young Bob" La Follette: A Biography of Robert M. La Follette, Jr., 1895–1953* (Columbia, Mo., 1978), 110, 87–88.

42. W. A. White to David Hinshaw, 13 February 1931, Fausold, *Hoover*, 131.

43. Richard W. Lowitt, *George W. Norris: The Triumph of a Progressive, 1933–1944* (Urbana, Ill., 1978), x; Maney, *La Follette*, 110.

44. Wilson, *Hoover*, 274.

45. Olson, *Hoover and the RFC*, 23.

46. Williams, *Some Presidents*, 39.

47. Burner, *Hoover*, 260.

48. Hawley, "Hoover and Modern American History," S 1931.

49. Wilson, *Hoover*, 229–230.

50. In his letter to William E. Borah, 28 February 1928.

51. Robert H. Ferrell, ed., *The Eisenhower Diaries* (New York, 1981). This volume, with an able introduction by Professor Ferrell, provides (apparently) the text of the several journals Eisenhower kept sporadically from 1939, when he went to serve General Douglas MacArthur in the Philippines, into the last years of his life. One must write "apparently" because the editor is not finally clear about deletions and omissions, noting only that a few entries were withheld because of alleged national security needs or because publication would violate the donor's deed of gift. Yet William B. Ewald in *Eisenhower the President: Crucial Days: 1951–1960* (Englewood Cliffs, N.J., 1981) prints passages for 8 October

1953 (81) and for 6 November 1957 (28) that are not to be found in the Ferrell edition. Stephen E. Ambrose in *Ike's Spies: Eisenhower and the Espionage Establishment,* with Richard H. Immerman (New York, 1981), reproduces an entry from Eisenhower's diary of 1 April 1968; the last entry in the Ferrell edition is for 14 March 1967. Fred Greenstein in *The Hidden-Hand Presidency: Eisenhower as Leader* (New York, 1982) similarly reprints diary items not to be found in the Ferrell text. Some clarification is surely in order.

52. Ferrell, ed., *Diaries,* 50.

53. Dwight D. Eisenhower, *Mandate for Change* (New York, 1963), 477–478.

54. Richard Nixon, *Six Crises* (1962; Warner paperback, 1979), 189.

55. W. C. Bruce, *John Randolph of Roanoke* (New York, 1922), II, 203.

56. Greenstein, *Hidden-Hand Presidency,* 57–58.

57. Ibid., 101.

58. Anne O'Hare McCormick, "Roosevelt's View of the Big Job," *New York Times Magazine,* 11 September 1932.

59. Arthur Larson, *Eisenhower: The President Nobody Knew* (1968; Popular Library paperback, n.d.), 123.

60. Stephen E. Ambrose, "The Ike Age," *New Republic,* 9 May 1981.

61. He sent the list on 18 October 1966 to James Hagerty, who kindly made it available to me.

62. Stephen E. Ambrose, *Eisenhower the President* (New York, 1984), 190.

63. Larson, *Eisenhower,* 122.

64. Ibid., 10.

65. Robert A. Divine, *Eisenhower and the Cold War* (New York, 1981), vii–viii.

66. Ferrell, ed., *Diaries,* 155–156, 160, 212.

67. Ewald, *Eisenhower,* 33, 242.

68. N. S. Khrushchev, *Khrushchev Remembers,* ed. Strobe Talbott (Boston, 1970), 397, 458; *Khrushchev Remembers: The Last Testament* (Boston, 1974), 487, 491.

69. Anthony Glees, "Churchill's Last Gambit," *Encounter,* April 1985, 30.

70. John Colville, *The Fringes of Power* (New York, 1985), 654, 672.

71. Ibid., 683.

72. Ibid., 673.

73. Divine, *Eisenhower and the Cold War,* 155.

74. Ibid., ix.

75. Kermit Roosevelt, *Countercoup: The Struggle for the Control of Iran* (New York, 1979), 107.

76. Anthony Eden, *Full Circle* (Boston, 1960), 235.

77. Ambrose, *Eisenhower the President,* 621.

78. Ibid., 197.

79. Ibid., 286.

80. See Brian Urquhart, *Hammarskjold* (New York, 1972), 121, and W. R. Corson, *The Armies of Ignorance* (New York, 1977), 365–366.

81. The source is a February 1957 report of the President's Board of Consultants on Foreign Intelligence Activities; Arthur M. Schlesinger, Jr., *Robert Kennedy and His Times* (Boston, 1978), 456. The 1952 figure is cited in J. L. Gaddis, *Strategies of Containment* (New York, 1982), 157. See also Ambrose, *Eisenhower the President,* 395.

82. William Manchester, *Portrait of a President* (Boston, 1962), 35.

83. David Bruce and Robert Lovett, "Covert Operations," report to President's

Board of Consultants on Foreign Intelligence Activities [1956], Robert F. Kennedy Papers; excerpted in Schlesinger, *Robert Kennedy,* 455–456.

84. Report to the Special Assistant for National Security, 12 February 1957, in Schlesinger, *Robert Kennedy,* 456.

85. White House meeting of the Board with Eisenhower, 16 December 1958, in Schlesinger, *Robert Kennedy,* 457.

86. Ambrose, *Eisenhower the President,* 506–507.

87. Report to Eisenhower, 5 January 1961, in Schlesinger, *Robert Kennedy,* 457–458.

88. Hearings of Cuba Study Group, 11 May 1961, in Schlesinger, *Robert Kennedy,* 458.

89. Ambrose, *Eisenhower the President,* 135.

90. Clark Clifford, "Memorandum on Conference between President Eisenhower and President-elect Kennedy and their Chief Advisers on January 19, 1961," in Schlesinger, *Robert Kennedy,* 444.

91. Gregg Herken, *The Winning Weapon* (New York, 1980), 345.

92. Henry A. Wallace, *The Price of Vision: The Diary . . . 1942–1946,* ed. John Morton Blum (Boston, 1973), 474, 530.

93. Herken, *Winning Weapon,* 373.

94. David Lilienthal, *Journals . . . The Atomic Energy Years 1945–50* (New York, 1964), 391.

95. Herken, *Winning Weapon,* 332–333.

96. Truman was reacting to the claim by General Mark Clark in *From the Danube to the Yalu* that bombing could have brought victory in Korea. Truman, *Off the Record: The Private Papers of Harry S. Truman,* ed. R. H. Ferrell (New York, 1980), 304.

97. Ambrose, *Eisenhower the President,* 658.

98. McGeorge Bundy, "Atomic Diplomacy Reconsidered," *Bulletin of the American Academy of Arts and Sciences,* October 1984, 30.

99. National Security Council meetings, 13 May, 20 May, 3 December, 1953, JCS-State Memorandum, 7 January 1954, *New York Times,* 8 June 1984.

100. Divine, *Eisenhower and the Cold War,* 49.

101. Ambrose, *Eisenhower the President,* 180.

102. Murray Marder, "When Ike Was Asked to Nuke Vietnam," *Washington Post,* 22 August 1982.

103. Divine, *Eisenhower and the Cold War,* 62.

104. Gaddis, *Strategies of Containment,* 170.

105. R. H. Immerman, "Diplomatic Dialings: The John Foster Dulles Telephone Transcripts," Society for Historians of American Foreign Relations *Newsletter,* March 1983.

106. Divine, *Eisenhower and the Cold War,* 65–66.

107. National Security Council meeting, 31 March 1953, *Foreign Relations of the United States 1952–1954, XV, Korea* (Washington, 1984), 827. Oddly these sentences are deleted (with deletion indicated) from the minutes of the meeting as reprinted in *FRUS 1952–1954, II, National Security Affairs,* 276.

108. Colville, *Fringes of Power,* 685; Colville, *Winston Churchill and His Inner Circle* (London, 1981), 139.

109. Ferrell, ed., *Diaries,* 202, 222.

110. Eden, *Full Circle,* 117; G. C. Herring and R. H. Immerman, "Eisenhower, Dulles, and Dienbienphu: 'The Day We Didn't Go to War' Revisited," *Journal of American History,* September 1984, 360.

111. Ambrose, *Eisenhower the President,* 225.

112. *London Times,* 3 January 1985.

113. Bundy, "Atomic Diplomacy Reconsidered," 32.

114. Ambrose, *Eisenhower the President,* 229.

115. Eisenhower to R. L. Simon, 28 March 1956, David Broder, "Eisenhower on the folly of nuclear war," *Boston Globe,* 7 September 1983.

116. Sherman Adams, *Firsthand Report* (New York, 1961), 87.

117. Gaddis, *Strategies of Containment,* 173.

118. Ambrose, *Eisenhower the President,* 493–494.

119. George B. Kistiakowsky, *A Scientist at the White House* (Cambridge, Mass., 1976), 293.

120. Ambrose, *Eisenhower the President,* 590.

121. Walter Pincus, "40 Years of the Bomb," *Washington Post Weekly,* 5 August 1985.

122. Ambrose, *Eisenhower the President,* 590.

123. Michael Howard, "Keeping the Team Together," *Times Literary Supplement,* 8 February 1985.

124. Schlesinger, *Robert Kennedy,* 702.

125. Ambrose, *Eisenhower the President,* 660–665; H. W. Brands, Jr., "Johnson and Eisenhower: The President, the Former President, and the War in Vietnam," *Presidential Studies Quarterly,* Summer 1985.

126. John Colville, *Footprints in Time* (London, 1976), 192.

127. Ronald Steel, *Walter Lippmann and the American Century* (Boston, 1980), 502.

128. Arthur M. Schlesinger, Jr., Journal, 12 February 1981.

129. Eric Hobsbawm, "Why America Lost the Vietnam War," *Listener,* 18 May 1972.

130. Richard M. Nixon, "Cuba, Castro, and John F. Kennedy," *Reader's Digest,* November 1964.

131. Elie Abel, *The Missile Crisis* (New York, Bantam paperback, 1966), 162.

132. Charles Dickens, *American Notes,* ch. xviii.

133. Arthur M. Schlesinger, Jr., *A Thousand Days: Kennedy in the White House* (Boston, 1965), 635.

134. Ibid., 1012.

135. Ibid., 941.

136. Ibid., 971.

137. John F. Kennedy, *Public Papers . . . 1963* (Washington, 1964), 469.

138. Schlesinger, *Robert Kennedy,* 358; Martin Luther King, Jr., *Why We Can't Wait* (New York, Signet paperback, 1964), 147.

139. *Look,* 17 November 1964.

140. Jack Anderson, "Conversation with an Author: Jack Anderson," *Book Digest,* May 1979.

141. Schlesinger, *Robert Kennedy,* 605.

142. Speech at University of Washington, 16 November 1961, John F. Kennedy, *Public Papers . . . 1961* (Washington, 1962), 726.

143. Schlesinger, *Robert Kennedy,* 713.

144. Ibid., 712.

145. Kenneth O'Donnell and David Powers, *"Johnny, We Hardly Knew Ye"* (Boston, 1972), 16; Schlesinger, *Robert Kennedy,* ch. 31; Jack Anderson, "The Roots of Our Vietnam Involvement," *Washington Post,* 4 May 1975.

146. Schlesinger, *A Thousand Days,* 331.

147. Address to Latin American diplomatic corps, 13 March 1962, John F. Kennedy, *Public Papers . . . 1962* (Washington, 1963), 224.

148. Castro said this to Jean Daniel and to Frank Mankiewicz; see Jean Daniel, "Unofficial Envoy," *New Republic,* 14 December 1963, and Frank Mankiewicz and Kirby Jones, *With Fidel* (Chicago, 1975), 200–202. Castro reiterated this judgment to me in conversations in May and October 1985.

149. Speeches at University of California, 23 March 1962, Kennedy, *Public Papers . . . 1962,* 265 and American University, 10 June 1963, *Public Papers . . . 1963,* 462.

150. Speech at United Nations, 25 September 1961, *Public Papers . . . 1961,* 618, 620.

151. Schlesinger, *A Thousand Days,* 831.

152. Press conference, 21 March 1963, *Public Papers . . . 1963,* 280.

153. Schlesinger, *A Thousand Days,* 904.

154. Norman Cousins, *The Improbable Triumvirate* (New York, 1972), 114.

155. Khrushchev, *Khrushchev Remembers,* 500; Khrushchev, *Khrushchev Remembers: The Last Testament,* 513–514.

156. Schlesinger, *A Thousand Days,* 110.

157. Herbert L. Mathews, *Fidel Castro* (New York, 1969), 225.

158. Robert F. Kennedy, Foreword to John F. Kennedy, *Profiles in Courage* (Memorial ed., New York, 1964), ix.

159. Arthur M. Schlesinger, Jr., *The Crisis of the Old Order* (Boston, 1957), ix.

14. Democracy and Leadership

This essay includes passages adapted from "On Leadership," the introduction to the Chelsea House series World Leaders: Past and Present *(New York, 1985); from "Politics and the American Language," Blashfield Address at the American Academy and Institute of Arts and Letters, reprinted in the* American Scholar, *Autumn 1974; from "The Decline of Greatness," Saturday Evening Post, 1 November 1958; from "On Heroic Leadership," Encounter, December 1960; and from "Creativity in Statecraft" (Occasional Papers of the Council of Scholars, No. 1, Library of Congress, 1983).*

1. *War and Peace,* Book Nine, ch. 1.

2. William James, "The Dilemma of Determinism," in *The Will to Believe and Other Essays in Popular Philosophy* (New York, 1897), 150.

3. Isaiah Berlin, *Four Essays of Liberty* (Oxford, 1969), 113, 72.

4. James, "Great Men and Their Environment," *Will to Believe,* 235.

5. Engels to Starkenberg, quoted in Sidney Hook, *The Hero in History* (1943; Beacon paperback, 155), 79.

6. Arthur M. Schlesinger, Jr., *The Crisis of the Old Order* (Boston, 1957), 466.

7. William James, "The Social Value of the College-Bred," in *Memories and Studies* (New York, 1911), 318.

8. James, *Will to Believe,* 227, 230.

9. William Wordsworth, "Preface to Poems" and "Essay Supplementary to Preface," in *Wordsworth's Literary Criticism,* ed. N. C. Smith (London, 1905), 150–151, 195, 198.

10. Henry Kissinger, "Domestic Structure and Foreign Policy," in *American Defense Policy,* ed. R. G. Head and E. J. Rokke (Baltimore, 1973), 20.

11. Alexis de Tocqueville, *Democracy in America,* I, ch. xiii.

12. Freud, in "Analysis Terminable and Interminable" (1937), quoted by Janet Malcolm, "The Impossible Profession," *New Yorker,* 24 November 1980.

13. Emerson, "Power," in *The Conduct of Life.*

14. Machiavelli, *The Prince*, ch. vi.
15. Joseph A. Schumpeter, *The Theory of Economic Development* (Cambridge, Mass., 1934), 85.
16. Ibid., 87.
17. J. M. Keynes, *The General Theory of Employment, Interest, and Money* (New York, 1936), 32. He should have added the Americans William Trufant Foster and Waddill Catchings.
18. Ibid., 33.
19. J. K. Galbraith, "Economics as a System of Belief," *Economics, Peace and Laughter* (Boston, 1971), 63, 65.
20. Tocqueville, *Democracy in America*, II, Third Book, ch. xxi.
21. James Bryce, *The American Commonwealth* (New York, 1888), II, 322–323.
22. Herbert Croly, *The Promise of American Life* (New York, 1909), 451.
23. Karl Popper, *The Open Society and Its Enemies* (Princeton, 1950), 154–155.
24. Alexis de Tocqueville, *Recollections*, ed. J. P. Mayer (New York, 1959), Part I, ch. v.
25. Henry Adams, *The Education of Henry Adams* (Boston, 1918), ch. xxiii.
26. Karl Popper, *The Poverty of Historicism* (Boston, 1957), 67.
27. Winston Churchill to Bourke Cockran, 12 April [1896], in Randolph Churchill, *Winston S. Churchill*, Companion Volume I, Part I (Boston, 1967), 668.
28. Locke, *Second Treatise on Civil Government*, ¶ 224.
29. Jefferson to Adams, 28 October 1813, in Jefferson, *Writings*, ed. Merrill D. Peterson (Library of America, 1984), 1305–1306.
30. Tocqueville to Mill, 5 December 1835, in J. P. Mayer, *Alexis de Tocqueville* (New York, 1960), 115.
31. Bryce, *American Commonwealth*, II, 460.
32. Emerson, "Napoleon; or, the Man of the World," in *Representative Men*.
33. Woodrow Wilson, *Leaders of Men*, ed. T. H. Vail Motter (Princeton, 1952), 53–54.
34. Jefferson, "Notes on the State of Virginia," in *Writings*, 290.
35. Emerson, "Language," *Nature*, ch. iv.
36. Tocqueville, *Democracy in America*, II, First Book, ch. xvi.
37. Joel Porte, ed., *Emerson in His Journals* (Cambridge, Mass., 1982), 421.
38. "Napoleon."
39. "Language."
40. Reinhold Niebuhr, *The Children of Light and the Children of Darkness* (1944; Scribner paperback, n.d.), xiii.
41. James, "The Importance of Individuals," *Will to Believe*, 261.
42. Emerson, "Uses of Great Men," in *Representative Men*.
43. Irving Babbitt, *Democracy and Leadership* (Boston, 1924), 167.

Index